T0261602

DEVELOPMENTS IN DATA STORAGE

DEVELOPMENTS IN DATA STORAGE

Materials Perspective

Edited by

S. N. Piramanayagam
Tow C. Chong

Data Storage Institute
Agency for Science, Technology and Research (A*STAR)
Singapore

IEEE Magnetics Society, *Sponsor*

IEEE PRESS

A JOHN WILEY & SONS, INC., PUBLICATION

For general information on our other products and services or for technical support, please contact our Customer Care Department within the United States at (800) 762-2974, outside the United States at (317) 572-3993 or fax (317) 572-4002.

Wiley also publishes its books in a variety of electronic formats. Some content that appears in print may not be available in electronic formats. For more information about Wiley products, visit our web site at www.wiley.com.

Library of Congress Cataloging-in-Publication Data:
Developments in data storage : materials perspective / [edited by] S.N. Piramanayagam, Tow C. Chong.
  p. cm.
   ISBN 978-0-470-50100-9 (hardback)
  1. Computer storage devices.   I. Piramanayagam, S. N.   II. Chong, Tow C.
  TK7895.M4D497 2011
  621.39'7–dc22

                                                                                2011006739

oBook ISBN: 978-1-118-09683-3
ePDF ISBN: 978-1-118-09681-9
ePub ISBN: 978-1-118-09682-6

10 9 8 7 6 5 4 3 2 1

To my mentors

Prof. Shiva Prasad,
Prof. S. N. Shringi,
Prof. Mitsunori Matsumoto and
The Late Ms. Terue Kamoi
who made a positive difference in my life

S. N. Piramanayagam

To my family and all the staff of Data Storage Institute, Singapore

Tow C. Chong

CONTENTS

PREFACE

It gives us great pleasure to present this book on the developments in data storage, from a materials perspective. This book has been designed to help the final year undergraduate and graduate students of physics, materials science, chemistry, electrical engineering, and other disciplines with an interest in the magnetic recording or other emerging alternative storage technologies. This book will also help new engineers as well as professionals in the recording industry to broaden their knowledge and serve as a useful reference.

It has been quite some time since a book on data storage was released and since then there have been several developments. The hard disk industry has moved from longitudinal recording technology to perpendicular recording. Even though the hard disk technology is more than 50 years old, the storage density of the hard disk drives has been increasing at a rate of about 30% per year. As of 2010, all the hard disk products are based on perpendicular recording technology. It is believed that some alternatives, such as heat-assisted magnetic recording or patterned media technology, are needed to maintain the growth of storage density which will enable the hard disk industry to maintain its superiority over competing technologies. Such growth has been (and will continue to be) brought on by various technological developments. We thought there was a need to condense these developments into a book that will benefit the readers for the next several years. With this aim, we requested several researchers from different backgrounds to write on the developments in their respective field. However, the book would not be complete if it did not provide the background information for a novice. With that in mind, we have also included some chapters that introduce the fundamentals. Chapters 1–3 provide the fundamentals and Chapters 4–9 provide the recent developments in several areas of hard disk drives. Chapters 10–12 cover the emerging technologies of hard disk drives.

Even though hard disk drives have enjoyed a successful advantage over the competing technologies in terms of cheaper costs and higher capacities, their superiority is threatened by the flash memory. Since there are several books on flash memory, we did not attempt to cover it here. However, flash memory will face its hurdles in the near future and several alternative memory technologies such as phase change random access memory (PCRAM) and magnetic random access memory (MRAM) are emerging as alternatives. Chapters 13–14 describe the fundamentals as well as the recent advances and challenges in these emerging memory technologies.

We believe the book will be useful to researchers and students and fulfill the aim with which we began this work.

S. N. PIRAMANAYAGAM
TOW C. CHONG

ACKNOWLEDGMENTS

Data storage—even if it has to be written purely from a materials perspective—is a multidisciplinary. It involves physics, chemistry, and materials science at the fundamental level; and mechanical, chemical, and electrical engineering at the application level. A book of such a multidisciplinary nature cannot be accomplished in an authoritative fashion without significant contributions of several kind hearts. First of all, we would like to thank all of the contributing authors: Shiva Prasad (IIT Bombay, India), Kumar Srinivasan (Western Digital, USA), Naoki Honda (Tohoku Institute of Technology, Japan), Kiyoshi Yamakawa (Akita Industrial Technology Center, Japan), Bruno Marchon (HGST, USA), Ganping Ju, William Challener, Yingguo Peng, Mike Seigler, and Ed Gage (Seagate Technology, USA); Jingsheng Chen (NUS, Singapore), Bruce Terris (HGST, USA), and Thomas Thomson (U. Manchester, UK), who represented authors from different parts of the globe; and Rachid Sbiaa, Guchang Han, Viloane Ko, Zaibing Guo, Hao Meng, Allen Poh, Thomas Liew, Jiangfeng Hu, Luping Shi, Rong Zhao, Randall Law, and Sunny Lua from Data Storage Institute (DSI), Singapore. They were very glad to contribute chapters and very cooperative in revising and improving the chapters. Our sincere thanks are due to these authors.

There are several others who provided the help and support at the initial stages which motivated us to take this job. Catherine Faduska (formerly of IEEE) and Liesl Folks (HGST, USA) were instrumental in helping with the review and selection of the book proposal. There are several authors who were interested in writing a chapter but could not write because of certain unavoidable circumstances. We acknowledge their support. We also would like to thank IEEE Press and Wiley for their support to publish this work.

Personally, S.N.Piramanayagam would like to thank his family members Preeti, Priya, and Pramesh, and colleagues and students in DSI for their support, understanding, and patience during this period. Tow C. Chong would like to dedicate this effort to his family and all the DSI staff.

S. N. P.
T. C. C.

CONTRIBUTORS

William Challener, Seagate Technology, USA

Jingsheng Chen, National University of Singapore, Singapore

Tow C. Chong, Data Storage Institute, Singapore

Ed Gage, Seagate Technology, USA

Zaibing Guo, Data Storage Institute, Singapore

Guchang Han, Data Storage Institute, Singapore

Naoki Honda, Tohoku Institute of Technology, Japan

Jiangfeng Hu, Data Storage Institute, Singapore

Ganping Ju, Seagate Technology, USA

Viloane Ko, Data Storage Institute, Singapore

Randall Law Yaozhang, Data Storage Institute, Singapore

Thomas Y. F. Liew, Data Storage Institute, Singapore

Sunny Y.H. Lua, Data Storage Institute, Singapore

Bruno Marchon, Hitachi GST, USA

Hao Meng, Data Storage Institute, Singapore

Yingguo Peng, Seagate Technology, USA

S. N. Piramanayagam, Data Storage Institute, Singapore

Allen Poh Wei Choong, Data Storage Institute, Singapore

Shiva Prasad, Indian Institute of Technology-Bombay, India

Rachid Sbiaa, Data Storage Institute, Singapore

Mike Seigler, Seagate Technology, USA

Luping Shi, Data Storage Institute, Singapore

Kumar Srinivasan, Western Digital, USA

Bruce D. Terris, Hitachi GST, USA

Thomas Thomson, The University of Manchester, UK

Kiyoshi Yamakawa, AIT, Akita Industrial Technology Center, Japan

Rong Zhao, Data Storage Institute, Singapore

1

INTRODUCTION

S. N. Piramanayagam

*Data Storage Institute, Agency for Science,
Technology and Research (A*STAR), Singapore*

1.1 INTRODUCTION

What is the earliest form of data storage used by human beings? When this question is posed, answers such as stone, paper, tape, and so on often come up before someone suggests "the brain." Although the brain is the data storage system that nature has provided us with, it is not sufficient for all purposes. Even though the brain can be used for storage of certain kinds of information, how reliably one can retrieve the information depends on the individual and the circumstances. Moreover, information stored in a person's brain cannot be transferred to others after the life of that person. We need data or information storage systems for at least two purposes: (1) to reliably preserve data and information for retrieval when it is needed, and (2) to spread or communicate information/knowledge to others. When humans realized this, they started inventing other means of storing information, such as using stone, clay, paper, and so on as media for data storage.

Magnetic recording was invented more than a century ago by Valdemar Poulsen [1]. It took about 30 years for magnetic tapes to be successfully commercialized [2]. Even though magnetic tapes were good for archival or sound recording, they did not possess random access capability, and hence access times were longer compared to other forms of recording available during that period, such as punch cards. To overcome the random-access problem of magnetic recording, IBM invented the first hard disk drive (HDD), which combined the advantages of magnetic recording (multiple read/erase cycles) with random acess capability, and suitably named it RAMAC (random access memory accounting system or random access method of accounting and control). The RAMAC (introduced in 1956) had a capacity of 5 MB, which was achieved using 50 magnetic disks with a diameter of 24 in.—each offering an areal density of 2 kilobits per square inch (kb/in.^{2}). Since then, HDDs have come a long way and now pack 1000 GB in two magnetic disks with a diameter of 2.5 in., each offering an areal density of over 600 gigabits per square inch (Gb/in.^{2}) as of 2011. An areal density increase of the order 10^8 times in a period of close to 50 years is simply remarkable and was possible because of the tremendous efforts to develop the technology behind each component of the HDD. Although most chapters of this book will cover in detail the technology behind the development of the HDD, this chapter will provide an overview of HDD technology, briefly covering the technology from a materials perspective, in line with the theme of this book. This chapter also provides a brief overview of memory technologies that are emerging as alternatives for future memory/storage applications.

1.2 BASICS OF DATA STORAGE

Any data storage system/device needs to satisfy certain basic criteria. The first basic requirement is a storage medium (or media). On this storage medium, the data will be written. The other requirements are that there should be ways to write, read, and interpret the data. For example, let us look at this book as a form of data storage containing the chapters written by the contributing authors. In the printed version of the book, paper is the storage medium. Writing the information (printing) is completed using ink, and reading is carried out with the user's eyes. Interpretation of the data and sometimes even error correction is carried out in the user's brain. Components with similar functions exist in an HDD, too.

Figure 1.1 shows the components of a typical HDD used in desktop personal computers (PCs). Some of the key components that make up an HDD are marked; an HDD has disk media, heads, a spindle motor, an actuator, and several other components. A disk is a magnetic recording medium that stores information, similar to the pages of a book. A head performs two functions, writing and reading information, corresponding to a pen and an eye in our example. A spindle motor helps to spin the disk so that the actuator, which moves along the radial direction, can carry the head to any part of the disk and read or write information. An HDD also has several circuitries in a printed circuit board that serve as its brain, controlling its activity, and receiving and conveying meaningful information from or to the computer or whatever device that uses the HDD.

Several disks (also called platters) may be stacked in an HDD in order to multiply the capacity. In almost all HDDs, the information is stored on both sides of the disks. Figure 1.2 shows the way the data are organized on magnetic disks. The data are stored in circular tracks. The number of tracks that can be packed closely within a given length

Figure 1.1. Picture of a hard disk drive and various components.

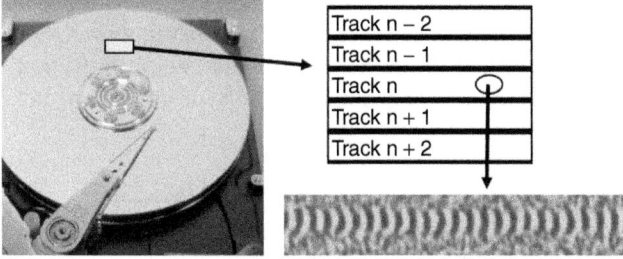

Figure 1.2. Illustration of hard disk media, various tracks, and the way the bits are arranged in tracks. The contrasting lines indicate the magnetic field emanating from the media.

is called track density and is expressed in tracks per inch (TPI). The number of bits that can be stored along the track is measured in terms of bits per millimeter (bits/mm) or bits per inch (bits/in.) and is called linear density. For a particular track density, media with better performance can achieve larger linear density than the inferior disk. The areal density, which is the number of bits that can be stored in a given area, is a product of the track density and the linear density, and is often expressed as bits per square inch (bpsi). Within the tracks there are addressed sectors in which the informa-tion can be written or read. The randomness in access or storage of information from or in an address provided by a central processing unit (CPU) comes from the ability to move the head to a desired sector. In state-of-the-art HDD, the total length of tracks on one side of a 65 mm disk covers a distance of 42 km, almost a marathon run. As of 2011, in each track the bits are packed at a density of 1.5–2 million bits in an inch.

1.3 RECORDING MEDIUM

There has to be a medium for storing information in a data storage device. In magnetic recording, a disk that comprises several magnetic and nonmagnetic layers serves as the recording medium [3]. Whether the medium is tape or disk, magnetic recording relies on two basic principles. First, magnets have north and south poles out of which its magnetic field emanates and can be sensed by a magnetic-field sensor. The sensing of a magnetic field by a magnetic-field sensor provides a way of reading information. Second, the polarity of the magnets can be changed by applying external magnetic fields, which is usually achieved using an electromagnet. This provides a way of writing information. Earlier magnetic recording media such as audio tapes, video tapes, and so on were mostly used for analog applications. HDDs are digital devices, which make use of strings of 1 and 0 to store information.

Figure 1.3 illustrates the recording process using longitudinal recording technol-ogy. In this technology the polarities of the magnets are parallel to the surface of the hard disk. When two identical poles are next to each other (S–S or N–N), a strong magnetic field will emerge from the recording medium, but no field will emerge when opposite poles (S–N) are next to each other. Therefore, when a magnetic-field sensor (a giant magnetoresistive [GMR] sensor, for example) moves across this surface, a voltage will be produced only when the GMR sensor goes over the transitions (regions where like poles meet). This voltage pulse can be synchronized with a clock pulse. If

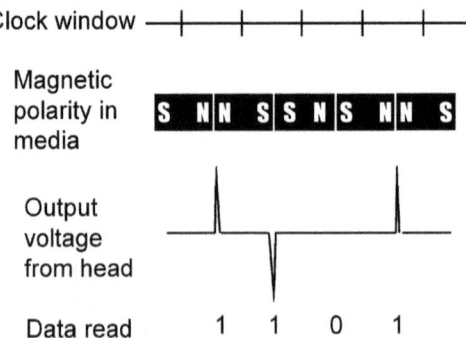

Figure 1.3. Illustration of the recorded pulses from magnetic transitions and the recording principle.

during the clock window the GMR sensor produces a voltage, the voltage is represented as "1." If no voltage is produced during the clock window, the absence of voltage is represented by "0." This is a simple illustration of how 1s and 0s are stored in hard disk media. The fundamentals of magnetism and the details of longitudinal recording technology, which will lay the foundation for most of the chapters in the book, will be discussed in Chapters 2 and 3, respectively. In perpendicular recording technology, which is the current way of recording information on HDDs, the magnetizations lie out of plane [3, 4]. In this technology the magnetic field emanates from the center of the bit cells rather than the transitions. More details about perpendicular recording media will be provided in Chapter 4.

1.4 HEADS

The head is a tiny device (as shown in Fig. 1.1) that performs the read–write operation in an HDD. Head technology has undergone tremendous changes over the years. In the past, both reading and writing operations were carried out using an inductive head. Inductive heads are transducers that make use of current-carrying coils wound on a ferromagnetic material to produce magnetic fields. The direction of the magnetic field produced by the poles of the ferromagnetic material can be changed by changing the direction of the electric current. This field can be used for changing the magnetic polarities of the recording media (writing information). Chapter 5 discusses the physics of write heads and the materials used for this purpose.

Inductive heads can also be used for reading information, based on Faraday's law, which states that a voltage will be generated in a coil if there is a time-varying flux (magnetic field lines) in its vicinity. When a magnetic disk with information rotates, the field emanating from the recording media bits will produce a time-varying flux, which will lead to a sequence of voltage pulses in the inductive head. These voltage pulses can be used to represent 1s or 0s. Inductive head technology was the prevailing technology for reading information until the early 1990s. However, in order to increase the bit density, the size of the bit cells had to be reduced. Moreover, the $M_r\delta$ (remanent moment-thickness product) also was reduced as technology progressed in order to reduce the medium noise, which resulted in a decrease in magnetic flux from the bits. The inductive heads were not sensitive enough to the increasingly reduced magnetic field from the smaller bits as technology progressed. To address this problem, more advanced read sensors were introduced into the head design. Modern HDDs have heads with two elements: one is a sensor for reading information (similar to an eye when reading a book), and the other is an inductive writer for writing information. Such components where the sensor and writer are integrated are called integrated heads or, simply, heads.

The HDDs used magnetoresistive (MR) heads for some time (early to late 1990s) before switching to the prevailing GMR sensors. Unlike inductive heads, MR and GMR heads work on the basis of change in the resistance of the sensor in the presence of a magnetic field. The GMR sensor is in fact made of several magnetic and nonmagnetic layers. GMR devices make use of the spin-dependent scattering of electrons. Electrons have "up" and "down" spins. When an electric current is passed through a magnetic material, the magnetic orientation of the magnetic material will favor the movement of electrons with a particular spin—up or down. In GMR devices, the magnetic layers can be designed in such a way that the device is more resistive or less resistive to the flow of electrons, depending on the direction of the field sensed by the sensors. Such a change in resistance can be used to define 1 or 0 for digital recording. Although write-head research is mostly limited to the companies that manufacture heads, read-sensor research is carried out widely. This is especially so because read sensors are not only technologically challenging but are also academically interesting. Therefore, this book has two chapters on read sensors: Chapter 6 focuses on the fundamentals of read sensors, and Chapter 7 provides an overview of future research and technologies for read sensors.

1.5 MATERIALS ASPECT OF THE HEAD–DISK INTERFACE

In an HDD, the head flies in close proximity to the media in order to read and write information. The component that carries the read sensor and the write head is called a slider. The slider has air bearings that provide the relevant aerodynamics for flyability at a specific height for which it has been designed. The flying height of the sliders has been reduced over the years to sub-10 nm levels [5]. In recent years, the sliders even comprise a technology called "thermal flying height control." This technology uses a microheater embedded in the slider that can be heated using a current to cause nanometer-level expansion near the reader and writer, allowing the possibility of reducing the flying height to sub-5 nm levels, especially when reading and writing operations are carried out [6]. When the head flies at close proximity to the disk medium, there may be intermittent contacts between the head and disk, which might cause damage to the head and/or hard disk medium, resulting in data loss. In order to minimize the damage involved, the hard disk medium is usually coated with a thin lubricant layer, which among many other advantages provides a way to reduce the friction and wear during sporadic contacts. However, there are many challenges in lubricant technology. Chapter 8 provides a detailed discussion of lubricants.

In addition to the lubricant layer, the hard disk medium also has an overcoat layer, which has been some form of carbon film for several years. The carbon overcoat protects the medium from corrosion and wear. The hardness of the carbon overcoat prevents the medium from wear, and the uniformity of the carbon coating helps the medium from being corroded. The overcoat also provides a surface that is suitable for the lubricant to adhere to. In the past, carbon overcoats were very thick (several hundred nanometers). However, tremendous improvement has been made in carbon overcoat technology, resulting in overcoats with thicknesses of about 2 nm and yet providing superior wear and corrosion protection. For future recording applications, it is necessary to obtain even thinner overcoats as an enabler for smaller magnetic spacing (the spacing between the top magnetic layer of the medium and the bot.tommost magnetic part of the read sensor) [7]. There are several challenges associated with the overcoat. These are covered in Chapter 9.

1.6 TECHNOLOGIES FOR FUTURE HDDS

In addition to the different aspects of technologies related to current and future HDD technology covered in Chapters 3–9, it is also essential to look at some technologies on the horizon that are unique and different from the existing technologies. It is widely accepted that the future HDDs may use heat-assisted magnetic recording technology, patterned media technology, or a combination of the two. The need for these technologies arises from the media trilemma issue to be discussed in detail in Chapter 4. However, in brief, the media trilemma is the difficulty faced in trying to optimize the signal-to-noise ratio (SNR), thermal stability, and writability. The SNR obtained from a recording medium should be kept high for reading information reliably, which requires small grains in the recording medium. However, the small grain size of the medium will cause thermal stability issues, whereby the magnetization of the grains may be susceptible to undergoing thermal reversals leading to data loss. The thermal stability problem may be overcome by using recording media with a high anisotropy constant, but this will result in writability issues. The trilemma is unavoidable at a certain stage, and hence researchers have to look at ways to overcome or delay them. Longitudinal recording technology reached its limit a few years back, and hence in 2006, perpendicular recording technology was introduced. However, perpendicular recording technology in its current form will also reach its limit soon. Therefore, alternative technologies such as heat-assisted (or energy-assisted) recording and patterned media are considered as they provide certain advantages.

In heat- or energy-assisted recording, the recording media material makes use of a high anisotropy material with a high thermal stability even for small grain sizes, thus providing a high SNR. Writing information on a high anisotropy material will not be possible with the existing write-head materials. Heat-assisted recording addresses this problem by making use of thermal energy to minimize the energy barrier for reversal at the time of writing. This may be achieved, for example, by focusing a small beam of laser to locally heat the samples. Since the disk is rotated away from the laser beam after the writing process, and the laser beam is off at times other than the writing time, the high anisotropy constant of the recording media material makes the information stable. Chapter 10 discusses heat-assisted recording technology from a system perspective, and Chapter 11 focuses on the materials aspect of heat-assisted recording. Together, these two chapters provide detailed information on heat- or energy-assisted magnetic recording.

Another unconventional scheme to tackle the media trilemma is to increase the volume (V) of the magnetic unit to tackle thermal stability problems. In conventional recording many magnetic grains store one bit, and the bit boundary is decided mainly by the grain boundary. Therefore, when the volume of the magnetic unit is increased, the bit boundary will be broader, limiting the areal density. However, bit-patterned media recording makes use of well-defined bit boundaries that could be made of non-magnetic materials or voids created by lithography or other procedures. In this case, the grains in the magnetic unit could be exchange coupled strongly to act as a single domain with high thermal stability. In conventional magnetic recording, strong exchange coupling could lead to bit boundaries that are very wide. However, the strong exchange coupling in the magnetic entity of a bit-patterned media does not affect the bit boundary because the bit boundary is defined by the lithography process. Since the volume of the magnetic entity in patterned media for a particular areal density is much larger than that of a grain in conventional recording, thermal stability and writability are not sacrificed. Chapter 12 gives a detailed coverage on patterned media technology. Whether heat- or energy-assisted recording or patterned media recording technology will take over perpendicular recording is not clear at this moment, but it is quite likely that the two technologies may be integrated at certain point of time.

1.7   MEMORY TECHNOLOGIES

HDDs enjoyed unmatched advantages over their competitors for several decades. Because of the high areal density (bits per area) growth achieved in early 2000s, it was possible for HDDs to be used for several applications, such as portable digital music and video players. HDDs with 1-in. disk media were made with compact-flash (CF) and custom-made interfaces, offering higher capacities at cheaper prices than that is possible with semiconductor memories. Apple™ made iPods using such a 1-in. small form factor (SFF) and 1.8-inch HDDs. However, the invasion of HDDs into areas occupied by semiconductor memory did not last long. iPod-Nano MP3 players, featuring semiconductor memories, were released in the next few years as a sign of the threat faced by HDDs. HDDs with 1-in. disk media were phased out in the next few years, and it seems that 1.8-in. HDDs are under threat from solid-state-memory-based storage. Although HDDs still enjoy a significant advantage in 2.5-in. and 3.5-in. disk drives because of their higher capacity and cheaper price, they face a steady threat from solid-state memory devices.

Flash memory—the current competitor for HDDs in certain areas—is also facing technological challenges beyond sub-22 nm scaling. It has been proposed that phase change memory or phase change random access memory (PCRAM) and/or magnetic random access memory (MRAM) may emerge as alternatives for flash memory. It has been proposed that PCRAM can be potentially scaled down to 5 nm, but the question remains as to whether the associated semiconductor technology can also be scaled down to that level. Not to fail in comparison, MRAM also has the potential (based on the thermal stability of FePt materials to be discussed in Chapter 11) to be scaled down to sub-5 nm, but several questions need to be answered before reaching such limits. Nevertheless, the potential scalability of these two candidates makes them good alternatives to flash memory in the long run. As there have been several books on semiconductor-based memories, this book does not cover flash memory. However, two chapters have been dedicated to PCRAM and MRAM. Chapter 13 reviews the developments and challenges of PCRAM, and Chapter 14 provides an overview of the developments and challenges of MRAM.

1.8   SUMMARY

To summarize, the book has been organized as follows: Chapters 2 and 3 discuss the fundamentals of magnetism, magnetic recording, and media technology, and lay the foundation to understand Chapters 4–12. Chapter 4 provides a discussion of the fundamentals and advances in perpendicular recording media technology. Chapter 5 discusses write-head technology, and Chapters 6 and 7 discuss the fundamentals of read technology and the challenges and advances in read technology. Chapters 8 and 9 deal with the head–disk interface aspects of HDDs, focusing on lubricants and overcoats, respectively. Chapters 10–12 concern the emerging technologies for HDDs, namely, heat-assisted magnetic recording and patterned media technology. Chapters 13 and 14 provide an overview of the fundamentals, challenges, and prospects of memory technologies such as PCRAM and MRAM, which are emerging as potential candidates for storage of information.

REFERENCES

1. F. Jorgensen, J. Magn. Magn. Mater. **193**, 1 (1997).
2. M. H. Clark, J. Magn. Magn. Mater. **193**, 8 (1997).
3. S. N. Piramanayagam, J.Appl. Phys. **102**, 011301 (2007).
4. S. Iwasaki and K. Takemura, IEEE Trans. Magn. **11**, 1173 (1975).
5. B. Marchon and T. Olson, IEEE Trans. Magn. **45**(10), 3608 (2009).
6. D. Meyer, P. E. Kupinski, and J. C. Liu, U.S. Patent 5991113 (1999).
7. A. Erdemer and C. Donnet, J. Phys. D Appl. Phys. **39**(18), R311 (2006).

2

FUNDAMENTALS OF MAGNETISM

Shiva Prasad

Indian Institute of Technology, Bombay

S. N. Piramanayagam

Data Storage Institute, Singapore

2.1 INTRODUCTION

Every one of us has found fascination in magnets in our childhood. What made them remarkable was that they showed both powers of attraction and repulsion. The "push" and "pull" exerted by magnets not only make them interesting but also useful in a variety applications. It is hard to imagine a world without magnets. From the fan of an air conditioner to the hard disk drive (HDD) where this chapter was stored while it was being written, many common appliances use magnets. This chapter will provide the fundamentals of magnetism at a beginner's level so that a person who is not familiar with magnetism can learn them and understand most of the other chapters, which assume a familiarity with basic magnetism. Concepts that are relevant to this book are being presented here rather than a comprehensive discussion of magnetism. A reader who wishes to learn more about magnetism might read the following books dedicated to this subject [1–4].

Developments in Data Storage: Materials Perspective, First Edition.
Edited by S. N. Piramanayagam, Tow C. Chong.
© 2012 Institute of Electrical and Electronics Engineers. Published 2012 by John Wiley & Sons, Inc.

2.2 THE ORIGIN OF ATOMIC MAGNETIC MOMENT

Magnets were known to us for ages in the form of permanent magnets. Eventually, they were used as navigation aids in the form of compass needles as magnets tend to align north–south. The end of the magnet which points toward North is termed its north pole, and the one that points toward South is called its south pole. Like poles of two different magnets repel each other, and unlike poles attract each other.

In classical electrodynamics, magnetism is caused by electric current. Two types of electric charges, traditionally termed "positive" and "negative," are found in nature. These charges can also show attraction and repulsion. Similar to magnetic poles, like charges repel whereas unlike charges attract each other. One of the major differences between electric charges and magnetic poles is that the charges can be isolated in the form of positive or negative charges, whereas the same cannot be done with magnetic poles. In any single magnet, if one end is its north pole, the other end is its south pole. If we break a magnet, we create two smaller magnets, each with both a north pole and a south pole. Hence, we often use the term "dipole" for a magnet.

Electric and magnetic forces are best visualized by introducing the concept of electric and magnetic fields. If there is a charge present in an isolated space, we visualize the presence of an electric field in space because of this charge. When any other charge is put in this field, it experiences a force via an interaction through the field. Similarly, if there is a magnetic dipole present in an isolated space, one can visualize the presence of a magnetic field in the space because of this. The concept of the field is basic and is important in higher physics.

When electric charges are set into motion as along a wire, an electric current is constituted. It has been found that magnetic forces are associated with these currents. The simplest magnet can be thought of in the form of a planar coil in which a current flows. Such a coil can be called a magnetic dipole. The north and south poles are situated in the opposite planes of the coil and depend on the current direction. They follow the right-hand rule. When we hold the thumb of the right hand up with all the other fingers folded such that the fingers point in the direction of flow of current in the coil, then the thumb shows the north pole (Fig. 2.1a). The magnetic field produced by this dipole emerges from the axis of the coil from north pole. The concept of magnetic field can be generalized, and one does not have to necessarily talk in terms of a single dipole.

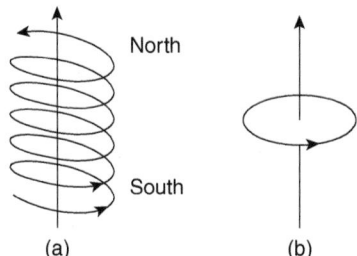

(a) (b)

Figure 2.1. Illustration of current flow in (a) a solenoid and (b) a current-carrying wire, and the magnetic field produced.

For example, we can even imagine a magnetic field from a single straight current-carrying wire. In this case, a magnetic field would be produced around the wire (Fig. 2.1b).

At an atomic level, most important magnetic dipoles are produced by electrons. Quantum mechanically, there are two types of angular momenta associated with electrons. First, the electrons have an orbital angular momentum, which classically can be imagined as their motion around the nucleus, like the motion of Earth around the sun. This orbital angular momentum produces a magnetic field, in a manner similar to that of a current-carrying coil. Another source of atomic magnetism is an inherent property of electrons called "spin." Spin can be imagined in a simplified classical manner as the rotation of a particle (e.g., an electron) around an axis passing through its center of mass, like the motion of the Earth around its own axis. There is also an angular momentum associated with spin that also produces its own field.

As there are many electrons in an atom, the net angular momentum of all the electrons, including spin and orbital contribution, would be responsible for making an atom magnetic. If the net angular momentum of all the electrons is nonzero, it behaves as a tiny magnet, the strength of which would be given by a quantity known as a magnetic moment, which depends on the value of the net angular momentum. Magnetic moment dictates the force between the gradient of magnetic field and the tiny magnet, and is expressed as emu (electromagnetic units) or erg/G in the cgs (centimeter gram second) unit system, and as $A \cdot m^2$ or J/T in SI (Système international) units. If the net angular momentum of all the electrons is zero, it will not have a magnetic moment of its own.

Atomic magnetic moments are measured in units called Bohr magnetons (μ_B); a Bohr magneton is given in terms of fundamental constants. It turns out from quantum mechanics that the orbital angular momentum and its z-components are quantized. The z-direction is taken as the direction of the applied magnetic field. The spin angular momentum has a fixed magnitude, but its z-component can take two values. The magnetic moments associated with these angular momenta will also be thus quantized. A Bohr magneton is approximately equal to (for most practical purposes) the magnitude of the magnetic moment associated with the z-component of the spin angular momentum of electron. It also turns out to be the magnitude of the magnetic moment associated with the lowest nonzero z-component of the orbital angular momentum of an electron.

The quantum states in an atom are given by four quantum numbers: the principal quantum number, n; the orbital quantum number, ℓ; the magnetic quantum number m_l;and the spin quantum number, m_s. Here n has to be a nonzero positive integer. The quantum number ℓ can have a positive integral or a zero value that has to be less than n. The third quantum number, m_l,can take an integral positive, negative, or zero value, but its magnitude has to be smaller or equal to ℓ. The ℓ values are often designated by the letters s, p, d, f, and so on, which means $\ell = 0, 1, 2, 3$, and so on. The fourth quantum number, m_s, known as the spin quantum number, can take only two values, plus half and minus half, independent of other quantum numbers. In an unperturbed hydrogen atom, the total energy is given by the principal quantum number, and the magnitude of the angular momentum of the electron is given by the quantum number ℓ. The magni-

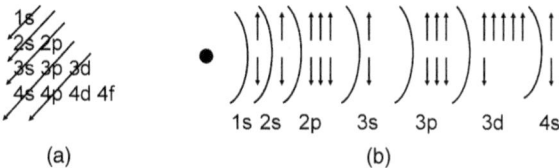

(a)   (b)

Figure 2.2. Schematic electron arrangement in different orbitals of an Fe atom.

tudes of the z-components of the orbital and the spin angular momenta of the electron are given by quantum numbers m_l and m_s, respectively.

In a multielectron atom, the arrangement of electrons follows Pauli's exclusion principle, which states that two electrons cannot occupy the same quantum state. This means that all four quantum numbers cannot be the same for any two electrons in an atom. For example, if we consider a helium atom with two bound electrons at ground state, they will occupy the lowest energy states (1s, i.e., $n = 1$, $\ell = 0$) with $m_l = 0$. They still obey the exclusion principle as the two electrons will have different spin quantum numbers m_s. As we go up in the periodic table looking at atoms with larger atomic numbers, the electrons start occupying states 2s ($n = 2$, $\ell = 0$), 2p ($n = 2$, $\ell = 1$), and so on, normally in the order shown by the arrows in Figure 2.2a. In other words, the shells are filled in the following order: 1s, 2s, 2p, 3s, 3p, 4s, 3d, 4p, and so on. The 3d transition metal atoms, from Sc to Mn, are the important ones for magnetism. In these atoms, electrons fill in the 4s ($n = 4$, $\ell = 0$) state before they fill the 3d ($n = 3$, $\ell = 2$) state. As we can see from the rule mentioned earlier, the 3d state can accommodate a maximum of 10 electrons, with 5 different values of m_l (-2, -1, 0, $+1$, $+2$), each with two different values of m_s. Fe, for example, has an atomic number of 26. An example of electron configuration in an isolated Fe atom is shown in Figure 2.2b. It has the electronic configuration $1s^2, 2s^2, 2p^6, 3s^2, 3p^6, 3d^6, 4s^2$, where the superscript gives the number of electrons for that particular n and l value. It tells that there are 6 electrons with $n = 3$ and $\ell = 2$.

The net angular momentum of an atom depends on the quantum numbers of the various electrons within the atom. A rule known as Hund's rule helps one to find out the net angular momentum of an atom. One also finds that the net angular momentum of electrons would be zero if electrons are occupying all possible m_l and m_s states for a given value of n and ℓ. We often term all the states for a given n and ℓ value as a shell. Hence, we need an unfilled shell in an atom if there is to have a net magnetic moment. As the 3d transition metal atoms have a partially filled 3d shell, they would possess a net angular momentum and thus a net magnetic moment.

2.3   MAGNETISM IN A SOLID

We have seen that the electrons in an isolated atom have a magnetic moment arising from the orbital as well as spin angular momentum. However, once an atom with a magnetic moment is put inside a solid, it is influenced by the field produced by neighboring atoms or ions, as the case may be. This leads to many new effects that must be taken into account before we fully understand the magnetism. Some of these effects are as follows:

1. In 3d transition elements, orbital motion no longer remains a major source of magnetism. The presence of neighboring atoms makes the orbital magnetism more or less ineffective, a phenomenon called quenching of orbital angular momentum. The orbital angular momentum nevertheless does contribute to overall magnetism in the case of rare earth materials. If the orbital angular momentum is quenched, then the magnetic moment of the atom would have to be revaluated by considering spin angular momentum only.

2. Because of the overlap of the wave functions of electrons, the energies of the atomic level are altered. The overlap is most dominant in the outermost shells, involving large quantum number n. The overall result of this interaction can be quite complicated, but in the simplest language, we get bands of allowed energies separated by band gaps instead of distinct energy levels. The electrons in the outer shells are no longer localized on a particular atom but are itinerant. As mentioned earlier, this broadening is most dominant in an outermost shell involving large "n" quantum numbers. If there is a significant broadening of the energy levels of the magnetic shells (i.e., the partially filled shells), the magnetic moment has to be treated in a totally different way as it is no longer localized at the atom. This effect is also quite dominant in 3d transition metals.

3. The magnetic moments of an atom or ion can interact with another either directly or mediated by another nonmagnetic atom through an "exchange interaction." This exchange interaction is purely a quantum mechanical effect and does not have a classical analog. The exchange effect can be present in a way so as to cause the magnetic moments to remain either parallel or antiparallel to each other. This effect is very important as it leads to some of the most widely used magnetic materials.

2.4 MAGNETIC SUSCEPTIBILITY

Within a finite-sized object, the total magnetic moment would depend on the total number of magnetic atoms or ions that it contains in addition to the magnetic moment of the individual atoms/ions and their relative orientation. Two different sizes of objects made of same material will have different moments. Therefore, in order to compare magnetic properties of different materials irrespective of their size, another term, magnetization, is used. Magnetization is the magnetic moment per unit volume of a material, expressed as emu/cm^3 in cgs and A.m^{-1} in SI units, respectively. Another thing that must be considered is that even though a finite material may have a large number of atomic moments, its entire magnitude cannot be measured or observed because the magnetic moments of individual atoms or of regions containing them may point out in different directions (as in paramagnetic materials or in the case of a demagnetized ferromagnetic (FM) material—to be discussed soon), leading to an overall zero magnetization. However, once this material were kept in a magnetic field, there would be in general some alignment of the moments in the direction of the field because this would lower the energy of the system. The result would be an induced magnetization of the material. The actual moment developed would depend not only on the applied magnetic field but also on the exchange interaction between the moments. We define the magnetic susceptibility χ as the ratio of the induced magnetization to the applied field. This quantity is thus a measure of how strong the induced magnetization is for a given magnetic field.

2.5 TYPES OF MAGNETIC MATERIALS

Strictly speaking, magnetic fields affect every solid, the effect being an induced magnetization on the solid. However, the induced magnetization is enhanced if the atoms or ions that form the solid have a permanent magnetic moment and, more so, if there is an exchange coupling between them. We now list some of the important types of magnetic materials, mainly based on their response to magnetic fields and interatomic interaction.

2.5.1 Diamagnetic Materials

Whenever any material is put in a magnetic field, the orbital motion of electrons is affected. This induces a magnetic moment in the material even when the atom has no net magnetic moment. The direction of this induced moment is such that it produces a field outside the material in a direction opposite to the applied field. Materials that exhibit only this kind of magnetic effect are called diamagnetic. If we imagine that a field is being applied on a diamagnetic material placed between the poles of an electromagnet, a north pole will be induced at the end closest to the north pole of the electromagnet, and the induced south pole will be closest to the south pole of the electromagnet. Thus, the material will tend to be repelled by the poles of the electromagnet. Of course, this force in most of the cases would be so small that it might be difficult to observe it. Since the induced magnetization in diamagnetic materials is weak and is opposite to the field direction, the susceptibility of diamagnetic materials is small and is defined as negative (Fig. 2.3a). This weak effect can generally be observed only in those materials where atoms do not have a net magnetic moment. Hence traditionally, only those materials whose atoms do not have a net magnetic moment are called diamagnetic materials.

2.5.2 Paramagnetic Materials

There are many materials which show a small induced moment in the same direction as the applied field. Such materials are called paramagnetic. Hence, if a paramagnetic material is put between the poles of an electromagnet, it would tend to be attracted toward the magnet pole nearer to it with a small force. The susceptibility of paramagnetic material is thus positive (Fig. 2.3b). Materials in which there is an atomic magnetic moment but no exchange interaction between the neighboring spins behave as

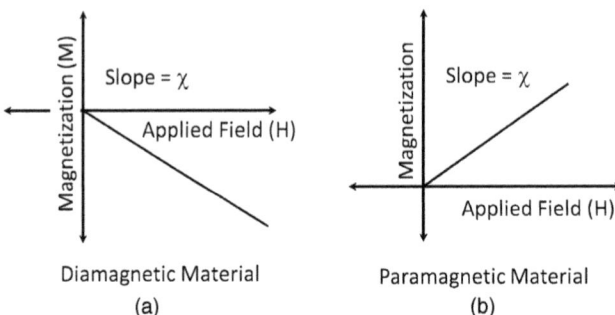

Figure 2.3. Magnetization behavior in (a) diamagnetic and (b) paramagnetic material. The slope of the M-H curve is the susceptibility.

paramagnets. The itinerant electrons in a partially filled band can also show paramagnetism. Several materials, such as Al, Ru, and Mg, are paramagnets.

When an external magnetic field is applied to a paramagnet, magnetic moments of the atoms or the electrons in the band, as the case may be, tend to individually align with it, based on quantum mechanical and statistical considerations. This leads to a net induced magnetization on the material as described before. However, the sample only remains magnetized so long as the field is present. After the removal of the field, thermal effects bring the material back to a state of zero net magnetization. Paramagnetic materials do not have significant applications in bulk as a result. However, thin layers of paramagnetic materials are still used, for example, in magnetic devices such as recording media to reduce exchange coupling between magnetic layers [5, 6].

2.5.3 Magnetically Ordered Materials

The most useful magnetic materials are those with a significant exchange interaction between the magnetic atoms. As mentioned earlier, the exchange interaction can favor both parallel and antiparallel alignments of the moments depending upon the material. If this interaction orders the magnetic moments parallel to each other, then we call such materials ferromagnets and the ordering ferromagnetic (FM). On the other hand, if the exchange interaction makes the magnetic moments order antiparallel to each other, the materials are known as antiferromagnets, and the ordering is called antiferromagnetic (AFM). The interesting aspect of ferromagnets is that magnetic moments remain aligned in them because of the exchange interaction even in the absence of an external magnetic field, resulting in a net magnetic moment. In that sense, the exchange interaction in these materials can be thought of as a strong internal magnetic field. In an antiferromagnet, on the other hand, the magnetic moments are antiparallel owing to exchange interaction, and the material does not have any net magnetic moment in the absence of the field.

There are some compound solids that contain more than one type of magnetic atom or ion, and whose magnetic moments are different. We may then come across a situation where the ordering between these moments is AFM, but their moments do not cancel out completely. These materials behave like ferromagnets but with a smaller effective moment. Such types of materials are known as ferrimagnets. Ferrimagnets in many ways behave like ferromagnets. Most of the discussions in the following sections about ferromagnets would also be applicable to ferrimagnets.

2.6 FERROMAGNETIC MATERIALS

The subsequent sections of this chapter are devoted mainly to discussion of FM materials because many devices and applications make use of them. Most of the permanent magnets are either ferromagnets or ferrimagnets. Loosely speaking, these materials are the ones often referred to as magnetic materials even though there are other types of magnetic materials, as described earlier. Ferromagnets are the materials that can remain magnetized even in the absence of an external magnetic field. Much before the process of exchange interaction was identified through quantum mechanics, Pierre-Ernest Weiss had formulated his theory of magnetism. According to him, FM materials possess an internal field that helps the magnetic moments to align parallel to each other. Thus FM materials are spontaneously magnetized. However, it is also possible to demagnetize a ferromagnet, a process by which the net moment is reduced to zero. To explain this, Weiss put forward the idea of magnetic domains. Magnetic domains, according to Weiss, could be spontaneously magnetized. However, it would be possible to align them in a way so that the material as a whole had a net magnetic moment of zero. Now these magnetic domains can be experimentally observed, and we know them to be a reality. In the following sections, we shall discuss some of the important aspects of FM materials. We shall also discuss magnetic domains in detail in a later section.

2.7 HYSTERESIS LOOPS

In materials other than ferrimagnetic or FM materials, induced magnetization shows a linear behavior with respect to the normal applied magnetic fields. Ferrimagnetic and FM materials, on the other hand, show hysteresis. In general, hysteresis is observed owing to the presence of energy barriers in a magnetic system and the need to overcome them during the magnetization or demagnetization processes. The way a system undergoes the magnetization/demagnetization process varies depending on the microstructure, size and shape, and various energies and is called a magnetization reversal mechanism. Let us postpone discussion of the magnetization reversal mechanism to a later section and focus our attention for a while on the parameters that we can obtain from the hysteresis loop.

An example of a hysteresis loop for an FM sample is shown in Figure 2.4. For an as-prepared sample that has never been placed in an external field or for a sample in a demagnetized state, the net magnetization will be zero (represented by O—the origin of the M-H plot). When a magnetic field (H) is applied in the positive direction, the magnetization (M) increases with the magnetic field and attains saturation. It may be noticed that the increase in the initial magnetization curve is nonlinear. Magnetization

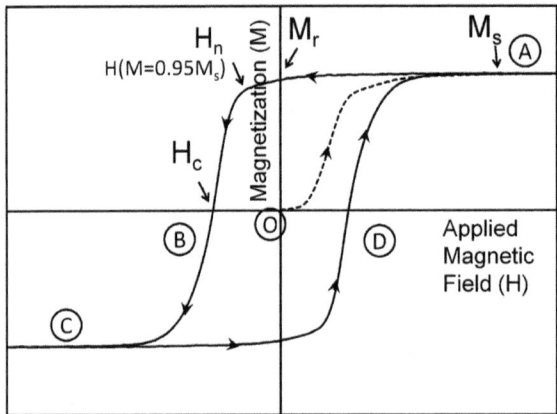

Figure 2.4. Hysteresis loop of a ferromagnetic sample and the various parameters that can be obtained from it. The dotted line shows the virgin (or) initial curve.

at a high field, observed at the saturated point (marked as A), is called saturation magnetization (M_s). In some materials, we see a small positive slope even at high fields. In such cases, the M_s is measured by extrapolating M to H = 0 and is called spontaneous magnetization.

When the field is reduced after saturation, magnetization does not follow the initial magnetization curve but goes via a different path (ABC), as shown in Figure 2.4. When the field is reduced to zero, the sample will still have a residual magnetization in the applied field direction, which is called remanent magnetization (M_r). The ratio M_r/M_s is called remanent squareness or simply, squareness (S). An S value of close to one indicates that the majority of the magnetic material retains its magnetization even after removing the magnetic field. An S value close to zero indicates that most of the magnetic material did not retain its magnetization after the removal of the applied field. For certain applications, such as a magnetic recording medium, it is good to have S close to one; it is, however, necessary to consider many other aspects as will be discussed in the chapters describing recording media. For certain applications, for example, transformers, electromagnets, and so on, an S close to zero is preferred as the core of the transformer/electromagnet should not retain a residual magnetic field.

When the field is reduced further to negative values (increasing magnitude but in the opposite direction to that of the saturating field), magnetization decreases and reaches zero at a certain field, called a coercive field. Coercivity (H_c) is a measure of the field needed to demagnetize a material. The value of H_c is an important parameter, and its desired value again depends on the application. Another useful parameter that can be measured from the hysteresis loop is called coercive squareness, S*, which is defined as $S^* = 1 - (M_r/(H_c(dM/dH)_{H=H_c})$. S* is a measure of exchange coupling in systems that consist of exchanged decoupled magnetic grains or units. In most practical cases, a high S* would mean stronger exchange coupling, and a low S* would mean a system where the magnetic units are less coupled to each other with a distribution in aniosotropy, and so on, although care needs to be taken in interpreting the results. Further application of the negative field reduces the magnetization to negative values, and at larger values of negative field, saturation is attained in the negative direction. When the field is swept from negative to positive values, magnetization changes direction from the negative to the positive direction, as shown in Figure 2.4. The path of this curve (CDA) almost mirrors that in the other direction (ABC) in most materials except in some special materials that have an exchange bias (to be discussed later).

2.8 HARD AND SOFT MAGNETIC MATERIALS

Based on the magnetization response to an applied field, FM materials can be classified broadly into two categories: soft and hard. The definition "soft" or "hard" is not related to their mechanical properties but to their magnetic properties. Soft magnetic materials are those that can be saturated or demagnetized with weaker magnetic fields. Their magnetization loop as a function of magnetic field would indicate that they have a low coercivity and a low residual magnetization, and the area occupied by the M-H loop is smaller. Commonly known materials such as Fe, steel, and permalloy belong to this category. Since soft magnetic materials have a high magnetization and consume relatively less energy in the magnetization and demagnetization cycles, they are used in high-frequency applications, in transformers, electromagnets, and write heads. For high-frequency applications, in addition to the soft magnetic property, minimizing losses from eddy currents is an important issue. Minimization of eddy currents is achieved using lamination or by using insulating magnetic materials such as ferrites. Since soft magnetic materials have a very low M_r, they do not generate a magnetic field around them. Moreover, their low coercivity means that they can easily be demagnetized. In this sense, the soft magnetic materials are not "permanent" magnets.

Hard magnetic materials, on the other hand, have a higher coercivity and relatively higher remanence. Therefore, saturating or demagnetizing hard magnetic materials requires a stronger magnetic field. Because of higher remanence, they are able to generate a significant magnetic field around them. In general, hard or permanent magnets are the magnets for laypersons because of their ability to retain magnetization and produce a magnetic field. Therefore, hard magnetic materials are used as permanent magnets in several applications, such as motors, speakers, refridgerator magnets, and so on. The hysteresis loops of hard magnetic materials have a larger area. The energy product, which is the maximum value of B.H in the second quadrant of the hysteresis loop and commonly expressed in G.Oe, is a measure of the hardness of a ferromagnet. Materials such as Barium or Strontium ferrites, AlNiCo, were used as permanent magnets in the past. In the last two decades, SmCo and NdFeB, which have much larger energy products, have emerged as hard magnets [7]. For such application as recording media, the hard magnetic property is a basic requirement but is not a sufficient requirement as will be discussed in later chapters.

2.9   MAGNETIZATION AND CURIE TEMPERATURE

We have discussed in an earlier section that we can saturate the magnetization of an FM sample by applying a large enough magnetic field. This saturation amounts to a near complete alignment of all the domains and thus all the magnetic moment contained in the sample in the direction of the magnetic field. This alignment becomes more and more complete as we lower the temperature and thus minimize thermal effects. Hence at very low temperatures, the net M_s we observe can be calculated from the individual moments of the atom. In the case of ferrimagnets, one has also to take into consideration the coupling. Still the magnetization can be evaluated from the magnetic moment of one unit cell. When one carries out such an exercise, one finds that the experimental and theoretical values of magnetic moment for 3d transition metals do not match. For example, if we apply Hund's rule and assume that orbital angular momentum is quenched, Fe, Co, and Ni atoms should have magnetic moments of 4, 3, and 2 μ_B, respectively. However, the measured values of M_s at 0 K turns out to be 2.2, 1.7, and 0.6 μ_B only, which are surprisingly non-integral. In case of FM oxides, which are insulating, the moment however indeed turns out to be the one expected. This difference is because in Fe, Co, and Ni metals, there is significant broadening of the 3d band, which makes these electrons itinerant. Magnetic moment in the presence of itinerant electrons has to be calculated from a band model to match the experimental results.

If a magnetically ordered material is heated, it loses its order at a particular temperature. This is because thermal energy starts dominating the exchange energy and destroys the order. In the case of an AFM material, this temperature is known as Néel temperature (T_N). For an FM material, this temperature is known as Curie temperature (T_C). Above these temperatures, the material behaves like a paramagnet.

2.10   VARIOUS ENERGIES INSIDE MAGNETIC MATERIAL

In this section we describe some of the energies involved in a magnetic material. It is quite important to know about these energies, as this knowledge will help to understand M-H loops, magnetic domains, and the behavior in general of magnetic materials.

2.10.1   Magnetostatic Energy

Magnetostatic energy is related to the presence of free poles or magnetic charges. If we were to magnetize a bar lengthwise (see Fig. 2.5a), poles would be induced at its ends. These poles would generate a field in space. Overall this magnetizing phenomenon would require an expenditure of energy, which can be understood in the following manner. Let us imagine a permanent magnet with a very low magnetization. This magnet would produce a small magnetic field near it. If we wanted to increase this field, one of the ways to do it would be to place another permanent magnet near the first magnet so that the north poles of the two magnets were close to each other and so were the south poles (Fig. 2.5b). But it would not be easy to bring a north pole closer to another north pole as like poles repel each other. Similarly a south pole repels a south

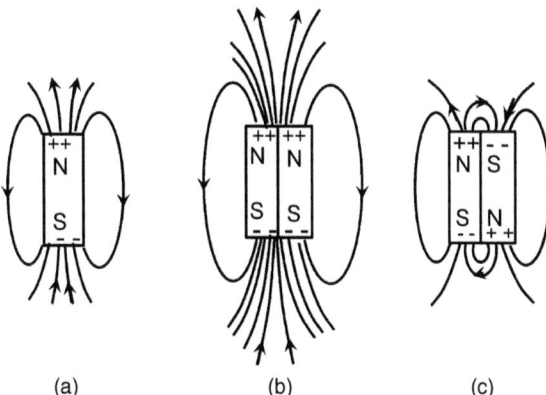

(a)   (b)   (c)

Figure 2.5. Illustration of magnetic fields from (a) single bar magnet, (b) two bar magnets with the like poles facing each other, and (c) two bar magnets with unlike poles facing each other.

pole. Hence, we will have to spend energy to bring these poles closer together and thus intensify the magnetic field. On the other hand, if we had placed the second magnet close to the first such that the north pole was near to the south pole, less energy would be spent. However, the field in the surrounding region would decrease (Fig. 2.5c). The above example demonstrates that in order to generate a field in space we must spend energy. We call this energy the magnetostatic energy associated with the field. This energy is less when the field generated in space is minimized.

2.10.2   Exchange Energy

As discussed earlier, the exchange interaction in an FM material tries to keep the directions of the atomic moments parallel to each other. Hence, if the magnetic moments of neighboring atoms are made to change their directions with respect to each other, it has to be at the cost of the exchange energy. In order to minimize expended energy, magnetic moments tend not to change the direction with respect to each other, and when they do change direction, they do it in a less abrupt manner.

2.10.3   Magnetic Anisotropy

Magnetic anisotropy refers to the differences in the magnetic properties of a material when measured along different axes. Many magnetic materials exhibit one or other form of anisotropy. The ability of a material to magnetize more easily in one direction than another is called magnetic anisotropy. The easy axis (or easy direction) is the one in which the magnetic saturation can be achieved with the smallest applied magnetic field in comparison to any other axis or direction. In the hard axis or direction, the largest field is needed to saturate the magnetic material. Moreover, the easy axis (or direction) retains more magnetization than the hard direction, in general, at remanence. This section will briefly highlight the different forms of anisotropy found in magnetic materials.

2.10.3.1 Magnetocrystalline Anisotropy. Any crystal by its own nature is anisotropic. In the simplest terms, if we move along any two arbitrary directions in a crystal, the distance between the atoms we encounter will be different. For example, consider a simple cubic structure of lattice constant "a." If we move along the [100] direction (i.e., along the cube edge), we will find the distance between lattice points as "a." On the other hand, if we move along the [111] direction (i.e., along the body diagonal), we will encounter points after distance "$\sqrt{3}$ a." Obviously, the physical properties along these two directions are also expected to be different. This applies to its magnetic properties also. We find that certain crystallographic directions become easy and others hard in a crystal.

In the case of Fe (body centered cubic structure), [100] is an easy direction, and [111] is hard. Of course we know that because of crystal symmetry, there are six equivalent <100> directions in a cubic crystal; therefore, in Fe all six of these would be easy directions. Similarly all eight equivalent <111> directions would be hard in Fe. In Ni, the situation is the opposite, where <111> directions are easy and <100> directions are hard.

One of the materials whose crystalline anisotropy is often put to use is hexagonal close packed Co. In Co, it is easier to magnetize the material along the c-axis than in any other direction. As there are only two equivalent c-directions (c and opposite to c) or a single axis, such a material is called a uniaxial material. The crystal anisotropy energy density E_a, for a uniaxial crystal material, depends on the angle θ between the direction of the magnetization and the c-axis, and is expressed by the equation,

$$E_a = K_1 \sin^2 \theta + K_2 \sin^4 \theta + \cdots, \tag{2.1}$$

where K_n ($n = 1, 2, \ldots$) represent the anisotropy constants. The contributions arising from K_2 and other higher order terms are usually small. Therefore, the strength of the magnetocrystalline anisotropy is expressed mainly by the magnitude of the anisotropy constant, K_1, in erg/cm³(cgs) or J/m³(SI). For uniaxial material, the symbols K_u or K_{u1} is often used instead of K_1. The magnetocrystalline anisotropy energy of a magnetic element with a volume V is proportional to $K_u V$ and it determines the energy spent, in general, to reverse the magnetization from one easy direction to the other.

2.10.3.2 Shape Anisotropy. As the name suggests, this is an anisotropy that is related to the shape of the sample. In a spherical sample, all the directions are equivalent. So if we try to magnetize a sphere, it can be magnetized with equal ease or difficulty in any direction, assuming no other anisotropy. But that is not the case if, for example, the sample is an ellipsoid with three axes of unequal length. In such a case, we will find that it is easy to magnetize it along the longest axis and most difficult to magnetize along the shortest axis.

Shape anisotropy is related to the demagnetization field, which can be explained as follows. Consider an ellipsoidal-shaped FM material that has been magnetized along the largest axis by an application of the external field, and the field has been removed after magnetization (Fig. 2.6). As the ellipsoid is magnetized, it implies that it has poles (or magnetic charges) at the two ends. The magnetization lies in the direction of its

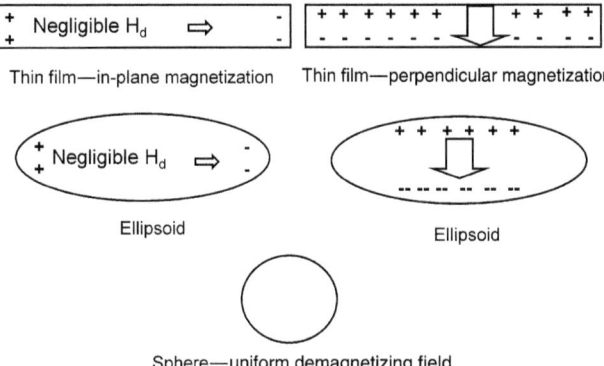

Sphere—uniform demagnetizing field

Figure 2.6. An illustration of demagnetizing fields from samples of different shapes magnetized in different configurations (bigger arrow represents a stronger demagnetizing field). The + and − signs indicate north and south poles, respectively.

south pole to its north pole inside the magnetic material. On the other hand, the poles on the ellipsoid would create their own field, which would be directed from its north pole to its south pole—both inside and outside it. As we can see clearly, inside the ellipsoid, this field would be in a direction opposite to that of magnetization and hence would try to demagnetize the ellipsoid.

The demagnetizing field for an arbitrarily shaped sample can be quite complex and most of the time is nonuniform. It is only for ellipsoidal-shaped samples that the demagnetizing field turns out to be uniform. One of the most common shapes of samples used in magnetic recording technology is thin films. This unfortunately is not a special case ellipsoid. However, if we assume that the thickness of the film is very small in comparison to other dimensions, we will be able to neglect the nonuniformity of the fields. In such a case, the demagnetizing field is zero in the direction of film plane, and it would be equal to magnetization along the normal to the film plane. In the absence of any other anisotropy, this would mean that magnetizing the sample in the plane of the film is easier than along the film-normal, just because of shape anisotropy. This is because as we try to magnetize the sample normal to the plane, the field required would be much larger since the induced poles would try to demagnetize the film. Figure 2.6 shows the directions where the demagnetization field would be the strongest for different cases. In the case of thin films, the demagnetizing field will be the strongest (shown by bigger arrows) when the magnetization is oriented perpendicular to the film-plane as compared to the case of in-plane magnetization. However, for a sphere, the demagnetizing field is uniform in all the directions.

It is interesting to note that shape anisotropy was the first to be exploited in the earlier generations of several devices or applications. For example, before the advent of stronger permanent magnets, such as AlNiCo, SmCo, or NdFeB, horseshoe magnets—which made use of shape anisotropy to retain magnetism—were used as permanent magnets. Similarly, magnetic recording media of the earlier days—whether in HDDs or tape recording—used magnetic particles in a needle shape to achieve shape anisotropy.

2.10.3.3 Interface Anisotropy. Interface anisotropy arises whenever there is an interface between two materials. The simplest interface is a magnetic material/nonmagnetic material interface. In such a case we call this form of anisotropy surface anisotropy. This anisotropy affects the surface atoms, as there is a change in their environment. In a bulk material, this anisotropy is hardly effective as the relative number of atoms affected by the surface effect is small. However, in the case of thin films, this anisotropy can play an important role. In many multilayered films, the changed environment of the atoms at the interface between two materials can give rise to strong interface anisotropy. This interface anisotropy has been used in multilayers with small film thicknesses effectively to create an overall anisotropy, which otherwise would not be present in the bulk materials. Co/Pd or Co/Pt multilayers are examples of such materials where a perpendicular magnetic anisotropy can be developed for thin layers of Co and Pd (or Pt) [8–10].

There is a special type of interfacial anisotropy, when certain FM and AFM materials are deposited one on top of the other. The resulting material is called an exchange biased film. In this material, a shift in the hysteresis loop of the FM material is seen when the material is cooled under a magnetic field from a temperature above the T_N of the antiferromagnet to a temperature below it. The exchange bias is also called "unidirectional anisotropy" because the magnetization will tend to point out in only one direction (and not along one axis as in uniaxial hexagonal materials). Unidirectional anisotropy and exchange bias can be qualitatively understood by assuming an exchange interaction at the FM/AFM interface. When materials with FM/AFM interfaces are cooled through the T_N of the AFM material, anisotropy is induced in the FM layer, especially when the T_C of the FM layer is higher than T_N. When a field is applied in the temperature range $T_N < T < T_C$, the FM spins align with the field, and the AFM spins remain random. When the system is cooled below T_N, in the presence of the field, the AFM spins next to the FM spins align in the same direction as those of the FM due to FM interaction. As a result of ordering below T_N, the other spin planes in the AFM will align antiferromagnetically so as to produce zero net magnetization. In the case of such structures, an extra field is needed to overcome the interfacial coupling, and hence the field needed to reverse the magnetization of the FM layer to the opposite direction (of the AFM layer closest to the interface) will be larger. On the other hand, no external field is necessary to keep the FM layer aligned in the direction of the interfacial AFM moment. Therefore, the FM spins have only one stable configuration and so demonstrate unidirectional anisotropy.

Figure 2.7 illustrates exchange bias where the field direction during the cooling process in Figure 2.7a and b are different. The easy direction of the FM layer lies along the applied field direction. It can be noticed that in both cases, the remanence magnetization is oriented only in one particular direction (determined by the applied field direction during the cooling process). This phenomenon has been exploited in several applications of magnetic recording, such as read sensors and the soft underlayer of perpendicular media. In read sensors of HDDs, for example, there are two FM layers. It is necessary to keep one layer fixed and let the other layer respond to the field coming from the recording media. Exchange bias is very helpful to fix or "pin" an FM layer in one particular direction (as in Fig. 2.7). In perpendicular media, exchange bias may be

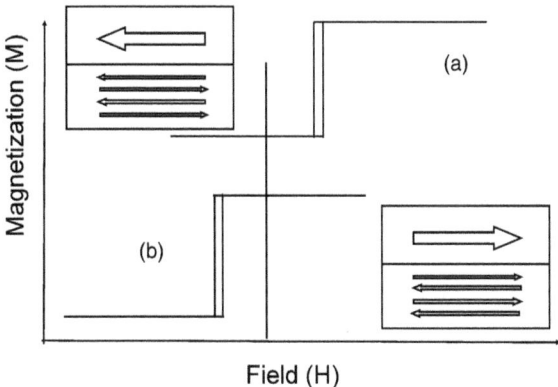

Figure 2.7. Exchange bias of a ferromagnetic film in two configurations. The offset of the hysteresis loop from the center (H = 0) depends on the field direction during the cooling process.

used to keep the magnetization of the soft underlayer in one direction so as to eliminate the formation of domains and thus stray fields [5, 11].

2.10.3.4 Growth-Induced Anisotropy. There is some anisotropy which is observed only when a thin-film material is grown using a particular method. This type of anisotropy is called growth-induced anisotropy. The origin of this anisotropy is not fully understood in many cases, but is believed to be related to the local arrangement of atoms. One of the classical cases of observation of this anisotropy was in structurally amorphous GdCo thin films, when deposited using sputtering. The garnet films deposited using liquid-phase epitaxy also showed a uniaxial anisotropy large enough to support magnetic bubbles.

2.11 MAGNETIC DOMAINS

The formation of magnetic domains is due to energy minimization. In an FM material, the magnetic moments of neighboring atoms would normally be aligned parallel to each other if exchange energy were the only energy playing a role. However, if this happens for the entire sample, free poles will be formed at the surface, which would mean larger magnetostatic energy (Fig. 2.8a). As the system tends to be at the state of lowest magnetic energy, minimization of the energy is achieved by the formation of domains. Figure 2.8b is an illustrative example of this phenomenon of minimizing magnetostatic energy. In short, magnetic domains are regions within which the directions of the neighboring magnetic moments are parallel. However, the magnetizations of different domains are oriented in different directions, thus reducing the magnetic energy. The magnetostatic energy can be minimized if no free poles are formed. Such domains are called closure domains.

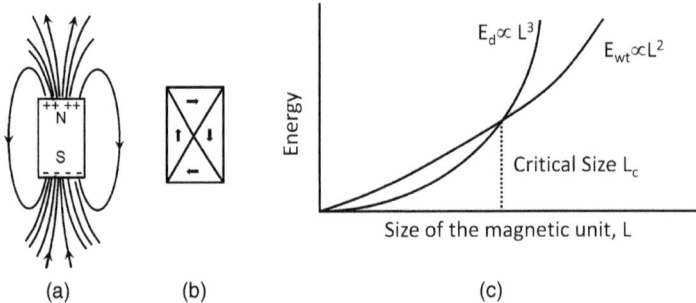

Figure 2.8. Illustration of (a) magnetized bar magnet and the field emanating from it, (b) the formation of a closure domain which minimizes the field, and (c) the dependence of magnetostatic energy and the domain wall energy as a function of lateral size, L, of a magnetic particle.

Although the formation of domains in a system reduces the magnetostatic energy, domain formation also results in the creation of an angle between the magnetic moments of the neighboring atoms as we move from one domain to another. As this change of magnetization works against the exchange forces, there will be a resultant increase in the energy of the system. In order to spend the least energy for the transition, the magnetic moments would change their directions only gradually. Thus, the change of direction of the magnetic moment from one domain to another will take place across many lattice constants. This transition region of atomic moments from one domain to another is referred to as a domain wall.

Domain wall formation increases the energy of the magnetic system, nevertheless, as the neighboring spins within a domain wall are oriented at an angle, which results in an increase in the exchange energy. Exchange energy tends to make the domain walls bigger as that will help in minimizing the energy. Moreover, the relative orientation of the spin with respect to the anisotropy direction (e.g., magnetocrystalline anisotropy) increases the anisotropy energy and is hence the second component of domain wall energy. The anisotropy component tends to reduce the thickness of the domain wall as anisotropy energy will be minimal if only a few spins are away from the easy direction. In general, the domain wall width is decided based on the balance between these two quantities.

Magnetic anisotropy can also play an important role in deciding the directions of the orientation of magnetic moments within a domain. If the magnetic anisotropy is very large, the magnetization in domains may point out only along the easy directions.

One special case of interest for many applications is that of small magnetic particles. If the particle size is very small, it tends to remain in a fully magnetized state (or a single domain state). This is because if domains have to form within the particle, the width of the wall has to be still smaller in size, which will be possible only by creating a large angle between the moments. This will become unfavorable from the exchange energy point of view. The above point can be explained using the graph shown

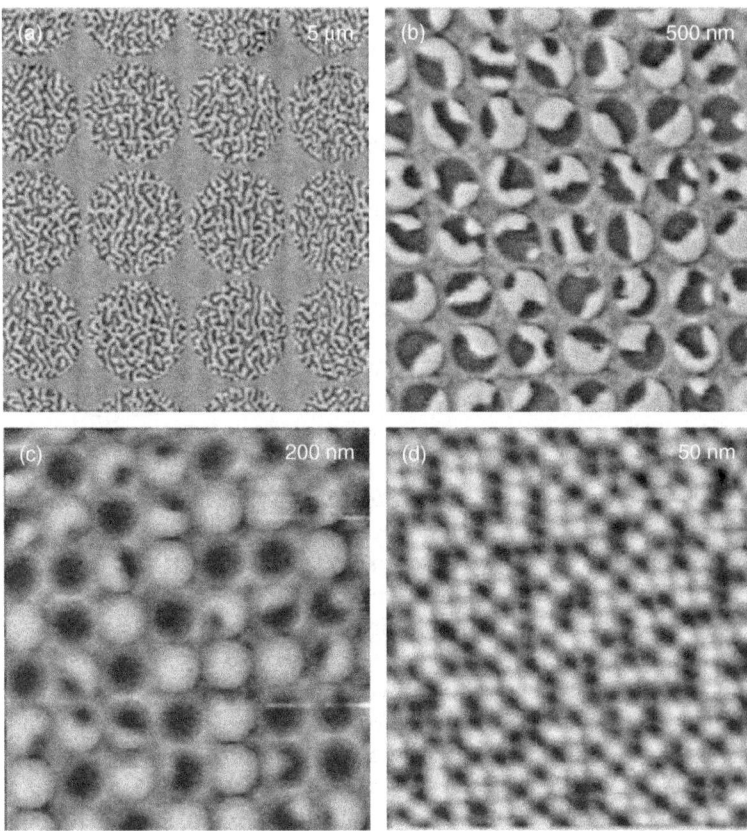

Figure 2.9. Magnetic force microscopy images of patterned Co/Pd multilayers with different lateral dimensions: (a)–(c) dots with a diameter greater than 50 nm show multidomains; (d) dots with a diameter of 50 nm show single domain. (Reprinted figure with permission from T. Thomson, J. Hu, and B. D. Terris, *Phys. Rev. Lett.* **96**, 257204 (2006). Copyright (2006) The American Physical Society.)

in Figure 2.8c, which shows the magnetostatic energy and domain wall energy as a function of the lateral size of a magnetic particle, L, in a cubic shape (for example). Magnetostatic energy scales with L^3, and domain wall energy scales as L^2. As a result, for smaller sizes L, the magnetic domains will be at single domain states. For sizes exceeding this critical size, magnetic domain formation will be favored. Figure 2.9 shows an example of domain formation in magnetic dots at different sizes fabricated using lithographic processes. The circled regions are magnetic, and the regions surrounding the dots are nonmagnetic. The black-and-white contrast indicates the magnetic flux coming out of the sample (north pole or south pole). The presence of both black and white regions inside the dot indicates the presence of magnetic domains. It can be noticed that the multidomain states are observed for feature sizes of 200 nm or larger.

However, when feature sizes are smaller (50 nm), the dots have a single domain structure (showing either black or white in the image) [12].

2.12 MAGNETIZATION PROCESSES

In Section 2.7, we learned that FM materials exhibit hysteresis. The mechanism behind the change of magnetization from one direction to the other in the presence of a magnetic field depends on the way the material was prepared. It is called a reversal mechanism, and understanding it is important in choosing a material for a specific application. This section will briefly discuss some reversal mechanisms.

As discussed earlier, magnetic materials may form domains if the energy spent in forming domain walls (domain wall energy) is less than the energy minimized in other ways (e.g., in the form of magnetostatic energy). In such multidomain materials, domain wall motion or domain wall pinning are the common magnetization mechanisms. When a multidomain sample is saturated, it contains only a single domain, the magnetization of which points out only along one direction. When such a sample is placed in a reversed magnetic field, nucleation of reversed domains occurs. When the reversal field increases further, the domain wall of the nucleated region may be swept away until it gets located in a position with a local minimum in energy state. Further increase in reversal field is needed to move the domain wall from such positions until the magnetization of the whole specimen is reversed. This process whereby the domain wall moves to accomplish the magnetization reversal is called the domain wall motion mechanism. Domain wall pinning occurs when the domain wall is pinned at a few sites. In the absence of a magnetic field, the domain wall is straight, and when a field is applied, the domain wall bulges until the applied field is strong enough to release the domain wall from the pinning sites. A domain-wall-related reversal mechanism occurs in materials where the whole of the material is exchange coupled strongly, such as an evaporated continuous thin film. Recording media of the earlier generations of thin-film media were of this type. They provided larger signals when the hard disk technology made a switch from particulate media to thin-film media. However, the drawback of materials with such a reversal mechanism is that the position of the domain walls cannot be precisely controlled, especially for applications in magnetic recording where the bit-to-bit transitions need to be controlled precisely [13].

If an FM material has many particles or grains that are single domains or contains only immobile domain walls, it can be magnetized or demagnetized only by rotation of the domain magnetization. Rotation of magnetization in a single-domain particle with a uniaxial anisotropy has been treated adequately by Stoner–Wolhfarth's model. According to this model, the energy barrier for magnetization reversal of such a particle with uniaxial anisotropy is proportional to the anisotropy constant K_u, and hence reversal occurs mainly at the anisotropy field, $H_k = 2K_u/M$. When the applied field is lower than H_k, the magnetization undergoes reversible rotation, and for field values larger than H_k, the magnetization overcomes the energy barrier and undergoes irreversible rotation. This theory, developed in the 1950s, provided a direction for the permanent magnet industry for choosing suitable materials and methods to improve the energy product. This theory is also quite handy to treat the particulate media, where the magnetic particles are isolated from each other and their reversals happen independently of each other. In polycrystalline materials such as the recording media of HDDs also, the magnetization of the grains follows this reversal mechanism although there are additional effects arising from the neighboring grains and the interaction between the grains. In magnetic recording, coherent rotation has been the preferred mechanism since the magnetization can be reversed more precisely at the desired bit boundary locations than is possible with domain wall mechanisms. Advance media of current hard disk products (as of year 2011) may not undergo coherent rotation. This is discussed in Chapter 4.

2.13 TIME-DEPENDENT EFFECTS

In the previous sections, we learned that a single domain particle reverses by coherent rotation and that the reversal happens at the anisotropy field, H_k. However, it was discovered several decades back that the switching field of a collection of magnetic particles depends upon the timescale of the applied reversal field [14]. This has been explained as arising from thermally induced magnetization reversals and is explained below.

The probability, P, for not reversing the magnetization, against the thermally induced reversals at temperature, T, is given by Néel–Arrhenius formulation as

$$P = \exp(-rt), \tag{2.2}$$

where t is the time, $r = \tau^{-1} = f_0 \exp(-E_B/k_B T)$ represents an inverse time constant, and E_B $(=K_u V(1 - H/H_0))$ is the energy barrier for the reversal of magnetization of a magnetic grain (as in a recording medium with segregated grain structure, for example). f_0 is called thermal attempt frequency, k_B is Boltzmann's constant, K_u is the anisotropy constant, V is the volume of the entity (particle or grain), H is the applied field, and H_0 is the switching field [15]. It has been reported that the H_0 in a collection of particles $(\sim K_u/M_s)$ is roughly half of the anisotropy field H_k of an individual particle $(\sim 2K_u/M_s)$. Alternatively, H_0 can be considered equivalent to the coercivity of a specimen measured at absolute zero.

Due to thermal agitation, the magnetization of a group of magnetic grains or entities decays as

$$m(t) = m_0[2\exp(-rt) - 1]. \tag{2.3}$$

Although an exponential decay of magnetization should be observed, the observed behavior may be different owing to the distribution in the size, shape, and composition of the magnetic grains or entitites in a system. Figure 2.10 is an example of magnetization decay in a recording media in the absence of an external magnetic field. It can be noticed that the magnetization decays as a function of time. This effect arises from thermal effects in particles with a smaller volume V, or in particles with a smaller anisotropy constant K_u, or both. The implication of this in a recording medium is that some FM grains that have a low $K_u V/k_B T$ may switch their magnetization, leading to

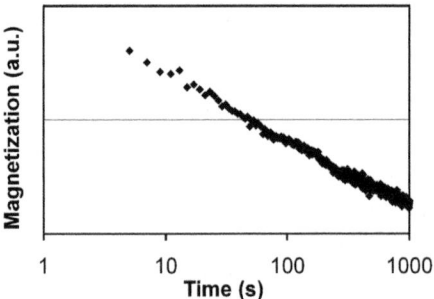

Figure 2.10. The magnetization decay of a thin polycrystalline magnetic film. The decay was observed without the application of an external magnetic field.

data loss. For preventing data loss for 10 years of storage life, a value of $K_u V/k_B T$ greater than 60 is preferred.

Based on the thermal effects discussed above, Sharrock has derived an expression for the time-dependent coercivity as

$$H_c(t) = H_0\{1 - [(k_B T/K_u V)\ln(\beta t)]^n\},\qquad(2.4)$$

where β and n are constants [16]. For a proper choice of these constants, information about H_0 and $K_u V/k_B T$ can be obtained by fitting the time-dependent coercivity. This equation has been quite extensively used for understanding the thermal stability of the magnetic particles/grains encountered in magnetic recording. This equation indicates that for a sufficiently smaller duration of applied field—such as a few nanoseconds, as is the case with hard disk magnetic recording—the switching field will be much larger than it is when the field is applied for a longer duration, say a few seconds. This time-dependence effect has a significant implication for magnetic recording: For example, a recording medium may exhibit a coercivity of 15 kOe when the timescale of the applied field is around 10 ns (as in the recording process of an HDD). Such a high switching field at smaller timescales indicates the need for a write head with stronger write fields. The same medium may exhibit a coercivity of 2 kOe when extrapolated to a timescale of 10 years, which is the minimum storage life. Such a low switching field along a longer timescale indicates that the switching field may be too small to hold the magnetization intact, resulting in data loss. Although time-dependent magnetization is illustrated here using a recording medium as an example, the effects will be different in different applications.

2.14 MAGNETIC CHARACTERIZATION TECHNIQUES FOR DATA STORAGE

Although the hysteresis loop is one of the major measurements that needs to be carried out to understand the properties of magnetic materials such as magnetic recording media, several other measurements have been used to characterize recording media, and this section briefly highlights some of them.

Direct current demagnetization (DCD) magnetization curves are useful in obtaining the remanent coercivity of magnetic systems. In DCD measurements, the film is saturated in one direction, a reverse field, H_r, is applied, and the value of M_r (magnetization in the absence of field) is noted using a magnetometric technique such as a vibrating sample magnetometer (VSM) or alternating gradient force magnetometer (AGM or AGFM). Several values of M_r are taken for different reversal fields (with or without saturating again) and are plotted as a function of H_r. The field, H_{cr}, at which $M_r = 0$, is called remanent coercivity. The difference between coercivity and remanent coercivity is that the reversible components of magnetization play no role in H_{cr}. Moreover, DCD measurements mimic a magnetic recording system closely—where the field is applied by the head and removed, and reading is taken at remanence state (in the absence of a field). The remanent coercivity can also be measured at different timescales, and the values fitted to Sharrock's equation to obtain the thermal stability factor, K_uV/k_BT.

The isothermal remanence magnetization (IRM) curve is also a plot of M_r versus H, but in this case, M_r is measured after alternating-current (AC) demagnetizing the sample for fields increasing from 0 to a finite value. Although much information cannot be obtained from IRM, DCD and IRM together can provide useful information about exchange coupling from a parameter called ΔM, defined as follows:

$$\Delta M(H) = M_d(H) - [1 - 2M_i(H)], \qquad (2.5)$$

where M_d and M_i represent the values of remanent magnetic moments obtained from DCD and IRM measurements, respectively [17]. The presence of a positive peak in the ΔM curve usually indicates strong exchange coupling, and a negative peak indicates the absence of exchange coupling and the presence of a magnetostatic coupling. However, this method is not free from ambiguities and artifacts, and therefore, care needs to be taken during the interpretation of the results.

Although many parameters such as M_r and H_c can be measured using a VSM or AGM, these methods are destructive, and the sample has to be cut to fit into the tools. At manufacturing sites, it is desirable to make these measurements without cutting the samples. As will be seen in Chapter 3, the signal from the recorded bits is proportional to $M_r\delta$, where δ is the thickness. The remanent coercivity, H_{cr}, determines the ability to store the information. Therefore, it is essential to monitor these values regularly and also to check the uniformity of these values over several areas of a disk. In the case of longitudinal recording, a device called a remanent moment magnetometer (RMM) has been used to achieve this purpose. This device mimics and scales the HDD operation at relatively lower speeds of disk rotation and larger dimensions of written bits. The signal from the larger bits can be read using a Hall sensor and converted to a signal, and the plot of the signal as a function of the applied field can give H_{cr}. Such systems can also be implemented for perpendicular recording media.

REFERENCES

1. S. Chikazumi and C. D. Graham, *Physics of Ferromagnetism*. Oxford: Oxford University Press, 1997.

2. D. C. Jiles, *Introduction to Magnetism and Magnetic Materials*. Boca Raton, FL: Chapman & Hall/CRC Press, 1998.

3. B. D. Cullity and C. D. Graham, *Introduction to Magnetic Materials*. Piscataway, NJ: IEEE-Wiley Press, 2009.

4. R. Bozorth, *Ferromagnetism*. Piscataway, NJ: IEEE Press, 1993.

5. S. N. Piramanayagam, J. Appl. Phys. **102**, 011301 (2007).

6. Y. Honda, K. Tanahashi, Y. Hirayama, A. Kikukawa, and M. Futamoto, J. Magn. Magn. Mater. **235**, 68 (2001).

7. H. R. Kirchmayr, J. Phys. D Appl. Phys. **29**(11), 2763 (1996).

8. H. Draaisma, W. Dejonge, and F. Denbroder, J. Magn. Magn. Mater. **66**, 351 (1987).

9. F. Greidanus, W. Zeper, B. Jacobs, J. Spruit, and P. Carcia, J. Appl. Phys. **28**, 37 (1989).

10. S. Hashimoto, Y. Ochiai, and K. Aso, J. Appl. Phys. **67**, 4429 (1990).

11. K. Tanahashi, R. Arai, and Y. Hose, IEEE Trans. Magn. **41**, 577 (2005).

12. T. Thomson, G. Hu, and B. D. Terris, Phys. Rev. Lett. **96**, 257204 (2006).

13. J. G. Zhu and H. N. Bertram, IEEE Trans. Magn. **24**, 2706 (1988).

14. R. Street and J. C. Woolley, Proc. Phys. Soc. A **62**, 562 (1949).

15. D. Weller and M. F. Doerner, Annu. Rev. Mater. Sci. **30**, 611 (2000).

16. M. P. Sharrock, IEEE Trans. Magn. **26**, 193 (1990).

17. R. W. Chantrell and K. O'Grady, J. Phys. D Appl. Phys. **25**(1), 1 (1992).

3

LONGITUDINAL RECORDING MEDIA

S. N. Piramanayagam

*Data Storage Institute, Agency for Science,
Technology and Research (A*STAR), Singapore*

3.1 INTRODUCTION

Chapters 1 and 2 briefly covered the background information on magnetic recording and magnetism in general. This chapter will discuss the fundamentals of magnetic recording media in detail. For this purpose, longitudinal recording technology—which has existed for about 50 years and is the base upon which our understanding and theories of magnetic recording were developed—is considered as the platform. This could be a farewell chapter for longitudinal recording, which has just been phased out from hard disk drive (HDD) technology and in all likelihood will not appear again (at least in rigid form). Section 3.2 covers the basics of longitudinal recording, and Sections 3.3 and 3.4 cover the influence of nanomagnetism on recording performance. Sections 3.5 and 3.6 discuss noise sources and ways to minimize them. Sections 3.7 and 3.8 describe the importance of grain-size reduction and its effect on thermal stability. Section 3.9 highlights how researchers pushed longitudinal recording technology to achieve better performance. Section 3.10 summarizes key processes involved in the manufacturing of longitudinal recording media.

3.2　BASICS OF MAGNETIC RECORDING

For a material to be used as a nonvolatile data storage medium, it should satisfy at least two criteria: (1) One should be able to store information (without the use of external power) in the medium reliably and (2) be able to sense the information using electrical or other means [1, 2]. We have seen in Chapter 1 that permanent magnets generate a field, and this field can be used as a means to sense information. The field is stronger around the two poles than anywhere else, which can be demonstrated by the ability of the magnets to attract magnetic materials mostly toward the poles. Bar magnets generate a magnetic field that is proportional to the remanent moment (which is a product of the remanent magnetization and the volume). Magnetic recording technology makes use of this magnetic field to read (or sense) information. For example, the magnetic field that comes out of a north pole can be considered as "1," and the field that is sensed out of a south pole can be considered as "0." It is good to repeat that the reading is done in a slightly different manner in HDDs (0 is represented by the absence of an emerging field from media and 1 by the presence of a field from transitions, N–N, or S–S arrangement of polarities) as discussed earlier in Chapter 1. In brief, the product of remanent moment M_r and the thickness of the magnetic material (δ), usually denoted as $M_r\delta$, is an important parameter of the recording media that determines the signal to be sensed from the media.

The other important aspect of nonvolatile recording media is the ability to store information in the absence of power. In the case of magnetic recording, the magnetization direction in the bit cells has to be retained over a long period (~10 years, in most practical cases) once the information is written. The hysteresis behavior of the magnetic material helps in achieving this criterion. As seen in Chapter 2, the magnetic material has an energy barrier arising from magnetocrystalline anisotropy, for example, which keeps the remanent magnetization stable. Such an energy barrier can prevent the magnetization from flipping in response to factors such as external magnetic fields, thermal agitations, and internal demagnetization fields. The ability of a magnetic material to retain information is typically indicated by its coercivity (H_c). In summary, $M_r\delta$ and H_c are key properties in choosing recording media material. However, as we will see in subsequent sections, there are many other criteria to be satisfied by a material to emerge as a candidate for storing information.

3.3　MAGNETISM AT NANOSCALE

In Chapter 1, magnetic recording is explained on the basis of each bit cell being represented by a magnet. However, this picture is oversimplified. In real hard disk media, a collection of grains are used for storing information as shown in Figure 3.1. The orientation of magnetization in the case of longitudinal recording is shown in the inset. Each bit cell contains a few grains, and the bit boundary is not straight. The need to use several grains to store information arises from the traditional methods in which media is fabricated and is due to the weak sensitivity of the heads which require a field from many grains to produce the needed voltage for readout. Suppose, however, that

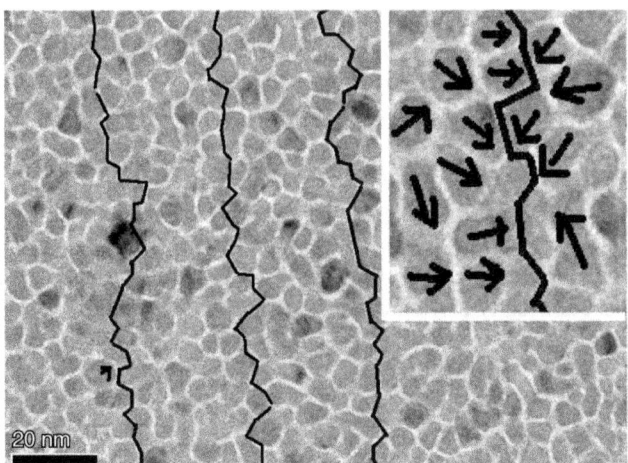

Figure 3.1. Illustration of bit boundary formation in granular recording media. (Inset) The magnetization orientation in the case of longitudinal recording media.

the recording medium were fabricated in such a way that tiny magnets of a few nanometers in diameter are uniformly placed all over the disk, and that the head is sensitive enough to pick up a signal from a tiny magnet, the scheme of using one magnet to store one bit would be plausible. In fact, this is discussed in Chapter 12, which focuses on bit-patterned media, an emerging alternative technology. However, this requires extensive patterning over a large area and hence is not yet cost advantageous. Moreover, there are several other technical challenges as well.

For more than 50 years, hard disk media have been making use of several grains to store one bit. Traditionally, thin-film coating has been used as the method to fabricate recording media. In the earliest generations of hard disk media, spin coating was used to deposit magnetic paint as the recording medium. In the 1980s, a switch was made to deposit the media by a sputtering process, to be discussed at the end of the chapter. In the case of sputtered films, for example, the resultant film is polycrystalline. In simple terms, a polycrystalline media material consists of several small crystallites or grains, and each grain can be considered a tiny magnet. In current technology, the size of the grain or the tiny magnet is below 8 nm, and the read sensor has a width of about 80 nm. In addition, the grains are in random positions and are of random sizes. Therefore, the read sensor cannot cover a single grain to access one bit of information. In addition, to sense the signal, the read sensor needs a significant amount of magnetic field, which can only be obtained from the magnetic field of several grains. Therefore, it is essential to use a collection of grains to store a single bit of information. In this scenario, even if two recording media A and B were prepared with identical values of H_c and $M_r\delta$, they might not exhibit similar recording performance. This is because H_c and $M_r\delta$, being macromagnetic properties, do not indicate how the recording material will behave at a nanometer scale level, where recording is achieved these days. Therefore, it becomes necessary to look at several other issues such as noise, pulse width, and bit error rate

(BER) that will depend on the micro- or nanostructural properties of the magnetic material and influence the performance of a recording medium. The following sections will describe these topics in detail.

3.4   RECORDING PERFORMANCE MEASUREMENTS

This section will briefly describe a few recording performance measurements before we discuss the influence of nanostructure on recording performance. The recording performance test is usually carried out in a device called a spin-stand. Because Guzik (http://www.guzik.com) is one of the popular manufacturers of spin-stands, a recording performance measurement is also sometimes called a "Guzik" test. A spin-stand can be considered a prototype HDD where several properties of the head and media can be tested. Spin-stands emulate HDDs and hence an understanding of how a particular medium or head will behave in a HDD can be gained. Therefore, in media and head research and development, the spin-stand is an essential tool. The spin-stand can also be used to study several other parameters related to signal processing, servo tracking, and so on.

The key components of a spin-stand system are the following: a spindle to place and rotate the disks, an actuator/head stage to hold and position the head, the relevant electronic circuits to provide voltage to the head and to pick up the signal from it, electronic circuits to analyze the information, and a computer to control and analyze the results. The rotation of the spindle and the head movement will enable one to move the head to the desired position and test the properties. The output signals from the head may be observed using a cathode-ray-oscilloscope (CRO) or analyzed using a spectrum analyzer. The input signals to the head may be fed using the controller of a spin-stand or using external signal generators. Figure 3.2 presents a block diagram to show the several components of a spin-stand tester. Although several measurements can be made using a spin-stand, let us discuss a few key measurements in this section.

The most significant test of a hard disk medium (besides reliability) is to find out how many errors are observed when information is written to a medium. This is called

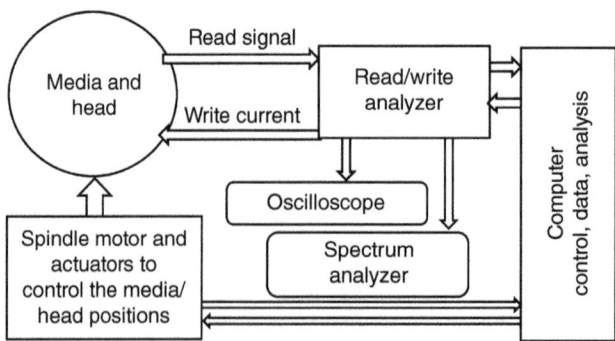

Figure 3.2. Schematic block diagram of a spin-stand setup and its various components.

the BER test, and the result is often expressed as errors out of successes, for example, 1e-6 to indicate 1 error for every million bits of information or 1e-4 to indicate 1 error for every 10,000 bits. For a fixed track density, BER is measured as a function of linear density. Achieving a low BER at a high linear density is essential to achieving a larger capacity per disk (assuming that high track density is not compromised). However, BER tests are time-consuming, and hence, most often, the signal-to-noise ratio (SNR) is measured as an indicator of BER. It should be pointed out that in the case of perpendicular recording, SNR may not be as good an indicator of media performance.

Pulse width (PW_{50}), typically the width of the pulse at 50% of its peak amplitude, is another important parameter measured using a spin-stand. PW_{50} is measured at very low densities, where the pulses from different bits are well isolated from each other; it serves as a measure of how much linear density can be achieved. We have seen in the previous section that the bit boundary in a recording medium is not straight but zigzags. The change in magnetization in the case of a straight bit boundary will be a step function, whereas a zigzag bit boundary produces a tanh (hyperbolic tangent) variation of magnetization. Similarly, a straight bit boundary will lead to a pulse of large amplitude and zero width (depends on sensor though); however, such a situation is too ideal and is never observed experimentally. A zigzag bit boundary, on the other hand, gives rise to a pulse with finite amplitude and finite width, which depends on the width of the bit boundary [3]. Figure 3.3 shows several cases. A transition that is wider leads to a larger PW_{50}. It is easy to understand from the figure that a lower PW_{50} is favorable for higher linear density; a lower PW_{50} indicates the possibility of writing smaller bit cells closer to each other without overlapping, whereas a larger PW_{50} indicates potential overlapping of pulses at relatively lower linear densities. Therefore, PW_{50} serves as a measure of the potential maximum linear density.

The SNR, as the name implies, indicates the quality of the signal against the noise present in the readout pulses. There are several definitions of SNR as desired by a hard disk media company or a customer (usually an HDD manufacturer) who orders hard disk media from a media manufacturing company. Whatever may be the definition, a higher SNR will help in retrieving the information reliably and hence should result in a lower BER. The SNR may be measured at different linear densities to analyze and understand the performance of a recording medium. Comparison of SNRs between media prepared under different conditions can be made to narrow down and choose the best recipe for a particular HDD product. Efforts are also made, based on spin-stand measurements, to improve the SNR of the next-generation medium that is under research and development in order to increase its areal density in future products.

The SNR of a medium can be increased by increasing the signal, by reducing the noise, or by doing both. The signal from a medium depends on factors intrinsic and extrinsic to the medium. For example, the signal is proportional to $M_r\delta$ of the medium and sensitivity of the read sensor. It is, on the other hand, inversely proportional to the spacing between the head and the medium. Since increasing the signal by increasing the $M_r\delta$ may also lead to a larger noise or a larger PW_{50}, the effort of increasing the SNR is directed toward reducing the noise of the recording medium. In practice, the medium $M_r\delta$ has been continually reduced to control the PW_{50} and the transition noise. The reduction of the signal arising from the reduction of $M_r\delta$ was compensated by

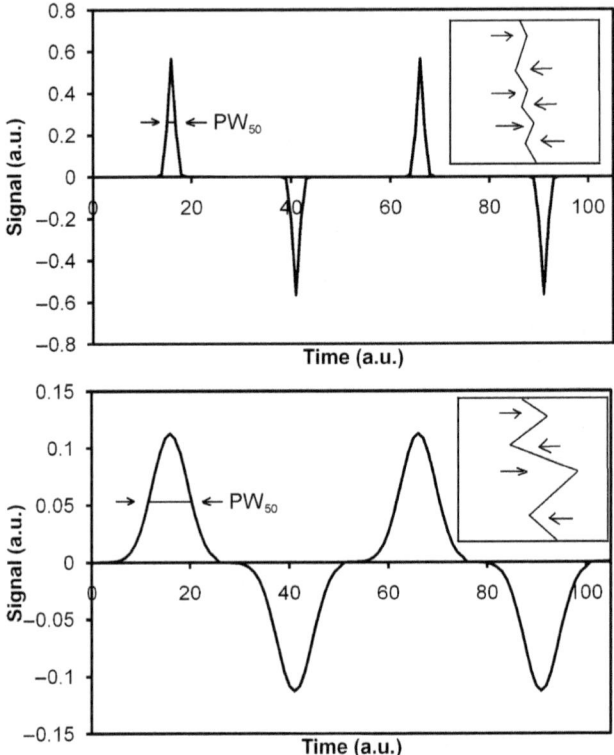

<u>Figure 3.3.</u> Illustration of waveforms from the recorded transitions of longitudinal recording media and PW$_{50}$. (Inset) Illustration of the corresponding bit boundaries.

improving the sensitivity of the read sensors (described in Chapter 6) or by reducing the magnetic spacing (as described in Chapters 8 and 9).

3.5 TYPES OF NOISE

In the previous section, we discussed that the way to obtain media with better recording performance is to minimize the noise of the recording medium. In this section, we will discuss the different types of noise in longitudinal recording media and their sources. In an ideal longitudinal recording, with straight bit boundaries, and magnetization perfectly aligned along the track and parallel to the disk surface, the noise will be the lowest. But, the ideal case is never achieved practically. Real recording media have zigzag bit boundaries because of the polycrystalline nature of the material used. The interaction between the magnetic grains (both magnetostatic and exchange interactions) will also play a role in the width and position of the zigzag boundaries. Moreover, the magnetization of the grains may not be as well aligned as desired. All these factors contribute to the noise in a recording medium. Direct current (DC) noise and transition noise are the two major sources of noise in a longitudinal recording medium.

3.5.1   DC Noise

DC noise is the background noise in a longitudinal recording medium. As an analogy, because this book is printed using black ink, the white paper produces very little background noise. On the other hand, if the paper had several black dots spread over the paper due to a problem with the printer or otherwise, it would be difficult to read the book. Especially where the printed letters were small, the presence of black dots in the background would make the text illegible. In a similar fashion, if the magnetic flux from the transitions is the needed signal, magnetic flux from other regions (the center of the bits, for example) contributes to the DC noise.

DC noise or DC erase noise is measured by erasing the disk using a DC on the write head and measuring the voltage produced in the read sensor after the erasure. DC erasure is equivalent to writing a string of 0s (no transitions). When the head is flying over a recording medium, applying DC to the write head for a period of time will produce a constant magnetic field. This will result in magnetizing all the grains of the medium in one direction. In the analogy of bar magnets, this is equivalent to placing the bar magnets in such a way that the north pole of a bar magnet meets the south pole of the next bar magnet and so on. In the ideal case, when bar magnets are arranged in this fashion, there should be no magnetic flux coming out of the surface, and if a read head flies over the surface, it will not produce any voltage. Therefore, in the ideal case, there will be no DC noise. However, in real recording systems, the read sensor will still exhibit some voltage signals that can be reproduced, indicating the emergence of magnetic flux from recording media even after DC erasure. These voltage signals constitute the DC noise as these signals do not come from writing any information.

Figure 3.4 shows an example of DC noise from a recording medium. The x-axis shows timescale/distance, and the y-axis shows the voltage from the read sensor,

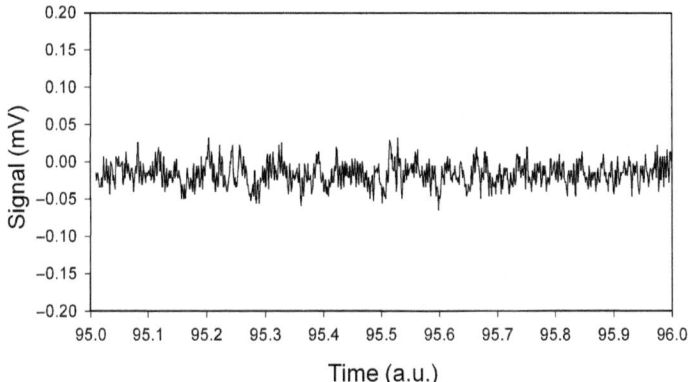

Figure 3.4. Illustration of noise from the recording media after DC erasure. A smooth line with no voltage signals indicates low DC noise in longitudinal recording.

representing the magnetic flux from different positions of a disk. In the ideal case, the read sensor voltage should be zero but we do observe a noise voltage. This noise voltage arises from the magnetic flux leaking from the recording medium even after DC erasure. As mentioned earlier using the bar magnet analogy, if strings of bar magnets are stuck to each other with opposing poles facing each other (as in Fig. 1.3 of Chapter 1), there will be no magnetic field coming out of the surface as the magnetic field from one magnet will enter into the other. However, the presence of any discontinuities or imperfect alignment will result in magnetic field leakage, as we are aware that a magnet left alone will produce a magnetic field around its poles. In a real recording medium, the magnetic grains may be isolated from each other intentionally to minimize the transition noise (to be discussed), leading to the emergence of weak magnetic flux. In addition, the recording medium will have voids, grains with different easy-axis orientations, and so on, as illustrated in Figure 3.5, which would all be sources of magnetic flux. The presence of such magnetic flux from the recording media results in a voltage in the read sensor and contributes to the DC noise.

3.5.2 Transition Noise

Transition noise is the noise that arises from the zigzag nature of the recorded transitions and is measured by writing a string of 1s. A spectrum analyzer, which can convert signals in the time domain to a frequency domain, is a useful tool to measure the transition noise. To understand the transition noise better, let us use the bar magnet analogy again. A string of 1s is equivalent to placing magnets with like poles facing each other, for example, S-N=N-S=S-N=N-S and so on. As shown in Figure 3.6, when a read sensor flies over these transitions, it would produce pulses at almost equal spacing. When this information is fed into a spectrum analyzer, it would convert the time-based signals into a frequency-dependent spectrum. For the ideal case with straight bit boundaries with no shift in the positions of the transitions, we would observe a strong δ-pulse at

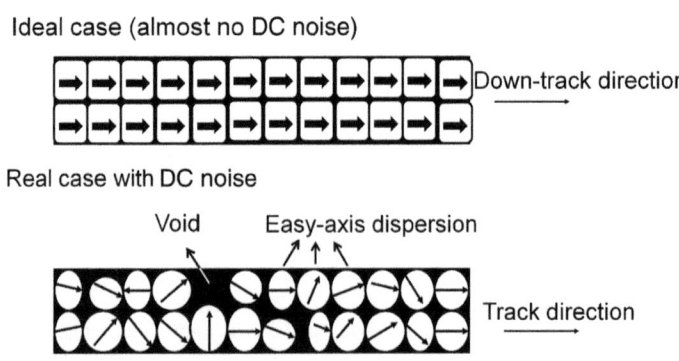

Figure 3.5. Schematic illustration of magnetization after DC erasure and its effect on DC noise from recording media: (a) Ideal case with almost no DC noise and (b) real case with a certain DC noise arising from various sources such as voids, easy-axis dispersion.

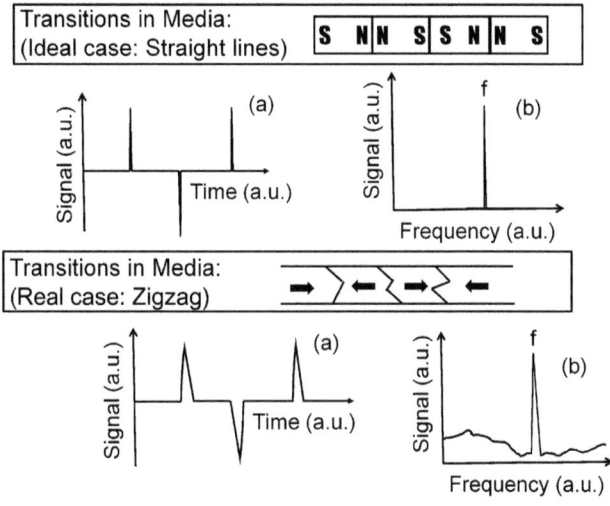

Signal from reader (a) Oscilloscope (b) Spectrum analyzer

Figure 3.6. Illustration of signals from the recorded transitions and the transitions: (Top) Ideal case where the transitions are straight lines and are at intended positions; (Bottom) real case, where the transitions are zigzag in nature and have a jitter. The symbols (a) and (b) represent the oscilloscope and spectrum analyzer output in the time domain and frequency domain, respectively.

a frequency, f, which is inversely proportional to the time, t, that it takes for the read sensor to traverse one bar magnet. There would be no voltage signals at any other frequency other than the higher harmonics of f (not shown in figure).

On the other hand, in real recording media based on polycrystalline materials, it is not possible to have straight bit boundaries. Therefore, when a read sensor flies over the written transitions, the spectrum analyzer would show a peak at a frequency f, corresponding to the spacing between the bits. This peak, unlike the ideal case, would be broader. Moreover, voltage signals would also be observed in all frequencies in a random manner. Since no information was written at these frequencies, the voltage at these frequencies is considered noise. Since this noise arises from the transitions, it is called transition noise. Transition noise arises from the nature of bit boundary formation. A write head produces a magnetic field to write information at a particular frequency. This corresponds to writing transitions at equal spacing. However, even in the best case, the bit boundary has to follow the grain boundary. As the grain positions in a polycrystalline film are random, the transitions do not happen exactly at the intended position. In addition, the magnetostatic and exchange interactions play a role in determining the position of the bit boundary (to be discussed in the subsequent section), resulting in the formation of bit boundaries with a slight deviation from the desired positions. As a result, the pulses which were supposed to be isolated from each other by an equal time, t (or equal distance, d), appear to be isolated from each other with dispersion in t (or distance d). This phenomenon is called transition jitter and is a source of noise.

3.6 SOURCES AND WAYS OF MINIMIZING NOISE IN LONGITUDINAL RECORDING

The previous section described DC and transition noise. This section will describe the potential sources and ways of minimizing noise in longitudinal recording. When the SNR of a recording medium is measured as a function of linear density, the SNR will decrease at higher densities. As the linear density is increased, the positive and negative pulses from the transitions will start overlapping in such a way that the peak amplitude is reduced. As the density at which they start overlapping depends on the PW_{50}, it is safe to state that the PW_{50} of the media is a good indicator of how the signal decreases as the density increases. DC noise, which can be considered noise at the lowest density, stays constant. However, transition noise increases as linear density is increased because of the larger number of transitions written on the media. As the total noise at a particular frequency is the sum of the DC noise and the transition noise, it is essential to understand the causes and find ways to minimize the noise. Hard disk media researchers have made tremendous progress in this direction, and the following section is a discussion of their efforts.

3.6.1 DC Noise in Longitudinal Recording

As discussed earlier, DC noise arises from voids/imperfections in the media materials, the intergranular spacing, and the dispersion in the magnetization orientation parallel to the disk as well as with respect to the track direction. Reducing the dispersion in the magnetization orientation is one key step toward minimizing DC noise. It also helps in increasing the signal as the signal produced by the longitudinal recording medium will depend on the component of magnetization that lies parallel to the disk and to the track direction. If the component of magnetization along the track direction or parallel to the disk can be enhanced, for instance, the SNR could be much larger than it would be in the case of random orientation for the same number of grains. Several researchers have carried out research work along these lines.

Let us discuss first the way to reduce DC noise by minimizing the randomness in the easy-axis orientation parallel to the film plane. Suppose a magnetic film is sputtered in unoptimized conditions, the resultant magnetic film will have crystallites with random easy-axis orientation. Some grains may have their easy axis oriented parallel to the film plane, whereas most of the other grains may have their easy axis directed at all different angles with respect to the film plane. Therefore, suitable methods are needed to increase the number of grains that have an easy axis along the film plane. Using suitable underlayers is one way to achieve this objective. When materials like Cr or Cr alloys are deposited at elevated temperatures, they develop a preferential crystalline orientation or texture [4]. For example, if Cr or Cr alloys are deposited at about 250°C, the Cr alloy can grow with a (200) texture. On a Cr surface with a (200)

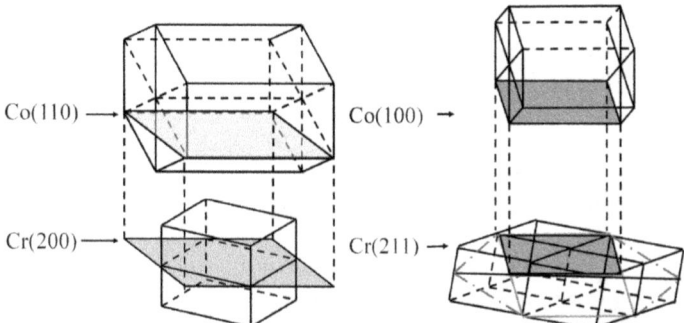

Figure 3.7. Illustrations of underlayers and the effect of their crystalline texture on the recording layer.

texture, a Co-alloy-based recording layer can grow with a (110) texture, as shown in Figure 3.7. Seed layers such as NiAl have also been proposed, which will induce a (211) texture, resulting in Co with a (100) texture (Fig. 3.7). Since the c-axis is the easy axis of Co crystal, the grains that have a (100) or (110) texture will have their magnetization parallel to the disk surface. However, from the point of view of orienting the easy axes of the grains along the down-track direction (to be discussed later), Co (110) texture is favored. Such grains would have a larger component of magnetization parallel to the substrate than the grains whose easy axes are tilted away from the disk surface. Several underlayers such as Cr, CrV, CrTi, CrMo, or combinations of these have been used by various researchers to improve the c-axis orientation parallel to the film plane [4, 5]. When such underlayers are used under suitable deposition conditions, the number of underlayer grains with a specific orientation can be enhanced.

It has also been reported that the use of intermediate layers helps to improve the easy-axis orientation by improving the lattice matching between the Cr underlayers and the CoCrPt-based magnetic layers. One way to achieve better lattice matching between Cr and CoCrPt alloys is to use a suitable material, such as a nonmagnetic CoCr alloy, with a lattice parameter that lies in between those of Cr and CoCrPt [6]. The introduction of such an intermediate layer would also help in reducing the dead-layer effect in Co alloys. It has even been reported that the introduction of a CoCr intermediate layer could improve the thermal stability of the media. Therefore, underlayers and intermediate layers in the longitudinal recording media help to reduce DC noise and improve the signal from the recording media.

In addition to using an underlayer and an intermediate layer to improve the in-plane easy-axis orientation, another way to minimize DC noise is to increase the number of grains that have an easy-axis orientation parallel to the track direction. For longitudinal recording media, such a partially ordered arrangement of easy axes was observed serendipitously. Hard disks used a mechanical texturing process that produced circular lines of a few tens of nanometers in width, to avoid stiction between the head and smooth disk. However, it was observed from the hysteresis loops of recording media

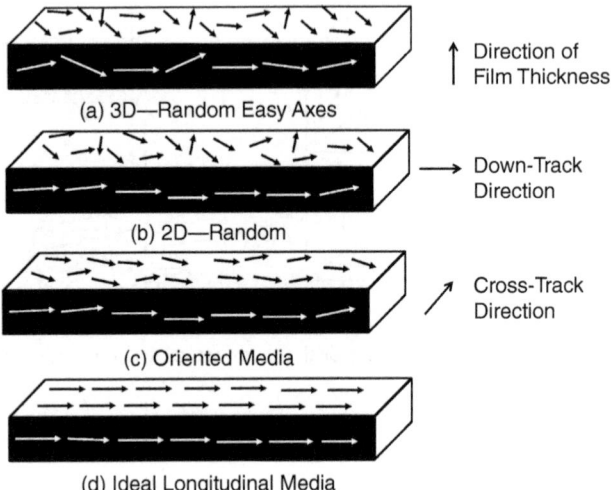

(a) 3D—Random Easy Axes

↑ Direction of Film Thickness

(b) 2D—Random

→ Down-Track Direction

(c) Oriented Media

↗ Cross-Track Direction

(d) Ideal Longitudinal Media

Figure 3.8. Schematic diagram of dispersion in the magnetization in various configurations: (a) 3d-random orientation of easy axes, where the magnetization is oriented at all possible angles; (b) 2d-random, where the magnetization is preferably oriented in plane; (c) oriented media, where the magnetization is preferably in plane and parallel to the down-track direction; and (d) ideal longitudinal media, which is the most desired configuration

on such mechanically textured substrates that the films could show different coercivity (H_c) and remanent moment (M_r) when measured along the track or radial direction (along or in the transverse direction of the texture lines, respectively). The ratio of H_c in the circumferential to that in the radial direction was called the orientation ratio (OR). Improvements made in the oriented media were one of the prime reasons for the increased life of longitudinal recording technology [7–9].

Figure 3.8 illustrates the magnetization orientation for different media configurations. A recording medium in which the magnetic moments are randomly oriented with respect to the plane and with respect to the track (Fig. 3.8a) would have the lowest SNR. This is because in such a recording medium, the component of magnetization that lies parallel to the disk surface or the track direction is low. This will lead to a reduction in the signal and an increase in the noise. However, the SNR can be increased by maximizing the number of grains that are oriented parallel to the disk surface (Fig. 3.8b). This is typically achieved by the use of underlayers such as Cr, as discussed previously. The SNR can be further increased by orienting the magnetization of the grains along the track direction (Fig. 3.8c). This is achieved by the texturing process, which can lead to an increased OR. Although the magnetization configuration as shown in Figure 3.8d is the ideal configuration for obtaining very high SNRs, it is not possible to achieve such orientations experimentally. However, a configuration closer to Figure 3.8d is the way to increase the SNR in longitudinal recording media.

3.6.2 Transition Noise in Longitudinal Recording

Pioneering micromagnetic simulations on recording media by Zhu et al. in the early 1990s indicated that the zigzag domain walls in longitudinal recording comes from the strong exchange coupling between the grains of a recording medium. Strong coupling leads to a larger bit boundary, resulting in a larger PW_{50} and a larger transition noise. Therefore, controlling exchange coupling between the grains is one of the key aspects of reducing transition noise. When the grains are completely isolated from each other, almost each grain switches independently of the other grains (except for the magneto-static interaction, which is long ranged). For isolated grains, the bit boundary follows the grain boundary. However, when the grains of a medium are not well isolated, the interaction between the grains is stronger, and the bit boundary is much larger than the grain boundary. In the extreme case of much stronger interaction, the switching mechanism itself could be different. In the earlier days of thin-film media, the magnetization reversal mechanism was by domain wall motion. In this case, the domain wall formation determined the bit boundaries, which were much broader.

It is essential to reduce the grain size and the intergrain interactions to obtain a narrower bit boundary. The interactions between the grains can be short ranged (exchange) or long ranged (magnetostatic interactions). Magnetostatic interaction is essentially determined by the $M_r\delta$: Reducing $M_r\delta$ is a way to minimize this effect. However, this will also reduce the signal available from the transitions as the signal is proportional to $M_r\delta$. To compensate for a reduction in $M_r\delta$, sensor sensitivity has to be improved. Over a few generations, read sensors have evolved from inductive to magnetoresistive (MR) transducers. Read sensors using MR transducers were developed further to incorporate giant magnetoresistive (GMR) and magnetic tunnel junction (MTJ) technologies.

Another interaction that needs to be reduced in order to achieve a narrower bit boundary is the exchange coupling between neighboring grains. While the challenge of reducing magnetostatic interaction was made possible by producing more sensitive read/write heads, the reduction of exchange coupling was largely focused on the recording medium itself. For the last several years, exchange decoupling of grains in longitudinal media has relied on compositional segregation in films deposited at high temperatures. It is also possible to sputter a thin film that will segregate into magnetic grains and nonmagnetic grain boundaries without resorting to high temperatures, for example, using a high-pressure deposition. If the core of the grain is magnetic and the grain boundary is nonmagnetic, exchange coupling between the grains is reduced. Earlier generations of longitudinal media used additive elements such as Ta to enhance the grain boundary along with nonmagnetic elements such as Cr, leading to better exchange decoupling. Later, additive elements such as B led to further improvement in grain isolation and much smaller grain sizes [10, 11].

3.7 INFLUENCE OF GRAIN SIZE ON RECORDING PERFORMANCE

The grain size of a recording medium plays a major role in the recording performance. The SNR of the recording medium depends on the number of grains in a bit cell. When the bit cells are smaller, media with smaller grains will have better performance than those with larger grains (assuming there is no deterioration in other properties such as thermal stability). When good exchange decoupling between the grains is achieved, the bit boundary follows the grain boundary. Therefore, the size of the grains also plays a major role in determining the transition jitter and the achievable linear density. As a consequence, grain-size reduction is always an important task on the agenda of a media researcher.

Grain-size reduction in longitudinal recording media was mostly based on the dopants used in the recording layer. Earlier generations of thin-film longitudinal media were binary alloys. Later additives such as Ta and Cr were found to improve grain segregation, and hence, CoCrPtTa alloy was one of the recording media candidates. It was discovered in the late 1990s that doping with B was much better at reducing the grain size and in improving segregation than doping with Ta. As a result, CoCrPtB alloy was used as recording layer in the 2000s. Other techniques, such as reducing the grain size of the layers below the recording layer and using dual recording layers with different functions, also helped to achieve optimized properties. For example, if the underlayer has a smaller grain size, the recording media that grows on the underlayer is also expected to have a smaller grain size. Therefore, reducing the grain size of the underlayer was considered as a way to obtain fine grains [10–13].

In the case of stacked magnetic layers, the proposed design was to have two recording layers (or more) in such a way that the bottom layer helped to obtain smaller grains. This could be achieved by doping it with more Cr and B, for example. However, such a layer alone had a poor recording performance as the grains were not thermally stable. When another layer with a lower concentration of Cr and B and a larger concentration of Pt, however, was deposited on top of the first layer, the stacked structure had optimized values of grain size and thermal stability. Techniques such as these were used in longitudinal magnetic recording media and are even adapted in perpendicular recording.

3.8 THERMAL STABILITY LIMITS

The evolution of the longitudinal recording technology from the 2 kb/in.^{2} of the random access memory accounting system or random access method of accounting and control (RAMAC) system in 1950s to the 2 Gb/in.^{2} demonstrations in the late 1990s was brought about by the improvement of several key technologies. The media technology had moved from particulate media to granular thin-film media, and the read sensor from inductive to MR and GMR technologies. As far as the media was concerned, the grain size kept reducing as the areal density progressed in order to improve the SNR and to reduce PW_{50}. In addition, the introduction of MR and GMR in hard drives also enabled the media to have lower $M_r\delta$, which would result in lower noise and PW_{50}. This resulted in a decrease in the volume of the grain as technology progressed.

As the grain volume (V) shrinks, the magnetizations of the grains are more prone to thermal agitation. This is because the anisotropy energy that helps to stabilize the magnetization and hence store information is proportional to K_uV, where K_u is the grain anisotropy constant. Thermal energy (k_BT), where k_B is the Boltzmann constant and T is temperature, tries to destabilize the magnetization. As the areal density of the hard disk grows, V gets smaller, leading to a reduction in the anisotropy energy. However, when V becomes too small, the k_BT starts competing with K_uV. When K_uV is 60 times higher than k_BT, the magnetization is stable for more than 10 years, which is preferable for hard disk technology, where a product becomes obsolete after 10 years. However, if K_uV/k_BT is smaller than 60, the magnetization will undergo reversals without the application of any external field. Even if only 5% of the grains change their magnetization, data integrity may be compromised. This was a serious problem, foreseen by Charap et al. [14]. They even proposed a limit of 40 Gb/in.[2] for longitudinal recording technology.

3.9 IMPROVEMENTS IN LONGITUDINAL RECORDING TECHNOLOGY

When longitudinal recording technology was gradually phased out in 2005 onward, an areal density of about 160 Gb/in.[2] had been achieved, which was four times larger than the proposed limit. Such a phenomenal growth beyond the superparamagnetic limit (discussed in Chapter 2) was possible owing to several factors. One major factor that helped to overcome the predicted limit was the intentional breakdown of the assumptions used in the prediction. Charap et al. assumed a bit aspect ratio (BAR) (ratio of the track width to the bit length) of 16, which was a common standard at that time. However, the HDD industry chose to narrow the tracks and increase the track density to increase the areal density [14]. For example, the 100 Gb/in.[2] demonstrations by several companies used a BAR of about 4. This led to the problem of reduction in signal as the reduction of bit width will result in smaller bits and hence reduced number of grains. However, this problem was compensated for by improved read heads, media, and signal-processing techniques. The improvements in the media mainly came in two innovations: (1) oriented media, which helped to reduce the DC noise and to increase the signal, and (2) antiferromagnetically coupled (AFC) media, which helped to maintain thermal stability even for lower values of $M_r\delta$. Since oriented media has already been discussed in the section on DC noise, we will discuss the AFC media briefly.

In conventional recording media, $M_r\delta$ reduction is achieved by decreasing the thickness, which leads to a reduction in K_uV. On the other hand, AFC media rely on two or more ferromagnetic layers that are coupled antiferromagnetically to each other through the use of a thin Ru layer to reduce the $M_r\delta$. The most common AFC design has two AFC magnetic layers, out of which one (recording layer) is much thicker than the other (stabilizing layer). In such a design, $M_r\delta$ reduction is achieved by the partial cancellation of $M_r\delta$ of one layer by that of the other. Although there are several theories proposed to explain the thermal stability of AFC media, the explanation in simple terms is that the thickness of the recording layers could be larger than they could be in conventional design, and thermal stability could be obtained [15–19]. As a summary, the improvements in oriented media, AFC media, and the combination of these two have made a significant contribution to increasing the areal density of longitudinal media from a recording media perspective. It is essential to note that the improvements in the head and other components and design of the system also played an important role.

3.10 LONGITUDINAL RECORDING MEDIA MANUFACTURING

This section briefly describes the process flow of manufacturing longitudinal recording media, most of which is also applicable to perpendicular recording media. Figure 3.9 shows a block diagram of the processes. The first step is substrate manufacturing. Two types of substrates—AlMg alloy and glass—are commonly used. AlMg alloy substrates are known for their ease of manufacturing and low cost. Typical disks used in desktop HDDs have an outer diameter (OD) of 95 mm and an inner diameter (ID) of 25 mm. Typical disks used in laptop drives have an OD of 65 mm and an ID of 20 mm. The AlMg substrates are usually coated with a thick layer (10–50 μm) of NiP in order to improve their mechanical properties. The substrates are subsequently polished to obtain smooth surfaces. In current technology, the average surface roughness (R_a) is below 0.2 nm for glass substrates and even lower for AlMg substrates.

Prior to sputtering, the disks may undergo a texturing process, which is important for longitudinal recording media. An optimized texturing process will enable a high OR, which leads to DC noise reduction and an improved resolution. After the texturing process, the disks undergo a cleaning and drying process before film sputtering.

Sputter deposition is a major process in recording media fabrication. Figure 3.10 illustrates the sputtering process. Sputtering, in simple terms, is a process of playing billiards with atoms to create thin-film layers. First, the sputtering chamber, where the thin-film deposition takes place, is pumped down to a low pressure. The objective of achieving this low pressure, called base pressure, is to minimize water vapor and other contaminating elements in the deposition chamber. After the required base pressure is

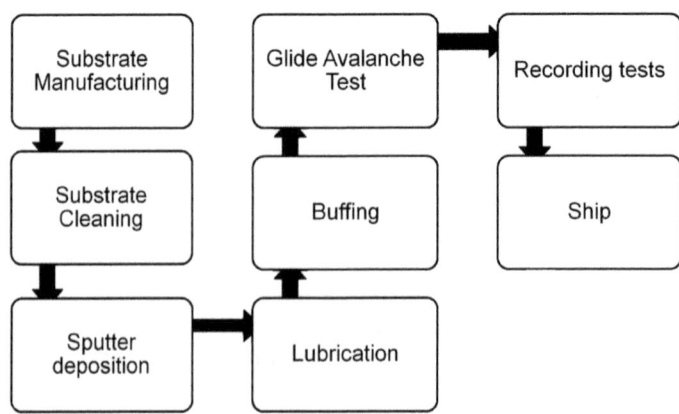

Figure 3.9. Illustrative process flow for recoding media fabrication.

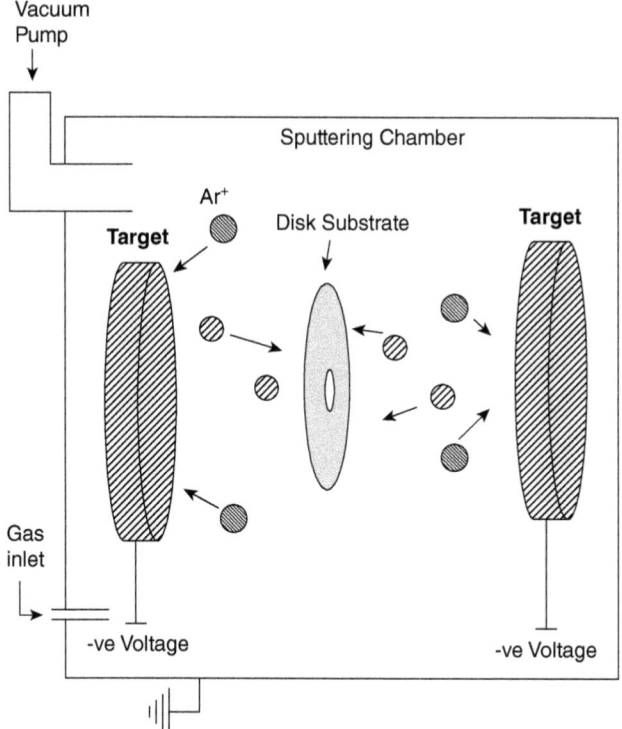

Figure 3.10. Illustration of sputtering process used for hard disk media.

achieved, Ar or some other inert gas is introduced into the chamber. When a high negative voltage is applied between the target (the material that needs to be deposited onto
the substrate) and the sputtering chamber (ground), a plasma discharge with Ar ions
and electrons is formed in the sputtering chamber from the inert gas. The Ar ions are
accelerated toward the target, knocking and releasing atoms from the target. These
atoms are scattered in different directions, and a significant portion arrives at the substrate (the disk that has to be coated). In Figure 3.10, the illustration is made for double-
sided deposition (sputtering on both sides of a substrate), whereas typical laboratory
deposition systems only coat one surface.

Several modifications can be made to the process described above to improve the
quality of the films. In modern sputtering machines used in the hard disk industry,
magnetron sputtering, where magnets are arranged below the targets, are used to deposit
thin film at faster deposition rates with good uniformity over the entire substrate. To
ensure uniform erosion of the targets and to achieve maximum utilization of the targets,
magnet assemblies behind the targets are designed in an asymmetric manner and are rotated.
Moreover, since the recording media has several layers, modern machines can have as many
as 20 or more sputtering chambers. All the layers are deposited sequentially without

exposing any intermediate layer to ambient conditions. In addition to the sputtering stations, sputtering systems may also be provided with chambers for heating, cooling, and chemical vapor deposition.

The sputtering process includes the deposition of several layers such as underlayers, magnetic layers, and one or several layers of carbon overcoat. The overcoats, as discussed in Chapter 9, protect the media from corrosion and mechanical failures. After the deposition of overcoat, the disk is unloaded from the sputtering machine and undergoes a lubrication process. The lubrication process may be a dip-and-raise process or drain process. In the dip-and-raise process, several disks are dipped into a solution containing a liquid lubricant at suitable speeds and raised, resulting in a thin coating of lubricant. In the drain process, a set of disks are immersed in lubricant, and the lubricant solution is drained, resulting in a coating of lubricant on the disk. In current technology, the lubricant thickness is about 1 nm. Chapter 8 describes lubricant technology in detail.

After the lubrication process, the disk undergoes a buffing process. The buffing process is a controlled abrasive process to remove asperities, the structures that are taller than the rest of the region and have a tendency to cause head crash. Removing the asperities that arise from the carbon overcoating or other layers helps to achieve a smooth surface, suitable for the head to fly over. After the buffing process, the disks are tested for smoothness and recording performance. The disks are then packaged and shipped.

3.11 SUMMARY

This chapter provided the fundamentals of magnetic recording technology using the longitudinal recording medium as the pedagogical example. The sources of noise in a recording medium, their significance, and the ways to minimize them were discussed. The processes involved in manufacturing the recording media were also briefly described.

REFERENCES

1. S. N. Piramanayagam, Perpendicular recording media for hard disk drives. J. Appl. Phys. **102**, 011301 (2007).

2. H. J. Richter, Recent advances in the recording physics of thin-film media. J. Phys. D-Appl. Phys. **32**, R147–R168 (1999).

3. J. Zhu, Noise of interacting transitions in thin-film recording media. IEEE Trans. Magn. **27**, 5040–5042 (1991).

4. D. E. Laughlin, L. L. Lee, L. Tang, and D. N. Lambeth, The control and characterization of the crystallographic texture of longitudinal thin film recording media. IEEE Trans. Magn. **32**, 3632–3637 (1996).

5. D. E. Laughlin, B. Lu, Y. N. Hsu, J. Zou, and D. N. Lambeth, Microstructural and crystallographic aspects of thin film recording media. IEEE Trans. Magn. **36**, 48–53 (2000).

6. S. Ohkijima, M. Oka, and H. Murayama, Effect of CoCr interlayer on longitudinal recording. IEEE Trans. Magn. **33**, 2944–2946 (1997).

7. G. Choe, J. N. Zhou, B. Demczyk, M. Yu, M. Zheng, R. Weng, A. Chekanov, K. E. Johnson, F. Liu, and K. Stoev, Highly in-plane oriented CoCrPtB longitudinal media for 130-Gb/in.[2] recording. IEEE Trans. Magn. **39**, 633–638 (2003).

8. X. Bian, K. Tang, A. Doerner, A. Mirzamaani, A. Polcyn, M. Mercado, Q. F. Xiao, J. Zhang, P. Dennig, J. Hagan, J. He, L. Tang, and T. Minvielle, Oriented longitudinal media on glass substrates. IEEE Trans. Magn. **39**, 2252–2257 (2003).

9. A. Ajan, E. N. Abarra, B. R. Acharya, A. Inomata, I. Okamoto, and M. Shinohara, Thermal effects and in-plane magnetic anisotropy in thin-film recording media. Appl. Phys. Lett. **82**, 1075–1077 (2003).

10. N. Inaba and M. Futamoto, Effects of Pt and Ta addition on compositional microstructure of CoCr-alloy thin film media. J. Appl. Phys. **87**, 6863–6865 (2000).

11. C. Paik, I. Suzuki, N. Tani, M. Ishikawa, Y. Ota, and K. Nakamura, Magnetic-properties and noise characteristics of high coercivity Cocrptb/Cr media. IEEE Trans. Magn. **28**, 3084–3086 (1992).

12. S. Yoshimura, D. D. Djayaprawira, T. K. Kong, Y. Masuda, H. Shoji, and M. Takahashi, Grain size reduction by utilizing a very thin CrW seedlayer and dry-etching process in CoCrTaNiPt longitudinal media. J. Appl. Phys. **87**, 6860–6862 (2000).

13. B. Ramamurthy, E. N. Abarra, and I. Okamoto, SNR improvements for advanced longitudinal recording media. IEEE Trans. Magn. **37**, 1475–1477 (2001).

14. S. H. Charap, P. L. Lu, and Y. J. He, Thermal stability of recorded information at high densities. IEEE Trans. Magn. **33**, 978–983 (1997).

15. E. N. Abarra, A. Inomata, H. Sato, I. Okamoto, and Y. Mizoshita, Longitudinal magnetic recording media with thermal stabilization layers. Appl. Phys. Lett. **77**, 2581–2583 (2000).

16. E. E. Fullerton, D. T. Margulies, M. E. Schabes, M. Carey, B. Gurney, A. Moser, M. Best, G. Zeltzer, K. Rubin, H. Rosen, and M. Doerner, Antiferromagnetically coupled magnetic media layers for thermally stable high-density recording. Appl. Phys. Lett. **77**, 3806–3808 (2000).

17. A. Inomata, B. R. Acharya, E. N. Abarra, A. Ajan, D. Hasegawa, and I. Okamoto, Advanced synthetic ferrimagnetic media (invited). J. Appl. Phys. **91**, 7671–7675 (2002).

18. S. N. Piramanayagam, J. P. Wang, C. H. Hee, S. I. Pang, T. C. Chong, Z. S. Shan, and L. Huang, Noise reduction mechanisms in laminated antiferromagnetically coupled recording media. Appl. Phys. Lett. **79**, 2423–2425 (2001).

19. E. Girt and H. J. Richter, Antiferromagnetically coupled perpendicular recording media. IEEE Trans. Magn. **39**, 2306–2310 (2003).

4

PERPENDICULAR RECORDING MEDIA

Kumar Srinivasan

Western Digital

S. N. Piramanayagam

Data Storage Institute, Singapore

4.1 INTRODUCTION

Until recently, longitudinal recording technology was the predominant mode for storing information in hard disk drives (HDD). In longitudinal recording technology, the magnetizations that lie longitudinally (parallel to the disk surface) are used for storing information. Alternative technologies such as perpendicular recording, in which magnetizations lie perpendicular to the disk surface, were proposed as early as the late 1970s to overcome some of the potential problems of longitudinal recording [1–3]. However, longitudinal recording remained a favorable candidate for about three decades and delayed the arrival of perpendicular recording. Meanwhile, perpendicular recording technology had several hurdles to overcome because the head and media design for perpendicular recording differs drastically from the head and media design associated with longitudinal recording technology. There were a number of challenges for recording media [4]. Finding a way to integrate a soft magnetic underlayer (SUL) without causing noise and adjacent track erasure was one of the issues. This will be discussed

Developments in Data Storage: Materials Perspective, First Edition.
Edited by S. N. Piramanayagam, Tow C. Chong.
© 2012 Institute of Electrical and Electronics Engineers. Published 2012 by John Wiley & Sons, Inc.

in a following section that is focused on SUL design. Identifying suitable recording media materials that could help to achieve fine grains that were thermally stable, suitably decoupled so as to keep noise low, and easily manufacturable were key problems in the recording layer design. Ultimately, it was only in 2006 that all these problems in production were overcome, and HDDs using perpendicular recording technology were successfully released by several manufacturers. This chapter discusses the progress made in SULs and recording media layers, and the technology and physics behind these layers. The discussion starts with the history and advantages of perpendicular recording technology in general. Then a brief overview is provided on the recording media. Following the overview are detailed discussions, first of SULs, and then of oxide-based perpendicular recording media.

4.2 HISTORY OF PERPENDICULAR MAGNETIC RECORDING (PMR)

Perpendicular recording technology was proposed in the mid-1970s as a method to overcome the problem of demagnetizing fields from recorded transitions. In any ferromagnetic or ferrimagnetic system, there exists a demagnetizing field that is oriented in the direction opposite to that of the magnetization. The demagnetization field, H_d, is expressed as

$$H_d = -N \cdot M, \tag{4.1}$$

where N is the demagnetization tensor, and M is the magnetization vector. N depends on the shape and direction of the magnet. The rule of thumb is that the demagnetization field is stronger when the magnetic charges or the magnetic poles are nearer. For example, the magnet shown in Figure 4.1a will have a stronger demagnetization field in direction x than in direction y, whereas the magnet in Figure 4.1b will be otherwise. The magnet in Figure 4.1c will have uniform demagnetization in all directions. In longitudinal recording, the distance between the magnetic charges or the magnetic poles decreases when the linear density increases. To give an analogy, the shape of the bit resembles the shape in Figure 4.1(b) at low densities and the shape Figure 4.1(a) at

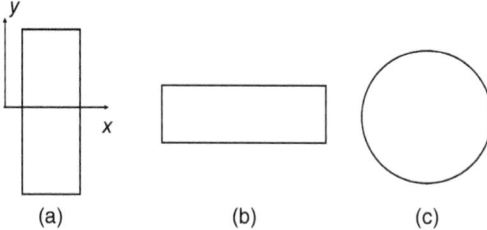

(a)   (b)   (c)

Figure 4.1. Illustration of demagnetizing fields for magnets of three different shapes. The magnets in (a) and (b) have less demagnetizing field in y and x-directions, respectively. The magnet in (c) has uniform demagnetizing field in all directions.

higher linear densities (while the magnetization lies in the x-direction). Therefore, an increased demagnetizing field that will oppose the magnetization direction is expected at higher linear densities of longitudinal recording media. In 1975, Iwasaki and Takemura experimentally observed that circular magnetization would be formed in longitudinal recording technology because of a stronger demagnetizing field when thicker films are used [1]. Such circular magnetization would not be able to produce high output voltage at high linear densities. They predicted and proposed that in perpendicular recording technology, the demagnetization field would be reduced at high linear densities, and therefore, perpendicular recording would be a superior technique to achieve high linear densities.

Professor Iwasaki and his team came up with many other inventions between 1975 and 1980 that laid the foundation for perpendicular recording technology [1–3, 5]. Media based on a CoCr alloy with a perpendicular anisotropy, double-layered perpendicular recording media with a CoCr recording layer and NiFe as the SUL, and designs of several types of heads for perpendicular recording were developed. Iwasaki and Nakamura developed a perpendicular recording medium based on CoCr and demonstrated that 30 kbpi (kilobits per inch) could be achieved with a 1000 nm-thick recording layer. This linear density was significantly larger than what could be supported by longitudinal recording at that time [6]. The technology evolved further over the past 30 years and was finally incorporated into HDDs by around 2005. Perpendicular recording technology has been the dominant technology since 2008.

4.3 ADVANTAGES OF PMR

Although Iwasaki et al. had proposed several configurations for perpendicular recording, the invention of the double-layered perpendicular recording medium and the single-pole head design turned out to be crucial for the superiority of perpendicular recording over longitudinal recording. The combination of a single pole head and the perpendicular medium with SUL provides superior writing performance in perpendicular recording than what is possible using longitudinal recording.

Figure 4.2 illustrates the writing process in longitudinal and perpendicular recording. If the fringing field from the head is higher than that of the coercivity of the grain, the magnetization will be reversed, and writing will be achieved in longitudinal recording. In the recording medium, the grains have different energy barriers because of the distribution in the size and anisotropy constant. Therefore, in order to reverse all the grains, the field from the head is made to be two to three times the coercivity of the material (the field required to reverse 50% of the magnetization). However, if a comparison is made between the fringing field and the field at the gap, the fringing field is less than the field available at the gaps by about 50%. In longitudinal recording, the weaker field is used for writing information. In perpendicular recording technology, the gap field is used for writing information. This is achieved by use of the SUL and the single-pole head. The single-pole head, the recording medium, and the SUL are illustrated in Figure 4.2b. The SUL, being highly permeable, can act as a magnetic mirror. In perpendicular recording, it can be visualized that the medium is

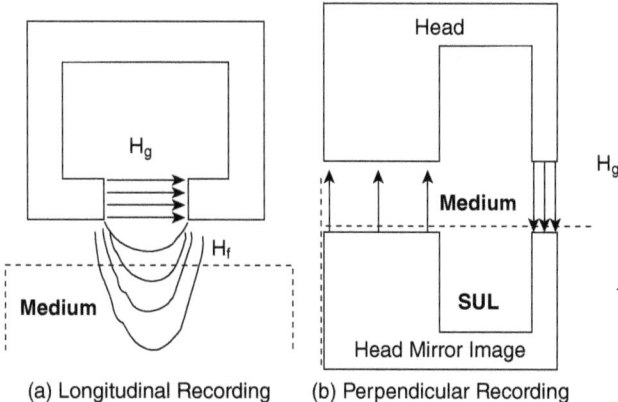

(a) Longitudinal Recording (b) Perpendicular Recording

Figure 4.2. Writing process in (a) longitudinal and (b) perpendicular recording. In perpendicular recording technology, the medium is virtually placed in the pole gaps between the head and the mirror image in the SUL.

virtually placed in the gaps between the poles. This function of the SUL is described in greater detail in a separate section below. Detailed information about the writing and reading processes of perpendicular recording can be obtained from the reviews by Khizroev and Litvinov [7, 8]. Besides the writing process, perpendicular recording technology also makes use of media with larger remanent moment–thickness product ($M_r \cdot t$), without degrading the sharpness of the magnetic transitions, which makes it attractive.

4.4 OVERVIEW OF PMR MEDIA

Perpendicular recording media consists of several layers of materials designed in order to improve the recording performance and reliability of storage. Although there are several layers, the heart of the medium is the magnetic layer that stores the information. The magnetic layer, produced by sputtering process, is a polycrystalline material. In other words, the magnetic layer consists of trillions of grains or crystallites that are densely and randomly packed in every square inch of the disk. The grains have crystallographic orientations randomly rotated with respect to the film normal. Moreover, they are arranged in random positions and sizes. Because of this randomness in the nature of the grains used in storing the information, a group of grains are used to store information. The write head can be moved over a specific area to make the polarity of the magnetization either in the up or down direction. When the read head flies over the recorded bit cells, the latter can produce signals based on the magnetization direction. The signal-to-noise ratio (SNR) during the readout is approximately proportional to the number of grains. In a simplistic model, the SNR is given by the following expression:

$$SNR = 10 \cdot \log(N) \text{ dB.} \tag{4.2}$$

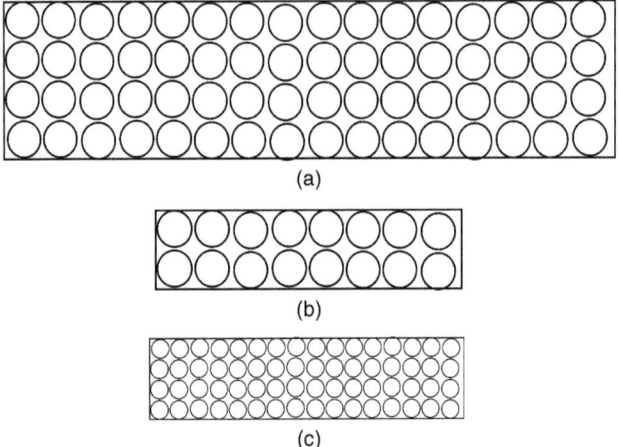

Figure 4.3. Bit cell of (a) an earlier generation HDD, where the grains are of a certain size. Illustration of bit cell of a later generation HDD, which needed to show four times the areal density, and cases where (b) grain size in recording media is not reduced and (c) grain size is also reduced significantly, leading to a similar number of grains per bit cell as in (a).

As discussed in Chapter 3, the SNR at a particular linear density is an indicator of how reliably the bits could be read out at that linear density. Therefore, the SNR is a key indicator of the recording performance of a recording medium. Media researchers always pay attention to improving the SNR of the recording medium at higher densities in order to achieve higher capacities per platter.

Since the SNR is proportional to the number of grains in a bit cell, it is possible to increase the SNR by increasing the number of grains per bit cell. However, when the areal density is increased, the size of the bit cell decreases. Therefore, it is quite difficult to increase the number of grains in a bit cell as the technology progresses. On the other hand, number of grains in a smaller bit cell can be maintained to be the same as the number in a bigger bit cell if the grain size is reduced. Figure 4.3 illustrates a scenario in which the size of a bit cell is reduced by four times to obtain an areal density increase of four times for two cases (i) without reduction in grain size (Fig. 4.3b) and (ii) with a reduction in grain size (Fig. 4.3c). It can be noticed that when the bit cell is reduced with a reduction in the grain size, an almost equal number of grains can be packed in the same bit area. However, when the bit size is reduced without reducing the grain size, fewer grains can be packed in the bit cell, which could cause a drastic reduction in the SNR. Therefore, one way to increase the SNR of the recording medium is to reduce the grain size and grain-size distribution, which would increase the number of grains in the bit area. A lot of research work has been carried out along this direction to increase the SNR. Grain-size reduction can be achieved by the use of seed layers or intermediate layers with small grain sizes, or from the magnetic layer itself [9–11].

Other possible ways to improve the SNR of the recording medium lie in looking beyond Equation 4.2. Equation 4.2 assumes that the SNR is proportional to the number of grains because of the randomness involved in the orientation of the easy axes, and the grain size. The signal produced by the recording medium will depend on the component of magnetization that lies parallel to the desired direction. If there are more grains with an easy axis perpendicular to the substrate, the component of magnetization along the perpendicular direction will also be higher. This will lead to an SNR that is enhanced beyond what is predicted by Equation 4.2 for the same number of grains. Several researchers have carried out research work along these lines. One way to minimize the randomness in perpendicular recording media is to improve the number of grains that have an easy axis along the perpendicular direction. This is achieved using intermediate layers in perpendicular recording media as will be discussed in a later section.

Theoretically, the linear density that can be supported by a longitudinal recording medium is proportional to the PW_{50}, which is the width of an isolated pulse at 50% height. Here, isolated pulse refers to readback from a transition that is far away from the other transitions so as not to be influenced by the magnetic interactions. In perpendicular recording technology, T_{50}, which is the width of the pulse from 25% to 75% of the pulse height, is commonly used to represent the pulse width. From a theoretical point of view, T_{50} depends mainly on the M_r, δ, and H_c, which are the remanent moment, thickness, and coercivity of the medium, respectively. Whereas the above is true for longitudinal recording, the correlations in perpendicular recording are more complicated and harder to establish. Nevertheless, some general conclusions can be reached, such as that the T_{50}, apart from the parameters mentioned above, also depends on the interaction between the grains. Therefore, controlling the exchange interaction between the grains would be another area of research. All these aspects related to oxide-based perpendicular media will be discussed in detail in the next few sections.

4.5 DESCRIPTION OF VARIOUS LAYERS AND THEIR FUNCTIONS

Figure 4.4 shows various functional layers, such as the SUL, the intermediate layer, and the recording layer of a typical double-layered perpendicular recording medium. Each layer has a specific function, and in most practical designs, there may be more than one layer involved for every function. For the sake of simplicity, only one layer is shown to illustrate the function of each layer. The recording media may be coated on an AlMg alloy or glass substrate of a dimension suitable for its particular application. At this point of time, server and desktop HDDs have disk substrates with an outer diameter (OD) of 95 mm. HDDs for laptops have disks with an OD of 65 mm and other form factors such as 1.8 in. are also common in consumer electronic applications such as MP3 players, and so on. Most of the layers in hard disk media are deposited by the sputtering process. Prior to the deposition of any layer, the substrates are cleaned to remove chemical and particle contaminants. Then, the substrate is first coated with an adhesion layer or interface layer, made of Ta, Ti, or an alloy of these materials. This layer helps in improving the adhesion of the SUL and all the other layers with the

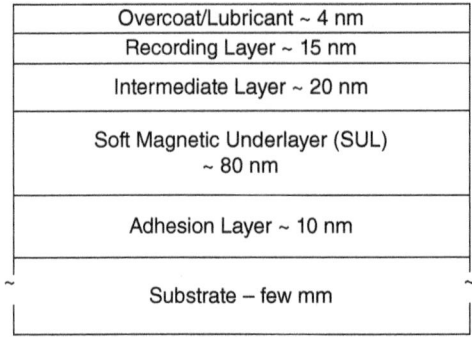

Figure 4.4. Different functional layers of perpendicular recording medium with approximate thickness (layers are not-to-scale). (Reprinted with permission from S. N. Piramanayagam, *J. Appl. Phys.* **102**, 011301 (2007). Copyright (2007) American Institute of Physics.)

substrate. The next layer deposited is the SUL. As discussed in the next section, the SUL helps in conducting the flux from the main pole of the write head to the auxillary pole.

On top of the SUL, some intermediate layers may be deposited with or without seed layers. The intermediate layers have at least two functions in perpendicular recording. Exchange decoupling the SUL and the magnetic layer, and providing epitaxial growth conditions for the recording layer are the two functions, and they will be described later. Sometimes, a seed layer may be deposited below the intermediate layer to enhance a preferred growth. The recording layer is a Co-based hexagonal close-packed (hcp) alloy for most of the designs carried out so far. The function of the recording layer is to store information for long periods of time (about 10 years) and to produce the signal when reading the information back. The disk will also be coated with carbon overcoats and lubricants to prevent the disk from failures caused by chemical reactions or mechanical impacts.

4.6 SUL IN PERPENDICULAR RECORDING

It is generally believed that the inclusion of an SUL in the perpendicular recording media generates the greatest benefits for perpendicular recording. Iwasaki et al. demonstrated in 1979 that a CoCr perpendicular recording medium also incorporating an Fe-Ni soft magnetic film requires less recording power (head field) and generates higher reproducing voltage (readback signal) than a single-layer medium [3]. This SUL is placed between the recording layer and the substrate, and serves to image the magnetic recording head. Figure 4.2 shows a single-pole head, double-layer perpendicular medium structure. In this structure, the SUL of the medium actually functions as part of the recording head. The functionality of the SUL is mainly as an imaging layer to increase the field gradient of the single-pole head. This is illustrated in Figure 4.5, where we treat

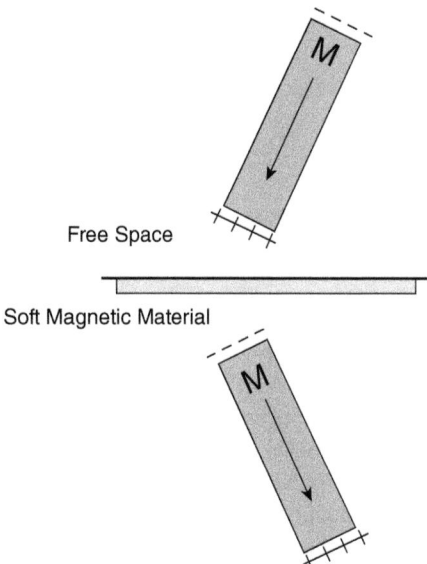

Figure 4.5. Schematic drawing explaining the functionality of the soft magnetic underlayer as an imaging layer.

the SUL as an infinite flat surface with very high permeability. If a magnetic source is brought near this surface, it will magnetize the soft layer, and the induced magnetization in the soft layer will then become a source of field itself. This can be illustrated using Maxwell's equations and simple electromagnetic theory as follows [12]:

Since

$$\vec{B} = \mu_0(\vec{H} + \vec{M}), \vec{\nabla} \cdot \vec{B} = 0, \tag{4.3}$$

we have

$$\vec{\nabla} \cdot \vec{H} = -\vec{\nabla} \cdot \vec{M} = \frac{\rho_m}{\mu_0}, \tag{4.4}$$

where ρ_m is the magnetic charge density.

For an infinitely large, very soft ($\mu \to \infty$) magnetic film, by using

$$\vec{\nabla} \cdot \vec{B} = 0, \vec{\nabla} \times \vec{H} = 0, \tag{4.5}$$

we can obtain

$$\vec{n} \cdot (\vec{B_o} - \vec{B_i}) = 0, \vec{n} \times (\vec{H_o} - \vec{H_i}) = 0, \tag{4.6}$$

where the suffixes o and i represent the outside and inside of the soft material, respectively.

Furthermore, using the linear constitutive relationship

$$\vec{B_o} = \mu_0 \vec{H_o}, \ \vec{B_i} = \mu_0 \vec{H_i}, \tag{4.7}$$

from Equation 4.6, we then have:

$$\mu_0 H_o^n = \mu H_i^n, \ H_o^t = H_i^t, \tag{4.8}$$

which means that

$$\frac{H_o^t}{H_o^n} = \frac{\mu_0}{\mu} \cdot \frac{H_i^t}{H_i^n} \to 0. \tag{4.9}$$

Therefore, the tangential component of H vanishes at the interface. This is a very important property since if only fields exterior to the soft material are considered, then this boundary condition will only be satisfied if the plane of the soft layer is thought to have a mirror image of the magnetic source. Thus, if $M(x, y)$ represents a magnetic dipole with x taken parallel to the plane of the soft layer, and the origin of y is at the soft layer surface (Fig. 4.5), then the mirror image of the magnetic source is given by

$$M_x^m(x, y) = -M_x(x, -y) \tag{4.10}$$

$$M_y^m(x, y) = M_y(x, -y). \tag{4.11}$$

Thus, the mirror imaging of the magnetic moment involves taking the magnetization at each $x, y > 0$ and placing the same magnetization at $(x, -y)$ in the soft layer but with the direction of the x component reversed.

So an SUL can effectively increase the head field in the perpendicular direction. Simulations have shown that a single-pole head—a medium with an SUL in perpendicular recording system—should enable write fields in excess of 80% of $4\pi M_s$ of the pole head/SUL material [13]. The increased head write fields opened the possibility to write on media with substantially higher anisotropy when compared to longitudinal media, and also led to better thermal stability. By acting as a magnetic mirror, the SUL effectively doubles the recording-layer thickness, facilitating substantially stronger readout signals [14, 15]. Also, this effective thickness increase leads to a reduction of the demagnetizing fields with a potential to further improve thermal stability.

While the use of perpendicular media with an SUL made it possible to postpone the superparamagnetic limit, the SUL introduced a number of technical challenges. The key factors of an SUL are its permeability, orientation, and magnetic moment. It was recognized early on that since reversal of the magnetization in the SUL is mainly realized by movement of the domain walls, this wall motion can potentially result in SUL playback noise ("spike" noise) originating from the Barkhausen effect [16]. The magnetization microstructure in an SUL, as also in the perpendicular recording medium, varies with the type of SUL material used. Media on amorphous SUL (a-SUL), such as CoTaZr, showed the smallest magnetization irregularities, whereas those on crystalline SUL, such as FeAlSi, showed large-scale magnetization irregularities which correlated with high medium noise [17, 18]. With regard to the SUL magnetization microstructure, even when the SUL is amorphous, stripe domain patterns can be observed, depending on the film thickness [19]. These stripe domains originate in the perpendicular anisotropy that is induced due to factors such as microshape anisotropy and magnetoelastic anisotropy [20]. In amorphous soft magnetic films that have a high magnetostrictive coefficient, such as FeCoB, compressive stresses during sputtering induce a perpendicular anisotropy and force the magnetization to oscillate out of the plane in a periodic manner to reduce the perpendicular anisotropy energy without paying a penalty in magnetostatic energy. Fringe magnetic fields emanating from the stripe domains cause SUL-induced direct current (DC) noise. Thermal annealing of the SUL was found to help in eliminating the stripe domain formation and reduce DC noise. Apparently, thermal annealing reduces the compressive stresses in the film and consequently, the perpendicular anisotropy [19].

Noise in the perpendicular recording medium could also be induced from surface roughness features or imperfect crystallographic features in the SUL since the former is fabricated over the latter. Another noise source is the funneling of stray fields into the media and head by the SUL. High permeability in the SUL allows a perfect imaging effect, but one solution that was proposed to control the noise from the SUL was to reduce its permeability [14]. Micromagnetic simulations [21] and finite element simulations [22] showed that perpendicular and in-track permeabilities as low as 50 did not significantly weaken the head fields or gradients.

Saturation of the SUL material by the high-moment magnetic recording head can lead to significant deterioration of the field gradient at the trailing pole [15]. While it was previously thought that the moment of the SUL material has to be higher than or equal to the moment of the recording pole tip material in order to avoid saturation effects in the SUL [15], magnetostatic arguments showed that it was sufficient if the moment of the pole tip not be more than twice the moment of the SUL [23]. This relaxation of restrictions allowed for a broad range of soft materials with moment in the range of 1–2 T to be considered.

Writability in perpendicular recording depends strongly on the spacing between the SUL and the writer pole [15, 24]. Better write field gradients and playback signals can be obtained by having the SUL as close to the air-bearing surface (ABS) of the recording head as possible. However, it is important to optimize the SUL-to-ABS distance because the value of the PW_{50} passes through a maximum as the SUL-to-ABS distance is varied [15]. Chang et al. reported that reducing head-to-keeper spacing from 45 to 35 nm can reduce the PW_{50} by 20% and enhance the head field from 11.9 to 13.9 kOe [19].

Stray fields generated by the recorded bit pattern in the recording layer can affect the imaging ability of the SUL [25]. This is a serious issue at high areal densities, where the ability of the SUL to respond to rapid spatial variations in the applied magnetic field becomes limited, or in other words, the effective permeability decreases. Conceptually, this is akin to an effective increase in the SUL-to-ABS distance. When this happens, the imaging performance can deteriorate, leading to loss of resolution (increased PW_{50} and decreased amplitude of the read sensitivity function) and distortions in the playback signal. This means that relatively high anisotropy SUL materials (anisotropy field $H_k > 50$ Oe) are desirable in order to optimize the performance of the recording system.

Another aspect affecting the performance of double-layered PMR media is the proper choice of the hard and easy axes of the SUL material [15]. If the easy axis of the SUL were to be radially aligned, then the magnetization switching during the write process would proceed by magnetization rotation instead of by a hysteretic process, which is inherently noisy owing to the Barkhausen effect. Even during the readback process, the application of the radial biasing field will efficiently wipe the domain walls out of the SUL. In modern PMR media, the radial anisotropy in the SUL is induced by means of the magnetic fields leaking from the magnetron cathodes used for sputtering from the targets.

Domain wall-induced noise has been mentioned above as a significant source of playback noise due to domain wall interaction with recorded bits or response to stray magnetic fields from the recording head. Early schemes to overcome this problem proposed magnetically biasing the SUL with a hard magnetic layer, such as SmCo, that could pin the domains via lateral exchange coupling [26, 27], or an externally placed permanent magnet, thereby sweeping the domain walls out of the SUL and forcing it into a single-domain state [15, 25]. A more practical (and economical) solution was proposed by Takahashi et al., who demonstrated that domains in the SUL could be pinned by exchange bias to an antiferromagnetic layer [28]. Exchange anisotropy is an interfacial phenomenon, and the strength of the exchange bias due to the antiferromagnetic layer falls off with the thickness of the ferromagnetic layer [29]. This means that for soft underlayers thicker than a few tens of nanometers, the entire SUL cannot be exchange biased using a single antiferromagnetic layer. However, the SUL cannot be merely exchange biased from the top because of the head-to-media spacing constraints. Multilayers composed of alternating ferromagnet–antiferromagnet films have been proposed to overcome some of these issues, and can provide significant exchange bias and reduction in integrated DC noise [28, 30, 31]. However, the manufacturing process for multilayer films is rather complicated, and as such, they are less desirable in the industry.

Synthetic antiferromagnetic (SAF) coupled films were later introduced as soft underlayers for perpendicular recording media [32–34]. SAF coupled thin films, in which two ferromagnetic layers are indirectly antiparallel coupled through a nonmagnetic spacer layer such as Ru [35], have already been studied extensively for applications such as spin-valve recording heads and longitudinal recording media. Compared to exchange-biased structures, the closed-loop structure resulting from the antiparallel coupling offers better thermal stability and near-zero edge demagnetization fields, and the thinner nonmagnetic spacer layers facilitate improved flux-carrying efficiency. At the same time, the two layers in the SAF structure cancel each other during the reading process, leading to zero remanent magnetization, and offering domain stability and low spike noise. During the write process, they function as conventional soft underlayers. Because of the exchange field, the saturation fields in both radial and circumferential directions are enhanced, which leads to reduced permeability levels. Additonally, the strength of the exchange coupling varies inversely proportional to the thickness of the individual SAF coupled layers, and the anisotropy field was observed to increase with increasing exchange coupling field [36]. Since the permeability depends on the strength of the exchange field, this provides a method of controlling permeability without changing material properties. Reduced DC noise, higher SNRs, and suppressed wide area adjacent track erasure have been demonstrated for perpendicular recording media on CoTaZr SAF coupled soft underlayers [36]. A nearly single-domain state with enhanced exchange and anisotropy fields, and high thermal stability have been achieved on SAF coupled dual and trilayer soft magnetic films [37], and on SAF coupled soft magnetic films pinned with an antiferromagnetic IrMn layer [38, 39]. SAF coupled soft underlayers pinned to a single domain state by hard magnetic layers have also been produced and optimized for recording performance [40, 41].

Since the introduction of SAF coupled SUL structures, investigations have also shown that their performance in terms of media writability and SNR was superior compared to antiferromagnet-pinned soft underlayers [42]. Current generation HDDs based on perpendicular recording media make use of SAF coupled soft underlayers with the composition, thickness, and exchange coupling of the layers tuned to achieve optimal SNRs.

4.7   CURRENT PERPENDICULAR RECORDING MEDIA

In spite of several advantages that perpendicular recording has over longitudinal recording technology, the former was not given serious thought until this century. There were several challenges with the media, including head design and the integration of a perpendicular recording drive. The areal density demonstrations on perpendicular recording were also lagging behind that of longitudinal recording. As far as the perpendicular recording medium itself is concerned, it had many problems that rendered it inferior to that of longitudinal recording. For example, in 2001 the recording medium for longitudinal recording had a grain size of about 8–9 nm, which was significantly smaller than what was possible then in perpendicular recording, which was about 12 nm. The problems with the introduction of soft underlayer technology were just discussed in the previous section. This section will briefly discuss the problems faced by earlier generation media and shift attention toward the oxide-based perpendicular media in more detail.

The material used for the recording layer of the perpendicular media has traditionally been a Co alloy. CoCr alloy thin film was the original media proposed by Iwasaki et al. in the late 1970s [3]. Since then, modifications of Co alloys, such as CoCrPt, CoCrTa, CoCrNb, CoCrPtNb, and CoCrPtB, have been used as the recording layer material [4]. Even though the material and processes used in the perpendicular recording media were similar to that used in longitudinal recording media, the former could not exhibit competing performance until the end of the last century. The requirements of perpendicular recording media and the way the oxide-based perpendicular media meets them are described in this section.

CoCrPt-oxide-based recording layers typically have Pt composition in the range of 10–20 at%, Cr in the range of 5–20 at%, and Co in the range of 60–80 at%. The oxide material could be a component in the target, for example, in the form of SiO_2,

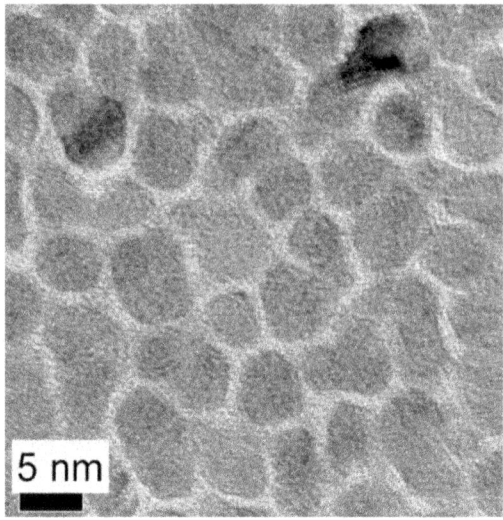

Figure 4.6. TEM planar view of a typical $CoCrPt:SiO_2$ perpendicular recording media. (Reprinted with permission from S. N. Piramanayagam, *J. Appl. Phys.* **102**, 011301 (2007). Copyright (2007) American Institute of Physics.)

Ta_2O_5, TiO_2, and so on. When such a composite target is sputtered, the resultant polycrystalline thin film has two regions: the grains that contain little or negligible oxygen and the grain boundary that has more oxygen. Since the grains are mainly made up of Co with Pt as the main elements, they are magnetic. The presence of Pt also increases the uniaxial anisotropy constant of the grain. The grain boundary that has excessive oxygen but may still have Co and Pt would turn out to be nonmagnetic. This nonmagnetic grain boundary helps to separate the magnetic grains from each other and to reduce the transition noise. Figure 4.6 is a transmission electron microscope (TEM) image of a typical oxide-based perpendicular media, which illustrates the grains and grain boundaries. The oxide material can also be formed by controlling the amount of reactive oxygen gas during the sputtering process, with or without the presence of oxide materials in the sputtering target. When there is no oxide material in the sputtering target, the resultant oxide in the grain boundary is mainly due to Cr. Recently, it has become quite common to use one or two oxide materials in the sputtering target.

4.7.1 Noise Issues

Design of recording media generally follows the famous media trilemma—which is to meet the required SNR, thermal stability, and writability simultaneously. The SNR can be improved by increasing the signal, reducing the noise, or doing both. Signal improvement can be achieved by several other means, such as reducing flying height, increasing the head sensitivity, and so on, besides improving the media design. However, for a properly written medium, reduced noise is mainly a function of media design. Therefore, noise reduction is one of the most important considerations in media design. As discussed in an earlier chapter, two types of noise are investigated. They are DC erase noise and transition noise. When a particular material is chosen for perpendicular recording media, they should also be able to achieve low DC and transition noise.

DC erase noise (or simply, DC noise) is measured after erasing a medium and measuring the output voltage of a flying head scanning over the medium. In the case of a longitudinal recording medium, there should be no stray field after erasing a particular track. Therefore, when the head flies over an erased track, no signal should be sensed by the read head. This would indicate zero DC noise. However, if there is some voltage in the read head when flying over an erased track, the voltage that is picked up by the head is called DC noise. One of the major requirements for recording media is that the DC noise should be low. This is because DC noise is like background noise in the system. In most recording media, the noise at highest density would be the sum of the DC noise and the transition noise. Therefore, it is essential to reduce the DC noise in order to achieve a low noise at high linear densities.

One of the major problems of earlier generation CoCr-alloy perpendicular media was that the DC noise of such media was high. When a perpendicular recording medium is DC erased, the magnetization of the erased track would be uniformly up or down depending on the polarity of the magnetic head during the writing process.When a read head flies over such a surface, the resultant output in the head would be a constant positive or negative voltage. However, if the recording medium is not designed well, it is quite likely that the magnetization is not uniformly up or down but interspersed with regions of opposite and zero remanent magnetization. Such regions of opposite and zero remanent magnetization would create DC noise. In perpendicular recording, regions of opposite magnetization are created by demagnetization effects on grains that would reverse the magnetization on their own when the applied field is removed.

In a typical perpendicular recording medium, the grains have a distribution in their size and in their anisotropy. Usually, the grains that are small in size or weak in anisotropy are in the superparamagnetic limit. Such grains cannot maintain their magnetization direction in the absence of an applied field. It is such grains that reverse their magnetization when the applied field is removed, leading to a lower value of remanent moment and to DC noise. As a matter of fact, such a behavior can be observed from magnetization curves, which can be easily obtained from a vibrating sample magnetometer (VSM) or polar Kerr magnetometer. The nucleation field (field required to switch 5% of the magnetization) of the recording layer is a useful parameter to get an idea of DC noise. A well-textured perpendicular medium in which the grains are thermally stable (which will have a negligible DC noise) will have its nucleation field in the second quadrant of the hysteresis loop. A medium in which a large percentage of grains are not thermally stable (with a large DC noise) will have its nucleation field in the first quadrant.

Figure 4.7 illustrates the behavior of two media with high and low DC noise. The grains are magnetized perpendicularly to the plane of the paper with an applied field (that goes into the paper). When the field is removed, all the grains are expected to maintain their magnetization state if they are thermally stable and their anisotropy energy is higher than that of the demagnetizing energy. If the anisotropy constant of

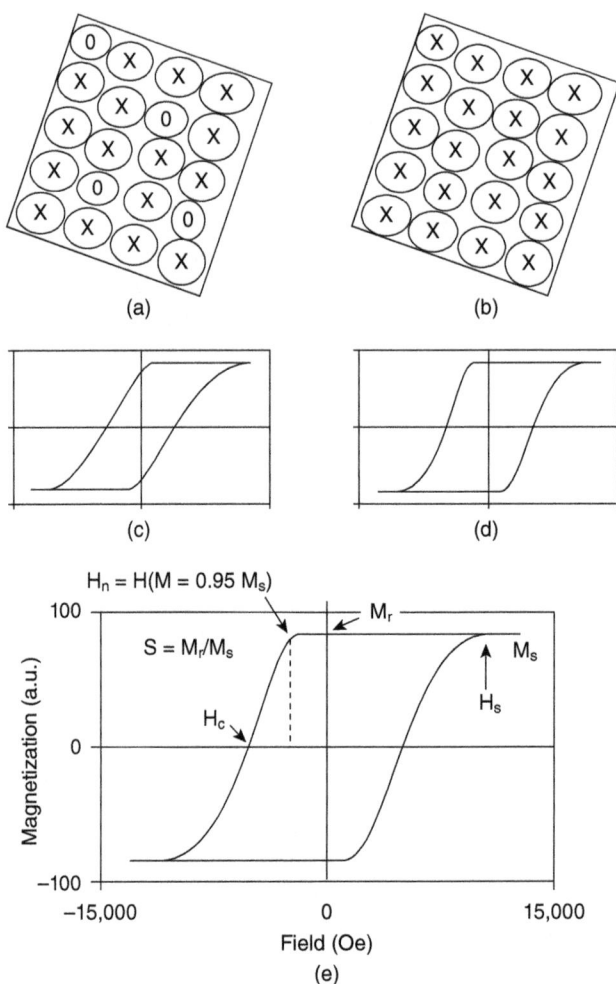

Figure 4.7. Illustration of (top) remanence magnetization state of grains of perpendicular media, after it was saturated with a field into the plane. Some grains on the left side show a reversal with remanent magnetization out of plane showing instability. (Bottom) Illustration of hysteresis loops of the respective media. (Reprinted with permission from S. N. Piramanayagam, *J. Appl. Phys.* **102**, 011301 (2007). Copyright (2007) American Institute of Physics.)

the media is rather low, the smaller grains would reverse, as in Figure 4.7a. On the other hand, if the anisotropy is high enough, all the grains would maintain their magnetization in the applied field direction, as in Figure 4.7b. This is seen in hysteresis loops with nucleation fields in the first quadrant (Fig. 4.7c) and second quadrant (Fig. 4.7d) for media with low K_u and high K_u, respectively. Therefore, media with a high anisotropy are needed to obtain a negative nucleation field and a negligible DC noise.

In the earlier days, it was difficult to obtain such media as Cr was used as an additive element to obtain the exchange decoupling. The process used then for making perpendicular media was similar to that of longitudinal recording media in the sense that the substrate was heated during the deposition of the medium. Due to the mobility obtained from heating, Cr would segregate to the grain boundary and form the nonmagnetic material needed to decouple the grains. However, such a process needed Cr concentrations of more than 14 at% to sufficiently decouple the grains. Since not all the Cr atoms would segregate to the grain boundary, the core of the grain would still be a CoCr alloy with a large amount of Cr (about 15 at%). Since the anisotropy constant of a Co alloy decreases in general with the amount of Cr in it, the presence of Cr in the core of the grain led to media with lower anisotropy energy [43], making them thermally unstable. To overcome this problem, Co/Pd multilayers were attempted as recording media for some period of time [44, 45]. Although Co/Pd multilayers showed unit squareness, indicating their promise for low DC noise, they exhibited high transition noise. Moreover, it was also considered difficult to fabricate Co/Pd multilayers, which required about 20 sputtering stations for the recording layer alone.

The problems mentioned above were made inconsequential with the arrival of CoCrPt-oxide-based perpendicular recording media. The key difference is in the way the nonmagnetic grain boundary is obtained. Unlike CoCrPt media, where a Cr-rich CoCr alloy forms the grain boundary, the grain boundary in oxide-based perpendicular media is an oxide material. The oxygen for oxide formation comes mainly from the oxygen introduced as reactive gas during the sputtering process, from the target, or both. Therefore, it is not necessary to have a high concentration of Cr in the sputtering target to obtain the nonmagnetic phase in the grain boundary. As a result, the concentration of Cr in the core of the grain is also reduced, leading to a grain with a large anisotropy constant. Thus, high thermal stability and low DC noise can be obtained with oxide-based media.

Transition noise depends on exchange coupling between the grains, and exchange coupling is a function of the thickness of the boundaries. Therefore, exchange coupling and hence transition noise can be reduced by separating the grains from each other either physically (voids) or by using nonmagnetic materials at the grain boundaries. In longitudinal recording media, a nonmagnetic Cr-rich CoCr alloy at the grain boundary helps to reduce the transition noise. In oxide-based recording media, lower transition noise is also obtained by segregating the grains from each other by forming a nonmagnetic oxide grain boundary. It has also been reported that better segregation between the magnetic grains can be obtained if the intermediate layers below (such as Ru) also have a better segregation. Therefore, it is common to see oxide-based media where the Ru layer next to the recording layer is sputtered at a high pressure.

Another significant aspect of oxide-based recording media is the ease of fabrication method. Unlike CoCrPt-based media, CoCrPt-oxide-based media do not need to be heated to form the grain boundary. Unlike its other competitors, such as Co/Pd multilayer-based media, the oxide-based media do not need several chambers to form the recording media structures. Because of such advantages, the oxide-based media have become the dominant choice in current perpendicular recording technology.

4.7.2   SNR Improvement

The previous section dealt with how the oxide-based perpendicular recording media overcame the problems encountered with the previous generations of perpendicular recording media. This section will describe how the improvement in SNR in oxide-based perpendicular media has been/can be achieved. As discussed earlier, the SNR of the recording medium depends on the grain size, grain-size distribution, proper exchange decoupling, and narrow distribution in c-axis orientation. All these aspects depend both on the recording and intermediate layers. Therefore, the roles of the intermediate layers and the recording layers are discussed simultaneously.

The primary function of the intermediate layer is to break the coupling between the SUL and the recording layer. When a magnetically soft layer and a hard layer are next to each other, the properties of both the layers change because of the exchange interaction. Such exchange interaction can reduce the coercivity of the recording layer, produce a large noise during the readout, and so on. Therefore, intermediate layers are necessary in perpendicular recording media design. In addition, the intermediate layers have supplementary functions, such as inducing textured growth in the recording layer and, more recently, in improving the exchange decoupling between the magnetic grains. Figure 4.8 represents the intermediate layer and recording layer configuration in a perpendicular recording medium. The details of the intermediate layers and the recording layers are presented together in this section.

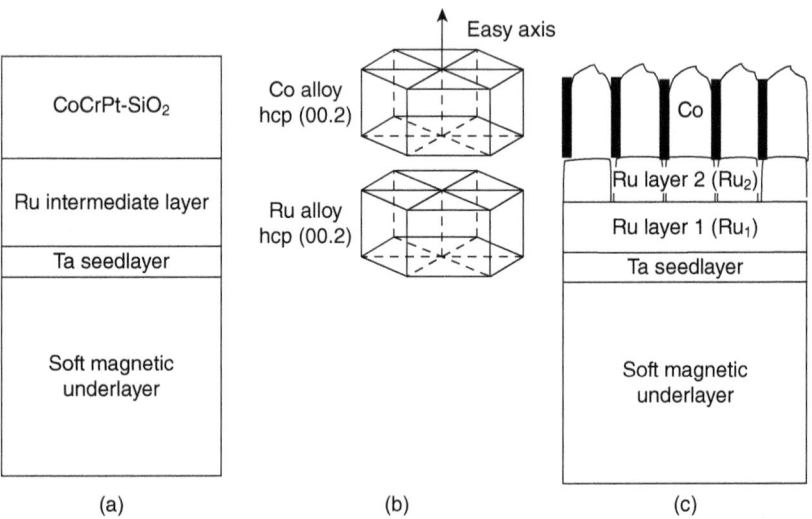

Figure 4.8. Illustration of (a) typical layers of current perpendicular recording media; (b) heteroepitaxial growth; and (c) design that involves dual Ru layers. (Reprinted with permission from S. N. Piramanayagam, *J. Appl. Phys.* **102**, 011301 (2007). Copyright (2007) American Institute of Physics.)

4.7.2.1 *Perpendicular c-Axis Orientation.*

As mentioned before, one of the functions of intermediate layers is to induce a perpendicular hcp (00.2) orientation in the Co-alloy-based recording layer. In Co-alloy-based perpendicular recording media, the easy axis (c-axis of the hcp crystal) needs to have a perpendicular orientation with respect to the substrate (as in Fig. 4.8b). When measured with X-ray diffraction (XRD), it will be seen as hcp (00.2) peaks in the θ-2θ scans at about 44°, depending on the constituents of the Co alloy. For Co alloys with Pt as an additive element, hcp (00.2) peaks will be seen at around 43° because the addition of Pt will lead to an expansion of the "c" parameter. As discussed in Section 4.6, in the current design of perpendicular recording media, amorphous materials such as CoTaZr or FeCoB are used as the SUL because they could provide a lower noise. Moreover, the a-SULs also exhibit a very low average roughness (closer to that of the substrate) of about 0.15 nm. When Co alloy is deposited directly on top of the a-SUL, hcp (00.2) texture is not developed with a low dispersion. Therefore, it is essential to grow intermediate layers that would induce an hcp (00.2) orientation on the Co-alloy-based recording layer. Several research efforts have been published since the 1980s. Most of the papers before 2002 were based on CoCrPt or CoCrPtB media and were deposited at high temperatures [4]. However, the present-day media based on CoCrPt-oxide are deposited at room temperature, and they need the presence of different kinds of seed layers and intermediate layers than considered before. The intermediate layers for CoCrPt-oxide-based media is discussed below.

In the pioneering work of Hikosaka et al. [46], an Ru intermediate layer was used for oxide-based perpendicular media. Since then, Ru is one of the most common materials used or investigated as the intermediate layer. This reality, in fact, led to a steady increase in the price of Ru (by 300–400%) in late 2006, when hard disk drives with perpendicular recording media were introduced in the market. Several researchers have investigated different materials as seed layer and intermediate layers for perpendicular recording media. From the literature available so far, Ta seems to be the most common seed layer material for an Ru intermediate layer in order to obtain a narrow c-axis orientation, but the industry players also use Ni-based nonmagnetic alloys. Choe et al. have studied Ta/Ru intermediate layers and have obtained a $\Delta\theta_{50}$ value (a measure of dispersion in the c-axis orientation) of 3° for the Co layer [47]. Although the surface energy of the seed layer and intermediate layer material could play an important role, it is not well known as to what factors induce the narrowest dispersion in the c-axis distribution of Ru intermediate layers. Considering the increase in the price of Ru and the scarcity of Ru, it is necessary to find alternative materials to Ru and alternative seed layer materials. Research efforts are also progressing in this direction.

Controlling the c-axis orientation dispersion with the intermediate layers is a focal area of perpendicular recording media research. Choe et al. have also indicated that the SNR of the media depends strongly (at the rate of 0.6 dB per −1°) on the $\Delta\theta_{50}$ [47]. In other words, the lower the $\Delta\theta_{50}$, the higher the SNR will be. The SNR depends inversely on $\Delta\theta_{50}$ for at least two reasons: (1) if all the Co grains are oriented with the c-axis perpendicular to the film plane, the component of M in the perpendicular direction will be higher, resulting in a larger signal and a lower noise; (2) if the easy axes of some small grains are oriented away from the perpendicular direction, their moments can be reversed by small external fields, which makes them susceptible to demagnetization and thermal effects. Such grains will be a source of noise. Therefore, it is clear that achieving a low value of $\Delta\theta_{50}$ is crucial for obtaining high performance from the recording media.

It has been generally observed that the $\Delta\theta_{50}$ depends on the thickness of the intermediate layers. Narrower $\Delta\theta_{50}$ values are possible with thicker intermediate layers. However, thicker intermediate layers also lead to reduced writing fields and increased PW_{50} values. Calculations by Chang et al., for example, indicate that lower head-to-keeper spacing will help to improve the writing and to reduce the PW_{50}. In double-layered perpendicular recording media, the thickness of the intermediate layer will contribute to the head-to-keeper spacing, and therefore, it is necessary to reduce the intermediate layer thickness [19]. Litvinov et al. also have reported that the head-to-keeper spacing will decide the amount of write field available for the writing process. In addition, it will also determine the width of the bits. Considering all the above factors, suitable design of intermediate layers is an ongoing research field.

To overcome the above problem, one possible approach is to find a suitable seed layer and intermediate layer combination that would lead to lower $\Delta\theta_{50}$, for thin intermediate layers. In such an approach, X/Pd/Ru intermediate layers have been studied and reported to have a dependence of $\Delta\theta_{50}$ on the material X [48].

Alternatively, another approach, which was also discussed in Section 4.6, involves reducing the intermediate layer thickness using crystalline SULs. By using a suitable combination of seed layers such as Ta/Ru, a face centered cubic (fcc)-based SUL such as FeCo could grow with a very good (111) texture (Fig. 4.9). When the intermediate

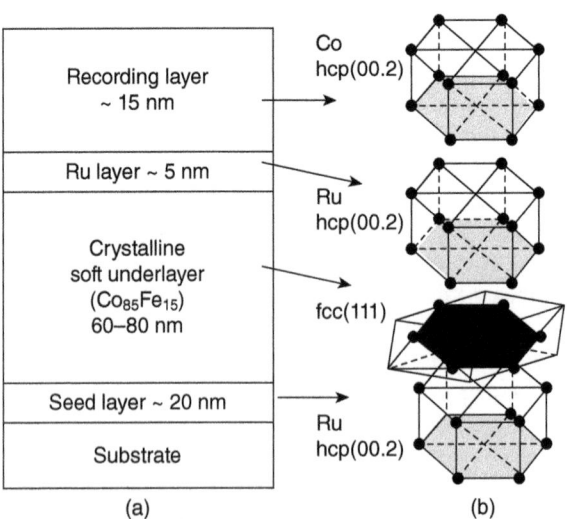

Figure 4.9. Illustration of (a) media layer structure and (b) epitaxial growth of Ru and recording layer on crystalline FeCo SUL. (Reprinted with permission from S. N. Piramanayagam, *J. Appl. Phys.* **102**, 011301 (2007). Copyright (2007) American Institute of Physics.)

layer and the recording layer are grown on fcc (111) template, the epitaxial growth condition for hcp (00.2) texture is achieved. The intermediate layer is needed only for exchange decoupling the SUL and the recording layer, and segregation of the grains. Therefore, the intermediate layer can be thinner than that needed with a-SULs.

A different take on the above approach involves a virtual way of reducing the intermediate layer thickness. In this case, the nonmagnetic Ru_1 layer, which is needed for producing the hcp (00.2) texture, is replaced with a magnetic layer such as CoCr. On the other hand, a part of the nonmagnetic Ru_1 layer can also be replaced with crystalline soft magnetic materials such as FeCo. In these cases, the magnetic-material-based intermediate layer would help to pass the flux from the head into the SUL. With such designs, the Ru-based intermediate layer is only needed for exchange decoupling and grain segregation. Media with magnetic intermediate layers showed recording performance comparable to that of media with conventional intermediate layers.

4.7.2.2 Nanostructure. An additional role of the intermediate layer could be to produce the right morphology to control the segregation of grains in the recording layer. For example, in the studies of Shi et al. and Park et al., it was noted that the deposition of Ru at higher pressures leads to an increase in the value of $\Delta\theta_{50}$ [49, 50]. On the other hand, sputtering Ru at higher pressures (Ru_2) leads to a segregated structure in both the Ru layer and in the recording layer, and leads to an improved coercivity (and a lower noise). Therefore, in order to achieve both narrow $\Delta\theta_{50}$ and a high coercivity, dual Ru intermediate layers have been studied (Fig. 4.8c). Shi et al. have varied the thickness ratio of Ru_1 and Ru_2 layers and have reported that coercivity, nucleation field, and $\Delta\theta_{50}$ are optimum for the intermediate values of thickness ratio when compared with pure Ru_1 or Ru_2 alone [51]. Shi et al. and Park et al. have also studied the effect of top Ru deposition pressure [49, 50]. In both studies, improved grain isolation is observed for films that were made with higher pressure Ru on the top. It is clear from these studies that sputtering the Ru layers at high pressures in the proximity of the recording layer is an approach that improves the exchange decoupling in the recording layer. It is common now to find such designs in hard disk media products.

Since the intermediate layers control the segregation of the recording layers to some extent, it might be a good idea to use the intermediate layers to control the grain size of recording media. Recently, studies have been carried out along these lines to reduce the grain size and increase the thermal stability of the recording layer using intermediate layers. Piramanayagam et al. have proposed an intermediate layer-based approach to reduce the grain size of the recording layer [52]. In this approach, the intermediate layer Ru_2 is not pure Ru but an alloy of RuCr. When the RuCr alloy is sputtered in the presence of reactive oxygen gas, Cr-based oxide forms the grain boundary. Using a suitable combination of pressure, and Cr and oxygen composition, the grain size could be tailored. Grain-to-grain distance of 6.4 nm based on this approach has been reported. Reducing recording layer grain size using the intermediate layer is one possible approach.

The authors also have proposed the use of a synthetic nucleation layer to control the grain size and the grain-size distribution [53]. Since the grain size depends on the number of nucleation sites, if there is a way to control the number and arrangement of the nucleation sites, the grain size and grain-size distribution can be controlled effectively. As such a control is lacking in current deposition schemes, the authors have proposed the use of a synthetic nucleation (SN) layer to achieve these objectives. This study on CoCrPt-oxide media using a special carbon layer has helped to achieve grain sizes below 6 nm with good crystallographic texture. Several materials could be tested as the SN layers to achieve lower grain sizes and grain-size distribution.

4.8 RECENT DEVELOPMENTS AND FUTURE TRENDS

The first-generation HDDs based on perpendicular recording technology, which were released around 2005–2006, could support areal densities of 100–150 Gb/in.^{2} Since then, advances in media have enabled areal densities upward of 500 Gb/in.^{2} in commercial HDDs (as of 2010). It is expected that PMR technology will continue to drive areal densities toward 1 Tb/in.^{2}, and possibly as high as 1.5 Tb/in.^{2} before the technology loses steam from inherent material limitations and gives way to more advanced technologies such as energy-assisted magnetic recording (EAMR) or bit-patterned media (BPM). This section is an attempt to provide a brief glimpse of the advances in media design that has enabled PMR to achieve its current status, and factors that will be crucial to extending its longevity.

Since the inception of PMR media, the most significant developments have been in the design of the magnetic recording layer. The first-generation PMR media consisted of only one or two CoCrPt-oxide magnetic recording layers; more recently, trends have been in the direction of multiple recording layers, with or without nonmagnetic layers inserted between them. The driving advantage behind this development has been the ability to reduce media switching fields and thus improve writability without degrading media thermal stability. In exchange-spring (ES) media [54, 55], the hard–soft perpendicular magnetic layers with very different oxide content and different anisotropy energy K_u are stacked next to each other, and the interlayer exchange coupling is strongest. The hard magnetic layer determines the thermal stability of the media, whereas the soft magnetic layer determines the switching field. In addition, the strong interlayer exchange coupling across the hard–soft interface also leads to narrower switching field distributions than in single-layer media, simply due to the fact that the hard-to-write media grains are switched more readily by ES effects than the already easy-to-write media grains. A narrower switching field distribution is essential to reduce medium noise. Modern PMR media, called exchange-coupled composite (ECC) media, make use of nonmagnetic spacer layers between the hard and soft magnetic layers. Usually only a few angstroms in thickness, these spacer layers help to exercise control over the degree of the interlayer exchange coupling and thus the switching field. Optimizing the coupling through the spacer layer in ECC media can significantly improve recording performance [56]. ES and ECC media designs have enabled media write fields to be reduced by a factor of two to four over single-layer media without losing thermal stability. Excellent overviews of ES and ECC media are provided by Victora and Shen, and Suess et al., referenced at the end of this chapter [54, 55]. It is expected that advanced ES and ECC media designs with several perpendicular magnetic layers, each having a different K_u, will be key to taking PMR media technology beyond 1 Tb/in.^{2}

Another important area of research and development in recent times concerns the interlayer and the SUL. While there have been only modest changes in the a-SUL and Ru interlayers since PMR media was first introduced, it is becoming imperative to further enhance write fields and gradients due to the SUL, and improve writability of perpendicular media by reducing the head-to-SUL spacing. In this regard, crystalline soft underlayers that have been previously proposed have gained renewed interest. If the crystallographic perpendicular orientation of the magnetic recording layer could be induced through the SUL instead of the thick intermediate layers, such as those of Ru currently in vogue, then the total interlayer thickness could be substantially reduced and writability improved. However, it is well known and was here previously discussed that crystalline soft underlayers tend to produce high levels of noise compared to a-SULs. Even when the noise was reduced by optimal design, large grain sizes in the crystalline SUL tended to induce large grain sizes in the recording layer [57]. A more promising design for improving writability involves an optimal combination of both amorphous and crystalline soft underlayers called hybrid soft underlayers [58]. In this design, by choosing a suitable ratio of amorphous to crystalline thickness, optimal surface smoothness and good perpendicular orientation for the recording layer along-side small and exchange-decoupled grains could be achieved on thinner interlayers, leading to smaller head-to-keeper spacing. Micromagnetic simulation has also demon-strated that the hybrid SUL scheme helps to improve writing field effectiveness and increase field gradient along down-track and cross-track directions [59]. In a variant of the hybrid SUL scheme, an antiferromagnetic IrMn layer was used above the crystalline SUL in order to pin the domains in the latter [60]. At the same time, the IrMn layer helps to promote the perpendicular orientation in the recording layer without the requirement of thick interlayers. With further optimization, this scheme could help to reduce crystalline SUL noise and improve writability.

A snapshot of recent developments and future directions for PMR media technol-ogy was provided above. Although a lot of effort has been devoted to optimizing the design of the recording layer, it will also require major advances in interlayer and SUL design to extend PMR media technology beyond 1–1.5 Tb/in.^{2}

4.9 SUMMARY

In this chapter, SUL design and the CoCrPt-oxide-based recording medium have been discussed in a systematic way.

- The incorporation of SULs in perpendicular recording gave it a significant boost in terms of writability on highly anisotropic, thermally stable perpendicular media.
- Early on, noise induced by domain wall motion in the SUL was identified as a serious problem in integrating the SUL into the media stack. Radially anisotropic,

a-SULs that were coupled in antiparallel direction through a spacer layer to overcome most of the noise-related issues.

- Oxide-based perpendicular recording media exhibit lower DC noise and transition noise than competitors such as CoCrPt alloys or Co/Pd multilayers. Moreover, the ease of fabrication has made them the best material for perpendicular recording as of now.
- Exchange-coupled composite media consisting of multiple magnetic recording layers, each with a different anisotropy constant K_u, have been key enablers as PMR media pushes beyond 500 Gb/in.^{2} In such a design, the soft(est) layer determines the switching field, and the hard(est) layer determines the thermal stability.
- Significant improvements in the SUL and intermediate layer design will be necessary in order to extend the CoCrPt-oxide-based PMR media longevity beyond 1–1.5 Tb/in.^{2}

REFERENCES

1. S. Iwasaki and K. Takemura, An analysis for the circular mode of magnetization in short wavelength recording. IEEE Trans. Magn. **11**, 1173 (1975).
2. S. Iwasaki and Y. Nakamura, The magnetic field distribution of a perpendicular recording head. IEEE Trans. Magn. **14**, 436 (1978).
3. S. Iwasaki, Y. Nakamura, and K. Ouchi, Perpendicular magnetic recording with a composite anisotropy film. IEEE Trans. Magn. **MAG-61**, 1456 (1979).
4. S. N. Piramanayagam, Perpendicular recording media for hard disk drives. J. Appl. Phys. **102**, 011301 (2007).
5. S. Iwasaki, Perpendicular magnetic recording—Evolution and future. IEEE Trans. Magn. **20**, 657 (1984).
6. J. H. Judy, Advancements in PMR thin-film media. J. Magn. Magn. Mater. **287**, 16 (2004).
7. D. Litvinov and S. Khizroev, Perpendicular magnetic recording: playback. J. Appl. Phys. **97**, 071101 (2005).
8. S. Khizroev and D. Litvinov, Perpendicular magnetic recording: writing process. J. Appl. Phys. **95**, 4521 (2004).
9. L. L. Lee, D. E. Laughlin, L. Fang, and D. N. Lambeth, Effects of Cr intermediate layers on CoCrPt thin film media on NiAl underlayers. IEEE Trans. Magn. **31**, 2728 (1995).
10. B. R. Acharya, E. N. Abarra, and I. Okamoto, SNR improvements for advanced longitudinal recording media. IEEE Trans. Magn. **37**, 1475 (2001).
11. S. N. Piramanayagam, Y. F. Xu, D. Y. Dai, L. Huan, S. I. Pang, and J. P. Wang, Ultrasmall grain size control in longitudinal recording media for ultrahigh areal densities. J. Appl. Phys. **91**, 7685 (2002).
12. J. D. Jackson, *Classical Electrodynamics*. New York: Wiley Text Books, 1998.
13. S. Khizroev, R. M. Chomko, Y. Liu, K. Mountfield, M. H. Kryder, and D. Litvinov, Perpendicular systems above 100 Gbits/in^2 density, No. CB-07, Intermag, 2000.
14. S. Khizroev, J. Bain, and M. H. Kryder, Considerations in the design of probe heads for 100 Gbits/in^2 recording density. IEEE Trans. Magn. **33**, 2893 (1997).

15. D. Litvinov, M. H. Kryder, and S. Khizroev, Recording physics of perpendicular media: soft underlayers. J. Magn. Magn. Mater. **232**, 84 (2001).

16. Y. Uesaka, M. Koizumi, and N. Tsumita, Noise from underlayer of perpendicular magnetic recording medium. J. Appl. Phys. **57**, 3925 (1985).

17. Y. Honda, A. Kikukawa, Y. Hirayama, and M. Futamoto, Effect of soft magnetic underlayer on magnetization microstructures of perpendicular thin film media. IEEE Trans. Magn. **36**, 2399 (2000).

18. A. Kikukawa, Y. Honda, Y. Hirayama, and M. Futamoto, Noise characteristics of double-layered perpendicular media using novel soft magnetic underlayer materials. IEEE Trans. Magn. **36**, 2402 (2000).

19. C. Chang, M. Plumer, C. Brucker, J. Chen, R. Ranjan, J. van Ek, J. Yu, D. Karns, Y. Kubota, G. Ju, and D. Weller, Measurements and modeling of soft underlayer materials for perpendicular magnetic recording. IEEE Trans. Magn. **38**, 1637 (2002).

20. S. X. Wang and J. Hong, Magnetic and microstructural characterization of FeTaN high saturation materials for recording heads. IEEE Trans. Magn. **35**, 782 (1999).

21. M. Khan and R. H. Victora, Micromagnetic model of perpendicular recording head with soft underlayer. IEEE Trans. Magn. **37**, 1379 (2001).

22. A. Shukh, 3D FEM modeling of keeper effect on perpendicular recording. J. Magn. Magn. Mater. **235**, 403 (2001).

23. J. Van Ek and M. Plumer, Magnetic moment of soft underlayers for perpendicular media, No. FQ-08, Intermag, 2002.

24. D. Litvinov, M. H. Kryder, and S. Khizroev, Recording physics of perpendicular media: hard layers. J. Magn. Magn. Mater. **241**, 453 (2002).

25. D. Litvinov, R. Chomko, L. Abelmann, K. Ramstock, G. Chen, and S. Khizroev, Micromagnetics of a soft underlayer. IEEE Trans. Magn. **36**, 2483 (2000).

26. T. Ando and T. Nishihara, Triple-layer perpendicular recording media for high SN ratio and signal stability. IEEE Trans. Magn. **33**, 2983 (1997).

27. T. Ando and T. Nishihara, Exchange-coupled CoZrNb/CoSm underlayer for perpendicular recording media. IEEE Trans. Magn. **37**, 1228 (2001).

28. S. Takahashi, K. Yamakawa, and K. Ouchi, A design of soft magnetic backlayer for double-layered perpendicular magnetic recording medium. J. Magn. Soc. Jpn. **23**(S2), 63 (1999).

29. J. Nogues and I. K. Schuller, Exchange bias. J. Magn. Magn. Mater. **192**, 203 (1999).

30. H. S. Jung and W. D. Doyle, FeTaN/IrMn exchange-coupled multilayer films as soft underlayers for perpendicular media. IEEE Trans. Magn. **37**, 2294 (2001).

31. K. W. Wierman, C. L. Platt, E. B. Svedberg, J. Yu, R. J. M. van de Veerdonk, W. R. Eppler, and K. J. Howard, Noise characteristics in exchange-biased soft underlayers for perpendicular media. IEEE Trans. Magn. **37**, 3956 (2001).

32. Y. Kawato, M. Futamo, and K. Nakamoto, Perpendicular magnetic recording medium and magnetic storage apparatus. U.S. Patent US2002/0 028 356 A1 (2002).

33. A. M. Shukh, E. W. Singleton, S. Khizroev, and D. Litvinov, Perpendicular recording medium with antiferromagnetic exchange coupling in soft magnetic underlayer. U.S. Patent US2002/0 028 357 A1 (2002).

34. M. J. Carey, Y. Ikeda, N. Smith, and K. Takano, Dual-layer perpendicular recording media with laminated underlayer formed with antiferromagnetically coupled films. U.S. Patent US2003/0 022 023 A1 (2003).

35. M. D. Stiles, Interlayer exchange coupling. J. Magn. Magn. Mater. **200**, 322 (1999).

36. B. R. Acharya, J. N. Zhou, M. Zheng, G. Choe, E. N. Abarra, and K. E. Johnson, Anti-parallel coupled soft under layers for high-density perpendicular recording. IEEE Trans. Magn. **40**, 2383 (2004).

37. S. C. Byeon, A. Misra, and W. D. Doyle, Synthetic antiferromagnetic soft underlayers for perpendicular recording media. IEEE Trans. Magn. **40**, 2386 (2004).

38. R.-F. Jiang and C.-H. Lai, Novel laminated antiferromagnetically coupled soft magnetic underlayer for perpendicular recording media. J. Magn. Magn. Mater. **272–276**, 2312 (2004).

39. K. Tanahashi, R. Arai, and Y. Hosoe, Exchange-biased soft underlayers for perpendicular recording. IEEE Trans. Magn. **41**, 577 (2005).

40. H. S. Jung, E. M. T. Velu, M. Avenell, S. S. Malhotra, and G. Bertero, Magnetic domain-free hard-magnet-biased soft magnetic underlayers for perpendicular media. J. Appl. Phys. **99**, 08Q901 (2006).

41. H. S. Jung, E. M. T. Velu, S. S. Malhotra, W. Jiang, and G. Bertero, Recording performance of CoCrPtO perpendicular media with single-domain hard magnet-biased soft magnetic underlayers. J. Appl. Phys. **99**, 08E702 (2006).

42. H.-S. Lee, S. Hong, and H. J. Lee, Comparison of recording performances between three different stabilizing schemes of soft underlayer. Phys. Stat. Sol. **204**, 4041 (2007).

43. T. Shimatsu, H. Uwazumi, Y. Sakai, A. Otsuki, I. Watanabe, H. Muraoka, and Y. Nakamura, Thermal agitation of magnetization in CoCrPt perpendicular recording media. IEEE Trans. Magn. **37**, 1567 (2001).

44. S. N. Piramanayagam, M. Matsumoto, A. Morisako, and D. Kadowaki, Controlling the magnetization reversal mechanism in Co/Pd multilayers by underlayer processing. IEEE Trans. Magn. **33**, 3247 (1997).

45. L. Wu, T. Kita, N. Honda, and K. Ouchi, Medium noise properties of Co/Pd multilayer films for perpendicular magnetic recording. J. Magn. Magn. Mater. **193**, 89 (1999).

46. T. Hikosaka, T. Komai, and Y. Tanaka, Oxygen effect on the microstructure and magnetic properties of binary CoPt thin films for perpendicular recording. IEEE Trans. Magn. **30**, 4026 (1994).

47. G. Choe, M. Zheng, E. N. Abarra, B. G. Demczyk, J. N. Zhou, B. R. Acharya, and K. E. Johnson, High-performance CoPtCrO perpendicular media: optimizing exchange coupling and anisotropy orientation dispersion. J. Magn. Magn. Mater. **287**, 159 (2004).

48. S. N. Piramanayagam, H. B. Zhao, J. Z. Shi, and C. S. Mah, Advanced perpendicular recording media structure with a magnetic intermediate layer. Appl. Phys. Lett. **88**, 092501 (2006).

49. J. Z. Shi, S. N. Piramanayagam, C. S. Mah, and J. M. Zhao, Influence of gas pressures on the magnetic properties and recording performance of CoCrPt–SiO$_2$ perpendicular media. J. Magn. Magn. Mater. **303**, E145 (2006).

50. S. H. Park, S. O. Kim, T. D. Lee, H. S. Oh, Y. S. Kim, N. Y. Par, and D. H. Hong, Effect of top Ru deposition pressure on magnetic and microstructural properties of CoCrPt–SiO$_2$ media in two-step Ru layer. J. Appl. Phys. **99**, 08E701 (2006).

51. J. Z. Shi, S. N. Piramanayagam, C. S. Mah, H. B. Zhao, J. M. Zhao, and Y. S. Kay, Influence of dual-Ru intermediate layers on magnetic properties and recording performance of CoCrPt–SiO$_2$ perpendicular recording media. Appl. Phys. Lett. **87**, 222503 (2005).

52. S. N. Piramanayagam, C. K. Pock, L. Lu, C. Y. Ong, J. Z. Shi, and C. S. Mah, Grain size reduction in CoCrPt:SiO$_2$ perpendicular recording media with oxide-based intermediate layers. Appl. Phys. Lett. **89**, 162504 (2006).

53. K. Srinivasan, S. K. Wong, S. N. Piramanayagam, and Y. S. Kay, Influence of synthetic nucleation layers on the microstructure, magnetic properties, and recording performance of $CoCrPt–SiO_2$ perpendicular recording media. J. Appl. Phys. **103**, 093912 (2008).

54. R. H. Victora and X. Shen, Composite media for perpendicular magnetic recording. IEEE Trans. Magn. **41**, 537 (2005).

55. D. Suess, J. Lee, J. Fidler, and T. Schrefl, Exchange-coupled perpendicular media. J. Magn. Magn. Mater. **321**, 545 (2009).

56. A. Berger, N. Supper, Y. Ikeda, B. Lengsfield, A. Moser, and E. E. Fullerton, Improved media performance in optimally coupled exchange spring layer media. Appl. Phys. Lett. **93**, 122502 (2008).

57. J. Z. Shi, S. N. Piramanayagam, S. Y. Chow, S. J. Wang, J. M. Zhao, and C. S. Mah, $CoCrPt–SiO_2$ perpendicular recording media with a crystalline soft underlayer. IEEE Trans. Magn. **42**, 2369 (2006).

58. S. N. Piramanayagam, K. Srinivasan, R. Sbiaa, Y. Dong, and R. H. Victora, CoCrPt-oxide based perpendicular recording media with hybrid soft magnetic underlayers. J. Appl. Phys. **104**, 103905 (2008).

59. Y. Dong and R. H. Victora, Micromagnetic simulation of hybrid soft underlayer for perpendicular recording media. IEEE Trans. Magn. **44**, 3527 (2008).

60. K. Srinivasan, S. N. Piramanayagam, R. Sbiaa, Y. S. Kay, H. K. Tan, and S. K. Wong, Antiferromagnetic iridium-manganese intermediate layers for perpendicular recording media (invited). J. Appl. Phys. **105**, 07B738 (2008).

5

WRITE HEADS: FUNDAMENTALS

Naoki Honda

Tohoku Institute of Technology, Japan

Kiyoshi Yamakawa

Akita Industrial Technology Center, Japan

5.1 INTRODUCTION

Write heads are significant components of magnetic recording that have an advantage over other competing storage technologies in terms of speed, larger capacity, and cost-effectiveness. The ability of magnetic recording to simultaneously satisfy requirements for both large capacity and low cost especially comes from the fact that recording media that does not need costly nanofabrication technology can still record nanobits. A precisely fabricated write head using a precision access mechanism (Fig. 5.1a) is the key to achieving nanobits, along with the recording medium, which should have a fine microstructure, as discussed in an earlier chapter. However, all recording bits are fabricated on a Si wafer in semiconductor memories, which inevitably increases the bit cost considerably (Fig. 5.1b). Therefore, the write head is one of the important devices that characterizes the magnetic recording system as a superior storage system.

Developments in Data Storage: Materials Perspective, First Edition.
Edited by S. N. Piramanayagam, Tow C. Chong.
© 2012 Institute of Electrical and Electronics Engineers. Published 2012 by John Wiley & Sons, Inc.

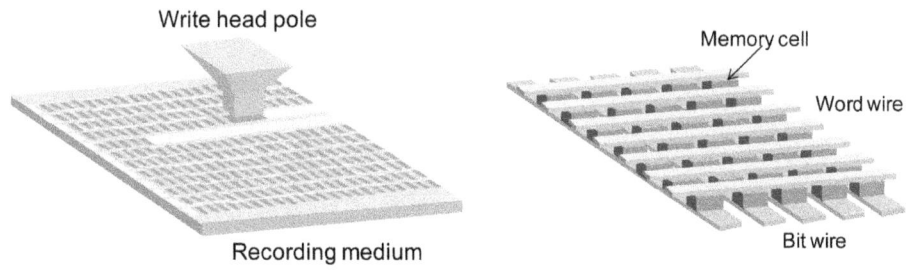

(a) Magnetic recording   (b) Semiconductor memory

Figure 5.1. Comparison of magnetic recording and semiconductor memories.

A write head could be used as a read head as well through electromagnetic induction. From the first designs of Valdemar Poulsen until the 1990s, inductive heads were commonly used for both writing and reading. Even in HiFi tape recorders, where separated write and read heads were used, both heads were of the inductive type. Pushed by the requirement of increased read sensitivity, read heads using magnetoresistive (MR) effect were incorporated into hard disk drive (HDD) design in the early 1990s. Since then, read and write heads have been separated with different working mechanisms but have remained part of an integrated head. This chapter focuses on the write part of the integrated head.

5.2 THE DAWN OF THE WRITE HEAD

The first magnetic heads proposed by Poulsen were perpendicular recording heads. As can be seen from his patent issue figures, shown in Figure 5.2 [1], the head was a single-pole type or dipole type, putting the wire recording medium on the pole edge or between the poles (Fig. 5.3a [2]). However, the perpendicular type was not efficient enough to generate a suitable write field for wire media. Fiber-shaped magnetic material is not easy to magnetize in a diametrical direction because of the large demagnetizing field acting in that direction. Soon the head was changed to a shifted-pole structure, which was more suited to generating a longitudinal field in the wire media shown in Figure 5.3b. Later a shift was made to a ring-type head, which was the most successful and suitable configuration for in-plane recording with a wider track width (Fig. 5.3c). The ring-type head is a simple but successful structure that was widely used until recently in HDDs because of its high efficiency for in-plane recording. In the current HDD technology, however, write heads have changed again to a perpendicular type, using recording media with perpendicular anisotropy but with a sophisticated structure.

Dansk Patent № 2653

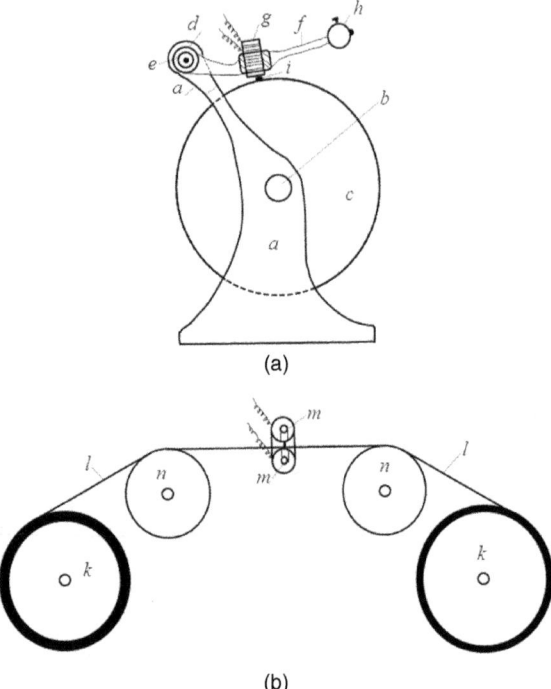

(a)

(b)

Figure 5.2. Figures of the first magnetic recording in the patent of V. Poulsen [1].

5.3 WRITE HEAD FUNDAMENTALS

A write head is a small electromagnet. One of its functions is to generate a high magnetic field that can sufficiently saturate the magnetization of the recording media. The recoding process is schematically illustrated in Figure 5.4. The field should usually be greater than 1.5 times the coercivity of the recording media so that all the grains can be magnetized in the desired direction. The head also should exhibit a steep field distribution, or high field gradient, at the trailing edge. The final magnetic state is determined by the trailing edge field. The role of the field gradient will be described later in detail in Section 5.7. A high field gradient is necessary to form a sharp magnetic transition, which is a key for obtaining high linear density recording. Moreover, narrower distribution in the cross-track direction is also required to obtain a narrow track width recording for high track densities.

From a materials perspective, a write head should make use of a material with a higher saturation flux density, B_s, with a high permeability, μ. The maximum magnetic

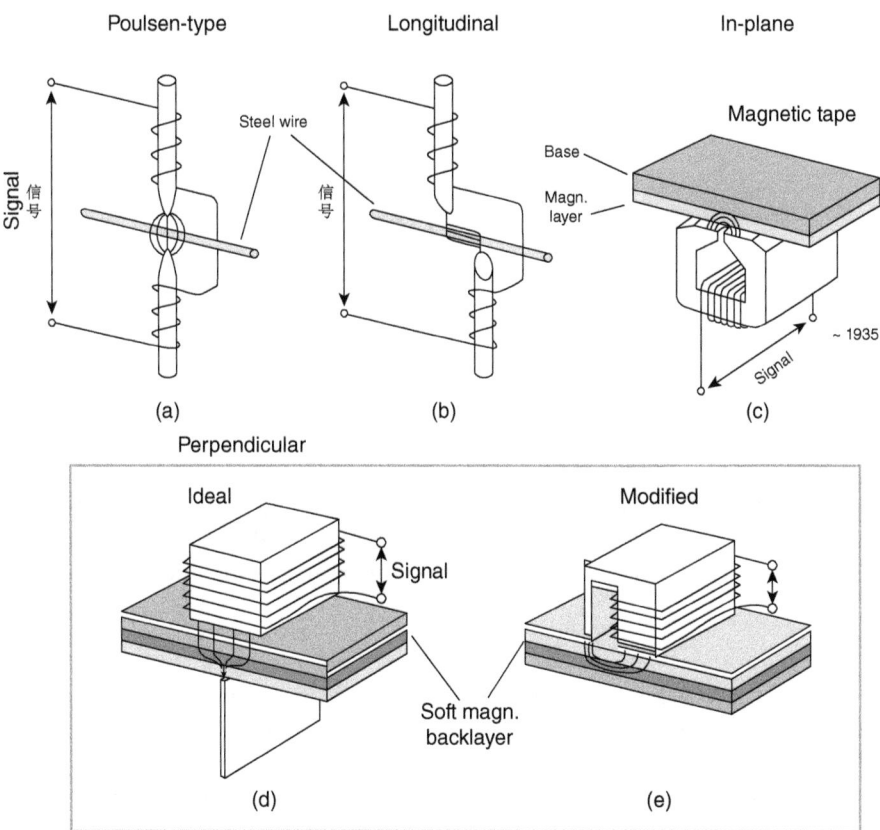

Figure 5.3. Transition of inductive heads in magnetic recording [2]. (Reprinted with permission from S. Iwasaki, *IEEE Trans. Magn.* **39**(4), 1868–1870 (2003). Copyright IEEE.)

field that a head can produce is limited by B_s of the material used. Higher B_s enables higher writing fields. Permeability of the head material determines efficiency of the head and affects sharpness of the field profile as well. The most common soft magnetic material used is permalloy, an Ni-Fe alloy containing about 80 at% of Ni. The alloy has a relatively large B_s of around 0.8 T and a high specific permeability of larger than 10^4. Use of the alloy, however, was restricted to audio tape recorders due to large eddy current loss at high frequencies. In the early days when bulk heads were used for data recording, Ni-Zn ferrite was commonly used for head material, which has high resistivity along with a high permeability. Higher resistivity is beneficial for use at high frequencies. However, as the areal density increased, the coercivity of recording media increased too, resulting in a requirement of higher flux from the heads. Therefore, metals regained their use again first as metal-in-gap (MIG) heads, where the metallic part was used only at the gap surfaces, avoiding eddy current loss. Then thin-film heads appeared as replacement for MIG heads as eddy current loss in thin-film heads was not significant. Until the middle of the 1990s, traditional permalloy was used commonly

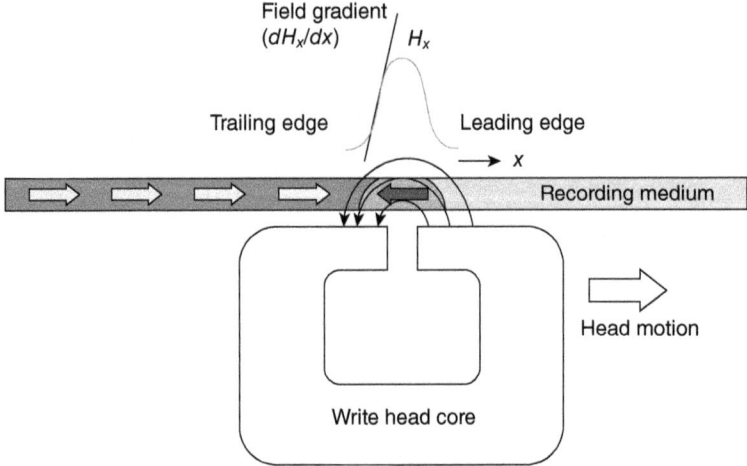

Figure 5.4. Recording process and the schematic profile of the longitudinal component of the magnetic field, H_x, near the gap. Recording is determined at the trailing edge of the field, and the field gradient, dH_x/dx, affects the sharpness of the magnetic transition in the medium.

in HDD heads. Owing to the demand for head materials with even higher B_s, $Ni_{45}Fe_{55}$ permalloy was introduced. The alloy has a higher B_s of around 1.5 T with a negligibly small increase in the coercivity. This material is used as a major material in head fabrication even today. Since about 2000, materials with an even higher B_s have been introduced but only to the tip of the pole(s) of the head, similar to that of the aforementioned MIG head. CoNiFe alloy has a higher B_s of around 2.0 T, and $Co_{35}Fe_{65}$ exhibits a higher B_s of 2.4 T, which is the material with the highest B_s that can be utilized today.

5.4 BASIC STRUCTURE OF THE WRITE HEAD

A ring head was used as a writer for a significantly long time in the history of magnetic recording. A ring head has the structure shown in Figure 5.5: a ring core wound with a coil, and a gap to extract the magnetic field from the core. The magnetic field strength, H, around the path $(l + g)$ is represented using Ampere's law,

$$\oint_{l+g} H \cdot dr = NI, \tag{5.1}$$

where N and I are the coil turns and the current, respectively. This equation is approximately represented as below, using the field strength in the core, H_l, and that in the gap, H_g

$$H_l l + H_g g \approx NI, \tag{5.2}$$

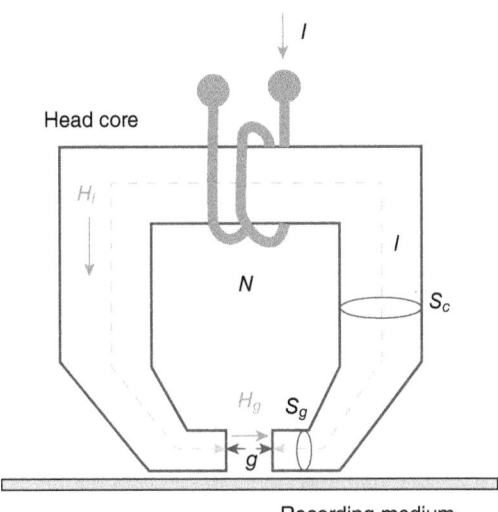

Figure 5.5. Structure of ring-type head.

and when the magnetic flux, Φ, almost flows only in the core and the gap, the relationship of the flux between the core and the gap gives

$$\Phi = \mu H_l S_c \approx \mu_0 H_g S_g, \tag{5.3}$$

where μ and μ_0 denote the permeability of the core and the vacuum, and S_c and S_g represent a cross-sectional area of the core and the gap, respectively. Equations 5.2 and 5.3 give the field H_g in the gap as

$$H_g \approx \frac{NI}{\dfrac{\mu_0 S_g}{\mu S_c} l + g}. \tag{5.4}$$

Equation 5.4 indicates that a larger H_g is obtained for a larger μS_c, and a smaller S_g, l, and g apart from a larger NI. In another words, a smaller magnetic resistance of the core, $R_m = l/\mu S_c$, is beneficial to obtain a higher field in the gap. Note that too small an S_g does not always work well because increased stray field around the gap increases effective cross-sectional area S_g. Equation 5.4 also gives a rough estimation of H_g for small magnetic resistance of the core as

$$H_g \sim \frac{NI}{g}. \tag{5.5}$$

This indicates that a smaller gap length directly increases the field in the gap, but it does not mean an increase in the field strength in the recording media. The stray field

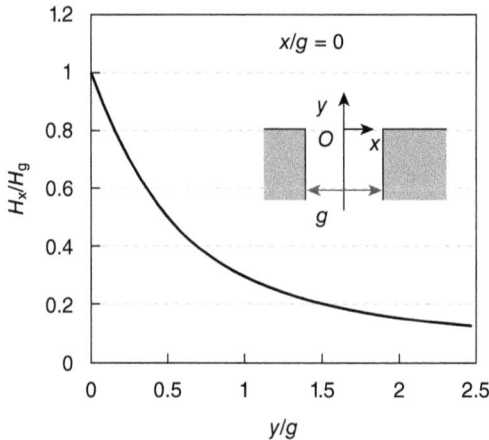

<u>Figure 5.6.</u> Normalized separation, y/g, dependence of the normalized field strength, H_x/H_g, at the center of the gap for a ring head.

strength near the gap of a ring head, H, drastically decreases with the distance from the gap surface, y, as

$$H \approx \frac{2H_g}{\pi} \tan^{-1}\left(\frac{g}{2y}\right). \tag{5.6}$$

As shown in Figure 5.6, Equation 5.6 means that the field is decreased to half when the distance, y, becomes half the gap length, g. The stray field strength at a constant distance from the gap surface is restricted by the gap length. A smaller gap length, however, is required to obtain a high field gradient at the trailing edge of the gap, which is preferable for achieving high linear density recording. Therefore, the gap length is optimized between required field strength and the field gradient. It should also be noted that a smaller track width of the core does not always result in a smaller cross-track field width nor larger field strength for ring heads.

5.5 THE RING HEAD FIELD NEAR THE GAP

In general, practical heads have track widths that are much longer than the gap length. Therefore, it is approximately correct to treat them as two-dimensional (2D). The 2D head field of a ring head is well analyzed and is represented with a relatively simple yet useful expression shown below. The field from such a 2D head is called a Karlqvist field. A ring head is assumed to be infinitely thick in z-direction and have a gap length of g (Fig. 5.7). The field components, H_x and H_y, for $y > 0$ is calculated by integrating the field from the magnetic charge, which is uniformly distributed on both ends of the gap [3]; the magnetic charge density is σ_m and $-\sigma_m$ at $x = -1/2$ and $1/2$, respectively:

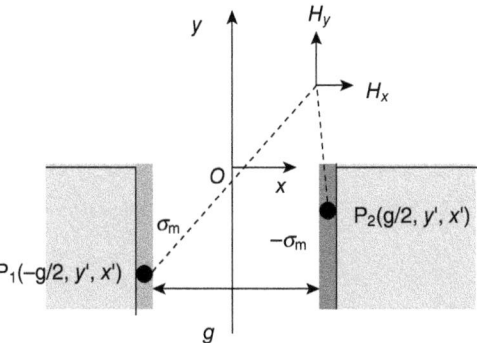

Figure 5.7. Two-dimensional ring head model near the gap.

$$H_x = \frac{1}{4\pi} \int_{z'=-\infty}^{\infty} \int_{y'=-\infty}^{0} \left[\frac{\sigma_m (x+g/2)}{\left\{ (x+g/2)^2 + (y-y')^2 + (z-z')^2 \right\}^{3/2}} \right.$$

$$\left. - \frac{\sigma_m (x-g/2)}{\left\{ (x-g/2)^2 + (y-y')^2 + (z-z')^2 \right\}^{3/2}} \right] dy'dz' \qquad (5.7)$$

$$= \frac{H_g}{\pi} \left\{ \tan^{-1} \frac{2/g+x}{y} + \tan^{-1} \frac{2/g-x}{y} \right\}$$

and

$$H_y = \frac{1}{4\pi} \int_{z'=-\infty}^{\infty} \int_{y'=-\infty}^{0} \left[\frac{\sigma_m (y-y')}{\left\{ (x+g/2)^2 + (y-y')^2 + (z-z')^2 \right\}^{3/2}} \right.$$

$$\left. - \frac{\sigma_m (y-y')}{\left\{ (x-g/2)^2 + (y-y')^2 + (z-z')^2 \right\}^{3/2}} \right] dy'dz' \qquad (5.8)$$

$$= \frac{H_g}{2\pi} \ln \left[\frac{(g/2-x)^2 + y^2}{(g/2+x)^2 + y^2} \right]$$

where $H_g = \sigma_m/2$ is the field in the head gap. The field profiles for H_x and H_y are shown in Figure 5.8. The field distribution approximately agrees with the precise field analyzed by Westmijze [4] or Fan [5] except for near the surface of the head ($y < 0.1g$). Equation 5.6 is derived from Equation 5.7 with $x = 0$. Three-dimensional distribution of a ring head was analyzed by Lindholm [6].

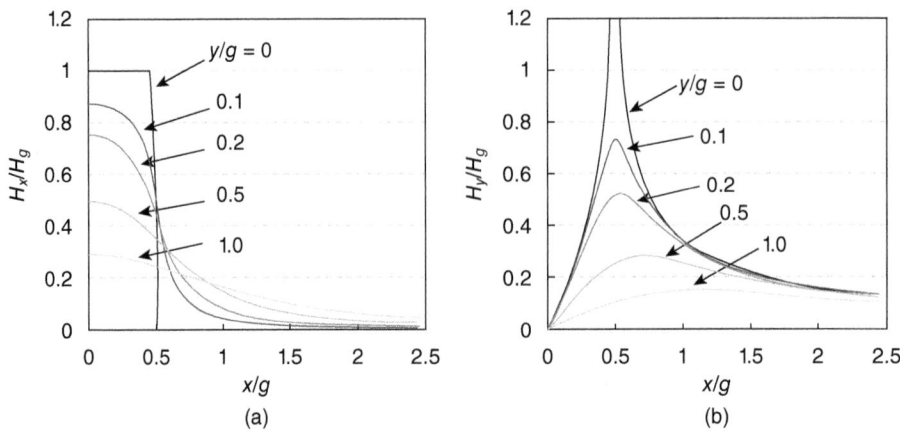

Figure 5.8. Field profiles of a two-dimensional ring head for H_x and H_y.

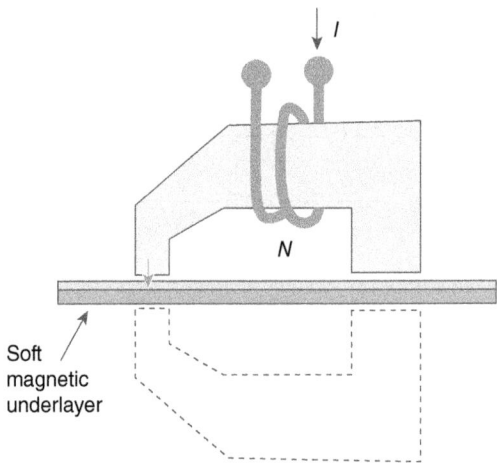

Figure 5.9. Single-pole-type head for perpendicular magnetic recording with double-layered medium.

5.6   THE PERPENDICULAR RECORDING WRITE HEAD

The modified perpendicular recording write head shown in Figure 5.3e is obtained from the ring-type head shown in Figure 5.5 by cutting it in half and rotating it 90° as shown in Figure 5.9. The soft magnetic underlayer of perpendicular magnetic recording media performs as a mirror surface for the half part of the head and constitutes a pseudo ring head as in Figure 5.9 but with the medium placed between the poles. The magnetic field of the head is approximately represented by that of a ring head rotated 90°. Therefore, Equation 5.7 can be used for the approximate field of a perpendicular head with exchanging x and y [7]. However, as mentioned above, the field distribution, H_x, in Equation 5.7 is not a good approximation for a small y or near the trailing edge of a perpendicular head pole. The perpendicular component of the perpendicular recording head, $H_y(x, y)$, may be expressed in polynomial with six terms using Fan's equation [5] as shown below:

$$\frac{H_y(x, y)}{H_g} = \frac{2}{\pi} \int_0^\infty \frac{\sin(kg/2)\cos ky}{k} e^{-kx} dk + \sum_{n=1}^{6} C_n 2n(-1)^n \int_0^\infty \frac{k\sin(kg/2)\cos ky}{k^2 - (2n\pi/g)^2} e^{-kx} dk,$$

$$(5.9)$$

with the following six coefficients:

$$C_1 = -0.0861157, \quad C_2 = 0.02915, \quad C_3 = -0.015254$$

$$C_4 = 0.0074, \quad C_5 = -0.0033, \quad C_6 = 0.0016$$

The first three coefficients are not from Fan's proposal, but from Wilton [8]. The fourth to sixth coefficients are obtained so that the truncation error is minimized. Equation 5.9 can be used even for $x = 0$.

The structure of the perpendicular head indicates that in-gap recording is realized in the head, with the result that the full field strength of H_g can act on the medium. This is one of the striking features of perpendicular magnetic recording along with the assisting properties of reversed magnetization in the media. The pole size of a perpendicular write head could be minimized with a minimum degradation in the field strength and distribution when the distance between the pole and the underlayer surfaces are simultaneously minimized. Therefore, a perpendicular write head can intrinsically produce a larger field strength even for a smaller track width pole, which is essential to realize high track densities.

5.7 ROLE OF THE HEAD FIELD IN PERPENDICULAR RECORDING

The recording process is schematically illustrated in Figure 5.10. The process for in-plane or longitudinal recording is similar to this if we treat them with longitudinal magnetization and a head field. Sharp transition in the medium magnetization is needed for high linear density recording. It has been well understood that the transition width, a_{50}, is affected by the field gradient of the head when the slope of the M-H loop of the media is finite. The M-H loop of perpendicular recording media is generally shifted or sheared due to the demagnetizing field acting in the media even when the magnetic property of the media exhibits no distribution. In the extreme case where the exchange coupling between the grains in the media is zero, the slope, $\alpha = dM/dH$ is $1/N = 1$ corresponding to the demagnetizing factor, N, of 1 for a film. The dependence of the transition width on the product of the M-H loop slope (α) and the head-field gradient (dH_y/dx)

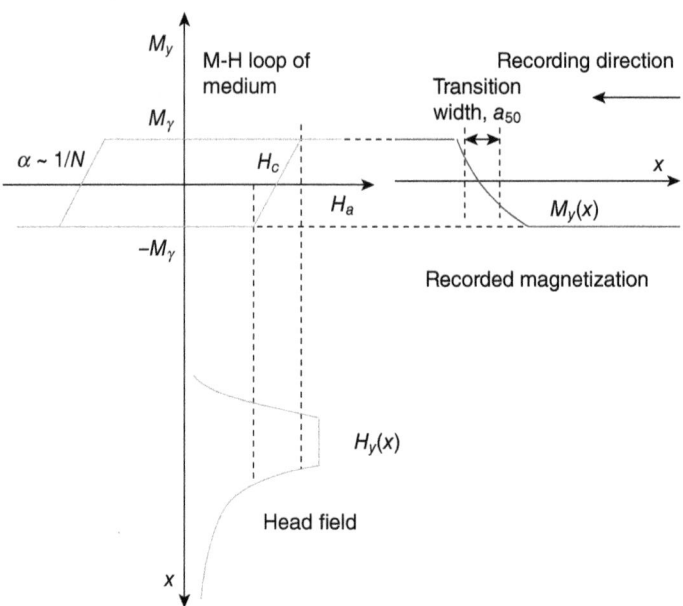

Figure 5.10. Schematic illustration of the recording process.

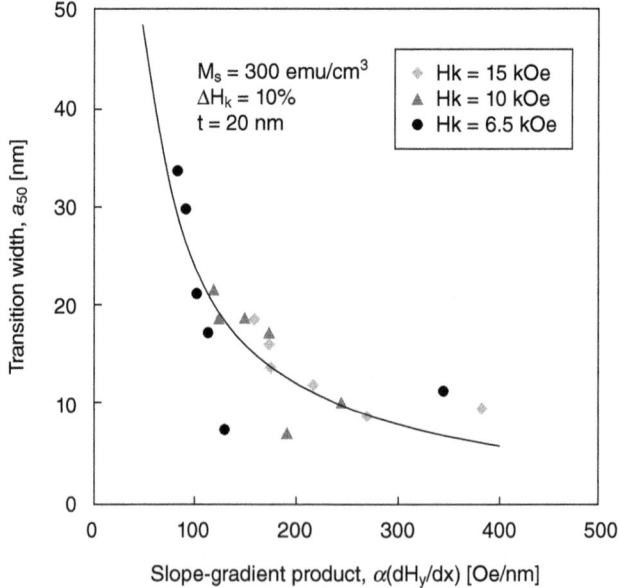

Figure 5.11. Dependence of the transition width on the product of M-H loop slope (α) and the head-field gradient (dH_y/dx).

is shown in Figure 5.11 [9]. The head field gradient is directly connected to the transition width. It is desirable for the head field to have as large a field gradient as possible.

The field gradient in the down-track direction is easily increased by putting a shield at the trailing edge of the pole, with only a slight decrease in the field strength, as shown in Figure 5.12a [10]. The stretched return yoke works as the shield for the main pole. The field gradient at $H = 4000$ Oe (318 kA/m in SI unit), dH_y/dx, 4000 Oe, could be increased with decreasing the separation between the main pole and the shield (return yoke), as seen in Figure 5.12b. However, the maximum field, H_y,max, is drastically decreased at too small separation lengths. This gradient increasing effect of the shield can be understood as the result of the shield acting like an opposite pole of a ring head, as suggested by the H_y component of Equation 5.8, which exhibits a large field gradient in the x or down-track direction, as seen in Figure 5.8b.

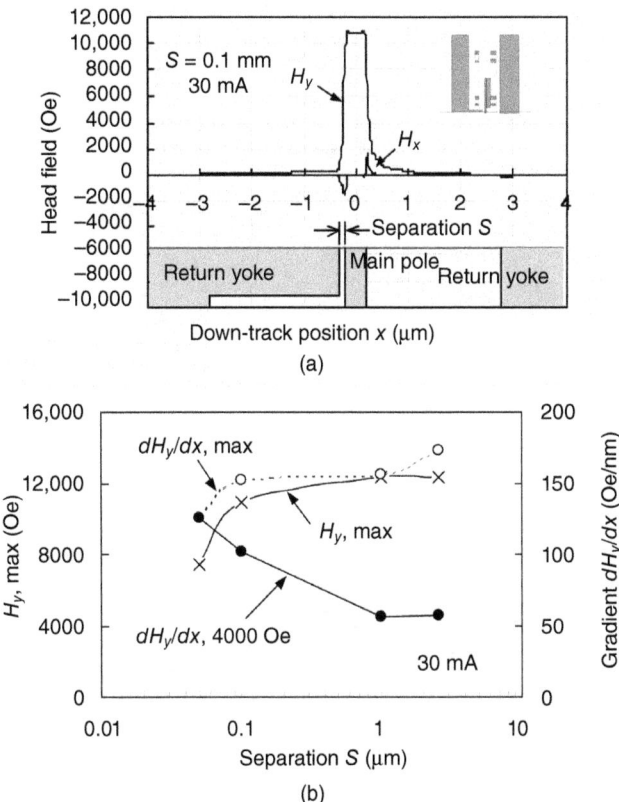

Figure 5.12. Trailing shielded single-pole head: (a) structure and the down-track field profile; (b) shield separation dependence of maximum field, H_y,max, and field gradient, dH_y/dx.

5.8 DEVELOPMENT OF THE PERPENDICULAR RECORDING HEAD

The first successful write head for perpendicular recording had an auxiliary pole, as shown in Figure 5.13 [11]. The field was excited by the auxiliary pole; therefore, it was called an "auxiliary pole driven head." The recording medium was placed between the main and auxiliary poles. This structure is ideal for magnetizing the magnetic pole near the surface facing the medium. However, the separated structure of the head placed at up and down surfaces of the medium is not easy to handle nor provides sufficient performance owing to a long magnetic circuit. To circumvent this problem, a single-sided head that utilized a soft magnetic underlayer as a part of the return yoke was subsequently developed (Fig. 5.14 [12]), and was one of the successful single-sided bulk heads. Soon after, the write heads advanced to the thin-film type.

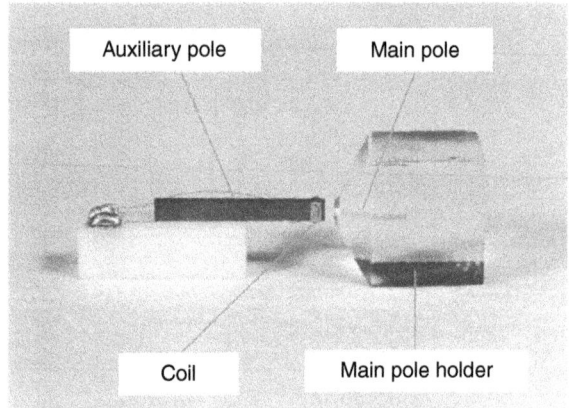

Figure 5.13. The first successful write head for perpendicular recording. (Courtesy of Dr. S. Iwasaki.)

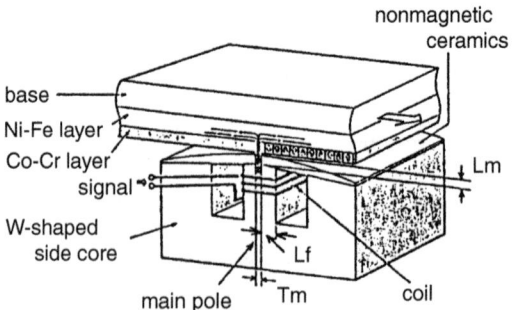

Figure 5.14. W-shaped single-pole head for single-side recording [12]. (Reprinted with permission from J. Hokkyo, K. Hayakawa, I. Saito, K. Shirane, *IEEE Trans. Magn.* **20**(1), 72–74 (1984). Copyright IEEE.)

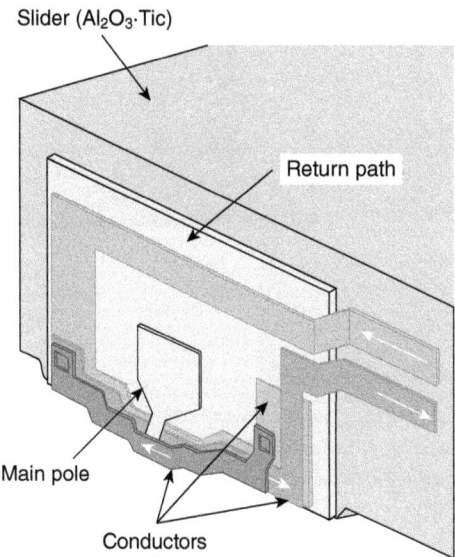

Figure 5.15. Main pole tip excited head [13]. (Reprinted with permission from H. Muraoka, K. Sato, Y. Nakamura, *IEEE Trans. Magn.* **34**(4), 1474–1476 (1998). Copyright IEEE.)

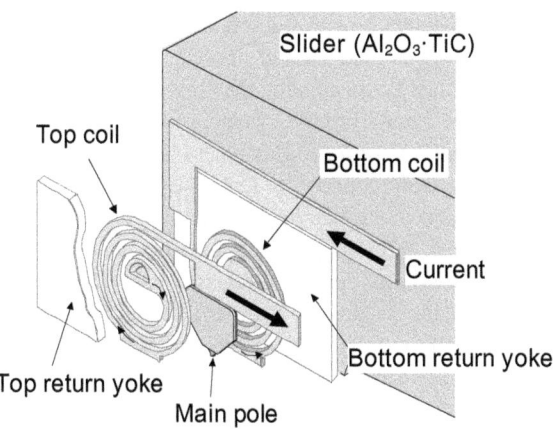

Figure 5.16. Structure of cusp-field single-pole-type (CF-SPT) head.

However, a single-sided structure is not suitable to excite the tip of the pole. The excitation coil should be placed as near as possible to the tip or surface of the pole. A main pole tip excited head was proposed by Muraoka et al., which is shown in Figure 5.15 [13]. It showed high write efficiency as well as a small inductance, which is required at high frequencies. Although the head pole is excited at the tip, the head generates enough write efficiency with its small coil turns (1.5 turns). Yamakawa et al. proposed improved structure for a tip excited head [10]. The improved design incorporated many coil turns using the cusp-field structure shown in Figure 5.16, yet with

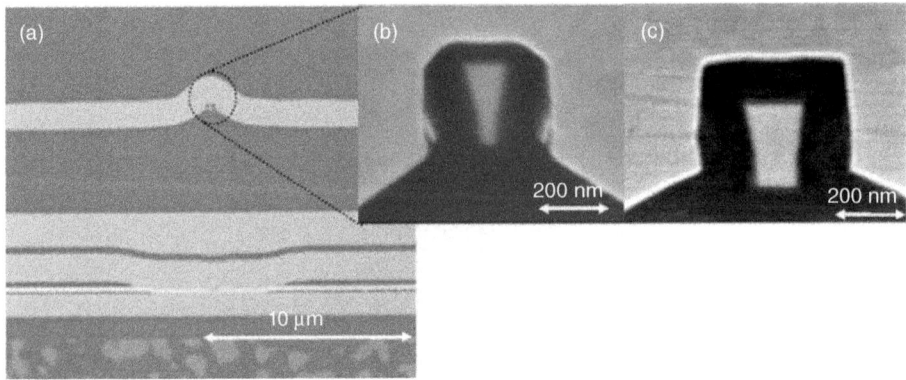

Figure 5.17. Air-bearing surface view of wraparound-shielded head [23]. (Reprinted with permission from T. Okada, I. Nunokawa, M. Mochizuki, M. Hatatani, H. Kimura, K. Etoh, M. Fuyama, K. Nakamoto, *IEEE Trans. Magn.* **41**(10), pp. 2899–2901 (2005). Copyright IEEE.)

a small inductance. A small inductance of less than 2 nH for 6 turns coil head due to its pancake coil structure was demonstrated [14].

Experimental models of practical perpendicular recording heads were reported to cause head-induced media erasure [15]. The most serious problem was the wide-area track erasure due to flux leakage through the soft magnetic underlayer [16, 17]. A similar wide area erasure problem was also known in write heads for longitudinal recording, where a fringing field from the write gap and the magnetic flux concentration at the edge of the wide head pole cause the erasure [18]. The erasure phenomena could be suppressed by improvements in the head design such as recessed yoke structure [19], surrounding the head pole with nonmagnetic conductive material, using a composite pole with high and low B_s materials [20], and so on. Similar approaches were applied to the perpendicular recording head. In addition, reduced perpendicular permeability in the soft magnetic underlayer of the media could also suppress the erasure in perpendicular recording [21]. Once the head-induced media erasure problem was solved with such techniques, HDDs using perpendicular magnetic recording were commercialized [22].

The practical structure of the shield in general is composed of a large soft magnetic layer placed at the trailing edge of the main pole. For narrow track width recording, field sharpness in the side direction is also required. A wraparound-shielded structure is proposed for this purpose (Fig. 5.17) [23]. However, the shield generally decreases the field strength in exchange for increased field gradient as described above. Optimization is needed to accommodate the magnetics of the media.

5.9 FUTURE DEVELOPMENTS

For future recording, increased areal density will require reduced track widths. In this case, the write head will be challenged by a small pole tip dimension. The head field is determined by the distance from the pole surface to the medium, which is normalized by the pole size. Therefore, relative head surface to medium surface spacing should be reduced when the pole size is reduced in order to achieve high fields. Alternatively, when the spacing does not scale with the change in the pole size, the head material should be changed. One option is to use a soft magnetic material with higher B_s to generate a higher field, but this option is limited by which materials are practical at an industrial scale. As mentioned in Section 5.3, present write heads for HDDs are already using FeCo-based alloy, which has the highest B_s among the materials we can use industrially today. An alternative path for write heads is to improve the design structure.

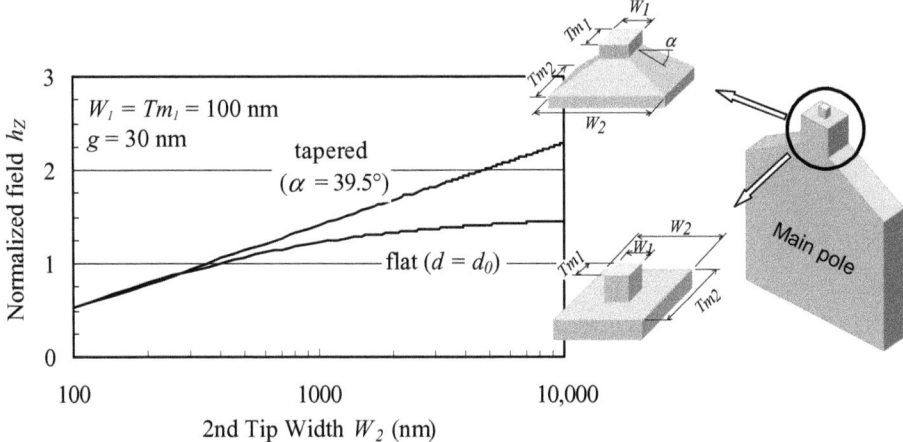

Figure 5.18. High magnetic field properties produced by heads with multicharged surfaces.

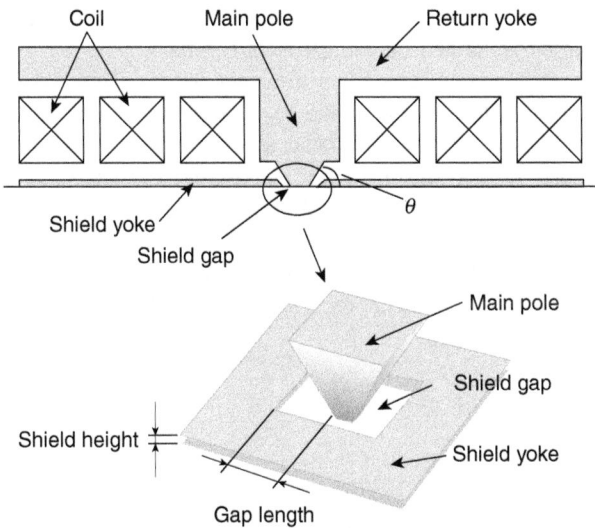

Figure 5.19. Structure of newly proposed shielded planar single-pole head.

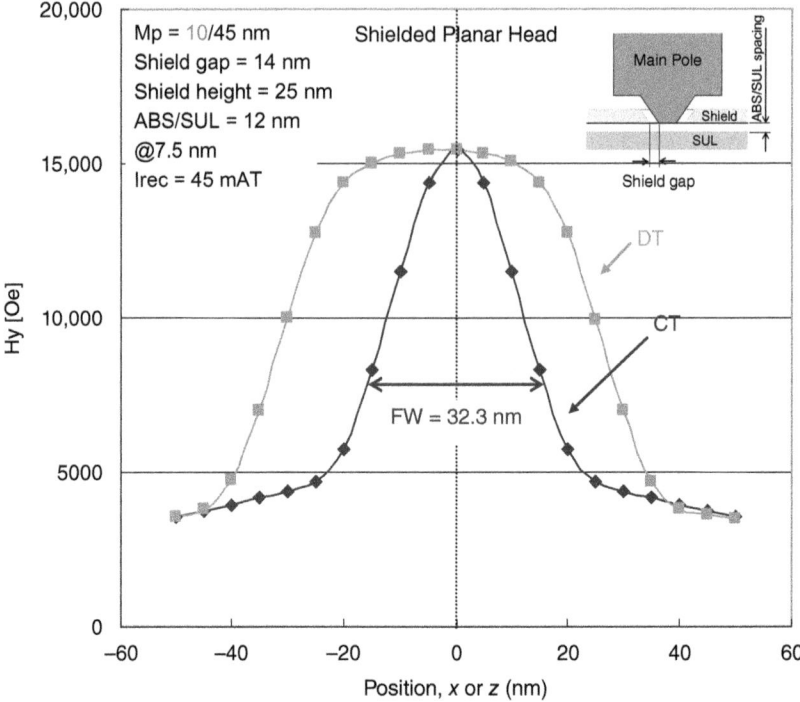

Figure 5.20. Down-track and cross-track field profiles of a shielded planar head with a narrow pole track width size of 10 nm.

An efficient structure for a single-pole-type (SPT) head is proposed by Ise et al. [24]. In this design, a magnetic field exceeding the limit imposed by the B_s of a magnetic pole material can be generated by using conically shaped pole pieces, which are typically used in electromagnets. The basic idea was proposed by Takahashi et al. [25], where high fields exceeding that from the B_s of the material are expected, as shown in Figure 5.18. In addition, the new SPT head is composed of a shield yoke surrounding a quadrangular-shaped pole piece, shown in Figure 5.19. The tapered surface of the main pole generates a large additional field, and the shield narrows the field distribution, resulting to a sharp, confined field with a high maximum field strength, as shown in Figure 5.20 [26]. Recent developments in shielded planar heads are discussed in References [27] and [28] to this chapter. These structures would pave the way for high areal densities beyond 1 Tb/in.^{2}

REFERENCES

1. H. Buhl, M. Clark, and H. Nielsen, The Telegraphone & The Arc Transmitter, Booklet of the International Conference on Magnetic Recording Media, Maastricht, 1998.

2. S. Iwasaki, Lessons from research of perpendicular magnetic recording. IEEE Trans. Magn. **39**(4), 1868–1870 (2003).

3. K. Nagai, S. Iwasaki, and K. Yokoyama, On the A. C. Bias of magnetic recording. J. IEE Jpn. **77**(825), 688–694 (1957).

4. W. K. Westmijze, Studies on magnetic recording. Philips Res. Rep. **8**, 148–157 (1953).

5. G. J. Y. Fan, A study of the playback process of a magnetic ring head. IBM J. Res. Dev. **5**, 321–325 (1961).

6. D. A. Lindholm, Magnetic fields of finite track width heads. IEEE Trans. Magn. **MAG-13**(5), 1460–1462 (1977).

7. H. N. Bertram and M. Williams, SNR and density limit estimates: a comparison of longitudinal and perpendicular recording. IEEE Trans. Magn. **36**, 4–9 (2000).

8. D. T. Wilton, Comparison of ring and pole head magnetic fields. IEEE Trans. Magn. **26**, 1229–1232 (1990).

9. N. Honda, K. Ouchi, and S. Iwasaki, Design consideration of ultrahigh-density perpendicular magnetic recording media. IEEE Trans. Magn. **38**(4), 1615–1621 (2002).

10. K. Yamakawa, K. Ise, S. Takahashi, and K. Ouchi, A new single-pole head structure for high writability. IEEE Trans. Magn. **38**(1), 163–168 (2002).

11. S. Iwasaki, Magnetism and information—significance of perpendicular magnetic recording. J. Magn. Soc. Jpn. **15**(S2), 1–14 (1991).

12. J. Hokkyo, K. Hayakawa, I. Saito, and K. Shirane, A new W-shaped single-pole head and a high density flexible disk perpendicular magnetic recording system. IEEE Trans. Magn. **20**(1), 72–74 (1984).

13. H. Muraoka, K. Sato, and Y. Nakamura, Extremely low inductance thin-film single-pole head on flying slider. IEEE Trans. Magn. **34**(4), 1474–1476 (1998).

14. P. George, K. Yamakawa, K. Ise, N. Honda, and K. Ouchi, High-frequency inductance measurements and performance projections made for cusp-field single-pole heads. IEEE Trans. Magn. **39**(4), 1949–1954 (2003).

15. W. Cain, A. Payne, M. Baldwinson, and R. Hempstead, Challenges in the practical implementation of perpendicular magnetic recording. IEEE Trans. Magn. **32**(1), 97–102 (1996).

16. A. S. Kao, H. J. Lee, G. Bekkers, and S. Hong, Wide-area track erasure in perpendicular recording. J. Magn. Magn. Mater. **287**, 175–480 (2005).

17. W. Jiang, G. Khera, R. Wood, M. Williams, N. Smith, and Y. Ikeda, Cross-track noise profile measurement for adjacent-track interference study and write current optimization in perpendicular recording. J. Appl. Phys. **93**, 6754–6756 (2003).

18. J. Feng, Long-range erasure of nearby recorded tracks. IEEE Trans. Magn. **40**(4), 2588–2590 (2004).

19. Y. K. Kim, S. Lee, and H. Lee, Design of recessed yoke heads for minimizing adjacent track encroachment. IEEE Trans. Magn. **36**(5), 2524–2526 (2000).

20. J. Feng, Magnetic write head design for reducing wide area track erasure. U.S. Patent US2007/0268623 A1 (2007).

21. A. Hashimoto, S. Saito, and M. Takahashi, A soft magnetic underlayer with negative uniaxial magnetocrystalline anisotropy for suppression of spike noise and wide adjacent track erasure in perpendicular recording media. J. Appl. Phys. **99**, 08Q907 (2006).

22. Y. Tanaka, Fundamental features of perpendicular magnetic recording and design considerations for future portable HDD integration. IEEE Trans. Magn. **41**(10), 2834–2838 (2005).

23. T. Okada, I. Nunokawa, M. Mochizuki, M. Hatatani, H. Kimura, K. Etoh, M. Fuyama, and K. Nakamoto, Newly developed wraparound-shielded head for perpendicular recording. IEEE Trans. Magn. **41**(10), 2899–2901 (2005).

24. K. Ise, S. Takahashi, K. Yamakawa, and N. Honda, New shielded single-pole head with planar structure. IEEE Trans. Magn. **42**(10), 2422–2424 (2006).

25. S. Takahashi, K. Yamakawa, and K. Ouchi, 2 steps type of single pole head for ultra narrow track. Technical Report of IEICE, MR2001-1, 1–8 (2001).

26. N. Honda, K. Yamakawa, and K. Ouchi, Simulation study of bit patterned media with weakly inclined anisotropy. IEEE Trans. Magn. **46**(6), 1806–1808 (2010).

27. K. Yamakawa, K. Ise, S. Takahashi, N. Honda, and K. Ouchi, Shielded planar write head. J. Magn. Magn. Mater. **320**, 2854–2859 (2008).

28. K. Yamakawa, Y. Ohsawa, S. Greaves, and H. Muraoka, Pole design optimization of shielded planar writer for 2 Tbit/in^2 recording, Abstracts of MMM 2008, DT-08, 2008.

6

MAGNETORESISTIVE READ HEADS: FUNDAMENTALS AND FUNCTIONALITY

Rachid Sbiaa

Data Storage Institute, Agency for Science, Technology and Research (A*STAR), Singapore

6.1 INTRODUCTION

In the area of digitalized information storage, the hard disk drive (HDD) retains its leading position among other memories and data storage devices. In the last decade, HDDs could be seen not just in computers but also in many other consumer electronics. Up to now, HDD and dynamic random access memory (DRAM) remain the major memory devices used in enterprise and desktop personal computers (PCs), and in other nonmobile consumer devices that require a large storage capacity. For mobile devices such laptop PCs, mobile phones, MP3s, and digital cameras, flash memory has a considerable market share. The mobile PCs using HDDs, including laptops and netbooks, are projected to reach 235 million units in 2011, and this sector will continue to grow with an estimated shipment of more than 350 million units by the year 2014. Figure 6.1 underlines the continuing strength of HDDs despite the phenomenal growth of newly popular tablets [1].

The success of HDD technology is mainly due to the large storage capacity it offers with low cost [2]. As can be seen from Figure 6.2, since the first HDD was introduced in the market by IBM in 1957, the areal recording density (ARD) has kept

Developments in Data Storage: Materials Perspective, First Edition.
Edited by S. N. Piramanayagam, Tow C. Chong.
© 2012 Institute of Electrical and Electronics Engineers. Published 2012 by John Wiley & Sons, Inc.

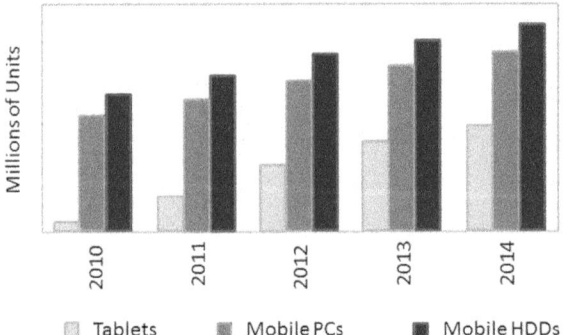

Figure 6.1. Global shipment of tablets, mobile PCs, and mobile HDDs. Even with the high growth of tablets, the mobile HDD segment will remain strong.

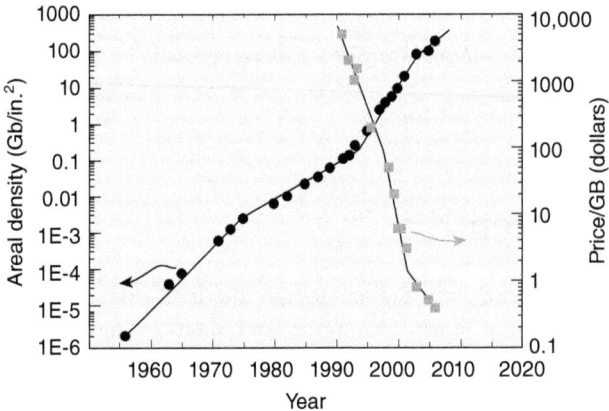

Figure 6.2. Evolution of areal density and price per gigabyte of magnetic HDD with time. The introduction of the first magnetoresistive (MR) and giant magnetoresistive (GMR) heads besides antiferromagnetically coupled media in 1991, 1997, and 2001, respectively contributed to this performance ([2]). (Reprinted with permission from Figure 6.1 of Reference 2. Copyright (2007) Bentham Science Publishers Ltd.)

increasing to reach 150 million-fold. (Today's HDDs available in the market have an ARD of about 625 Gb/in.^{2} [3].)

The first HDD, called RAMAC, which is an abbreviation of random access method of accounting and control, had an ARD of 2 kb/in.^{2} It needed fifty 24-inch-diameter plates to reach the capacity of 4.4 MB. An inductive write head was used to change the magnetization direction of the media so that bits of information "0" and "1" could be recorded. In the same manner, an inductive "read" head was used to read this information by sensing the magnetic flux from the bit-transition area.

The tremendous increase in the ARD of HDDs is in part due to exploitation of advancements in the field of spintronics, which started first in 1991 with the introduction of the anisotropic magnetoresistive (AMR) read head. The AMR read head had a higher sensitivity compared to the inductive read head, resulting in better readback signals from thinner recording media. The readback signal of an AMR head is proportional to the magnetoresistance, which represents the resistance change between maximum and minimum resistances ($\Delta R = R_{max} - R_{min}$) normalized by the minimum resistance value. The AMR read head had a relative magnetoresistance of about 1% only, but it was enough to increase the annual growth rate of HDD ARD from 30% to 60%.

Obviously, there is a continuous need for higher ARD, which requires a high sensitivity read head able to detect the magnetic fields from recorded bits of the recording medium. The giant magnetoresistive (GMR) effect, discovered in 1988 by Fert's group at the University of Paris in France [4] and Grünberg's group at the Julich Institute in Germany [5], represents a new phenomenon that contributed to the continued success of HDD technology. The observed large change in resistance, called "giant," was possible due to the existence of the antiferromagnetic coupling between two ferromagnetic Fe layers separated by a thin layer of Cr. The discovery of GMR (the Nobel prize was awarded for it in 2007) has stimulated intensive studies aiming to increase further the MR value and to lower the field needed to achieve higher resistance change—that is, the field needed to change the magnetizations of the two adjacent ferromagnetic layers from parallel to antiparallel. This will allow better differentiation between two resistance states with smaller applied magnetic fields originating from the written bits in the HDD media.

The first big change in HDD technology was introduced in 1991, when the inductive read head was replaced by an AMR read head. The later technology provided a higher readback signal, and thus the size of the recorded bits could be reduced further, leading to high ARD. At the same time, intense investigation and development of more sensitive read heads based on the GMR effect discovered in 1988 were carried out.

Six years later, the first GMR read head was implemented in a commercial HDD by IBM with an ARD of slightly more than 2 Gb/in.[2] Different generations of GMR read heads were used until 2005 when the tunnel magnetoresistive (TMR) type was introduced. TMR technology offers higher magnetoresistance than GMR technology, and it is most likely to be used for more than 1 Tb/in.[2] areal recording density. Even though TMR read heads can produce a larger readback signal compared to GMR read heads, its higher resistance limits its operation frequency.

In this chapter, we will discuss the history of GMR and TMR, and follow with the principles of retrieving data recorded on a medium. Table 6.1, on page 123, summarizes the history of the development of HDD.

In Sections 6.4 and 6.5, different GMR and TMR read head structures will be presented and described.

6.2 PRINCIPLES OF THE READOUT PROCESS

Figure 6.3 shows schematically the principles of magnetic recording in an HDD, where the data are stored in a thin magnetic recording layer (up and down magnetizations shown by the arrows in the figure). In a perpendicular magnetic recording (PMR) scheme, the recording layer is sputter-deposited on a lamination of nonmagnetic intermediate layers, as shown in Figure 6.3. The intermediate layers have more than one function: they promote proper crystallographic growth for the recording layer, induce its grain isolation, and exchange decouple the recording layer from a magnetic soft underlayer (SUL) [6–10]. The SUL enables the increase of write field efficiency by imaging the write head. Consequently, higher anisotropy recording media can be used that could be with earlier longitudinal magnetic recording (LMR). Details on PMR and the principles of magnetic recording are discussed in Chapters 3 and 4 of this book.

Data to be recorded can be written and erased by a write head. The principles of the writing process has not changed much from the early days of HDDs, except that the ring head is now replaced by a single pole head or shielded pole head in PMR [11, 12]. PMR can deliver a higher magnetic field because the recording layer is located in the gap between the write pole and its image in the SUL.

For reading the recorded data, a change in the resistance in GMR or TMR sensors due to media magnetic field can be used to determine the magnetic orientation of the bit just below the sensing layer. Figure 6.3 shows the case of GMR or TMR where the current flows perpendicular to the film plane. The same principle applies for cases of current-in-plane.

It can be seen from Figure 6.3 that the current i flows through the film multilayer structure from one electrode to the other. The read head is located between two shields

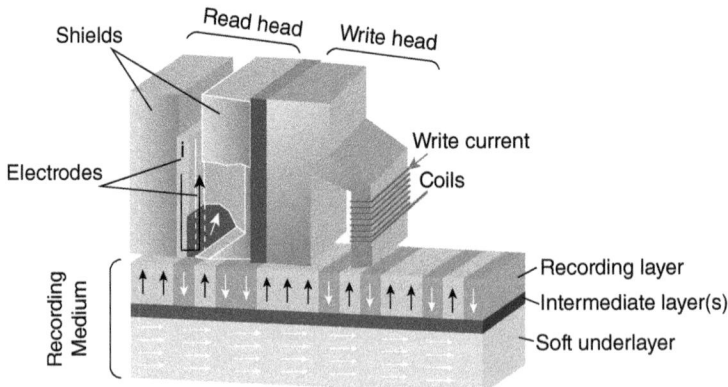

Figure 6.3. Schematic diagram of read head with current perpendicular to plane, write head, and recording medium. The read head is separated from the write head by a thin insulating layer called a gap. In this figure, perpendicular magnetic recording media is shown, and the read head is a TMR sensor where the current is flowing perpendicular to the film plane. Only the free layer "sensor" is shown for clarity.

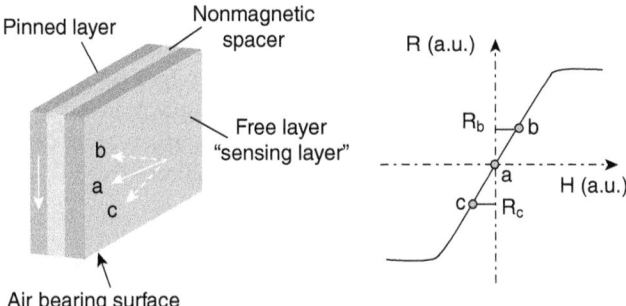

Figure 6.4. When the magnetic field from the recorder bits is sensed by the free layer, its magnetization rotates up (state b) or down (state c). The pinned layer magnetization is fixed by an antiferromagnetic layer. If no field is coming from the media, the free layer magnetization is orthogonal to the pinned layer magnetization (state a). Depending on the angle between the two magnetizations, a change in resistance can be measured.

made of high permeability magnetic materials and serve to deflect the magnetic field originating from the bits adjacent to the one just below the sensing layer. In Figure 6.3, only the magnetization of the sensing layer, also called the free layer, is shown for clarity. The fixed layer, also called the pinned layer, has its magnetization fixed and pointing either in the up or down direction, that is, perpendicular to the air-bearing surface (ABS), which is the bottom surface of the read head and is facing the recording media.

If no magnetic field is sensed by the free layer, its magnetization will remain orthogonal to the pinned layer, as represented by state (a) in Figure 6.4. Depending on whether the magnetic field emanating from the bit to be read is in the up direction "state b" or down direction "state c," the free layer magnetization will rotate accordingly, and a change in resistance or voltage will be measured.

In the case of the spin valve (SV), which is composed of a pinned layer, a non-magnetic spacer such as Cu, and a free layer, the angular dependence of the multilayer stack resistivity can be well described by the phenomenological expression

$$\rho(\theta) = \rho_0 + \frac{1}{2}\Delta p . \cos(\theta), \tag{6.1}$$

where θ is the angle between the magnetization directions of the free and pinned layers. $\Delta\rho$ is the resistivity change when the magnetizations are parallel and antiparallel, and ρ_0 is the resistivity when θ equals 90°.

The read head operates in the linear regime of Equation 6.1 (i.e., near $\theta = 90$°) in order to detect a media field smaller than the free layer coercivity. Usually the efficiency of the read head is around 20%, as can be seen in Figure 6.4. This means that when the free layer is under the media field, its magnetization rotates from its initial state by a small angle, and it is not fully saturated in the same direction as the pinned-layer magnetization.

Until now, GMR and TMR read heads have been based on free and pinned layers with in-plane anisotropy. It is necessary to align the free layer magnetization perfectly orthogonal with respect to the pinned layer. Also, the free layer should be free from magnetic domains, which generate noise to the readback signal. For these reasons, a hard-bias material is deposited at both sides of the free layer. More details of the GMR and TMR structures will be discussed in the following sections.

6.3 A BRIEF HISTORY OF THE GMR AND TMR EFFECTS

Long before the discovery of the GMR and TMR effects, it was known that some magnetic materials can exhibit an MR effect, called anisotropic magnetoresistance [13–15]. Anisotropic magnetoresistance is a characteristic of some materials whereby they exhibit a change in resistance depending on the direction of electrical current with respect to external magnetic field. A high resistance can be measured due to frequent collision of the conduction electrons when they travel parallel to the film magnetization. On the other hand, lower resistance can be measured when they travel perpendicular to the magnetization. A typical example is NiFe, which shows a maximum magnetoresistance of about 2%. It has been widely used for read head based on the AMR effect.

GMR is a change in electrical resistance in response to an applied magnetic field. However, as the change in magnetoresistance is quite huge, it is termed GMR to distinguish it from the small changes observed with AMR materials. It was first observed in Fe/Cr multilayers and was explained as arising from changes in the relative orientation of the magnetization in the adjacent ferromagnetic layers [4, 5] as a function of magnetic field. For a specific thickness of the Cr layer, the magnetizations of the adjacent Fe layer are aligned antiparallel to each other in the absence of an external magnetic field, as can be seen from Figure 6.5a. This leads to a high resistive state as more electrons get scattered when passing through the layers with antiparallel alignment, which will be explained in a subsequent section. A drop in resistivity was measured when the magnetic moments of all ferromagnetic layers are aligned parallel to each other, which can be realized by applying an external magnetic field (Fig. 6.5b). This change in resistivity is much larger than the anisotropic magnetoresistance. The antiferromagnetic coupling between Fe layers separated by a thin Cr layer was found in 1986 by Peter Grünberg [16], and the study of the transport properties of these structures by Peter Grünberg and Albert Fert was behind the discovery of the GMR effect. Figure 6.6 shows the variation in the resistance of the Fe/Cr multilayers from the paper of Baibich et al. The maximum GMR measured was 80% at a temperature of 4.2 K. Magnetoresistance is defined as the difference between R_{AP} and R_P divided by R_P. R_{AP} (R_P) is the resistance when the magnetizations of the ferromagnetic layers are antiparallel (parallel). In the case of Grünberg's experiments, a magnetoresistance of 1.5% was measured in the Fe/Cr/Fe trilayer (Fig. 6.7). The large magnetoresistance observed in Fert's experiments compared to Grünberg is due to the use of multilayer structure in addition to low temperature measurements. It was also observed that in the Fe/Cr/Fe trilayer, the required field to align magnetizations in the same direction is much lower than in case of the Fe/Cr multilayer.

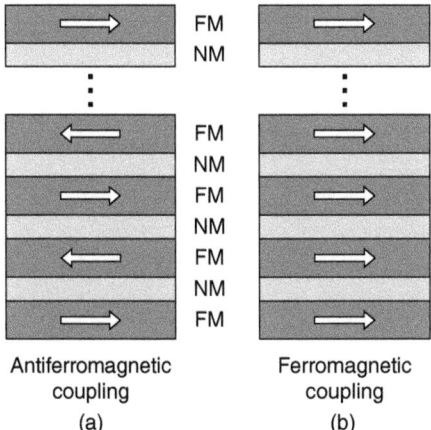

Figure 6.5. Magnetic multilayer where the ferromagnetic (FM) layers are separated by non-magnetic (NM) spacer layers. In case (a), the adjacent FM layers are antiferromagnetically coupled. The antiferromagnetic (AFM) coupling strength depends on the thickness of the NM layers. In case (b) the FM layers are parallel. This can be achieved by applying a magnetic field higher than the magnitude of the AFM coupling field. This structure was the basis of the discovery of the GMR effect where FM and NM were Fe and Cr, respectively.

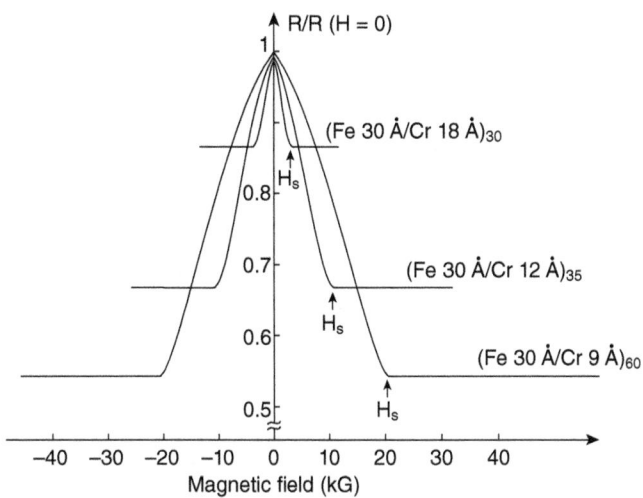

Figure 6.6. Original measurement of giant magnetoresistance from Baibich et al. [4]. Normalized resistance versus applied magnetic field for different (Fe/Cr) multilayers at 4.2 K with a current flowing in plane of the films. When there is no applied magnetic field, the adjacent Fe layers have their magnetization antiparallel. The saturation field, H_s, is the field needed to overcome the antiferromagnetic exchange coupling and align their magnetizations parallel. (Reprinted with permission from Figure 6.3 of Reference 4. Copyright (1988) American Physical Society.)

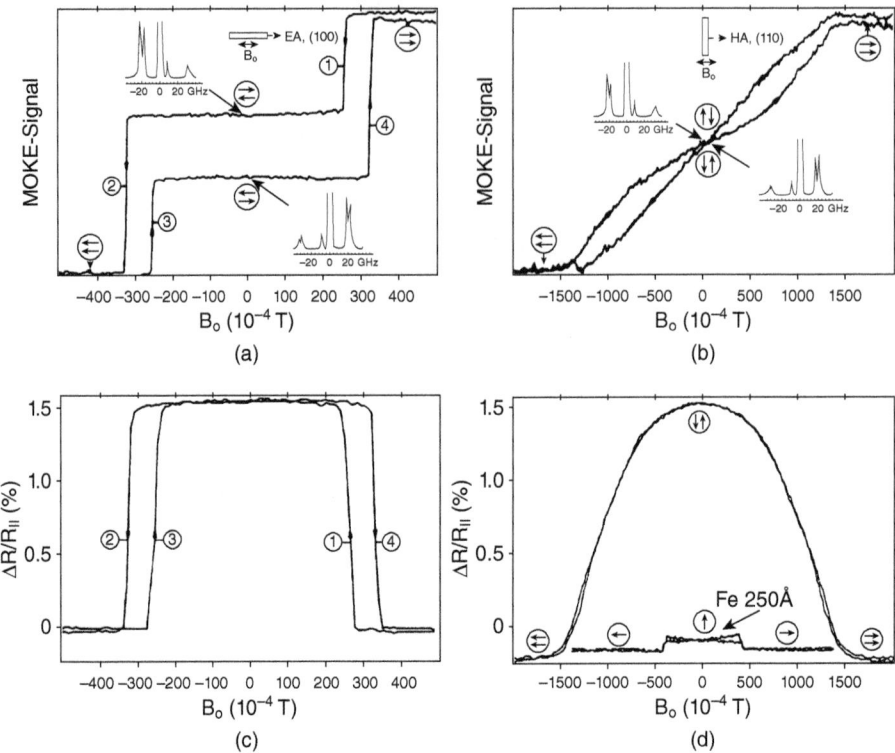

Figure 6.7. Original measurement of giant magnetoresistance from Grünberg et al. [5]. The samples were trilayer of Fe(12 nm)/Cr(1 nm)/Fe(12 nm). The left and right panels show the results with the magnetic field applied along the easy and hard axes, respectively, in the plane of the multilayer. The upper graphs (a) and (b) show the magnetization curves measured using the magneto-optic Kerr effect, and the lower graphs (c) and (d) are the magnetoresistance measured with the current in the plane of the layers and at room temperature. The insets to the magnetization curve in graphs (a) and (b) show the light scattering from spin waves signifying antiferromagnetic coupling. Graph (d) also shows the anisotropic magnetoresistance measured on a 250 Å Fe film. (Reprinted with permission from Figure 6.2 of Reference 5. Copyright (1989) American Physical Society.)

Besides being observed in Fe/Cr multilayers, the GMR effect was later observed in Co/Cu, NiFe/Ag, NiFe/Au, Fe/Au, Co/Ag, and other systems [17–22]. The Co/Cu and CoFe/Cu show an even higher MR ratio, and a Cu spacer was adopted for GMR devices and later in spin-valve structures, which will be discussed later.

In all these multilayers, the antiferromagnetic coupling between the adjacent ferromagnetic (FM) layers leads to a high resistivity of the multilayer, and a ferromagnetic coupling leads to a significant reduction of its magnitude. However, the antiferromagnetic coupling between the adjacent FM layers through a nonmagnetic (NM) spacer is not the only condition for the GMR effect to occur. By choosing two FM layers with

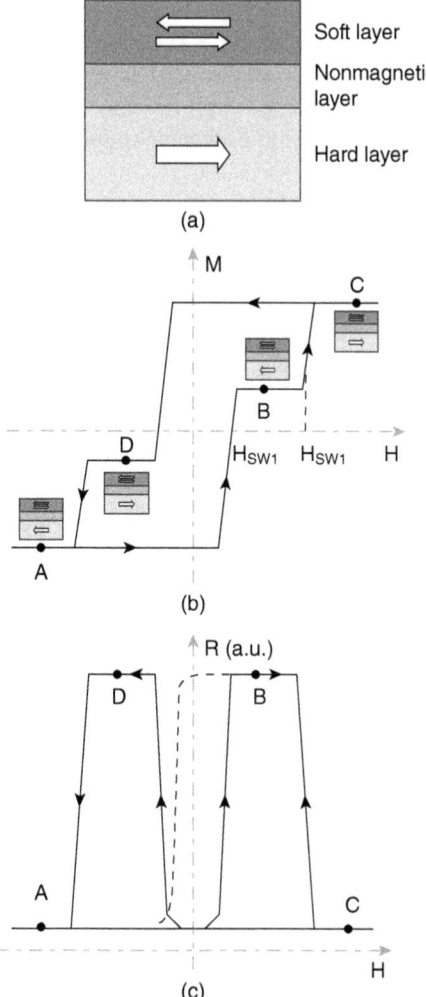

Figure 6.8. Schematic representation of a simple GMR structure where one ferromagnetic layer, called hard, has higher coercivity than the other ferromagnetic layer. A conductive nonmagnetic spacer is inserted between them (a); magnetization versus external magnetic field plot for the GMR structure (b); the corresponding resistance versus magnetic field with minor loop in dotted line (c).

different coercivities—that is, one is soft and the other is hard, as schematically represented in Figure 6.8—it is possible to align the magnetizations of the two FM layers antiparallel to each other in a range of applied fields, depending on the differences in the layers' coercivities [23, 24]. In that case, the soft and hard layers have their magnetizations antiparallel for an applied magnetic field between their respective switching fields H_{SW1} and H_{SW2} of the soft and hard layers. A high resistance can then be measured in a field range between H_{SW1} and H_{SW2}. Furthermore, if we consider the minor loop represented by the dotted line of the R-H curve (after reversal of magnetization in soft layer and before switching of the hard layer magnetization), we can have only two states, A and B, with low and high resistance, respectively. The shift in the minor hysteresis loop depends on the exchange coupling between the soft and hard layers.

The TMR effect is manifested in the same way as the GMR effect. The device has a low resistance when the two adjacent ferromagnetic layers have their respective magnetizations parallel to each other and high resistance when they are antiparallel. In the case of TMR, the nonmagnetic spacer is a thin insulator such as AlO_2, TiO_2, or MgO, for example. In contrast, the spacer in GMR devices is a conductive thin layer such as Cu or Cr. Even though GMR and TMR effects look similar, their physics and origins are quite different.

6.3.1 The GMR Effect

From the moment of the discovery of the GMR effect, the theoretical understanding of its origin became the subject of intensive studies. The development of band structure theory gave a realistic model to describe GMR effect. However, a qualitative explanation of the GMR effect can be understood using the Mott model, which was proposed in 1936 [13]. The key idea of Mott's model is that the electrical conductivity in ferromagnetic metals can be described in terms of two independent conducting channels, corresponding to the spin-up and spin-down electrons. The spin dependence of the conductivity can be understood from the typical band structure of a ferromagnetic metal, as shown in Figure 6.9a. In ferromagnetic materials such Fe, Co, Ni, and their alloys, there is a splitting in the density of states of the d-band spin-up and spin-down electrons. As a result, the spin-up and spin-down electrons at the Fermi level, which carry the electrical current, are in different states and exhibit different conduction properties. Mott's theoretical work has been confirmed experimentally 30 years later by Fert et al. [14] and Loegel et al. [15] in different magnetic materials. From Mott's model, the mobility of the electrons is spin dependent, and the resistance of the two channels is different, as shown schematically in Figure 6.9b.

Using Mott's argument, the GMR effect can be qualitatively explained using Figure 6.10. When the magnetic moments of the two ferromagnetic layers are parallel, the spin-up electrons pass through the structure almost without scattering because their spin direction is parallel to the magnetization of the two layers. On the other hand, the spin-down electrons are scattered strongly within both ferromagnetic layers because their spin direction is antiparallel to their magnetizations. Since the two conducting channels are independent, and conductivity occurs at the same time for both of them, the total resistivity of the multilayer shown in Figure 6.10a is determined mainly by the spin-up electrons and appears to be low.

On the other hand, when the magnetic moments in the two ferromagnetic layers are antiparallel, the electrons of each spin channel are scattered by one of the two ferromagnets, as can be seen in Figure 6.10b. This situation will lead to a high resistivity of the multilayer F/NM/F.

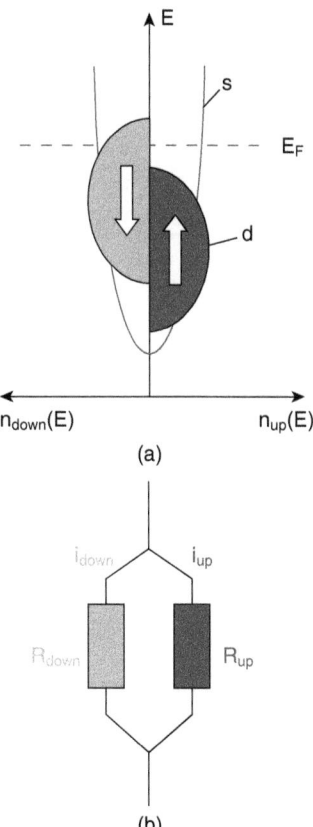

Figure 6.9. Schematic band structure of a ferromagnetic metal showing a splitting in spin-up and spin-down band energies. The difference between the number of electrons with spin up and spin down below Fermi level is not zero, leading to net spin polarization. Based on two-current model current, there are two conduction channels, "spin up" and "spin down," that are independent and have two different resistances.

The spin polarization P defined by the difference between the number of spin-up, n_{up}, and spin-down, n_{down}, electrons (normalized by $n_{up} + n_{down}$) is an important parameter in electrical transport. The higher the value, the larger is the GMR effect. Most of the studies in spintronics focused on increasing the spin polarization with an ultimate target of 100%. That can be achieved by using half metals, which is another hot topic in spintronics [25–28]. For these materials, one of the conducting channels is above Fermi level, and the other is below. In contrast, nonferromagnetic materials have the same number of spin-up and spin-down electrons, and hence there is no spin polarization.

In ferromagnetic materials, it has been reported that Fe has a larger spin polarization than Co at 4.2 K, which itself has a larger spin polarization than Ni [29]. However, at room temperature, replacing only Fe with Co (by 10% or more) leads to a better

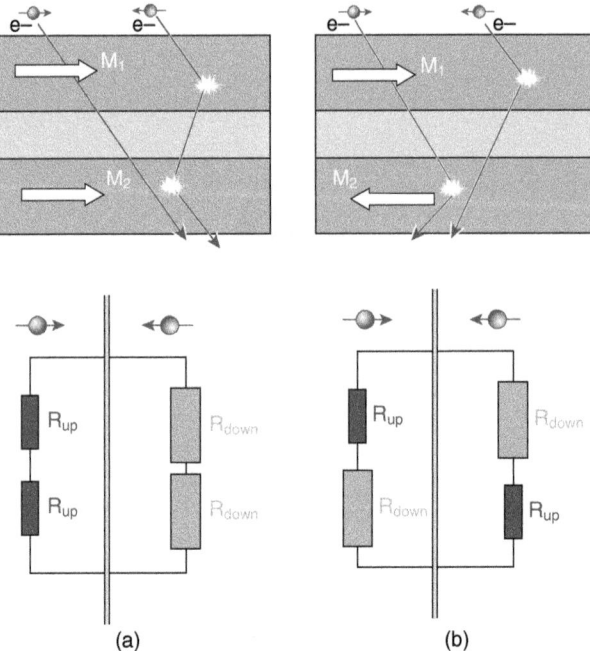

Figure 6.10. Two-current model and equivalent resistor network with two parallel resistance branches for each spin (majority and minority) channel.

GMR value, which could be attributed to the larger spin polarization of Co compared to Fe. It is also important in spintronics to consider the interface between the ferromagnetic and nonmagnetic spacer. Experiments showed that Co/Cu is better than Co/Cr or Co/Ag [18, 22, 30]. Furthermore, the Co alloys give a larger GMR than pure Co; for example, CoFe alloys with different compositions are widely used in GMR and also TMR devices. Because many requirements must be met for good read head operation, combinations of more than one ferromagnetic layer with different alloys are used [31–36]. For instance, CoFe has better spin polarization and low anisotropy compared to pure Co. On the other hand NiFe has low magnetostriction and lower anisotropy than CoFe alloys.

6.3.2 The TMR Effect

If the two ferromagnetic layers, as discussed in the previous section, are separated by a thin insulating layer, the electrons cannot across the barrier; however, if the insulating layer is thin enough, typically a few atomic layers, then the electrons are able to tunnel from one ferromagnetic layer to the other, provided there are available electron states on the other side. The tunneling of electrons from one ferromagnetic layer to the other depends on the available states. The TMR effect is very sensitive to the matching between spin-selective bands, which is not the case with the GMR effect; but both effects depend on the orientation of the magnetization (magnetic moments) of the two ferromagnetic layers. In other words, when the two ferromagnetic layers have their magnetization parallel, the resistance of the TMR structure is minimal; when they are antiparallel it is maximal.

Jullière's formalism is based on the change of conductance between the state where the magnetizations in the two ferromagnetic layers are parallel and the state where they are antiparallel [37]. In Jullière's model, it is assumed that electrons tunnel without spin flip. The TMR ratio is then given by the relation,

$$TMR = \frac{2P_1P_2}{1 - P_1P_2},$$ (6.2)

where P_i (i = 1 or 2) is the polarization in each of the ferromagnetic layers. It can be seen from Equation 6.2 that if P_1 and P_2 are closer to 100%, the TMR can reach very high values. This is possible using half metal materials, which are under intensive investigation.

Jullière's model predicted the spin-valve effect, where the resistance can be changed by manipulating the relative orientations of the magnetizations in the two ferromagnetic layers. Although the first observation of TMR in Fe/Ge/Fe thin films was made by Jullière in 1975 [37], there was not much research activity in this field until the middle of 1990s.

The revival of TMR exploration was due to the volume of research conducted in electrical transport in magnetic multilayers and SV after the discovery of GMR effect.

In addition, there was improvement in thin-film growth and the performance of materials, that is, high-spin polarization, which led to high TMR. It was revealed by many groups that the growth of the tunnel barrier and the oxidation process are crucial for achieving a high TMR effect [38–43].

The golden age of TMR started in 1995 after the first reports of high TMR values at room temperature by Moodera et al. [38] and Miyazaki et al. [39]. After that, there were many reports on a higher TMR that could reach 70% using amorphous Al_2O_3 as the tunnel barrier [44, 45]. Theoretical studies predicated that a single crystal barrier can produce a very high TMR [46–48]. As predicted, a TMR of more than 200% was observed by Parkin et al. [49] and Yuasa et al. separately [50]. More recently Ikeda et al. reported a TMR value of about 600% at room temperature and 1140% at 5 K by improving the quality of the MgO barrier [51]. TMR effect is an important research field that has potential applications in magnetoresistive random access memories (MRAMs) despite the shortcomings of the effect for high-frequency read sensors.

6.4 SVS AND THE READ HEAD

The evolution of an invention from scientific discovery to product generally involves improvements to make it practical. This section describes the evolution of GMR heads in HDD applications. To use the GMR effect in real devices, there are a few requirements that should be fulfilled for suitable performance. In HDDs, the read head sensor has to sense the flux from a selected recorded bit and should not be affected by flux from neighboring bits. This is achieved by placing the read sensor between two magnetic shields made of a highly permeable material that shunts the field from the neighboring bits. For high areal densities, the bits get closer to each other, and therefore, it is necessary to reduce the shield-to-shield spacing. This means that the spacing between the bottom and top shields of the reader is determined by the linear density. The width of the head itself is chosen to match the track density. In addition to the physical dimension, which has to match the bit dimensions, the sensitivity of the head has to match the field emanating from the media. As the ARD increases, the field that comes from the media decreases, and hence, the head should have a signal response for smaller magnetic fields. As discussed earlier, the original GMR structure, which was made of a multilayer of Fe/Cr, had a high saturation field H_S (i.e., the field needed to align the magnetizations in all the ferromagnetic layers). This structure is not able to provide enough resistance change for less than 200 Oe, which is the range of the field that can be generated by one magnetic recorded bit. This value may even become lower as the bit size shrinks to follow the increase in the ARD.

The hard/soft structure was not practically useful because it was not possible to have a hard layer of more than 500 Oe, using Co alloys with good spin polarization. For a very good resistance-field response, it is necessary that the hard layer magnetization does not switch during the readout process and that the soft layer magnetization responds linearly to the field. In addition, spin polarization is important to achieve a better GMR effect. Increasing the thickness of Co may help to increase the coercivity but not enough, and increasing the thickness of the magnetic layer will cause current shunting, thus lowering the resistance change in the geometry where the electrical current flows in the multilayer plane. Therefore, a breakthrough was required to take advantage of the GMR effect for applications in HDDs.

To exploit the GMR effect in read head sensors, an elegant structure was proposed by Dieny et al. [52]. This structure is shown in Figure 6.11a. The key feature of this structure is that instead of using a hard ferromagnetic layer, they proposed to have the ferromagnetic layer exchange coupled to an antiferromagnetic layer in order to fix its magnetization direction (pinned). Since the exchange bias pins the magnetization of one layer strongly, only the soft layer responds to the field as desired. This structure, called an SV, made the GMR effect practical for spintronic devices. In their initial experiments, Dieny et al. used 15-nm-thick NiFe ferromagnetic layers (Fig. 6.12), which are quite thick, and consequently the MR ratio was low [14]. However, several improvements have been made in this scheme, which was implemented in HDDs from 1997 to 2005 until TMR read heads were introduced. The research and development of GMR read heads focused on: (1) optimal reduction of the thickness of the ferromagnetic layers as the sensitivity of the sensor is proportional to the product $t.M_S$, where t and M_S are the thickness and saturation magnetization of the soft layer; (2) optimal increase of the antiferromagnetic exchange coupling (H_{ex}) so that the magnetization direction of the pinned layer will not change under the media magnetic field during the reading process; (3) optimal reduction of the anisotropy of the soft layer since for low

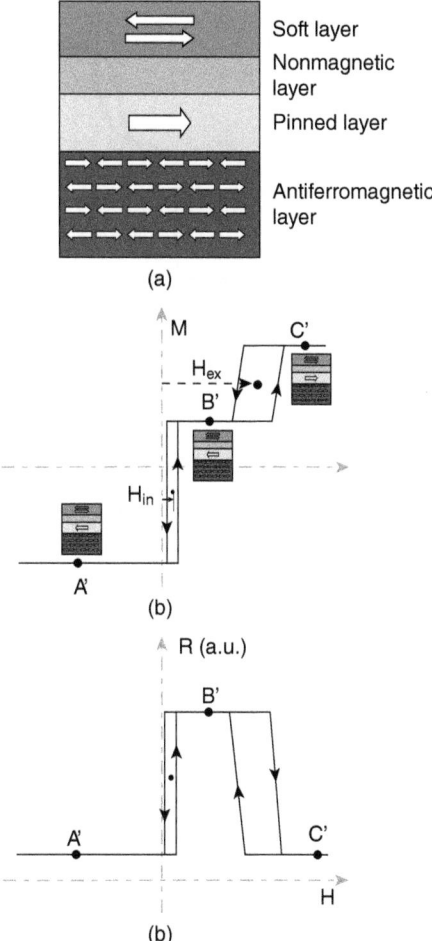

Figure 6.11. Schematic representation of an exchange biased spin-valve structure where one ferromagnetic layer, called hard, has its magnetization fixed by exchange coupling to an antiferromagnetic layer, and the other ferromagnetic layer has its magnetization direction changed by an external magnetic field (a); magnetization versus external magnetic field plot for the spin valve (b); and the corresponding resistance versus magnetic field with minor loop in dotted line (c).

anisotropy materials, the magnetization can rotate easily when it is subject to an external field in its hard axis direction; (4) optimal reduction of the magnetostriction of the soft layer so there will be no increase in the effective anisotropy field due to magnetostrictive effect; (5) optimal reduction of the thickness of antiferromagnetic layer without compromising its stability—that is, keeping the blocking temperature T_B as high as possible [53].

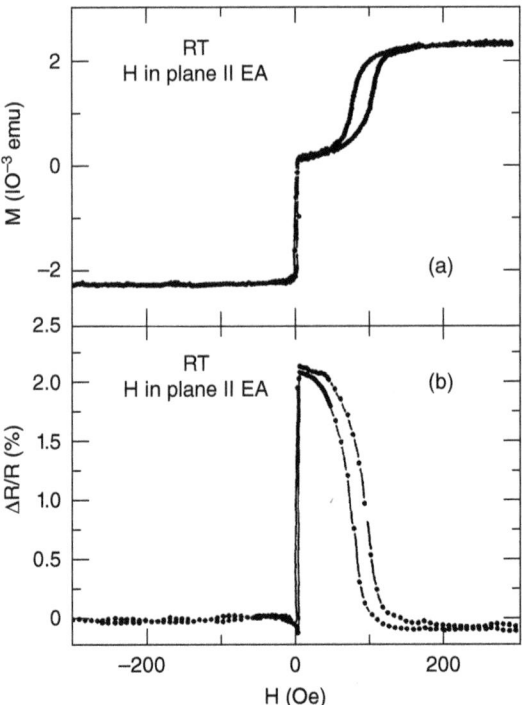

Figure 6.12. Magnetization curve (a) and magnetoresistance (b) for a spin valve made of NiFe (150 Å)/Cu(26 Å)/(NiFe 150 Å)/FeMn (100 Å)/Ag (20 Å). The magnetic field is applied parallel to exchange anisotropy field created by the AFM layer FeMn. (Reprinted with permission from Figure 6.1 of Reference 52. Copyright (1991) American Physical Society.)

The exchange coupling can be estimated from the shift in the hysteresis loop of the layer that is in contact with the antiferromagnetic layer (Fig. 6.11b,c). The value of H_{ex} is strongly dependent on the interface quality between the antiferromagnetic and the ferromagnetic layers. Also, growing a good antiferromagnetic layer is one of the key challenges, and the choice of the seed layer is important to favor the desired crystallographic texture of the antiferromagnetic layer.

The schematic hysteresis loops shown in Figure 6.11b,c, correspond to magnetization versus field, and resistance versus field, respectively, and were obtained when the applied field is parallel to the easy axis of the two ferromagnetic layers. The unidirectional anisotropy for the antiferromagnetic layer is achieved by annealing the multilayer above the T_B of the antiferromagnetic layer and simultaneously applying a magnetic field. When the multilayer is cooled down to room temperature, the unidirectional exchange bias can be achieved.

For making read heads, another annealing step is necessary at a temperature below the T_B of the antiferromagnetic layer and at a field much lower than the first step in order to induce a 90° orientation for the free layer magnetization. It is worthy to note that in the early 1990s, NiO, NiMn, and FeMn materials were widely used as antiferromagnetic layers [52, 54–61]. NiO, which is an electrical insulator is suitable for current-in-plane (CIP) SVs because it helps to increase the electron scattering, and consequently a higher MR ratio could be achieved [59]. However, these materials were abandoned as they provide a lower exchange coupling field compared to PtMn [60] and IrMn [61]. In the case of an IrMn antiferromagnetic layer, the first-step annealing can be carried out under high vacuum at 280°C to 350°C with an applied field of 6 to 10 kOe. The second step can be carried out at around 100°C or less and with an applied magnetic field of a few hundred Oe to set the free layer magnetization perpendicular to the pinned layer. In both steps, the magnetic field is applied in the film's plane. With the free layer easy axis orthogonal to the pinned layer, a linear readback signal can be obtained.

In current products, FeMn has been changed to IrMn, which can offer H_{ex} of more than 1000 Oe even with 5-nm thickness. At this thickness, the antiferromagnetic layer of IrMn has a T_B of less than 250°C but still high enough for stable and reliable read head operation. Furthermore, IrMn can grow on a thin seed layer such as 5-nm NiCr or NiFeCr, or a 3-nm lamination of NiCr followed by 1-nm lamination of FeCo. This helps to reduce the shield-to-shield spacing required for small bit size.

6.4.1 Types of SV Structures

In a read head sensor, it is important to eliminate the interaction between the free and pinned layers. The interaction can be exchange or magnetostatic coupling, and the presence of a Cu layer eliminates the exchange coupling. The magnetostatic coupling cannot be eliminated but can be evaluated from the interlayer coupling H_{in} depicted in Figure 6.11. The free layer magnetization should ideally be uniform, free from any magnetic domain, and perfectly aligned at 90° to the pinned layer when it is not under any external magnetic field.

One way to reduce H_{in} is to increase the NM spacer thickness, but this will reduce GMR as increase of the spacer layer will lead to reduction of spin scattering. In order to achieve a high GMR, the spacer layer along with the free layer and pinned layer thicknesses should be smaller than the mean free paths of electrons when the current flows in the film plane. In addition, it is also essential to reduce the thickness of all the layers as much as possible in order to decrease the shield-to-shield spacing. From these two considerations, it is important to find a way to reduce the thickness of the NM spacer layer without compromising the MR ratio. The MR ratio can be expressed as a function of the NM layer thickness by the phenomenological equation [62]:

$$\frac{\Delta R}{R} = \left(\frac{\Delta R}{R}\right)_0 \left[\exp\left(-\frac{t_{NM}}{\lambda_{NM}}\right) \middle/ \left(1 + \frac{t_{NM}}{t_0}\right) \right]. \tag{6.3}$$

In this equation, t_{NM} is the thickness of the nonmagnetic layer, λ_{NM} is the mean free path of the electrons in the nonmagnetic layer, t_0 is the effective thickness of the rest of the multilayer causing shunting of the electrical current, and $(\Delta R/R)_0$ is a normalization coefficient.

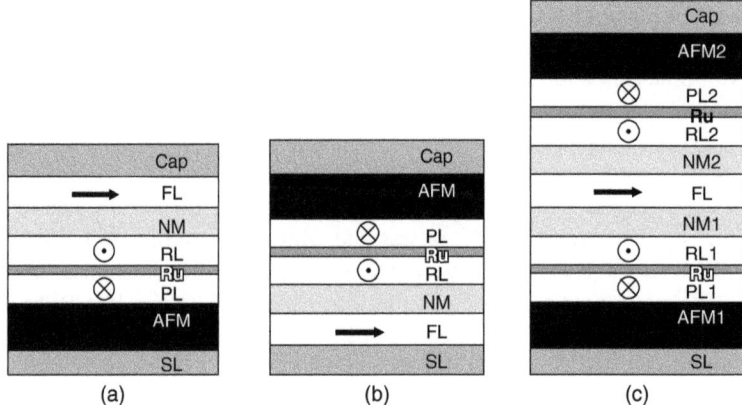

Figure 6.13. Different types of spin valves: bottom type (a); top type (b); and dual type (c). FL is the free layer, PL is the pinned layer, RL is the reference layer, SL is the seed layer, and Cap is the capping layer.

Much care should be taken during the growth of not only of the NM spacer layer but also all other layers, such as the seed layer, the antiferromagnetic layer, the pinned layer, and others. The roughness, for example, causes an increase of the interlayer coupling, through orange-peel coupling or Néel coupling [63–66]. The existence of pinholes can also induce the same effect and degrade the reliability of each read head device.

One way to reduce H_{in} is to use a synthetic antiferromagnetically coupled (AFC) pinned layer [67]. This structure can also stabilize both pinned and free layers by reducing or even totally canceling the stray field coming from the pinned layer (Fig. 6.13a). Antiferromagnetic coupling between two ferromagnetic pinned layers is achieved by inserting a thin Ru layer of about 8 Å between them. Materials such as Ru, Rh, and so on have been reported to induce high values of antiferromagnetic coupling between two ferromagnetic layers. The value of the antiferromagnetic exchange coupling field oscillates as a function of the thickness of Ru or Rh, similar to the Ruderman–Kittel–Kasuya–Yoshida (RKKY) interaction. In fact, higher values of the antiferromagnetic coupling field can be obtained for 4 Å-thick Ru corresponding to the first peak in the interlayer exchange coupling [30]. However, the range of thickness where the exchange coupling peaks is very narrow, so even a small difference in the thickness of Ru of 1 Å or 2 Å can cause a drastic change in the antiferromagnetic exchange coupling. This kind of thickness variation throughout a whole substrate would be unavoidable during the mass production of head wafers and hence would result in device-to-device variation in performance. Since that is not desirable for head applications, the second peak in the RKKY oscillation is preferred.

At least three types of SVs have been proposed for read head and other spintronic devices. The first type is called a bottom SV, where the pinned layer is deposited first, followed by the NM spacer and free layer. The reversed structure, called a top SV, has the free layer deposited first (Fig. 6.13b). The dual SV is a combination of both top and bottom SVs where the free layer is located between two pinned layers and two NM spacers (Fig. 6.13c). The dual SVs can offer higher MR than the single type. It was used in early generations of GMR read heads because of the higher signal that can be achieved with it but was later abandoned due to the need for a smaller shield-to-shield spacing. The shield-to-shield spacing is approximately 50% larger than the width of the bit in the recording media. Currently, the separation between the two shields of the read head is around 30 nm, and this value should be reduced further to around 20 nm for 1-Tb/in.[2] ARD. Therefore, reducing the thickness of the layers of an SV device is an important area of research. In the latest generation of read heads with single-type SV, a lot of studies were devoted to find a thinner seed and antiferromagnetic layers, and to continuous optimization of other layers to reduce the total thickness of the SV.

6.4.2 Read Head Configurations

The first-generation GMR read head was used to sense recorded information from LMR media as shown in Figure 6.14. In an LMR scheme, the magnetic flux originates from the bit transitions. When the magnetizations in two neighboring bits are aligned in the opposite directions, the flux is either up or down, depending on whether their magnetic moments are pointing at or away from each other. As the read head flies over the media along a defined track, the magnetization of the free layer rotates while the

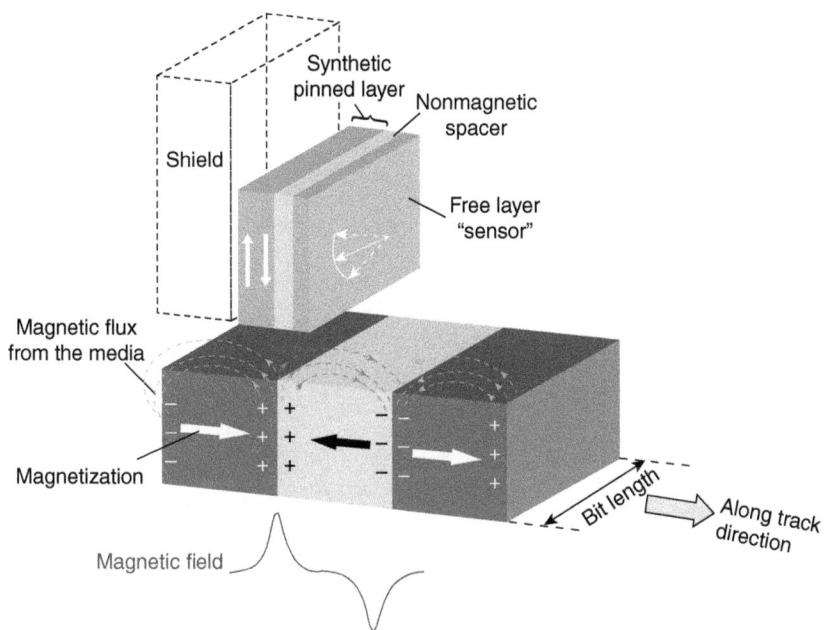

Figure 6.14. View of read head and LMR media. The magnetic flux from the media is originating from bit transitions.

magnetization of the pinned layer maintains its direction. Sometimes the pinned layer closer to the NM spacer is called the reference layer. The resistivity of the SV changes with the magnetization angle, θ, between the free and the reference or pinned layers according to relation (1).

With a current source, called the sense current, connected to the sensor, the passage of the free layer over a bit transition yields a voltage pulse with the polarity determined by the sign of the magnetic field at the transition, as shown in Figure 6.14. In this figure, only the free layer, the synthetic pinned layers, and the NM spacer are shown for clarity. It is important to mention that a hard bias is always deposited at the side of the free layer in order to keep it in a single domain state. Domain walls within the free layer can cause noise during the readback process. The bias field from the hard bias should be just enough to align all the magnetic moments in the free layer in one direction (orthogonal to pinned layer magnetization direction). If the hard bias field is too strong, it may change the stiffness of the free layer and will affect its sensitivity—that is, its response to media magnetic fields. The materials commonly used for hard bias are mainly based on high coercivity CoPt and FePt.

The same GMR read head configuration discussed earlier for LMR media is used for PMR media (Fig. 6.15). The only difference is that the readback signal originates from the recorded bit itself and not the transition. A high signal from the media is another advantage of PMR besides improvement in writability, as is discussed in detail in Chapter 4. The magnetic field from PMR media is stronger because of the SUL. This

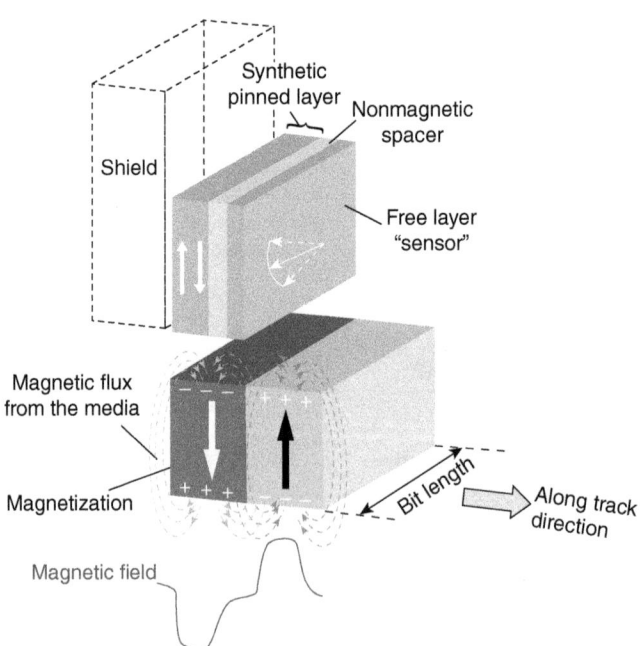

Figure 6.15. View of read head and PMR media. The magnetic flux from the media is originating from the recorded bit.

leads to larger rotation of the free layer magnetization, that is, better efficiency. Major changes in PMR technology were introduced to the media and writer design, but no change in read head design and structure was required except for the continuous improvement in materials performance.

PMR technology enables the reduction of bit size to smaller measures than is possible with LMR technology. The reduction of the bit size was accompanied by a requirement to shrink the read head size. As a result, the readback signal from a GMR read head operating in a CIP scheme was not enough to differentiate the recorded data. This problem was overcome with the TMR head, which was introduced for the first time in 2005.

Nevertheless, conscious of the challenges facing the technology, researchers and engineers are still developing a GMR SV with current perpendicular to plane, which will be discussed later in this section.

6.4.2.1   CIP Read Head. The discovery of the GMR effect was made upon observations of electrical current flowing along a Fe/Cr multilayer plane (CIP). After that, experiments on GMR were intensively carried out using a CIP scheme until 1993, when the first experiments with current perpendicular to plane were performed. From a practical point of view, all GMR read head were operating with a CIP scheme until the first TMR read head was commercialized in 2005. The GMR element shown in Figure 6.16 represents the structure with an SV composed of a synthetic pinned layer, separated from the free layer by a nonmagnetic conductive spacer. An antiferromagnetic layer was deposited in contact with the first pinned layer.

Figure 6.16 shows the cross-sectional view of the read head sensor viewed from the media surface, which is called ABS. A bottom gap made from an insulating material is deposited on a bottom shield. The gap insulates the ferromagnetic layers from the shields. The shields are deposited by electroplating and are composed of highly permeable and magnetically soft material such as NiFe. They have the main function of shunting the magnetic field from the adjacent recorded bits away from the read sensor. The thickness of the insulating gap layers should be as thin as possible to reduce the spacing between the bottom and top shield but should be uniform. Insulating layers without pinholes require a minimum thickness, which could be around 5–8 nm. On top of the bottom gap, the SV (GMR) structure is deposited with a capping layer.

Either electron beam lithography or KrF photolithography is used with ion milling to fabricate GMR devices with the desired size. After the ion milling process, and without breaking the vacuum, deposition of hard bias materials is carried out. For better growth and consequently better performance of the hard bias, at least one seed layer is deposited on the bottom gap while the GMR element is protected by a resist mask. After that, the leads or electrodes are made using an additional process step. Finally, a top gap similar to the bottom is deposited followed by top shield. The two gaps are used to avoid current from flowing through the shields.

There has been continuous improvement in both materials performance and device fabrication. The GMR and electrode contact area has to be large enough to avoid read head damage due to high current, and it has to be small enough to follow the reduction of the track density.

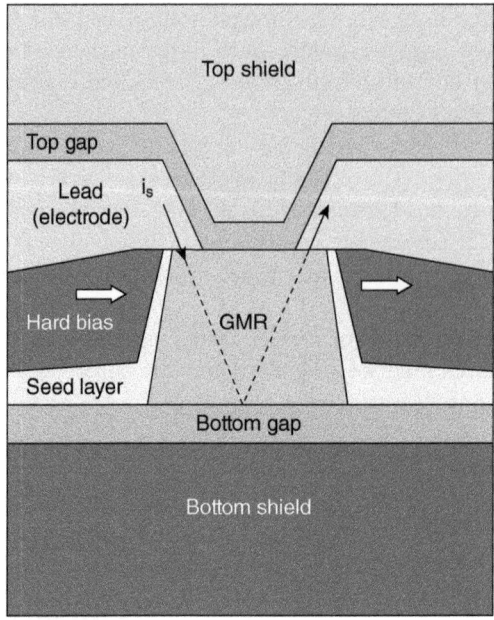

Figure 6.16. Cross-sectional view of the GMR read head in CIP scheme, Also called air-bearing surface. Two insulating layers, and bottom and top gaps are used to prevent the current from flowing through the shields. A hard bias is used to stabilize the free layer and align its magnetization in plane at 90° from the pinned layer magnetization. This [later] is fixed perpendicular to the air-bearing surface by an antiferromagnetic layer.

6.4.2.2 Current-Perpendicular-to-Plane (CPP) Read Head.

Even though CIP-GMR technology was intensively investigated and successfully implemented in read heads for many generations, there was a strong concern about its limits as many challenges were foreseen. Both CPP-GMR and TMR heads were investigated as strong candidates to replace the CIP-GMR read head. Among the key issues affecting the CIP read head are the following:

1. The existence of two insulators in the gap between the SV and the two shields increases the shield-to-shield spacing and hence these two gaps are not desirable for high bit density recording;

2. The contact area between the electrodes and the SV becomes smaller and smaller as the width of the read head is reduced to cope with the increase in track density. The later generations of CIP read head showed an increase in damage at the contact area with the electrodes due to overheating induced by the sense current.

In a CPP-GMR read head, these two key issues are nonexistent. First, there is no need for the two gaps as the current flows through the whole stack of the SV. Second, the

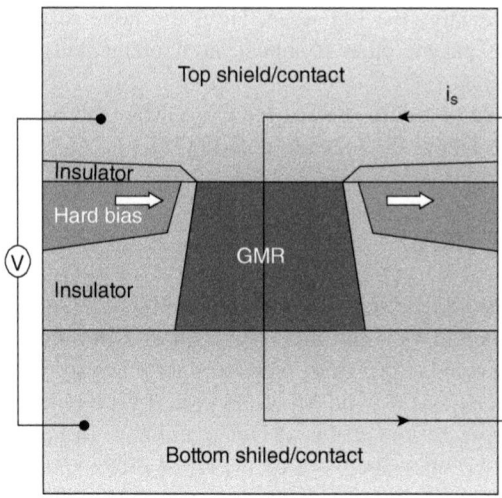

<u>Figure 6.17.</u> GMR read head in CPP scheme, also called air-bearing surface. Two insulating layers, and bottom and top gaps are used to prevent the current from flowing through the shields. A hard bias is used to stabilize the free layer and align its magnetization in plane at 90° from the pinned layer magnetization. This later is fixed perpendicular to the air-bearing surface by an antiferromagnetic layer.

contact area is the area of the SV which is much larger than in the CIP scheme (Fig. 6.17). Furthermore, according to the two-current model calculation, CPP-GMR technology provides a higher intrinsic MR ratio compared to CIP-GMR technology. The intrinsic MR ratio is magnetoresistance calculated from the free layer and pinned layer, separated by an NM conductive layer such as Cu. The extrinsic MR ratio includes in addition the effect of the seed layer, the capping layer, and the antiferromagnetic layer. The extrinsic MR ratio is lower than the intrinsic one.

In CPP-GMR technology, the two shields can be used as electrodes for sensing current, but depending on the requirements, additional electrodes may be deposited on top of the bottom shield and below the top shield. It is important to mention that in order to avoid the electrical current from flowing at the side of the SV, an insulator layer is needed. The insulator on the top of the bias shown in Figure 6.17 is an additional insulator that helps to make sure that the current will not circulate in the hard bias.

Unfortunately, even after several years of development, the output signal of CPP-GMR technology was still below the required value of 1 mV. The main problem with current CPP-GMR technology is its low resistance, and consequently, the resistance change ΔR remains low, too. Up to now, an MR ratio of only less than 5% has been achieved, which is not enough for an ARD exceeding 300 Gb/in.[2] [68–71]. Relatively high CPP-giant magnetoresistance was reported where the Cu spacer was replaced by a mixture of Cu and an insulator such as alumina to create a current-confined path in the CPP-GMR read head [72–74]. In this scheme, controlling the number of current paths between the free and pinned layers through the spacer matrix ($Cu\text{-}Al_2O_3$) in a reproducible way remains the big issue. Until the large difference in GMR values between one device and the other is solved, its implementation in a commercial read head is not possible.

As an alternative to and to replace the CIP-GMR read head, the TMR read head was implemented in HDDs by Seagate in 2005 [75].

6.5 TMR READ HEAD

The first work on the TMR effect was reported in 1972 by Gittelmar et al. on granular Ni-SiO$_2$ films [76] and in 1975 by Jullière in a stack of thin films [37]. Because of the low TMR values reported at that time, there was not much work carried out until 1995, when both Moodera et al. [38] and Miyazaki et al. [39] reported independently a significant TMR value of 12% in CoFe/Al$_2$O$_3$/Co and 18% in Fe/Al$_2$O$_3$/Fe, respectively. At that time, there was intensive work on the GMR effect and that probably helped to achieve large TMR values. It is worth noting the strong similarities between TMR and GMR layer structures.

As mentioned earlier, only the NM conductive spacer used in GMR technology is replaced by an insulating barrier to make a TMR device. One of the major challenges in TMR structures is growing the thin insulating tunnel barrier uniformly and without or at least with minimal pinholes. The first high TMR values reported at room temperature were on structures having an Al$_2$O$_3$ tunnel barrier, which is amorphous in nature. It was possible to achieve TMR values as high as 70% with an Al$_2$O$_3$ tunnel barrier [45]; however, a single crystal MgO barrier provides much larger values of more than 600% [51].

TMR structure is similar to CPP-GMR structure with a current flowing perpendicular to the film planes. Consequently, there are no major changes in the read head design. A TMR read head offers much higher readback signals due to its larger TMR values as compared to a CPP-GMR read head. However, the major challenge facing TMR heads is the high resistance, which poses a limitation on the operating frequency.

Research in TMR read head application aimed at the reduction of the device resistance (impedance) by reducing the insulating layer thickness. It was possible to obtain reasonable TMR values with a low resistance. This was possible in first-generation TMR devices with an amorphous Al$_2$O$_3$ barrier and later with crystalline MgO [77–81]. Because there was no breakthrough in increasing the readback signal in CPP-GMR read heads, it was not surprising to see the first TMR head in 2005 manufactured with these two types of insulators at the same time.

In order to reduce the resistance in TMR devices, the insulating tunnel barrier thickness should be reduced. However, this leads to the formation of pinholes that affect the performance of the devices. There was enormous work to minimize the number of pinholes in TMR devices by improving the deposition of the tunnel barrier, reducing the roughness of each layer in the stack, and so on. When compared to the CIP-GMR head, the reliability of the TMR read head remains low.

The research on TMR effect has been very active and conducted in parallel to research into CPP-giant magnetoresistance. Some theoretical works predicted that much higher TMR is possible by using a single crystal barrier. By using an epitaxial MgO barrier, S. Yuasa et al. and Parkin et al. were able to deposit magnetic tunnel junctions by sputtering with an over 200% MR ratio. More interestingly, for Yuasa's devices, the MgO tunnel barrier was grown on an amorphous CoFeB ferromagnetic thin layer. The achieved results were another big breakthrough in spintronics research, and since those results were published, more investigations have been carried out on MgO-based TMR devices. In these TMR devices, the single crystal barrier plays the role of a filter of the symmetry of the wave functions of the tunnelling electrons. As has been described by Zhang and Butler, the TMR effect depends on the spin polarization of the electrodes for the selected symmetry only [48]. Different wave functions can be selected depending on the barrier and the magnetic electrode. This reveals the fact that there is no intrinsic spin polarization of the ferromagnetic electrodes. The effective spin polarization depends on the symmetry selected and the barrier used. Consequently, huge TMR can be achieved and even negative values are also possible [82–84]. More recently, a tunnel magnetoresistance of 600% has been achieved by Ikeda et al. [51].

6.6 FUTURE PERSPECTIVES

Considering the road map of HDD technology in the coming years, some believe that there is a rough ride ahead. To keep up with the current growth in ARD per year of 30–40%, 1 Tb/in.^{2} should be available in products in 2013. This is a challenge not only for read head researchers but also for media technology. We should also consider the extendibility of ARD beyond 1 Tb/in.^{2}

For recording media, granular-film-based perpendicular media technology can probably be extended to 1 Tb/in.^{2}, but beyond that, alternative technologies such as heat-assisted magnetic recording or discrete track recording/bit-patterned media (DTR/ BPM) will be adopted. The current bit length is around 17 nm; this will be reduced as linear density increases further. These values put a strict constraint on shield-to-shield spacing, which in that case should be between 20 and 25 nm. In other words, the reduction of almost all the layers in the TMR structure should be obtained without sacrificing the TMR effect. The concern here is not the TMR value because using MgO or other crystalline tunnel barriers could maintain or even increase the value further. The main problem is that as the thickness of the layers is reduced, stability and reliability will be compromised. For example, IrMn with less than 5 nm in thickness will not be stable as the T_B depends strongly on the film thickness. Another major concern with TMR-based devices is their high resistance values. For head application, the thickness of the MgO tunnel barrier is only a few Angstroms. Reducing the thickness further will be challenging.

An additional scaling problem is encountered when the width of the read head has to be reduced to follow the reduction in track pitch. In both GMR and TMR read heads, the free and pinned layers have their magnetizations lying in the film plane. Reducing the width of the head will not be sustainable below 50 nm as the magnetization will not be uniform and will be in a curling shape. Overcoming this problem using a stronger hard bias will have the drawback of negatively affecting the sensitivity of the free layer. Scaling of track width is more of a challenge in the case of BPM. For example, 1 Tb/in.^{2} with a bit aspect ratio (BAR) of 1 requires a bit width of 25 nm.

A further physical problem that has to be solved or minimized by researchers working on GMR read head sensors is the spin transfer noise. It is known that polarized electrons can transfer their momentum to the free layer magnetic moment as has been predicted theoretically by Slonczewski [85] and Berger [86]. This phenomenon, called the spin transfer effect, can switch magnetization of the free layer or generate spin waves [87–91]. It is useful for MRAM and microwave emitters but not for read head application. Spin transfer can generate a noise in the readback signal and should be minimized [92–95]. As the sizes of GMR and TMR devices are continuously reduced, spin transfer is becoming stronger.

These are only a few issues that are now considered by researchers in this field. If we look back at the late 1990s, the ARD was expected to stagnate at around 40 Gb/in.^{2} because of the limitation imposed by the superparamagnetic effect on LMR media. But 10 years later, the prospect of reaching even 10 Tb/in.^{2} and beyond is being considered. There have been many breakthroughs in HDD technology; the use of the GMR read head, AFC media, perpendicular media, and TMR read heads are just a few examples. There have been also many breakthroughs in read head design, nanofabrication, and materials optimization.

It is worth mentioning that the development of CPP-GMR technology is not over, and researchers still believe it will be the future technology for read head as it has much lower resistance values compared to tunnel magnetoresistance. It is not necessary to have a very high MR ratio, just reasonably compatible with 1 mV readback signal.

Another scheme which is the subject of intense investigation is the use of perpendicular anisotropy free layer [96–98]. This scheme has the advantage of avoiding the use of hard bias because the free layer magnetization can be uniformly aligned in the easy axis direction for small size (single domain). Furthermore, the size of the device can be made small (sub-10 nm diameter) without compromising thermal stability, provided the free layer anisotropy field is slightly higher than the demagnetizing field. However, spin-torque induced noise in this structure is not yet studied, and this effect is expected to be one of the challenges facing attempts to reduce the size of the read head sensor.

6.7 CONCLUSION

Since the first RAMAC HDD, there has been a continuous increase in the ARD of HDDs, making this technology one of the most successful ones. Besides improvements in media and other technologies, the read head has had and still continues to make important contributions to this success. The introduction in 1991 of the AMR read head was the first real application of spintronics in HDD. The discovery of the GMR effect helped to bring the ARD to the Gb/in.^{2} range with no major changes in head design. In 2005 the TMR read head was commercialized as an answer to limitations in the output signal delivered by GMR read heads. Table 6.1 summarizes the history of the

TABLE 6.1. The Areal Density of HDD and the Major Technology Involved for Different Years

Year	Areal Density Mb/in.^{2}	Technology
1957	2×10^{-3}	RAMAC (first HDD) inductive read head
1991	130	First anisotropic magnetoresistive (AMR) read head
1997	2.6×10^3	First giant magnetoresistive (GMR) read head
2001	25×10^3	First antiferromagnetically coupled (AFC) media
2005	130×10^3	First tunnel magnetoresistance (TMR) read head and first perpendicular magnetic recording (PMR) media
2008	375×10^3	Improved TMR head and PMR media

development of HDD. However, intensive development of the CPP-GMR read head is still continuing in hopes that a breakthrough in output signal and MR ratio can be achieved. The major advantage of CPP-giant magnetoresistance compared to tunnel magnetoresistance is its low resistance values and consequently its high frequency operation.

TMR read technology is most likely to still be used in HDD for 1 Tb/in.^{2} or so, but for higher ARD, many issues need to be solved, such as reduction of shield-to-shield spacing, reducing free layer thickness, improving thermal stability, and minimizing spin-torque induced noise. These issues are discussed in detail in Chapter 7.

Development of the perpendicular anisotropy free layer, deposition of very thin tunnel barriers with no pinholes, and other types of crystalline barriers are among the schemes investigated by researchers and engineers in order to expand the capacity of GMR and TMR read heads to reach 10 Tb/in.^{2} In today's read heads, there is only improvement in film growth, represented especially by the MgO barrier, which can allow the reduction of thickness without producing many defects and pinholes.

REFERENCES

1. IHS isuppli Research, February 2011. http://www.isuppli.com.
2. R. Sbiaa and S. N. Piramanayagam, Recent Pat. Nanotechnol. 1, 29–40 (2007).
3. http://www.seagate.com.
4. MN Baibich, JM Broto, A Fert, F Nguyen Van Dau, F Petroff, P Etienne, G Creuzet, A Friederich, and J Chazelas, Phys. Rev. Lett. 61, 2472 (1988).
5. G. Binasch, P. Grunberg, F. Saurenbach, and W. Zinn, Phys. Rev. B 39, 4828 (1989).
6. J. Ariake, N. Honda, K. Ouchi, and S. Iwasaki, IEEE Trans. Magn. 36, 2411 (2000).
7. Y. Honda, A. Kikukawa, Y. Hirayama, and M. Futamoto, IEEE Trans. Magn. 36, 2399 (2000).
8. T. Oikawa, M. Nakamura, H. Uwazumi, T. Shimatsu, H. Muraoka, and Y. Nakamura, IEEE Trans. Magn. 38, 1976 (2002).
9. B. R. Acharya, J. N. Zhou, M. Zheng, G. Choe, E. N. Abarra, and K. E. Johnson, IEEE Trans. Magn. 40, 2383 (2004).
10. S. N. Piramanayagam, J. Appl. Phys. 102, 011301 (2007).

11. M. Mallary, A. Torabi, and M. Benakli, IEEE Trans. Magn. **38**, 1719 (2002).

12. K. Ise, K. Yamakawa, N. Honda, K. Ouchi, H. Muraoka, and Y. Nakamura, IEEE Trans. Magn. **39**, 2374 (2003).

13. F. Mott, Proc. R. Soc. Lond. A **153**, 699 (1936).

14. A. Fert and I. A. Campbell, Phys. Rev. Lett. **21**, 1190 (1968).

15. B. Loegel and F. Gautier, J. Phys. Chem. Solids **32**, 2723 (1971).

16. P. Grünberg, R. Schreiber, Y. Pang, M. B. Brodsky, and H. Sowers, Phys. Rev. Lett. **57**, 2442 (1986).

17. P. Grünberg, S. Demokritov, A. Fuss, M. Vohl, and J. A. Wolf, J. Appl. Phys. **69**, 4789 (1991).

18. S. S. Parkin, R. Bhadra, and K. P. Roche, Phys. Rev. Lett. **66**, 2152 (1991).

19. B. Rodmacq, G. Palumbo, and P. H. Gerard, J. Magn. Magn. Mater. **118**, L11 (1993).

20. S. S. Parkin, R. F. S. Farrow, R. F. Marks, A. Cebollada, G. R. Harp, and R. J. Savoy, Phys. Rev. Lett. **72**, 3718 (1994).

21. K. Shintaku, Y. Daitoh, and T. Shinjo, Phys. Rev. B **47**, 178584 (1993).

22. S. Araki, J. Appl. Phys. **73**, 3910 (1993).

23. T. Takahata, S. Araki, and T. Shinjo, J. Magn. Magn. Mater. **82**, 287 (1989).

24. C. Dupas, P. Beauvillain, C. Chappert, J. P. Renard, F. Triqui, P. Veillet, E. Velu, and D. Renard, Phys. Rev. B **67**, 5680 (1990).

25. P. Seneor, A. Fert, J.-L. Maurice, F. Montaigne, F. Petroff, and A. Vaures, Appl. Phys. Lett. **74**, 4017 (1999).

26. P. A. Dowben and R. Skomski, J. Appl. Phys. **95**, 7453 (2004).

27. Y.-H. A. Wang, A. Gupta, M. Chshiev, and W. H. Butler, Appl. Phys. Lett. **92**, 062507 (2008).

28. W. Wang, H. Sukegawa, R. Shan, and K. Inomata, Appl. Phys. Lett. **93**, 182504 (2008).

29. R. J. Soulen, J. M. Byers, M. S. Osofsky, B. Nadgorny, T. Ambrose, S. F. Chong, P. R. Broussard, C. T. Tanaka, J. S. Moodera, A. Barry, and J. M. D. Coey, Science **282**, 88 (1998).

30. S. S. P. Parkin, N. More, and K. P. Roche, Phys. Rev. Lett. **64**, 2304 (1990).

31. H. Kanai, K. Yamada, K. Aoshima, Y. Ohtsuka, J. Kane, M. Kanamine, J. Toda, and Y. Mizoshita, IEEE Trans. Magn. **32**, 3368 (1996).

32. A. Veloso and P. P. Freitas, J. Appl. Phys. **87**, 5744 (2000).

33. H. Fukuzawa, Y. Kamiguchi, K. Koi, H. Iwasaki, and M. Sahashi, J. Appl. Phys. **91**, 3120 (2002).

34. M. Li, T. C. Horng, and R.-Y. Tong, U.S. Patent 7,323,215 (2008).

35. K. Zhang, M. Li, R. Sbiaa, S. Liao, and Y. Liu, U.S. Patent 7,141,314 (2006).

36. R. Sbiaa and H. Morita, Appl. Phys. Lett. **84**, 5139 (2004).

37. M. Jullière, Phys. Lett. **54A**, 225 (1975).

38. J. S. Moodera, L. R. Kinder, T. M. Wong, and R. Meservey, Phys. Rev. Lett. **74**, 3273 (1995).

39. T. Miyazaki and N. Tezuka, J. Magn. Magn. Mater. **139**, 231 (1995).

40. S. Tehrani, J. M. Slaughter, E. Chen, M. Durlam, J. Shi, and M. De Herrera, IEEE Trans. Magn. **35**, 2814 (1999).

41. W. F. Egelhoff, P. J. Chen, R. D. McMichael, C. J. Powell, R. D. Deslattes, F. G. Serpa, and R. D. Gomez, J. Appl. Phys. **89**, 5209 (2001).

42. Z. Zhang, S. Cardoso, P. P. Freitas, X. Batlle, P. Wei, N. Barradas, and J. C. Soares, J. Appl. Phys. **89**, 6665 (2001).

43. K. Tsunekawa, D. D. Djayaprawira, M. Nagai, H. Maehara, S. Yamagata, N. Watanabe, S. Yuasa, Y. Suzuki, and K. Ando, Appl. Phys. Lett. **87**, 072503 (2005).

44. H. Kikuchi, M. Sato, and K. Kobayashi, J. Appl. Phys. **87**, 6055 (2000).

45. D. Wang, C. Nordman, J. M. Daughton, Z. Qian, and J. Fink, IEEE Trans. Magn. **40**, 2269 (2004).

46. J. Mathon and A. Umerski, Phys. Rev. B **60**, 1117 (1999).

47. P. Mavropoulos, N. Papanikolaou, and P. H. Dederichs, Phys. Rev. Lett. **85**, 1088 (2000).

48. X. G. Zhang and W. H. Butler, Phys. Rev. B **70**, 172407 (2004).

49. S. S. P. Parkin, C. Kaiser, A. Panchula, P. M. Rice, B. Hughes, M. Samant, and S. H. Yang, Nat. Mater. **3**, 862 (2004).

50. S. Yuasa, A. Fukushima, T. Nagahama, K. Ando, and Y. Suzuki, Nat. Mater. **3**, 868 (2004).

51. S. Ikeda, J. Hayakawa, Y. Ashizawa, Y. M. Lee, K. Miura, H. Hasegawa, M. Tsunoda, F. Matsukura, and H. Ohno, Appl. Phys. Lett. **93**, 082508 (2008).

52. B. Dieny, V. S. Speriosu, S. S. P. Parkin, B. A. Gruney, D. R. Wilhoit, and D. Mauri, Phys. Rev. B **43**, 1297 (1991).

53. K. Imakita, M. Tsunoda, and M. Takahashi, J. Appl. Phys. **97**, 10K106 (2005).

54. K. Nishioka, T. Iseki, H. Fujiwara, and M. R. Parker, J. Appl. Phys. **79**, 4970 (1996).

55. R. W. Cross, Y. K. Kim, J. O. Oti, and S. E. Russek, Appl. Phys. Lett. **69**, 3935 (1996).

56. S. L. Burkett, S. Kora, J. L. Bresowar, J. C. Lusth, B. H. Pirkle, and M. R. Parker, J. Appl. Phys. **81**, 4912 (1997).

57. S. Mao, N. Amin, and E. D. Murdock, J. Appl. Phys. **83**, 6807 (1998).

58. R. F. C. Farrow, R. F. Marks, S. Gider, A. C. Marley, and S. S. P. Parkin, J. Appl. Phys. **81**, 4986 (1997).

59. W. F. Egeihoff, T. Ha, R. D. K. Misra, Y. Kadmon, J. Nir, C. J. Powell, M. D. Stiles, and R. D. McMichael, J. Appl. Phys. **78**, 273 (1995).

60. M. Saito, N. Hasegawa, F. Koike, H. Seki, and T. Kuriyama, J. Appl. Phys. **85**, 4928 (1999).

61. H. Fuke, K. Saito, Y. Kamiguchi, H. Iwasaki, and M. Sahashi, J. Appl. Phys. **81**, 4004 (1997).

62. B. Dieny, V. S. Speriosu, S. Metin, S. S. P. Parkin, B. A. Gurney, P. Baumgart, and D. R. Wilhoit, J. Appl. Phys. **69**, 4774 (1991).

63. L. Neel, C. R. Acad. Sci. **255**, 1676 (1962).

64. J. C. S. Kools et al., IEEE Trans. Magn. **31**, 3918 (1995).

65. J. L. Leal and M. H. Kryder, J. Appl. Phys. **79**, 2801 (1996).

66. C.-L. Lee, J. A. Bain, S. Chu, and M. E. McHenry, J. Appl. Phys. **91**, 7113 (2002).

67. S. S. Parking, Phys. Rev. Lett. **67**, 3598 (1991).

68. Y. Jiang, S. Abe, T. Nozaki, N. Tezuka, and K. Inomata, Appl. Phys. Lett. **83**, 2874 (2003).

69. S. Maat, J. Checkelsky, M. J. Carey, J. A. Katine, and J. R. Childress, J. Appl. Phys. **98**, 113907 (2006).

70. K. Yakushiji, K. Saito, S. Mitani, K. Takanashi, Y. K. Takahashi, and K. Hono, Appl. Phys. Lett. **88**, 222504 (2006).

71. Y. Sakuraba, T. Iwase, K. Saito, S. Mitani, and K. Takanashi, Appl. Phys. Lett. **94**, 012511 (2009).

72. H. Fukuzawa, H. Yuasa, S. Hashimoto, K. Koi, H. Iwasaki, M. Takagishi, Y. Tanaka, and M. Sahashi, IEEE Trans. Magn. **40**, 2236 (2004).

73. H. Fukuzawa, H. Yuasa, K. Koi, H. Iwasaki, Y. Tanaka, Y. K. Takahashi, and K. Hono, J. Appl. Phys. **97**, 10C509 (2005).

74. K. Hoshino and H. Hoshiya, J. Appl. Phys. **99**, 08T103 (2006).

75. S. Mao, Y. Chen, F. Liu, X. Chen, B. Xu, P. Lu, M. Patwari, H. Xi, C. Chang, B. Miller, D. Menard, B. Pant, J. Loven, K. Duxstad, S. Li, Z. Zhang, A. Johnston, R. Lamberton, M. Gubbins, T. McLaughlin, J. Gadbois, J. Ding, B. Cross, S. Xue, and P. Ryan, IEEE Trans. Magn. **42**, 97 (2006).

76. J. Gittleman, Y. Goldstein, and S. Bozowski, Phys. Rev. B **5**, 3609 (1972).

77. J. J. Sun, N. Kasahara, K. Sato, K. Shimazawa, S. Araki, and M. Matsuzaki, J. Appl. Phys. **89**, 6653 (2001).

78. J. Wang, P. P. Freitas, E. Snoeck, X. Batlle, and J. Cuadra, IEEE Trans. Magn. **38**, 2703 (2002).

79. J. Wolfman, D. Mauri, T. Lin, J. Yang, and T. Chen, J. Appl. Phys. **97**, 123713 (2005).

80. Y. Nagamine, H. Maehara, K. Tsunekawa, D. D. Djayaprawira, N. Watanabe, S. Yuasa, and K. Ando, Appl. Phys. Lett. **89**, 162507 (2006).

81. S. Isogami, M. Tsunoda, K. Komagaki, K. Sunaga, Y. Uehara, M. Sato, T. Miyajima, and M. Takahashi, Appl. Phys. Lett. **93**, 192109 (2008).

82. J. M. De Teresa, A. Barthélémy, A. Fert, J. P. Contour, F. Montaigne, and A. Vaures, Science **286**, 507 (1999).

83. J. P. Velev et al., Phys. Rev. Lett. **95**, 216601 (2005).

84. M. Bowen et al., Phys. Rev. B **73**, 140408 (2006).

85. J. C. Slonczewski, J. Magn. Magn. Mater. **159**, L1 (1996).

86. L. Berger, Phys. Rev. B **54**, 9353 (1996).

87. M. Tsoi, A. G. M. Jansen, J. Bass, W. C. Chiang, M. Seck, V. Tsoi, and P. Wyder, Phys. Rev. Lett. **80**, 4281 (1998).

88. J. A. Katine, F. J. Albert, R. A. Buhrman, E. B. Myers, and D. C. Ralph, Phys. Rev. Lett. **84**, 3149 (2000).

89. J. Grollier, V. Cros, A. Hamzic, J. M. George, H. Jaffres, A. Fert, G. Faini, J. Ben Youssef, and H. Legall, Appl. Phys. Lett. **78**, 3663 (2001).

90. B. Özyilmaz, A. D. Kent, J. Z. Sun, M. J. Rooks, and R. H. Koch, Phys. Rev. Lett. **93**, 176604 (2004).

91. S. I. Kiselev, J. C. Sankey, I. N. Krivorotov, N. C. Emley, R. J. Schoelkopf, R. A. Buhrman, and D. C. Ralph, Nature **425**, 380 (2003).

92. M. Covington, M. AlHajDarwish, Y. Ding, N. J. Gokemeijer, and M. A. Seigler, Phys. Rev. Lett. B **69**, 184406 (2004).

93. N. Smith, J. Appl. Phys. **99**, 08Q703 (2006).

94. A. V. Nazarov, H. M. Olson, H. Cho, K. Nikolaev, Z. Gao, S. Stokes, and B. B. Pant, Appl. Phys. Lett. **88**, 162504 (2006).

95. R. Sbiaa and S. N. Piramanayagam, J. Appl. Phys. **101**, 073911 (2007).

96. Y. Ding, J. H. Judy, and J. P. Wang, Appl. Phys. **97**, 10N704 (2005).

97. S. van Dijken and J. M. D. Coey, Appl. Phys. Lett. **87**, 022504 (2005).

98. R. Sbiaa, I. Sato, and H. Morita, U.S. Patent 7602591 (2009).

7

READ SENSORS FOR GREATER THAN 1 Tb/in.^{2}

Guchang Han, Viloane Ko, Zaibing Guo, and Hao Meng

Data Storage Institute, Agency for Science,
Technology and Research (A*STAR), Singapore

7.1 CURRENT-IN-PLANE (CIP) GIANT MAGNETORESISTIVE (GMR) READ HEAD

In previous chapters, we have studied GMR effect and its application in magnetic read heads. Here we provide further details into the reader's structure along with the trend in technical evolution. Probably because of the simplicity of GMR characterization, the first-generation GMR head used CIP geometry, where current flows parallel to the plane of the sensor layers. In CIP geometry, the bulk properties of a GMR sensor can be easily measured, and the results can be extrapolated to the sensor level.

A typical CIP reader is illustrated in Figure 7.1. The read head is composed of two magnetic shields, two gap layers, and a multilayered GMR spin-valve sensor structure. The GMR sensor consists of a seed layer, an antiferromagnetic (AFM) pinning layer, a pinned ferromagnetic (FM) layer, a spacer layer (SL) (usually it is Cu whose conducting electron has a long mean free path), a free FM layer, and a cap layer. The magnetization of the pinned FM layer is fixed perpendicular to the easy axis of the free layer (FL), which is along the sensor height direction (normal to the plane of the paper in Fig. 7.1a), by the exchange coupling between the pinned FM and AFM layers. In practical

Developments in Data Storage: Materials Perspective, First Edition.
Edited by S. N. Piramanayagam, Tow C. Chong.
© 2012 Institute of Electrical and Electronics Engineers. Published 2012 by John Wiley & Sons, Inc.

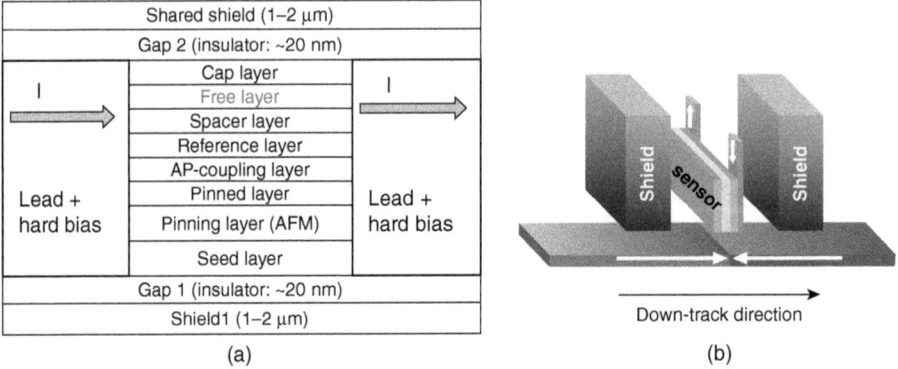

Shared shield (1–2 μm)		
Gap 2 (insulator: ~20 nm)		
	Cap layer	
I	Free layer	I
→	Spacer layer	→
	Reference layer	
	AP-coupling layer	
Lead +	Pinned layer	Lead +
hard bias	Pinning layer (AFM)	hard bias
	Seed layer	
Gap 1 (insulator: ~20 nm)		
Shield1 (1–2 μm)		

(a)   (b)

Figure 7.1. Schematic of a CIP reader structure. (a) Cross-sectional view of multilayer sensor stack. (b) Three-dimensional view of a reader over a magnetic track.

application, a more robust synthetic spin-valve structure in which the pinned layer is antiferromagnetically coupled (AFC) to a reference magnetic layer is used to increase the sensor magnetic stability [1]. The thickness of the pinned layer and reference layer (RL) is designed so that the magnetostatic field of each is canceled at the FL.

The magnetization of the FL can be rotated from a parallel to an antiparallel orientation with respect to the magnetization of an RL when the external field (e.g., from the media) changes from one direction to the opposite direction. The magnetization of the FL is magnetically biased by a hard bias, which is formed by a permanent magnet (PM) at both sides of the sensor so that the magnetic easy axis of the FL is perpendicular to the magnetization of the reference/pinned layers so as to generate a linear response to the field from the media. In addition, the PM is also designed to keep the FL in a single domain state, thus eliminating Barkhausen noise. The cap layer is used to protect the whole film stack from oxidation/corrosion and also serves as a good adhesive layer for resist during read head fabrication. Ta and/or NiFeCr are often used as the seed layer to develop the textured structure of other sensor layers.

The sensor output signal is read by applying a current through a pair of conductive leads overlaid on the PM and partially on the sensor. To prevent shunting by the magnetic shields, a layer of insulator (typically Al_2O_3) has to be inserted into the gaps between the sensor and the shields. As the linear density of a reader is mainly determined by the distance between the two shields, the insertion of these two gap layers largely limits the linear density of the read head. Therefore, the gap layer should be as thin as possible. The thinnest gap layer thickness is determined by the roughness of the shield, the insulating properties of the material, and the robustness to the electrostatic discharge.

Figure 7.1a shows a typical layer structure of a GMR spin-valve read head operating in CIP geometry. The current flows from the left lead (or right), passes through the sensor layers parallel to the layer plane, and goes back through the right lead (or left). In this geometry, the sensor resistance and output signal are proportional to the sensor width between the two current leads. As shown in Figure 7.1b, the sensor width will determine the track width of a reader.

As is apparent from Figure 7.1, in CIP geometry we have

$$R = \rho_{\text{eff}}.(w/ht) \text{ and } \Delta R = \Delta\rho.(w/ht), \tag{7.1}$$

where ρ_{eff} is the effective resistivity; $\Delta\rho$ is the change of resistivity due to the GMR effect; and w, h, and t are the track width, the height, and the thickness of the element respectively. The output voltage of a reader is:

$$V_{\text{out}} = \eta I \Delta R = \eta.J.MR.R_s. w/t, \tag{7.2}$$

where I (J) is the operating current (density); MR (or magnetoresistive) is the GMR ratio of the sensor; η is the head efficiency; and R_s is the sheet resistance.

One can see that the output signal is proportional to the sensor width, which is again determined by the distance between the two leads overlaid on the sensor. As the areal density increases, the sensor track width has to be scaled down accordingly to provide sufficient track resolution as shown in Figure 7.1b. To maintain the signal amplitude in order to achieve the required bit error rate (BER), one has to increase either the operating current or MR ratio. However, the MR ratio is technically limited to about 10% due to the limited electrons traveling through the interfaces between the spacer and electrodes (FL and RL) in CIP geometry. A higher MR ratio of 20% is achieved by using a nano-oxide layer to increase the electron specular scattering [2] and thus increase the electrons passing through the interfaces. On the other hand, high current will cause Joule heating and eventually lead to electromigration. Hence, the minimum track width is determined by the requirement of signal output to achieve the required BER. This limitation in turn sets the highest track density of a read head. Together with the limitation of linear density imposed by the gap length, the areal density of the CIP read head is limited to about 100 Gb/in.[2]

7.2 CPP-GMR READ HEAD

For an areal density beyond 100 Gb/in.[2], implementation of a current-perpendicular-to-plane (CPP) geometry was proposed. Figure 7.2 shows a typical structure for a CPP-GMR spin-valve head.

Figure 7.2 shows a typical layer structure for a GMR spin-valve read head operating in CPP geometry. The current flows from the top (or bottom) shield, passes through the sensor stack perpendicular to the layer plane, and goes back through the bottom (or top) shield.

As it is apparent from Figure 7.2, the output amplitude in the CPP geometry can be written as

$$R = \rho_{\text{eff}}.(t/hw),$$
$$\Delta R = \Delta\rho.(t/hw), \tag{7.3}$$
$$V_{\text{out}} = \eta I.\Delta R = \eta I.MR.RA/A = \eta J.MR.RA = \eta J.\Delta R.A = \eta J.\Delta\rho.t,$$

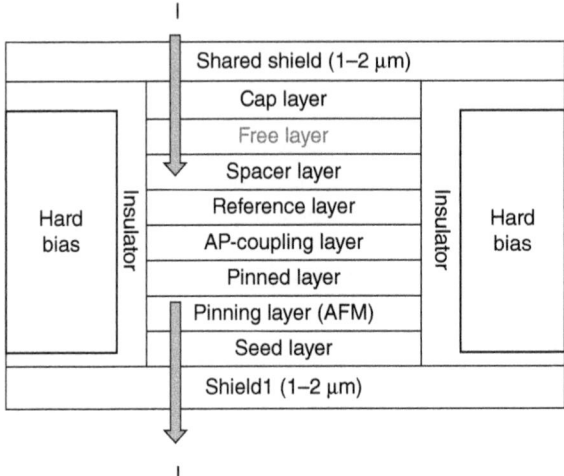

Figure 7.2. Schematic of a CPP reader structure.

where R and A are the resistance and the cross-sectional area of the sensor, respectively. Again, one sees that the output signal is proportional to the operating current density, which is in turn determined by the material properties of the sensor. It is interesting to note that the signal is not only proportional to the MR, but also to RA. To increase the signal, there is a need to increase the GMR ratio by increasing spin-dependent scattering, or the total resistance or both. Actually, the GMR ratio is directly linked to the total resistance through GMR = $\Delta R/R$; as a result, the signal is eventually determined by ΔRA. Therefore, if the current density is kept constant, the ΔR should be increased to compensate for the loss of cross-sectional area to accommodate the higher areal density.

In contrast to the CIP mode, the CPP-GMR read head has two gaps at both sides of the sensor stack to prevent shunting by the hard bias. The shield can be directly used as an electrode for the operating current. The current flows from the top (or bottom) shield, passes through the sensor stack perpendicular to the layer plane, and goes back through the bottom (or top) shield. The sensor stack is essentially the same as in the CIP mode. CPP read head geometry has numerous advantages that a sensor using CIP-GMR read does not have: The first advantage of CPP mode is that the read gap is no longer necessary. The shield-to-shield distance is now only determined by the sensor thickness. As a result, the linear density can be greatly increased. Second, the intrinsic GMR ratio of a CPP-GMR sensor for the active layers defined by RL, SL, and FL is much larger than that of a CIP-GMR sensor, because in CPP geometry, all polarized electrons contribute to the spin-dependent transport through the sensor layers and interfaces. The third advantage is that the downsizing of the CPP-GMR sensor will not reduce the output signal. This is because in CPP geometry, the sensor resistance change is inversely proportional to the sensor width and stripe height. As can be seen from

Equation 7.3, V_{out} will be independent of the sensor longitudinal dimensions. Therefore, CPP-GMR sensors have the potential for application in extremely high-density recording. Finally, the cross-sectional area in CPP geometry is determined by the stripe height and the physical track width of the sensor (sensor width), which is much larger than that in CIP geometry, where the cross section is determined by the stripe height and the thickness of the sensor. As a result, CPP-GMR geometry supports a much larger current without inducing heat or electromigration problems.

It is worthwhile to point out that although both CIP and CPP modes have a similar structure, the influence of each layer to the sensor performance is quite different. In the CIP mode, all inactive layers such as the AFM and cap layers act as a current-shunting path for the active layers. The total resistance and thus GMR ratio decrease as the resistance of the inactive layers decreases. As a result, materials with high resistivity are desired for these inactive layers. On the other hand, each layer in CPP mode is connected in series for current transportation. The resistance of each layer contributes to the total resistance directly. The GMR ratio decreases with the increase of the resistance of each layer. Therefore, it is desirable to select materials for the inactive layers with low resistivity.

A CPP-GMR sensor using a conventional spin-valve structure as shown in Figure 7.2 suffers from its inadequate output to meet the BER requirement. To understand this low output, we give a simple calculation. Suppose that the sensor is composed of only active layers, and the thickness of the RL, SL, and FL is 3 nm, 2 nm, and 3 nm, respectively. Using an average resistivity of 30 $\mu\Omega$cm, the resistance for a sensor of 100×100 nm is only 240 mΩ. Even for a GMR ratio of 30% ($\Delta RA = 0.72$ m$\Omega\mu$m^2), an operating current of 1×10^8 A/cm^2, and 100% efficiency, the output signal is only 0.72 mV. From this simple calculation, one can see that the issue for a CPP-GMR spin valve is that its resistance is too low. Even if a high GMR ratio (30%) could be obtained, the output signal is still too low. To understand what voltage amplitude is required, let us look at the signal-to-noise ratio (SNR) of a reader. Being a resistance device, the read head signal consists of at least Johnson noise, which can be written as $(4k_B T.R.\Delta f)^{1/2}$, where T is the temperature, R is the resistance of a device, and Δf is the bandwidth. For a reader typically having 50 Ω and operating at a bandwidth of 1 GHz, the Johnson noise is 14.5 μV. Even exclusive of other noise sources such as shot noise, the SNR is only about 36 dB for an output of 1 mV.

Suppose now the sensor size is reduced to 50×50 nm, the total resistance of the active layers is increased to 960 mΩ. However, if we keep the GMR ratio of 30%, then ΔRA will be the same as above (i.e., 0.72 m$\Omega\mu$m^2). For the same current density, the output will be kept to 0.72 mV. From the above calculation, we can see that in CPP sensors, a high ΔRA is the most important factor in increasing the signal output. It should be pointed out that a CPP-GMR sensor is generally composed of several other inactive layers, as shown in Figure 7.2. The total resistance is much larger than that calculated above. As the resistance change is only determined by the active layers, the presence of the inactive layers reduces the GMR ratio significantly. That is why the reported GMR ratio of a CPP spin valve is generally much smaller than the expected value. In contrast to CIP geometry, where the inactive layers shunt the signal of the sensor, and thus high resistivity is favored for inactive layers, in CPP mode, low resistivity of the inactive layers is desired for a high GMR ratio. On the other hand, high resistivity is desired for the active layer so that the sensor resistance can be high and thus increase ΔR.

7.3 CPP-TMR READ HEAD

A tunnel magnetoresistive (TMR) sensor is another type of CPP sensor. The difference between a CPP-TMR sensor and a CPP GMR sensor is that the SL in a TMR sensor is an insulator instead of metal, as it is in a GMR sensor. For read head application, the SL is usually very thin (<1 nm) to provide a low tunnel resistance. In spite of the structural similarity, the transport mechanisms in GMR sensors and TMR sensors are very different. In a GMR head, the GMR effect is from the spin-dependent scattering (for a review, see Bass and Pratt [3]), but in a TMR sensor, the electrons are transported by tunneling across the tunnel barrier (SL). As a result, the resistance of a TMR sensor is mainly determined by the SL. Following the first demonstration of the TMR head in magnetic recording [4], TMR became widely used in read heads because it provides a large signal output, particularly TMR sensors using MgO as the barrier layer which offers a TMR ratio in excess of 100%. With a resistance-area (RA) product of 2 $\Omega\mu m^2$, this gives an ΔRA of about 2 $\Omega\mu m^2$, which is three orders of magnitude larger than than the figure generated in sensors using CPP-GMR technology. However, this type of sensor also suffers from high impedance due to the usage of an "insulating" SL. Typically, for RA = 2 $\Omega\mu m^2$, the resistance of the sensor with dimensions of 50 × 50 nm will be 800 Ω, much larger than the usual value of 50 Ω. High impedance will limit the bandwidth of the read channel.

The impedance of a TMR sensor is reduced usually by reducing the thickness of the spacer (barrier) layer, which brings along great technical challenges as the thickness of the barrier layer has been reduced to below 1 nm to achieve an RA of several $\Omega\mu m^2$. The higher resistance in TMR sensors does not only induce large noise, but also causes a high resistance-capacitance (RC) time constant, reducing the data rate. For an areal density of 1 Tb/in.^{2}, if the bit aspect ratio (BAR) is 3.5, then the linear and track density will be 1872 kbpi (kilobits per inch) and 535 ktpi (kilotracks per inch), respectively. To achieve such a high linear density, the average data rate will be 1.28 GB/s, that is, a bandwidth of 0.64 GHz, for a 2.5-inch disk rotating at 7500 rpm. Although the required bandwidth can be reduced either by reducing the spindle speed or by using a small form factor disk, this is generally undesirable because the data rate would be also reduced accordingly. If we assume that the head has a parasitic capacitance (C) of 1pF, the head resistance should be less than 249 Ω [R < 1/(2πfC)] to keep the required data rate. On the other hand, as the required track pitch for 1 Tb/in.^{2} is about 48 nm, the physical track width of the sensor should be less than 0.7 × track pitch = 34 nm. Assuming a similar stripe height of 34 nm, if the RA of the TMR sensor is 1 $\Omega\mu m^2$, the total resistance of the sensor will be 865 Ω, much larger than the required 249 Ω. According to the above simplified calculations, one can see that the resistance of the TMR sensor would be too high to provide a sufficient data rate. Two methods have been proposed to reduce the impedance of TMR sensors in terms of the head structure.

One is to connect a shunting resistance to the read head circuit so as to reduce the resistance of the head [5]. This approach can easily reduce the head overall resistance but would sacrifice signal output due to the shunting effect of the shunting resistor.

To reduce the resistance without decreasing too much of the signal or increasing the SNR, a large stripe height (LH) sensor structure has been proposed [6]. For a fixed RA value, the resistance of a TMR head can be reduced to meet the requirements for operation of TMR heads by increasing the sensor stripe height. As a result, in LH sensor design, the sensor stripe height is generally much larger than the read track width. An apparent advantage of the LH sensor is that it will loosen the stringent requirement of the lapping process control to define the sensor height. As the LH sensor has a larger volume of the FL, one would also expect a lower thermal magnetization fluctuation noise (mag-noise) [7]. However, an LH sensor will also have a sensor bias problem as the shape anisotropy will favor the magnetization along the stripe height instead of the stripe width. Readers are referrred to Reference 6 of this chapter for further details.

7.4 CONFINED CURRENT PATH (CCP)-CPP GMR READ HEAD

From the above discussion, we see that CPP-GMR sensors using all-metal design suffer from low resistance and ΔRA, while CPP-TMR sensors have too high a resistance to meet the high data rate requirement. To overcome this problem, Fujiwara et al. [8] proposed a CCP-CPP spin-valve structure. In this type of the sensor, the SL is neither an insulator nor a metal, but a combined layer that consists of insulator and metal alternately. The current is thus confined to flow through the metal paths. Figure 7.3 shows a typical CCP-CPP structure, where the CCP layer is inserted into the SL. In this structure, the current density is much larger at the interfaces between the SLs and RLs/FLs than that flowing through the other inactive parts of the sensor, thus increasing ΔRA.

To evaluate the CCP effect, let us consider a simple two-current model and define the resistances for "parallel" and "antiparallel" channels as R_1 and R_2, respectively. For a CPP device, referring to Figure 7.4, we have:

$$
\begin{aligned}
R_P &= [(1/2R_1)+(1/2R_2)]^{-1} \\
R_{AP} &= (R_1 + R_2)/2 \\
\Delta R &= R_{AP} - R_P = (\alpha-1)^2 R_1/(2(\alpha+1)),
\end{aligned}
\tag{7.4}
$$

where R_P and R_{AP} are the resistances for the parallel and antiparallel magnetization arrangement of the FLs/RLs, respectively; $\alpha \equiv R_2/R_1$ is the scattering asymmetry parameter.

For CCP-CPP device, defining that $\beta = A_c/A$, where A_c is the area of the conducting parts of CCP layer, and A is the total area of the CCP layer, we have

$$
\Delta R = R_{AP} - R_P = (\alpha-1)^2 R_1/[(\alpha+1).(1+\beta)].
\tag{7.5}
$$

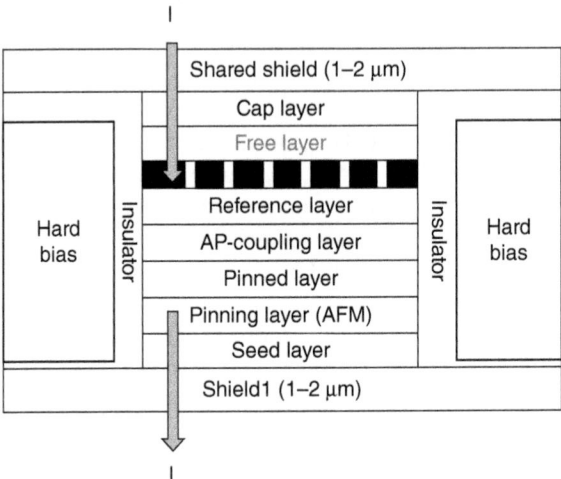

Figure 7.3. A typical current confined path CPP spin-valve structure.

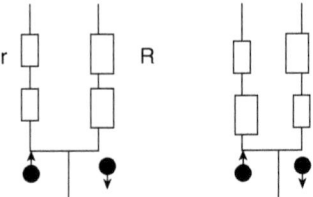

Figure 7.4. Two-current model to illustrate the resistance change for different magnetic configurations.

Comparing Equation 7.5 with Equation 7.4, one can easily find that as β decreases from 1 (in the CPP case), the ΔR increases monotonically. That implies that one would be able to increase ΔR by increasing the area of the nonconductive part of the CCP layer. The maximum variation is a factor of 2 from $\beta = 0$ (in MTJ case) to $\beta = 1$ (in the pure CPP case). It should be mentioned that in the above simple estimation, we ignored the TMR effect through the insulating part of the CCP layer. Therefore, Equation 7.5 is invalid for ΔR calculation at $\beta = 0$. It should be noted that as β decreases, the total resistance of the CCP-CPP device also increases, which will eventually limit the application of CCP-CPP design in read heads.

The application of CCP-CPP GMR structure in the read head has been much debated. One of the serious problems is the uniformity of the current confined path. As the sensor dimension decreases, the number and the size of the conductive parts will vary from device to device, causing a production yield problem. Another issue is its low GMR ratio, which is typically less than 10%.

Recently, lot of progress has been made in CCP-CPP structures. A GMR ratio as high as 18% was achieved with RA~0.2 $\Omega\mu m^2$ (ΔRA~36 m$\Omega\mu m^2$) in a CCP-CPP structure through careful control of the area of the nanoholes [9]. More recently, a similarly larger ΔRA of 30 m$\Omega\mu m^2$ with a GMR ratio of up to 20% has been reported by Peng et al. [10]. Such a low RA value makes CCP-CPP GMR technology very promising for application beyond 1 Tb/in.^{2}. However, some challenges remain to be solved before realizing the application of CCP-CPP GMR design. The most important challenge is that the sensor should be able to provide sufficient signal output for high SNR to ensure the required BER with small sensor size. As the sensor size decreases, noise will become a major issue. As pointed out by Smith et al. [7], the amplitude of magnetic noise arising from thermally activated magnetization fluctuations is inversely proportional to the sensor volume. At the same time, as the current density is increased to increase the signal amplitude, the large spin-torque effect may either induce magnetization switching or increase spin transfer noise. A more detailed discussion of this issue will be given in the last section of this chapter.

7.5 DIFFERENTIAL DUAL SPIN-VALVE (DDSV) HEAD

As shown in Figure 7.2, a typical CPP sensor is composed of a seed layer, an AFM pinning layer, a pinned layer (PL), an AP-coupling layer (AL), an RL, an SL, an FL, and a capping layer (CL). The thickness of these layers ranges from 0.8 nm for the AL to 10 nm for the AFM pinning layer. As the total thickness of the sensor poses a minimum limitation of the shield-to-shield distance, which in turn limits the linear density (bit length) of the recording head, the thickness of each layer has to be reduced to increase linear density. The thickest layer in a reader is the AFM pinning layer. For PtMn and IrMn, the critical thickness above which a sufficiently strong pinning field can be achieved is about 14 nm and 8 nm, respectively. To reduce the sensor thickness, an AFM-free sensor structure has been proposed [11], where the AFM pinning layer is removed. To make the sensor magnetically stable, a so-called hard/soft structure is employed [11]. However, even using this AFM-free structure, the total thickness may exceed 15 nm (e.g., for a typical structure of SL(3)/PL(2.5)/AL(0.8)/RL(2.5)/SL(2.5)/FL(2.5)/CL(2), where the numbers in brackets represent the thickness of each layer in nm, the total thickness is 15.8 nm). This will limit the bit length to around 7–8 nm, corresponding to a linear density of 3359–3840 kbpi. To further increase the linear density, a differential dual spin-valve head structure has been proposed [12]. As shown in Figure 7.5, the sensor consists of two spin valves with their magnetization of RL biased in opposite directions. Two spin valves are conductively connected in series through a gap layer. The gap layer magnetically separates two FLs so that both spin valves operate independently. Since their RLs are biased oppositely, for the field from the media for which the magnetic fields from the adjacent bits are always in opposite directions, the total signal output will be the sum of the output from the two spin valves. For the field from other sources, there will be no output due to the compensating effect. Therefore, in this structure no shield layers are required. The linear density or linear resolution is determined by the thickness of the gap layer (GL) and FL only, thus

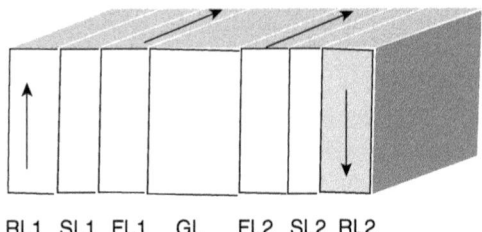

RL1 SL1 FL1   GL   FL2 SL2 RL2

Figure 7.5. Schematic diagram of a differential dual spin-valve structure. CL, AL, PL, and AFM for both spin valves are not shown for simplicity.

increasing the linear density significantly. However, as the DDSV does not respond to a uniform field, the reading performances can be evaluated only at the system level, which will risk raising the fabrication cost. In addition, although a DDSV can provide twice the signal amplitude that a single spin valve does, the signal amplitude may still be too low. Researchers are now working on spin valves with high GMR ratios, using high polarization materials.

7.6 NOISE ISSUES

Noise exists universally in any MR device with a definite length. Some of them are magnetic in nature, and some are purely electrical. According to their origins, the noise can be classified as thermal resistance noise (Johnson noise), shot noise, random telegraph noise, 1/f noise, mag-noise, and spin-torque noise. Johnson noise exists in all dissipative devices and is basically independent of frequency. This noise originates from the thermal fluctuations in electron density within a resistor itself. Johnson noise can be expressed as

$$V_{nJ}(rms) = \sqrt{4kTR\Delta f},$$

where k is Boltzmann's constant, R is total device resistance in ohms, T is the absolute temperature in Kelvin, and Δf is the bandwidth in Hz. Shot noise exists generally in a TMR device in which only a finite number of electrons can tunnel through the barrier. The shot noise can be expressed as

$$V_{sn}(rms) = R\sqrt{2qI\Delta f}, \tag{7.6}$$

where q is electron charge, I is electrical current, R the resistance, and Δf is the bandwidth. The shot noise is also independent of frequency.

Flicker Noise, also known as 1/f noise, usually dominates in low frequency ranges. The power spectral density of this noise follows the well-known Hooge relation:

$$S_{1/f} = \frac{\alpha_H V^2}{N f^\gamma}, \tag{7.7}$$

where, α_H is the Hooge constant, N is the number of charge carriers, f is frequency, and γ is usually close to 1. If charge carrier density is assumed constant, then N can be replaced by sample volume, V. So 1/f noise is inversely proportional to sensor size. The root sources of 1/f noise are generally explained using the two-level fluctuation model conceived by Dutta and Horn [13]. As this noise is only important at low frequencies (<50 kHz) and can be neglected in magnetic recording [14], we will not discuss this noise further.

7.7 THERMAL MAGNETIZATION FLUCTUATION NOISE (MAG-NOISE)

It is well known that the frequency of the thermally activated magnetization fluctuation is $f = f_0 \exp(-\Delta E / k_B T)$, where f_0 is the attempt frequency (~10^9 Hz), $\Delta E = K_u V$ is the energy barrier for the magnetization fluctuation, K_u is the anisotropy constant, and V is the volume of the FL.

As the size of devices shrinks with the increase in storage density, the energy barrier for the magnetization fluctuations decreases significantly. Because the magnetization of the FL is designed to be sufficiently sensitive to the external field to provide the desired SNR, the K_u cannot be too large. Therefore, the value of $\Delta E = K_u V$ will eventually meet the superparamagnetic limitation as the sensor size decreases. As the output signal of the sensor is proportional to the magnetization angle of the FL, the magnetization fluctuation of the FL will induce a noise with an amplitude proportional to the signal as both the noise and signal are proportional to the magnetization angle of the FL. There will be no mag-noise without signal at zero bias. If the total noise of a reader is dominated by the mag-noise, the conventional technique to increase the signal output and thus the SNR by enhancing the GMR ratio will fail to work. Therefore, efforts should be made to reduce mag-noise.

The amplitude of mag-noise can be expressed as

$$V_{mag} = I \frac{\Delta R \cos \phi}{H_{stiff}} \sqrt{\frac{\alpha k_B T}{\mu_0 M_s V \gamma}}, \tag{7.8}$$

where γ is the gyromagnetic constant ($\gamma = 2.21 \times 10^5$ m/As), α the damping parameter, M_s and V are the saturation magnetization and the volume of the FL, ϕ is the angle of the FL magnetization deviated from its easy axis, μ_0 is the vacuum permeability, I is the bias current, ΔR is the saturation-to-saturation sensor resistance change, and H_{stiff} is effective stiffness field acting on the magnetization of the FL.

Equation 7.8 illustrates that the magnitude of magnetic noise is inversely proportional to the volume of the head. Hence, mag-noise becomes more and more prominent as devices shrink. To reduce the mag-noise, an effective way is to increase the effective stiffness field H_{stiff}, which is determined by the hard bias and the anisotropy of the FL magnetization, in particular, the shape anisotropy. The increase of H_{stiff} will decrease the sensitivity of the read head. However, it does not necessarily imply a decrease in signal output. The reason is that the field from the hard bias increases as the sensor width decreases, and thus H_{stiff} increases. In the mean time, the sensor height needs to be scaled down to keep proper shape anisotropy. The smaller sensor height increases the sensor efficiency and thus the signal amplitude. As it can be clearly seen, another way to reduce the mag-noise might be to use an FM material with a low damping constant and a high magnetization M_s. However, a low damping constant may induce another type of magnetic instability noise, which is the spin-transfer-torque-induced noise.

7.8 SPIN-TORQUE NOISE

As shown in Equation 7.3, in CPP readers, a large transport current density is required to provide a sufficient output signal. However, when a large current flows through the CPP structure as shown in Figure 7.2, the interaction of the electron spin with the FL and RL magnetization can result in spin-torque-induced instability. To understand this effect, let us simply look at the CPP structure shown in Figure 7.6a. Suppose that the FL magnetization is driven at an angle from the RL magnetization by an external field, and a current is flowing from the FL to RL (electrons flow from RL to FL). After passing through the FL, the electron spin is aligned to be collinear with the FL magnetization. In other words, the electron spin is polarized after passing through the RL. As these polarized electrons pass through the FL, the electron spin now aligns collinearly with the FL magnetization, which means that the spin direction changes after passing through FL.

As a result, there is a spin momentum change when the electrons pass through the FL. Since the total momentum of the system is conserved, the change in electron spin momentum must be compensated by an equal but opposite spin-torque transfer to the FL magnetization. It is this torque that results in a variety of magnetization dynamics in the FL layer. Depending on the strength of the spin torque and relative magnetization orientation of the FL and RL, the magnetization dynamics can either generate a so-called spin-torque noise due to the spin wave excitations and chaotic magnetization or irreversible magnetization reversals [15, 16]. Therefore, in the field of developing CPP readers, there is an intensive interest in enhancing the critical current (J_c) above which the spin-torque-induced instabilities occur so that the device can be operated below J_c without the spin-torque issues.

It is not difficult to understand that the critical current for switching from the parallel-to-antiparallel configuration, J_c (P-AP), is larger than that for switching from the antiparallel-to-parallel configurations, J_c (AP-P), due to the difference of the spin-polarized electrons acting on the FL. When the magnetizations of the FL and the RL are parallel, and if the electrons flow from the RL to the FL, the spin torque acting on the FL tends to enhance the magnetization stability because the spin-polarized electrons have the same spin direction as in the FL. The magnetization instability of the FL will be induced when the electrons flow from the FL to the RL. As shown in Figure 7.6b,

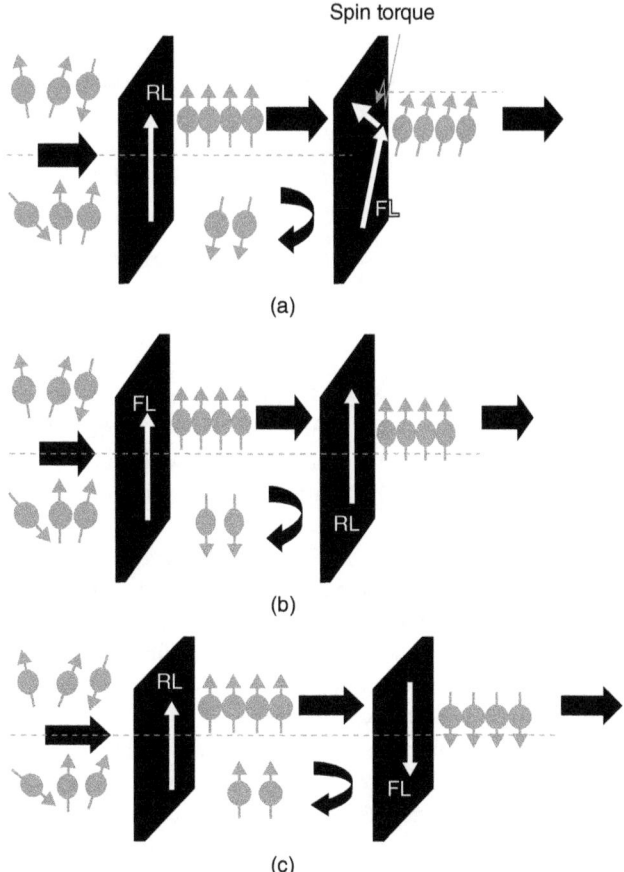

(a)

(b)

(c)

Figure 7.6. (a) Spin-torque transfer at any magnetization configuration; (b) the magnetization instability of the FL induced by spin-torque transfer at parallel magnetization configuration; (c) the magnetization instability of the FL induced by spin-torque transfer at antiparallel magnetization configuration.

in this case, the spin-up electrons from the FL will pass through the RL without any effect on the FL. However, the spin-down electrons from the FL will be reflected by the RL, as their spin directions are opposite to the magnetization of the RL. Therefore, there is a spin torque acting on the FL when the reflected spin-down electrons pass through the FL. This spin torque tends to switch the FL magnetization from upward to downward. However, as the spin-down electrons are much fewer than the spin-up electrons, more current is required to transfer sufficient spin torque to the FL for its switching.

On the other hand, for switching from AP to P, as shown in Figure 7.6c, the spin torque is from the spin-up electrons polarized by the RL magnetization. The spin-torque effect is stronger, and thus J_c (AP-P) is smaller. The critical currents for reversal can be estimated from a stability analysis of the Landau–Lifshitz–Gilbert (LLG) equations of motion, including the Slonczewski form of the spin transfer torque [15]. They are [17]

$$J_c(P-AP) = \frac{A\alpha M_S V}{g(0)P}(H + H_{dip} + H_k + 2\pi M_S), \text{ and} \tag{7.9}$$

$$J_c(AP-P) = \frac{A\alpha M_S V}{g(\pi)P}(H + H_{dip} - H_k - 2\pi M_S), \tag{7.10}$$

where P is the spin polarization of the current. The factor g depends on the relative angle of the RL and FL magnetizations. The factor A is dependent on the specifics of the transport model but is of the order of 3×10^{11} mA Oe^{-1} emu^{-1}. H, H_{dip}, and H_K are the in-plane applied field, the dipole field from the RL acting on the FL, and the uniaxial in-plane anisotropy field, respectively. The factor $2\pi M_S$ arises from the demagnetizing field of the thin-film geometry.

To reduce the spin-torque effect, a high critical current is desired. However, as shown in Equations 7.9 and 7.10, as the sensor size scales down with the need to increase the storage density, J_c will decrease proportionally. Several ways have been proposed to suppress the spin-torque-induced noise. The first is to use a dual spin-valve structure with a symmetric arrangement of two FLs as first proposed by Zhu et al. [18] and later confirmed experimentally by Childress et al. [19]. The dual spin-valve structure allows the cancellation of the spin torque from two RLs acting on the FL. However, this structure is not suitable for extremely high-density recording due to its thicker sensor stacks and the resultant increase in shield-to-shield spacing. Another way is to use AFC FLs [20]. In an AFC FL structure, the total volume of the FL is increased without increasing the switching field, thus increasing magnetic stability. The disadvantage is that the total thickness of the AFC FL increases and thus reduces the linear resolution. Finally, it is helpful to use high damping materials to reduce the spin-torque effect and thus reduce the spin-torque noise. However, as discussed in the previous section, the high damping constant results in high mag-noise.

In TMR readers, since bias current density is relatively low, the noise from the spin transfer torque might not be as significant as in a CPP-GMR reader. However, it would be a big issue in CCP-CPP GMR readers, where the current density is extremely high through the confined paths.

7.9 SYSTEM NOISE

In a recording channel, noise arises from various sources. It can arise from the media, the head, the preamp, and so on. In today's hard disk drives, media noise is dominant. However, head noise becomes more and more significant as the dimensions of recording heads are reduced to push for higher recording areal density. Therefore, minimizing head noise has been an important area of research in the past few years.

7.10   FUTURE READ HEAD TECHNOLOGIES

To push the recording density toward 10 Tb/in.^{2} or beyond, several storage technologies are currently being explored [21, 22]. For example, energy-assisted recording enables the use of media with a high anisotropy constant (K_u) to achieve high thermal stability. At the same time, bit-patterned media increases magnetization stability by using a single larger magnetic feature to store a bit, and reduces the noise by isolating each bit physically. However, it is not necessary to change the basic structure and functionality of the read head, irrespective of the technology used. This is because the read sensor reads the data by detecting the vertical component of the magnetic field from the media. The central problem lies in the continued decrease in the dimensions of the read sensors to accommodate increasing storage density. Typically, for an areal density of 10 Tb/in.^{2}, the sensor size will be about 10 nm. Even for a CCP-CPP sensor with an RA of 0.2 $\Omega\mu m^2$, the read resistance will be about 2000 Ω, limiting the band width below 159 MHz (assuming C = 0.5 pf). To overcome this problem, a CPP-GMR design using all metallic layers has to be used. However, as discussed above, the current CPP-GMR sensors suffer from a low ΔRA. To provide sufficient output, new materials with high polarization should be used in the sensor. Full Heusler alloys are one of the best candidates toward this end.

Figure 7.7a,b shows a typical Co_2MnSi Heusler $L2_1$ ordered structure (X_2YZ) and density of states (DOS), respectively. In this $L2_1$ ordered structure, there are four interpenetrating face-centered cubic (fcc) structures with atoms at $Co_1(0,0,0)$, $Co_2(1/2,1/2,1/2)$, $Mn(1/4,1/4,1/4)$, and $Si(3/4,3/4,3/4)$. From Figure 7.7b, one can clearly see that there is a band gap for minority-band and finite density for majority-band electrons at the Fermi surface. As a result, all conducting electrons are from the majority band, resulting in half metallicity—that is, a 100% polarization. As the GMR ratio is proportional to the polarization of the two FM electrodes, half metals are a very promising means

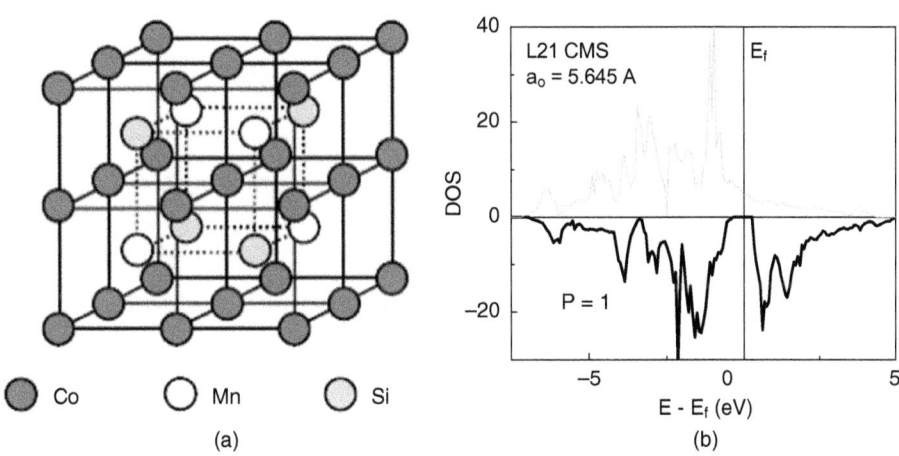

Co   Mn   Si

(a)   (b)

Figure 7.7. A typical Heusler $L2_1$ structure (a) and the corresponding band structure (b), showing half metallicity.

to provide the large signal output required for extremely high-density recording. Recently, a GMR ratio of 28.8% was reported for FM Heusler alloys used with Ag as the SL [23].

Other than the conventional MR technologies (including TMR, CPP, CIP, and CCP-CPP), new read technologies are continuing to be explored. One of the candidates is multiferroic (MF) materials to read the magnetic field [24]. The technology is based on the magneto-electric (ME) effect, which is the generation of an electric field in the presence of a magnetic field. As a result, the data are read back directly as an induced voltage; no direct current (DC) is required to detect the signal, which thus removes the thermal issues and power consumption by the bias current. However, since the ME reader operates via a stress-mediated ME effect, this type of sensor is very sensitive to mechanical head/medium contact, which may suppress its application in 10-Tb/in.² recording due to the requirements of head/media contact. In addition, significant challenges remain to achieve sufficient ME effect in proper thin-film-based MF structures.

Another candidate may be from spintronics devices such as the spin-valve transitor and magnetic tunnel transistor. However, these spintronics devices offer a total resistance similar to that produced in TMR sensors, thus losing their advantages. Finally, ballistic magnetoresistance (BMR) may be a promising avenue for read sensor application. An extremely large (above 100,000%) MR effect was achieved in stable Ni nanocontacts at room temperature [25]. However, these types of devices suffer from reliability and uniformity issues. So far, there remains much debate on the MR effect. It is argued that the observed magnetoresistance may not be from a BMR but a mechanical effect. (For a detailed review, see Reference 26).

REFERENCES

1. J. G. Zhu, IEEE Trans. Magn. **35**(2), 655 (1999).

2. H. Fukuzawa et al., J. Magn. Magn. Mater. **235**, 208 (2001).

3. J. Bass and W. P. Pratt Jr., J. Magn. Magn. Mater. **200**, 274 (1999).

4. S. N. Mao et al., IEEE Trans. Magn. **42**, 97 (2006).

5. J. G. Zhu, INSIC Meeting, March 2006.

6. Y. K. Zheng, G. C. Han, and B. Liu, J. Magn. Magn. Mater. **320**, 2850 (2008).

7. N. Smith and P. Arnett, Appl. Phys. Lett. **78**, 1448 (2001).

8. H. Fujiwara, T. Zhao, G. J. Mankey, K. Zhang, W. H. Butler, and S. Matsunuma, Trans. Magn. Soc. Jpn. **3**, 95 (2003).

9. H. Katada et al., J. Magn. Magn. Mater. **320**, 2975 (2008).

10. X. L. Peng et al., J. Magn. Magn. Mater. **321**, 1889 (2009).

11. Y. H. Wu et al., Appl. Phys. Lett. **80**, 4413 (2002).

12. I. G. Trindade, U.S. Patent US6643103B1 (November 4, 2003), and S. N. Mao et al., U.S. Patent US7016160B2 (March 21, 2006).

13. P. Dutta and P. M. Horn, Low-frequency fluctuations in solids: 1/f noise, Rev. Mod. Phys. **53**(3), 497 (1981).

14. S. Wang and A. M. Taratorin, *Magnetic Information Storage Technology*, Academic Press, 1999.

15. J. C. Slonczewski, J. Magn. Magn. Mater. **159**, L1–L7 (1996).

16. L. Berger, Phys. Rev. B **54**, 9353–9358 (1996).

17. S. Mangin et al., Nat. Mater. **5**, 210 (2006).

18. J. G. Zhu et al., IEEE Trans. Magn. **40**, 2323 (2004).

19. J. R. Childress et al., IEEE Trans. Magn. **42**, 2444 (2006).

20. M. J. Carey et al., Appl. Phys. Lett. **93**, 102509 (2008).

21. J. J. M. Ruigrok et al., J. Appl. Phys. **87**, 5398 (2000).

22. D. Weller et al., IEEE Trans. Magn. **35**, 4423 (1999).

23. T. Iwase et al., Appl. Phys. Express **2**, 063003 (2009).

24. M. Vopsaroiu et al., J. Phys. D-Appl. Phys. **40**, 5027 (2007), and J. Appl. Phys. **103**, 07F506 (2008).

25. S. Z. Hua et al., Phys. Rev. B **67**, 060401 (2003).

26. B. Doudin and M. Viret, J. Phys. Condens. Matter **20**, 083201 (2008).

8

THIN-FILM MEDIA LUBRICANTS: STRUCTURE, CHARACTERIZATION, AND PERFORMANCE

Bruno Marchon

Hitachi GST, San Jose Research Center, San Jose, CA

8.1 INTRODUCTION

Tribology encompasses the physics and chemistry of two contacting surfaces in relative motion, and it is often described as the science of friction, wear, and lubrication. In a disk drive, the read and write elements are embedded at the tip of a ~millimeter-size slider that is shaped such as it self-generates an air bearing and flies at a given height over the disk while spinning (Fig. 8.1). During power-off, the air bearing is lost, and the slider automatically moves to the outside of the disk and comes to a rest on a dedicated ramp. Upon power-up, the slider is loaded back onto the disk. An alternative to this load–unload (L/UL) technology involves a dedicated zone at the inner diameter of the disk where the slider gently lands on power-off. A well-controlled topography made of 10- to 30-nm-high bumps is usually introduced on this landing zone in order to prevent stiction. The major challenge for the head/disk tribologist is to enable a head-to-disk spacing (also called magnetic spacing) that is commensurate with the size of the bit while at the same time improving reliability. In a typical head–disk system, magnetic spacing consists of disk variables (topography, overcoat, and lubricant thickness), flying height, and slider variables (topography and overcoat thickness) (see Fig. 8.1). Historically, this magnetic spacing has been set by design to about half the bit

Developments in Data Storage: Materials Perspective, First Edition.
Edited by S. N. Piramanayagam, Tow C. Chong.
© 2012 Institute of Electrical and Electronics Engineers. Published 2012 by John Wiley & Sons, Inc.

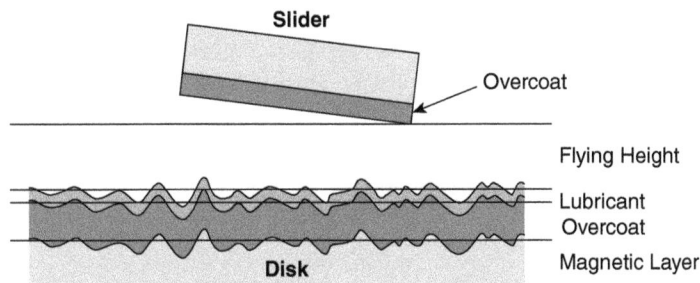

Figure 8.1. Schematics of the head–disk interface.

length. It is believed that in order to achieve the terabit per square inch mark, the total magnetic spacing needs to be in the 6–8 nm range.

This chapter is dedicated to the topic of disk lubricant. In the early days of thin-film disk technology, disks were not always intentionally lubricated, and they probably relied on adventitious lubrication from ambient organic contaminants. In today's technology, an approximately 0.8- to 1.5-nm-thick lubricant film is applied over the disk overcoat layer for several reasons: it considerably reduces friction and wear during head–disk contacts, it lowers the overall surface energy, it protects the disk during the manufacturing process, it adds protection against corrosion, and it passivates the surface against adsorption from organic contaminants.

The head–disk lubricant system is unlike traditional lubrication technologies, as typical separation distances (nanometers) and contact speeds (10–40 m/s) collude to exhibit shear rates in the range of 10^{10} s^{-1}, which is far beyond what is experienced in what was considered a "harsh" environment before, such as in engines and turbines. In addition, the molecularly thin lubricant layer is expected to keep its beneficial characteristics in a wide range of temperatures and humidity levels, and for at least 10 years! As a result, contributions from this field to molecular tribology in the last two decades or so have been substantial.

In this chapter, the physics and chemistry of disk lubricants will be reviewed. We will discuss their molecular attributes (backbone, endgroups), and the use of additives. We will describe how they are typically characterized, both in bulk and film. Emphasis will be given to the thermodynamics (e.g., stability) and dynamics of the film under typical disk drive usage. In particular, chemical stability, evaporation, spin-off, reflow, and perturbation by the slider will be reviewed.

8.2 LUBRICANT STRUCTURES

8.2.1 Backbone

Hydrocarbon oils, which represent the large majority of industrial lubricants, are not adequate as disk lubricants as they are not chemically stable enough under oxidative environments. The same applies to silicone oils, which have an added drawback as their

Fomblin Z

$$R-[O-CF_2-CF_2]_m-[O-CF_2]_n-O-R$$

Asahi

$$R-[O-CF_2-CF_2]_m-O-R$$

Demnum

$$R-[O-CF_2-CF_2-CF_2]_m-O-R$$

Figure 8.2. Commercial PFPE lubricant chain structures.

oxidation product is silica. Perfluorinated alkanes, on the other hand, have much stronger chemical stability and very low surface tension. However, these molecules are quite rigid and tend to all be solid at room temperature. Introducing ether linkages throughout the backbone adds great torsional flexibility, and the resulting class of lubricants called perfluoropolyethers (PFPE) has been the mainstay of the disk industry for many years now. We will describe $[-CF_2-]_n$ segments as C1, C2, and C3 units for $n = 1$, 2, and 3, respectively. Three commercial linear PFPE series are available today that exhibit small structural variations in the amount of C–C to O–C bond ratio: Fomblin Z series from Solvay-Solexis (random C1 and C2 units, C1:C2 ratio ≈ 1); Asahi Glass PFPE (C2 units), and Demnum from Daikin (C3 units) (Fig. 8.2). As expected, the lubricant backbone's stiffness increases with increasing –CF$_2$– segments from C1 to C2 to C3, increasing the resulting surface viscosity accordingly. Of the three lubricant types mentioned here, the Fomblin Z series is the most widely used in the thin-film disk industry today.

One chemical drawback of the Fomblin Z family is the existence of the acetal linkage O–CF$_2$–O, which has been proven to be readily decomposed under the presence of Lewis acids [1]. This was deemed relevant to the head–disk interface, since aluminum oxide is a major component of the slider body. This reaction pathway is probably much more prevalent in the contact-start-stop (CSS) mode, when the head is allowed to slide and land at the inner diameter of the disk upon power-off, in contrast to load/unload technology, when the heads are parked on a dedicated ramp outside of the disk stack. In today's head technology, the air-bearing surface (ABS) is coated with 1–3 nm of diamond-like carbon to protect the sensor against corrosion and mechanical damage, and this degradation in the presence of Lewis acids is probably not very significant.

8.2.2 Functional Groups

The previous section described how to tailor the molecular backbone structure in order to optimize the desired chemical and physical properties of the lubricant. The resulting PFPE molecules, though, offer little affinity to the disk overcoat surface, and they would

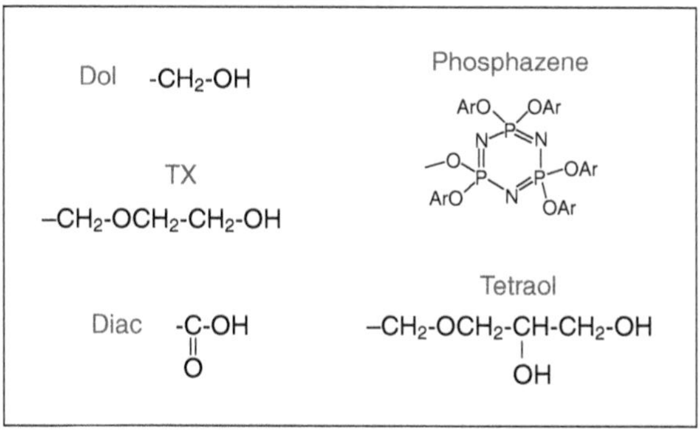

Figure 8.3. Functional groups.

be readily evaporated or spun off from the disk surface. It is therefore necessary to provide attachment moieties to the chain ends in order to provide strong anchor points. In Figure 8.3, some typical chemical groups (endgroups) that are commercially available on PFPE backbones are reproduced. Although the exact nature of the chemical affinity to the carbon overcoat surface is not yet fully understood, it is generally accepted that hydrogen bonding through alcohol $-OH$ or amine $-NH_2$ bonds provides the necessary bonding scheme. In today's disk technology, alcohol endgroups on a Fomblin Z backbone are by far the most popular, with Zdol and Ztetraol being widely used. Typically, bonding strength scales with the number of hydroxyl groups, with Ztetraol exhibiting far greater affinity to the carbon surface as compared to Zdol. Finally, phosphazene endgroups in a product called A20h from the Japanese company Moresco are believed to provide some additional chemical stability against Lewis acid degradation at the expense, perhaps, of weaker bonding. It is sometime used as an additive in some applications, and this will be discussed further, later in this section.

8.2.3 Importance of Molecular Weight (MW) Distribution

The lubricant synthesis reaction involves some sort of polymerization, and this leads to a fairly broad MW distribution (Fig. 8.4). Since the physical properties of lubricant polymers depend greatly on their MW, it is sometimes important to purify and narrow the MW of the lubricant. For instance, the low MW tail often leads to undesired evaporation/transfer to the slider, whereas the high MW tail exhibits a longer backbone length, which can interfere with proper head–disk clearance [2]. The purification process is typically done using supercritical fluid extraction (SFE), in which the PFPE is dissolved in supercritical CO_2, and separated according to different solubility of the various MW at different temperatures. The resulting MW distribution has enhanced tribological properties. Commercial firms such as Phasex (http://www.phasex.com) and Separex (http://www.separex.fr) have optimized separation conditions for Fomblin lubricants, and are routinely offering their services to the disk industry.

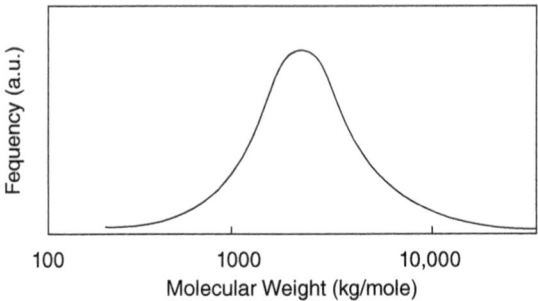

Figure 8.4. Molecular weight distribution of Zdol2000.

8.2.4 Additives

As mentioned earlier, and despite an overall chemically robust structure, PFPE lubricants with acetal linkage ($O-CF_2-O$) could suffer from catalytic degradation induced by sliding contact against the slider alumina (aluminum oxide) body. It was found, perhaps serendipitously, that a phospazene-containing lubricant called X1p from Dow Chemical, when added in just a few percent to Fomblin Zdol, greatly enhanced the chemical stability and overall disk reliability [1]. This molecule was used extensively in the industry in the mid-1990s, in the late stages of inductive head technology, when sliders where allowed to fly near zero clearance (near-contact) against mechanically textured disks. This lubricant mixture was not without challenges as it could lead to phase separation on the disk under high humidity. In the past decade or so, the Japanese company Moresco has made available a phosphazene endgroup attached to a Fomblin backbone, as mentioned earlier. The resulting molecule, named A20h and now fully miscible with Zdol and Ztetraol, is sometimes used as an additive to hydroxylated PFPEs.

8.2.5 Novel Backbone Structures

With the advent of thermal flying height control (TFC), where a thermal actuator located near the slider read/write elements allows subnanometer in-situ flying height adjustment [3], it is now possible to reliably fly under extremely low head–disk clearance (<2–3 nm). Under these conditions, it was found that the length of the lubricant chain could start interfering with the flying slider [2]. As a result, a new class of lubricants is starting to emerge, where in addition to functional groups located at the end of the chain, attachment moieties are incorporated in the middle of the chain in a linear fashion ("multidentate"), or in several distinct segments ("multifunctional"), as illustrated in Figure 8.5. An example of this class of molecules has been called Ztetraol Multidentate, or ZTMD, where two short-chain Ztetraol-1000 units have been coupled together to form a molecule containing a total of 8-hydroxyl moieties, with two on each end, and four in the middle of the chain. The resulting surface structure in effect forces

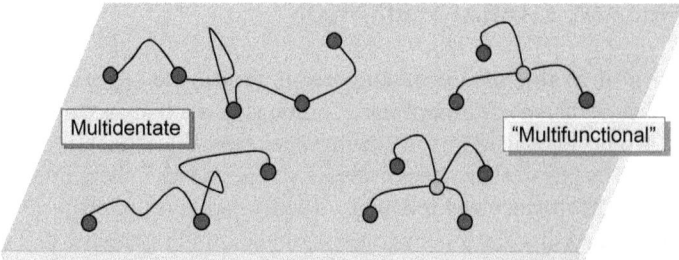

Figure 8.5. Multidentate and multifunctional lubricants.

the lubricant chain against the disk surface, allowing the slider to fly about half a nanometer lower [4].

8.3 LUBRICATION PROCESS

8.3.1 Deposition

The deposition of a circa 1 nanometer-thin lubricant film on a surface seems like a process that would require expensive vacuum equipment. In fact, it turns out to be a fairly straightforward procedure. The lubricant is dissolved in a fluorinated solvent, and disks are simply dip-coated in the solution. Thickness is adjusted by changing withdrawal speed and/or lubricant concentration. An optimized soak time is sometimes added that allows polar lubricants to make their way and bond to the disk surface while immersed in the solvent solution. Typical solvents in use today are for instance HFE, PF5060 (3M), Vertrel (DuPont), or AK-225 (Asahi). Recently, a commercial unit capable of depositing lubricant from vapor phase has been made available (http:// www.intevac.com). This equipment is compatible with the media sputter-deposition process, and it could therefore be a potential cost-saving device, as it does not involve solvent usage. It is too early to predict whether this technology will displace the traditional dip-coating method.

8.3.2 Post-Processing

Asperities on a hard disk surface can lead to damage to the head sensor or even crashes if they are taller than the slider flying height, and hence they should be removed. To do so, a tape buffing process is used. In the tape buffing process, the disk is rotated, and an abrasive tape is pressed against the rotating disk at a suitable loading force. This results in the removal of the asperities, leading to a smoother surface. Burnishing, where the asperities are removed by a low-flying hard slider, is also commonly used. These processes are somewhat aggressive, perhaps even more than head–disk interactions in regular drive operations. As a result, it is important to optimize overcoat and lubricant properties in to order to sustain this operation with little damage to the disk integrity.

8.4 LUBRICANT CHARACTERIZATION

The ultimate goal of the lubrication engineer is to provide superior drive reliability under a number of harsh environmental conditions (e.g., temperature and humidity). Ideally, one would endeavor to fully understand how the structure of the lubricant molecule affects its physical and chemical properties, and how these properties eventually affect field performance and reliability. To this end, a set of characterization tools have been developed that allows one to get a handle on the structure–property–performance relationship.

8.4.1 Structural Characterization

By far the most useful technique for the characterization of the lubricant structure is nuclear magnetic resonance (NMR) of the Fluorine 19 isotope [5]. Depending on the chemical environment of the fluorine atom in the PFPE molecule, small but measurable chemical shift of the 19F nucleus resonance can be detected, allowing the estimation of such quantities as average MW, endgroup purity, and C1/C2 ratio of methylene oxide to ethylene oxide units as depicted in Figure 8.2. A typical NMR spectrum of Ztetraol2000, with corresponding peak assignment is illustrated in Figure 8.6.

8.4.2 Bulk Characterization

Besides mean MW, it is very important to know the actual MW distribution, as mentioned earlier. Gel permeation chromatography is an effective technique to obtain this information [5]. As far as physical and chemical stability are concerned, thermal gravimetric analysis (TGA) is the characterization tool of choice that allows the prediction of evaporative and degradation-loss channels in the drive. For pure evaporation, it is

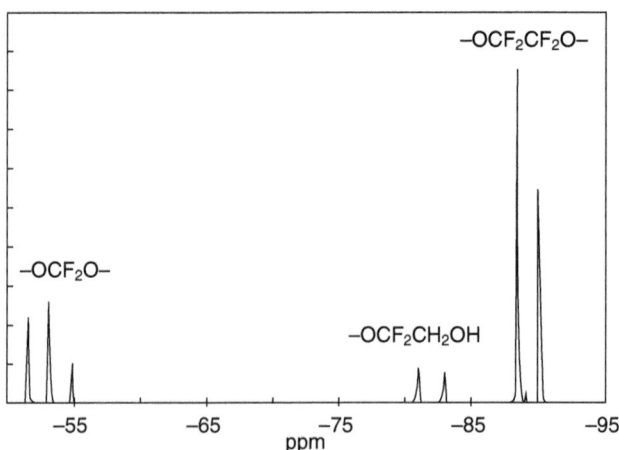

Figure 8.6. NMR spectrum of Ztetraol2000.

customary to run TGA measurements in a vacuum or under inert gas. For oxidative stability measurements, oxygen can be introduced to the sample vial, and it has also been demonstrated that mixing a small amount of a Lewis acid powder (e.g., Al_2O_3) can significantly enhance chain scission and mass loss [1]. A number of other bulk characterization techniques have also been used (viscosity, light scattering) with some success. However, surface characterization on actual disk provides by far the most useful set of information relevant to reliability performance. This is discussed in the next section.

8.4.3 Surface Characterization

8.4.3.1 Thickness.
The thickness of the lubricant film on a disk surface is of utmost importance as deviations as small as an Angstrom or less can undermine head–disk stiction, wear, or proper flyability. As a result, the control and accurate measurement of its thickness in the manufacturing environment is extremely critical. The three main lubricant thickness techniques used today are X-ray photoelectron spectroscopy (XPS or ESCA), Fourier-transform infrared spectroscopy (FTIR), and X-ray reflectivity (XRR).

XPS is a surface sensitive technique that relies on the interaction between X-ray photons and the core electrons of the sample under investigation. These core electrons get ejected with an escape depth of a few nanometers, hence providing the surface selectivity. They are then analyzed as a function of their energy, and the resulting spectrum gives qualitative and quantitative information about the nature and chemical bonding of the atomic species at the surface. For instance, the 1s core electron of the carbon atom yields a peak at about 284 eV if it is part of a C–C or C–H bond. However, the same C(1s) electron exhibits a peak at approximately 285–288 eV when bonded to oxygen, and about 286–294 eV when in a C–F bond. It is, therefore a convenient technique to estimate the thickness of the lubricant film, as the C(1s) signals from the lubricant molecule (mostly C–F bonds) and the disk overcoat (mostly C–C bonds) are well separated. Their respective intensities allow the determination of the lubricant thickness t as $t = \lambda \ln(aR + 1)$, where a is the ratio of the C(1s) intensity from the pure carbon overcoat to that of the bulk lubricant, R is the intensity ratio of the C–F to C–C peak intensities, and λ the electron escape depth, typically equal to 2.5 nm for this system.

FTIR performed at grazing angle is very suitable to lubricant thickness measurement, as C–F bond stretching vibration peaks at around 1200 cm^{-1} are very intense, owing to the polar attribute of the C–F bond. This C–F stretching peak absorbance scales with the lubricant thickness, and this measurement technique is therefore quick, accurate, and fairly easy to implement in a manufacturing environment. For these reasons, it is widely used today in the disk industry. An unlubricated reference disk is usually used as background. This technique, however, is not absolute, and proper calibration needs to be carried out for every product type.

XRR is probably the most exact and accurate of all the thickness measurement techniques, as it does not require any calibration or fitting parameters. The technique consists of measuring the surface reflectivity as a function of the angle of incidence of an X-ray beam at near grazing angle (0–5°). The scattered signal is the combination of the beam reflecting off the top of the lubricant film, and the beam reflecting off the lubricant–disk interface. As a result, a series of constructive and destructive interference signals is produced when the angle of incidence is changed, following Bragg's law. These oscillations of the X-ray signal are then analyzed, and the thickness and density of the lubricant film, as well as interfacial roughness can be obtained.

It is worth mentioning that ellipsometry is also widely used today, not for the control of the mean film thickness but rather for the observation of small lubricant nonuniformity across the disk surface. Fast two-dimensional lubricant maps of the disk surface can therefore be obtained with circa 10 µm lateral resolution, and sub-Angstrom thickness accuracy [6]. This technique allows the observation and study of slider-assisted lubricant dynamics, a topic which will be discussed later in this chapter.

8.4.3.2 *Surface Chemical Structure.* As mentioned earlier, the hydroxyl endgroups depicted in Figure 8.3 provide strong adhesion of the lubricant molecule to the carbon overcoat surface, and they are often depicted as anchored to it (Fig. 8.7). This is obviously an oversimplification as a broad range of chemical and physical interactions do take place (this will be described in more detail in the next section on lubricant bonding). Nevertheless, the interaction energy of the endgroup to the disk surface is far greater than that of the backbone. As the thickness is increased, the surface density of the endgroup increases until a point when no more room is left, and steric hindrance prevents any further crowding (Fig. 8.7). This critical thickness is called dewetting thickness as additional molecules do not wet the surface, segregating instead on top of the first molecular layer. Further thickness increase can even lead to a complete second layer formed of lubricant dimers whose thickness is approximately twice that of the first layer (see Fig. 8.7; also Fig. 8.14, later in this chapter). This layering can be observed by monitoring the slow spreading of a lubricant step, using a micro-ellipsometer [7]. As expected from geometric arguments, the dewetting thickness scales monotonically with the MW of the lubricant. For a MW of 2000 Daltons, a typical dewetting thickness is in the 2.0–2.5 nm range. Care must be taken to adjust lubricant MW and film thickness in order to operate below the dewetting transition. Typically, a circa 8–15 Å-thick film of Zdol or Ztetraol (2000 Daltons) is applied, which is well within the wetting regime.

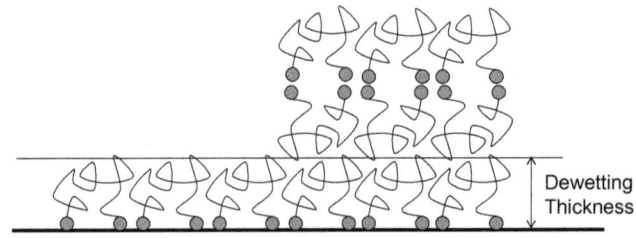

Figure 8.7. Schematics of lubricant multilayers on the disk surface.

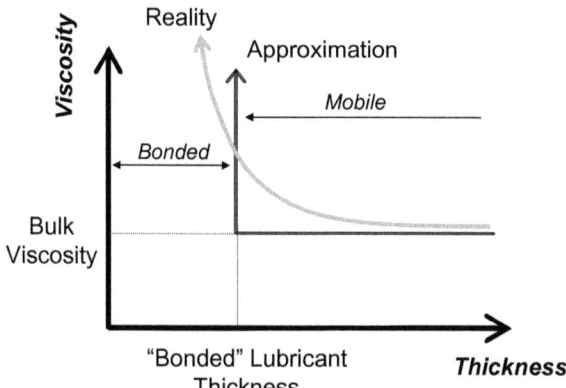

<u>Figure 8.8.</u> Bonded versus free lubricant.

8.4.3.3 Bonding. It is customary for media lubricant engineers to estimate the degree of mobility of the lubricant film by rinsing the disk with a solvent. The amount of lubricant that cannot be removed by rinsing is designated as "bonded," whereas the lubricant that is removed is deemed as "mobile." As it involves hydrogen bonding between the hydroxyl endgroups and the active sites of the overcoat surface, bonding usually scales with the density of endgroups in the lubricant molecule. A typical ratio of bonded lubricant amounts to about 40–60% for Zdol, 60–80% for Ztetraol, and 80–90% for ZTMD. Interestingly, the kinetics of lubricant bonding is fairly slow: at ambient temperature, it takes up to several weeks to reach a steady state. This bonding time can be reduced to less than an hour by thermal activation. For this reason, some sort of thermal curing is sometimes performed on commercial disks. Another way to chemically enhance lubricant bonding is to expose the lubricant film to ultraviolet light [8]. As will be discussed in the following sections, the trend to lower slider flying height tends to exacerbate air shear effects on the lubricant film, leading to possible reliability issues. For this reason, higher lubricant bonding is increasingly necessary.

It is important to draw a parallel between the chemical bonding of the lubricant and its effective surface viscosity. The oversimplified description of a "mobile" and a "bonded" layer implies that the mobile or free layer has a viscosity close to the bulk viscosity of the lubricant, whereas the bonded layer is of infinite viscosity. In reality, it is likely that a continuous transition from bulk/liquid-like to solid-like exists, as illustrated schematically in Figure 8.8.

8.4.4 Thermodynamics: Film Energy and Wetting

Many of the surface and tribological phenomena associated with nanometer-scale lubricant thickness can be derived and quantitatively explained from the knowledge of its thermodynamic properties. From a macroscopic viewpoint (large thickness), it is convenient to introduce the concept of surface energy, corresponding to the energy per

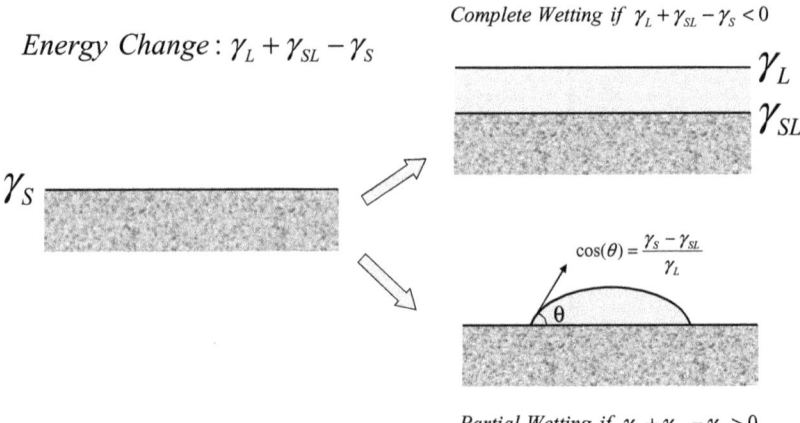

$$\textit{Energy Change}: \gamma_L + \gamma_{SL} - \gamma_S$$

Complete Wetting if $\gamma_L + \gamma_{SL} - \gamma_S < 0$

$$\gamma_L$$
$$\gamma_{SL}$$

$$\cos(\theta) = \frac{\gamma_S - \gamma_{SL}}{\gamma_L}$$

$$\gamma_S$$

$$\theta$$

Partial Wetting if $\gamma_L + \gamma_{SL} - \gamma_S > 0$

Figure 8.9. Thermodynamics of wetting.

unit area that it takes for a given solid to create a surface. It is measured in in Joules per square meter, or simply Newtons per meter. The analog for a liquid is called surface tension. The thermodynamics of wetting a solid surface is depicted in Figure 8.9. Wetting a liquid film onto a solid of surface energy γ_S requires the elimination of the solid surface, the formation of a liquid surface, and a solid–liquid interface. As a result, the net change in energy per unit area is $\delta E = E_{final} - E_{initial} = \gamma_L + \gamma_{SL} - \gamma_S$, where γ_L is the liquid surface tension and γ_{SL} the liquid–solid interfacial energy. If δE is negative, wetting is energetically favored and it is total. If it is positive, wetting is not favored, and the liquid will only partially wet with an angle of contact given by Young's equation:

$$\cos(\theta) = \frac{\gamma_S - \gamma_{SL}}{\gamma_L}. \tag{8.1}$$

In the nanometer scale, however, the behavior of the film will be dictated by the shape of the energy curve and, more specifically, how it goes from γ_S (limit of zero thickness) to $\gamma_{SL} + \gamma_L$ (infinite thickness). In the case of purely dispersive, or Van der Waals interactions, $E(h)$ follows:

$$E(h) \sim \frac{A}{12\pi(h + r_0)^2}. \tag{8.2}$$

A is called the Hamaker constant of the solid/liquid system, and r_0 is a the distance of closest approach, typically about 3.2 Å, corresponding to the sum of the atomic radii in contact between the disk (carbon) and the lubricant molecule (fluorine). This distance of closest approach r_0 keeps $E(h)$ from being unbounded in the limit of zero thickness. The Hamaker constant A is an estimate of the interaction between the lubricant molecule and the surface (adhesive interaction) versus itself (cohesive interaction). If adhe-

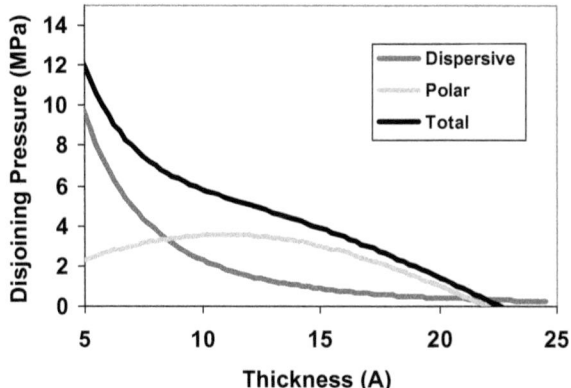

<u>Figure 8.10.</u> Example of polar and dispersive lubricant film energy (for Zdol2000).

sive interactions are stronger than cohesive interactions, the molecules would want to wet the surface, and A is positive. Conversely, if cohesive interactions dominate, the lubricant molecule will prefer to be associated with itself, and it will not wet the surface. Equation 8.2 is a fairly good description of surface interactions concerning the non-functional Fomblin Z system.

For polar lubricants like Zdol or Ztetraol, however, a strong oscillatory polar term that reflects their tendency to strongly interact with polar surface species or with themselves, as depicted schematically in Figure 8.7, needs to be taken into account. The period of these energy oscillations is a function of the chain length or MW. A simple example of the dispersive and polar components for Zdol lubricant is depicted in Figure 8.10.

In practice, the negative of the first derivative of the interface energy with respect to film thickness is a more useful concept. Similar to an energy gradient creating a force, this energy gradient per surface area creates an interface pressure. It is called disjoining pressure since it tends to disrupt wetting films. From Equation 8.2, it is easy to derive its expression for the case of purely dispersive interactions:

$$\Pi(h) = \frac{A}{6\pi(h+r_0)^3}. \tag{8.3}$$

This disjoining pressure can be viewed as the force per unit area that keeps the lubricant film against the disk surface, and it is a key contributor to lubricant distribution on a rough disk surface as it counterbalances capillary pressure $P_c = 2\gamma/d$ in cavities or pores, where γ is the surface tension of the lubricant, and d is the diameter of the cavity (Fig. 8.11a). During power-off in CSS drives, this effect also mitigates slider stiction at the "landing zone" at the inner diameter of the disks, where a well-controlled array of bumps is introduced using a pulsed laser. The resulting contact points with the slider tend to draw lubricant from the smooth disk surface, creating possible stiction issues (Fig. 8.11b). However, lubricant migration to the contact points stops when the

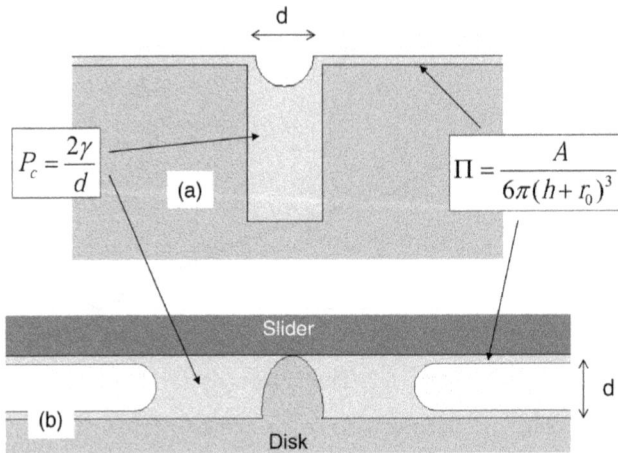

Figure 8.11. Lubricant distribution of a disk surface: disjoining versus capillary pressure (a) in a disk cavity; (b) at slider disk contact in the landing zone.

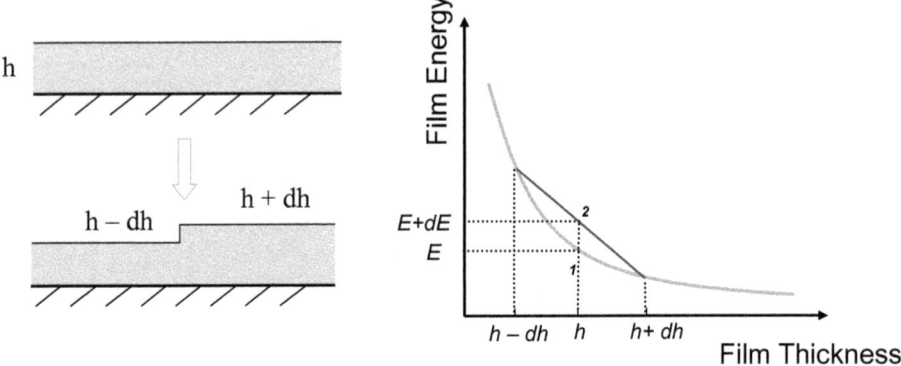

Figure 8.12. Film energy versus thickness, demonstrating wetting stability.

resulting capillary pressure equals the disjoining pressure on the smooth area of the disk. Stiction is hence avoided by a careful optimization of lubricant thickness, viscosity ("bonding"), asperity density, and geometry [9].

A useful feature of the disjoining pressure concept is that lubricant wetting stability is directly associated with its first derivative with respect to film thickness. This can be easily understood by the following argument: if a small perturbation of the film of thickness h happens, it leads to an area where half the film is at a thickness $h—dh$, whereas the other half is at $h + dh$ (Fig. 8.12). If $d\Pi/dh$ is negative (i.e., d^2E/dh^2 is positive, or the E vs. h curve is convex), the resulting energy (average of the energy at $h—dh$ and $h + dh$, or point 2 in the curve) is higher than the initial energy of the unperturbed film (point 1 in the curve), and hence the transition is energetically unfavorable, and the system is stable. Conversely, although not shown here, if $d\Pi/dh$ is negative ($E(h)$ concave), the perturbed state is more stable than the unperturbed one, and the film dewets. For purely dispersive interactions, it can be shown that wetting will only depend on the sign of the Hamaker constant, as Equation 8.2 predicts that the second derivative d^2E/dh^2 is proportional to the Hamaker constant A. As discussed above, modeling of polar lubricants such as Zdol or Ztetraol requires the introduction of a polar term to the expression of the film energy. Doing so leads to the actual prediction of the dewetting transition at the critical thickness mentioned above in Section 8.4.3.2.

8.5 DYNAMICS/FLOW

Whereas the previous section was devoted to the static, thermodynamic aspect of the lubricant film, this section describes the dynamic behavior of the film when subjected to various forces. We will review the general equations that govern the lubricant flow, and investigate some of the details of spin-off, spreading, and slider-induced lubricant motion.

8.5.1 General Equations: Couette versus Poiseuille

Figure 8.13 illustrates the two types of flow systems that are relevant to today's disk drives, where η is the effective viscosity of the lubricant film, and h is the film thickness. The Couette (shear-induced) flow originates from air-velocity effects acting on the lubricant film. As the velocity field is linear, the flow varies as the thickness squared, after integration. It is also proportional to the air shear stress σ. The lubricant motion induced from a pressure gradient dP/dx, or Poiseuille flow, has a parabolic velocity field, and hence its flow varies as the cube of the film thickness. Earlier studies have demonstrated that for all practical purposes, the Poiseuille flow only applies to lubricant reflow (also referred to spreading or diffusion) under its own disjoining pressure gradient, whereas all spin-off and slider effects can be described accurately in the Couette-flow framework [10]. These phenomena will be described in more details in the next

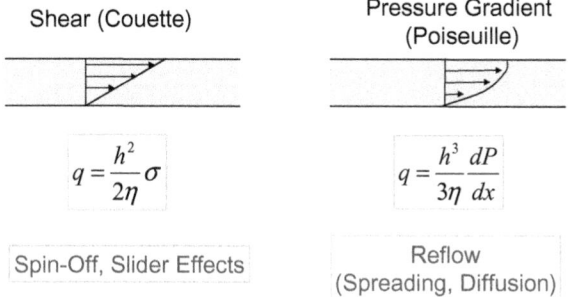

Figure 8.13. Schematics of shear-driven versus pressure-gradient-driven flow.

few sections. Once the details of the lubricant flow are known, the time dependent thickness variations can be obtained using the continuity equation: $dh/dt = -dq/dx$.

Flow equations shown on Figure 8.13 only apply rigorously to a multilayer regime where flow can be approximated in the framework of continuum physics. It has been demonstrated, however, that this formalism still applies to monomolecular films when used with the concept of effective surface viscosity.

8.5.2 Spreading

In the case of CSS technology, lubricant can get sheared off from the top of the disk texture asperities under the rubbing slider during take-off and landing. In addition, local lubricant movement also results from slider effects, as very low slider-disk spacing creates extremely high shear forces (see further in the text). It is therefore important to model and predict film "self-healing" behavior. As mentioned earlier, replenishment flow is provided through film spreading, driven primarily by its disjoining pressure gradient [11]:

$$q = \frac{h^3}{3\eta}\frac{d\Pi}{dx}. \tag{8.4}$$

Using the continuity equation, Equation 8.4 leads to

$$\frac{dh}{dt} = \frac{d}{dx}\left(-\frac{h^3}{3\eta}\frac{d\Pi}{dh}\frac{dh}{dx}\right). \tag{8.5}$$

Equation 8.5 is essentially equivalent to a diffusion equation corresponding to a thickness-dependent diffusion coefficient $D(h)$ equal to

$$D(h) = -\frac{h^3}{3\eta}\frac{d\Pi}{dh}. \tag{8.6}$$

For dispersive interactions where the disjoining pressure can be expressed analytically (Eq. 8.3), $D(h)$ becomes, as shown in Reference 12:

$$D(h) = \frac{Ah^3}{6\eta(h+r_0)^4}. \tag{8.7}$$

Most of the experimental studies of Fomblin spreading have been conducted by monitoring the time evolution of a lubricant step on a smooth surface [7]. A remarkable feature of the spreading characteristics is that nonfunctional Fomblin Z obeys continuum physics (Eq. 8.7) quite well for thickness values as thin as 10 Å and below, whereas Zdol shows a characteristic terraced profile (Fig. 8.14) with step heights corresponding to the molecular layers depicted in Figure 8.7. Another fact of interest is that the mere addition of the hydroxyl endgroups on Zdol slows down surface spreading by an order of magnitude or so.

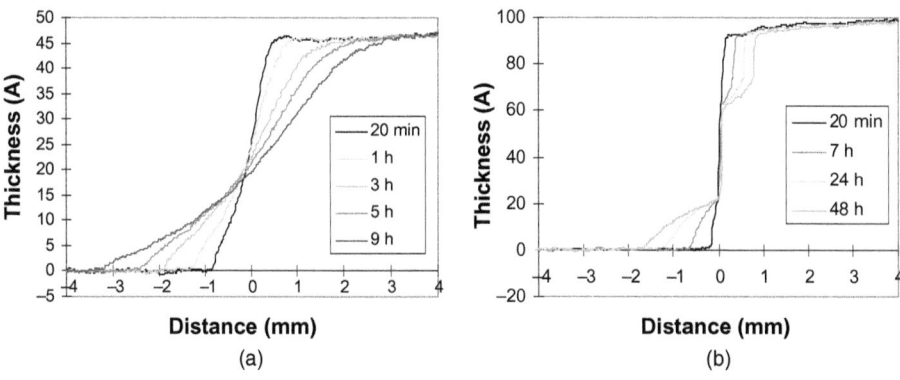

Figure 8.14. Spreading of Z (a) and Zdol (b).

8.5.3 Spin-off

Fast access to user data on a given disk requires increasing rotational speed. In the last two decades or so, the fastest disk drives have seen their rotational speed climb from 3600 rpm to 15,000 rpm today. Under these stringent requirements, lubricant spin-off could become an issue, and care must be taken that it does not amount to any significant loss during a 5- to-10-year lifetime. For very thin liquid layers, it turns out that spin-off forces from air shear are predominant, compared to centrifugal effects. The equation governing the rate of lubricant loss dh/dt from an unbounded spinning disk surface is as follows [13]:

$$\frac{dh}{dt} = -\omega\sqrt{\eta_a \rho_a \omega}\,\frac{h^2}{2\eta}, \tag{8.8}$$

where ω is the angular rotational speed of the disk, and η_a and ρ_a are the viscosity and specific gravity of air. The factor of 2 in the denominator is an approximation of a numerical coefficient of approximately 1/0.51. Numerical solutions to Equation 8.8 would predict that Z lubricant would tend to exhibit significant spin-off when subjected to 15,000 rpm rotational speed. Addition of hydroxyl endgroups in Zdol and Ztetraol to enhance surface viscosity is therefore a necessary requirement for proper drive reliability.

8.6 SLIDER EFFECTS

As the slider flies ever closer to the disk surface, its effect on the integrity of the head–disk interface becomes more pronounced. In particular, lubricant transfer to the slider can create a number of possible problems. In Section 8.6.1, a short review of possible reliability issues stemming from lubricant pickup is described. Section 8.6.2 enumerates the various physical mechanisms of lubricant disk-to-slider transfer that have been identified. Finally, Section 8.6.3 discusses how the lubricant can be engineered and tailored to minimize or even eliminate these problems.

8.6.1 Lubricant Pickup: Reliability

8.6.1.1 Fly-Stiction. The stiction effect when the slider rests on the landing zone of the disk surface has already been partially described in Section 8.4.4 and Figure 8.10b. It could affect disks that have too much mobile lubricant or inadequate topography. Another compounding aspect of head–disk stiction could happen when lubricant slowly transfers from the disk to the slider during regular drive operations, as this transfer can lead to dramatically enhanced stiction after a drive is powered-off, when the lubricant is allowed to migrate back to the contacting area of the slider–disk interface. This phenomenon has been called "fly-stiction," and it is stiction resulting from flying the slider over the disk.

8.6.1.2 Skip Write or High Fly Write. Another possible detrimental effect of lubricant pickup on the slider happens when so much lubricant has been picked up by the slider that macroscopic droplets get released onto the disk, creating a puddle of liquid higher than the slider flying height. When the slider subsequently flies over that area, the resulting sudden friction increase jolts the slider upward by several tens of nanometers (Fig. 8.15). If the head just happened to be writing data at that moment, the higher spacing would result in a loss of data integrity, and hard errors.

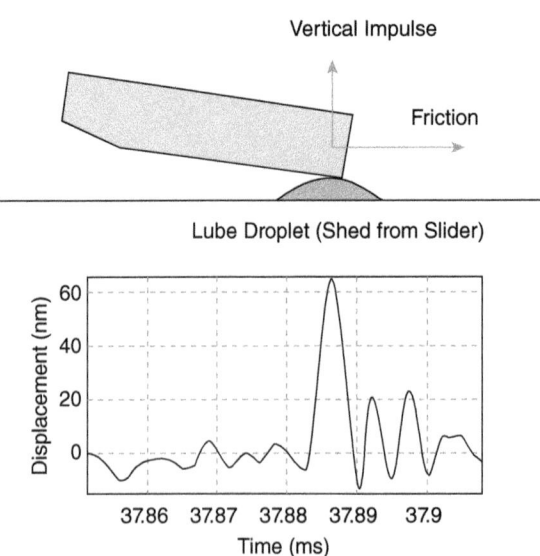

Figure 8.15. "Skip write" or "high fly write" effect. Top: Schematics. Bottom: Actual vertical slider motion.

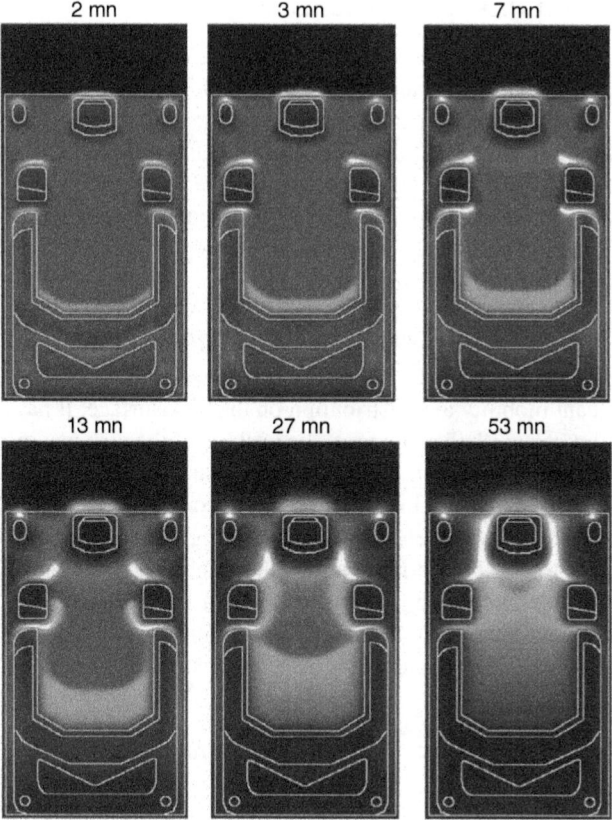

Figure 8.16. Evolution of a 0.5-nm lubricant film on a slider surface.

8.6.1.3 *Spacing Increase.* In today's head–disk system, where total magnetic spacing is below the 10 nm mark, every Angstrom change causes a measurable recording signal alteration, whether from the write (overwrite) or read (signal amplitude) process. As a result, a thin lubricant film on the slider can now cause a measurable magnetic spacing increase, leading to possible reliability failures. A growing number of publications are now focused on understanding and modeling lubricant flow on the slider surface itself. A typical approach is to solve the air-bearing equation using a standard industry solver (e.g., http://cml.berkeley.edu/), and then apply the resulting air shear map to an initial lubricant distribution. An example of lubricant map evolution on a slider surface is reproduced in Figure 8.16. In this figure, the evolution of an initial 0.5-nm lubricant film on a slider is shown. The colorscale spans 0–2 nm, with regions of higher thickness being shown brighter. A fine examination of the lubricant film thickness on the air-bearing pads, its effect on magnetic spacing increase, and its time evolution allows one to better understand this type of problem and to act on it.

8.6.2   Lubricant Pickup: Mechanisms

8.6.2.1   Evaporation. It has been found that evaporation and transfer of lower molecular fractions of the lubricant from the disk to the slider was dramatically increased when the slider-to-disk distance crosses the mean-free path of air of about 60 nm (Fig. 8.17). The reason for this is that the lubricant molecule now encounters far fewer collisions with air molecules in its attempts to evaporate, in effect undergoing a transition from the regimes of ambient to vacuum evaporation, and enhancing rates manyfold [14]. As discussed in Section 8.2.3, a solution to this problem relies on eliminating the low tail of the lubricant MW distribution.

8.6.2.2   Shear Effects: "Moguls" and "Ripples". When the slider flying height crosses the approximately 20 nm barrier, air shear effects start to significantly affect the lubricant mobility and distribution on the disk surface. It has been found that the lubricant film gets pushed away from the upslope of the disk waviness in the down-track direction, to accumulate in the downslope areas. The resulting lubricant pooling is correlated to disk waviness in incoherent patterns coined "moguls" [15]. Furthermore, coupling with the natural frequency of the air-bearing or head suspension can result in a coherent "rippling" of the lubricant in a well-defined corrugation pattern, similar to washboarding on dirt roads [16]. It was also found that this coherent, self enhanced modulation of the air bearing could lead to instabilities below a critical flying height. An example of actual moguls and ripple structures is reproduced in Figure 8.18.

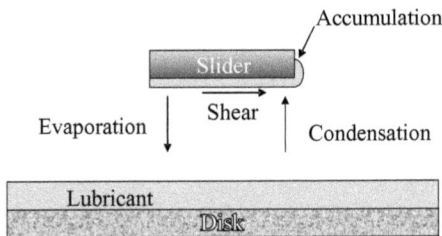

Figure 8.17. Disk to slider lubricant transfer by evaporation.

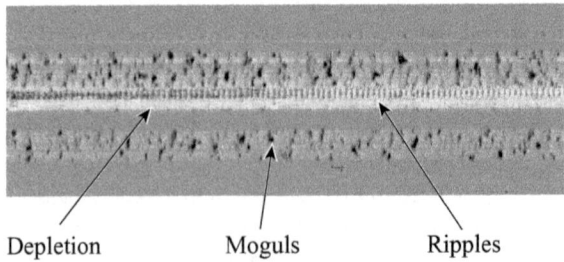

Figure 8.18. Lubricant map showing moguls, ripples, and depletion. The gray scale contrast is darkest for thicker lubricant film.

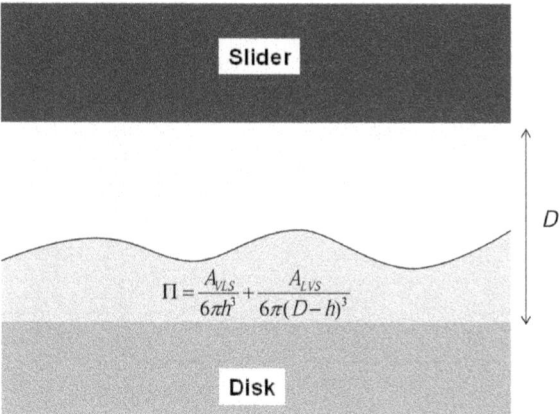

Figure 8.19. Intermolecular effects at the head–disk interface, leading to lubricant dewetting. *AVLS* is the Hamaker constant for the lubricant–disk interactions, and *ALVS* corresponds to the lubricant–slider interactions through the air gap.

These shear-induced lubricant features are detrimental to proper drive reliability because they add to the disk topography, in effect increasing flying height and signal amplitude modulation. They could also lead to another channel path to lubricant transfer to the slider, with the unwanted consequences discussed above.

8.6.2.3 Intermolecular Effects. The latest to date (and possibly last) of the disk–slider effects has been shown to originate from molecular interactions at slider-to-disk distances below circa 2 nm [17]. For these separations, the Van der Waals interaction field from the slider starts to exert a measurable tensile attraction to the lubricant film, leading the resulting disjoining pressure to enter the dewetting regime as described in Section 8.4.4, and causing lubricant to transfer to the slider (Fig. 8.19). A critical flying height whose value scales with the thickness of the lubricant film has been experimentally found and modeled.

8.6.3 Lubricant Pickup: Remedies

In Figure 8.20, we have summarized the various "barriers" that have been crossed over the years, opening up the different physical channels to slider lubricant transfers. In order to mitigate these effects, disk lubricant engineers have been steadily reducing lubricant thickness and enhancing bonding. The overall goal is obviously to increase surface viscosity and enhance disjoining pressure attributes. As mentioned earlier, lubricant fractionation has also dramatically reduced evaporative pickup. Another aspect discussed earlier is the length of the free polymer chain and its effect in reducing clearance. It is believed that a combination of multifunctional/multidentate structures (Fig. 8.5) coupled with stiffer backbones, increased endgroup to backbone ratio, and thermal or UV-assisted bonding will pave the way to tomorrow's disk lubricants for

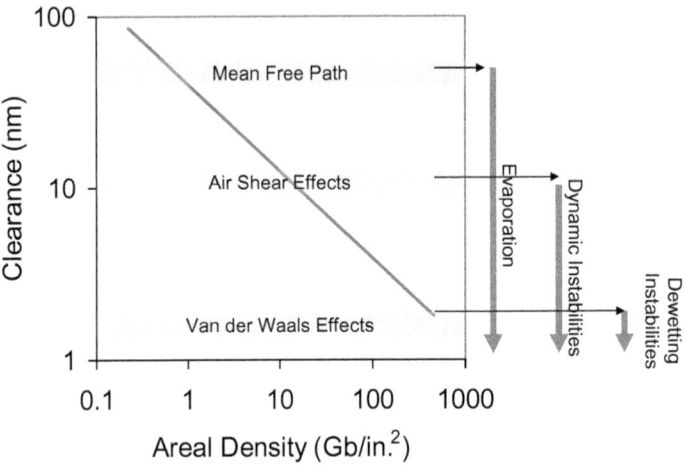

Figure 8.20. Summary of disk-to-slider lubricant transfer mechanisms.

subnanometer clearance. Finally, although it is not a specific topic of this chapter, it is believed that several slider attributes also contribute to lubricant pickup, both from a physical as well as chemical viewpoint.

8.7 LUBRICANTS FOR BIT-PATTERNED MEDIA (BPM) AND HEAT-ASSISTED RECORDING (HAMR)

DTM (discrete track media) and BPM media topography consist of well-defined magnetic structures separated by narrow (<30-nm) gaps of 5- to 30-nm depth. It is possible that these magnetic structures will need to be planarized in order to achieve proper air bearing, flying height, or corrosion properties. In that case, no DTM or BPM-specific lubricant attributes are expected to be required. On the other hand, if the structure is not planarized, care will have to be taken to avoid lubricant or condensing water from filling the gaps in an uncontrolled fashion.

For HAMR, short laser pulses will momentarily heat a small lubricant spot to a temperature in the 200–500°C range. Even though the timescale (nanosecond) of this thermal excursion is small in comparison to the relaxation time of the lubricant molecule (microsecond), it is believed that lubricant evaporation or decomposition will be enhanced under this severe condition, leading to reliability issues [18]. It is likely that the same lubricant attributes that were discussed above in the context of slider-induced effects will still be applicable under thermal transients. In other words, the same molecular interactions that govern adhesion and viscosity also apply to vapor pressure and evaporation processes.

8.8 CONCLUSION

The technological challenges presented by the disk drive industry have spurred a number of fundamental studies that have contributed notably to the field of molecular tribology. As empirical findings build our understanding, gaps in our knowledge are narrowing, and scientifically based advances can be made. As the areal density in actual disk drives is fast approaching the terabit per square inch mark, requiring a subnanometer slider–disk clearance, it is essential that a full, comprehensive knowledge of the fine tribomolecular processes taking place at the flying interface be well understood. This chapter was an attempt to review the state-of-the-art in disk lubrication technology. The grand challenge for the disk drive engineer is to incorporate this fundamental understanding of the physical and chemical phenomena taking place at the sliding interface into materials and process variables that will eventually be integrated into reliable products.

ACKNOWLEDGMENTS

The author would like to acknowledge Jing Gui, Xiaoding Ma from Seagate Technology, and Mathew Mate, Robert Waltman, Qing Dai, Bernhard Knigge, and Ferdinand Hendriks from Hitachi GST, for valuable discussions and input.

REFERENCES

1. P. H. Kasai, Degradation of perfluoropoly(ethers) and role of X-1P additives in disk files. Adv. Inform. Storage Syst. **1**, 23–31 (1999).
2. A. Khurshudov and R. J. Waltman, The contribution of thin PFPE lubricants to slider-disk spacing. Tribology Lett. **11**, 143–149 (2001).
3. M. Suk, K. Miyake, M. Kurita, H. Tanaka, S. Saegusa, and N. Robertson, Verification of thermally induced nanometer actuation of magnetic recording transducer to overcome mechanical and magnetic spacing challenges. IEEE Trans. Magn. **41**, 4350–4352 (2005).
4. X. C. Guo, B. Knigge, B. Marchon, R. J. Waltman, M. Carter, and J. Burns, Multidentate functionalized lubricant for ultralow head/disk spacing in a disk drive. J. Appl. Phys. **100**, 044306 (2006).
5. T. E. Karis, B. Marchon, D. A. Hopper, and R. L. Siemens, Perfluoropolyether characterization by nuclear magnetic resonance spectroscopy and gel permeation chromatography. J. Fluor. Chem. **118**, 81–94 (2002).
6. S. W. Meeks, W. E. Weresin, and H. J. Rosen, Optical-surface analysis of the head-disk-interface of thin-film disks. J. Tribology-Trans. ASME **117**, 112–118 (1995).
7. X. Ma, J. Gui, L. Smoliar, K. Grannen, B. Marchon, M. S. Jhon, and C. L. Bauer, Spreading of perfluoropolyalkylether films on amorphous carbon surfaces. J. Chem. Phys. **110**, 3129–3137 (1999).
8. D. D. Saperstein and L. J. Lin, Improved surface-adhesion and coverage of perfluoropolyether lubricants following far-Uv irradiation. Langmuir **6**, 1522–1524 (1990).

9. J. Gui and B. Marchon, A stiction model for a head-disk interface of a rigid disk-drive. J. Appl. Phys. **78**, 4206–4217 (1995).

10. B. Marchon, Q. Dai, B. Knigge, and R. Pit, Lubricant dynamics in the sub-nanometer clearance regime. IEEE Trans. Magn. **43**, 3694–3698 (2007).

11. C. M. Mate, Application of disjoining and capillary-pressure to liquid lubricant films in magnetic recording. J. Appl. Phys. **72**, 3084–3090 (1992).

12. B. Marchon and T. E. Karis, Poiseuille flow at a nanometer scale. Europhys. Lett. **74**, 294–298 (2006).

13. T. E. Karis, B. Marchon, V. Flores, and M. Scarpulla, Lubricant spin-off from magnetic recording disks. Tribology Lett. **11**, 151–159 (2001).

14. B. Marchon, T. Karis, Q. Dai, and R. Pit, A model for lubricant flow from disk to slider. IEEE Trans. Magn. **39**, 2447–2449 (2003).

15. R. Pit, B. Marchon, S. Meeks, and V. Velidandla, Formation of lubricant "moguls" at the head/disk interface. Tribology Lett. **10**, 133–142 (2001).

16. Q. Dai, F. Hendriks, and B. Marchon, Modeling the washboard effect at the head/disk interface. J. Appl. Phys. **96**, 696–703 (2004).

17. R. P. Ambekar, D. B. Bogy, Q. Dai, and B. Marchon, Critical clearance and lubricant instability at the head-disk interface of a disk drive. Appl. Phys. Lett. **92**, 033104 (2008).

18. Y. S. Ma and B. Liu, A theoretical study of vapor lubrication for heat assisted magnetic recording. Tribology Lett. **32**, 215–220 (2008).

9

OVERCOAT MATERIALS FOR MAGNETIC RECORDING MEDIA

Allen Poh Wei Choong, S. N. Piramanayagam,
and Thomas Y. F. Liew

*Data Storage Institute, Agency for Science,
Technology and Research (A*STAR), Singapore*

9.1 INTRODUCTION

Hard disk drive (HDD) technology has been advancing at an incredible pace since its first introduction in 1956 by IBM (Fig. 9.1). The IBM 350 Disk Storage Unit consisted of fifty 24-inch disks (each of 2-kb/in.^{2} areal density; at 100 bits/in. and 20 tracks/in.) with a total capacity of 4.4 MB. Such storage units were used in the refrigerator-sized IBM 305 RAMAC (random access memory accounting system or random access method of accounting and control), which weighed 971 kg and occupied almost the whole room. Since the invention of the HDD, it has undergone both evolutionary and revolutionary changes at a very fast pace that has led to the tremendous increase in storage capacity. As depicted from the areal density perspective in Figure 9.1, such evolutionary and revolutionary changes enabled the areal density to increase by a factor of as much as 260 million since the introduction of the IBM 350 Disk Storage Unit. Some of the contributing factors to this rapid growth are the transition from particulate media (mixture of magnetic particles in organic binders) to thin-film media (continuous magnetic thin films); the transition from longitudinal magnetic recording (LMR) to perpendicular magnetic

Developments in Data Storage: Materials Perspective, First Edition.
Edited by S. N. Piramanayagam, Tow C. Chong.
© 2012 Institute of Electrical and Electronics Engineers. Published 2012 by John Wiley & Sons, Inc.

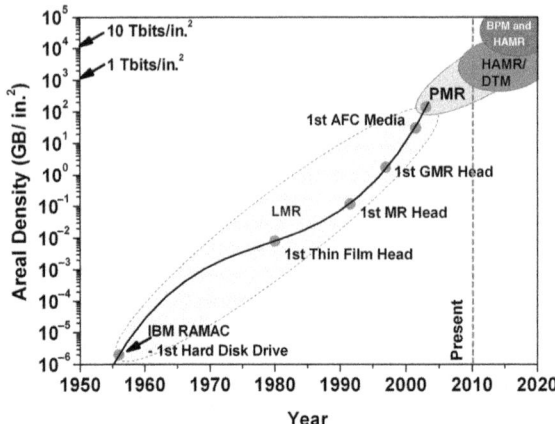

Figure 9.1. Areal density perspective. (Adapted from References 1, 38, and 39.)

recording (PMR) media; improved deposition techniques; magnetic thin-film structure; and the transition from using an induction read head to a GMR read head, and similar advancements in all the components. These factors have enabled the HDD to store larger amounts of information while their size becomes smaller in the attempt to fulfill the demand of today's booming consumer electronics industry. Note that progress in coding and signal processing, actuators, sliders, and other aspects, not included in this book, also played an equally important role.

Future development of HDDs may occur due to new technologies such as heat-assisted magnetic recording (HAMR), patterned media, or a combination of them [1]. Increasing recording density requires a look into several aspects of HD technology. The subject of tribology in HD technology deals with the motion of head over the media and the issues associated with it. This field is important as writing and reading information not only depends on the head and media but also on the spacing. A stable and reliable flying height of the head will ensure reliable writing and reading. In the view of tribology researchers, reduction of the spacing between the magnetic layer and the magnetic read head (or the magnetic spacing) in order to enable ultrahigh-density recording is an important task. The main components that make up the magnetic spacing are the media overcoat, the lubricant, the flying height, the slider overcoat, and the pole tip recess (PTR).

In this chapter, emphasis will be placed on advancements in media overcoat technology. Here we will look first at the history and the evolution of the media overcoat, which will also include the desired properties, chemical/electrochemical reactions, effects of deposition conditions, and how the media overcoat evolved into the present-day carbon overcoat material and configurations. After that, an insight into the state-of-the-art deposition techniques will be presented. In order to make this chapter more comprehensive, highlights of some emerging media overcoat materials and the media overcoat designs for future HD media technology will also be discussed.

9.2 EVOLUTION OF HD TRIBOLOGY

The main purpose of the media overcoat is to provide chemical and mechanical protection for the media from corrosion agents and accidental head–disk contact, respectively. However, the thickness of the media overcoat contributes significantly to the magnetic spacing. Hence one way of reducing the magnetic spacing is to reduce the thickness of the media overcoat. Flying height is another parameter that adds to the magnetic spacing that needs to be reduced. The trend of changes in magnetic spacing, flying height, and media overcoat thickness with respect to areal density is shown in Figure 9.2. The spacing/overcoat thickness versus areal density perspective in Figure 9.2 shows that the magnetic spacing, the flying height, and the media overcoat thickness decrease as areal density increases. The plot also shows that the magnetic spacing of the first HD, the IBM 350 Disk Storage Unit used in the first computer, the IBM 305 RAMAC, is very large (about 25.4 μm) compared to present day HDDs with a magnetic spacing below 10 nm. Likewise, Figure 9.2 also shows that the thickness of the media overcoat decreases (from its initial adoption) as areal density increases. It is important to note that a media overcoat was not used for particulate media as the magnetic particles were encapsulated in a polymer matrix, and the magnetic spacing was still very large. The use of a media overcoat was only adopted when media technology changed from particulate media to thin-film media, as magnetic thin films are prone to both chemical corrosion and mechanical damage owing to head–disk contact. As shown in Figure 9.2, as areal density approaches Tb/in.^{2}, the thickness of the media overcoat needs to be in the sub-2 nm range in order to get good readback signals from such ultrahigh recording density HD media. At the same time, these ultrathin media overcoats have to be able to protect the HD media against both chemical corrosion and mechanical damage.

Presently, amorphous carbon (in particular, diamond-like carbon [DLC]) is still the material of choice for media overcoats due to its unique mechanical, physical, and chemical properties. Amorphous carbon is chemically inert; it does not have grain

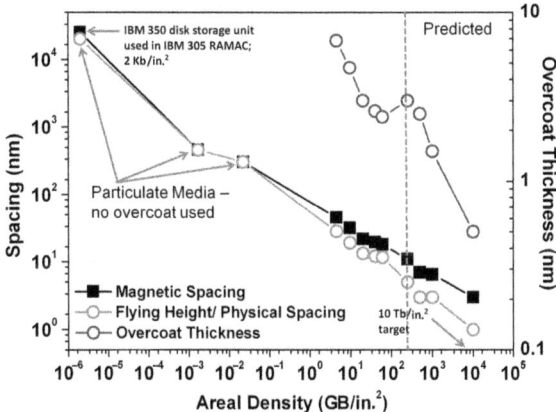

Figure 9.2. Spacing/overcoat thickness versus areal density perspective. (Adapted from References 1, 2, 17, 38, 40–45.)

boundaries and has excellent topographical conformity enabling it to act as a natural corrosion barrier for magnetic HD media. Amorphous carbon is extremely smooth and continuous, adding to its attractiveness as a candidate for HD media overcoat material. In addition, its hardness can also be tailored to approach that of a diamond to act as a wear resistant overcoat.

However, the HD media overcoat has seen many changes since the introduction of the first HDD in the mid 1950s. In the early days, media overcoats were made of spin-coated silicon oxide. Later, with the introduction of physical vapor deposition (PVD), such as sputtering, various types of HD media overcoat materials (such as zirconia (ZrO_2), yttria (partially) stabilized zirconia [$ZrO_2-Y_2O_3$], and SiO_2) were also used. But due to defects (such as sputter debris, arc marks, or spits) formed during deposition, oxide compounds became less attractive as HD overcoat materials and in turn made amorphous carbon the preferred material for media overcoats. This will be discussed in detail in the following sections.

9.3 DESIRED PROPERTIES OF OVERCOATS

Before beginning the discussion on the history and evolution of media overcoats, it is important to highlight the desired properties of an ideal media overcoat. This section starts with a discussion of the desired properties of an ideal media overcoat and the rationale behind them. First and foremost, the primary role of the media overcoat is to protect the HD against corrosion [2]. In order to achieve this, the media overcoat has to be chemically inert, continuous, densely packed, free of pinholes, and also act as a barrier separating the recording layer (usually a Co-based alloy) and the read/write head from the external environment.

In the earlier stage of corrosion, Co migration to the surface predominates. This is because Co (in a Co-based magnetic layer) is nearer to the surface and has positive oxidation potential ($E^0 = 0.28$ V); hence, it has a tendency to oxidize (lose electrons) to form Co^{2+}, and if the recording layer is not well protected, the Co in the recording layer will be exposed to ambient conditions (which contain oxygen and water vapor) and corrode to form corrosion products such as cobalt hydroxides ($Co(OH)_2$). This happens more strongly near the pinholes, as schematically illustrated in Figures 9.3 and 9.4. The oxidation and reduction (redox) reactions shown in Figure 9.3 are favorable as the overall redox reaction potential has a positive value of 0.68 V. A positive value indicates that the reaction is more likely to occur.

Under prolonged exposure to corrosive conditions, Ni from the NiP layer of the substrate will also tend to migrate to the surface at the later stage of corrosion. Likewise, Ni has a positive oxidation potential ($E^0 = 0.25$ V), and hence also has a tendency to oxidize to form Ni^{2+}. Hence, at the later stage of corrosion, nickel hydroxides ($Ni(OH)_2$) will also be formed. Similarly, this redox reaction is favorable as the overall redox reaction potential has a positive value of 0.65 V.

For the redox reaction to take place in HD media, there has to be (1) a direct contact of the environment with the magnetic layer; and (2) there has to be an electronic path to facilitate charge transfer [3]. With the fulfillment of these two criteria, corrosion will

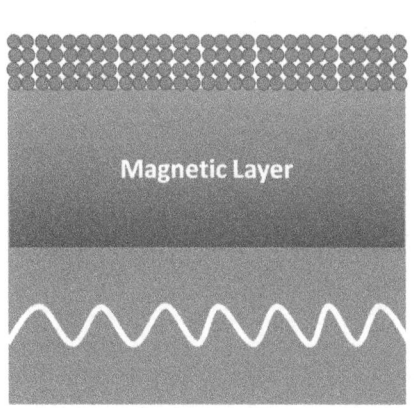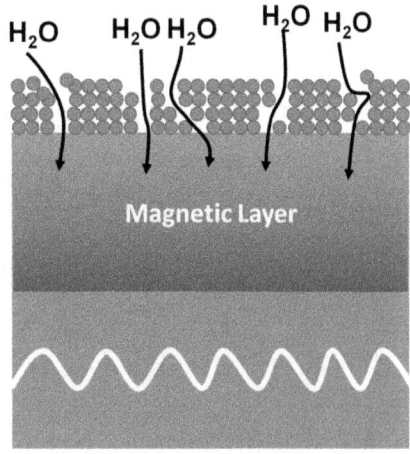

(a) Densely packed overcoat structure

(b) Overcoat structure with pin holes

Figure 9.3. Schematic diagram showing media overcoat that is (a) continuous, densely packed, and pinhole free, and (b) porous and full of pinholes.

take place, and the formation of corrosion products such as $Co(OH)_2$ particles on the surface will in turn cause crashing of the head onto the HD media. When such a crash occurs, important data that were stored in the HD can be lost, and the HDD may become unusable. To effectively suppress the onset of media corrosion, either of the conditions stated above has to be substantially suppressed [3]. Hence, with the use of an HD media overcoat that is continuous, densely packed, and free of pinholes, environmental agents will not be able to come in contact with the recording layer, which means that the redox reaction (one of the conditions for corrosion) will cease to occur, and corrosion of the recording layer will be prevented (see Fig. 9.3a).

Another property that is expected from a good HD media overcoat is the ability to bond well with the lubricant and be chemically inert. As discussed in Chapter 8, the lubricant is used to protect the HD media against wear, reduce friction, and provide additional corrosion protection. In an ideal situation, a monolayer of the lubricant molecules is bonded tightly onto the HD media overcoat, and the rest of the molecules are free to flow to fill voids between the lubricated and nonlubricated HD surface or located at the top of the lubricant, resulting in a "carpet" of lubricant molecules. Hence, if the HD media overcoat and the lubricant used are not compatible, the lubricant will not be able to bond tightly with the HD media overcoat, and it may not be able to fully cover the surface of the HD media overcoat. As a result, the wear prevention, friction reduction, and additional corrosion protection properties of the lubricant will be compromised. In addition, the HD media overcoat has to be chemically inert so that it will not react with other materials, which sometimes form products that may be detrimental to the HD media (such as those causing corrosion). This may also lead to wear and

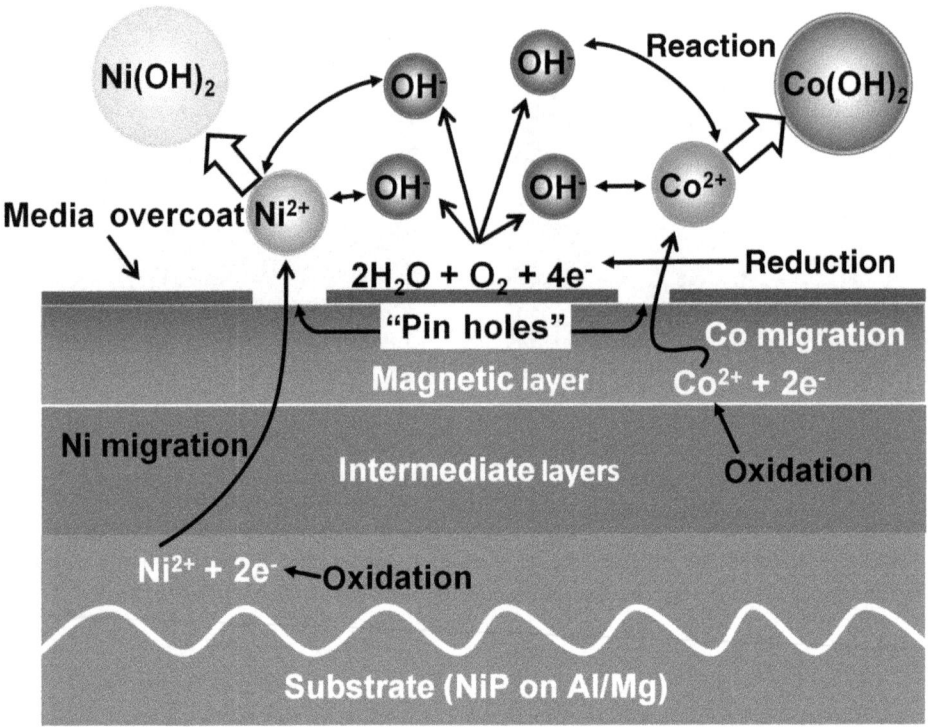

Figure 9.4. Schematic diagram showing the corrosion mechanism and the chemical equation of the reduction/oxidation reaction. (Note: Co migration is predominant at the earlier stage of corrosion, and Ni migration is predominant at the later stage of corrosion.)

corrosion of the HD media, which may eventually cause crashing of the HDD. This will be highlighted in detail in a later section.

The roughness of surface of the media overcoat is also an important consideration because it is closely linked to the coverage of the film; the other source of pinholes in a film is extrinsic particulates. Roughness may be attributed to the probability distribution of film thickness across the film surface (R(r)). Hence, in an analysis, if the measured R(r) value exceeds the mean film thickness, h, giving a negative h–R(r) at position r, it means that the position correspond to a hole. An actual pinhole will result if this hole exists over a large enough area. In order to have good coverage, one main criterion to meet in terms of roughness is that the expression h–R remain significantly in the positive range. This condition has to be met even as h decreases, as required in the case of ultrahigh-density recording. Thin-film growth obeys certain mathematical laws of fractal growth, such that the roughness varies as the power law with mean film thickness [2, 4–7]:

$$R \propto h^{\beta},\tag{9.1}$$

where β is a fundamental parameter describing the growth process. For random, ballistic deposition or "hit and stick," $\beta = 0.5$. Diffusion without island formation gives $\beta = 0.25$ or less. A low value of β favors a smooth film formation without pinholes. In addition, a smooth surface will ensure that the head will be able to fly over the HD media without hitting any protrusions or any uneven surfaces. The HD media overcoat must also be particle and asperity free so that head will be able to fly over the HD media unhindered because if the head hits a particle while flying over an HD medium, scratching of the medium may occur, and sometimes crashing of the HDD may also result.

Wear resistance is also another factor to consider. A well-engineered HD media overcoat must possess reasonable hardness, low friction, and sufficiently high elasticity. The HD media overcoat must have enough hardness to withstand accidental head–disk contact, so that the recording layer and the layers beneath will not be damaged as a result of such contact. With a low friction, the HD media overcoat (usually aided with suitable lubricant) allows smooth gliding of the slider. The HD media overcoat must also have sufficiently high elasticity to minimize the generation of debris during accidental head–disk contact; which would otherwise be generated if an inelastic (brittle) HD media overcoat is used. An HD media overcoat with poor wear resistance will certainly be damaged (needless to mention the other layers under the media overcoat) during accidental head–disk contact, and debris will be generated that will affect the smooth flying of the head and eventually lead to the crashing of the entire HDD.

Another important side effect arises dominantly from the deposition process rather than from a property inherent in the media overcoat itself; this is magnetic layer poisoning, which may happen as a result of high energy collisions. This means that during deposition of the HD media overcoat, the selected techniques or the parameters (e.g., power and applied bias) used during the deposition of the overcoat have to be carefully optimized such that impinging ion particles will not be so energetic that some of them are implanted into the recording layer (Fig. 9.5). Such implantation leads to the

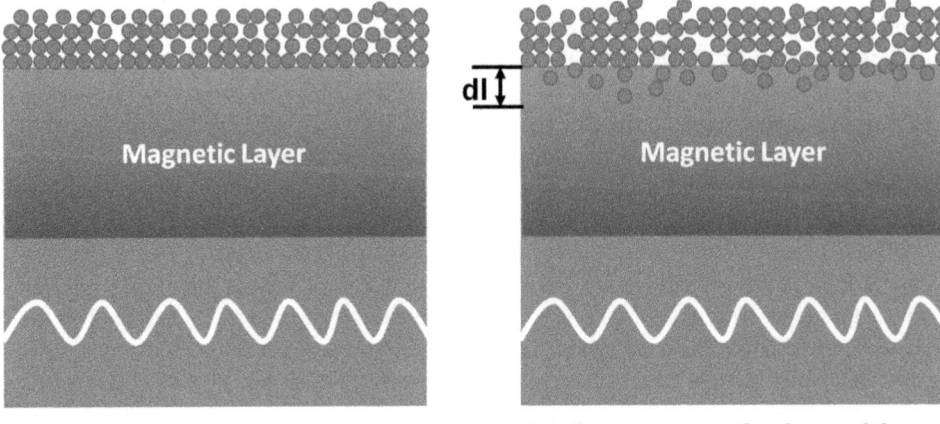

(a) Minimum impingement   **(b) Overenergetic deposition**

Figure 9.5. Schematic diagram showing (a) ideal deposition conditions, and (b) extremely high energetic deposition conditions.

formation of a dead layer (DL) in the affected part of the recording layer that is degraded magnetically or is nonmagnetic. Table 9.1 below summarizes the desired properties.

9.4   EVOLUTION OF THE MEDIA OVERCOAT

As mentioned earlier, the HD media overcoat has seen many changes since the introduction of the first HDD in mid-1950s. In the early days, HD media overcoats were deposited by spin-coating silicon oxide (SiO_2) onto the HD media surface. Later, with the introduction of PVD, such as sputtering, spin-coating the HD media overcoat was phased out. Although the deposition of HD media overcoats had changed, SiO_2 [8] continued to be an HD media overcoat material together with emerging materials at that time, such as zirconia (ZrO_2) [9, 10], yttria (partially) stabilized zirconia (ZrO_2–Y_2O_3), and carbon. But due to defects formed during deposition (such as sputter debris, arc marks, or spits), oxide compounds became less attractive as HD overcoat materials [10].

With increases in the recording density, continuous reduction of the thickness of the HD media overcoat became essential. This in turn made carbon the material of choice for HD media overcoating. For the past three decades, amorphous carbon, usually in the form of pure DLC, nitrogenated carbon (a-C:N) or hydrogenated carbon (a-C:H) films deposited by sputtering is used for coating in the magnetic recording industry. This is because amorphous carbon has unique mechanical, physical, and chemical properties. The amorphous carbon is able to act as a natural corrosion barrier for magnetic media due to its chemical inertness, lack of grain boundaries, and excellent topographical conformity. In addition, it is extremely smooth and continuous, with a surface roughness well below 1 nm. Hence, up until recently amorphous carbon remained as the main media (or head) overcoat material. But as areal density approaches 1 Tb/in.^{2}, given a magnetic spacing of 6.5 nm, the expected thickness of the amorphous carbon is 1 nm. Therefore, fabricating amorphous carbon films that are well covered with a minimum of pinholes or none may be very challenging with present sputtering technology. It was reported by Gui [3] that the thickness of the film with pinhole-free coverage is limited by its porosity; hence, if carbon atoms were laid down in a truly random fashion in accordance to Poisson's distribution, a 1-nm carbon film would leave almost 2% of surface area uncovered by any carbon atoms, and it is through these atomic channels, or pinholes that corrosion attack could initiate and propagate. In response to this problem, many researchers have been working on improving techniques to deposit amorphous carbon films, with the hope of being able to find ways to deposit thinner, pinhole-free amorphous carbon films. On the other hand, improving deposition techniques is not the only solution to the problem of depositing ultrathin amorphous carbon films that are free of pinholes. Some researchers have attempted to find alternative materials, such as silicon nitride (SiN_x) [11, 12], that are similar to or have even better properties than amorphous carbon. These will be discussed in the later section.

9.5 DLC FOR MEDIA OVERCOAT

DLC is considered a type of amorphous carbon (a-C), also known as tetrahedral amorphous carbon (ta-C). It consists of a high concentration of sp^3 hybridized carbon atoms. Amorphous carbon also consists of several types of others types of carbon. When a-C is hydrogenated or nitrogenated it is known as hydrogenated amorphous carbon (a-C:H) or nitrogenated amorphous carbon (a-C:N).

In magnetic recording, a-C is widely used as an overcoat material. The types of bonding in a-C give it versatility and its other physical properties (such as mechanical and structural properties). Such properties are strongly dependent on the ratio of the sp^2 (graphite-like) and sp^3 (diamond-like) bonds in the a-C film. In general, it is possible to have a mixture of sp^3, sp^2, and to some extent sp^1 sites in an a-C film. In addition, incorporation of hydrogen and nitrogen during the deposition process of a-C is also adopted in the fabrication of HD media to prevent corrosion of the magnetic layer, enhance the mechanical hardness of the media overcoat, and improve the adhesion of the lubricant to the media overcoat.

As mentioned earlier, the DLC is a form of a-C that contains a significant amount of sp^3 hybridized carbon in which the carbon atoms are bonded via a sigma (σ) or single bond. Sometimes hydrogen may also be incorporated in DLC to yield hydrogenated amorphous carbon a-C:H. The phase diagram of a-C shown in Figure 9.6a is one of the best ways to represent the composition of DLC. The fraction of sp^3 bonding in a-C may vary from almost 0% (as with graphitic carbon) to around 90% (as with tetrahedral carbon [ta-C]). On the other hand, the hydrogen content may vary from 0% to about 60%. A hydrogen content of greater than 60% will render the film polymeric, and with an excessive amount of hydrogen, a carbon film will not be able to form.

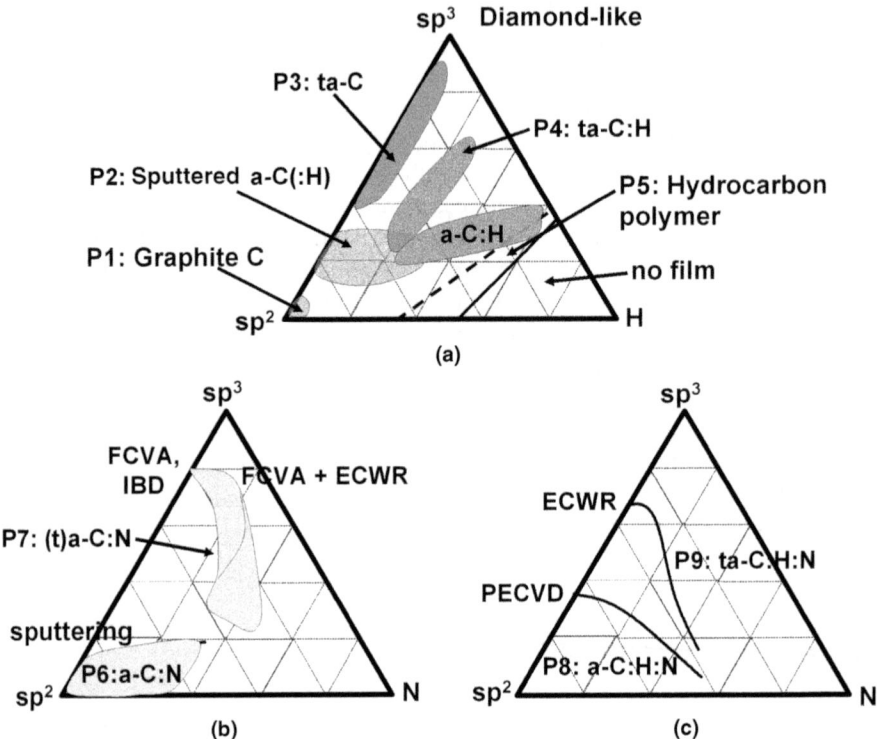

Figure 9.6. ternary phase diagram of amorphous carbon. The three corners correspond to diamond, graphite, and hydrocarbons, respectively. Ternary phase diagrams of amorphous carbon nitride alloys, without hydrogen (b) or with hydrogen (c), showing sp C, sp C, and N. (Adapted from Reference 2.)

The commonly used direct current (DC) or radio-frequency (RF) magnetron sputtered a-C is mainly made up of sp^2 bonded carbon atoms and about 20–30% sp^3 bonded carbon atoms (see Fig. 9.6a). In sputter deposition of a-C:H, the role of hydrogen is to increase the fraction of sp^3 C–C bonding. It is important to note that through the addition of hydrogen, the amount of C–H (the carbon is also sp^3 hybridized) also increases, but only the C–C bonding is the main contributor to the hardness or elastic modulus of the deposited film. Hence, if excess hydrogen is incorporated, resulting in the formation of a larger amount of C–H bonding than C–C bonding, the sputter-deposited film will become "softer." The density and hardness of a-C:H film will pass through a maximum as a function of hydrogen content. It has to be noted that plasma-enhanced chemical vapor deposition (PECVD) using hydrocarbons (such as toluene as precursor) has been increasingly used to deposit a-C:H instead of sputter deposition owing to the ability of PECVD to fabricate denser film with a higher sp^3 content as it is able to generate a higher amount of high-energy ionized species.

As mentioned earlier, tetrahedral a-C (ta-C) is also a form of DLC that has a very high sp^3 content of 80–90% (see Fig. 9.6a), and the hydrogenated form is ta-C:H. The fabrication of such films with very high sp^3 content requires high-energy deposition techniques such as filtered cathodic vacuum arc (FCVA) for ta-C and PECVD for ta-C:H. Although several research groups have highlighted that the role of the DLC is to provide mechanical protection for the HD media; there is no correlation between the mechanical properties of DLC and the density and coverage. In fact, it was found that the optimum hydrogen content for ta-C:H for a good HD media overcoat is greater than the amount of hydrogen that yields maximum hardness. It was suggested by Robertson et al. [6] that the optimum hydrogen content may arise because a slightly hydrogen-rich surface is preferred when working with lubricant. In addition, there is also no correlation between the density and hardness (which is dependent on the sp^3 C–C content) of the film. Hence, Robertson et al. [6], further suggested that the primary role of the carbon film is to be continuous. This is to prevent corrosion of the media and also to act as a barrier for the Co-based magnetic layer against the environment.

Another form of carbon that is commonly used by many HD media manufacturing companies is nitrogenated a-C (a-C:N). Like a-C and a-C:H, a-C:N may also be classified into four types: (1) a-C:N with 80–100% sp^2 and 0–20% sp^3 bonding, usually produced by reactive sputtering of graphite in an Ar/N_2 gas mixture; (2) ta-C:N with a very high sp^3 content, usually produced using the FCVA technique; (3) a-C:H:N with moderately high sp^3 content, usually produced by plasma deposition, such as PECVD; and (4) ta-C:H:N with higher sp^3 content and lower hydrogen content, usually produced by a higher plasma density source like electron cyclotron wave resonance (ECWR). The above is shown in the ternary phase diagrams in Figure 9.6b,c.

In particular, attention should be paid to the commonly used DC- or RF-magnetron sputtered a-C:N in HD media. Such a-C:N films have a high content of sp^2 hybridized carbon atoms. However, when a-C:N films are deposited at around 200°C, they are found to have increased mechanical hardness and large elastic recovery [2] with an increase in density. This is due to the increase in strong cross-linkages or bonds forming between the graphite planes within the internal structure of a-C:N. Hence, unlike the increase in sp^3 content (as in Fig. 9.6b), which usually improves the mechanical hardness and large elastic recovery in a-C and a-C:H, the increase in disorder contributes to this phenomenon in a-C:N films. This is exploited in the fabrication of HD media as a mechanically strong a-C:N overcoat may be fabricated at a temperature that will not affect the magnetic properties of the media (max. about 200°C). On the other hand, if N is incorporated into carbon with high sp^3 content, the opposite effect will result (i.e., a reduction in mechanical hardness).

As shown in Figure 9.7a, when H atoms are incorporated into two graphitic sheets with sp^2 bonding, the reaction is merely an addition of H atoms into the π (C=C) bonds, forming C–C and C–H bonds. As mentioned earlier, it is the formation of more C–C bonds that result in the increase in mechanical hardness. On the other hand, an N atom, having five valence electrons, has one more valence electron than a C atom, which has four valance electrons. Hence, the addition of N will result in forming species such as R-C≡N, R_3N, or incorporating itself into the aromatic rings that make up the graphitic sheets, similar to that of the pyridine, as shown in Figure 9.7b. In such case, the substitution of the C atoms with an N atom will result in the cleavage of the π (C=C) bonds, leaving an unpaired π electron (•) on the adjacent C atom and a filled π orbital

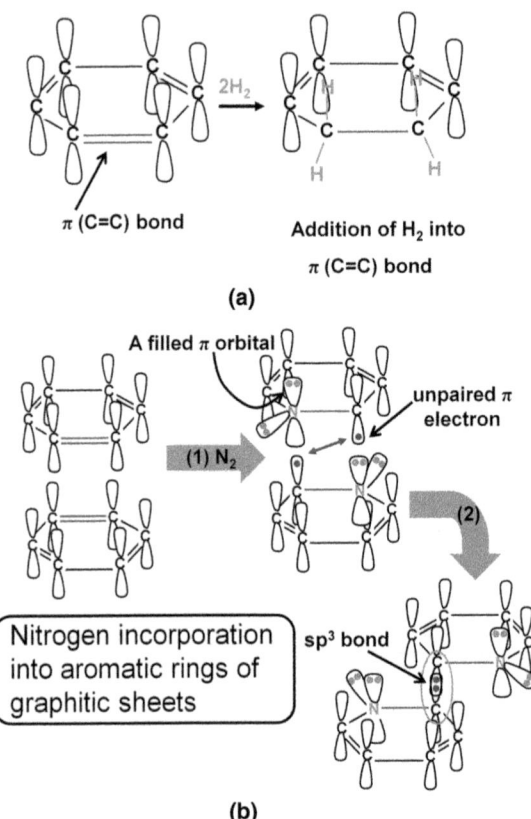

Figure 9.7. Schematic diagrams comparing the bonding changes when (a) hydrogen and (b) nitrogen is introduced into a C–C bond.

($\bullet\bullet$) on the N atom (see Fig. 9.7b). Subsequently, two such Cs on adjacent graphitic layers may join to form a C–C bond between the layers, resulting in the creation of an sp^3 bond. This process results in an increase in mechanical hardness, larger elastic recovery, and higher density. In addition, this incorporation of N also increases the disorder (through more cross-linkages between the aromatic rings within the graphitic planes) which contributes significantly more to the improvement of mechanical properties on top of the increase in sp^3 content. In contrast, the addition of N into C with a high sp^3 content (e.g., ta-C) will only promote sp^2 bonding and clustering of sp^2 sites, resulting in a reduction in mechanical hardness, smaller elastic recovery, and lower density.

Typical HD media does not rely on a single a-C:H or a-C:N layer but on a dual-layer design that has an a-C:H layer closer to the magnetic layer and an a-C:N layer closer to the lubricant. The a-C:H layer helps in providing the coverage needed to protect the media from corrosion. In a dual-layer carbon overcoat system, a-C:N- is used for its advantages related to the overcoat/lubricant interaction and as a barrier between the lubricant and the a-C:H overcoat layer (above the magnetic layer). Under stressful conditions introduced by head–disk contact, the perfluoro-polyether (Z-DOL —HO–CH$_2$–CF$_2$–O–[–CF$_2$–CF$_2$–O–]$_m$–[–CF$_2$–O–]$_n$–CF$_2$–CH$_2$–OH) lubricant molecules tend to degrade with the emission of fluorine compounds, such as carbonyl difluoride (CF$_2$=O) [13] or other compounds with florocarbonyl functional groups [14], which are able to extract H from the a-C:H under localized heating (due to friction), leading to the formation of HF. As HF is an acid, it will react aggressively with the Al$_2$O$_3$ (from Al$_2$O$_3$-TiC slider material) and underlying metals in the HD media. The catalytic decomposition mechanism of Z-DOL on an Al$_2$O$_3$–TiC surface has been investigated by Chen et al. [15]. The step-by-step description of the decomposition and reaction mechanisms of Z-DOL and the overcoat is shown in Figure 9.8. In contrast, heating of a-C:N releases only N$_2$ gas upon degradation, which will not give rise to HF [2, 16]. Therefore, a-C:N is used as an interface layer for lubricant.

The decomposition and reaction mechanisms of Z-DOL and the overcoat

Step 1: Z-DOL decomposes and forms CF–O under friction stimulation while the a-C:H film degrades and produces H$_2$ gas.

$$-O-/-CF2-O-/-CF2-CF2-O-/-CF2- \rightarrow CF2=O +-CF2-CF2-O- \text{ (lubricant)}$$
$$-CH_x \rightarrow -CH_{x-2} + H_2 \text{ (media overcoat)}$$

Step 2: Complex chemical reactions of Z-DOL decomposition products occur with H$_2$ and produce HF and CF$_2$H.

Step 3: CF$_2$–O and HF react with Al$_2$O$_3$ (from Al$_2$O$_3$–TiC slider material) to produce a strong Lewis acid (electron deficient sites), AlF$_3$.

$$Al_2O_3 + 6HF \rightarrow AlF_3 + 3H_2O$$
$$Al_2O_3 + 3CF_2O \rightarrow 2AlF_3 + 3CO_2$$

Step 4: The rapid decomposition reactions along the main Z-DOL chain take place on the AlF$_3$ surface to form methoxy (CF$_3$–O–) and ethoxy (CF$_3$CF$_2$–O–) compounds, and acyl fluoride (R–CF=O).

9.6 DEPOSITION OF CARBON OVERCOATS

Earlier sections have shown that in order to increase the areal density, there must be a corresponding decrease in magnetic spacing to maintain well-defined readback signals. As the HD media overcoat is a main component of the magnetic spacing, a way to decrease the magnetic spacing is by reducing the thickness of the HD media overcoat. In general, the approaches taken by researchers to improve the HD media overcoat may be divided into two main groups. As discussed earlier, one of the approaches generally focuses on improving deposition techniques by developing new or modified techniques to fabricate thin carbon films with enhanced properties. The other approach is by concentrating efforts on looking for alternative overcoat materials.

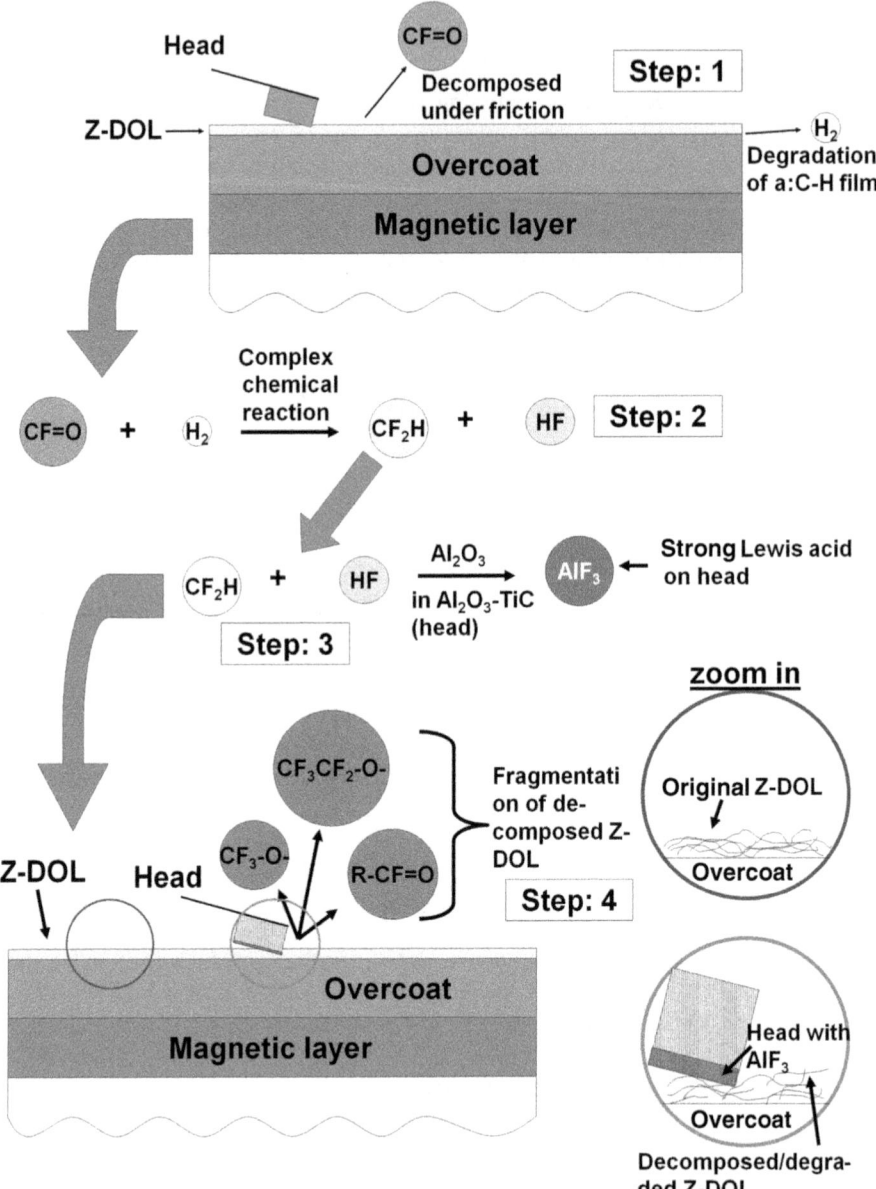

Figure 9.8. Schematic diagrams showing the decomposition and reaction mechanisms of Z-DOL and the overcoat.

In the earlier years of HDD technology, the HD media overcoat materials that were of commercial importance were not only limited to carbon but also included others of noncarbon origin, such as SiO_2 and ZrO_2 [8–10], but due to defects (such as sputter debris, arc marks, or spits) formed during deposition, they are less attractive as HD media overcoats [10]. This is why carbon has been the preferred material.

The main deposition technique used to deposit the carbon overcoat is magnetron sputtering [2, 5, 17, 18]. Magnetron sputtering methods are preferred by industry because of their versatility, high deposition rate, and the ease they offer to scale up. In addition, deposition conditions can be controlled by the plasma power, DC bias voltage, and gas pressure, and are reproducible.

The previous sections have shown that carbon overcoating has evolved from using only a- C to a-C:H to a-C:N or even a combination of two layers carbon films. Based on the above, if one is to consider only a single type of carbon media overcoat, a-C:N seems to have most of the desired properties that may render it a suitable overcoat material. However, there is a thickness limit to the beneficial properties of a-C:N films. It is found that a-C:N films below 3-nm thickness are not able to protect the magnetic layer sufficiently against corrosion [16, 18–20]. In fact, it is known that when using magnetron sputtering, both a-C:N and a-C:H cease to provide protection against corrosion and wear below 2- to 3-nm thickness. This is because in conventional magnetron sputtering, most of the species being generated are mainly neutral atoms. Hence, even if a bias is being applied to the substrate, only a small amount of charged species (ions) have the ability to accelerate toward the substrate with higher energies under the influence of the electric field. As a result of this, a small amount of high-energy ions are able to reach the substrate, and the carbon overcoat being formed will not be as dense as desired [4]. In order to form a dense overcoat, species arriving at the substrate must have sufficient energies to rearrange themselves for local relaxation, and more importantly, to penetrate the existing carbon film and fill in the holes, resulting in a much denser structure. Such subimplantation of carbon atoms also enhances the formation of sp^3 bonding due to localized high pressure, making the film more "diamond-like" [3]. For this reason, increasing attention has been devoted to developing better techniques to deposit ultrathin carbon overcoats that have uniform coverage, ability to protect against corrosion, ultrasmooth surfaces, and reasonable mechanical properties down to a thickness of 1 nm. In this connection, ion beam deposition (IBD), PECVD, electron cyclotron resonance plasma chemical vapor deposition (ECR-CVD), and FCVA have been developed as alternatives to sputtering deposition.

Although the deposition techniques mentioned above have the ability to deposit an ultrathin carbon film, they have their limitations too. These limitations have to be overcome in order to use them for HD media overcoat deposition. The following discussion will highlight some of the advantages and disadvantages of some of the techniques mentioned above.

In IBD [17], methane gas is fed through a cylindrical ion source and is ionized by energetic electrons produced by a hot-wire filament. Ionized species then pass through as grid with a bias voltage of about 50 V, where they gain high acceleration energy. The kinetic energy of the accelerated species may range from 50 eV to 500 eV. With such high kinetic energy of the approaching species, it is possible to form a carbon overcoat with good coverage and hardness. However, the drawbacks of this method are that the deposition rate is slow (about 0.1 nm/s using kinetic energy of about 50 eV) and if higher kinetic energy is used, impingement into a magnetic layer may result in the deterioration of the magnetic properties of the HD media. In addition, the use of IBD also tends to introduce defects into the HD media.

In PECVD, the hydrocarbon species are produced by the RF plasma decomposition of hydrocarbon precursors such as acetylene (C_2H_2) [21–24]. Instead of requiring thermal energy as in thermal CVD, the energetic electrons in the plasma (typically at pressures of less than 10 Pa) can activate almost any reaction among the gases in the glow discharge at relatively low substrate temperatures ranging from 100 to 600°C (typically less than 300°C). But even such temperatures may be too high for HD media application as high temperature may affect the magnetics of the recording layer. Hence, in order to use CVD in HD media fabrication, proper optimization of deposition conditions is required.

In FCVA-based coatings [6, 17, 18, 20], a vacuum arc plasma source is used to form carbon film. In this technique, energetic carbon ions are produced by a vacuum arc discharge between a planar graphite cathode (graphite disk) and a grounded anode. The plasma being generated is guided by a magnetic field that transports current between the electrodes to form tiny, rapidly moving spots on the cathode surface. The source is coupled to a 90° bent or an S-shaped magnetic filter to remove the macroparticles produced concurrently with the plasma in the cathode spots. The ion current density at the substrate is in the range of 10–50 mA cm^{-2}. The base pressure is usually less than 10^{-4} Pa. It is known that FCVA is able to produce carbon ion with kinetic energy between 100–2500 eV, which is the highest among the techniques discussed. Hence, this technique is able to deposit very dense carbon film. However, it also has a drawback which is the simultaneous production of macroparticles which will be deposited together with the other energetic species. This happens because the techniques such as the 90° bent or the "S" shaped magnetic filter are not be able to totally remove them. Since it is important for the HD media overcoat to be very smooth and be free from particles or protrusions, overcoat depositing using FCVA (which has a few macroparticles) may result in a higher possibility for HD crashes. However, further advancements and improvements are required for FCVA to be viable. Summaries of the most commonly used deposition techniques and some of the advantages and the disadvantages are shown in Tables 9.2 and 9.3.

It has also been reported that facing targets sputtering can provide energetic deposition [25, 26] to achieve denser carbon films. However, facing targets sputtering is not commonly used in the production of recording media as it is still mainly used in research and is yet to be developed with full automation, suitable for commercial application. In a recent study by Poh et al. [27], a novel hybrid facing targets sputtering (HyFTS) was proposed, and it has been indicated that this technique is able to achieve denser carbon films with good corrosion resistance and scratch resistance. Figure 9.9 shows a schematic of the magnetron arrangement in conventional DC-magnetron sputtering (CMS) and HyFTS. In the HyFTS arrangement, the magnets in the center are stronger than those at the periphery. Also, the polarities of the magnets on the two sides are opposite to each other. This arrangement results in a flow of magnetic flux from one side to the other. The magnetron is designed such that the flux is concentrated near the substrate. Because of

TABLE 9.1. Summary of the Desired Properties of an Ideal Media Overcoat (Adapted from Reference 6)

Property	Description
Corrosion protection	Chemical inertness, complete coverage (pinhole free), and high density (high cross-linkages)
Chemistry	Lubricant compatibility, stability, and low adsorption
Surface topography	Smoothness, complete coverage, and absence of particles and asperities
Wear resistance	Sufficient hardness, low friction, and high elasticity
Maintenance of magnetic layer integrity	Dead layer that is created by impinging ion particles is minimized by optimization of the deposition process parameters

this, the electrons spiral around the flux lines and create more ionization. By applying a moderate negative substrate bias between 100 V and 500 V (to minimize the heating up of the substrate due to very high energy ions approaching the surface), these ions can be made to bombard the substrate at sufficiently high energies, and therefore the film can be made dense. In contrast, the CMS is not able to produce species of high energies (only a few eV). Hence, it is not able to deposit the dense continuous carbon layer in ultrathin films that the HyFTS is capable of depositing.

9.7 EMERGING MEDIA OVERCOAT MATERIALS AND DESIGNS FOR THE FUTURE

As mentioned, another focus of some researchers to achieve thinner overcoats is to look for HD media overcoat materials other than carbon (Table 9.4). In the past, researchers have investigated the possible use of materials such as silicon oxide (SiO_2), aluminium oxide (Al_2O_3), and zirconia (ZrO_2) as possible HD media overcoat materials. In recent years, the use of silicon nitride (SiN_x) by Yen et al. [11, 12], boron carbide (B_4C) and boron carbon nitride ($B_xC_yN_z$) by Chen et al. [28], titanium carbide (TiC) by Svedberg et al. [29], and zirconia (ZrO_2) on silicon boride (SiB_x) dual-layer by Wu et al. [30] as possible HD media overcoat materials have also been proposed. Some of the more recent research in this direction will be highlighted in this chapter.

The investigations reported by Yen et al. [11, 12] showed that an RF-reactively sputtered 1.5-nm a-SiN_x overcoat not only had a lower coverage limit, but it also significantly outperformed thicker 4.5-nm a-CN_x in terms of better corrosion protection. Their investigations included the determination of pinhole defect density of the overcoat by immersing the disk in an etchant containing 3 wt% $Ce(NH_4)_2(NO_3)_6$ and 97 wt% H_2O, which is known to attack the underlying CoPtCr alloy, and employed X-ray photoelectron spectroscopy (XPS) to determine the oxidation state of the Co magnetic layer. The longer accelerated flyability test results showed that the SiN_x films had better durability. In fact, it was also reported that the 1.5-nm a-SiN_x overcoat outperformed

TABLE 9.2. Summary of Most Commonly Used Deposition Techniques, Species Generated, and Kinetic Energy of Depositing Species and Deposition Rates

Deposition Technique	Process	Species Generated	Kinetic Energy (eV)	Deposition Rate (nm s^{-1})
Filtered cathodic vacuum arc (FCVA)	Energetic carbon ions produced by a vacuum arc discharge between a graphite cathode and a grounded anode accelerated toward a substrate using bias	Ions	100–2500	0.1–1 (slow)
Ion beam deposition (IBD)	Carbon ions produced from methane gas in an ion source and accelerated toward a substrate using bias	Ions	50–500	0.1–1 (slow)
Plasma-enhanced chemical vapor deposition (PECVD)	Hydrocarbon species produced by plasma decomposition of hydrocarbon gases (e.g., acetylene) are accelerated toward a DC-biased substrate	Mainly ions	1–30	1–10 (fast)
Electron cyclotron resonance plasma chemical vapor plasma deposition (ECR-CVD)	Hydrocarbon ions produced by decomposition of ethylene gas in the presence of a plasma in electron cyclotron resonance condition are accelerated toward an RF-biased substrate	Mainly ions	1–50	1–10 (fast)
DC/RF magnetron sputtering	Sputtering of graphite target by argon ion plasma (bias may be applied to substrate)	Mainly atoms and some ions	1–10	1–10 (fast)

TABLE 9.3. Summary of Most Commonly Used Deposition Techniques and Their Advantages and Disadvantages

Deposition Technique	Advantages	Disadvantages
Magnetron sputtering	• High sputtering rate at low gas pressure • Low temperature vaporization	• Plasma confined to a small volume near sputtering target surface • Mostly neutral atoms are generated • Produces less dense film • Unable to provide sufficient activation of reactive gas near substrate for reactive deposition, or ions for bias sputtering
Ion beam deposition (IBD)	• Produces dense coatings with high ion concentrations	• Irradiation induced defects • High temperature may affect substrate and magnetics of the recording media
Chemical vapor deposition (CVD) with/ without plasma enhancement	• Process is gas phase • Uniform temperature within the coating retort • Uniform concentrations of the depositing species • Similar deposition rate on all surfaces	• Relatively high temperatures • High temperature may affect substrate and magnetics of the recording media
Filtered cathodic vacuum arc (FCVA)	• Highly ionized evaporated material • High energy (about 50 eV) species reach the substrate surface. • Produces dense carbon films	• 0.1–10 μm microdroplets emitted from arc spot • Embedded in film; creates bums and pinholes

the thicker 4.5-nm a-CN$_x$ overcoat in terms of lasting longer in the accelerated flyability test. Yen et al. attributed the improvement in performance in part to the high hardness of SiN$_x$.

Boron carbide (B$_4$C) and boron carbon nitride (B$_x$C$_y$N$_z$) deposited by DC-magnetron sputtering were two possible materials that were suggested by Chen et al. [28]. They found, under the conditions specified in their article, that B$_4$C has a greater hardness (about 30 GPa) than B$_x$C$_y$N$_z$ (20 GPa). They also reported that given suitable substrate tilt (45°), rotation (20 rpm), and high frequency pulsed bias (−100 V), B$_x$C$_y$N$_z$ of less than 10 nm is smoother and provides better corrosion protection than B$_4$C and CN$_x$ of equivalent thickness. They concluded that the use of B$_x$C$_y$N$_z$ is quite promising and should be further explored.

Wu et al. [30] suggested in a patent the use of an 8 Å silicon boride (SiB$_x$; where $3 \leq x \leq 6$) as an intermediate layer with a 4 Å zirconia (ZrO$_2$) protective layer on top.

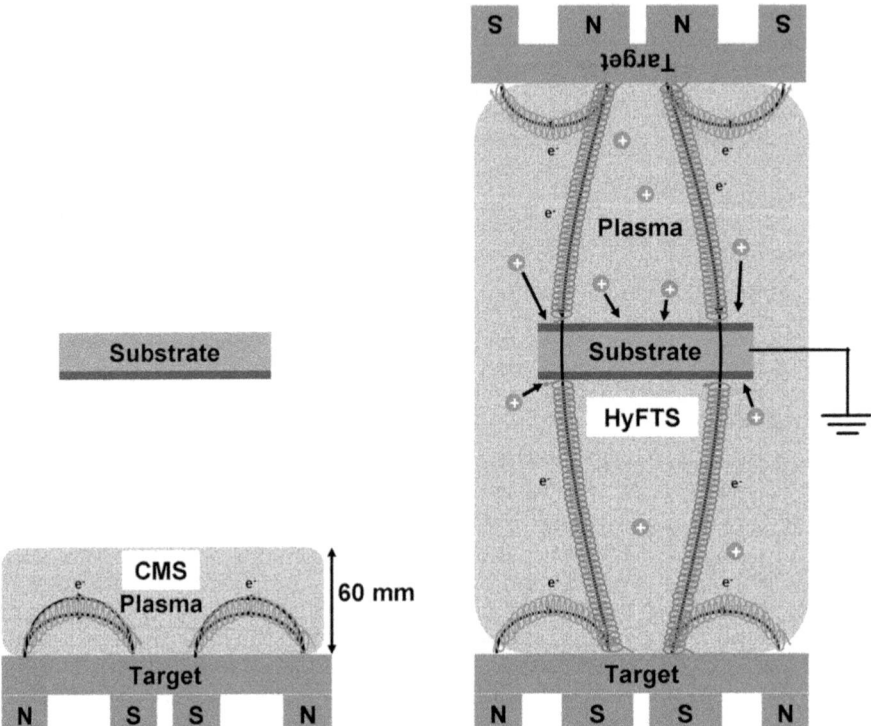

<u>Figure 9.9.</u> Schematic diagrams showing conventional magnetron sputtering (CMS) (left) and hybrid facing targets sputtering (HyFTS) (right) arrangement. (Adapted from Reference 5.)

These two layers were deposited by DC-magnetron sputtering. In this patent, they claimed that with a total thickness of 12 Å, the SiB_x/ZrO_2 dual layer was able to protect the Co-based magnetic layer from corrosion after four days of high temperature/high humidity treatment at 80°C and 80% humidity. To verify this claim, they used XPS analysis to determine the oxidation state of the Co $2p_{3/2}$ peak, which showed no sign of oxidation before and after the high temperature/high humidity treatment.

Other than using purely new materials, some researchers have also suggested the use of an intermediate layer (made of a new material) between the magnetic layer and the carbon protective layer. Such layers were also known as flash layers, capping layers, sealing layers [31], corrosion barrier layers [32], or simply interlayers [33]. The combined use of the intermediate and the carbon layer improves corrosion reliability of the ultrathin carbon overcoat while retaining good wear protection. More recent examples of materials used for the intermediate layer are refractory metals and their alloys in their metallic oxide or nitride forms, such as an Ru/carbon combination and Cr, Mo, CrMo, CrW/carbon combinations such as reported by Thangaraj et al. [31, 32], and an Ni_xSi_y composite reported by Yang et al. [33].

TABLE 9.4. Summary of Possible Overcoat Materials and Their Deposition Techniques

Media Overcoat Material	Deposition Techniques	Reference
Using material as media overcoat		
Amorphous carbon: diamond-like-carbon (DLC), or tetrahedral carbon/hydrogenated carbon/nitrogenated carbon	• DC or RF magnetron sputtering • Chemical vapor deposition (CVD) w/o plasma enhanced (PE) • Ion beam deposition (IBD) • Filtered cathodic vacuum arc (FCVA) • Hybrid facing targets sputtering (HyFTS) • Facing targets sputtering (FTS)	[2, 5, 16–27]
-a-C, ta-C, a-C:H_x, ta-C:H, a-C:N_x, ta-C:N, a-C:N:H, ta-C:N:H		
Boron carbide (B_4C) and boron carbon nitride ($B_xC_yN_z$)	• Pulsed DC magnetron Sputtering	[28]
Silicon nitride (SiN_x)	• RF reactive sputtering • Chemical vapor deposition (CVD) w/o plasma enhancement (PE)	[11, 12]
Silicon boride (SiB_x) on zirconia oxide (ZrO_2)	• DC magnetron sputtering	[30]
Silicon oxide (SiO_2)	• RF magnetron sputtering • Spin coating	[8]
Titanium carbide (TiC)	• RF Sputtering	[29]
Zirconia (ZrO_2)	• RF magnetron sputtering	[9, 10]
Using interlayers between the magnetic layer and the carbon overcoat		
Carbon/refractory metal or their alloys and its oxides or nitrides	• DC or RF magnetron sputtering • Chemical vapor deposition (CVD) w/o plasma enhanced (PE)	[31, 32]
Carbon/Ni_xSi_y	• DC magnetron sputtering	[33]

In an article by Yang et al. [33], it was reported that samples using a DC-magnetron sputtered C:N/Ni_xSi_y overcoat layer as thin as 50 Å (C:N [10 Å] and Ni_xSi_y [40 Å]) is more effective at resisting corrosion than those using an C:N/a-C overcoat of equivalent thickness when they were subjected to an accelerated corrosion test at 80°C and 80% humidity for 24 hours, and 60°C and 80% humidity for 96 hours. They further demonstrated that the samples using 50 Å C:N/Ni_xSi_y were as durable as those using 50 Å C:N/a-C through a hot/dry contact-start-stop (CSS) test carried out for 50,000 CSS cycles, which resulted in no visible disk wear in either type of sample. These observations were attributed to a layer of nonstoichiometric silicon nitride formed at the C:N/Ni_xSi_y interface in the form of Si_xN_y or C_xSi_yN where the carbon layer covers, and in the form of Si_xN_y where the pores are. The strong bonding at the interface of C:N/Ni_xSi_y provides improved wear and corrosion reliability for magnetic HD media.

On the other hand, Thangaraj et al. [31, 32] suggested the use of refractory metals and their alloys in their metallic, oxide, or nitride forms as the intermediate layer. They had demonstrated using the potentiostatic polarization technique that the use of CrMo and CrW [31], and also Cr, Ru, Pd, and Pt (in particular Ru) [32] of less than 10 Å below a carbon protective overcoat of 50 Å or less is able to provide sufficient corrosion protection to the magnetic recording medium. It was claimed in both patents that the films may be deposited by using DC- or RF-magnetron sputtering, or PECVD.

However, the work on B_4C [28], $B_xC_yN_z$ [28], and $C:N/Ni_xSi_y$ [33], and the use of refractory metals and their alloys in their metallic, oxide, or nitride forms as the intermediate layer [31, 32] may not be suitable for use with today's ultrahigh-density recording media as such media would require overcoats in the sub-3-nm range. Hence, efforts have been focused on the more promising materials and deposition techniques, or to finding other possible solutions that have the potential to fabricate ultrathin media overcoats.

In order to give a more comprehensive overview of possible ways to reduce the thickness of media overcoats, it is also important to mention some of the very recent novel approaches. One is the use of low molecular weight molecules that are inert and hydrophobic in nature to seal pinholes in carbon overcoats by UV irradiation [34], and the other is the use of a hybrid magnetic overcoat (Hy-MOC), which makes it possible to reduce the magnetic spacing by using a magnetic overcoat (MOC) below an ultrathin carbon layer [35, 36].

Liu et al. [34] reported in a patent that they were able to improve the corrosion protection ability of carbon overcoats by the use of low molecular weight molecules that are inert and hydrophobic in nature to seal the pinholes in carbon overcoats by UV irradiation. Such chemicals may be in the family of perfluoropolyethers, fluoroethers, chlorofluoroalkanes, and chlorofluoroethers. It was suggested that by using UV irradiation in an inert hydrophobic chemical environment, moisture on the surface and the channels of the carbon overcoat may be removed. The surface is rejuvenated by the replacement of the moisture in pinholes in the carbon overcoat with inert and hydrophobic low molecular weight molecules, sealing it against moisture penetration through to the magnetic layer (which is a cause of corrosion onset in HD media). In addition, it was also reported that Z-DOL lubricated samples treated with such a process have a larger water contact angle than those that are not treated by it.

Another deviation from some of the more common approaches previously mentioned is the proposal of the magnetic overcoat [37], which utilizes an oxide-based material for the overcoat. But this solely oxide-based magnetic overcoat has a limitation, which is that the oxide material is not compatible with the presently used lubricants. Although finding lubricants for oxide-based magnetic overcoats is a solution, a simpler but effective approach that does not involve too many changes in the existing processes in recording media is more desirable.

With the above consideration, Poh et al. [35, 36] proposed a novel Hy-MOC containing two layers with different purposes. Schematic diagrams comparing the media with a 3-nm overcoat to that with the Hy-MOC is depicted in Figure 9.10. As can be seen from Figure 9.10b, the Hy-MOC is a dual-layer overcoat consisting of an ultrathin amorphous carbon overcoat (1 nm) at the top and a magnetic overcoat at the bottom.

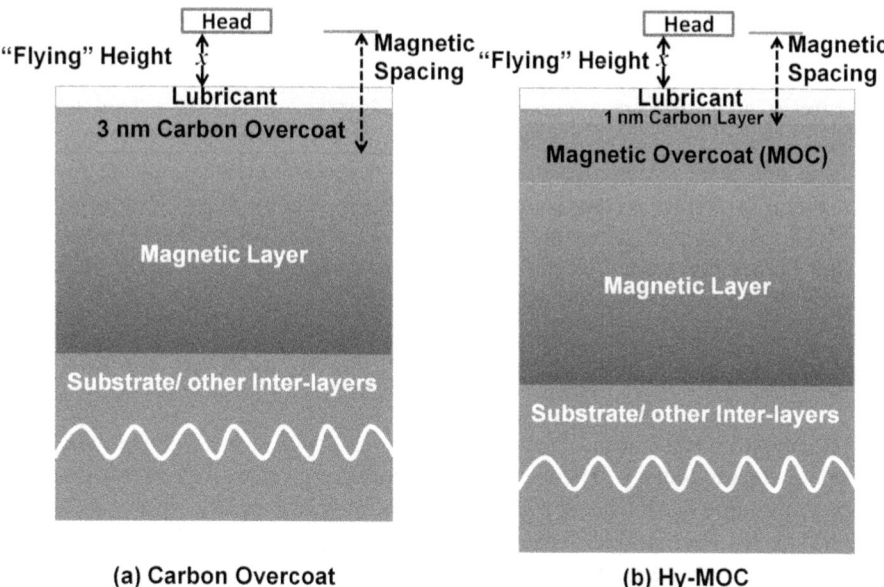

Figure 9.10. Schematic diagrams of the structures of media with (a) carbon overcoat and (b) hybrid magnetic overcoat (Hy-MOC). (Adapted from Reference 35.)

Like the conventional carbon overcoat, the Hy-MOC system must have the desired properties as stated earlier. In addition, being an Hy-MOC system, having magnetic properties is a primary requirement. Hence, it is appropriate to discuss the functions of each layer that constitutes the Hy-MOC system here.

The purpose of the MOC is to provide both corrosion protection and mechanical properties. At the same time, the MOC should have permeability as high as that of the recording layer in order to reduce the magnetic spacing. It should also couple with the magnetic layer without degrading the magnetic properties of the HD media. In addition, it should not affect the microstructure of the recording layer, as the signal-to-noise ratio (SNR) of the media is determined by factors such as grain size and grain-size distributions.

On the other hand, the main function of ultrathin carbon is to provide a good overcoat–lubricant interaction. The ultrathin carbon may also act as a reinforcement for corrosion protection and enhancement of the mechanical properties of the whole Hy-MOC system.

As shown in Figure 9.10, the magnetic spacing is the distance between the magnetic layer and the head. At a given flying height of x nm and a constant lubricant thickness, the magnetic spacing for the Hy-MOC media (Fig. 9.10b) is greatly reduced as a result of using a 4-nm MOC; but the magnetic spacing for the conventional carbon overcoat media (Fig. 9.10a) is comparatively larger although it is using a typical overcoat thickness of about 3 nm. This is because the MOC forms a corrosion barrier with the advantage that it still contributes magnetically. Therefore, improved performance (e.g. better readback signal in ultrahigh-density recording HD media) is expected in the media with a dual overcoat.

Investigation shows that samples using the Hy-MOC system have good corrosion protection ability, and although magnetic in nature, the Hy-MOC couples to the recording layer and does not interfere with the good magnetic properties of the recording layer. It may be further postulated that with the use of suitable magnetic material(s) for the MOC together with a compatible lubricant(s), it will be possible to remove the ultrathin carbon layer, and the lubricant(s) may be coated directly onto the MOC, thus reducing the magnetic spacing further.

9.8 SUMMARY

The evolution of HD media overcoats and various deposition techniques were highlighted. In order to prolong the use of DLC overcoats, researchers have been looking into various deposition techniques to improve the protectiveness of DLC overcoats at ultrathin thicknesses. An example of some of the more promising deposition techniques that are compatible with today's HD media manufacturing are facing targets sputtering (FTS) and the newly developed HyFTS. However, some of the recent works on the use of other possible materials, such as SiN_x, have also been intensively researched. The novel concept of the Hy-MOC is also a prospective overcoat candidate for use in ultrahigh-density HD media. In addition, it may be possible to remove the ultrathin carbon layer in the Hy-MOC if suitable magnetic material is used for the MOC, and this concept may be further applied to future 10-Tb/in.^{2} extreme high-density HD media.

REFERENCES

1. R. Wood, Future hard disk drive systems. J. Magn. Magn. Mater. **321**, 555 (2009).
2. A. C. Ferrari, Diamond-like carbon for magnetic storage disks. Surf. Coat. Technol. **180–181**, 190 (2004).
3. J. Gui, Tribology challenges for head–disk interface toward 1 Tb/in^2. IEEE Trans. Magn. **39**(2), 716 (2003).
4. S. S. Das and P. Tamborenea, A new universality class for kinetic growth: one-dimensional molecular-beam epitaxy. Phys. Rev. Lett. **66**(3), 325 (1991).
5. J. Robertson, Amorphous carbon. Adv. Phys. **35**, 317 (1986).
6. J. Robertson, Requirements of ultrathin carbon coating for magnetic storage technology. Tribol. Int. **36**, 405 (2003).
7. A.-L. Barabasi and H. E. Stanley, *Fractal Concepts in Surface Growth*. New York: Cambridge University Press, 1995.
8. M. Yanagisawa, Tribological properties of spin-coated SiO_2 film on plated magnetic recording disks. Tribol. Mech. Magn. Storage Syst. I **SP-19**, 21–26 (1985).
9. T. Yamashita, G. T. Chen, J. Shir, and T. Chen, Sputtered ZrO_2 overcoats with superior corrosion protection and mechanical performance in thin film rigid disk application. IEEE Trans. Magn. **24**(6), 2629 (1988).

10. K. J. Schulz and K. V. Viswanathan, A comparison of film structure and surface chemistry of carbon and oxide disk overcoats. IEEE Trans. Magn. **27**(6), 5166 (1991).

11. B. K. Yen, R. L. White, R. J. Waltman, C. M. Mate, Y. Sonobe, and B. Marchon, Coverage and properties of a-SiN$_x$ hard disk overcoat. J. Appl. Phys. **93**, 8704 (2003).

12. B. K. Yen, R. L. White, R. J. Waltman, Q. Dai, D. C. Miller, A. J. Kellock, B. Marchon, P. H. Kasai, M. F. Toney, B. R. York, H. Deng, Q. F. Xiao, and V. Raman, Microstructure and properties of ultrathin amorphous silicon nitride protective coating. J. Vac. Sci. Technol. A **21**(6), 1895 (2003).

13. B. B. Baker and D. J. Kasprzak, Thermal degradation of commercial fluoropolymers in air. Polym. Degrad. Stab. **42**, 181 (1993).

14. P. H. Kasai, Perfluoropolyethers: intramolecular disproportionation. Macromolecules **25**(25), 6791 (1992).

15. C. Y. Chen, W. Fong, D. B. Bogy, and C. S. Bhatia, Initiation of lubricant catalytic decomposition by hydrogen evolution from contact sliding on CHx and CNx overcoats. Tribol. Lett. **8**, 25 (2000).

16. B. Tomcik, S. C. Seng, B. Balakrishnan, and J. Y. Lee, Electrochemical tests on the carbon protective layer of a hard disk. Diamond Relat. Mater. **11**, 1409 (2002).

17. A. K. Menon, Interface tribology for 100 Gb/in^2. Tribol. Int. **33**, 299 (2000).

18. P. Bernhard, C. Ziethen, R. Ohr, H. Hilgers, and G. Schönhense, Investigations of the corrosion protection of ultrathin a-C and a-C:N overcoats for magnetic storage devices. Surf. Coat. Technol. **180–181**, 621 (2004).

19. R. Ohr, B. Jacoby, M. V. Gradowski, C. Schug, and H. Hilgers, Analytical and functional characterization of ultrathin carbon coatings for future magnetic storage devices. Surf. Coat. Technol. **173**, 111 (2003).

20. C. Casiraghi, A. C. Ferrari, J. Robertson, R. Ohr, M. V. Gradowski, D. Schneider, and H. Hilgers, Ultra-thin carbon layer for high density magnetic storage devices. Diamond Relat. Mater. **13**, 1480 (2004).

21. L. Holland and S. M. Ojha, Deposition of hard and insulating carbonaceous films of an rf target in butane plasma. Thin Solid Films **38**, L17 (1976).

22. L. P. Andersson, A review of recent work on hard i-C films. Thin Solid Films **86**, 193 (1981).

23. A. Bubenzer, B. Dischler, G. Brandt, and P. Koidl, R.F. plasma deposited amorphous hydrogenated hard carbon thin films, preparation, properties and applications. J. Appl. Phys. **54**, 4590 (1983).

24. A. Grill, B. S. Meyerson, and V. V. Patel, Diamond-like carbon films by rf plasma-assisted chemical vapor depostion from acetylene. IBM J. Res. Dev. **34**, 849 (1990).

25. J. R. Shi and J. P. Wang, Diamond-like carbon films prepared by facing-target sputtering. Thin Solid Films **420**, 172 (2002).

26. J. R. Shi, Y. J. Xu, and J. Zhang, Corrosion resistance of nitrogenated amorphous carbon films prepared by facing target sputtering. Surf. Coat. Technol. **198**, 437 (2005).

27. W. C. Poh, S. N. Piramanayagam, J. R. Shi, and T. Liew, Novel hybrid facing target sputtered amorphous carbon overcoat for ultra-high density hard disk media. Diamond Relat. Mater. **16**(2), 379 (2007).

28. Y. F. Chen, Y. W. Chung, and S. Y. Li, Boron carbide and boron carbonitride thin films as protective coatings in ultra-high density hard disk drives. Surf. Coat. Technol. **200**(12–13), 4072 (2006).

29. E. B. Svedberg and N. Shukla, Adsorption of water on lubricated and non lubricated TiC surfaces for data storage applications. Tribol. Lett. **17**(4), 947 (2004).

30. M. Wu, J. K. Howard, and P. M. Jones, Protective overcoat materials. United States Patent Application US 2003/0228497 A1 (2003).

31. R. Thangaraj, K. Chour, X. Ma, H. Tang, and J. Gui, Component of a magnetic recording medium with sealing layer for corrosion protection. United States Patent US 6660413 B1 (2003).

32. R. Thangaraj, C. F. Brucker, H. Tang, J. Gui, and G. Rauch, Magnetic recording media with Ru corrosion barrier layer. United States Patent US 6680106 B1 (2004).

33. M. M. Yang, D. Spaulding, J. L. Chao, and M. A. Russak, Use of Ni_xSi_y as an interlayer for wear and corrosion resistance. IEEE Trans. Magn. **36**(5), 2702 (2000).

34. J. Liu, M. J. Stirniman, and L. Wang, System and method for improving corrosion resistance of magnetic media. United States Patent US 7244521 B2 (2007).

35. W. C. Poh, S. N. Piramanayagam, and T. Liew, Novel hybrid magnetic overcoats: a prospective solution for low magnetic spacing. J. Appl. Phys. **103**(7), 07F523 (2008).

36. W. C. Poh, S. N. Piramanayagam, and T. Liew, Magnetic properties and corrosion resistance studies on hybrid magnetic overcoats for perpendicular recording media. IEEE Trans. Magn. **46**(4), 1069 (2010).

37. S. N. Piramanayagam and J. P. Wang, Magnetic recording media with a magnetic overcoat layer. Patent No.: SP2002005123-3 (2002). (Publication No. 118153).

38. R. Wood, The feasibility of magnetic recording at 1 Terabit per square inch. IEEE Trans. Magn. **36**(1), 36 (2000).

39. A. Currie Munce and J.-U. Thiele, Hitachi's overseas research on hard disk drive. Hitachi Rev. **55**, 150 (2006).

40. S. Iwasaki, Past and present of perpendicular magnetic recording. J. Magn. Magn. Mater. **320**, 2845 (2008).

41. D. Abramovitch and G. Franklin, A brief history on disk drive control. IEEE Control Syst. Mag. **22**(3), 28 (2002).

42. E. S. Murdock, R. F. Simmons, and R. Davidson, Roadmap for 10 Gbit/in^2 media: challenges. IEEE Trans. Magn. **28**(5), 3708 (1992).

43. J. H. Judy, Past, present, and future of perpendicular magnetic recording. J. Magn. Magn. Mater. **235**, 235 (2001).

44. B. Marchon and T. Olson, Magnetic spacing trends: from LMR to PMR and beyond. IEEE Trans. Magn. **45**(10), 3608 (2009).

45. B. Bhushan, *Tribology and Mechanics of Magnetic Storage Devices*, 2nd ed. New York: Springer Verlag Inc., 1996.

10

HEAT-ASSISTED
MAGNETIC RECORDING

Ganping Ju, William Challener, Yingguo Peng,
Mike Seigler, and Ed Gage

Seagate Technology

10.1 INTRODUCTION

With the continuous growth of demand for digital-content storage in the information age, the areal density of the data storage for both magnetic recording and solid-state memory continues to increase at a rapid pace of about 30–40% per year. However, the superparamagnetic limit imposes a signal-to-noise ratio, thermal stability, and writability trade-off that limits the ability to continue to scale traditional magnetic recording technology to higher storage densities. Further increase of the areal density calls for smaller grains that will require higher magnetic anisotropy to remain thermally stable; however, this pose a major writability challenge due to limited saturation magnetization ($B_S \sim 2.4$–2.5 Tesla) for the write pole materials. Among several other technologies discussed in this book, heat-assisted magnetic recording (HAMR) offers a potential solution to such a dilemma by introducing a new degree of freedom: a write temperature that holds the promise of extending the areal density of magnetic data storage well beyond 1 Tb/in.^{2} By temporarily heating the media during the recording process, the media coercivity can be lowered below the available applied magnetic write field, allowing higher media anisotropy and therefore smaller thermally stable grains. The

Developments in Data Storage: Materials Perspective, First Edition.
Edited by S. N. Piramanayagam, Tow C. Chong.
© 2012 Institute of Electrical and Electronics Engineers. Published 2012 by John Wiley & Sons, Inc.

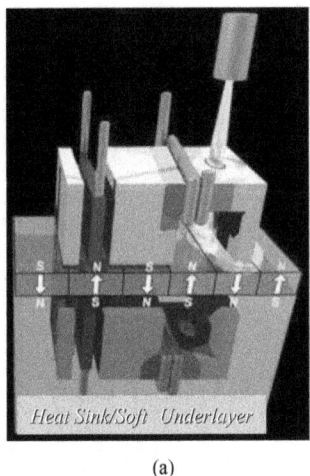
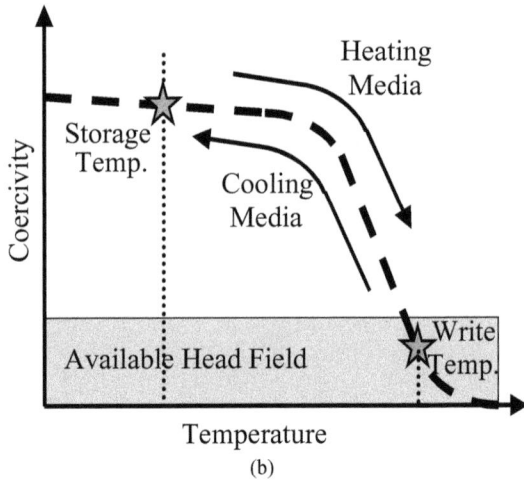

(a)   (b)

Figure 10.1. (a) Schematics of a HAMR system include thermal and magnetic field delivery, as well as properly designed HAMR media; (b) illustration of HAMR recording scheme [57].

heated region is then rapidly cooled in the presence of the applied head field, whose orientation encodes the recorded data. A sketch illustrating the HAMR writing process is shown in Figure 10.1b. With a tightly focused laser beam heating the media, the write process is similar to magneto-optical (MO) recording, but in an HAMR system, the readout is performed with a magnetoresistive element.

As illustrated in Figure 10.1a, HAMR requires the development of a number of novel components. These include the light delivery system, the thermomagnetic writer, a robust head disk interface, and high anisotropy media with proper thermal design. Designing these components into a high performance data storage system requires system level optimization. The ability to record on very high anisotropy materials holds the promise of allowing an order of magnitude increase in areal density over perpendicular recording, but a number of technical challenges must first be addressed. The unique physics of recording by rapidly freezing the magnetic state in a modulated head field will be discussed in Section 10.2. It is shown that optimizing thermal gradients and the applied field are important to recording quality transitions. The optical design must produce spot sizes that are far below the conventional diffraction limit to confine the thermal heating. As discussed in Section 10.3, efficient light delivery systems, from laser diode to a near field optical transducer, are needed. If possible, HAMR should leverage the extremely successful hard disk drive (HDD) thin-film head experience to produce the optical and magnetic fields. The media challenges for creating smooth, high anisotropy materials with the appropriate microstructure for low noise at high densities will be discussed in Section 10.4. This section will cover the various media candidates for HAMR media, the challenges in controlling Curie temperature, the thermal design, and alternative media designs for lowering the recording temperature. The repeated thermal cycling brings new challenges to the head–disk interface and the mechanical requirements of the drive. The unique challenges of a high-temperature robust head–disk interface (HDI) will be presented in Section 10.4.4. A few examples of HAMR recording will be addressed in Section 10.5. This chapter will finish with a summary and outlook of this recording technology. We will consider conventional, nonthermally assisted magnetic recording to be the reference case for discussion of HAMR [1, 2]. In this chapter, we focus on the significant *differences* between HAMR and conventional recording physics.

10.2 HAMR RECORDING PHYSICS

In HAMR, the temperature of a high anisotropy (usually perpendicular) recording medium is locally elevated to facilitate the writing process by significantly reducing the magnetization switching field needed, and then dropped abruptly to "freeze in" stable recorded information. The medium is understood to be a granular ensemble, in which the grains are more or less magnetically isolated, closely packed particles of average volume V, each of which has a sufficiently high uniaxial magnetocrystalline anisotropy K so that the ambient temperature stability factor $KV/k_B T$ is greater than or equal to 70, so that the written information can remain stable for 10 years. The heating and cooling process is executed rapidly, on the same time scale as used in conventional magnetic recording (~1 ns). A principal attraction of heat-assisted recording (along with high anisotropy) is that a very high effective writing field gradient can be achieved with little or no required contribution from the magnetic field gradient from the magnetic poles. This is understood in terms of the simple relation

$$\frac{dH_{write}}{dx} \sim \frac{dH_k}{dT} \cdot \frac{dT}{dx}, \tag{10.1}$$

where the first factor on the right side is the slope of the medium's temperature-dependent anisotropy field $H_k(T)$ just below the Curie temperature T_C (the critical temperature at which the medium magnetism and H_k vanish), and the second factor is the gradient of the thermal profile in the medium at the freezing temperature (down-track or cross-track). Using expected values on the right side yields an effective writing gradient 3×–20× larger than direct field gradients from inductive head designs, with details as illustrated in the next paragraph. Such large writing field gradients can more easily carry one toward the grain size limit for recorded magnetization transition length, a key for attaining maximum down-track recording density in a given medium design. Additionally, a high cross-track gradient can help not only minimize adjacent track erasure effects, a prime ingredient for high-track-density recording but also reduce the cross-track correlation length. The discussion above implies that the temperature dependence of the medium magnetic properties, particularly around T_C, will be critical for HAMR performance. Along with the slope of $M_S(T)$ and $H_K(T)$ just below T_C, it is the deeper understanding of the underlying recording physics near Curie temperature, that is, the disappearance and reformation of the memory layer magnetization as T passes through T_C (increasing and decreasing), that are crucial for recording rate limitations and recording quality in HAMR. That is, we need to understand what factors limit the

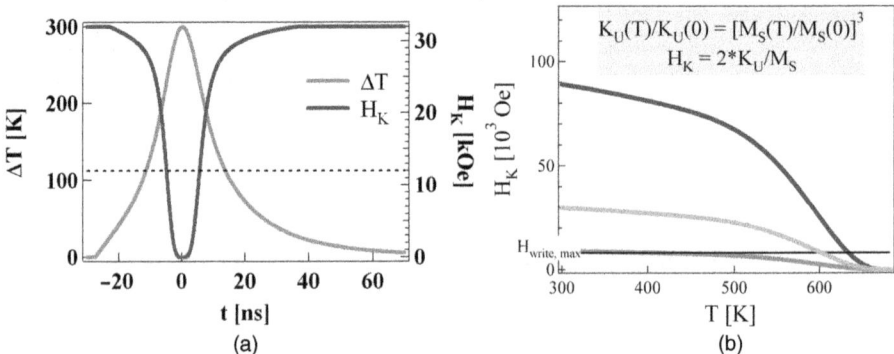

Figure 10.2. (a) Temperature profile in the media and the resultant temporary reduction of anisotropy field; (b) typical temperature dependence of anisotropy of several types of media with different anisotropy. (Courtesy of Jan-Ulrich Thiele.)

rate of magnetization collapse and reformation, and also the quality of the magnetization formation during freezing (e.g., whether saturated remanence is achieved or not). A failure to achieve saturated remanent magnetization during rapid medium cooling is a superparamagnetic effect. In this situation, the population of grains that freeze into the desired magnetic polarity (i.e., align with the head field) can be below 100%, and the theory of superparamagnetism describes this alignment probability distribution in terms of the system temperature and applied magnetic field [3].

Estimation of effective field gradient strongly depends on the media anisotropy and its temperature dependence. As illustrated in Figure 10.2, media with high anisotropy (such as FePt) shows a large slope of dH_K/dT, which could be as high as 900 Oe/K [4]; in contrast, media with low anisotropy (CoCrPt alloy) show a much smaller slope of dH_K/dT, approximately 30–100 Oe/K. This also illustrates the importance of high anisotropy media for HAMR, not only for enabling the thermally stable smaller grains needed for high density recording, but also enabling a large effective field gradient. Combine this with the temperature gradient of 5–10 K/nm, and the result could be an effective field gradient of 1000–9000 Oe/nm, much bigger (3–20×) than the field gradient of state-of-art perpendicular recording, which is approximately 300–400 Oe/nm. In this aspect, HAMR scales more favorably than conventional perpendicular recording for higher areal density recording: higher anisotropy and smaller spot size means higher effective field gradient in HAMR; in contrast, conventional perpendicular writers lose field amplitude when the pole dimensions are reduced, and it is also difficult to increase field gradient due to field divergence from reduced pole dimensions.

10.3 HAMR OPTICS AND HEAD

HAMR at $Tb/in.^2$ densities requires the ability to heat a spot in the recording medium to its Curie point that is no larger than 50-nm cross-track and to simultaneously apply a recording field to the heated region of the medium. Even with the recent development of high power semiconductor lasers with a wavelength of 405 nm, a sub-50-nm optical spot is well below the diffraction limit. The diffraction limit is the smallest optical spot size to which light can be focused by standard far-field optics like lenses and mirrors. In terms of the full width at half maximum (FWHM), this spot diameter is

$$d = \frac{0.51\lambda}{NA},$$

(10.2)

where λ is the wavelength of the light, and NA is the numerical aperture of the focusing element. In order to obtain optical spot sizes below the diffraction limit, it is necessary to make use of near field optics. A wide variety of near-field transducers (NFTs) have been described and developed over the past 15 years to address the problem of confining an optical spot below the diffraction limit. In this section we discuss what is important for a HAMR NFT and some of the design criteria for optimizing this NFT. We then describe a NFT that has been fabricated according to these criteria and has been successfully used to demonstrate HAMR.

10.3.1 Three Categories of NFTs

Many of the NFTs discussed in the literature are based on apertures that confine light by the size of the hole. As the hole diameter is reduced, there is frequently an exponential decrease in the transmitted optical power. A variety of clever techniques have been developed to enhance the throughput by making use of propagating surface plasmons (SPs) on the surface of the aperture and localized SPs inside the hole. With an optimum design, the optical energy can be collected over a wide area of the surface and funneled into and through the hole with a high degree of efficiency. A recent example of this consisted of a 100-nm aperture in an aluminum film surrounded by concentric grooves [5]. A UV laser at a wavelength of 365 nm was focused onto the aperture, exciting SPs that propagated along the surface towards the aperture. An 80-nm optical spot was measured at the output of the aperture with a theoretical field intensity enhanced by a factor of ~100 relative to the hole without the grooves. This device was incorporated into a flying recording head and used to expose an 80-nm track in a TeO_x thermal photoresist on a rotating disk.

There is another category of NFT that is based on antennas. The bow-tie antenna, for example, has received a great deal of attention [6, 7]. Composed of two metallic triangles, point-to-point, with a small gap between them, this antenna captures optical energy over both metal surfaces and generates a concentrated field intensity within the gap. The theoretical field intensity in the gap can be over three orders of magnitude larger than that of the incident field [7]. A single-triangle antenna with a "beak" can also be extremely effective at concentrating the incident optical energy at the point of the beak [7, 8]. The beaked triangle antenna has also been incorporated into a recording head and used to record magnetic marks of 20–25-nm diameter in a recording medium, by scanning the media with piezoelectric scanners. The beaked triangle antenna is an "apertureless" recording technique. Apertureless near-field microscopy has been able to resolve features much smaller than aperture-based near-field microscopy [9].

Apertureless NFTs are characterized by a sharp metallic point that confines and concentrates the optical power in the near field.

Other NFTs lie in an intermediate category, partly related to apertures and partly to apertureless antennas. An example of this is the C-aperture [10–12].When light at a wavelength of 1 μm is incident upon a C aperture with optimized dimensions, the field intensity in the region of the ridge can theoretically be enhanced by at least a factor of 40 and confined to a region that is approximately a tenth of a wavelength [13]. A simple test to determine the category of a NFT is to consider the location of the peak field. If it occurs underneath a metallic element, then it is an antenna. If it occurs underneath a dielectric region (aperture or gap), then it is an aperture. The highest field intensity of the C aperture occurs at the edge of the ridge, between the dielectric and the metal, so it is an intermediate type of NFT. The peak field intensity of the bow-tie antenna also occurs at the edges of the tips.

The category of NFT is important because it provides a general rule of thumb regarding the spot size that can be generated by the NFT. In the case of apertures, as the aperture or gap is reduced, the amount of optical power which can be conveyed through the NFT to the region of exposure will drop exponentially. Even when a SP effect is used to enhance the throughput, for sufficiently small apertures, the throughput becomes negligible. Typically this occurs for aperture diameters of $\sim\lambda/10$. To generate optical spot sizes smaller than this, it is generally better to switch to either an antenna or intermediate NFT geometry. The latter are often efficient for spot sizes down to $\sim\lambda/20$. The results of optical modeling indicate that smaller spots sizes can only be obtained efficiently by an apertureless NFT.

10.3.2   An NFT Figure of Merit

The transducers that have been discussed up to this point have been characterized by such parameters as "throughput" in the case of apertures and "peak field intensity" in the case of antennas. For a HAMR system, it is important to ask if either of these parameters is a useful figure of merit. In a HAMR system, the NFT is placed in proximity to a recording medium. The medium itself is generally composed of an alloy or a multilayer of transition and noble metals such as Co, Fe, Pd, and Pt along with other additives. Therefore, the media is a lossy metal and can be expected to interact electromagnetically with the NFT. Moreover, the recording layer is deposited onto either a metallic substrate like aluminum or a dielectric substrate like glass. In either case the presence of the substrate modifies the near-field of the NFT. Therefore, any figure of merit must include the effect of the recording medium and substrate. A parameter such as the peak field intensity of the NFT when surrounded by free space is in fact largely irrelevant for HAMR. It has been shown [14], for example, that the bow-tie antenna, when placed adjacent to a recording medium, will couple energy into the medium—not in the gap between the triangles, but rather directly underneath each triangle, generating two very large hot spots in the medium and not at all suitably for an HAMR transducer. The NFT "throughput" of light into free space, though often quoted for apertures, does not include the effect of the recording medium and is also not a useful HAMR figure of merit. For example, although a circular aperture may generate a confined near-field spot on the opposite side of the aperture in free space, in the presence of a recording medium, the light that passes through the aperture is often "wicked" away from the aperture via the waveguide that is formed between the metal film of the aperture and the recording medium. The resulting hot spot within the medium is extended into a region that is much larger than the aperture itself.

For HAMR we are particularly interested in two things: (1) the size of the optical spot within the recording medium and (2) the amount of optical power that is absorbed by the medium within this spot. A single figure of merit cannot really capture both parameters simultaneously, but different NFTs can be compared for a specific optical spot size in the recording medium by measuring the optical coupling efficiency of the NFT into the recording medium within that spot. This is determined from the ratio of the power dissipated within the optical spot in the medium to the power incident upon the NFT. The power dissipated within the recording medium is given by the volume integral,

$$P_{diss} = \frac{1}{2} \int_{medium} \mathrm{Re}(\sigma)|E|^2 \, dV, \tag{10.3}$$

where $\mathrm{Re}(\sigma)$ is the real part of the conductivity of the recording medium at the frequency of the incident light and $|E|^2$ is the local field intensity. The total incident power is well defined for an incident focused beam of light but not for an incident plane wave. Fields generated by an NFT when illuminated by a plane wave, therefore, are generally not useful as a HAMR figure of merit.

10.3.3 Six NFT Design Principles

We now consider the design principles that can be used to optimize the HAMR NFT. There are at least six principles that we have found to be useful:

(1) A NFT should make use of the localized SP resonance effect. The localized SP resonance can enhance the field intensity within a recording medium by a factor of five or more. This translates directly into enhanced power dissipation via Equation 10.3 and enhanced coupling efficiency. Therefore, the NFT must be composed of a plasmonic metal. It should also have good corrosion resistance and a high melting point. Because the NFT is a dissipative object at the focus of a high intensity laser beam, it will get very hot. There are a few options to consider for the NFT material. For visible light, gold, silver, copper, and aluminum are all able to generate SP resonances. In the infrared, there are several other metals that can be considered. Aluminum has a very low melting point and is probably not suitable. The practical importance of corrosion resistance for the reliability of a commercial product greatly restricts the choice of metal, and gold seems to be the most suitable candidate for the NFT material.

(2) The wavelength for exciting the SP resonance of the NFT should be that of a low cost, high power semiconductor laser. Fortunately, there are many options.

If the NFT is composed of gold, however, the strong SP effects are restricted to wavelengths longer than ~700 nm.

(3) An apertureless antenna design is preferable to an aperture design. The goal for HAMR is to reach storage densities of 10 Tb/in.[2] or higher, which will require delivering optical power into a spot in the medium that is much smaller than 50 nm. Because a 50-nm spot size is already less than $\lambda/10$, an aperture-based NFT is marginal for even a first generation HAMR product with a storage density of 1 Tb/in.[2]

(4) The shape of the NFT should be optimized to obtain the best possible coupling from the incident optical power. Obviously, this is in part a function of the method of focusing light onto the NFT. Different focusing elements will generate different focused field distributions, which in turn will couple differently to specific NFT designs. Therefore, the design of the NFT must be chosen in conjunction with the choice of the focusing element, and both should be adjusted and optimized together for highest coupling efficiency.

(5) It has been found that the fields generated by nanoparticles can be greatly enhanced by bringing two nanoparticles close together. This is sometimes called the "dual dipole" effect [15] and is thought to be very important in surface enhanced Raman spectroscopy. The bow-tie antenna in free space employs the dual dipole effect and this contributes to its very large field enhancement.

(6) Finally, it is also important from the standpoint of high volume and low cost manufacturing for any NFT design to be compatible with standard thin-film and lithographic fabrication processes.

10.3.4 An HAMR Near-Field Transducer

Having discussed the proper figure of merit for HAMR and the basic design principles for a NFT, we are now ready to consider a particular example, the "lollipop" NFT that is shown in Figure 10.3.

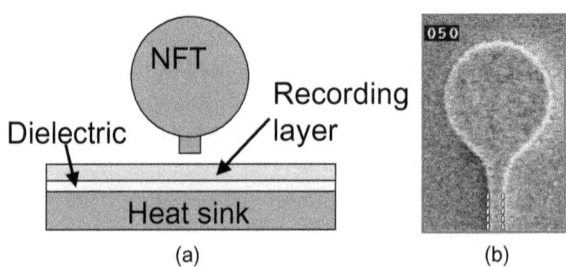

(a)   (b)

Figure 10.3. (a) A schematic of a lollipop NFT in proximity to a HAMR recording medium; (b) a gold lollipop NFT fabricated.

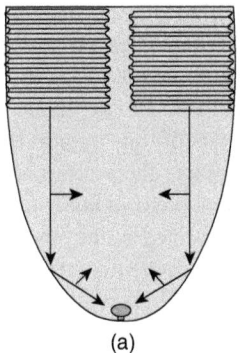 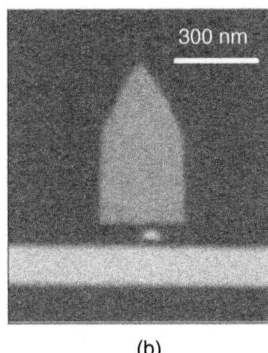

(a)   (b)

Figure 10.4. (a) Parabolic waveguide with two diffraction gratings at the top for coupling the incident laser light into the waveguide, and the NFT located at the focus; (b) air bearing surface view of NFT HAMR head, consisting of the core layer of the waveguide (white stripe), bottom cross section of the peg of the NFT (small white rectangle), and the recording pole (trapezoid) [71].

The lollipop NFT is lithographically patterned in a thin film of gold. It has a diameter of ~200 nm and a thickness of 25 nm. The peg of the lollipop, shown in Figure 10.3b after lapping, is 15 nm long and its width is adjusted to be slightly smaller that the desired recording track width. The NFT itself is located at the focus of a waveguide with a parabolic shape as shown in Figure 10.4a.

The gold lollipop NFT is a fairly complex structure and exhibits multiple SP resonances in the visible and near infrared spectra. The diameter of the disk, thickness of the film, and especially the location of the NFT within the waveguide are all chosen so that the most efficient SP resonance is excited at the selected laser wavelength. The mode index of the waveguide in which the NFT is located has a strong influence on the resonance wavelength. The NFT need not be placed at the center of the core of the waveguide, but can even be placed within one of the cladding layers as shown in Figure 10.4b to adjust the resonance wavelength. The peg of the lollipop acts like the needle in apertureless microscopy to confine and concentrate the optical near field in the medium.

The polarization of the light focused onto the NFT is also important. If the incident electric field is vertically polarized, the NFT couples energy into the medium. If it is horizontally polarized, the NFT is ineffective. The two coupling gratings at the top of Figure 10.4a are offset vertically from each other by half a grating period. This causes the light that is coupled into the waveguide to be 180° out of phase on either side of the parabola. When the light is recombined at the focus, it generates an electric field that is correctly polarized in the vertical direction.

The dual dipole effect can also be incorporated into this NFT design by way of the HAMR medium. As shown in Figure 10.3a, the recording medium includes a heat sink. The heat sink can be a plasmonic metal like copper. By placing a highly conductive metal below the recording layer, an electromagnetic image plane is created that essentially places the recording layer between the lollipop and its electromagnetic image. This plasmonic image plane in the medium generates a *virtual* dual dipole effect to further confine and enhance the field intensity in the recording layer. All six design criteria are thus satisfied by the lollipop NFT and HAMR medium!

The theoretical coupling efficiency into a 50×50-nm^2 region in the medium for this transducer design is about 5%. In actual practice there are many things that can reduce this efficiency. For example, up to this point we have not considered the recording pole. It is essential that a recording pole be located within the recording head in proximity to the NFT so that the magnetic field is sufficiently strong within the heated region of the medium to set the magnetic state of the bit. A recording pole is composed of optically lossy metals such as Fe and Co, and when brought into the near field of the NFT, it absorbs some of the optical power and damps the SP resonance. Fortunately, in the design shown in Figure 10.4b the pole is located outside the core of the waveguide and most of the optical power traveling down the waveguide and interacting with the NFT does not strongly interact with the recording pole even when the gap between the NFT and pole is only 50 nm.

10.3.5 Light Delivery to the Transducer

According to the NFT design principles previously outlined, a laser light source is required with a wavelength longer than 700 nm. High power, single mode, and low cost semiconductor lasers are already available at many wavelengths, including 785, 830, and 904 nm. Delivering the laser light to the NFT, however, is a significant challenge, and a variety of concepts have been proposed. In Figure 10.4a the laser light is delivered through free space, focused by a low numerical aperture lens onto a coupling grating on the recording head. The theoretical efficiency of a coupling grating can be as high as 70% [16, 17], but it is difficult to achieve this in practice. It is also possible to convey the light to the recording head via an optical fiber [18]. Alternatively, the laser diode can be embedded directly in or attached to the recording head. There are alignment issues in both approaches, and heat sinking issues if the laser is part of the recording head assembly since all of the electrical power dissipated within the laser will generate heat within the head. Though light delivery is a very challenging engineering task, several research groups have been actively engaged in solving this problem and there will likely turn out to be several viable approaches.

Once the optical energy has been introduced into the recording head, it must still be transported to and concentrated upon the NFT. Here again a variety of techniques have been suggested. Solid immersion lenses [19, 20] have been a favorite approach for achieving small optical spots. In this case the light is brought to a focus within a high index lens so that the numerical aperture can significantly exceed the value of 1. According to Equation 10.2, the spot size can be much smaller than the incident wavelength. A related approach makes use of a three-dimensional solid immersion mirror [21, 22] or planar solid immersion mirror [23] (shown in Fig. 10.4a) to concentrate the optical energy onto the NFT. Tapered waveguides [24] can be used, or in the case of apertures, grooves around the hole can direct the incident optical power towards the aperture [5, 25].

10.4 HAMR MEDIA

10.4.1 Overview

Because of the utilization of thermal assistance during the recording process, an integrated HAMR medium capable of supporting high density not only requires the fabrication of thermally stable media with high anisotropy and small grain size but also proper thermal design for heat confinement in the media. This section will focus on the HAMR media overview and thermal aspect of the media design, and the details of media processes and microstructure will be discussed in the next chapter.

A schematic of a typical HAMR media structure is illustrated in Figure 10.5. Many of the components are also commonly used in perpendicular recording media, such as a lubricant, an overcoat (OC), a recording layer, a properly designed soft underlayer (SUL), and an interlayer for magnetic property and microstructure control. However, there are many unique aspects of the HAMR media structure as well. First of all, in order to support high recording densities while also providing thermal stability [26], the recording layer must have high anisotropy and small grain sizes. Second, the use of heat during the recording process requires that the media OC and lubricant be thermally stable. Moreover, in order to optimize the thermal response of the media, a heat sink of proper thermal properties must be provided. This may be incorporated into the interlayer and/or SUL or a separate heat sink layer may be utilized. The design of these layers will be discussed in sections below. There are several potential magnetic material systems for HAMR such as $L1_0$ FePt, FePd, CoPt, and MnAl, all of which offer high magnetic anisotropy [26–28]. However, in order to induce the ordering required to achieve the high anisotropy, a high processing temperature is required. This high processing temperature requirement makes it extremely challenging to obtain low noise recording media with a suitably small grain size, as the high processing temperature causes not only the chemical ordering, but may also cause grain growth to adversely affect media microstructure [29].

$SmCo_5$ [30–32] and $Fe_{14}Nd_2B$, represent another class of materials that has been studied for permanent magnet applications and which also exhibits extremely high

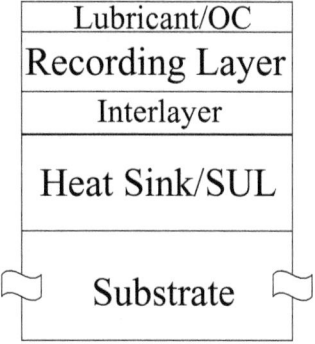

Figure 10.5. Schematic drawing of a typical layered structure for HAMR media.

anisotropy. In order to have the desired high anisotropy, however, the materials must be made in the proper phase, which is not typically easily achieved via sputtering. Moreover, these materials have a high potential for corrosion due to their rare-earth content.

Co/Pt and Co/Pd mutilayers represent yet another potential class of materials [33, 34]. Here one has to be rather careful with the very high anisotropy values reported in the literature because it is usually normalized to the Co volume instead of the total Co/Pt multilayer volume, but the latter is critical for thermal stability considerations. They can be designed with anisotropy (normalized to total media thickness) around 1×10^7 erg/cm^3 [35, 36], due to the interfacial anisotropy in the multilayer structure. However, achieving a low noise is a significant problem in these materials, and therefore, they offer rather limited potential advantage over conventional perpendicular media based on CoCrPt:oxide.

There have also been several attempts to utilize perpendicular MO media for HAMR-type applications [37–39]. Such media can be written at high temperatures; however, the "readout" layers of these media have been optimized for the MO Kerr-effect readout and do not typically have the large magnetization saturation (M_s) required for magnetoresistive readout. Nemoto [40] on the other hand proposed a double-layer MO-type medium for heat-assisted writing and readout at room temperature. It consisted of a low-coercivity, high-magnetization TbDyFeCo readout layer exchange coupled to a TbFeCo memory layer with high coercivity near room temperature. The magnetization of almost 300 emu/cm^3 of the readout layer at room temperature could be used with magnetoresistive readout. Katayama et al. [41] of Sharp proposed a single-layer MO-type of medium for heat-assisted writing and reading. The compensation temperature of the rare-earth transition-metal (RE-TM) alloy chosen, $Tb_{23}Fe_{22}Co_{55}$, is close to room temperature, and thus it is necessary that the media be heated during both writing and reading. Corrosion is a serious concern for all these MO media because they contain rare earths, and the OC must be very thin for such high density near-field recording and readout. Moreover, the relatively large minimum stable domain size in such media probably limits the potential of such media to relatively low areal densities.

The basic material properties of the potential candidates for HAMR media, and the calculated thermally stable grain size, assuming columnar grains with 10-nm thickness, are listed in Table 10.1. The areal density potential of these materials, based upon the requirement that the thermal energy barrier

$$E_B = K_U V \left(1 - \frac{4\pi M_S}{H_K} \right)^2 \tag{10.4}$$

must be at least equal to 60 k_BT.

The Curie temperature, T_C, is an important parameter in the design of HAMR media since it largely determines the necessary recording temperature and, consequently, the materials used for OCs and lubricants. Modeling has suggested that recording close to or above the Curie temperature is required to achieve the highest areal-density advantage for HAMR [3, 42]. The Curie temperature varies with the material systems.

TABLE 10.1. List of Properties of High Anisotropy Magnetic Materials Including Reference on Conventional CoCrPt Alloy. This Table Is Modified after Klemmer et al. [31] and Weller et al. [30]

Type	Material	K_1 (10^7 erg/cm^3)	M_S (emu/cm^3)	H_K (kOe)	T_C (K)	D_P (nm)
Co alloy	CoCr20Pt15	0.3	330	18.2		14.4
	Co3Pt (L1$_2$)	2	1100	36.4		6.9
	(CoCr)3Pt	1	800	25.0		10.2
	CoPt3	0.5	300	33.3	600	9.7
Multilayer	Co2/Pt9	1	360	55.6	500	6.6
	Co2/Pd9	0.6	360	33.3	500	9.1
L1$_0$	FePd	1.8	1100	32.7	760	7.8
	FePt	7	1140	122.8	750	2.6
	CoPt	4.9	800	122.5	840	3.0
R.E.	SmCo5	20	910	439.6	1000	1.4

SmCo$_5$ and CoPt show high T_C around 840–1000 K, $L1_0$ FePt shows a modest T_C of 750 K, and Co/Pt and Co/Pd mutilayer systems offer great flexibility in tuning T_C with the thickness ratio of Co/Pt(Pd).

Rare earth Co-based materials have also made good progress recently, with high perpendicular anisotropy being achieved in thin films of SmCo deposited on Cu/Ti and Cu/Pt dual underlayers [32–34]. Sayama et al. [32] reported that SmCo$_5$ films on Cu underlayers with a Ti buffer layer show a coercivity of 12 kOe and an anisotropy of up to 4×10^7 erg/cm^3, even though the film morphology was continuous. A recent study by Sayama et al. [34] showed that adding Cu produces substantially improved corrosion resistance.

For the Co/Pt mutilayer type of media, Kuo et al. reported anisotropy above 1×10^7 erg/cm^3 can be achieved with optimal thickness and process optimization [43]. Meanwhile, Kawada et al. reported that Co layers with added SiO_2 were applied to Co/Pt multilayer media to enhance the grain isolation and reduce the media noise [37]. Typical magnetic properties of the media with 0.29-nm Co layer thickness and 0.12-nm Pt layer thickness were coercivity $H_C = 6.2$ kOe, saturation magnetization $M_S = 540$ emu/cm^3, and the perpendicular anisotropy energy $K = 6.0 \times 10^6$ erg/cm^3. Average grain size and grain boundary of those media were 6.6 nm in diameter and about 2 nm in width, respectively. The media exhibited both excellent recording performance and good thermal stability. However, the limited gain in anisotropy will limit the potential of such multilayer media.

Another class of the technologically important magnetic alloys has $L1_0$ structure and tends to form in alloys that contain light 3d transition metals (A = Mn, Fe, Co, and Ni) and heavy 4d/5d transition metals (B = Rh, Pd, Ir, and Pt). The ones that are ferromagnetic and have high magnetocrystlline anisotropy are FePt, FePd, and CoPt. The 4d/5d moment contributes little to the magnetization and Curie temperature, but it plays a key role in the realization of the magnetic anisotropy. The room-temperature-as-deposited state of such alloys is disordered A1 phase with face-centered cubic (fcc) structure, where the placement of the A and B atoms for the disordered phase is random. Upon heating during deposition or post annealing, such alloys form a chemical ordered state called $L1_0$ that demonstrates high anisotropy. $L1_0$ is the Strukturbericht designation for the crystallographic structure. For convenience, the structure is often depicted as face centered tetragonal although the real basis is body centered tetragonal. This chemically ordered structure forms in substitutional binary AB alloys owing to a tendency for nearest neighbors to prefer bonds between unlike atoms (A–B, B–A) over the bonding between similar atoms (A–A, B–B) [44]. One out of three nearest neighbors are of similar atoms and tend to arrange in atomic sheets giving rise to a multilayered structure of single atomic planes containing either all A atoms or all B atoms stacked along the vertical direction in the figure (traditionally called the c-axis). This stacking breaks the cubic symmetry and gives rise to anisotropy in many of the properties determined by the crystalline nature such as magnetism.

Despite the very large potential of high anisotropy materials such as $L1_0$ FePt for high density magnetic recording media, there are many challenges to make it practical. The high process temperature required to induce the $L1_0$ chemical ordering makes it difficult to use conventional substrates and to achieve the grain size, 001 texture, and grain isolation that are required. Nevertheless, progress relevant to each of these challenges has been made through the efforts of several different groups [45, 46]. It has been reported that the ordering temperature could be reduced by the addition of Ag and Cu [47, 48] and by ion irradiation [49]. However, the texture was undesirably random. Low-temperature fabrication and texture control of $L1_0$ FePt films were achieved by alternate monoatomic layer deposition [50] and stress/strain assistance [50–52]. In addition, $L1_0$ FePt films with small grain size and (001) texture were obtained by post-deposition annealing of multilayer films at temperatures higher than 550°C [53, 54]. More recently, Chen et al. reported depositing $L1_0$ FePt (001) oriented films with coercivity higher than 14.4 kOe and well-isolated 7.5-nm grains onto glass substrates at 350°C by using a MgO intermediate layer and doping C into the FePt films [45, 46]. Well-isolated columnar grains can be seen in the cross-section TEM for the media sputtered at relatively higher power with 15 v% of carbon doping. The plan view images show that better grain decoupling is achieved for media made with higher sputtering power, while further optimization is needed to improve the uniformity of the grain decoupling. It is also claimed that the lattice mismatch is optimized for the CrRu seed layer to lower the ordering temperature [45, 46]. Although the process involved deposition onto only one side of the substrate while the back side was heated and is, therefore, not suitable for manufacturing, these results appear to represent a significant step toward developing FePt with good magnetic properties and microstructure using modest processing temperatures.

More recent progress have been reported by Perumal et al. on the study of $L1_0$ FePt–C nanogranular perpendicular anisotropy films fabricated on oxidized Si substrates with a (100) textured MgO intermediate layer. The addition of a small amount of C (<12%) to an FePt (4-nm) film results in the formation of interconnected FePt particles, whereas a higher C addition leads to the formation of well-isolated $L1_0$ FePt nanoparticles with a c-axis texture. The FePt particle size can be reduced to 5.5 nm with a size distribution of 2.3 nm in variance by adjusting FePt thickness. Perpendicular

TABLE 10.2. Magnetic Properties of the Series of Highly Chemically Ordered, High Anisotropy $Fe_{55-x}Ni_xPt_{45}$ Films ($0 \leq x \leq 30$ at. %)

x [at. % Ni]	M_S [emu/cm³]	K_1 [10^7 erg/cm³]	$H_{K,RT}$ [kOe]	T_C [K]	D_P [nm]	$dH_K/dT|_{Hk=10\ kOe}$ [Oe/K]
0	1125	4.6	82	770[a]	2.8	[b]
5	1110	4.4	79	750[a]	2.85	[b]
10	1100	4.0	73	690	2.9	900
15	990	2.6	53	650	3.4	220
20	900	1.8	40	580	3.8	200
30	795	1.3	33	490	4.3	90

Saturation magnetization, M_S; magneto-crystalline anisotropy constant, K_1; switching field, $H_K = 2 \times K_1/M_S$; Curie temperature, T_C ([a] the values for the films with $x = 0$ and $x = 5$ at. % were obtained by extrapolation); minimum stable grain size, $D_P = (65\ k_BT/K_U)^{1/3}$ (storage time = 10 years); temperature coefficient of the switching field at $H_K = H_W$ (=10 kOe), $dH_K dT|_{Hk=10\ kOe}$ ([b] only extrapolated data available at $H_K = H_W$).
Source: J.-U. Thiele et al. [4]

coercivity is controllable between 8 and 15 kOe with high squareness. These results demonstrate that the FePt–C system can accomplish a nanogranular structure suitable for ultrahigh density recording media [55].

Yang et al. reported that perpendicular $L1_0$ ordered FePt-oxide two-phase thin films with an average grain size of ~7 nm were prepared by alternate sputtering of FePt and SiO_2 at 475°C. Very uniform and well-isolated columnar grains were obtained but coercivity is only about 7 kOe [56].

The Curie temperature of the recording layer can also be tuned with doping. In one example, shown in Table 10.2, Thiele et al. [4] have shown that the Curie temperature of FePt can be reduced with Ni doping. However, at the same time, the anisotropy also decreases. Thus, at least in this example, reducing the Curie temperature requires a design trade-off between Curie temperature and anisotropy. On the other hand, $L1_0$ FePt has a sufficiently high anisotropy, that there is some operating space for such a trade-off to be made. The doping will also have adverse effects on the effective field gradient due to reduction of dH_K/dT with reduction of anisotropy and changes in form of $H_K(T)$.

10.4.2 HAMR Media Thermal Design and Characterization

10.4.2.1 HAMR Media Thermal Design.
As illustrated in Section 10.2, the well-confined thermal spot is essential not only for defining the recording track width and avoiding adjacent track erasure (ATE) but also for the large effective field gradient needed for high linear density recorded transitions. The optimum mode for HAMR is to assure that the medium thermal profile T(x,y,z,t) has such a high spatial gradient that it creates a dominant recording field gradient, thus determining the recording process. In conventional recording, the spatial and temporal variation of the recording head magnetic field H(x,y,z,t) is the driving factor, but in HAMR the H-field simply provides the bias for the final magnetization polarization. The principal requirement for the

H-field is that its strength throughout the heated zone during the medium cooling phase be sufficient to ensure well-saturated recording in the face of highly variable demagnetization and exchange fields, as well as thermal fluctuations. In HAMR the spatial variation of H(x,y,z,t) is of limited importance when the thermal profile is adequate (large gradient at the medium's freezing temperature), as indicated by Equation 10.1.

To say that T(x,y,z,t) determines the HAMR process means several things. First, its cross-track width determines the recorded track profile and does not perturb adjacent track recorded information. Further, the down-track profile should establish as high a value of dT/dx as possible to assure that a minimally narrow magnetization transition is written. Lastly, one does not want the medium temperature to wastefully exceed the necessary thermal demagnetization temperature $T \sim T_C$ in order to avoid depositing unneeded energy that can damage medium materials (degrade magnetics, damage OC materials, and deplete lubricants). Two factors govern efficient heating and cooling of the medium—(1) the mode of thermal energy deposition, and (2) the thermal design of the recording medium. A suitable average temperature elevation for good quality HAMR writing is most efficiently achieved by pulsing the heating source with a duty cycle commensurate with the recording rate rather than heating continuously. The time-average energy deposition can be several times less when the heating is modulated in time. Additionally, careful tailoring of the medium thermal diffusion performance is necessary. Achieving these dual objectives involves a design process combining thermal modeling analysis and proper material selection.

Temporal modulation of the thermal excitation of the magnetic medium plays an important role in determining the cooling rate of the information storage material. This is readily understood in terms of the relation

$$\frac{dT(x, t)}{dt} = \frac{\partial T(x, t)}{\partial t} + \frac{\partial T(x, t)}{\partial x} \frac{dx}{dt}. \tag{10.5}$$

When the medium heating is performed with a continuous source, the cooling of magnetic grains as the imposed thermal profile passes by is determined entirely by the second term on the right in Equation 10.5. That is, the cooling rate is the product of the down-track thermal gradient at the magnetic "freezing temperature" and the speed of the thermal profile along the track. On the other hand, if the heating source is pulsed on and off, there is the possibility that a significant fraction of the magnetic particles within the area of thermal profile warm enough to enable the HAMR process to experience a cooling rate determined entirely by the first term on the right in Equation 10.5. Let us compare the magnitude of the two terms. Experiment and modeling give us the usable ranges for the important variables $\partial T/\partial t$ and $\partial T/\partial x$ for our estimation. While the linear speed in hard drives would be expected to lie in the range of ~10–50 m/s, $\partial T/\partial t$ for thermal profile widths in the 40–200-nm range might be 400–2000 K/ns, and $\partial T/\partial x$ is estimated to be 3–10 K/nm. Consequently, the second term on the right could range over 30–500 K/ns. We thus see that the explicit cooling rate of grains $\partial T/\partial t$ due to the thermal response time of a well-engineered medium following sudden removal of the heat source can be dominant, particularly for the large majority of grains that would cool due to source modulation rather than translation through the trailing edge of the profile (comparing the relative areas of the those thermal zones).

The major issues in the film stack design for good thermal confinement involve providing for rapid heat diffusion out of the memory layer in the axial direction, while greatly restricting lateral heat spreading. One is trying to achieve (1) rapid thermal response time, commensurate with the recording rate, and (2) good lateral heat confinement to the recording zone without interference with the adjacent tracks. Numerical simulation of heat flow under different scenarios of disk film stack geometry and material selection, combined with a description of the thermal excitation (whether optical or otherwise) has proven invaluable in understanding proper thermal design of media, as it did previously in optical data storage [28].

The thermal properties of the thin-film stack for HAMR media must be designed to cool the medium very quickly in the presence of the recording field. Typically the thermal time constant of the medium should be less than 1 ns. This ensures that the down-track thermal gradient in the medium is large, which in turn causes there to be a large gradient in the coercivity of the medium. A large gradient supports a sharp bit edge definition during recording. It also ensures that the magnetic state that gets recorded at high temperature does not demagnetize from superparamagnetic effects during cooling to ambient temperature. The aggressive heatsinking of the HAMR medium is another reason that the NFT must be designed for high efficiency so that it can deliver a sufficient amount of optical power into the recording medium in a very short time interval to heat the medium to its Curie point.

Another approach to thermal management is to pulse the laser in synchronization with the magnetic recording signal and with a pulse width that is much shorter than the time constant of the medium [57]. It is possible to obtain the same peak temperatures in the medium with a much smaller time-averaged optical power by pulsing the laser. There are many advantages to doing this, including the ability to use a less expensive, lower power laser and having a smaller temperature rise in the recording head. Finally, the thin-film structure of the recording medium can often be engineered to have very anisotropic thermal properties. If the recording layer has a much higher thermal conductivity in the direction normal to the plane of the film than within the plane of the film, this helps to restrict the lateral heat flow that causes thermal bloom of the tracks.

10.4.2.2 *Thermal Characterization.* The thermal characterization is critical for obtaining proper thermal properties of media stacks for thermal design, among which the measurement of thermal conductivity and minimization of lateral thermal diffusion are the most critical elements for optimizing the media thermal design

To study the effect of different underlayer designs on the cooling rate, time-resolved pump-probe techniques utilizing a pulsed laser (100–150 fs) were used as shown in Figure 10.6a. An intense pump pulse is used to heat the medium while a time-delayed probe pulse is used to monitor the temperature change as function of time using the change of reflectivity of the sample. As shown in Figure 10.6b, with proper design of heatsink, the cooling times can be reduced by an order of magnitude from 1ns to ~100 ps, and with proper design of interlayers, the media cooling times can be tuned accordingly, ranging from 100 ps to several nanoseconds.

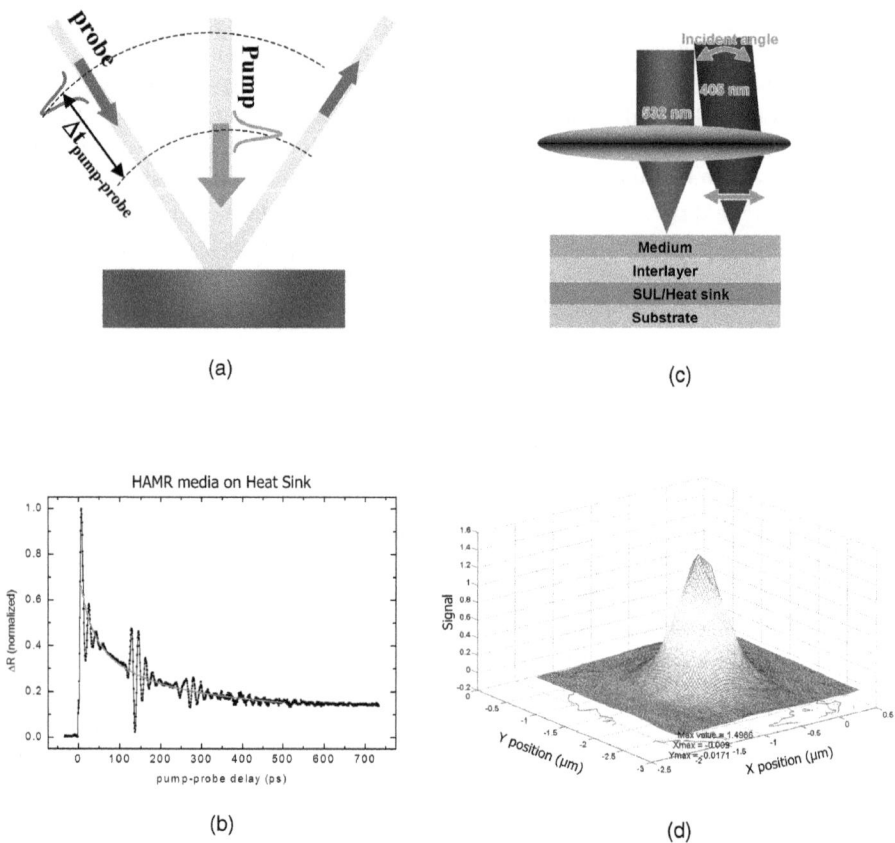

Figure 10.6. Thermal characterization: (a) schematics of time-resolved pump probe for thermal conductivity; (b) an example of pump-induced change of reflectivity of HAMR media on heatsink, from which thermal conductivity can be extracted; (c) schematics of scanning pump probe for lateral thermal mapping; (d) an example of scanning pump probe mapping of temperature profile on a HAMR media. (Courtesy of Duane Karns and Julius Hohlfeld.)

Another important aspect of media thermal design is to avoid lateral thermal diffusion. Consequently, a spatially scanning pump-probe set up was established by Karns et al. and utilized to study the effects of thermal design and disc motion on lateral thermal spreading [58], as illustrated in Figure 10.6c. A pump laser was focused and used to heat the media while a probe pulse was scanned spatially around the heated spot to study the temperature distribution, again using changes of reflectivity to monitor the temperature [58], with a typical temperature profile as shown in Figure 10.6d. The thermal profile was studied for media with and without a heatsink, and the effect of media velocity. Mapping of the equivalent temperature profile upon heating with a focused laser beam using the scanning pump-probe technique is shown in Figure 10.7, for several different cases: (1) stationary media without heatsink; (2) spinning media without heatsink; (3) stationary media with heatsink; and (4) spinning media with

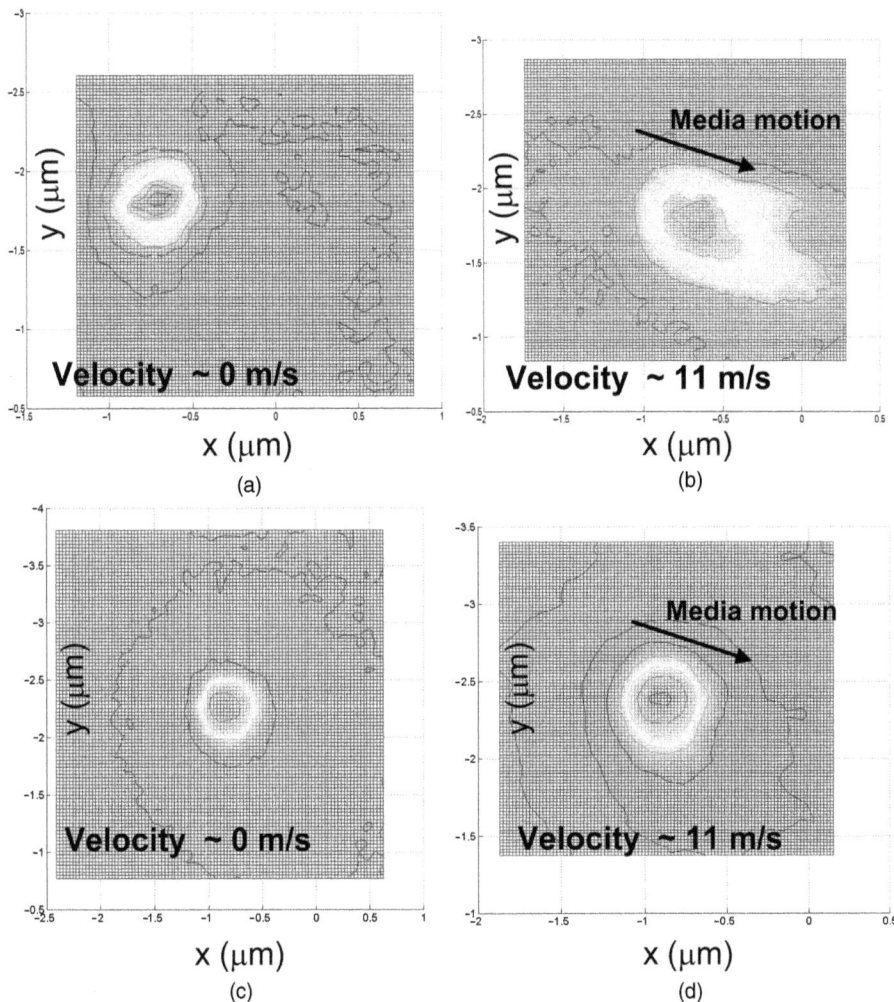

Figure 10.7. Mapping of the equivalent temperature profile upon heating with a focused laser beam using the scanning pump-probe technique for several different cases: (a) stationary media without heatsink; (b) spinning media without heatsink; (c) stationary media with heatsink; and (d) spinning media with heatsink. (Courtesy of Duane Karns.)

heatsink. With the disk at stationary state, a confined symmetric thermal spot was found for both cases, as shown in Figure 10.7a,c. However, when the disk was spinning at 10 m/s, the media without a heatsink exhibited a thermal profile with a tear-drop-like shape and with elongation along the disk motion direction, as shown in Figure 10.7b. On the other hand, for the media with a good heatsink, the thermal profile shows negligible broadening, as shown in Figure 10.7d. Such thermal confinement is very important for achieving the small written track widths and large thermal gradients necessary for high-density recording with HAMR. This illustrated the importance of proper thermal design for media temperature confinement while the media is moving at relatively high velocity (~10 m/s) during recording.

10.4.3 Alternative HAMR Media Design

As discussed earlier, in order to write well, conventional HAMR media must typically be heated close to the Curie temperature, T_C. At high write temperatures, significant challenges with the head–disk interface of the recording system, such as lubricant degradation and large thermal stresses, must be overcome. Hence it would be very desirable to develop advanced media designs that would enable recording at lower temperatures. Many designs have been proposed to make this possible. Thiele et al. proposed an "exchange spring" bilayer system based on FePt/FeRh [59, 60]. The proposed bilayer structure consists of a first layer made from a ferromagnetic high anisotropy alloy (FePt) that is exchange coupled to a second layer consisting of FeRh. At close to equiatomic compositions, FeRh is an antiferromagnet (AF) at room temperature. Interestingly, upon heating beyond the Néel temperature, T_N, FeRh undergoes a phase transformation and becomes ferromagnetic (FM) for temperatures $T_N < T < T_C$. The temperature-induced FM FeRh layer assists the switching of the hard layer via an exchange-spring effect where a domain wall forms at the interface and applies a torque on the hard layer. This enables the switching of the FePt layer at considerably reduced temperatures compared to the T_C of FePt. The transition temperature can be tuned by changes in the Fe/Rh ratio or by small additions of other elements such as Ir or Pt. Significant challenges are still present, however, to fabricate such bilayer structures as both layers require high process temperatures (>450°C) to induce chemical ordering, and interlayer diffusion is hard to control. It has also been found that the thickness of the FeRh layer needs to be larger than 10–20 nm in order to minimize thermal hysteresis in the AF-FM-AF transition upon heating and cooling. This makes it challenging to fabricate bilayers with high grain aspect ratio (thickness/grain size) [60].

Other advanced bilayer HAMR media designs such as thermal spring media [61], and low T_C and high T_C composite media have also been proposed. All of them are directed at the possibility of recording at reduced temperatures. A concept of an exchange-coupled magnetic multilayer was presented by Kikitsu et al. [62], where magnetic layers with different Curie temperatures and similar coercivities were obtained via exchange coupling. The coercivity of the double layer changes abruptly near T_C of one of the layers. It was argued that the recording temperature could be reduced with little reduction in the thermal stability in such multilayers. An example of such a medium was fabricated using two Co/Pd multilayers.

10.4.4 HAMR Media Tribology

As described in earlier sections, HAMR requires the heating of the magnetic media to or above the Curie temperature (T_C) of the media magnetic material within a nanosecond, using a special magnetic recording head that can deliver thermal energy to the media. Properties of some of the possible media candidates are shown in Table 10.1, where Dp is the minimum thermally stable grain size, assuming each grain is a 10-nmtall pillar or column. Since it is necessary to utilize smaller grain size to maintain signal-to-noise ratio at higher densities, it is seen that $L1_0$ FePt, $L1_0$ CoPt, and even SmCo$_5$ are attractive media for high density applications. These materials have T_C around 750 K, 840 K, and 1000 K, respectively, as indicated in Table 10.1.

With such high temperatures required for recording, the lubricant used to coat the magnetic media could desorb from the media surface or degrade leading to other detrimental side effects like corrosion [63–65]. Moreover, at such high temperatures, the currently used PECVD carbon OC could also change properties leading to poor corrosion protection and bad tribology performance. Associated with these high temperatures, other effects such as thermal pole tip protrusion and transient elastic thermal distortion of the media surface [66] could further exacerbate the head–media interface stability.

Conventional perfluoropolyether (PFPE) lubricants such as [Z-Dol 4000 or Z-Tetroal], which are used to coat current magnetic recording media surfaces cannot withstand the HAMR recording temperatures [65, 67, 68]. This has been demonstrated experimentally with results obtained from thermal gravimetric analysis (TGA) and temperature programmed desorption studies. Moreover, it is well documented by former industrial companies Quinta and Terastor that if the lubricant is not properly designed, the lubricant can easily be evaporated and/or degraded in the presence of large temperature excursions. Finding a reliable HAMR lubricant that can sustain the elevated recording temperature remains as a challenge before HAMR can be practically utilized [63–65, 67].

10.5 HAMR RECORDING AND MAGNETIC FORCE MICROSCOPY IMAGES

In order to evaluate the recording performance of a HAMR system, an integrated HAMR head capable of delivery of both magnetic field and thermal spots and flyable media with proper magnetic and thermal properties are both essential. The fully integrated HAMR heads were tested on a specially designed HAMR spinstand [27] that allows for full operation of the magnetic read and write head with light delivery that couples the laser light with the wavelength of selection into the integrated HAMR head while flying on the media with controlled flight heights.

The first type of HAMR recording experiments were shown with a HAMR head with asolid immersion mirror (SIM) where a 488-nm laser light is coupled into the waveguide, and a thermal spot size of about 120–140 nm can be achieved. The effect of heat-assisted writing can be clearly shown by comparing the recording with and without the laser radiation. A magnetic-force microscopy (MFM) image of the media after both non-HAMR (no laser power) and HAMR writing is shown in Figure 10.8a. It can be seen that with a write current of 70 mA, no transitions were written using non-HAMR recording in column 1. With a write current of 120 mA, there are still no clear transitions written in column 2. With the laser turned on for HAMR recording, bits were easily written with a 70 mA write current as seen in columns 3 through 7. Columns 3, 5, and 7 are tones at increasing linear densities, while columns 4 and 6 are pseudorandom bit sequences at increasing frequencies [69]. Figure 10.8b shows MFM

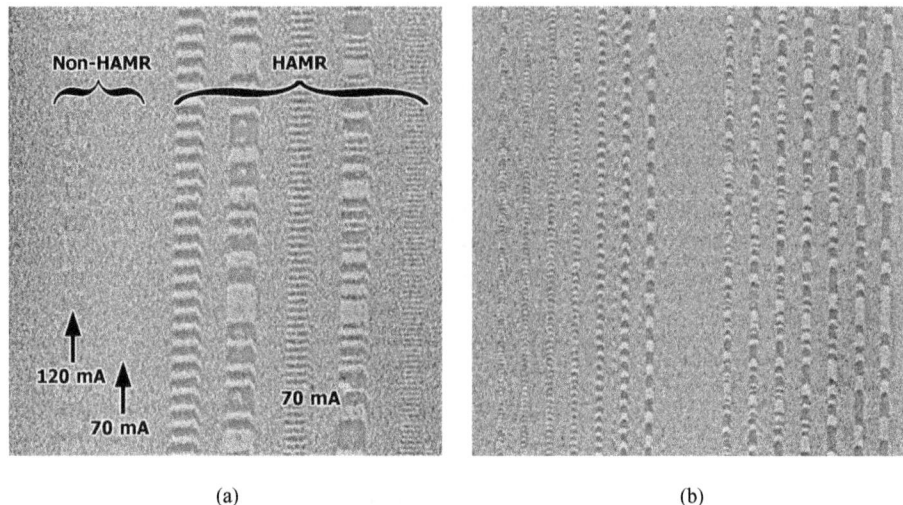

(a)　　　　　　　　　　　　　　　　　　　　　　　　(b)

Figure 10.8. (a) MFM images of high coercivity media being written without heat assist and with heat assist; (b) MFM images for HAMR recorded tracks of single frequency and pseudo-random bit sequences on a media with high anisotropy, where it is dominated by thermally assisted recording (Courtesy of Xiaobin Zhu) [57].

images for HAMR recorded tracks of single frequency tone and pseudorandom bit sequences on a FePtX medium with high anisotropy, where it is more dominated by thermally assisted recording. The track width is very close to the optical spot size, and the recorded tracks also show a curved transition, as is expected for HAMR in the thermally dominated regime.

As illustrated in Section 10.2, the HAMR recording head with NFT are developed to further reduce the optical/thermal size, hence enabling recording capability at high track density. To demonstrate the recording with an integrated HAMR head with NFT, a recording medium of 7.5-nm-thick FePt was used with a coercivity of 20.2 kOe [70, 76, 77], which was too large for a conventional perpendicular recording head to switch. Various underlayers were deposited on the substrate for epitaxial growth of the magnetic grains in the recording layer in the $L1_0$ crystalline structure. During recording, a constant 80 mW of laser power at a wavelength of 830 nm was incident upon the coupling grating, and the electrical heater current was adjusted to maintain a constant head-to-medium spacing of ~15 nm. This spacing corresponded to a physical air gap of ~2 nm between the bottom of the carbon OC on the recording head and the top of the lubricant on the disk. Differential thermal expansion from laser heating may have also caused a small protrusion of the NFT, reducing the NFT-to-medium spacing during recording as previously described. The coils around the recording pole were driven with 59 mA of current that was modulated at the data rate. A MFM image of a recorded track is shown in Figure 10.9. Because the recording layer is so thin, the magnetic signal from the recorded track is very small and the image is rather noisy. While using a state-of-art reader, an autocorrelated signal-to-noise ratio (ACSN) for a pseudoran-

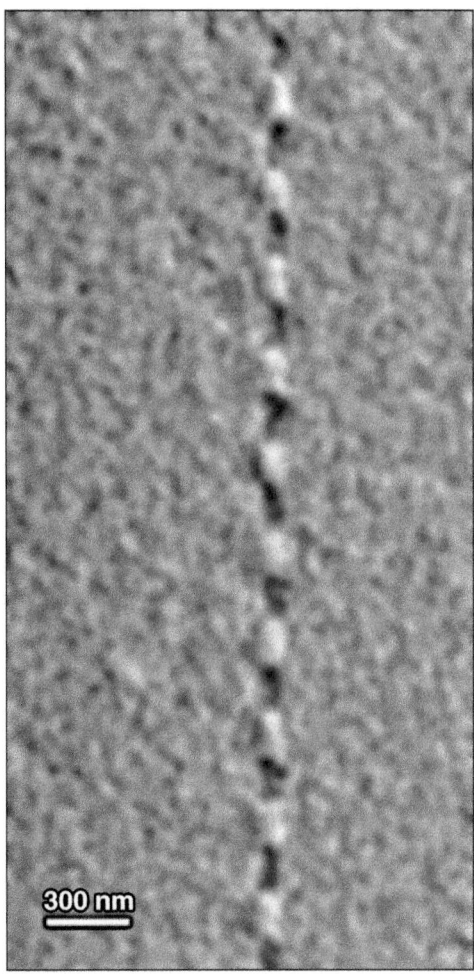

Figure 10.9. MFM image of a recorded track using near-field transducer (NFT) HAMR head on FeCuPt Media. The track width is ~70 nm. The scale bar is 300 nm (Courtesy of Xiaobin Zhu) [71].

dom bit sequence in which the background electronic noise was removed by averaging was 15.5 dB for a FWHM track width of 74 nm and a down-track linear density of 36 nm per flux change. This track width is much smaller than the region of the medium that experiences the full-applied magnetic field from the 310-nm-wide recording pole. The ACSN of a central recorded track was also measured as neighboring tracks were recorded on either side of it with varying offsets from the central track. Not until the track offset dropped below 80 nm was a sudden drop in ACSN measured. Therefore, it is reasonable to estimate an areal density of ~375 Tb/m^2 for these HAMR results by multiplying the measured FWHM track width by the minimum bit length for which an acceptable signal-to-noise ratio of at least 15 dB was obtained.

10.6 SUMMARY AND OUTLOOK

In summary, we have discussed in this chapter the concept of HAMR and different aspects of this technology, including design for an [optical and magnetic head] for thermal and magnetic field delivery, proper thermally designed high anisotropy media with small grain size, and production of a thermally robust and reliable head–media interface compatible with the corresponding recording temperature.

In general, it is projected that perpendicular recording will be limited to about 1 Tb/in.^{2}, because the write field that can be produced by a magnetic write head is limited to about 2.5 Tesla by the maximum saturation flux density of known magnetic materials. This limitation makes it impossible to scale the head field with the media coercivity, which is required if the linear density is to be increased while maintaining thermal stability in the media.

HAMR utilizes thermal energy produced by a laser incorporated into the write head to overcome this limitation. Heat generated by absorption of the laser light in the medium reduces the anisotropy of the medium during the write process, making it possible to record with available head fields. Moreover, the effective head-field gradient, which determines the width and precision of the written bit, is considerably higher with HAMR than can be achieved with a magnetic head alone. This high effective head-field gradient results in both better-defined written transitions and narrower and more well-defined track widths.

HAMR recording and readback has been demonstrated on a spinstand at state-of-the-art densities, and the measured performance is encouraging. Although HAMR involves thermal processes, which are often expected to be slow, proper design of the media with a heatsink of high thermal conductivity facilitates heating and cooling speeds much less than 1 ns, potentially enabling data rates in the gigahertz range. HAMR thus appears promising as a candidate technology to replace perpendicular recording as we know it today. There remains, however, considerable work to be done to ready this technology for mass production.

The need for a HAMR write head to provide both magnetic fields and optical energy to the media places new requirements on the write-head design. Although numerous approaches are possible, the current integrated write-head designs utilize a planar waveguide, which is incorporated into the gap of the write head to transmit the optical energy down to the media. To place the thermal spot close to where the field is highest, it is desirable that this waveguide be close to the magnetic pole of the head; however, placing it too close can disturb the optical transmission of the waveguide. For areal densities beyond 1 Tb/in.^{2}, the track pitch needs to be less than 50 nm, assuming a 4:1 bit aspect ratio. Since such a spot size is far beyond the limits of a diffraction-limited optically focused spot in free space, some sort of near-field transducer is required at the air-bearing surface of the head. This is perhaps one of the most challenging aspects of HAMR head design, but modeling has indicated that spot sizes as small as 10 nm are theoretically possible, enabling track density well above 1000–2000 ktpi. Detailed design considerations and guiding principles for such NFT heads has been discussed in Section 10.2. There has also been quite some excitement recently over the experimental demonstration of NFT head recording on high anisotropy media

[8, 71, 72], showing clear recording transition with narrow track width, on both continuous granular media and bit-patterned media as well. This is an important milestone for HAMR technology as it paves the way for demonstrating recording at high track density, not just based on theoretical modeling but in working models.

The design and processing of HAMR media is also a challenge, but again, progress has been made, and there are certainly magnetic materials that offer sufficiently large anisotropy to support recording at densities far beyond 1 Tb/in.^{2} $L1_0$ FePt and $L1_0$ CoPt in bulk form, for example, offer anisotropies adequate to provide thermal stability in grains down to 2.4 nm and 2.8 nm in diameter, respectively. $SmCo_5$ could support an even smaller grain size of 1.3 nm, but corrosion is a concern with any material containing rare-earth metals. Whether this anisotropy can be maintained in small grain materials remains an issue. Although early attempts to make low-noise small-grain $L1_0$ FePt were largely unsuccessful, recently good progress was made by using a MgO intermediate layer and doping C into the films [46] [55]. Further improvements are being made to improve media microstructure and magnetics to enable the high media signal-to-noise ratio needed to realize high-density HAMR recording (for further details on progress with FePt media, see the next chapter).

Optimal writing requires that HAMR media be heated near to their Curie temperatures, which are 750 K and 840 K for $L1_0$ FePt and $L1_0$ CoPt, respectively. Achieving such high temperatures requires significant laser power at the head–disk interface, which in turn may cause pole-tip protrusion as well as media deformation and damage to the lubricant, unless lubricants that are more resistant to such high temperatures can be found. Hence, finding a thermally stable lubricant that will withstand such high temperatures without degradation is a goal [63–67]. Alternatively, multilayer exchange-spring media may offer a path to writing at much lower temperatures.

Overcoming these challenges will require a dedicated effort, but modeling has indicated that if HAMR is combined with bit-per-grain recording such as might be achieved with bit-patterned media, HAMR could enable densities two orders of magnitude higher than in current products. At the present time, nothing indicates that the physics of HAMR imposes a barrier to attainment of an areal density of ~4–10 Tb/in.^{2} or beyond. Certainly, employment of bit-patterned media with HAMR enables an extension of both technologies, with projections of areal density reaching ~20–100 Tb/in.^{2} based on the thermal stability of known magnetic materials [73, 74].

HAMR is expected to have a role in extending the areal density potential of magnetic recording after conventional perpendicular recording reaches expected performance limits. HAMR, with its dual strengths of providing writability and extremely stable media, has considerable promise when employed alone [3, 73], and even more if used in conjunction with other approaches such as bit-patterned media [72, 75]. Extendibility of HAMR is based on two facts: (1) there is potential to elevate the magnetocrystalline anisotropy of magnetic storage materials [2, 28] well beyond that in use at present, and that is expected to deliver a factor of 10 in areal density based on maintenance of thermal stability KV of granular magnetic media as grain volume is reduced; and (2) it appears that local heating of the magnetic medium (optically or otherwise) can be extended well below that afforded by the diffraction limit of conventional optics. The combination of media with high anisotropy of smaller grain size and large effective field gradient gives HAMR technology the advantage in enabling ultra-high-density magnetic recording.

ACKNOWLEDGMENTS

The authors would like to thank their many colleagues at Seagate Research and the universities associated with the ATP program for their help. Although too numerous for all to be mentioned, particular acknowledgement is given to Bill Crue, Nils Gokemeijer, Kaizhong Gao, Cal Hardie, Yiao-Tee Hsia, Julius Hohlfeld, Amit Itagi, Bill Jensen, Paul Jones, Darren Karns, Duane Karns, Timothy J Klemmer, Mark Kryder, Lei Li, Terry McDaniel, Kalman Pelhos, Chubing Peng, Tim Rausch, Mark Re, Werner Scholz, Dieter Weller, Jeff West, Xiaobin Zhu, Xiaowei Wu, Min Xiao, XiaoMin Yang, Hua Zhou, and Xiaobin Zhu of Seagate; Jim Bain and Ed Schlesinger of Carnegie Mellon University, and Tom Milster of the University of Arizona. Some of this work was performed as part of the Information Storage Industry Consortium (INSIC) program in Heat Assisted Magnetic Recording (HAMR), with the support of the U.S. Department of Commerce, National Institute of Standards and Technology, Advanced Technology Program, Cooperative Agreement Number 70NANB1H3056.

REFERENCES

1. H. N. Bertram, *Theory of Magnetic Recording*. Cambridge, NY: Cambridge University Press, 1994.

2. M. Plumer, J. van Ek, and D. Weller, eds. *The Physics of Ultra-High Density Magnetic Recording*. Berlin, Germany: Springer, 2001.

3. A. Lyberatos and K. Y. Guslienko, Thermal stability of the magnetization following thermo-magnetic writing in perpendicular media. J. Appl. Phys. **94**, 1119–1129 (2003).

4. J.-U. Thiele, K. R. Coffey, M. F. Toney, J. A. Hedstrom, and A. J. Kellock, Temperature dependent magnetic properties of highly chemically ordered $Fe_{55-x}Ni_xPt_{45}$ $L1_0$ films. J. Appl. Phys. **91**, 6595–6600 (2002).

5. W. Srituravanich, L. Pan, Y. Wang, C. Sun, D. B. Bogy, and X. Zhang, Flying plasmonic lens in the near field for high-speed nanolithography. Nat. Nanotechnol. **3**, 733–737 (2008).

6. R. D. Grober, R. J. Schoelkopf, and D. E. Prober, Optical antenna: towards a unity efficiency near-field optical probe. Appl. Phys. Lett. **70**, 1354–1356 (1997).

7. T. Matsumoto, T. Shimano, H. Saga, H. Sukeda, and M. Kiguchi, Highly efficient probe with a wedge-shaped metallic plate for high density near-field optical recording. J. Appl. Phys. **95**, 3901–3906 (2004).

8. T. Matsumoto, K. Nakamura, T. Nishida, H. Hieda, A. Kikitsu, K. Naito, and T. Koda, Thermally assisted magnetic recording on a bit-patterned medium by using a near-field optical head with a beaked metallic plate. Appl. Phys. Lett. **93**, 031108–031103 (2008).

9. A. Hartschuh, E. J. Sánchez, X. S. Xie, and L. Novotny, High-resolution near-field Raman microscopy of single-walled carbon nanotubes. Phys. Rev. Lett. **90**, 095503 (2003).

10. X. Shi, R. L. Thornton, and L. Hesselink, A nano-aperture with 1000× power throughput enhancement for Very Small Aperture Laser system (VSAL), in *Proc. SPIE*, p. 320 (2002).

11. T. E. Schlesinger, T. Rausch, A. Itagi, J. Zhu, J. A. Bain, and D. D. Stancil, An integrated read/write head for hybrid recording. Jpn. J. Appl. Phys. **41**, 1821–1824 (2002).

12. K. şendur, C. Peng, and W. Challener, Near-field radiation from a ridge waveguide transducer in the vicinity of a solid immersion lens. Phys. Rev. Lett. **94**, 043901/043901–043904 (2005).

13. X. Shi, L. Hesselink, and R. L. Thornton, Ultrahigh light transmission through a C-shaped nanoaperture. Opt. Lett. **28**, 1320–1322 (2003).

14. W. A. Challener, E. Gage, A. Itagi, and C. Peng, Optical transducers for near field recording. Jpn. J. Appl. Phys. **45**, 6632–6642 (2006).

15. M. Moskovits, Surface-enhanced spectroscopy. Rev. Mod. Phys. **57**, 783–826 (1985).

16. C. Peng and W. Challener, Input-grating couplers for narrow Gaussian beam: influence of groove depth. Opt. Express **12**, 6481–6490 (2004).

17. C. Peng, Apparatus and method for coupling light to a thin film optical waveguide, U.S. Patent 7792402 (2008).

18. M. Hirata, M. Oumi, K. Nakajima, and T. Ohkubo, Near-field optical flying head with protruding aperture and its fabrication. Jpn. J. Appl. Phys. **44**, 3519–3523 (2005).

19. S. M. Mansfield and G. S. Kino, Solid immersion microscope. Appl. Phys. Lett. **57**, 2615–2616 (1990).

20. M. Shinoda, K. Saito, T. Kondo, T. Ishimoto, and A. Nakaoki, High-density near-field readout over 50 GB capacity using solid immersion lens with high refractive index. Jpn. J. Appl. Phys. **42**, 1101–1104 (2003).

21. K. Ueyanagi and T. Tomono, Proposal of a near-field optical head using a new solid immersion mirror. Jpn. J. Appl. Phys. **39**, 888–891 (2000).

22. Y.-S. Kim, S.-J. Lee, Y.-J. Kim, N.-C. Park, and Y.-P. Park, Design of a super-paraboloidal solid immersion mirror for near-field recording. Jpn. J. Appl. Phys. **43**, 5756–5760 (2004).

23. W. Challener, C. Mihalcea, C. Peng, and K. Pelhos, Miniature planar solid immersion mirror with focused spot less than a quarter wavelength. Opt. Express **13**, 7189–7197 (2005).

24. F. Tawa, S. Hasegawa, and W. Odajima, Optical head with a butted-grating structure that generates a subwavelength spot for laser-assisted magnetic recording. J. Appl. Phys. **101**, 09H503/501–503 (2007).

25. T. Ishi, J. Fujikata, and K. Ohashi, Large optical transmission through a single Subwavelength hole associated with a sharp-apex grating. Jpn. J. Appl. Phys. **44**, L170–L172 (2005).

26. M. A. Seigler, W. A. Challener, E. Gage, N. Gokemeijer, B. Lu, K. Pelhos, C. Peng, R. E. Rottmayer, X. Yang, H. Zhou, X. Zhu, and T. Rausch, Heat assisted magnetic recording with a fully integrated. Recording head, in *ODS 2007* (2007).

27. T. Rausch, C. D. Mihalcea, K. Pelhos, C. Peng, E. C. Gage, K. Mountfield, M. A. Seigler, and W. A. Challener, Spin stand characterization of dielectric optical waveguides fabricated on AlTiC sliders for heat assisted magnetic recording, in *Proc. SPIE—Optical Data Storage 2004*, pp. 40–46 (2004).

28. D. Weller and A. Moser, Thermal effect limits in ultrahigh-density magnetic recording. IEEE Trans. Magn. **35**, 4423 (1999).

29. Y. Peng, J.-G. Zhu, and D. E. Laughlin, L1$_0$ FePt–MgO perpendicular thin film deposited by alternating sputtering at elevated temperature. J. Appl. Phys. **99**, 08F907 (2006).

30. D. Weller et al., High K_u materials approach to 100 Gbits/in². IEEE Trans. Magn. **36**, 10–15 (2000).

31. T. Klemmer, D. Hoydick, H. Okumura, B. Zhang, and W. A. Soffa, Magnetic hardening and coercivity mechanisms in $L1_0$ ordered FePd ferromagnets. Scripta Metallurgica et Materialia. **33**, 1793–1805 (1995).

32. J. Sayama, K. Mizutani, T. Asahi, and T. Osaka, Thin films of $SmCo_5$ with very high perpendicular magnetic anisotropy. Appl. Phys. Lett. **85**, 5640 (2004).

33. Y. K. Takahashi, T. Ohkubo, and K. Hono, Microstructure and magnetic properties of $SmCo_5$ thin films deposited on Cu and Pt underlayers. J. Appl. Phys. **100**, 053913 (2006).

34. J. Sayama, K. Mizutani, T. Asahi, J. Ariake, K. Ouchi, S. Matsunuma, and T. Osaka, Magnetic properties and microstructure of $SmCo_5$ thin film with perpendicular magnetic anisotropy. J. Magn. Magn. Mater. **287**, 239 (2005).

35. G. A. Bettero and R. Sinclair, (Pt/Co/Pt)/X multilayer films with high Kerr rotations and large perpendicular magnetic anisotropies. Appl. Phys. Lett. **64**, 3337–3339 (1994).

36. J. M. MacLaren and R. H. Victora, Theoretical predictions of interface anisotropy in the presence of interdiffusion. J. Appl. Phys. **76**, 6069–6074 (1994).

37. Y. Kawada, Y. Ueno, and K. Shibata, Magnetic properties, microstructure, and read-write performance of $CoSiO_2$-Pt granular multilayer perpendicular recording media. IEEE Trans. Magn. **40**, 2489–2491 (2004).

38. Y. Kawada, Y. Ueno, and K. Shibata, Co-Pt multilayers perpendicular magnetic recording media with thin Pt layer and high perpendicular anisotropy. IEEE Trans. Magn. **38**, 2045–2047 (2002).

39. J. J. M. Ruigrok, R. Coehoorn, S. R. Cumpson, and H. W. V. Kesteren, Disk recording beyond 100 Gb/in.²: hybrid recording? J. Appl. Phys. **87**, 5398 (2000).

40. H. Nemoto, H. Saga, H. Sukeda, and M. Takahashi, Exchange-coupled magnetic bilayer media for thermomagnetic writing and flux detection. Jpn. J. Appl. Phys. **1**, 1841–1842 (1999).

41. H. Katayama, S. Sawamura, Y. Ogimoto, J. Nakajima, K. Kojima, and K. Ohta, New magnetic recording method using laser assisted read/write technologies. J. Magn. Soc. Jpn. **23**, 233 (1999).

42. J. J. M. Ruigrok, Limits of conventional and thermally-assisted recording. J. Magn. Soc. Jpn. **25**, 313 (2001).

43. V. Guo, B. Lu, X. W. Wu, G. Ju, and D. Weller, A survey of anisotropy measurement techniques and study of thickness effect on interfacial and volume anisotropies in Co/Pt multilayer media. J. Appl. Phys. **99**, 08E918 (2006).

44. W. Shockley, Theory of ordering for the copper gold alloy system. J. Chem. Phys. **6**, 130–144 (1938).

45. J. S. Chen, B. C. Lim, J. F. Hu, B. Liu, and G. M. Chow, High coercivity $L1_0$ FePt films with perpendicular anisotropy deposited on glass substrate at reduced temperature. Appl. Phys. Lett. **90**, 042508 (2007).

46. J. S. Chen, B. C. Lim, J. F. Hu, B. Liu, G. M. Chow, and G. Ju, Low temperature deposited $L1_0$ FePt-C (001) films with high coercivity and small grain size. Appl. Phys. Lett. **91**, 132506 (2007).

47. T. Maeda, T. Kai, A. Kikitsu, T. Nagase, and J. Akiyama, Reduction of ordering temperature of an FePt-ordered alloy by addition of Cu. Appl. Phys. Lett. **80**, 2147 (2002).

48. C. L. Platt, K. W. Wierman, E. B. Svedberg, R. V. D. Veerdonk, J. K. Howard, A. G. Roy, and D. E. Laughlin, $L1_0$ ordering and microstructure of FePt thin films with Cu, Ag, and Au additive. J. Appl. Phys. **92**, 6104 (2002).

49. D. Ravelosona, C. Chappert, V. Mathet, and H. Bermas, Chemical order induced by ion irradiation in FePt (001) films. Appl. Phys. Lett. **76**, 236 (2000).

50. T. Shima, T. Moriguchi, S. Mitani, and K. Takanashi, Chemical order induced by ion irradiation in FePt films. Appl. Phys. Lett. **80**, 288 (2002).

51. T. Suzuki, K. Harada, N. Honda, and K. Ouchi, Preparation of ordered Fe-Pt thin films for perpendicular magnetic recording media. J. Magn. Magn. Mater. **193**, 85–88 (1999).

52. Y. N. Hsu, S. Jeong, D. N. Lambeth, and D. Laughlin, Effects of Ag underlayers on the microstructure and magnetic properties of epitaxial FePt thin films. J. Appl. Phys. **89**, 7068 (2001).

53. M. L. Yan, R. F. Sabirianov, Y. F. Xu, X. Z. Li, and D. J. Sellmyer, $L1_0$ ordered FePt:C composite films with (001) texture. IEEE Trans. Magn. **40**, 2470 (2004).

54. K. Kang, Z. G. Zhang, C. Papusoi, and T. Suzuki, Composite nanogranular films of FePt-MgO with (001) orientation onto glass substrates. Appl. Phys. Lett. **84**, 404 (2004).

55. A. Perumal, Y. K. Takahashi, and K. Hono, $L1_0$ FePt-C nanogranular perpendicular anisotropy films with narrow size distribution. Appl. Phys. Express **1**, 101301 (2008).

56. E. Yang and D. E. Laughlin, $L1_0$ FePt-oxide columnar perpendicular media with high coercivity and small grain size. J. Appl. Phys. **104**, 023904 (2008).

57. M Kryder, EC Gage, TW McDaniel, WA Challener, RE Rottmayer, G Ju, Y-T Hsia, and MF Erden, Heat assisted magnetic recording, in *Proc. IEEE 96*, pp. 1810–1835 (2008).

58. D. Karns et al., Design and characterization of a media thermal stack for confining lateral thermal heat flow, in *Intermag 2008* (2008).

59. J.-U. Thiele, S. Maat, and E. E. Fullerton, FeRh/FePt exchange spring films for thermally assisted magnetic recording media. Appl. Phys. Lett. **82**, 2859–2861 (2003).

60. J.-U. Thiele, S. Maat, E. E. Fullerton, and J. L. Robertson, Magnetic and structural properties of FePt-FeRh exchange spring films for thermally assisted magnetic recording media. IEEE Trans. Magn. **40**, 2537 (2004).

61. K. R. Coffey, J.-U. Thiele, and D. Weller, "Thermal spring" magnetic recording media for writing using magnetic and thermal gradients, U.S. Patent 6881497 (2005).

62. A. Kikitsu, T. Kai, T. Nagase, and J.-I. Akiyama, A concept of exchange-coupled recording medium for heat-assisted magnetic recording. J. Appl. Phys. **97**, 10P701 (2005).

63. H. Chiba, Y. Oshikubo, K. Watanabe, T. Tokairin, and E. Yamakawa, Synthesis of Trifunctional PFPE lubricants and its spreading characteristics on a hard disk surface, in *Proceedings of the 2004 International Symposium on Micro-Nanomechatronics and Human Science*, pp. 261–264 (2004).

64. J. Zhang, R. Ji, J. W. Xu, J. K. P. Ng, B. X. Xu, H. X. Yuan, and S. N. Piramanayagam, Lubrication for heat-assisted magnetic recording media. IEEE Trans. Magn. **42**, 2546–2548 (2006).

65. M. S. Lim and A. Gellman, Kinetics of laser induced desorption and decomposition of Fomblin Zdol on carbon overcoats. Tribol. Int. **38**, 554–561 (2005).

66. W. Peng, Y. T. Hsia, S. Kursat, and T. McDaniel, Thermo-magneto-mechanical analysis of head-disk interface in heat assisted magnetic recording. Tribol. Int. **38**, 588–593 (2005).

67. L. Li, C. L. Platt, and Y. T. Hsia, *Head disc interface design*, in *United States Patent Application* (2006).

68. L. Wu, Modelling and simulation of the lubricant depletion process induced by laser heating in heat-assisted magnetic recording system. Nanotechnology **18**, 215702 (2007).

69. M. A. Seigler, W. A. Challener, E. Gage, N. Gokemeijer, G. Ju, B. Lu, K. Pelhos, C. Peng, R. E. Rottmayer, X. Yang, H. Zhou, and T. Rausch, Integrated heat assisted magnetic recording head: design and recording demonstration. IEEE Trans. Magn. **44**, 119–124 (2008).

70. T. Klemmer, Y. Peng, X. Wu, and G. Ju, Materials processing for high anisotropy $L1_0$ granular media. IEEE Trans. Magn. **45**, 845–849 (2009).

71. W. A. Challener, C. Peng, A. V. Itagi, D. Karns, W. Peng, Y. Peng, X. Yang, X. Zhu, N. J. Gokemeijer, Y. T. Hsia, G. Ju, R. E. Rottmayer, M. A. Seigler, and E. C. Gage, Heat-assisted magnetic recording by a near-field transducer with efficient optical energy transfer. Nat Photon. **3**, 303–303 (2009).

72. B. C. Stipe, T. C. Strand, C. C. Poon, H. Balamane, T. D. Boone, J. A. Katine, J.-L. Li, V. Rawat, H. Nemoto, A. Hirotsune, O. Hellwig, R. Ruiz, E. Dobisz, D. S. Kercher, N. Robertson, T. R. Albrecht, and B. D. Terris, Magnetic recording at 1.5 Pb m^{-2} using an integrated plasmonic antenna. Nat. Photon. **4**, 484–488 (2010).

73. T. W. McDaniel, Ultimate limits to thermally assisted magnetic recording. J. Phys. Condens. Matter **17**, R315–R332 (2005).

74. E. Gage et al., An integrated recording head for heat assisted magnetic recording, presented at ISOM Conference, Singapore, October 2007, paper We-H-05 (2007).

75. K. Şendur and W. Challener, Patterned medium for heat assisted magnetic recording. Appl. Phys. Lett. **94**, 032503–032503 (2009).

76. Y. Peng, G. Ju, X. Wu, X. Zhu, T. Klemmer, D. Karns, D. Buechel, L. Li, E. Gage, M. Seigler, W. A. Challener, Y-T. Hsia, and R. Hempstead, High anisotropy L10 media development for heat assisted magnetic recording, in 19th Magnetic Recording Conference (TMRC2008), Singapore, 2008.

77. Y. Peng et al., Heat assisted magnetic recording on high anisotropy nanocomposite media, in NANO'08, August 18–21, 2008, pp. 603–604.

11

$L1_0$ FePt FOR MAGNETIC RECORDING MEDIA APPLICATION

Jiangfeng Hu

Data Storage Institute, Singapore

Jingsheng Chen

National University of Singapore

Ganping Ju

Seagate Technology

11.1 INTRODUCTION

It was learned in the previous chapters that the media trilemma will pose limitations on the areal density achieved using the existing granular perpendicular media technology. Although technologies such as exchange-coupled composite (ECC) media may extend the areal density beyond 1 Tb/in.^{2} in perpendicular media, significant progress in research over the last several years has brought the introduction of alternative technologies such as heat-assisted magnetic recording (HAMR). Chapter 10 introduced the concept of HAMR at a systems level. This chapter will discuss the recording media

Developments in Data Storage: Materials Perspective, First Edition.
Edited by S. N. Piramanayagam, Tow C. Chong.

candidate material $L1_0$ FePt for HAMR. Section 11.2 will provide an overview of $L1_0$ FePt alloys. Section 11.3 focuses on the magnetic anisotropy and chemical ordering that makes $L1_0$ FePt unique. Section 11.4 discusses the techniques adopted to control the microstructure and texture of FePt to suit the media requirements, and Section 11.5 summarizes the discussions.

11.2 OVERVIEW OF FUNDAMENTAL OF $L1_0$ FePt

Owing to their large magnetocrystalline anisotropy, $L1_0$ magnetic alloys are promising candidates for the next generation of magnetic recording media. The high magnetic anisotropy of $5–10 \times 10^7$ erg/cc (1 erg/cc $= 10^{-1}$ J/m^3) makes FePt grains thermally stable for grain diameters of less than 3 nm with film thickness of about 10 nm. This section will provide a brief introduction to $L1_0$ FePt alloys.

$L1_0$ is a crystalline structure derived from face-centered cubic (fcc) structure where the corner and the corresponding face in the same plane are occupied by one type of atoms, and the other faces between two planes are occupied by a second type of atoms. The structure is fcc if the two types of the atoms are randomly distributed. The $L1_0$ is a chemical ordering or atomic ordering obtained by stacking alternating single-different atomic layers. Fcc and $L1_0$ structures are shown in Figure 11.1.

The prototype structure of $L1_0$ is the tetragonal CuAu (I)-type structure. The stability of this structure depends on the atomic size difference between the two atom components, which is normally less than 15%. For example, FePt shows a chemically disordered fcc structure at high temperatures, as shown in the phase diagram (Fig. 11.2) [1]. At lower temperatures, the Fe and Pt atoms are ordered in an atomic multilayer structure, known as $L1_0$ chemical ordering. The temperature of fcc to $L1_0$ transformation is ~1300°C; the fcc phase is stable at temperatures above 1300°C. $L1_0$ FePt is a thermodynamically stable phase at room temperature. However, a disordered phase is commonly obtained when FePt film is deposited at room temperature. The reason is that the energy barrier is too high for atomic diffusion at low temperature to

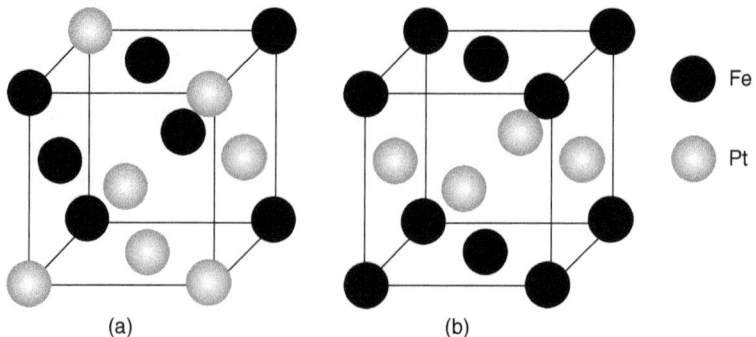

Fe

Pt

(a) (b)

Figure 11.1. Schematics of (a) fcc and (b) $L1_0$ structures.

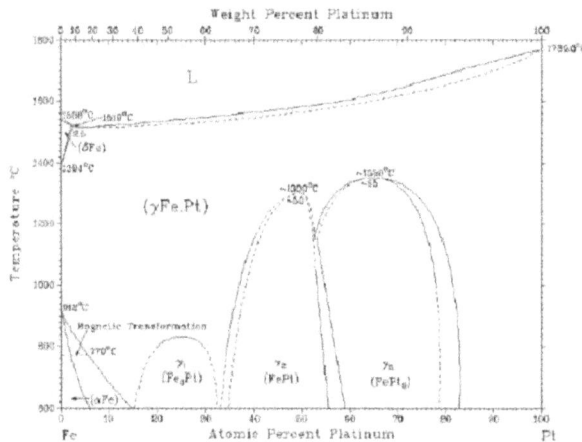

Figure 11.2. Phase diagram of FePt alloy. (Reprinted with permission from Reference 1, ASM International. All rights reserved. http://www.asminternational.org)

enable the formation of chemically ordered $L1_0$ FePt. As the magnetocrystalline anisotropy of $L1_0$ FePt is about 100 times greater than that of fcc FePt, it is crucial to get $L1_0$ FePt for recording applications. Although this is a first-order transition, the phase transformation can occur even when the temperature is away from the equilibrium phase boundary and below the instability temperature for the disordered alloy [2]. The long-range order of $L1_0$ phase can be quantified [3, 4] by the order parameter

$$S = (\gamma_{Fe} - x_{Fe})/y_{Pt} = (\gamma_{Pt} - x_{Pt})/y_{Fe}, \tag{11.1}$$

where $x_{Fe(Pt)}$ is the atomic fraction of Fe (Pt) in the sample, $y_{Fe(Pt)}$ the fraction of Fe (Pt) sites, and $\gamma_{Fe(Pt)}$ the fraction of Fe (Pt) sites occupied by the correct atom. For $Fe_{50}Pt_{50}$ alloy, when the long range order is perfect, and the Fe (Pt) sites are occupied by the correct atoms, S is equal to 1. When the atomic arrangement is completely random, $\gamma_{Fe} = x_{Fe} = 50\%$ or $\gamma_{Pt} = x_{Pt} = 50\%$ according to statistical theory and thus S equals 0 [5].

11.3 MAGNETIC ANISOTROPY OF $L1_0$ FePt AND CHEMICAL ORDERING

FePt gains its prominence mainly because of its high magnetic anisotropy. This high anisotropy is obtained only in the chemically ordered state. Therefore, this section deals with the magnetic anisotropy and the chemical ordering of FePt.

Magnetic anisotropy is one of the intrinsic properties of magnetic materials, originating in atomic magnetism and closely related to quantum phenomena such as exchange, crystal field, interatomic hopping, and spin–orbit coupling. In most cases, magnetic anisotropy reflects the competition between the crystal-field interaction and spin–orbit coupling, which is called magnetocrystalline anisotropy. Generally, magnetocrystalline anisotropy is caused by strong coupling among spin, orbital, and lattice degrees of freedom.

FePt is a binary alloy, and in general, its phase behavior is determined by a balance among the interactions AA, BB, and AB in a binary A–B system. The energy of the interactions is typically on the order of 1 eV. However, the effective pair interactions are small and typically on the order of several 10 meV, and thus can compete with thermal excitations in the system [6, 7]. In FePt the stability of a specific phase depends on a balance of three different types of energies: (1) the formation enthalpy of the ordered structure, (2) the mixing enthalpy of the random alloy, and (3) the strain energy from atomic size mismatch.

It is known that high magnetic anisotropy only exists in the $L1_0$ ordered FePt. In fcc FePt, the probability of each site being occupied by Fe or Pt is the same, which means the Fe and Pt atoms are randomly distributed. The phase transformation from fcc to $L1_0$ is accompanied by the rearrangement of Fe and Pt atoms, where two of the faces are occupied by one type of atom, and the corner and other faces are occupied by another type of atom. Therefore, the translational symmetry decreases by a factor of two when the fcc structure transforms to $L1_0$ structure. Laughlin et al. has reported the formation of both translational and orientational domains in $L1_0$ FePt due to the variation in symmetry [2]. Two possible ordering structures were observed due to the loss of the translational symmetry of the elements after the atomic ordering (as shown in Fig. 11.3a). The interface between these two structures is called the antiphase boundary. At this boundary, the local atomic bonding is disrupted, and hence the local magnetocrystalline anisotropy energy is expected to vary. There is also another type of domain; it is called an orientational domain or variant as shown in Figure 11.3b. The formation of these domains is due to the reduction of the fourfold axes from three to one when FePt undergoes fcc to $L1_0$ transformation. The axis can be orientated along any of the original cubic <100> axes. Each orientational domain can have two translational domains. Therefore, there can be six distinct domains in FePt when fcc to $L1_0$ transformation occurs.

The ordering of FePt from A1 to $L1_0$ is accompanied by a variation of the crystalline structure, and hence a variation in the crystal field and the spin–orbit coupling. Theoretical work to investigate the origin of the high magnetic anisotropy in $L1_0$ FePt has been done. Simulation work based on first principle using the full-potential linear muffin-tin orbitals method has also been done [8, 9]. In the case of FePt, it is believed that the large magnetic anisotropy is caused by a delicate interaction between Fe and Pt atoms, where the large spin–orbit coupling of the Pt site and the hybridization between Fe $3d$ and Pt $5d$ states is crucial. Experiments done by X-ray magnetic circular dichroism (XMCD) have shown that the microscopic origin of perpendicular magnetic anisotropy is related to $3d$ and $5d$ orbital moment an isotropies such as out-of-plane components of the orbit moments being higher than the in-plane components [10]. It

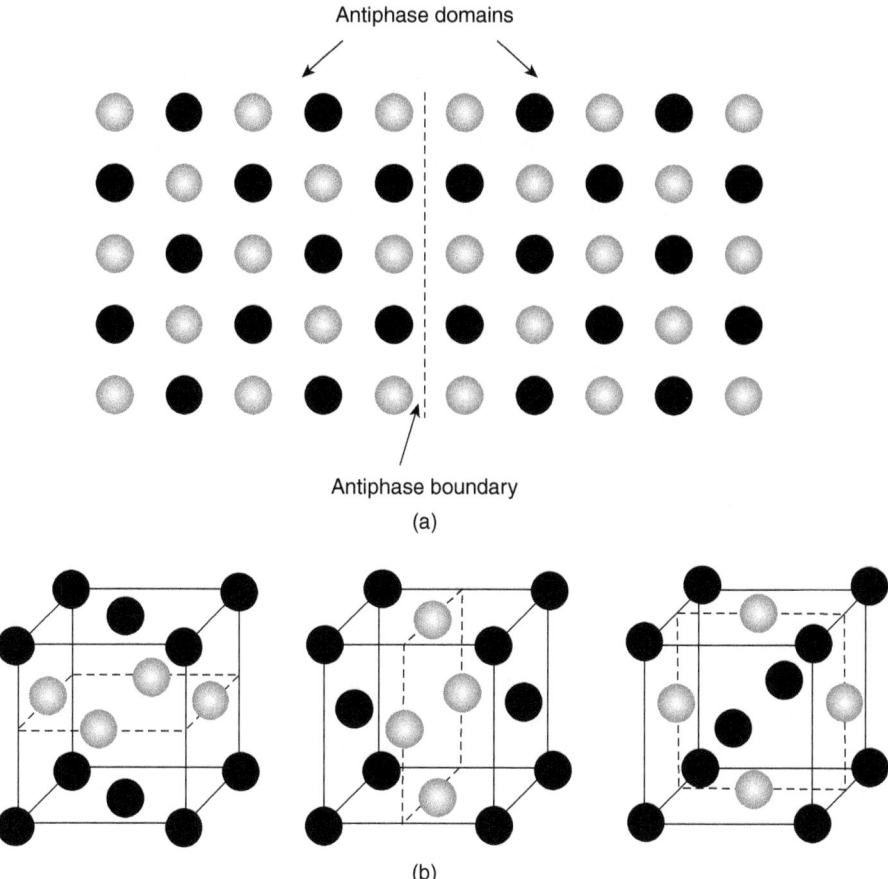

Figure 11.3. The translational domains and the antiphase boundary (a); and the orientational domains of $L1_0$ structure (b).

is believed that the magnetic easy axis coincides with the direction having the largest orbital moment. An XMCD study of Co/Pt multilayers indicated that the perpendicular magnetic anisotropy is caused by anisotropy in orbital moments and originates from Pt $5d$-Co $3d$ hybridization [11]. It seems that the anisotropy in FePt mainly originates from Pt in FePt. Therefore, the large magnetic anisotropy in FePt originates from both the large spin–orbit interaction and the anisotropy in the orbital moment at the Pt site in FePt. Crystal-field splitting induced by the reduction in symmetry of the systems when going from A1 to $L1_0$ also contributes to the lager magnetic anisotropy in FePt, which is proved by a strong dependence of the magnetic anisotropy on the c/a ratio. Although the $L1_0$ is a low-temperature ordered phase, FePt thin films or particles fabricated by vapor deposition methods such as sputtering, evaporation, and pulsed laser deposition can only be formed in the disordered fcc phase. In order to obtain $L1_0$ ordered FePt, a high temperature process such as postannealing and/or in-situ substrate heating is required. Therefore, it is very important to understand the kinetics of the ordering as a function of the thermal process. To obtain $L1_0$ FePt with a high ordering parameter, a temperature more than 550°C for the postannealing process and 400°C for in-situ substrate heating is normally required. However, such a high temperature process is not favorable for real magnetic recording applications. On one hand, the high temperature is not favorable for obtaining small grains, which is a critical requirement for HAMR media for future ultrahigh density magnetic recording. On the other hand, high temperature is not compatible with the equipment, the substrates, and the processes currently used in the hard disk industry. Therefore, the techniques to achieve $L1_0$ FePt at lower temperatures are very important to achieve smaller grain sizes and to suit manufacturing processes. From the viewpoint of signal-to-noise ratio (SNR) of the media, it is desirable to obtain $L1_0$ FePt with high K_u and small K_u dispersion at a relatively low process temperature. Therefore, we need to have a clear picture about the factors that may affect the K_u and thus the K_u distributions.

11.3.1 Factors That Affect the Chemical Ordering of FePt

Based on the phase diagram of FePt, temperature and stoichiometry are two important factors of the ordering parameter S. In the case of thin films, the film thickness is also very important since it affects atomic diffusion and thus the S at a given temperature. Moreover, the crystallographic texture appears to play a role in the ordering parameter too. The S for two FePt films with different textures has been studied as a function of the deposition temperature, and the results are shown in Figure 11.4 [12]. It can be seen that the S increases with increasing substrate temperature in both the cases, but with a different absolute value and trend for two different textures. It has to be noted that other

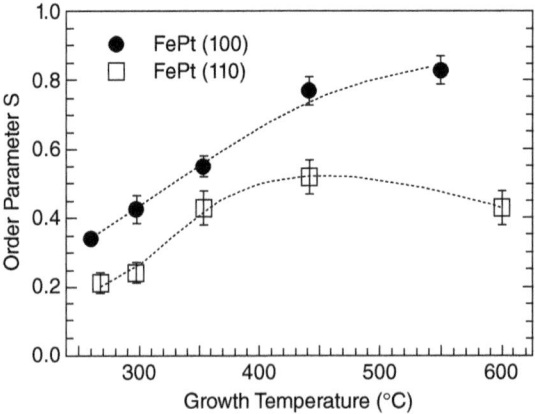

Figure 11.4. The average ordering parameter S as a function of growth temperature for FePt films grown on MgO (100) and MgO (110) single crystal substrates. (Reprinted with permission from Reference 12, M. M. Schwickert, et al., *J. Appl. Phys.* **87**, 6956 (2000). Copyright (2000) American Institute of Physics.)

factors such as deposition method, deposition rate, the substrates being used, and so on also affect the final S of the FePt thin films.

The ordering process of sputtered FePt thin films deposited on a heated Corning glass substrate at 300°C with different film thicknesses was studied by Takahashi et al. [13]. Magnetic properties indicated that the film was a disordered one when the film thickness was thinner than 50 nm. The ordering parameter S increased from near zero to about 0.8 with increasing film thickness up to 300 nm. The variation of the S with increasing film thickness was attributed to the recrystallization that occurred for film thickness over 100 nm. The effect of the film thickness on chemical ordering of the FePt thin films was also found for postannealed FePt-alloy thin films [14]. It was found that the ordering process in the thick samples occurred at much lower temperature in comparison to the thinner ones.

The stoichiometric effects of FePt films deposited by sputtering on a MgO (200) single crystal substrate at 300°C were investigated by Seki et al. [15]. The Fe concentration was varied from 19 to 68 at%. The X-ray diffraction (XRD) (001) and (003) superlattice peaks were observed at a Pt-rich composition range, indicating formation of $L1_0$ ordered structure. The maximum values of the S and K_u were 0.6 ± 0.1 and 1.8×10^7 erg/cm^3, respectively for 38 at% of Fe. The low value of S in this study is mainly due to the low substrate temperature (only 300°C). The order parameters S and anisotropy constants of a series of epitaxial $L1_0$ FePt films deposited on MgO (001) single crystal substrate at 620°C by co-sputtering with compositions in the range of 45–55 at% Fe and nominal thicknesses of 50 nm have been characterized by Barmak et al. [16]. It was found that the S had a maximum for the film composition closest to the equiatomic composition, whereas the magnetocrystalline anisotropy increased as the Fe content increased from below to slightly above the equiatomic composition. These results imply that nonstoichiometric FePt compositions with a slight excess of Fe may in fact be preferred for applications that require high anisotropy. Some parameters to illustrate the effect of the Fe concentration are listed in Table 11.1.

TABLE 11.1. Measured Composition, Thickness, Lattice Parameters a and c, c/a and Order Parameter, S, for FePt(001) Films. S_{max} Is the Maximum Order Parameter for the Given Composition. See Text for More Details. Also Listed Is Whether Or Not in-Plane c-Axis Variants Were Present. The Substrate Temperature, T_s, for Seed Layer and Film Deposition Was 620°C. The Relatively Large Error in the Actual Compositions (±2.0%) and Thicknesses (±5.0 nm) Measured by Rutherford Backscattering Are a Result of the Presence of the Bilayer Fe/Pt Seed

Material	Composition x (at. %)	Thickness (nm)	a	b	c/a	S	S_{max}	In-plane c-axis Variant
Fe$_x$Pt$_{100-x}$	46.0	50.6	3.870	3.721	0.961	0.89 ± 0.02	0.92	No
/Pt(1 nm)	51.0	57.7	3.863	3.710	0.960	0.93 ± 0.05	0.98	No
/Fe(1 nm)	51.9	53.6	3.857	3.706	0.961	0.89 ± 0.06	0.96	No
	55.3	47.8	3.839	3.704	0.965	0.72 ± 0.05	0.89	Yes

The stoichiometric effects on ordering and magnetic anisotropy had also been investigated in FePt nanoparticles by Klemmer et al. [17]. It was reported that variation of the Fe/Pt atomic ratio near equilibrium demonstrated a strong influence on the lattice parameters of $L1_0$ FePt nanoparticles. It was found that the c parameter mostly changes in the Pt-rich compositions, and the a parameter mostly changes in the Fe-rich composition with respect to the equiatomic composition. This causes the tetragonality of the $L1_0$ structure to be maximized near the equilibrium composition. It was also found that the magnetic anisotropy is strongly correlated with the c/a ratio, and the peak anisotropy coincides with the maximum tetragonality. It was believed that the chemical ordering is a driving force for the structural changes and maximum tetragonality reflects the highest degree of the layered chemical order.

11.3.2 Promotion of Chemical Ordering by Element Doping

It has been reported that the element doping can enhance the chemical ordering in FePt, which enables obtaining $L1_0$ ordered FePt at a relatively low process temperature. Elements such as Cu, Au, Ag, and Cr are effective dopants to promote ordering of FePt, thus decreasing the ordering temperature for the formation of the $L1_0$ FePt. It was found that the ordering temperature for FePt alloy with 15% Cu doping was reduced from 400°C (pure FePt) to 300°C [18]. The promoted ordering was attributed to the formation of FePtCu ternary alloy, which was experimentally confirmed [19], where the Fe site in the lattice was substituted by Cu. It was believed that the Gibbs free energy of the FePtCu alloy was smaller than that of FePt, thus a larger driven force for the fcc–$L1_0$ transformation [20]. Similar results were reported that the ordering temperature of FePtCu film was reduced from 600°C to 400°C [21]. FePtCu film with a coercivity of 8 kOe was obtained after annealing at 400°C. The optimized composition was found to be $(FePt)_{96}Cu_4$. However, some research works pointed out that the impact of the Cu on the ordering temperature of FePt depended greatly on the initial Fe/Pt atomic ratio [22, 23]. For films starting with an equiatomic Fe and Pt composition, the doped Cu does not significantly promote $L1_0$ ordering [24]. It was suggested that the decrease of ordering temperature by Cu doping was due to deviation from the equiatomic FePt composition, which would alter the ordering kinetics [25].

The effects of Ag and Au doping on the $L1_0$ ordering of thin FePt films have also been reported [26, 27]. It was found that the Ag and Au additives affected the structure and magnetic properties of FePt in a similar manner. Both Ag and Au tended to chemically segregate from FePt instead of forming a ternary alloy as happened in the case of FePt film with Cu additive. The dark-field transmission electron microscopy (TEM) images of FePt thin films with different additives are shown in Figure 11.5. The average grain size for the FePt + 20% Cu sample was 50 nm, compared to 24 nm for the FePt + Ag, 14 nm for the FePt + Au, and 20 nm for the reference pure FePt sample. Au additive demonstrated a better grain refinement for FePt. As to the $L1_0$ ordering process, the most significant improvement was found in film with Cu additions above 20%. The promoting of the $L1_0$ ordering was attributed to the formation of the FePtCu alloy.

The comparison of the magnetic properties of the Ag- and Au-doped FePt film with pure FePt demonstrated an increased anisotropy field and the magnetic anisotropy.

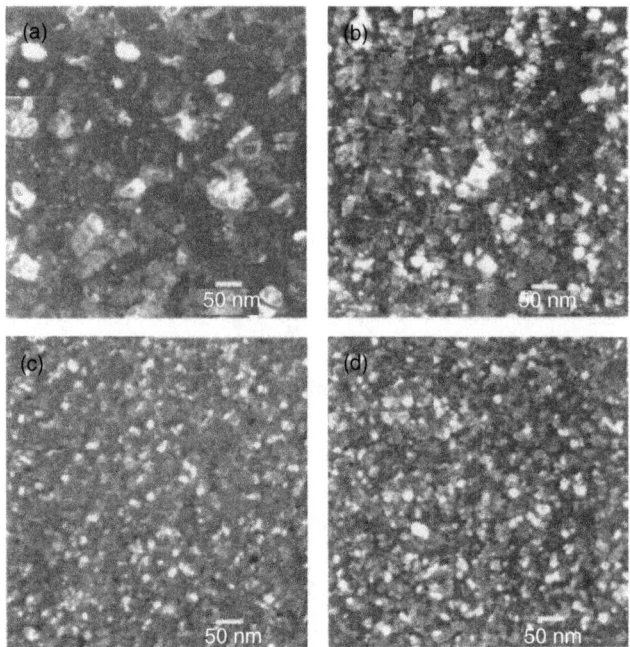

Figure 11.5. Plan-view dark-field TEM images of 450°C/10 min annealed MgO (5 nm)/ FePt + 20% additive (20 nm) films with (a) Cu, (b) Ag, (c) Au, and (d) reference. (Reprinted with permission from Reference 26, C. L. Platt, et al., *J. Appl. Phys.* **92**, 6104 (2002). Copyright (2002) American Institute of Physics.)

Results suggested both Au and Ag enhanced the $L1_0$ ordering of FePt thin films. The coercivity significantly increased from 5.4 to 9.4 kOe for Au doping and to 20.5 kOe for Ag doping, as shown in Figure 11.6. The improved ordering process was attributed to the variation of the melting point of FePt alloy by alloying with Au and Ag, thus resulting in the enhancement of the atomic mobility. The accelerated atomic diffusion promotes the ordering process. However, the formation of the FePtAu (Ag) ternary alloy was not confirmed.

The influence of Ag on the ordering process of FePt was also demonstrated in FePt nanoparticles. FePt nanoparticle assemblies with and without Ag additions were annealed at 500°C [28]. Without the addition of Ag, the coercivity of FePt nanoparticle assembly was only 2 kOe, but exceeded 10 kOe after adding 15% Ag in FePt nanoparticles. Since both FePt and FePt-Ag nanoparticles were well separated, exchange decoupling may not be the reason for the increase in coercivity. The increase in H_C of FePt-Ag could therefore be attributed to an increase of $L1_0$ ordering and magnetocrystalline anisotropy. The possible mechanisms for the promotion of $L1_0$ ordering with Ag doping were attributed to the low surface energy (promotes Ag segregation) and the low solubility of Ag with both Fe and Pt [29, 30]. When Ag is incorporated in FePt nanoparticles, it diffuses out of the particles upon heating, resulting in creation of

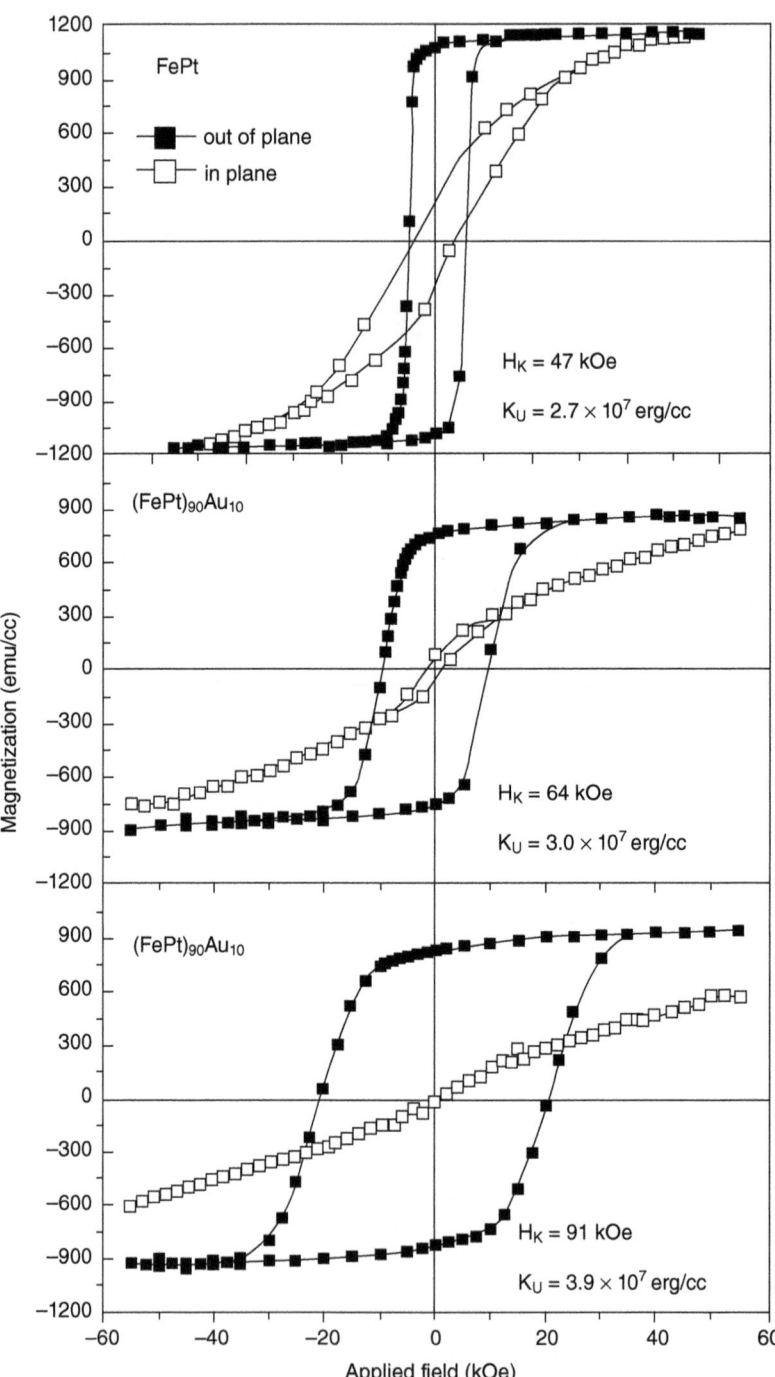

Figure 11.6. M-H loops of the FePt, (FePt)$_{90}$Au$_{10}$, and (FePt)$_{90}$Ag$_{10}$ films. (Reprinted with permission from Reference 27, C. Y. You, et al., *J. Appl. Phys.* **100**, 056105 (2006). Copyright (2006) American Institute of Physics.)

vacancies in the FePt lattices. This in turn enhances the kinetics of $L1_0$ ordering and thus decreases the ordering temperature. The effect of the Ag doping on reducing the ordering temperature of $L1_0$ FePt nanoparticles was investigated by differential scanning calorimetry (DSC) at different scanning rates [31]. The activation energy was reduced for Ag-doped FePt nanoparticles from 251 to 219 kJ/mol. Ag diffusion and segregation to form the Ag phase during the annealing process will generate vacancies at the FePt lattices. The reduction of the activation energy was due to the increase in the number of vacancies, thus the reduction of the $L1_0$ ordering temperature in doped FePt nanoparticles. Based on the Arrhenius-type relationship, the diffusion coefficient of the Fe and Pt atoms will be much larger owing to the increasing vacancy concentration. The enhanced diffusion coefficients of the Fe and Pt atoms thus promote the transformation from A1 to $L1_0$ structure. It was also reported that the ordering temperature of Ag- and Au-doped self-assembled FePt nanoparticles can be effectively reduced to 400°C due to the formation of high concentration vacancies during the annealing process [32, 33]. The chemical ordering enhancement was also found in Sb-doped FePt nanoparticles, where the ordering temperature was reduced to 300°C [34]. The dramatic reduction in the ordering temperature was attributed to enhancement of the Fe and Pt diffusion resulting from the excess vacancies generated due to the low solubility and the lower interfacial energy of Sb.

Other additives, such as Zr, also enhanced the chemical ordering kinetics for annealed polycrystalline films prepared by sputtering [35]. It appears that Zr doping introduces point defects and lattice strain in the FePt matrix because of its larger atomic radius compared to that of Fe and Pt. These lattice defects are believed to act as activated nucleation sites for the ordered phase, and as a result, the kinetics of the ordering process is enhanced. However, Zr may form an intermetallic compound with Pt, thus making the FePt ordered phase unstable.

11.3.3 Promotion of Chemical Ordering by Strain or Stress

The transformation of FePt from A1 to $L1_0$ is accompanied by a variation of the crystalline structure, thus an increase of the lattice constant a, and a decrease of the lattice constant c. Therefore, if one can apply a force either along or normal to the cube surface direction, the cube may deform to a tetragonal shape and achieve $L1_0$ ordering.

It was reported that the compressive stress along the c-axis during high gas-pressure (100 Pa) sputtering could promote the ordering process $L1_0$ FePt films [36]. $L1_0$ FePt film was also prepared at 275°C by so-called dynamic stress [37]. In this method, FePt films were deposited on a Cu underlayer/HF-cleaned Si (100) substrate, followed by postdeposition annealing. With increasing annealing temperature up to 250°C, the stress increased due to the difference in thermal expansion coefficients between the Cu film and the Si substrate. It was demonstrated that the $L1_0$ ordering of FePt films was closely related to the change of the stress.

When a thin film with a certain lattice mismatch with the substrate is deposited, the lattice parameter of the film can either expand or shrink in the film direction, depending on whether the mismatch is negative or positive. For a negative lattice mismatch, that is, the lattice constant of film is less than that of the substrate; the lattice

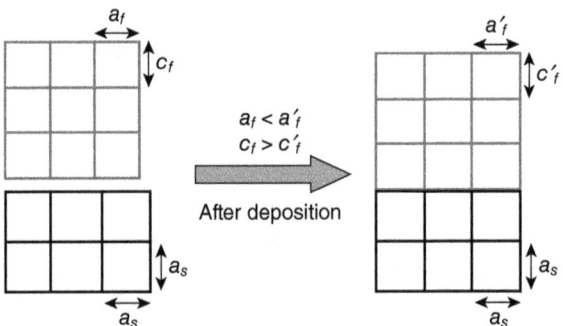

Figure 11.7. Schematic drawings of strain- or stress-induced *L*1$_0$ ordering.

constant could be expanded in the film direction and shrunk in the film normal direction. The schematic drawings of this principle are shown in Figure 11.7 [38].

There exists a critical film thickness for lattice mismatch between the film and substrate. Below the critical thickness, the lattice constant of the film will match that of the substrate. Beyond the critical thickness, the strain induced by the lattice mismatch would be relieved by the formation of defects such as dislocations, and the lattice constant of the top part of the film will revert to the unstrained value. It has been suggested that lattice mismatch at the interface between FePt film and the underlayer may expand the *a*-axis and shrink the *c*-axis of the FePt film, favoring the ordering at low temperatures. The *L*1$_0$ phase was obtained for FePt films deposited on a CrX (X = Ru, Mo, W, Ti) underlayer at low temperatures [38, 39]. It was found that a lattice mismatch of about 6.33% is most effective to reduce the ordering temperature.

Other approaches have also been investigated to decrease the ordering temperature and increase the *S*. The ordering process of FePt films was investigated using 130 keV He ion irradiation [40]. The *S* increased up to 0.3 and 0.6, respectively when the disordered (S~0) and partially ordered (S~0.4) FePt films were irradiated by He ions with fluences of 4×10^{16} ions/cm^2 at 280°C. The ion beam led to atomic displacements, and the heating promoted atomic rearrangements and lattice relaxation. With increasing energy of He ions (2MeV) and beam current (1.25–6 μA), highly ordered *L*1$_0$ FePt films were obtained [41]. The films demonstrated coercivity exceeding 5700 Oe after the disordered FePt was irradiated at beam current 1.25 μA with ion fluencies of 2.4×10^{16} ions/cm^2. The high beam current caused direct beam heating on the sample. In addition, the irradiation-induced heating provided efficient microscopic heating transfer and created excess point defects, significantly enhancing diffusion and thus promoting formation of *L*1$_0$ ordered FePt films. It was also reported that the FePt/Au multilayers deposited on a MgO single crystal substrate followed by annealing can effectively reduce the ordering temperature by 150°C [42]. It was found that the additional FePt/Au interface energy, the stress energy due to the lattice mismatch, and the diffusion of the Au atoms all promote the ordering process of FePt film. The *L*1$_0$ ordered FePt film could also be obtained by annealing at 350°C the FePt film deposited on a AuCu underlayer [43]. The ordering of the AuCu underlayer at low temperature coherently induced the disorder-order transformation of FePt films. The ordering temperature can be even reduced to 300°C for FePt films deposited on a AgCu underlayer followed by postannealing [44]. The low temperature ordering of the FePt thin films was attributed to the dynamic stress induced by phase separation in the AgCu underlayer and Cu diffusion during the annealing process.

11.3.4   Kinetics and Thermal Processing

As mentioned earlier, FePt thin films deposited at room temperature nominally adopts a soft-magnetic A1 phase. Either a subsequent annealing or in-situ substrate heating is required to obtain the desired $L1_0$ phase. Although the phase transformation from A1 to $L1_0$ is a simple polymorphic one (a variation in crystal symmetry and not composition), the mechanism for A1 to $L1_0$ ordering can be complex. The mechanism of $L1_0$ ordering kinetics of FePt thin films is normally dependent on the approaches used to obtain the ordered phase. Films deposited at room temperature followed by subsequent annealing have been reported to proceed via a discontinuous or first-order (nucleation and growth) process [45–49], whereas films deposited on heated substrate are claimed to proceed via a continuous-type reaction [50, 51].

FePt films prepared by molecular beam epitaxy on a MgO single crystal substrate with a Pt seedlayer at different substrate temperatures ranging from 100°C to 500°C have been studied [50]. Partially ordered films grown in the temperature range 100–300°C show no evidence of a first-order reaction since no splitting of the (002) Bragg peak into distinct ordered and disordered components was observed. The transformation is a continuous type instead of the first-order type observed in annealed FePt films. Since the deposition temperature was below 600°C, which is much lower than the order–disorder temperature of 1300°C, the bulk diffusion was slow. Therefore, it was assumed that the FePt films were partially ordered (small S), and the dependence of S on temperature should exhibit an Arrhenius behavior with the activation energy that is the diffusion barrier height. The Arrhenius equation gives the dependence of the rate constant of chemical ordering on the temperature and activation energy. Fitting the ordering parameter as a function of the process temperature into the Arrhenius equation gives the activation energy (diffusional barrier height) of about 0.2 ± 0.04 eV, which is quite close to the energy barrier (~ 0.2 eV) for adatom diffusion from a terrace to a lower terrace for Ag/Pt (111) [52]. The ordering process seems to be surface diffusion dominated through surface segregation of Pt and Fe atoms onto adjacent terraces to form the $L1_0$ superlattice. Kim et al. also observed the $L1_0$ ordered structure at a temperature of 200°C on a MgO (100) substrate. The ordering phase was formed via a second-order type transformation [51]. For FePt films deposited at room temperature, films adopt the A1 phase. Therefore, the A1 to $L1_0$ transformation is normally thermodynamically first order, occurring by nucleation and growth of the ordered phase in the disordered matrix during the annealing process. The changes of the disordered A1 phase were observed prior to the transformation to the ordered $L1_0$ phase [53]. It was found that the short-range order increased in the disordered fcc phase with increasing annealing temperature. Therefore, the ordering kinetics was dependent on the initial state of the disordered A1 phase in the films prepared under different conditions.

The ordering kinetics depends on the Fe/Pt atomic ratio in the film. The A1 to $L1_0$ ordering transformation in binary FePt films with composition in the range of 47.5~54.4 at% Fe have been studied [54]. It was found that the kinetic ordering temperature decreases from 447°C to 357°C as the increase of the Fe content. However, the Curie temperature (T_C) of the $L1_0$ ordered phase increases from 384°C to 455°C. The lattice parameter of the A1 phase and the c/a ratio of the $L1_0$ phase decrease with increasing Fe content.

The substrate material also affected the ordering kinetics of FePt thin films. FePt thin films deposited on $SrTiO_3$, MgO, and a 2-nm FeO_x, underlayer on a Si substrate at room temperature followed by postannealing at elevated temperatures have been investigated [55]. It was found that the ordering temperature for the FePt film deposited on the nonepitaxial Si/FeO_x, substrate is about 150°C lower than the epitaxial FePt films deposited on MgO and $SrTiO_3$ substrates. The difference in the ordering kinetics was attributed to the stresses arising from lattice defects, recrystallization, and the thermal strain resulting from the different thermal expansion between substrates and film.

The A1 to $L1_0$ ordering process in FePt granular films was dependent on the particle size of FePt in the films [56]. Granular films were annealed at 600°C for 1 hour in a vacuum. It was found that the $L1_0$ ordered phase was not obtained in granular film with FePt particle size smaller than 4 nm, while the granular film with particle size larger than 7 nm was fully ordered. The size dependence of the phase transformation from A1 to $L1_0$ in FePt nanoparticles with different initial size has been investigated [57, 58]. It was found that the grain boundaries as nucleation sites played a critical role in the ordering process of the FePt nanoparticles. The results suggested that the transformation kinetics of the A1 to $L1_0$ transformation in FePt nanoparticles is limited by slow nucleation and relies on pre-existing nucleation sites formed before annealing. In order to obtain ordered FePt nanoparticles without sintering, the nucleation-site density has to be increased. Li et al. [59] recently reported dark field TEM images for FePt thin films annealed in time scales of seconds that indicated that the ordering initiated at the grain boundaries. Grain boundaries are sources and sinks for vacancy migration that assists in the diffusion processes necessary for atomistic rearrangement.

The ordering kinetics of FePt depended on a lot of factors such as the Fe/Pt atomic ratio, substrates, doping materials, and so on. Since A1 and $L1_0$ phase transformation is accompanied by the rearrangement of the Fe and Pt atoms, the differences in the ordering kinetics are mainly due to the different diffusion ability of the atoms or diffusion barrier energy. It is known that the bulk diffusion for an annealed sample is slower than the surface diffusion; therefore, the $L1_0$ ordered structure can be obtained at a relatively low heating temperature for FePt thin film deposited on heated substrate compared to that of the annealed FePt thin films. Introducing the additives can effectively reduce the ordering temperature. The main reasons are that either the doped element forms the ternary alloy with FePt, thus lowering down the melting temperature of ternary alloy, or the doping element segregates from the FePt and creates excess vacancies during the thermal process. Both cases will improve the diffusion ability of the Fe and Pt atoms. Thus a much faster ordering process or much lower ordering temperature could be achieved. For FePt film prepared via different approaches, the diffusion barrier is different, thus the variation of the ordering kinetics. For FePt nanoparticles, the size refinement also affects the ordering kinetics.

11.4 MICROSTRUCTURE CONTROL OF $L1_0$ FePt

The magnetic recording media in commercialized hard disk drives is granular film with magnetic grains separated by grain boundary materials (nonmagnetic). In order to increase the recording areal density further, the magnetic grains have to be further reduced to maintain a sufficient SNR. Besides grain size reduction, the intergranular exchange coupling also needs to be well controlled. However, unlike the current Co-alloy-based magnetic recording media fabricated at room temperature or slightly elevated temperatures, the formation of $L1_0$ phase ordering needs a high temperature process. A high temperature process provides a higher Ku but increases the grain growth. Therefore, achieving small grain size in FePt thin films is a major challenge. This section will discuss some of the major progress in the reduction of grain size in FePt thin films.

11.4.1 Granular $L1_0$ FePt Films via Postannealing Process

In order to obtain granular $L1_0$ FePt films with small, uniform and isolated grains, postannealing of room-temperature-deposited FePt-based composite films or FePt/X multilayer films has been studied. FePt thin films doped with various nonmagnetic additives such as C [60, 61], AlO_x [62], AlN [63], SiN_x [64], BN [65], Zr [66], ZrO_x [67], Cr [68], Au, Cu, Ag [26, 69], W, Ti [70], HfO_2 [71], and Ni [72] were prepared at room temperature followed by a postannealing process. It was found that some dopants, C, AlO_x, ZrO_x, SiN_x, HfO_2, Au, and Ag, were effective to suppress the growth of FePt grains during subsequent annealing. B doping could reduce the exchange coupling but showed little effect on control of the grain size [73, 74]. For granular film prepared by postannealing of as-deposited composite films, the grain size and intergranular exchange coupling could be controlled by changing the concentration of the additives, annealing temperature, and duration. The preferred perpendicular magnetic anisotropy was not obtained in most cases, but (001) textured FePt-B_2O_3 or FePt-C nanocomposite films with well-separated grains (less than 10 nm in diameter) were obtained by postdeposition annealing of FePt/B_2O_3 and FePt/C multilayers [75, 76]. Films also showed a large in-plane magnetic anisotropy. In order to improve the FePt (001) texture, postannealing of [FePt/MgO]$_n$ multilayers was studied, and granular FePt-MgO films with (001) texture were obtained [77]. The basic idea was to use the MgO (001) texture to induce the heteroepitaxial growth of the FePt during the annealing process. It has been shown that grain size can be well controlled by varying the thickness of every single layer of MgO and/or FePt.

The fcc FePt (200) films were deposited on a 10-nm MgO (200) underlayer and the FePt (001) textured films were obtained by postdeposition annealing at high temperatures [78–81]. It was found that the texture of the FePt film after annealing depended on the film thickness. The (001) texture was obtained for 5-nm FePt film on a MgO

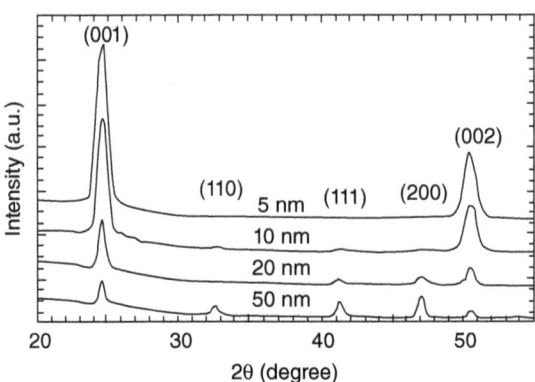

Figure 11.8. XRD scans of MgO (5 nm)/FePt + 20% Cu Films with varying total thickness annealed 650°C/10 minutes. (Reprinted with permission from Reference 26, C. L. Platt, et al., *J. Appl. Phys.* **92**, 6104 (2002). Copyright (2002) American Institute of Physics.)

underlayer after annealing. FePt films with thicknesses of 20–40 nm showed predominance of in-plane *c*-axes. FePt films with an additive (such as Cu, Ag, Au) on a MgO underlayer were also investigated [26]. It was found that Cu doping favored the FePt (001) orientation on a MgO underlayer after postdeposition annealing at 650°C. As the thickness of the FePt-20 vol% Cu film ranged from 5 to 20 nm, the FePt (001) texture was maintained, as shown in Figure 11.8.

A good FePt (001) texture and perpendicular magnetic anisotropy were obtained by postdeposition annealing of FePt/MgO multilayers on a glass substrate or SiO_2 seed layer [82–84]. The full-width-at-half maximum (FWHM) of the rocking curve of FePt (001) peak was 3.7°. When the surface roughness of the substrate or seed layer increased from 0.74 to 2.35 nm, the FWHM increased to 4.2° correspondingly. Likewise, when doping a certain amount of Cu in the FePt layer in an optimized FePt/MgO multilayer structure with subsequent annealing at high temperature, the FWHM of the rocking curve of FePt (001) peak was as narrow as 2.1° [85]. It was also reported that FePt (001)-textured films were obtained by annealing Pt (100)/Fe (100) bilayered films deposited on glass substrate. It was suggested that the initial growth layers, which consisted of Fe oxides formed in the interface of the substrate and the Fe oxide layer, affected the texture [86]. It was also confirmed by experiments that the Fe-O underlayer was the main reason for the FePt (001) texture [87].

Although the grain size and the intergranular exchange coupling could be well controlled by using above mentioned approaches, the FePt granular films prepared by postannealing have some disadvantages such as (1) the packing density of the magnetic grains is normally low, which is not favorable for future ultrahigh density magnetic recording; (2) the FePt grains normally have a spherical shape to minimize the surface energy, which causes *c*-axis dispersion in most cases; and (3) the temperature for the postannealing process is normally higher than 550°C—such a high process temperature is not compatible with fabrication processes in the hard disk industry.

Evaporation or sputter deposition of the FePt and doping materials on a heated substrate enables one to obtain $L1_0$ ordered FePt at a relatively low temperature. This is due to the fact that the rearrangement of the Fe and Pt atoms happens mainly through surface or interface diffusion on the heated substrate instead of by bulk diffusion of the atoms, as is the case with the postannealing method. Since the surface diffusivity is orders of magnitude higher than the volume diffusivity, deposition on heated substrates offers clear advantages. Therefore, in the next few sections, we will focus on microstructure control of the $L1_0$ FePt based HAMR media by sputtering deposition on heated substrate.

11.4.2 Texture Control and Seedlayer

In order to obtain the FePt with (001) texture, either the substrate or a suitable underlayer which has a similar atomic configuration to that of the FePt (001) plane and small-lattice misfit is required. Substrates or underlayers such as MgO (100), $SrTiO_3$ (100), Cr (200), Ag (200) are normally used to induce the FePt (001) texture. The corresponding epitaxial relationship is FePt (001) <100> || MgO (100) <001>, FePt (001) <100>||$SrTiO_3$ (100) <001>, FePt (001) <100> || Ag (100) <001>, and FePt (001) <100> || Cr (100) <110>, respectively. The lattice misfit of FePt with respect to MgO (100), $SrTiO_3$ (100), Ag (200), and Cr (200) is 8.5%, 2%, 7.1%, and 5.8%, respectively. Growth of FePt films with (001) texture on the MgO (100) and $SrTiO_3$ (100) single substrates has been achieved using different film-deposition technologies such as, molecular beam epitaxy (MBE), sputtering, and laser ablation [88–91]. Single crystal substrates are too expensive to be used for practical application. FePt (001) textured thin films have also been grown on a Ag (100) underlayer/Si (100) substrate [92, 93], where the Ag films were very thick. Since Ag has very good thermal conductivity, it can act as a heatsink layer for HAMR media application. The major problem with using Ag as the underlayer and/or heatsink layer is that the film surface is too rough. This happens mainly due to the large grain size of Ag at high temperature resulting from its low melting point and low surface energy.

The MgO (100) and CrX (200) (X = Ru, Mo, W, Ti) underlayers are very promising for practical applications. MgO thin films usually obtain (200) texture when deposited at room temperature because of their NaCl structure. A Cr underlayer can also be used to control the (001) texture of FePt film. The development of Cr (200) texture is the key to obtaining FePt (001)-textured film. Cr is body-centered cubic (*bcc*), and Cr films usually have a (110) texture when deposited at room temperature. Cr (200) texture can be obtained at elevated temperature. The lattice mismatch between Cr (200) and FePt (001) is ~5.8%. It has been reported that a lattice mismatch of 6.33% can effectively promote the chemical ordering of $L1_0$ FePt with Ru doping into Cr film to adjust the lattice constant. The substrate temperature and sputtering power were the key factors affecting the (200) texture of $Cr_{90}Ru_{10}$ film on glass [38]. CrMo (200)-textured film directly deposited on a heated glass substrate has been achieved [94].

The XRD [θ-2θ] patterns of 30-nm CrRu films deposited at different temperatures are shown in Figure 11.9. The inset shows the $\Delta\theta_{50}$ of the CrRu (200) diffraction peak at different substrate temperatures. The CrRu (110) diffraction peak is dominated at a

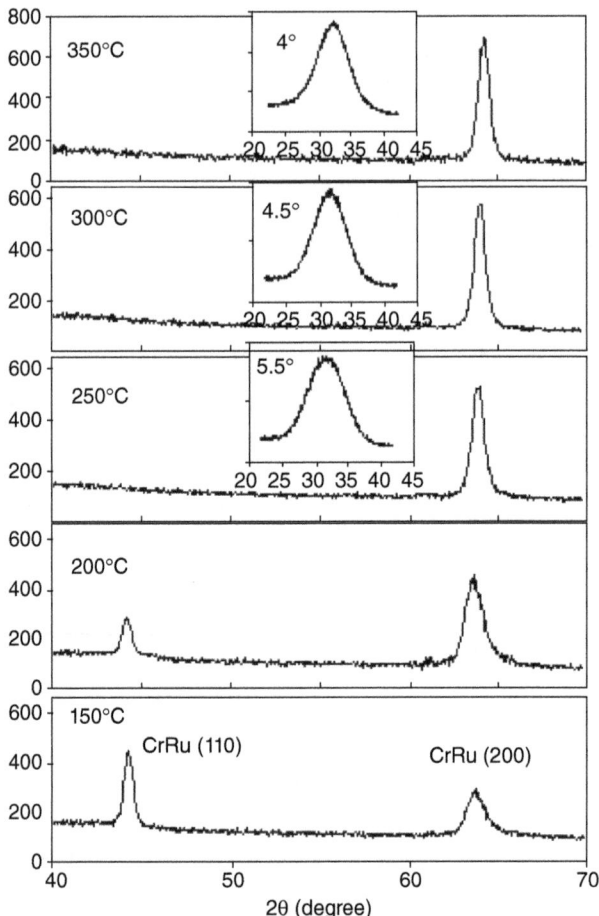

Figure 11.9. XRD θ-2θ scans of CrRu films with different temperatures. (Reprinted with permission from Reference 38, J. S. Chen, et al., *J. Magn. Magn. Mater.* **303**, 309 (2006). Copyright (2006) Elsevier.)

substrate temperature of 150°C. The intensity of the Cr (110) peak decreases, and the Cr (200) peak increases with increasing temperature. The Cr (110) peak disappears, and only the Cr (200) peak can be observed when the substrate temperature is over 250°C. The FWHM of the rocking curve of the Cr (200) peak decreases with increasing substrate temperature, indicating the well-formed Cr (200) texture.

For (200)-textured CrRu, the in-plane spacing along the CrRu [110] direction is close to the spacing along FePt [100]. Therefore, FePt [100] would lie in the film plane by matching the Cr [110] direction. The in-plane FePt [100] direction means the perpendicular FePt (001) and (002) texture. A schematic diagram of the lattice relationship is shown below in Figure 11.10.

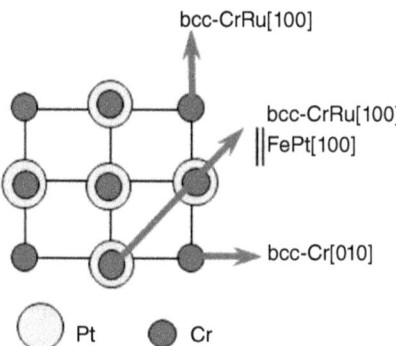

Figure 11.10. Schematic diagram of the lattice relationship between CrRu underlayer and perpendicular-textured FePt thin film. (Reprinted with permission from Reference 38, J. S. Chen, et al., *J. Magn. Magn. Mater.* **303**, 309 (2006). Copyright (2006) Elsevier.)

One issue that needs to be addressed before using Cr-alloy based underlayers to induce the growth of $L1_0$ FePt at elevated temperature is the Cr diffusion, which will cause the deterioration of the magnetic properties of the $L1_0$ ordered FePt. Therefore, an intermediate layer or a buffer layer to prevent the Cr diffusion is required. MgO and Pt can be used as a buffer layer.

Besides utilization of an underlayer with similar atomic configuration to that of the FePt (001) plane, nonepitaxial growth methods have also been used to develop the FePt (001)-textured films [95, 96]. $(Fe/Pt)_n$ multilayer films were deposited on glass substrate or thermally oxidized Si substrate, followed by rapid thermal annealing (RTA) in forming gas $(Ar + 4\%H_2)$. It was found that the FePt (001) texture depended on parameters such as annealing time, temperature, and thickness of each Fe or Pt layer [97]. For FePt films annealed at different temperatures, only the (111) peak was observed at temperatures below 350°C. The (111) peak decreased, and the FePt (001) peak increased with increasing temperature. Good $L1_0$ FePt (001)-textured films were obtained when 550°C was exceeded. Further increase of the temperature to above 750°C reverted the films to (111) texture again. The investigation of the annealing duration illustrated that the FePt (001) texture was only obtained with a moderate annealing time, but a strong FePt (111) peak was observed for a short (2 seconds) or long (30 minutes) annealing time [75]. To obtain the FePt (001) texture, the thickness of each Fe and Pt layer should be not thicker than 1.38 nm and 1.2 nm, respectively. Otherwise, the FePt film becomes (111)-texture predominated. The mechanisms of nonepitaxial growth could be understood by combining the kinetics and thermodynamics of film growth, with the initial nucleation of FePt (001) grain due to the stress resulting from the difference in thermal expansion coefficients between the substrate and FePt films [98]. Thermodynamically, FePt (111) is preferred since the (111) plane is the closest packed and has the lowest energy. Therefore, films deposited at low temperature have (111) texture since the thermal stress is insufficient for nucleation of (001) grains. Films deposited at high temperature or annealed for a long time favored the

(111) texture due to predominant thermodynamics. At moderate temperatures or moderate annealing times, FePt (001) textured films were obtained. This was possibly because the thermal stress sufficiently caused nucleation of (001) grains with favorable kinetics for diffusion to occur. For thicker Fe and Pt layers, the (111)-preferred orientation could be due to insufficient diffusion length at that temperature and annealing time.

Nanocomposite FePt:SiO$_2$ films have been fabricated by annealing the as-deposited FePt/SiO$_2$ multilayers at temperatures from 450°C to 650°C [99]. These films consist of high-anisotropy tetragonal $L1_0$ FePt particles embedded in a SiO$_2$ matrix. It was found that coercivity and grain size are highly dependent on the annealing temperature and SiO$_2$ concentration. Films with coercivities in the range from 2 to 8 kOe and grain sizes of 10 nm or less were obtained.

11.4.3   Granular *L1₀* FePt Films via in-situ Substrate Heating

The most common approach to obtain $L1_0$ FePt-based granular films is to introduce the additives into the film. The additives are chosen in such a way that they do not mix with FePt, but segregate to the grain boundaries. FePt granular films with different additives such as SiO$_2$, Al$_2$O$_3$, MgO, C, Ta$_2$O$_5$, TiO$_2$, AgC, Ag, and Au have been studied [100–106]. $L1_0$-ordered FePt-SiO$_2$ granular films by cosputtering Fe, Pt, and SiO$_2$ on heated MgO (001) substrates were investigated by Chen et al. [100]. They have reported that FePt-SiO$_2$ granular film with an average grain size of 15 nm and a relatively narrow size distribution was obtained at a substrate temperature of 700°C. The average grain size was further reduced to 6.2 nm by reducing the substrate temperature to 500°C. However, the FePt particles remained as an $A1$ disordered phase. Introduction of Ag to the FePt particles and increasing the Ar gas pressure in the sputtering chamber were found to be both beneficial for enhancing the $L1_0$ ordering while keeping the fine granular structure. The grain size was further reduced to 5.8 nm with a standard deviation of 1.5 nm. However, the magnetic properties were deteriorated.

FePt:C films with a structure of FePt:C (4–12 nm)/Pt or MgO (2 nm)/CrRu (30 nm)/glass were prepared by a magnetron sputtering system. The volume fraction of C is in the range of 0 to 20%. Figure 11.11a,b show the plan-view TEM images of FePt:C film with 10 and 20 vol% C grown on Pt intermediate layer, respectively [102]. For 10 vol% C, granular film was formed with some grain aggregation. The grain size roughly followed a Gaussian distribution with a mean diameter 9.9 nm and a standard deviation of 2.3 nm. When C was increased to 20 vol%, well-separated grains with relatively uniform grain size were obtained. The average grain size and standard deviation were 5.6 and 1.6 nm, respectively.

The magnetic properties of FePt:C films with 10 vol% and 20 vol% C doping indicated a perpendicular magnetic anisotropy. However, the slopes of hysteresis loops at coercivity remained very steep, which implied the existence of a strong intergranular exchange coupling even for the FePt + 20 vol% C film with well-isolated FePt grains [107]. It was found that the strong exchange coupling is due to the two-layer structure of the FePt:C films composing one continuous FePt layer on top of the Pt buffer layer and one granular film with well-isolated FePt:C on the continuous FePt layer (as shown in Fig. 11.12). It seems that the FePt:C composite films prefer layer-by-layer growth

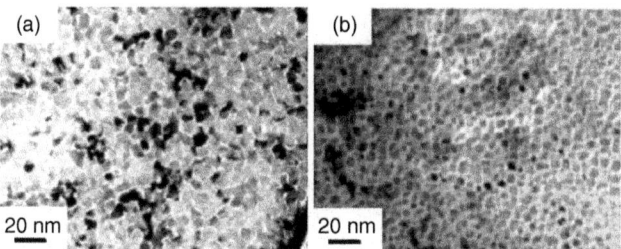

Figure 11.11. Plan-view transmission electron microscopy images of FePt:C films on Pt intermediate layer with (a) 10 vol% and (b) 20 vol% C doping. (Reprinted with permission from Reference 102, J. S. Chen, et al. *IEEE Trans Magn.* **45**, 839 (2009). Copyright (2009) Institute of Electrical and Electronics Engineers.)

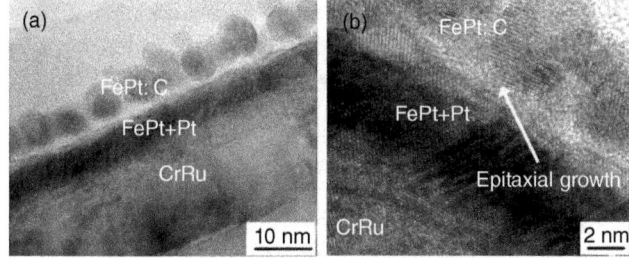

Figure 11.12. Cross-section transmission electron microscopy images of FePt:C Films on Pt intermediate layer with 20 vol% C doping: (a) low magnification and (b) higher magnification. (Reprinted with permission from Reference 102, J. S. Chen et al. *IEEE Trans Magn.* **45**, 839 (2009). Copyright (2009) Institute of Electrical and Electronics Engineers.)

in the initial stage accompanied by the C diffusion up to the film surface. As the thickness of composite film becomes thick, the C accumulated on the film surface will cause the formation of the granular structure.

The existing continuous FePt layer at the initial stage was attributed to the surface energy and interfacial energy of FePt and Pt buffer layers. It was proposed to use a MgO intermediate layer to replace the Pt layer and as a result, a FePt:C composite film with granular structure was obtained. Firstly, a MgO buffer layer prevents the diffusion of the Cr into the FePt layer, and hence prevents the deterioration of the magnetic properties of the $L1_0$ ordered FePt. Second, the small surface energy of MgO and the larger interfacial energy between MgO and FePt enable the formation of the columnar structure in FePt-based composite films. The surface energies of the FePt, MgO is about 2.9 J/m^2 and 1.1 J/m^2, respectively. The surface energy of the interface between a metallic material and an oxide material is normally large. Therefore, island growth of the FePt film during the film growth process is preferred.

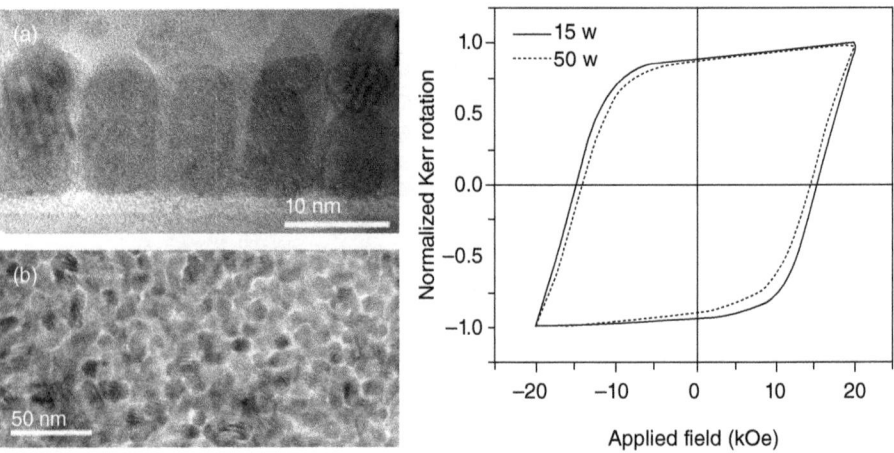

Figure 11.13. (a) Cross-section transmission electron microscopy image. (b) Plan-view images of FePt-C film on MgO intermediate layer with carbon concentration of 15 vol%. (Reprinted with permission from Reference 102, J. S. Chen et al. *IEEE Trans Magn.* **45**, 839 (2009). Copyright (2009) Institute of Electrical and Electronics Engineers.)

The cross-section TEM image of the FePt:C film with C concentration of 15% deposited by cosputtering FePt and carbon targets is shown in Figure 11.13a. Granular film with well-isolated columnar FePt grains of 7.5 nm in diameter was epitaxially grown on the MgO intermediate layer. The plane-view TEM images (Fig. 11.13b) of the sample deposited at high sputtering power showed that the grain boundaries were more distinguished, indicating that the exchange coupling was further reduced. The coercivity of the composite film is about 14.4 kOe.

Hono et al. investigated the effect of C doping content on the microstructure and magnetic properties of FePt films [103]. FePt:C composite films were deposited on a thermally oxidized Si substrate with a 10 nm (100)-textured MgO intermediate layer. The MgO layer was deposited on thermally oxidized Si substrates at 100°C by radio-frequency (RF) sputtering, and the FePt (4 nm):C(x vol%) films and FePt(y nm):C (50%) films with x = 0–50 and y = 4–10 were deposited by cosputtering of Fe, Pt, and C targets at 500°C. The bright field TEM images of FePt films with different volume fractions of C doping are shown in Figure 11.14.

For the FePt film without carbon, a particulate structure with an average particle size of 17 nm with a wider distribution was observed. Well-isolated and interconnected grains were observed for film with 12 vol% C doping. A particulate structure with reduced grain size (9.5 nm) and grain size distribution (variance = 17.1) was observed for 37 vol% C-doped film. With C-volume fraction further increasing to 50%, a granular-type structure with a unique average particle size of about 6.5 nm and a size distribution of 4.08 was obtained. For FePt film with thick layer thickness, although the plan-view TEM image shows a granular structure with well-isolated FePt grains, the cross-sectional TEM images reveals that the FePt:C composite film is a two-layer structure,

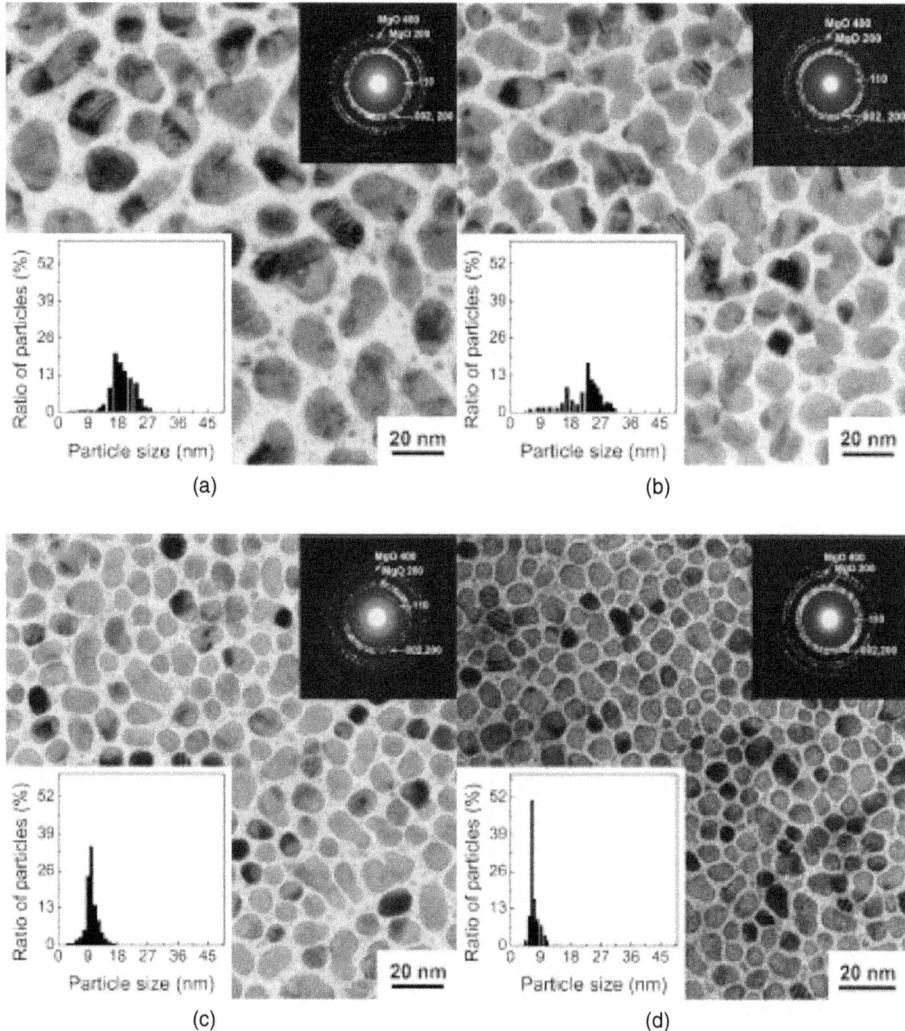

Figure 11.14. TEM bright field images, SAED patterns and particle size distribution Histograms of FePt (4 nm):C (x%)/MgO (10 nm) films grown on an oxidized Si substrate with various volume fractions of C [x = (a) 0, (b) 12, (c) 37, and (d) 50]. (Reprinted with permission from Reference 103, A. Perumal, et al., *Applied Physics Express* **1**, 101301(2008). Copyright (2008) Japan Soc of Applied Physics.)

which is consistent with the previous work with much lower C concentration [102]. The coercivity decreases from 10.5 to 7.6 kOe by increasing the FePt thickness from 4 to 10 nm, while the squareness remains about 100% for the film with a thickness up to 6 nm and decreases to 80% for the FePt(10 nm):C (50%) film. In addition, the in-plane M–H loops show a coercivity of 2.8 kOe for the FePt (10 nm):C (50%) film, which could be due to the random orientation of the FePt particles in the second layer.

Figure 11.15. Cross-section TEM image (a) pure FePt film and (b) FePt film doped with 20 vol% Ta$_2$O$_5$. (Reprinted with permission from Reference 104, B. C. Lim, et al., *J. Appl. Phys.* **105**, 07A730 (2009). Copyright (2009) American Institute of Physics.)

Ta$_2$O$_5$-doped FePt films with Ta$_2$O$_5$ volume fraction varying from 0 to 30 vol% were investigated by Lim et al. [104]. The film structure is Corning glass/CrRu/MgO/FePt:Ta$_2$O$_5$.

The microstructure of FePt:Ta$_2$O$_5$ film was investigated by the cross-section TEM images as shown in Figure 11.15. A continuous film was observed for the pure FePt layer without dopant, as shown in Figure 11.15a. For the 20 vol% Ta$_2$O$_5$-doped FePt film, well-isolated columnar FePt grains of grain size about 10 nm were formed, as shown in Figure 11.15b. The CrRu, MgO and FePt-Ta$_2$O$_5$ layers could be clearly seen. The light contrast regions at the grain boundaries of the FePt layer were believed to be Ta$_2$O$_5$. This may be due the fact that Ta$_2$O$_5$ could have a large affinity to bond with the MgO buffer layer as the surface of the RF-sputtered MgO layer would possess unfulfilled bonds. In addition, Ta$_2$O$_5$ tends to remain at the FePt grain boundaries as it does not preferentially form compounds with Fe or Pt. The perpendicular anisotropy of FePt was maintained even when doped with 20 vol% Ta$_2$O$_5$ and possessed high H$_c$ exceeding 10 kOe. Well-isolated FePt grains of columnar structure were formed when the magnetic layer thickness was 12 nm.

FePt:TiO$_2$ films doped with various TiO$_2$ contents had been studied by Ding et al. [105]. Figure 11.16 shows the out-of-plane hysteresis loops of the FePt:TiO$_2$ films doped with various TiO$_2$ contents as measured by polar Kerr. FePt:TiO$_2$ films that were 20 vol% or less TiO$_2$ doped demonstrated a perpendicular anisotropy. The *Hc* increases with increasing TiO$_2$ content up to 20 vol%, which is mainly due to the reduced exchange coupling as indicated from the loop slope and TEM images.

The cross-sectional TEM images of the FePt:TiO$_2$ films with 10 and 20 vol% TiO$_2$ contents are shown in Figure 11.17a,b.

FePt:TiO$_2$ films with 10 vol% and 20 vol% TiO$_2$ contents show a granular microstructure. The grain size is 10 nm for 10 vol% TiO$_2$-doped sample, the grain size is further reduced to about 5 nm with further increase of the TiO$_2$ contents to 20%. The

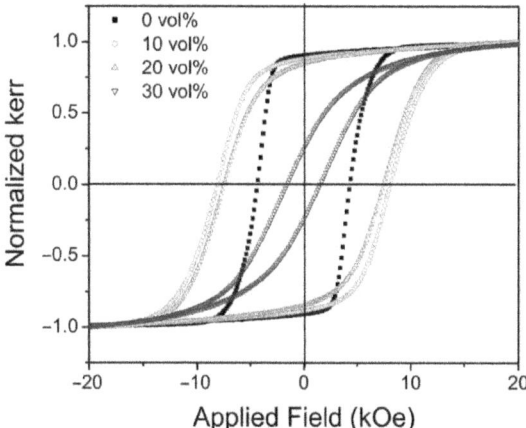

Figure 11.16. Out-of-plane hysteresis loops of FePt:TiO_2 films with different TiO_2 content. (Reprinted with permission from Reference 105, Y. F. Ding, et al., *Appl. Phys. Lett.* **93**, 032506 (2008). Copyright (2008) American Institute of Physics.)

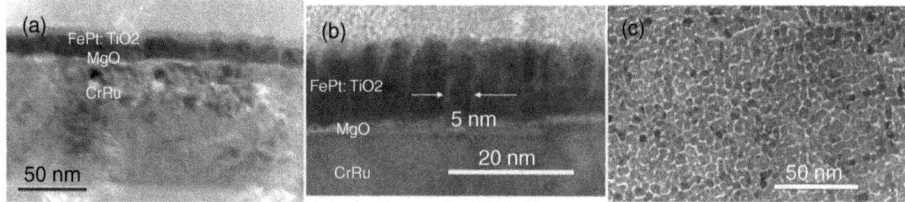

Figure 11.17. The HRTEM cross-sectional images of FePt films doped with (a)10 vol%, (b) 20 vol% TiO_2, and (c) plane-view TEM images of FePt films with 20 vol% TiO_2. (Reprinted with permission from Reference 105, Y. F. Ding, et al., *Appl. Phys. Lett.* **93**, 032506 (2008). Copyright (2008) American Institute of Physics.)

plane-view TEM image of the FePt:TiO_2 film with 20 vol% TiO_2 shown in Figure 11.17c confirmed that the mean FePt grain size is about 5 nm. It is worth noting that there is no continuous FePt layer and double-layer structured FePt found in these FePt:TiO_2 films, unlike that observed in the FePt:C system [103], indicating that TiO_2 is more efficient than C for grain size and kinetic control in FePt system.

Perpendicular $L1_0$ ordered FePt-oxide composite films were prepared by alternate sputtering of FePt and oxide at 475°C [106]. Figure 11.18 shows the TEM images and magnetic properties of FePt:30% oxide thin films.

The effects of different oxide materials on the microstructure of FePt codeposited with MgO, Al_2O_3, and SiO_2 were investigated. Among different dopants, SiO_2 works better than MgO as the amorphous oxide, which provides for magnetic isolation of the

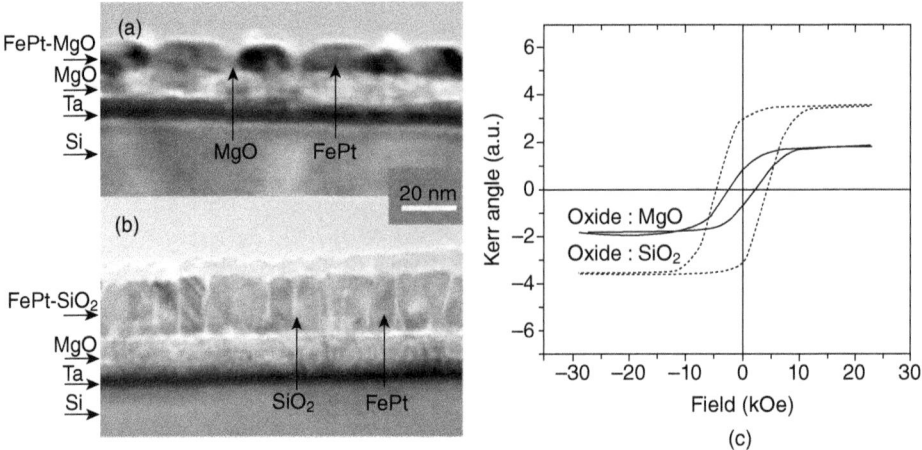

Figure 11.18. TEM cross-sectional images of FePt:30% oxide thin films using MgO (a) and SiO₂ (b) as oxide. The perpendicular hysteresis loops as measured by MOKE are plotted in (c). (Reprinted with permission from Reference 106, En Yang, and D. E. Laughlin, *J. Appl. Phys.* **104**, 023904 (2008). Copyright (2008) American Institute of Physics.)

FePt grains. Very uniform and well-isolated columnar grains with an average grain size of 7 nm were obtained with coercivity as high as 7 kOe for FePt films with 38% SiO₂ doping. The coercivity of the films increases with increasing grain size and thinner alternately sputtered single layers. Reducing the grain size to 2.9 nm produces granular grains with a coercivity of 3.5 kOe. It was found that the morphology of the FePt films varied with the codeposited oxides. The FePt layers were continuous and segmented by stacking faults aligned at 54° to the surface. Films with SiO₂ added, besides the oriented columnar FePt grains, exhibited a fraction of misoriented crystallites due to random repeated nucleation. Al₂O₃ addition resulted in a layered structure, that is, an initial continuous epitaxial FePt layer covered by a secondary layer of FePt:Al₂O₃ composite. Both components (FePt and MgO) of the MgO-added samples were grown epitaxially on the MgO intermediate layer, so that a nanocomposite of intercalated (001) FePt and (001) MgO was formed.

It can be seen from the results mentioned above that the microstructure of the L1₀ FePt composite films depends on the doping materials and their volume fractions, the underlayer/intermediate layer used, the preparation technologies, and so on. In order to achieve a desired microstructure (isolated columnar grains) in the L1₀ FePt composite films, the film growth mechanism and the control of dopant diffusion are two main issues that need to be considered. It is well known that the microstructure of a deposited film depends greatly on surface energies of a substrate or the intermediate layer, the deposited film and the interfacial energies between the film and substrate or intermediate layer. Selection of the intermediate layer is based on surface energies of FePt, the intermediate layer itself and the interface between them. The basic idea is to promote island growth instead of layer by layer growth mode. However, promoting only the island growth is not enough to obtain columnar structure. Diffusion of the dopants is another critical issue in microstructure control of $L1_0$ FePt composite films, which includes lateral diffusion of the dopant to grain boundaries and diffusion of the dopant along the grain boundaries with increasing film thickness. The combination of dopant material selection and experimental conditions for preparation of the $L1_0$ FePt-based composite film is very critical for obtaining the desired microstructure. The desired microstructure with columnar grains has been reported. However, further improvement of the microstructure of $L1_0$ FePt composite films with further reduced grain size and grain size distribution is required for ultrahigh density magnetic recording. Moreover, all these advancements have to be integrated with a suitable soft underlayer material and intermediate layer thickness, which are critical to achieving a high SNR.

11.4 CURIE TEMPERATURE (T_C)

T_C is one of the intrinsic magnetic properties of magnetic materials. The T_C is determined by the spin–spin exchange interaction and closely related to the so-called magnetic order in magnetic materials. The competition between interatomic exchange and thermal disorder leads to the vanishing of spontaneous magnetization at a well-defined sharp T_C. The T_C of the $Fe_{50}Pt_{50}$ fct phase is reported to be 477°C [108]. For HAMR media application, the media need to be heated up beyond the T_C to erase the bit, followed by a writing process at a temperature lower than T_C to store the information. The high T_C of FePt will impose technical constraints regarding the design of the thermal system integrated with the slide. Furthermore, the carbon overcoat and the lubricant cannot withstand such a high temperature, which means a novel overcoat and/or lubricant needs to be developed that is compatible with the high-temperature writing process. Therefore, if the T_C of FePt could be reduced, the writing process thus could be conducted at a relatively low temperature.

It is known that intrinsic magnetic properties depend greatly on the local atomic environment. Therefore, variation of the intrinsic properties is expected in the cases of alloying or surrounding by a matrix since the electronic structure of the magnetic grains will be changed. Regarding the T_C of FePt, several different FePt-based thin films should be discussed: (1) pure FePt (composition, phase, etc.); (2) FePtX alloy; and (3) FePtX composite films (where X is oxides or other doping materials).

The relationship of T_C to Fe content in FePt films with compositions in the range of 47.5–54.5 at% Fe has been described [54]. It was found that T_C increased from 384 to 455°C with increasing Fe content. An FePt thin film with 40 at% Fe deposited on a MgO (100) substrate has been investigated [109]. The T_C for FePt with 40 at% Fe content is around 325°C according to the nearly zero M_s measured at that temperature. It is known that the T_C of the FePt face-center tetragonal (fct) phase is strongly dependent on the alloy composition. The T_C of $L1_0$ FePt could be reduced by element doping. It was reported that the diffusion of Cu and Cr into the FePt layer could effectively reduce the T_C of $L1_0$ FePt [110]. The estimated T_C values based on the intersection of the straight line in the M (T) curve are 427°C and 337°C, respectively, which are much smaller than the reported value of 477°C. The replacement of the Fe atoms with a nonmagnetic atom in the fct phase will reduce the exchange interactions of Fe–Fe and Fe–Pt, leading to a reduction of T_C. Both Ni and Cu can lower the T_C with Cu additions being more effective than Ni, which suggests the superiority of FeCuPt for use in HAMR applications [111].

The substitution of Fe atoms by Ni atoms changes the spin–orbit interaction in the FePtNi films, thus causing a decrease in the magnetic anisotropy, the saturation magnetization, and the T_C [112]. A systematic study of the influence of the substitution of Ni for Fe in epitaxial FeNiPt film was presented [113]. The basic magnetic properties such as M_s, K_u, and T_C were found to be controlled by changing the Ni content in the film. The T_C showed an almost linear reduction with the Ni content, where a high K_u can still be maintained for FePt film with 10 at% Ni. The anisotropy field also demonstrated a strong temperature dependence, which makes these materials promising candidates for media application in HAMR.

The effect of Cu on the Al to $L1_0$ transformation in FePt thin films had been studied by using DSC [24]. It was found that the substitution of nonmagnetic Cu into the structure significantly reduces the T_C, with higher Cu contents corresponding to larger decreases. Cu additions have been shown to reduce the magnetocrystalline anisotropy, but this decrease is small and linear for small amounts of Cu. Thus, additions of Cu may be useful for engineering the T_C of FePt-based $L1_0$ alloys for HAMR.

Besides doping metallic elements into FePt to tune the T_C to be compatible with the future high capacity magnetic storage, the matrix material in FePt granular films also can be exploited to tune the T_C. The demand for ultrahigh-density magnetic recording will push the grain size of the $L1_0$ ordered FePt to become smaller and smaller. The finite size effect will cause the depression of the T_C, as reported for granular $Ni-Al_2O_3$ thin film [114].

In order to evaluate the finite size effect on small FePt grains, investigation of the T_C of FePt nanoparticles will give us useful information. The T_C of $L1_0$ FePt nanoparticles was studied by different research groups. The chemically synthesized Fe_xPt_{100-x} nanoparticles with controlled compositions were annealed to transfer from the disordered fcc structure to the ordered structure. It was found that the $L1_0$ FePt structure can be formed in the wide compositional region x = 40–68, and lower or higher Fe content leads to the formation of the $L1_2$ $FePt_3$ or Fe_3Pt phase, respectively. The T_C of $L1_0$ FePt is strongly composition and size dependent [115]. For FePt nanoparticles, besides the factors that may affect the T_C in FePt thin films, the T_C also depended on the size of the nanoparticles. The effect of nanoparticle size on T_C has been studied [116]. T_C decreases remarkably with decreasing particle size, especially when d < 6 nm. To understand the strong particle size dependence of the T_C, the finite-size-scaling theory was used to fit the behavior of T_C.

$$\frac{Tc(\infty) - Tc(d)}{Tc(\infty)} = \left(\frac{d}{d_0}\right)^{-1/v},$$ (11.2)

where $T_C(d)$ is the T_C as a function of d, $T_C(\infty)$ is the bulk T_C, d_0 is a constant and v is the critical exponent of the correlation length. After considering the chemical ordering effect on T_C, the shift of T_C could be described by the finite-size-scaling theory. It was proposed that the T_C depression originated from the surface layer with the coordination number imperfection compared to that of the bulk [117].

Although the T_C is one of the intrinsic properties of magnetic materials, it originates from the atomic spin–spin interaction. Therefore, T_C depends greatly on the crystalline structure and the electronic structure of the magnetic materials. It has been shown that we can tailor the T_C of $L1_0$ ordered FePt to be in a wide range from 477°C to lower than 300°C. However, the reduction of the T_C was accompanied by decrease in magnetic anisotropy in most of the cases. A high magnetic anisotropy is the key requirement for magnetic recording media for ultrahigh-density application. Therefore, there is a trade-off between the high magnetic anisotropy and low T_C. Another concern is the T_C distribution of HAMR media. The distribution of the T_C will cause data erasure and also affect the sharpness of the transition, thus also affecting the recording performance. As mentioned above, the T_C is a function of the composition, particle size, ordering parameters, and so on. Therefore, it is very critical to control the microstructure of $L1_0$ FePt-based granular film to have a small distribution of composition, grain-size distribution, and similarly ordered parameters among enormous magnetic grains.

11.5 SUMMARY

In this chapter, we have described some fundamental properties of $L1_0$ FePt and the techniques used to achieve suitable magnetic anisotropy and microstructure for recording media applications. It was discussed that the chemical ordering degree depends greatly on process temperature, stoichiometry, and film thickness. The ordering kinetics of $L1_0$ FePt has been discussed for different thermal processes in thin film and nanoparticles as well. The ordering kinetics mainly depends on the diffusion barrier energy that needs to be overcome in order to rearrange the Fe and Pt atoms, which depends on different thermal processes for $L1_0$ FePt formation and the film preparation conditions. In order to implement $L1_0$ FePt for recording media application, several issues, such as ordering temperature reduction, (001) texture control, microstructure control, have to be addressed. Different approaches to reducing the ordering temperature for $L1_0$ FePt have been reviewed. Element doping and utilization strain induced from the lattice mismatch between the underlayer and $L1_0$ FePt are the most promising methods to reduce the ordering temperature. Granular $L1_0$ FePt with different doping materials has been reviewed for both postdeposition annealing and in-situ substrate heating processes. The texture and microstructure control of $L1_0$ FePt composite films prepared on heated substrate has been discussed. The desired microstructure with columnar grains has been achieved by several research groups. However, for real magnetic recording media application, further improvement of the microstructure, and reduction of the $L1_0$ FePt grain size and grain size distribution are required. To develop $L1_0$ FePt films for HAMR media application, there are still a lot of issues that need to be addressed such as reducing the switching field distribution, $L1_0$ FePt-based HAMR media design with heatsink layer, T_C control and proper writing process, and thermal profile optimization with proper thermal design, and so on.

REFERENCES

1. T. B. Massalski, H. Okamoto, P. R. Subramanian, and L. Kacprzak, *Binary Alloy Phase Diagrams*. Materials Park, OH: ASM International, 1990.

2. D. E. Laughlin, K. Srinivasan, M. Tanase, and L. Wang, Scr. Mater. **53**, 383 (2005).

3. A. Cebollada, D. Weller, J. Sticht, R. Harp, R. F. C. Farrow, R. R. Marks, R. Savoy, and J. C. Scott, Phys. Rev. B **50**, 3419 (1994).

4. B. E. Warren, in *X-Ray Diffraction*. Reading, MA: Addison-Wesley, p. 208, 1969.

5. B. D. Cullity and S. R. Stock, *Elements of X-ray Diffraction*, 3rd ed. Pearson Education International, 2001.

6. D. D. Fontaine, Solid State Phys. **34**, 73 (1979).

7. F. Ducastelle, *Order and Phase Stability in Alloys*. Amsterdam: North-Holland, 1991.

8. P. Ravindran, A. Kjekshus, H. Fjellvag, P. James, L. Nordström, B. Johansson, and O. Eriksson, Phys. Rev. B **63**, 144409 (2001).

9. T. Burkert, O. Eriksson, S. I. Simak, A. V. Ruban, B. Sanyal, L. Nordström, and J. M. Wills, Phys. Rev. B **71**, 134411 (2005).

10. W. Grange, J. P. Kappler, M. Maret, J. Vogel, A. Fontaine, F. Petroff, G. Krill, A. Rogalev, J. Goulon, M. Finazzi, and N. Brooks, J. Appl. Phys. **83**, 6617 (1998), and Phys. Rev. B **58**, 6298 (1998).

11. N. Nakajima, T. Koide, T. Shidara, H. Miyauchi, H. Fukutani, A. Fujimori, K. Ito, T. Katayama, M. Nyvlt, and Y. Suzuki, Phys. Rev. Lett. **81**, 5229 (1998).

12. M. M. Schwickert, K. A. Hannibal, M. F. Toney, M. Best, L. Folks, J.-U. Thiele, A. J. Kellock, and D. Weller, J. Appl. Phys. **87**, 6956 (2000).

13. Y. K. Takahashi, M. Ohnuma, and K. Hono, J. Appl. Phys. **93**, 7580 (2003).

14. P. T. L. Minh, N. P. Thuy, and N. T. N. Chan, J. Magn. Magn. Mater. **277**, 187 (2004).

15. T. Seki, T. Shima, K. Takanashi, Y. Takahashi, E. Matsubara, and K. Hono, Appl. Phys. Lett. **82**, 2461 (2003).

16. K. Barmak, J. Kim, L. H. Lewis, K. R. Coffey, M. F. Toney, A. J. Kellock, and J.-U. Thiele, J. Appl. Phys. **95**, 7501 (2004).

17. T. J. Klemmer, a) N. Shukla, C. Liu, X. W. Wu, E. B. Svedberg, O. Mryasov, R. W. Chantrell, D. Weller, M. Tanase and D. E. Laughlin, Appl. Phys. Lett. **81**, 2220 (2002).

18. T. Maeda, T. Kai, A. Kikitsu, T. Nagase, and J. I. Akiyama, Appl. Phys. Lett. **80**, 2147 (2002).

19. T. Kai, T. Maeda, A. Kikitsu, J. Akiyama, T. Nagase, and T. Kishi, J. Appl. Phys. **95**, 609 (2004).

20. T. Maeda, A. Kikitsu, T. Kai, T. Nagase, H. Aikawa, and J. Akiyama, IEEE Trans. Magn. **38**, 2796 (2002).

21. Y. K. Takahashi, M. Ohnuma, and K. Hono, J. Magn. Magn. Mater. **246**, 259 (2002).

22. K. W. Wierman, C. L. Platt, and J. K. Howard, J. Magn. Magn. Mater. **278**, 214 (2004).

23. X. C. Sun, S. S. Kang, J. W. Harrell, D. E. Nikeles, Z. R. Dai, J. Li, and Z. L. Wang, J. Appl. Phys. **93**, 7337 (2003).

24. D. C. Berry, J. Kim, K. Barmak, K. Wierman, E. B. Svedberg, and J. K. Howard, Scr. Mater. **53**, 423 (2005).

25. K. W. Wierman, C. L. Platt, J. K. Howard, and F. E. Spada, J. Appl. Phys. **93**, 7160 (2003).

26. C. L. Platt, K. W. Wierman, E. B. Svedberg, R. van de Veerdonk, J. K. Howard, A. G. Roy, and D. E. Laughlin, J. Appl. Phys. **92**, 6104 (2002).

27. C. Y. You, Y. K. Takahashi, and K. Hono, J. Appl. Phys. **100**, 056105 (2006).

28. S. S. Kang, D. E. Nike, and J. W. Harrell, J. Appl. Phys. **93**, 7178 (2003).

29. C. Chen, O. Kitakami, S. Okamoto, and Y. Shimada, Appl. Phys. Lett. **76**, 3218 (2000).

30. O. Kitakami, Y. Shimada, Y. Oikawa, H. Daimon, and K. Fukamichi, Appl. Phys. Lett. **78**, 1104 (2001).

31. Y.-M. Sung, M.-K. Lee, K.-E. Kim, and T. G. Kim, Chem. Phys. Lett. **443**, 319 (2007).

32. S. S. Kang, Z. Y. Jia, D. E. Nikles, and J. W. Harrell, IEEE Trans. Magn. **39**, 2753 (2003).

33. S. S. Kang, J. W. Harrell, and D. E. Nikles, Nano Lett. **2**, 1033 (2002).

34. Q. Yan, T. Kim, A. Purkayastha, P. G. Gansan, M. Shima, and G. Ramanath, Adv. Mater. **17**, 2233 (2005).

35. S. R. Lee, S. Yang, Y. K. Kim, and J. G. Na, Appl. Phys. Lett. **78**, 4001 (2001).

36. T. Suzuki, K. Harada, N. Honda, and K. Ouchi, J. Magn. Magn. Mater. **193**, 85 (1999).

37. C. H. Lai, C. H. Yang, C. C. Chiang, and T. K. Tseng, Appl. Phys. Lett. **85**, 4430 (2004).

38. J. S. Chen, B. C. Lim, Y. F. Ding, and G. M. Chow, J. Magn. Magn. Mater. **303**, 309 (2006).

39. Y. F. Ding, J. S. Chen, E. Liu, C. J. Sun, and G. M. Chow, J. Appl. Phys. **97**, 10H303 (2005).

40. D. Ravelosona, C. Chappert, V. Mathet, and H. Bermas, Appl. Phys. Lett. **76**, 236 (2000).

41. C. H. Lai, C. H. Yang, and C. C. Chiang, Appl. Phys. Lett. **83**, 4550 (2003).

42. C. Feng, Q. Zhan, B. H. Li, J. Teng, M. H. Li, Y. Jiang, and G. H. Yu, Appl. Phys. Lett. **93**, 152513 (2008).

43. Y. Zhu and J. W. Cai, Appl. Phys. Lett. **87**, 32504 (2005).

44. Y. S. Yu, H.-B. Li, W. L. Li, M. Liu, and W. D. Fei, J. Magn. Magn. Mater. **320**, L125 (2008).

45. R. A. Ristau, K. Barmak, L. H. Lewis, K. R. Coffey, and J. K. Howard, J. Appl. Phys. **86**, 4527 (1999).

46. J. G. Na, J. Mater. Sci. Lett. **19**, 1171 (2000).

47. T. J. Klemmer, C. Liu, N. Shukla, X. W. Wu, D. Weller, M. Tanase, D. E. Laughlin, and W. A. Soffa, J. Magn. Magn. Mater. **266**, 79 (2003).

48. W. A. Soffa and D. E. Laughlin, Acta Mater. **37**, 3019 (1989).

49. K. Barmak, a) J. Kim, and S. Shell, E. B. Svedberg and J. K. Howard, Appl. Phys. Lett. **80**, 4268 (2002).

50. R. F. C. Farrow, D. Weller, R. F. Marks, M. F. Toney, S. Hom, G. R. Harp, and A. Cebollada, Appl. Phys. Lett. **69**, 1166 (1996).

51. M.-G. Kim and S.-C. Shin, J. Appl. Phys. **90**, 2211 (2001).

52. K. Brune, K. Bromann, and K. Kern, Mater. Res. Soc. Symp. Proc. **399**, 213 (1995).

53. F. E. Spada, F. T. Parker, C. L. Platt, and J. K. Howard, J. Appl. Phys. **94**, 5123 (2003).

54. K. Barmak, J. Kim, D. C. Berry, and W. N. Hanani, J. Appl. Phys. **97**, 024902 (2005).

55. C. L. Zha, S. H. He, B. Ma, Z. Z. Zhang, F. X. Gan, and Q. Y. Jin, IEEE Trans. Magn. **44**, 3539 (2008).

56. Y. K. Takahashi, T. Ohkubo, M. Ohnuma, and K. Hono, J. Appl. Phys. **93**, 7166 (2003).

57. Y. Ding and S. A. Majetich, Appl. Phys. Lett. **87**, 022508 (2005).

58. Y. Ding and S. A. Majetich, IEEE Trans. Magn. **43**, 3100 (2007).

59. X. H. Li, B. T. Liu, W. Li, H. Y. Sun, D. Q. Wu, and X. Y. Xhang, J. Appl. Phys. **101**, 093911-1 (2007).

60. Y. Huang, H. Okumura, G. C. Hadjipanayis, and D. Weller, J. Magn. Magn. Mater. **242**, 317 (2002).

61. J. A. Christodoulides, Y. Huang, Y. Zhang, G. C. Hadjipanayis, I. Panagiotopoulos, and D. Niarchos, J. Appl. Phys. **87**, 6938 (2000).

62. D. H. Ping, M. Ohnuma, K. Hono, M. Watanabe, T. Iwase, and T. Masumoto, J. Appl. Phys. **90**, 4708 (2001).

63. S. C. Chen, P. C. Kuo, C. T. Lie, and J. T. Hua, J. Magn. Magn. Mater. **236**, 151 (2001).

64. C. M. Kuo and P. C. Kuo, J. Appl. Phys. **87**, 419 (2000).

65. M. Daniil, P. A. Farber, H. Okumura, G. C. Hadjipanayis, and D. Weller, J. Magn. Magn. Mater. **246**, 297 (2002).

66. S. R. Lee, S. H. Yang, Y. K. Kim, and J. G. Na, J. Appl. Phys. **91**, 6857 (2002).

67. K. R. Koffey, M. A. Parker, and J. K. Howard, IEEE Trans. Magn. **31**, 2737 (1995).

68. P. C. Kuo, Y. D. Yao, C. M. Kuo, and H. C. Wu, J. Appl. Phys. **87**, 6146 (2000).

69. S. C. Chen, P. C. Kuo, A. C. Sun, C. T. Lie, and W. C. Hsu, Mater. Sci. Eng. B **88**, 91 (2002).

70. C. M. Kuo, P. C. Kuo, W. C. Hsu, C. T. Li, and A. C. Sun, J. Magn. Magn. Mater. **209**, 100 (2000).

71. C. L. Platt, K. W. Wierman, J. K. Howard, A. G. Roy, and D. E. Laughlin, J. Magn. Magn. Mater. **260**, 487 (2003).

72. M. L. Yuan, Y. F. Xu, X. Z. Li, and D. J. Sellmyer, J. Appl. Phys. **97**, 10H309 (2005).

73. N. Li, B. M. Lairson, and O. H. Kwon, J. Magn. Magn. Mater. **205**, 1 (1999).

74. N. Li and B. M. Lairson, IEEE Trans. Magn. **35**, 1077 (1999).

75. M. L. Yan, H. Zeng, N. Powers, and D. J. Sellmyer, J. Appl. Phys. **91**, 8471 (2002).

76. M. L. Yan, R. F. Sabirianov, Y. F. Xu, X. Z. Li, and D. J. Sellmyer, IEEE Trans. Magn. **40**, 2470 (2004).

77. K. Kang, T. Suzuki, Z. G. Zhang, and C. Papusoi, J. Appl. Phys. **95**, 7273 (2004).

78. S. Jeong, Y.-N. Hsu, D. E. Laughlin, and M. E. McHenry, IEEE Trans. Magn. **36**, 2336 (2000).

79. S. Jeong, Y.-N. Hsu, D. E. Laughlin, and M. E. McHenry, IEEE Trans. Magn. **37**, 1299 (2001).

80. S. Jeong, M. E. McHenry, and D. E. Laughlin, IEEE Trans. Magn. **37**, 1309 (2001).

81. S. Jeong, T. Ohkubo, A. G. Roy, D. E. Laughlin, and M. E. McHenry, J. Appl. Phys. **91**, 6863 (2002).

82. K. Kang, Z. G. Zhang, C. Papusoi, and T. Suzuki, Appl. Phys. Lett. **82**, 3284(2003).

83. K. Kang, Z. G. Zhang, C. Papusoi, and T. Suzuki, Appl. Phys. Lett. **84**, 404 (2004).

84. Z. G. Zhang, K. Kang, and T. Suzuki, Appl. Phys. Lett. **83**, 1785 (2003).

85. C. L. Platt and K. W. Wierman, J. Magn. Magn. Mater. **295**, 241 (2005).

86. S. Nakagawa and T. Kamiki, J. Magn. Magn. Mater. **287**, 204 (2005).

87. A. Yano, T. Koda, and S. Matsunuma, IEEE Trans. Magn. **41**, 3211 (2005).

88. B. M. Lairson and B. M. Clemens, Appl. Phys. Lett. **63**, 1438 (1993).

89. M. R. Visokay and R. Sinclair, Appl. Phys. Lett. **66**, 1692 (1995).

90. T. Yang, E. Ahmad, and Y. Suzuki, J. Appl. Phys. **91**, 6860 (2000).

91. Y. F. Ding, J. S. Chen, and E. Liu, J. Cryst. Growth **276**, 111 (2005).

92. Y.-N. Hsu, S. Jeong, D. Laughlin, and D. N. Lambeth, J. Appl. Phys. **89**, 7068 (2001).

93. Y.-N. Hsu, S. Jeong, D. E. Laughlin, and D. N. Lambeth, J. Magn. Magn. Mater. **260**, 282 (2003).

94. Y. F. Ding, J. S. Chen, and E. Liu, Appl. Phys. A **81**, 1485 (2005).

95. C. P. Luo, S. H. Liou, L. Gao, Y. Liu, and D. J. Sellmyer, Appl. Phys. Lett. **77**, 2225 (2000).

96. H. Zeng, M. L. Yan, N. Powers, and D. J. Sellmyer, Appl. Phys. Lett. **80**, 2350 (2002).

97. M. L. Yan, N. Powers, and D. J. Sellmyer, J. Appl. Phys. **93**, 8292 (2003).

98. P. Rasmussen, X. Rui, and J. E. Shield, Appl. Phys. Lett. **86**, 191915 (2005).

99. C. P. Luo and D. J. Sellmyer, Appl. Phys. Lett. **75**, 3162 (1999).

100. T. O. Seki, Y. K. Takahashi, and K. Hono, J. Appl. Phys. **103**, 023910 (2008).

101. G. Sáfrán, T. Suzuki, K. Ouchi, P. B. Barna, and G. Radnóczi, Thin Solid Films **496**, 580 (2006).

102. J. S. Chen, J. F. Hu, B. C. Lim, Y. F. Ding, G. M. Chow, and G. Ju, IEEE Trans. Magn. **45**, 839 (2009).

103. A. Perumal, Y. K. Takahashi, and K. Hono, Appl. Phys. Express **1**, 101301 (2008).

104. B. C. Lim, J. S. Chen, J. F. Hu, P. W. Lwin, Y. F. Ding, K. M. Cher, and B. Liu, J. Appl. Phys. **105**, 07A730 (2009).

105. Y. F. Ding, J. S. Chen, B. C. Lim, J. F. Hu, B. Liu, and G. Ju, Appl. Phys. Lett. **93**, 032506 (2008).

106. E. Yang and D. E. Laughlin, J. Appl. Phys. **104**, 023904 (2008).

107. N. Honda, K. Ouchi, and S. Iwasaki, IEEE Trans. Magn. **38**, 1615 (2002).

108. H. Zeng, R. Sabirianov, O. Mryasov, M. L. Yan, K. Cho, and D. J. Sellmyer, Phys. Rev. B **66**, 184425 (2002).

109. Y. C. Wu and C. H. Lai, IEEE Trans. Magn. **43**, 822 (2007).

110. W. Y. Zhang, H. Shima, F. Takano, H. Akinaga, X. Z. Yu, T. Hara, W. Z. Zhang, K. Kimoto, Y. Matsui, and S. Nimori, J. Appl. Phys. **106**, 033907 (2009).

111. D. C. Berry and K. Barmak, J. Appl. Phys. **102**, 024912 (2007).

112. R. V. P. Montsouka, J. Arabski, A. Derory, J. Faerber, G. Schmerber, and V. Pierron-Bohnes, Mater. Sci. Eng. B **126**, 236 (2006).

113. J.-U. Thiele, K. R. Coffey, M. F. Toney, J. A. Hedstrom, and A. J. Kellock, J. Appl. Phys. **91**, 6595 (2002).

114. A. Gavrin and C. L. Chien, J. Appl. Phys. **73**, 6949 (1993).

115. C. B. Rong, Y. Li, and J. P. Liu, J. Appl. Phys. **101**, 09K505 (2007).

116. C.-B. Rong, D. Li, V. Nandwana, N. Poudyal, Y. Ding, Z. L. Wang, H. Zeng, and J. P. Liu, Adv. Mater. **18**, 2984 (2006).

117. H. M. Lu, Z. H. Cao, C. L. Zhao, P. Y. Li, and X. K. Meng, J. Appl. Phys. **103**, 123526 (2008).

12

PATTERNED MAGNETIC RECORDING MEDIA: PROGRESS AND PROSPECTS

Thomas Thomson

The University of Manchester, UK

Bruce D. Terris

Hitachi Global Storage Technologies

12.1 INTRODUCTION

Magnetic recording, invented over 100 years ago, has played a key role in the development of information storage technologies, including analog audio, video, and digital data recording. Since the sale of the first magnetic hard disk drive (HDD) by IBM in 1956, the capacity and storage density, that is, the number of bits per square inch (b/in.^{2}), has increased by a factor of more than 200 million from 2 kb/in.^{2} to 500 Gb/in.^{2}. The increase in density has required continuous scaling of the critical components and dimensions of the disk drive to ever smaller values. As a result of scaling, the head flies closer to the disk, write and read resolution is increased, write fields and field gradients from the head increase, the grains in the medium become both thinner and smaller in diameter, and the medium anisotropy is increased, all allowing for a growth in areal density and a corresponding increase in data rate [1, 2].

Developments in Data Storage: Materials Perspective, First Edition.
Edited by S. N. Piramanayagam, Tow C. Chong.
© 2012 Institute of Electrical and Electronics Engineers. Published 2012 by John Wiley & Sons, Inc.

Recording demonstrations at densities of 412 Gb/in.^{2} [3] and 519 Gb/in.^{2} [4] have been reported on conventional perpendicular continuous granular media (CGM), and system designs have been discussed for Tbit/in.^{2} densities [5–8]. As described in earlier chapters, this increase in density has been achieved by scaling the grain size in the media with the bit size, thus keeping the number of grains/bit approximately constant (not strictly true in recent years) and maintaining a sufficient signal-to-noise ratio (SNR). In order to prevent long-term signal decay caused by thermally activated magnetization reversal, the magnetic anisotropy must increase with decreasing grain size. Ultimately, the recording density will be limited by the inability of the write element to reverse grains having the required anisotropy for thermal stability.

In order to push recording densities beyond the limits of conventional CGM, two classes of approaches have been proposed. In the first class, an additional source of energy is introduced to assist the applied magnetic field in reversing the bit magnetization, thus allowing higher anisotropy media to be used. Until recently, "energy assisted recording" was synonymous with heat-assisted recording where locally heating the bit [9] lowered the anisotropy during writing. However, additional energy can also be provided by adding a radio-frequency magnetic field [10]. The higher anisotropy enables smaller grains to be thermally stable, and adding a new energy source to the write element enables bits to be written with heads fabricated from existing pole materials. The second class of approaches involves the use of lithographically patterned media. This has the advantage that head designs similar to those in production today can still be used, but with radically different media. Two forms of lithographically patterned media have been proposed: discrete (or patterned) track media (DTM) and bit-patterned media (BPM) [11–14].

DTM is a modified form of CGM in which the magnetic film has been lithographically patterned into tracks separated by nonmagnetic material or empty gaps. In DTM, the bit transitions along the track are still defined by the grain structure, exchange coupling between the grains, and the field gradient from the write head as in conventional CGM. This chapter, however, will focus primarily on the challenges for BPM, which will offer a larger density gain than DTM. In BPM, each bit is lithographically patterned to be one grain, or more precisely, one magnetic switching volume (which may consist of a few strongly coupled grains), referred to as an "island." The magnetic anisotropy energy, K_uV, is thus no longer governed by the grain volume but rather by the entire island volume. Hence the anisotropy can be reduced due to the increased magnetic switching volume to achieve both thermal stability and writability at high density.

Although BPM may be a route to thermally stable recording, such a recording system differs substantially from a CGM system. For example, the SNR and data error rate in a CGM system depend on transition jitter, which is strongly affected by the media grain (or cluster) size and distribution (as well as switching field distribution and write-field gradient). In contrast, for BPM a major source of errors is the patterning tolerance in the island fabrication process. Another striking difference between CGM and BPM is the need for synchronized writing. In BPM, it is critical to synchronize the write clock to the passage of individual islands under the write head, which is not necessary for the featureless CGM.

12.2 BIT-PATTERNED MEDIA AND DISCRETE TRACK MEDIA

One of the key advantages of conventional magnetic recording over other data storage technologies, such as DRAM and flash, is the use of a continuous featureless recording medium. The magnetic write/read head is fabricated using conventional lithography processes, but even here the processing steps at the finest lithographic resolution are few compared to the number of steps required for semiconductor-based storage. For example, in the case of a 520-Gb/in.^{2} disk, roughly the highest product density at the end of 2009, the bit dimensions are on the order of 15 nm × 81 nm, where 15 nm is the downtrack spacing between transitions, and 81 nm is the track pitch. The ratio of track pitch to downtrack bit period is referred to as the bit aspect ratio (BAR), and is 5.4 in this case. The short, downtrack dimension is not lithographically defined but is rather defined by the thin-film deposition processes used to form the write and read elements in the head. The track width is set by lithography and typically requires only a few steps at the critical feature size of approximately 40 nm (half track pitch). Thus, to address the 125 Gb of data on a single side of the disk, only a few lithographically defined features at the critical dimension are required, all of which are on the recording head. Heads are typically manufactured using 5-inch diameter wafers, on which there are roughly 40,000 heads. Since each head requires only a few features at the minimum size, a single wafer contains approximately 10^5 features at the smallest dimension. This compares to 10^{10} features that are typically required on a semiconductor memory wafer. Therefore, to the extent that the device price will depend on fabrication costs, disk drives have a huge advantage over semiconductor memory. This is borne out in the market place, where the price for disk drives is approximately $0.20/Gb, and for flash memory, around 20 times more, or $4/Gb. This cost disparity is even more remarkable when one considers the mechanical complexity of a disk drive.

Given the inherent cost advantage of continuous unstructured media used in magnetic recording, the question arises as to what compelling advantage nanofabrication of media might bring. There are currently two types of patterning under consideration, patterned discrete tracks and patterned bits, as shown schematically in Figure 12.1. We introduce each of these below in order of increasing advantage or gain, and likely also in order of increasing cost.

12.2.1 Discrete or Patterned Tracks

In conventional magnetic recording, both the bit length (along the track) and the bit width (across the track), are defined by the write-field gradient from the recording head—assuming that the grains are small and they are well exchange-decoupled. The track locations are defined by the prewritten servo marks. However, due to mechanical vibrations and nonperfect track following of the head, there is some misregistration of the head to the track locations from revolution to revolution. The errors introduced by this misregistration of either the write element or the read element to the track location can be reduced by physically defining the track locations on the disk and thus no longer relying solely on the mechanical positioning capability of the disk drive. The regions between the tracks should be either nonmagnetic or recessed from the head such that

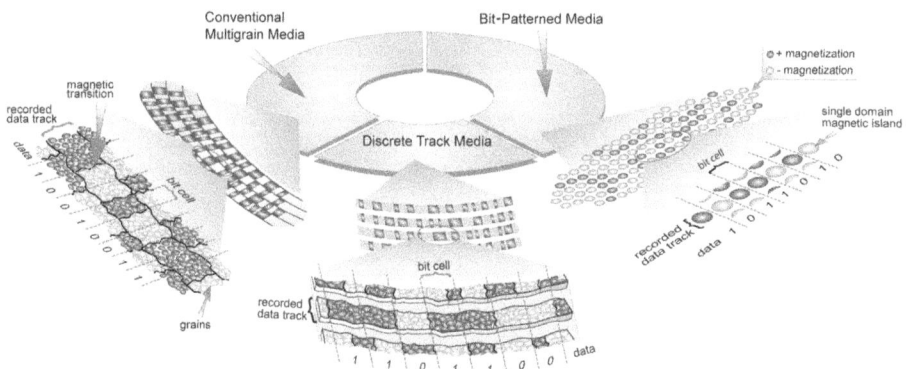

Figure 12.1. Schematic of continuous media bits, discrete track bits. and patterned media bits.

the read element senses little or no magnetic response from them. This approach reduces the problem of poorly written and partially erased information at the edges of the track, which is a significant source of noise. The use of discrete tracks allows the read element to be made wider than is possible with CGM and comparable to the write-element width, as so-called side reading is no longer an issue. With the track widths physically defined in the medium, the requirements on head tolerances may be eased, thus improving manufacturing yield.

In DTM, the track width is defined by lithography, but the downtrack bit transitions are still defined by the field and field gradient from the write element, as in conventional magnetic recording. The bit transition is thus still determined by the reversal of magnetization direction in adjacent grains [15]. Hence material requirements for DTM are very similar to those of continuous media.

In principle, the fabrication processes for DTM share common features with BPM which we discuss in the next section. However, the extent of this overlap has yet to be determined as the optimal process for each class of patterned media remains to be defined and is currently the subject of a highly active research effort. There are two basic approaches to creating patterned structures in magnetic media—prepatterning substrates followed by deposition of a magnetic thin film (an additive process), and deposition of the magnetic film followed by some etch process to remove the unwanted material between the desired tracks or islands (a subtractive process). Schematics of these processes are shown in Figure 12.2.

12.2.2 Patterned Bits

The most demanding application of nanofabricated media is BPM. As magnetic grain sizes in conventional media are reduced, the magnetic energy per grain becomes too small to prevent thermally activated reversals. In order to keep thermally activated reversal at an acceptable level, $K_u V/k_B T$, where K_u is the unaxial magnetic anisotropy,

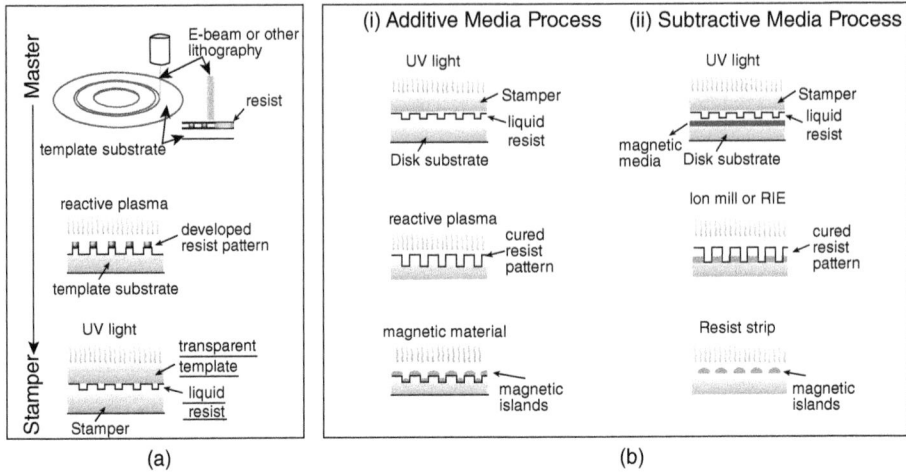

Figure 12.2. Schematic of example process for (a) fabricating stamper from a master and (b) fabricating disks from stamper using (i) additive processing and (ii) subtractive processing.

V the magnetic switching volume, k_B Boltzmann's constant, and T the absolute temperature, must remain greater than approximately 60 for both longitudinal and perpendicular granular media [16]. To maintain sufficient SNR, it is desirable to conserve the number of grains per bit as the density is increased, and hence the grain volume must be reduced. In passing we note that some additional gain in areal density is realized through improved data coding and error correction techniques, which reduce the number of grains required per bit. In order to maintain $K_u V$, the value of K_u cannot be increased without bound, since the magnetic field required to write a bit increases with K_u. The write processes and head designs for perpendicular media that includes a soft magnetic underlayer are reviewed by Khizroev and Litvinov [17, 18], who concluded that the fields available to reverse the recording layer are approximately 15 kOe. Piramanayagam [19] has reviewed advanced perpendicular media, and Greaves et al. [20] have shown that recording at 1 Tb/in.^{2} is theoretically possible on exchange-spring media with 6-nm-diameter grains, where each bit contains only a few grains. However, compared with today's 520-Gb/in.^{2} media, significantly tighter anisotropy and grain-size distributions will be required.

In the case of BPM, the SNR argument is very different from that for CGM. Here the number of grains (or more correctly, the number of magnetic switching volumes) per bit is reduced to 1, and there is no statistical averaging over many grains/clusters to reduce noise. The transitions, both downtrack and crosstrack, are now defined exclusively by the patterning and not by the head field. The switching volume is now equal to the bit size, and thus islands (bits) as small as 10 nm and below will be thermally stable and still writeable with current recording heads.

TABLE 12.1. Dimensional Requirements (Downtrack) for BPM with Bit Aspect Ratio (BAR) of 1 and 4

Density (Tb/in.^{2})	Bit Period (nm) BAR = 1	Bit Period (nm) BAR = 4
0.5	36	18
0.75	29	14.5
1	25.4	12.7
5	11	5.5
10	8	4
40	4	2

In a BPM recording system, the relative orientation of the magnetic easy axes of the islands and head field must be the same for every bit on the disk. This requirement strongly favors the use of materials with a perpendicular easy axis since the condition is then met automatically, and almost all research aimed at finding suitable magnetic materials for BPM is now concentrated on thin films with perpendicular anisotropy. An additional motivation for perpendicular BPM is the change from longitudinal to perpendicular media in conventional magnetic recording that has occurred since 2006 as larger write fields and hence higher areal densities are possible with perpendicular recording.

As discussed in previous chapters, it is likely CGM will approach 1 Tb/in.^{2}, but to reach higher densities, a new technology will likely be required. This density thus defines a possible entry point for BPM, and as shown in Table 12.1, the island dimensions can then be calculated. For 1 Tb/in.^{2}, the bit cell area is 625 nm^2, which for a square bit corresponds to 25 × 25 nm. If we assume equal islands and spaces, this results in a minimum feature size of 12.5 nm. However, a square bit with a bit aspect ratio (BAR) of 1 is undesirable from a recording systems point of view. HDD systems generally benefit from a higher BAR, which relieves the stress on track servo, increases lithographically defined reader and writer widths, and enables higher data rates. Current technology in HDDs uses BARs in the range 5–8. Of course, for BPM, increasing the BAR results in reducing the bit size in the along down-track direction, and thus reduces the required minimum lithography feature size. It is likely some compromise between a BAR of 1 and a BAR of 5 will need to be reached. However, in the most optimistic case, for 1 Tb/in.^{2}, 12.5-nm lithography will be required, and how to accomplish this in a manufacturable process is discussed in the following section.

12.3 FABRICATION OF PATTERNED STRUCTURES

There are many methods for fabricating nanometer-scale magnetic elements, and these have been recently reviewed [21, 22]. The requirements include inexpensive fabrication capable of producing patterns with circular symmetry having the potential for sub-10 nm resolution and resulting in a clean surface on which a head might fly.

The patterning process typically consists of several steps, including lithography to define the pattern, transfer of the pattern into a substrate or thin film, thin-film deposition, and various ancillary processes such as resist spinning, resist developing, residue cleaning, and so on.

Electron beam (e-beam) lithography is probably the most widely used method for fabricating sub-100 nm patterns, and magnetic elements of many sizes and shapes have been created using a variety of pattern transfer processes, a number of examples of which have recently been reviewed [21–23]. The resolution is determined not only by the e-beam diameter, but also by the exposure and development processes in the resist. It should be noted that the very high isolated feature resolution, as small as a few nm, is not the most important figure of merit for BPM applications where dense features of roughly equal bits and spaces are required. In this case, the proximity effect due to overlapping low-level exposures from adjacent features will limit how close features can be placed and thus will limit the achievable density. In addition, since e-beam lithography is a serial writing process, it is expensive and slow. It is most unlikely to have the low cost and high throughput required for direct writing of patterned media [24], but it may have application in the fabrication of masks for master/replication methods, such as nanoimprinting. In addition, nontraditional processes, such as self-assembly of nanometer-scale particles, may also be used to create patterned magnetic entities.

The fabrication process currently envisioned for BPM would combine the use of e-beam lithography, possibly self-assembly, and nanoimprint lithography for the creation and replication of patterns. As shown in Figure 12.2, a single topographic master pattern, generated at considerable expense, is replicated by a two-generation nanoimprint lithography process, first to create a number of imprinting templates that are copies of the master pattern, and then to replicate the patterns from the imprinting templates onto millions of disks.

In order to create master templates for BPM, a new generation of rotary-stage e-beam writers will be essential. Rotary-stage writers produce large circular patterns with a continuously rotating stage, which avoids the stitching errors between exposure fields inherent to conventional Cartesian (X–Y) e-beam lithography tools. Resolving the feature sizes needed for BPM (e.g., 12.5-nm diameter islands with a 25-nm period for an areal density of 1 Tb/in.^{2}) pushes the limits of e-beam lithography. Although chemically amplified resists would allow reduced dose and faster overall pattern writing time, their resolution is generally not sufficient for BPM needs; nonchemically amplified resists such as poly-methyl-methacrylate (PMMA), ZEP [25], or hydrogen silsesquioxane (HSQ) provide the best resolution but can require extraordinarily long times to pattern a complete 65-mm disk (from around 100 hours to >1000 hours, depending on pattern size, beam current, and resist). Pattern densities as high as 4.5 Tb/in.^{2} have been shown [26], but requirements for island uniformity and placement tolerance may ultimately limit e-beam lithography to ~1 Tb/in.^{2}

Once the e-beam pattern has been written into the resist, a pattern transfer process is used to convert it into a topographic pattern in the substrate, which will become the imprint stamper. Following development of the resist and possible deposition of a hard mask to provide better etch contrast, the pattern is typically transferred to the substrate by reactive ion etching (RIE). This topographic pattern can then be inexpensively replicated into imprint stampers using UV-cure nanoimprint lithography [27, 28], in which ultraviolet light is used to cure a liquid imprint resist, rapidly converting it to a solid. Alternatively, thermoset polymers can also be used in thermally activated nanoimprinting processes. In one example of the uv process, the resist is dispensed onto the disk substrate using an ink jet process. As the topographic master pattern is brought into contact with the resist, the resist flows and conforms to the pattern. After a brief (~1 second) exposure to uv light, the resist solidifies into a permanent negative copy of the topographic master pattern. This resist pattern then serves as a mask for subsequent pattern transfer into the substrate/stamper.

The process described to this point is common to any patterned-media processing scheme, whether it be for DTM or BPM, that uses expensive masters to generate mass-produced and inexpensive replicas. The imprint process is then repeated using the stamper to define the pattern to be transferred into the recording medium. If a subtractive processing scheme is used, then the resist is coated onto a medium that has been prepared by depositing a magnetic thin film, and possibly some additional sacrificial etch/ion mill mask layers, onto an unpatterned disk substrate. The etch/ion mill step then converts the continuous magnetic film into tracks or islands.

However, most of the published work to date, particularly for BPM, has concentrated on additive processing. Here a reactive ion etch step is used to clear any residual layer and etch a specified depth into the disk substrate, leaving an array of pillars protruding from a recessed background on the substrate. A magnetic thin film, such as Co/Pd multilayers, can then be blanket deposited on the patterned disk (Fig. 12.3). Material deposited on the pillar tops forms isolated magnetic islands, and the remaining material falls into the trenches, which may become a source of readback noise.

The remaining steps in media fabrication include planarization, in which the trenches between islands are filled with nonmagnetic material, and application of a suitable overcoat and surface lubricant. Planarization, while not mandatory in an absolute sense, is highly beneficial in creating a disk surface well suited to flying an air-bearing slider at low flying height (<5 nm) with high stiffness and tight flying height tolerance.

12.3.1 Enhanced Methods of Ultra-high Density Patterned Creation

As noted in the previous section, e-beam lithography may not have sufficient resolution and tolerance control to create master templates with areal densities significantly greater than 1 Tb/in.^{2} If patterned media is to be an extendable technology, then new methods of creating large area arrays of magnetic islands must be explored. Block copolymer self assembly provides a route to achieving resolutions in the range of 10–100 nm [29–31], and recent work has suggested even higher resolution may be possible. Linear diblock copolymer molecules consist of two immiscible chains joined by a covalent bond. The immiscible materials microphase separate to minimize the number of contacts between the incompatible blocks [32] forming ordered arrays with a well-defined periodic structure. The resulting morphology (most commonly spherical, cylindrical, or lamellar) is dictated by the volume fraction of the individual blocks in the copolymer

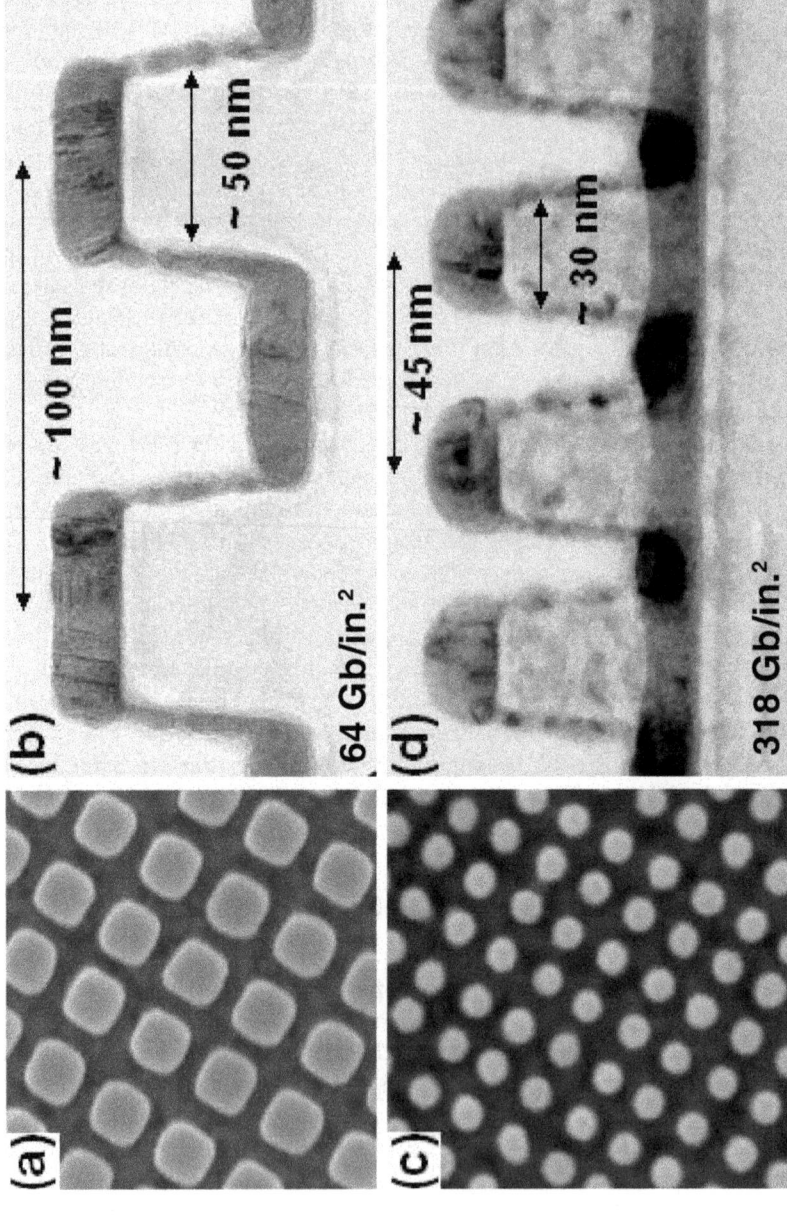

Figure 12.3. Plan-view scanning electron microscope (SEM) (a, c) and cross-sectional-view (b, d) TEM images of pre-patterned substrates after magnetic media deposition for 50-nm islands on 100-nm pitch (64 Gb/in.²) (a, b) and 30-nm islands on 45-nm pitch (318 Gb/in.²) (c, d) (from Reference 14).

chain, and the degree of polymerization, N, determines the characteristic periodic distance between features, L_o.

The block copolymer pattern would serve as a mask for transferring the pattern into an imprint master, most likely by etching. Typically, the pattern transfer process involves selective removal of one of the two copolymer blocks by use of an appropriate solvent or developer. The remaining template is then used as a sacrificial mask in a variety of ways that range from reactive ion etching (RIE) [30, 31, 33, 34] to lift-off [35] or ion milling [36, 37].

A guided self-assembly method is more likely to succeed than a pure bottom-up approach in addressing challenges such as long-range ordering, placement jitter, feature size distribution, and pattern registration needed to meet the specifications for patterned media applications. An example of guided self assembly is that of chemically prepatterning the substrate as shown by recent results from Ruiz et al. [38] (Fig. 12.4). Here e-beam lithography is used to create a chemically prepatterned surface. The prepatterning changes the local surface energy, and can be used to impose long-range order as well as allowing e-beam patterning at a lower density than the final self-assembled pattern (i.e., with a lattice constant $L_s = nL_o$, where n is an integer greater than 1). A block copolymer film can then use the prepattern lattice as a guiding template, effectively multiplying the feature density while maintaining long-range coherence.

An additional advantage of block copolymer patterns is their ability to keep a uniform spacing and size distribution even in the presence of feature size fluctuations on the

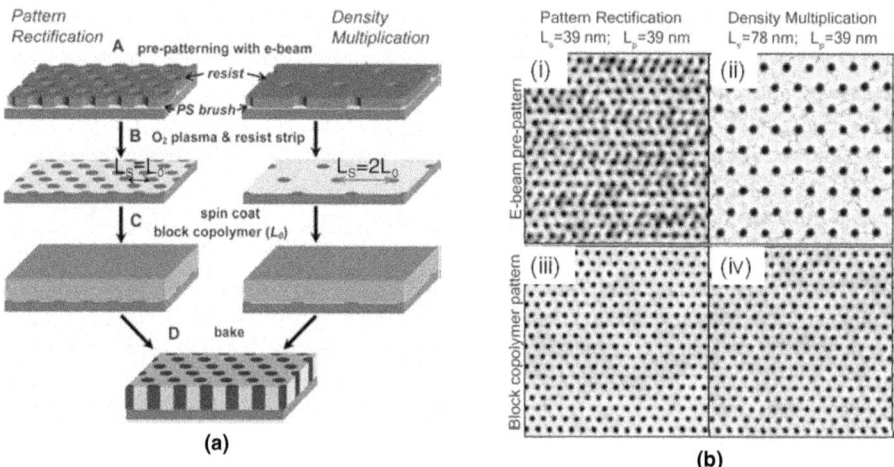

(a)

(b)

Figure 12.4. (a) Process to create lithographically defined chemically prepatterned surfaces and subsequent directed assembly. (A) Electron-beam lithography patterns at Ls = L₀ (left) and Ls = 2L₀ (right). (B) Chemical contrast on the substrate after O₂ plasma exposure on the electron-beam–defined spots above. (C) Block copolymer thin film. (D) Guided self-assembly in registration with the underlying chemical pattern. (b) SEM images of developed electron-beam resist with Ls = 39 and 78 nm. SEM images of the block copolymer film on top of the prepattern defined by the corresponding electron-beam pattern above (from Reference 38).

chemically prepatterned substrate. The bit size distribution is thus limited by the degree of size dispersion in the block copolymer components and not by the e-beam patterning, allowing some relaxation of tolerances for the e-beam lithography step. The ability of self assembly to maintain a uniform lattice helps to reduce downtrack and crosstrack jitter.

The approach of using lithography to maintain long-range pattern registration and self- assembly to impose short-range order may prove a good candidate to efficiently use the available area. Chemical prepatterning does not come at the expense of data storage area (as opposed to graphoepitaxy) and can provide a uniform guide for the self-assembled pattern. However, recent work has suggested topographic approaches with sparse guiding structures [39] may also prove promising.

12.3.2 Addressability of Patterned Media

Data storage systems must be able to write and read information at low error rates, and current standards demand raw (uncorrected) rates of around 10^{-4} to 10^{-6}. In magnetic recording, the binary data are encoded by the presence or lack of a transition at a given clock cycle (Fig. 12.1). This is true for CGM and DTM, and will likely be true for BPM as well. For example, in analogy to CGM, in BPM a "1" may be stored as a change in the magnetization between successive islands and a "0" as no change. However, there is a fundamental difference between continuous media and BPM in the method used for writing data to the disk. In CGM, the media are isotropic with the only structure due to grain-to-grain variations that occur on a 10-nm-length scale. Hence all locations on the disks are equivalent. Data are written to the disk by the write-field gradient from the head, with the field gradient and media switching-field distribution (SFD) defining the bit locations. On a blank disk, the system can start recording data at any position on the disk. Recording on DTM media is similar to this in terms of the head defining the transitions. The track positions in DTM are, of course, defined by the disk patterning, but along the track all the data locations are still defined by the head gradient and media SFD.

In contrast, for BPM all the bit locations are defined by the disk although the data values (such as magnetization up or down) are still written by the head field. In this case, in order to correctly address the pre-existing island locations, the head write field must be synchronized to the island locations. This synchronization process will be described below, but the implications for patterning are that the distributions of island sizes and positions must be tightly controlled. The head write field will ideally reverse when the head is located at the center of the gap between two islands. If islands are misplaced or improperly sized, then they will not experience the intended field amplitude for the desired time duration and may either not reverse at all or may reverse when not intended. Micromagnetic models of BPM systems imply the standard deviations of the distributions for island size and center-to-center distance need to be below 10% to achieve the desired error rates of 10^{-4} to 10^{-6} at 1-Tb/in.^{2} density [40–42]. The requirements on these distributions will, of course, only become more stringent as densities increase toward 10 Tb/in.^{2}

Another requirement to ensure the addressability of patterned media is the need to fly the recording head in a stable manner within a few nanometers of the disk surface, a requirement also placed on CGM and DTM systems. In patterned media this requirement is more onerous than for CGM since after patterning the disk surface is no longer flat and smooth, which leads to changes in fly height. Simulations and experimental results show that sliders flying over the surface of a DTM suffer a flying height loss compared to flight over a smooth medium [43]. The reduction in fly height is approximately proportional to the ratio of area of the land (island) to area of trench. This reduction in average fly height could be compensated for by adjusting the air bearing design. However, the fluctuations in fly height that arise from instabilities in the air bearing as the head flies over a patterned surface are a much more serious problem. If these instabilities cannot be tolerated or overcome, then it is likely that planarization of the disk surface after patterning will be required. One possible solution would involve the use of chemical mechanical polishing (CMP), but cost and manufacturability are serious concerns. Planarization might be achieved using a purely chemical approach. Here the gaps between tracks (DTM) or islands (BPM) can be at least partially filled with a viscous liquid such as spin-on glass or disk lubricant that would flow, thereby planarizing the surface. Significant work still needs to be done in this area in order to demonstrate a manufacturable approach that would allow patterned disks surfaces to be sufficiently planar to support a flying recording head with the required tolerances.

12.3.3 Magnetic Requirements for Patterned Media

The magnetic requirements for DTM and BPM are very different. Essentially DTM properties are similar to conventional perpendicular media, with a small (<10 nm), heterogeneneous granular structure. Since DTM largely solve the problem of adjacent track interference through physical patterning, the medium can be optimized for maximum linear (downtrack) density. An example of this optimization might be increased intergranular exchange coupling since the track patterning eliminates the possibility of crosstrack interference, thus permitting a reoptimization of the balance between exchange and magnetostatic interactions.

The magnetic properties needed for BPM are very different. Here the entire bit must switch as a unit rather than the individual grains. This leads to the requirement that the medium must be highly exchange coupled, which is the antithesis of all conventional magnetic media developed to date. The other critical feature of patterned media is that each individual bit (island) switches at very similar values of applied field—that the switching field distribution (SFD) is very narrow. This requirement has been discussed in detail by Schabes [42], Richter et al. [41], and Degawa et al. [40]. Schabes showed that successfully writing data at densities of 2 Tb/in.^{2}, and assuming a lithography jitter of 1 nm, required anisotropy distributions ($\sigma H_k/H_k$) in the range 4–7% depending on challenging but realistic choices of head field gradient.

Several factors contribute to the SFD; there are intrinsic contributions owing to material variations within the magnetic island under consideration, and extrinsic contributions due to the fields from other islands in the array. The applied field needed to reverse a particular island depends on the sum of the magnetostatic fields produced by the other islands in the BPM array. The contribution of these fields to the total SFD depends only on the geometry of the patterned array and the saturation magnetization (M_s) of the medium. An example of a measured SFD for Co/Pd islands is shown in Figure 12.5 [44]. The magnetostatic contribution to the SFD can be calculated by summing over all neighboring islands and can also be extracted from measured minor hysteresis loops [45]. In the case of arrays where the island size is half the period, the contribution of magnetostatic interactions to the total SFD increases significantly as island size (and period) decreases, ultimately approaching a sizeable fraction of $4\pi M_s$

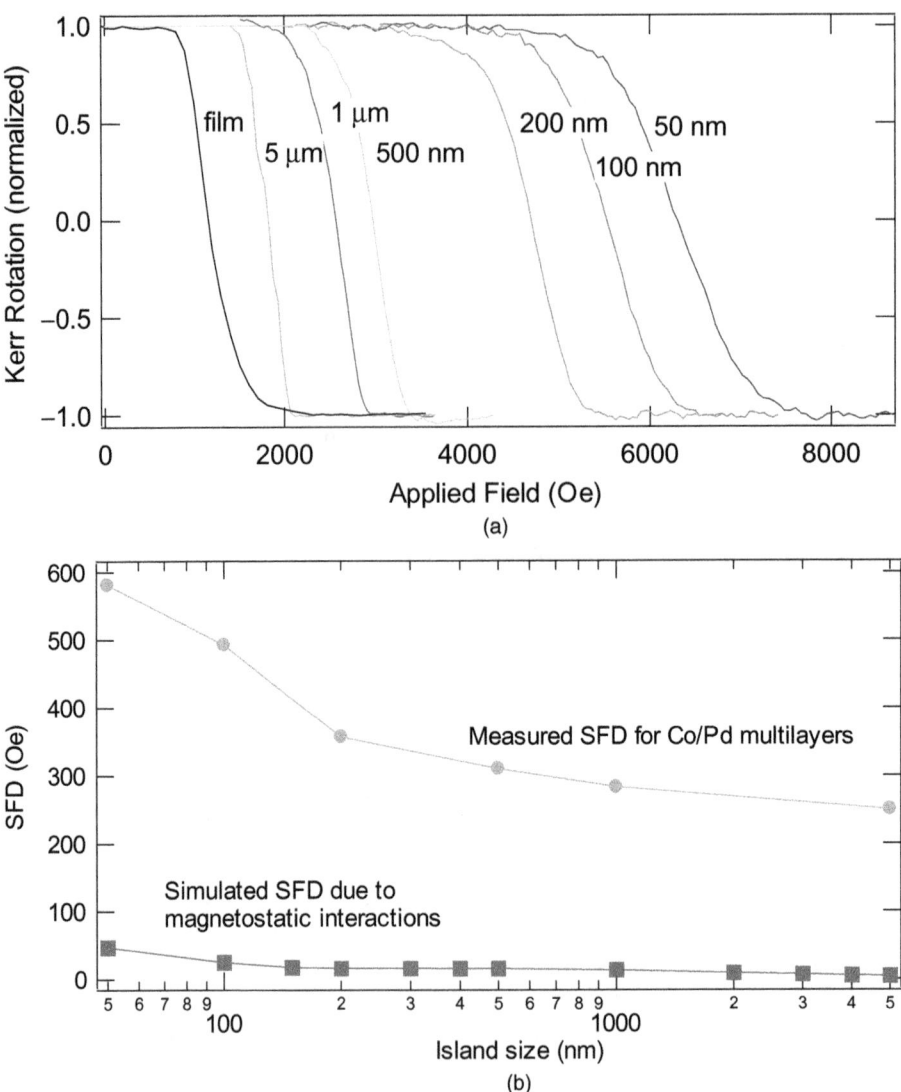

Figure 12.5. (a) Kerr rotation vs. applied magnetic field for a Co (0.33 nm)/Pd (0.96 nm)x8 film and a variety of Co/Pd islands sizes. Both the switching field and switching field distribution increase as the island size decreases, as shown in (b). Also shown in (b) is the calculated contribution to the SFD from the dipolar fields emanating from neighboring islands. See Reference 44 for details.

for small (nm) island spacing. Although it is possible to control the magnetostatic part of the SFD by reducing M_s, this approach is limited by the fact that the same magnetostatic stray fields are responsible for the signal detected by the read element, hence decreasing the signal and leading to reduced SNR. Perturbations to the magnetostatic fields from soft underlayers as well as from head write poles and shields will also need to be included in any system design.

While magnetostatic fields set the limit on the smallest SFD that can be obtained, island-to-island variation of magnetic properties provides the greatest challenge to creating patterned media with narrow SFDs. These island-to-island variations currently account for the largest fraction of the SFD. They originate from microscopic variations in the local anisotropy. In highly exchange coupled continuous thin films (films with an area greater than a few tenths of a mm), reversal occurs by nucleation of a small reversed site, following which, the remaining film is reversed by domain wall motion. In this case, the reversal field of the thin film is dependent on both the lowest nucleation reversal field in the film and on the depinning field needed to displace a domain wall. Thus, unless this minimum nucleation field is changed, local variations of magnetic anisotropy do not affect the reversal of the film. The length scale over which variations in anisotropy affect nucleation is set by the exchange length, which for the high perpendicular anisotropy, high exchange-coupled thin films needed for patterned media is on the order of 20 nm.

Single domain islands with small subexchange length dimensions reverse in a very different manner. In this case the islands cannot support domain walls and so reverse by rotation. The reversal field is therefore determined by the average anisotropy of the island and, of course, the temperature of the sample through thermal activation. Creating patterned media from an exchange-coupled film results in a large number of nanoscale islands, each of which now roughly corresponds to a nucleation volume in the original film [44]. If the local anisotropy of the full film varies as a function of position, then the field required to switch individual islands will also vary. This intrinsic distribution of anisotropy is always present to a greater or lesser extent in magnetic thin films. The significance of this intrinsic distribution only becomes manifest as magnetic structures and devices approach the nanometer scale, of which BPM for densities > 1 Tb/in.^{2}, are an extreme example. Thus determination of underlying physical mechanisms and control of intrinsic anisotropy distributions will be a key enabling element in virtually all nanomagnetic devices.

In addition, the lithography and patterned processes can also introduce variations in the island anisotropy. For example, in islands created by ion milling a Co/Pd multilayer, damage at the island edges can result in reduced anisotropy and a broadening of the switching field distribution [46]. This edge damage is particularly severe for multilayer films, where the perpendicular anisotropy originates from the interfaces which are easily modified by stray ions from the milling process. One should not conclude that all etch process are detrimental, but rather that the materials and fabrication processes must be optimized in concert with each other.

In addition to possessing a narrow SFD, the media must also support bits that will remain thermally stable for the lifetime of the product. Unlike CGM, where one unstable grain degrades the SNR, in BPM an unstable island results in an error, and thus the stability requirement is much more stringent for BPM than for CGM.

The individual magnetic islands must remain outside the superparamagnetic limit determined by the ratio of the anisotropy energy to that of the thermal environment $K_u V/k_B T$. In the simplest possible case, the probability of thermal activated reversal is given by:

$$P(t) = 1 - e^{-t/\tau}$$

$$\text{where } \frac{1}{\tau} = f_0 e^{-\frac{K_u V}{k_B T}}.$$

Here f_0 is the "attempt frequency," with values typically taken as in the range 10^9 to 10^{12} Hz. In order to have a robust medium, we must ensure that $K_u V$ is large enough to keep any thermally activated reversal events to within a limit that allows the coding and error-correction channel to retrieve the data without corruption. Together, thermal activation and the write field available from a recording head set quite strict limits on the magnetic anisotropy for BPM. If the anisotropy is too high (needed to ensure thermal stability) then the head field may not be able to reverse the magnetization of the islands and write data. Conversely, too low an anisotropy leaves the islands vulnerable to thermally activated reversal although the writing becomes easier. Optimizing the trade-off between the various parameters requires detailed micromagnetic and recording system modeling. Recent work in this area suggests that recording at >1 Tb/in.^{2} should be possible using BPM with challenging but realistically attainable materials and processes. Recording densities significantly greater than 1 Tb/in.^{2} may also be possible by taking advantage of new developments such as exchange spring media, similar to that proposed for conventional granular perpendicular recording. The advantage of these materials is that the exchange spring allows the reversal mechanism to be engineered so that a high anisotropy thin film can be reversed at moderate applied fields, thereby maintaining thermal stability while ensuring writability. Even higher densties, approaching 10 Tb/in.^{2}, may be possible by combining BPM with energy assisted recording, such as thermal and microwave sources, in order to write the high anisotropy media required for thermal stability (Fig. 12.6).

12.4 RECORDING SYSTEMS

Recording on DTM requires very similar writing, signal processing, error correction, coding, and data recovery schemes to that of continuous perpendicular media. The signal is determined by the number of grains that compose the bit, and the medium noise is due to the uncertainty in the bit position (jitter) and the width of the transition, both of which are essentially controlled by the grain size and grain-size distribution along with the head-field gradient. In addition, direct-current noise due to media inhomogeneities, that is, fluctuations in the remanent magnetization, may also be present.

However, both the writing and reading processes for BPM are very different compared to CGM. The writing process, as discussed above, involves synchronizing the head write field to the island location. This will likely be achieved using a sector synchronization scheme, where the write pulses are frequency and phase synchronized to a field of patterned islands. The data would then be written in an open loop fashion,

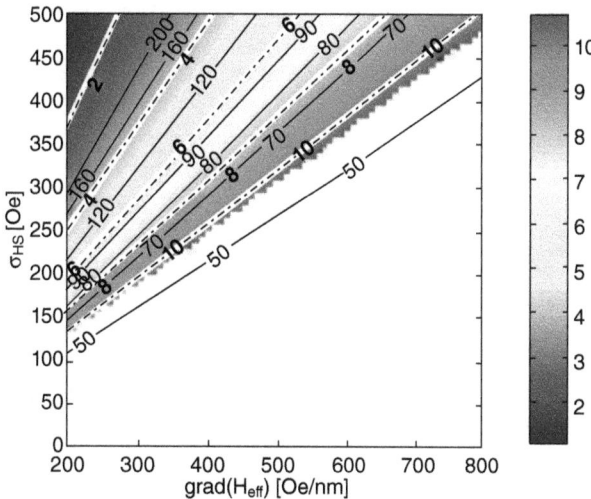

Figure 12.6. Design chart for lithography and synchronization $\sigma = 0.4$ nm, Ms = 430 emu/cm^3, K$_1$ = 2.7 × 10^6 erg/cm^3, and write BER = 10^{-6}. The color scale encodes the areal density in Tbt/in.^{2} The dashed contours with labels in bold font are areal-density contours in Tb/in.^{2} Other contours are thermal energy-barrier contours of the islands at the underlying areal density and temperature T = 350 K (from Reference 42).

where the head field is switched according to the frequency and phase determined from the synchronization field. This would proceed until the head reaches the next synchronization field, and there could be several hundred of such fields around the circumference of the disk. The better the long range order of the patterned bits, the fewer synchronization fields will be needed, and the higher the areal utilization of the disk.

In BPM an error in writing, that is, failure to reverse an island as intended, gives a hard error, as discussed above. Read recovery is clearly not possible, and hence the data coding scheme must be sufficiently robust so as to accommodate the expected hard error rate. In addition to hard-write errors, imperfections in the patterning process result in variations in the size of the magnetic islands and displacements from their intended positions—that is, size jitter and position jitter. While such variations have a larger effect on write errors, these sources of jitter also give rise to read errors and should not be ignored. This jitter in physical parameters affects the waveform obtained from the read element and makes data recovery difficult. Suzuki et al. [47] studied the effect of this jitter noise on the recording performance of BPM and concluded that for patterning jitter of <8%, BPM offered a performance advantage over conventional recording media. It was also found that improvements in error rates can be obtained by increasing the land-length to bit-length ratio, that is, the duty cycle. Overall, the requirements for heads and media tolerances that lead to acceptable error rates have been explored using micromagnetic simulations by Schabes [42]. This work focused on the requirements for recording at 1.3 Tb/in.^{2} and demonstrated the importance of write synchronization and the need for tight control over the switching-field distribution, such that $\sigma H_k/H_k$ is ~5–10%, along with a σ of 5–10% for the size and position of the islands (Fig. 12.6).

In all HDD systems, the radial position of the head on the surface of the disk is controlled by a servo system (for correct positioning on the intended track), which uses a position error signal (PES) and synchronization marks to define the start of a sector along a track. Servo bursts and synchronization marks are normally created in a time-consuming operation at the final stages of manufacturing. One of the advantages that physical patterning of the medium offers is the ability to create the necessary servo bursts and synchronization schemes at the same time as either the data tracks in the case of DTM or bits in BPM. This potentially offers significant manufacturing cost savings that could offset some of the greater expenses incurred in producing patterned media.

Recovering data from the replay signals produced by patterned media has been investigated by Hughes [48]. It was assumed that the patterned media had magnetically active trench material that produced significant replay signals. A read response from the trenches is highly undesirable since this directly increases the noise in the system. The need to reduce this noise favors the use of subtractive processing or schemes to substantially reduce the moment of the trench material through magnetic poisoning [49]. The readback signal jitter due to lithographic imperfections has been investigated by Ntokas et al. [50]. They demonstrated that coding schemes based on low-density parity-check (LDPC) codes together with iterative decoding enhanced the read channel bit-error-rate (BER) performance in the presence of lithography jitter.

Another readback feature of BPM is that the spacings between adjacent tracks and adjacent bits are similar, and this can result in significant intertrack interference (ITI). A method to mitigate the effects of ITI, a modified trellis coding scheme using the Viterbi algorithm (VA), has been proposed by Nabavi et al. [51], who showed through simulation that improved bit error rates and more tolerance to track misregistration were possible using a modified read channel. It is also possible to utilize the proximity of adjacent tracks by creating a two-dimensional (2D) channel code [52]. This treats the data as a 2D pattern so that a block of data is read rather than a single track. However, the code rate of 7/9 gives a redundancy of 22%, which represents a significant overhead and consequent loss of user areal density.

12.5 PRODUCING A PATTERNED MEDIA DRIVE

The prospects for commercialization of patterned media into HDD products will depend on scientific discovery, engineering innovation, and the ability to create cost effective manufacturing processes. These are all formidable challenges, and at the time of writing (2010), progress is needed in each of these areas. In order to determine whether or not HDDs based on patterned media can become a commercial reality significant resources are now being deployed and some important advances have been made. It appears that conventional perpendicular recording will approach 1 Tb/in.^{2}, and thus a clear technology path to higher densities in the range of 5–10 Tb/in.^{2} should exist in order to justify the large investments in new manufacturing technology and equipment that will be needed.

In general, the solutions for DTM are easier than those for BPM. However, the advantage to be gained from DTM has still not been established unambiguously. One attractive feature of DTM from a commercial and manufacturing point of view is that it allows some of the technology elements needed for BPM to be introduced at lower risk. This, of course, presupposes that similar methods will be employed to manufacture DTM and BPM. Scientifically, this has not yet been established, and it is possible that DTM media may be successfully manufactured using a subtractive process, for example, but BPM may be most advantageously produced using an additive process that uses a prepatterned substrate. It seems likely that if DTM are introduced as the first patterned media, efforts to maximize the overlap in processes between DTM and BPM will be essential in order to ensure a reasonable chance of commercial success.

Scientific discovery is needed for pattern master creation and to narrow the switching field distribution, especially at densities above 1 Tb/in.^{2} In the case of DTM, the development of a high-precision rotary stage e-beam tool may be sufficient to create master templates with the required track periodicity and width. However, for BPM it is unlikely that e-beam alone will be sufficient at higher densities. In this respect, the recent advances in guided diblock copolymer lithography may offer a route to creating the required high-density patterns, but there is still much work to be done in order to create patterns over disk-sized areas. In addition, the necessary servo and formatting patterns will need to be developed. It is also possible to contemplate master-pattern creation by other lithographic means, such as scanning-probe techniques and X-ray interference lithography [53–55]. However, here too, much work needs to be done to demonstrate manufacturable processes. Reducing SFDs requires understanding of the physical mechanisms responsible for these distributions at the nanometer scale. Determining and controlling the variations found in magnetic properties over nanometer-length scales is an important scientific challenge, requiring new insights into material properties, both for patterned media and more widely for any nanomagnetic device where switching characteristics must be controlled.

Innovation in engineering is needed in the area of nanoimprint lithography and pattern transfer. Imprint lithography has made steady progress with a number of companies producing prototype imprint machines and processes [56]. The pattern transfer process, unlike the nanoimprint and master-template creation processes, depends critically on the material into which the pattern is to be transferred. If the pattern is to be transferred directly into the recording layer, then a process capable of etching a magnetic material, that has close to zero impact on the remaining unetched material, must be developed. This is certainly the case for BPM where the process must remove material from the entire perimeter of a nanomagnetic island without significantly altering its switching properties or thermal stability. In DTM this condition is slightly more relaxed since only the track edges are etched. It is clearly an engineering and scientific challenge to determine the optimal pattern transfer route and then to implement the process. While many of these processes can build on tooling from the semiconductor industry, one significant difference is that disks will require patterning on two sides, unlike silicon wafers.

Metrology for nanometer-scale features will also need to be developed. In order to have a robust manufacturing process it is vital to monitor progress as the disk progresses through the manufacturing stages. This clearly requires the development of new tools to quickly determine pattern quality, possibly based on light or X-ray scattering. This complementary activity is just one of the components that will be necessary to develop the manufacture technology necessary to mass produce patterned media.

Finally, we need to consider what changes will be required at a disk manufacturing plant in order to produce patterned media. Manufacturing patterned media would be the largest single change ever undertaken in disk manufacturing since at a minimum it would introduce two new processes, (i) nanoimprint, and (ii) pattern transfer, together with the associated testing procedures needed to ensure quality control (since very few master templates are needed, this step does not necessarily have to be done in a disk manufacturing facility). In order to be economically viable, equipment capable of processing several hundred disks per hour will be required (currently, a typical disk-sputtering machine produces around 600 disks/h). This additional processing would clearly take significant extra floor space in the production facility and involve tens of millions in investment currency for new equipment, process development, and training. Therefore, if HDDs based on patterned media are to become commercially successful, innovation in scientific and technological areas will have to be complemented by cost-competitive manufacturing. Patterned media is only one of several potential data storage technology paths; however, from today's (2010) perspective, it offers one of the best chances of success in providing the increased data storage capacity demanded by the information society in the years ahead.

REFERENCES

1. H. J. Richter, Recent advances in the recording physics of thin-film media. J. Phys. D-Appl. Phys. **32**(21), R147–R168 (1999).

2. A. Moser et al., Magnetic recording: advancing into the future. J. Phys. D-Appl. Phys. **35**(19), R157–R167 (2002).

3. Seagate, in presented at Idema Discon, Sept 2006.

4. S. Mao, *from Westen Digital presented at PMRC*, 2007, Tokyo Japan.

5. X. Shen et al., Issues in recording exchange coupled composite media. IEEE Trans. Magn. **43**(2), 676–681 (2007).

6. J. J. Miles et al., Parametric optimization for terabit perpendicular recording. IEEE Trans. Magn. **39**(4), 1876–1890 (2003).

7. K. Z. Gao and H. N. Bertraum, Magnetic recording configuration for densities beyond 1 Tb/in^2 and data rates beyond 1 Gb/s. IEEE Trans. Magn. **38**(6), 3675–3683 (2002).

8. H. J. Richter, The transition from longitudinal to perpendicular recording. J. Phys. D-Appl. Phys. **40**(9), R149–R177 (2007).

9. T. W. McDaniel, Ultimate limits to thermally assisted magnetic recording. J. Phys.-Condens. Matter **17**(7), R315–R332 (2005).

10. J. G. Zhu, X. C. Zhu, and Y. H. Tang, Microwave assisted magnetic recording. IEEE Trans. Magn. **44**(1), 125–131 (2008).

11. S. Y. Chou, P. R. Krauss, and L. S. Kong, Nanolithographically defined magnetic structures and quantum magnetic disk. J. Appl. Phys. **79**(8), 6101–6106 (1996).

12. R. M. H. New, R. F. W. Pease, and R. L. White, Lithographically patterned single-domain cobalt islands for high-density magnetic recording. J. Magn. Magn. Mater. **155**(1–3), 140–145 (1996).

13. B. D. Terris and T. Thomson, Nanofabricated and self-assembled magnetic structures as data storage media. J. Phys. D Appl. Phys. **38**, R199–R222 (2005).

14. T. R. Albrecht et al., *Bit Patterned Magnetic Recording*. Dordrecht: Springer, 2009.

15. H. N. Bertram, *Theory of Magnetic Recording*. Cambridge: Cambridge University Press, 1994.

16. D. Weller and A. Moser, Thermal effect limits in ultrahigh-density magnetic recording. IEEE Trans. Magn. **35**(6), 4423–4439 (1999).

17. S. Khizroev and D. Litvinov, Perpendicular magnetic recording: writing process. J. Appl. Phys. **95**(9), 4521–4537 (2004).

18. D. Litvinov and S. Khizroev, Perpendicular magnetic recording: playback. Journal Applied Physics. **97**, 7 071101 (2005).

19. S. N. Piramanayagam, Perpendicular recording media for hard disk drives. J. Appl. Phys. **102**(1), 011301 (2007).

20. S. J. Greaves, H. Muraoka, and Y. Kanai, Simulations of recording media for 1 Tb/in^2. J. Magn. Magn. Mater. **320**(22), 2889–2893 (2008).

21. C. Ross, Patterned magnetic recording media. Annu. Rev. Mater. Res. **31**, 203–235 (2001).

22. J. I. Martin, et al., Ordered magnetic nanostructures: fabrication and properties. J. Magn. Magn. Mater. **256**(1–3), 449–501 (2003).

23. J. C. Lodder, Methods for preparing patterned media for high-density recording. J. Magn. Magn. Mater. **272–276**, 1692–1697 (2004).

24. A. A. Driskill-Smith, Electron-beam and emerging lithography for the magnetic recording industry. Emerging Lithographic Technologies VIII. Edited by Mackay, R. Scott, in *Proceedings of the SPIE*, 5374: pp. 16–30 (2004).

25. ZEP520A electron beam resist, Zeon Chemicals, L. P., available at http://www.zeon.co.jp/index_e.html.

26. X. Yang et al., Challenges in 1 Teradot/in^2 dot patterning using electron beam lithography for bit-patterned media. J. Vac. Sci. Technol. **25**(6), 2202–2209 (2007).

27. M. Colburn et al., Step and flash imprint lithography: a new approach to high resolution patterning, in *Proc. SPIE*, 3676: p. 379 (1999).

28. D. Lentz et al., Whole wafer imprint patterning using step and flash imprint lithography: a manufacturing solution for sub-100-nm patterning, in *Proc. SPIE*, 6517: p. 65172F (2007).

29. T. L. Morkved et al., Mesoscopic self-assembly of gold islands an diblock-copolymer films. Appl. Phys. Lett. **64**(4), 422–424 (1994).

30. P. Mansky, P. Chaikin, and E. L. Thomas, Monolayer films of diblock copolymer microdomains for nanolithographic applications. J. Mater. Sci. **30**(8), 1987–1992 (1995).

31. M. Park et al., Block copolymer lithography: periodic arrays of ~10^{11} holes in 1square centimeter. Science **276**(5317), 1401–1404 (1997).

32. F. S. Bates and G. H. Fredrickson, Block copolymer thermodynamics: theory and experiment. Annu. Rev. Phys. Chem. **41**(1), 525–557 (1990).

33. T. Thurn-Albrecht et al., Nanoscopic templates from oriented block copolymer films. Adv. Mater. **12**(11), 787–791 (2000).

34. K. Asakawa and T. Hiraoka, Nanopatterning with microdomains of block copolymers using reactive-ion etching selectivity. Jpn. J. Appl. Phys. 1-Regular Pap. Short Notes Rev. Pap. **41**(10), 6112–6118 (2002).

35. K. W. Guarini et al., Nanoscale patterning using self-assembled polymers for semiconductor applications. J. Vac. Sci. Technol. B **19**(6), 2784–2788 (2001).

36. J. Y. Cheng et al., Magnetic properties of large-area particle arrays fabricated using block copolymer lithography. IEEE Trans. Magn. **38**(5), 2541–2543 (2002).

37. K. Naito et al., 2.5-inch disk patterned media prepared by an artificially assisted self-assembling method. IEEE Trans. Magn. **38**(5), 1949–1951 (2002).

38. R. Ruiz et al., Density multiplication and improved lithography by directed block copolymer assembly. Science **321**(5891), 936–939 (2008).

39. I. Bita et al., Graphoepitaxy of self-assembled block copolymers on two-dimensional periodic patterned templates. Science **321**(5891), 939–943 (2008).

40. N. Degawa et al., Optimisation of bit patterned media for 1 Tb/in.^{2}. J. Magn. Magn. Mater. **320**(22), 3092–3095 (2008).

41. H. J. Richter et al., Recording on bit-patterned media at densities of 1 Tb/in.^{2} and beyond. IEEE Trans. Magn. **42**(10), 2255–2260 (2006).

42. M. E. Schabes, Micromagnetic simulations for terabit/in^2 head/media systems. J. Magn. Magn. Mater. **320**(22), 2880–2884 (2008).

43. J. H. Li, J. U. Xu, and Y. Shimizu, Performance of sliders flying over discrete-track media. J. Tribol.-Trans. Asme **129**(4), 712–719 (2007).

44. T. Thomson, G. Hu, and B. D. Terris, Intrinsic distribution of magnetic anisotropy in thin films probed by patterned nanostructures. Phys. Rev. Lett. **96**, 257204 (2006).

45. O. Hellwig et al., Separating dipolar broadening from the intrinsic switching field distribution in perpendicular patterned media. Appl. Phys. Lett. **90**, 162516 (2007).

46. J. M. Shaw et al., Reversal mechanisms in perpendicularly magnetized nanostructures. Phys. Rev. B **78**(2), 024414 (2008).

47. Y. Suzuki et al., Reproduced waveform and bit error rate analysis of a patterned perpendicular medium R/W channel. J. Appl. Phys. **97**(10), 10P108 (2005).

48. G. F. Hughes, Read channels for patterned media. IEEE Trans. Magn. **35**(5), 2310–2312 (1999).

49. O. Hellwig et al., Suppression of magnetic trench material in bit patterned media fabricated by blanket deposition onto prepatterned substrates. Appl. Phys. Lett. **93**(19), 192501 (2008).

50. I. T. Ntokas et al., Improved data recovery from patterned media with inherent jitter noise using low-density parity-check codes. IEEE Trans. Magn. **43**(10), 3925–3929 (2007).

51. S. Nabavi, B. Kumar, and J. G. Zhu, Modifying viterbi algorithm to mitigate intertrack interference in bit-patterned media. IEEE Trans. Magn. **43**(6), 2274–2276 (2007).

52. J. P. J. Groenland and L. Abelmann, Two-dimensional coding for probe recording on magnetic patterned media. IEEE Trans. Magn. **43**(6), 2307–2309 (2007).

53. J. L. Martin, J. Nogues, K. Liu, J. L. Vicent and I. K. Schuller, Ordered magnetic nanostructures: Fabrication and properties. J. Magn. Magn. Mater. **256**(1–3), 449–501 (2003).

54. A. A. Tseng, A. Notargiacomo, and T. P. Chen, Nanofabrication by scanning probe microscope lithography: A review. J. Vacuum Sci. Technol. B **23**(3), 877–894 (2005).

55. V. Auzelyte, C. Dais, P. Farquet, D. Grutzmacher, L. J. Heyderman, F. Luo, S. Olliges, C. Padeste, P. K. Sahoo, T. Thomson, A. Turchanin, C. David, and H. H. Solak, J. Micro/Nanolithography MEMS MOEMS. **8**(2), 021204 (2009).

56. L. J. Guo, Nanoimprint lithography: Methods and material requirements. Adv. Mater. **19**(4), 495–513 (2007).

13

PHASE CHANGE RANDOM ACCESS MEMORY

Luping Shi, Rong Zhao, and Tow C. Chong

Data Storage Institute, (A*STAR) Agency for Science Technology and Research, Singapore

13.1 INTRODUCTION

Memory technology is one pillar for IT technology and is also widely used in consumer electronic products. The growth of the memory market has been driven by the personal computer revolution fueled by the multimedia revolution, wireless mobile phone, and internet applications. Currently the mainstream memory technologies and systems include solid-state memory, hard disk drive, and optical disk. Each technology has its special market and application although there is some overlap [1–3]. Solid-state memories, which have high speed and compact size, are mainly used as primary (internal) memories, and magnetic and optical storage devices are typically used as secondary storage devices for computer systems. Semiconductor memories have become the most attractive segment in the global semiconductor market: they have taken one third of the whole semiconductor market in revenue with the fastest growth rate.

Generally speaking, there are two camps of semiconductor memories: volatile memories and nonvolatile memories. Volatile memories are the memories that would lose data without a power supply. The main members are DRAM (dynamic random-access memory) and SRAM (static random-access memory). High-end DRAMs are cost-effective and space efficient because each DRAM cell consists of only one

Developments in Data Storage: Materials Perspective, First Edition.
Edited by S. N. Piramanayagam, Tow C. Chong.

transistor and one capacitor. Till now, DRAMs have taken the largest market segment of semiconductor memories for more than 10 years. SRAM is a faster memory with lower standby current compared to DRAM. However, in SRAM, a single memory cell includes four or six transistors, resulting in a lower chip density and a much higher cost in comparison to DRAM.

Recently, with the rapidly growing demand for portable and mobile products, such as digital cameras and cellular phones, the demand for solid-state nonvolatile memory (NVM) has greatly increased [4, 5]. NVMs are memories that can retain stored information even when the power supply is off or removed. A representative of NVM is flash memory, which can keep data for about 10 years. One flash memory cell typically consists of only one transistor, enabling high memory density. Because of its nonvolatile and high-density capabilities, flash memory is widely used in portable devices such as handphones, camcorders, and high-end laptops.

However, although flash memory is rapidly growing, it will be facing technological and physical constraints that make their further scaling more difficult even if the scaling limits are still under debate. The current visibility allows predicting a scenario where the floating-gate concept is a valuable solution till even a 25-nm technology node [6]. Although much effort has been put into implementing new structures and new materials to extend the scaling limitations of flash memory, at this moment it is believed that scaling beyond 20 nm is very challenging. Therefore much effort has been made looking for alternative solutions that exploit new materials and concepts to go beyond flash technology, such as magnetoresistive random access memory (MRAM), ferroelectric random access memory (FeRAM) chalcogenide-based phase change random access memory (PCRAM), organic thin-film memory, molecular memory, nonvolatile silicon memory, and so on [7–17].

PCRAM, also known as OUM (ovonic unified memory), is based on the original invention by S. R. Ovshinsky in 1970s, which used phase change alloy materials to store information [18–20]. Those early devices developed in 1970s were not commercial because of their slow speed, high power consumption, and tendency to degrade owing to the large currents needed to write and erase data. Most of these technical problems were related to the materials. The success of rewriteable optical disk storage, where most of the problems related to materials were solved, was indirectly responsible for PCRAM's second wind. During the 1970s and 1980s, several companies were interested in rewriteable optical disks and developed materials with very fast crystallization speeds, including the germanium-tellurium-antimony alloy. The new material benefited both optical and electronic memory because it requires much less time and energy to program a bit. That made it possible to program a PCRAM cell with a short current pulse, which is needed to produce a commercially competitive NVM.

PCRAM is considered as one of the best candidates for the next generation NVM due to its near-ideal NVM advantages: high scalability, low power, fast access time, long endurance, good data retention, and low cost [21]. The most important advantage of this technology is its high scalability. The critical characteristic of phase change materials is its switching property between amorphous and crystalline states by using electrical pulses. Because the energy needed for operating this memory decreases with cell size, the writing current decreases with cell-size scaling and thus facilitates memory scaling.

Density, data transfer rate, and performance such as overwrite cycle are the most important technological criteria for PCRAM. For PCRAM, density is highly related to cell size. To achieve high density, minimizing the size of recording bits is one of the most effective approaches. The data transfer rate of PCRAM depends highly on the crystallization speed of the phase change materials.

In this chapter, we will introduce the key technologies for PCRAM, including phase change, PCRAM read/write, phase change materials, and the solutions to achieve high density and high speed. Further consideration and future research issues for PCRAM will also be presented.

13.2 PCRAM PRINCIPLES

In the last few decades, chalcogenide-based phase change materials have been widely investigated. These materials have two phase structures, amorphous and crystalline phases, as shown in Figure 13.1. The transformation between these two phases can be induced either by laser light or electric pulses.

13.2.1 Electric Current Induced Phase Change

The effect of electrically induced phase change in chalcogenide materials was discovered in the 1960s. It was found that the application of electric pulses caused changes in the material atomic structures. These different atomic structures have different characteristic physical properties, including different values of electrical conductivity. Relative to the amorphous state, the crystalline state has a lower resistance.

Memory switching is a switching that allows a change in the conduction state of the bistable phase-change materials even in the absence of a current or voltage to sustain

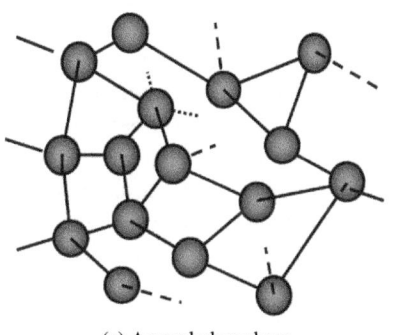 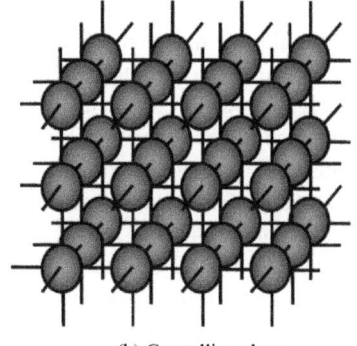

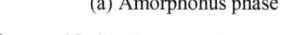

(a) Amorphohus phase   (b) Crystalline phase

Figure 13.1. The two phases of phase change materials: (a) amorphohus phase; (b) crystalline phase.

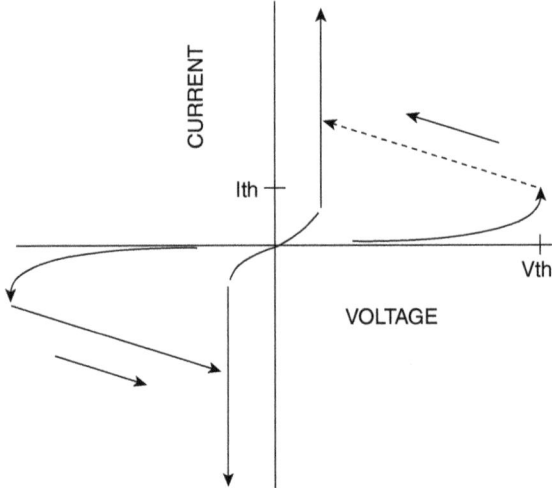

Figure 13.2. Memory switching in phase change material.

it. In Figure 13.2, it can be seen that the curve for memory switching continues through the origin of the graph demonstrating that once in a low resistance state, a sustaining current or voltage is not required. This is because the resistance drop of memory switching is caused by a material atomic structure change during the electrical pulses. These different atomic structures have different characteristic physical properties, including different values of electrical conductivity. This effect was originally observed using a suitable metallized electrode of memory-switch material that was demonstrated at a lecture given at the Detroit Physiological Society Meeting in 1959 [22]. A pulse of one polarity set the memory, and a pulse of different amplitude or opposite polarity shut it off. Therefore, the devices could remain indefinitely either in the ON or OFF state without any sustaining energy input. The ON state (low resistance) is normally the crystalline state with ordered atomic structure, and the OFF state (high resistance) is normally the amorphous state with disordered atomic structure.

The debate about the mechanism of the threshold switching of phase change materials has been continuing [23, 24]. It is now believed that predominantly electronic effects may be involved [25] although some initial models were mostly based on fully thermal phenomena. Instead of happening as a uniform change throughout the phase change material, it has also been recognized that the switching may occur along narrow "filaments" [24]. Recently Karpova et al. proposed a simple physical model of threshold switching in PCRAM cells based on the field-induced nucleation of conductive cylindrical crystallites [26]. The model was solved analytically and led to a number of predictions, including correlations between the threshold voltage V_{th} and material parameters, such as the nucleation barrier and radius, amorphous layer thickness, as well as V_{th} versus temperature and switching delay time. The predictions were verified by experimental results, and good agreement was achieved. In general, the basic nature of threshold switching has not been well understood yet. Moreover, it must be kept in mind that the switching phenomena observed may present a variety of mechanisms at the nanoscale, depending on various factors such as film thickness, volume, and the surrounding materials.

13.2.2 The Principle of PCRAM

PCRAM, as shown in Figure 13.3, works based on a rapid reversible phase change effect in phase change materials. Normally phase change materials have two states, a crystalline state with lower resistance and an amorphous state with higher resistance.

The most commonly used phase change material is GeSbTe alloy, which is the same family of materials used in optical rewritable discs. During operation, the phase change material switches between its high conductive amorphous and low conductive crystalline states by the Joule heating induced by electrical pulses. The rapid and reversible structural change results in a change in material resistivity. The transition from the amorphous state to the crystalline state is generally referred to as "set," and the transition from the crystalline state to the amorphous state is referred as "reset," as shown in Figure 13.4. The small volume of active media acts as a programmable resistor. Its

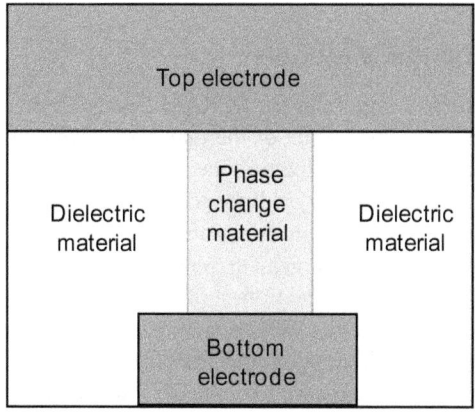

Figure 13.3. Schematic cross-section of PCRAM structure.

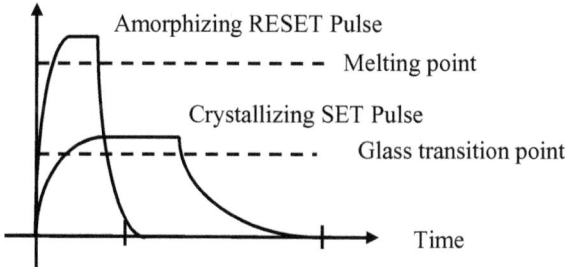

Figure 13.4. Graph of phase transformations of PCRAM.

high and low resistances are measured and recorded as data "1" and "0." To switch to the amorphous state, a short reset pulse with high current increases the temperature to a value above the melting point. After the pulse, the molten state cools rapidly (10^{11} K/s) and is quenched into the amorphous state. To convert the material back into a crystalline state, a relatively longer set pulse with medium current is applied to heat the material above its crystallization temperature but below the melting point. The duration of the set pulse is longer than the material-dependent crystallization time. A much lower current with essentially no Joule heating is used for reading the cell.

In view of the high amorphous resistance, a relatively longer set pulse is expected to dissipate enough energy to induce crystallization. Therefore, it is crucial that the phase change material used show "threshold switching." This means that when the electric field over the amorphous volume exceeds the threshold field, highly conductive filaments are formed within the amorphous material. Within these filaments, Joule heating will occur inducing the desired phase transition at relatively low voltages.

Since the energy required for phase transformation decreases with cell size, the write current scales with cell size and thus facilitates memory scaling. PCRAM has many advantages, such as fast access time, long endurance, and good data retention. It also can be programmed to intermediate resistance values, such as for multistate storage application.

13.2.3   Phase Change Materials

Phase change materials are important for PCRAM. Many phase change materials have been developed. Table 13.1 lists some of the materials developed to date.

According to the classic crystallization theory, crystallization involves two distinct processes, the nucleation of small crystallites followed by the subsequent growth. Both the nucleation rate and growth rate are functions of temperature. In view of the contribution of nucleation and subsequent growth, phase change materials have been categorized into two types, so-called nucleation-dominated material and growth-dominated material [27]. If the nucleation rate of a material is higher than its growth rate, this material is called nucleation-dominated material. If the nucleation rate of a material is lower than its growth rate, this material is called growth-dominated material.

It is always very attractive to utilize molecular engineering to design and model new phase change materials with excellent structure and performance, and meet some

TABLE 13.1. Phase Change Materials

Binary	Ternary	Quaternary
GaSb	$Ge_2Sb_2Te_5$	AgInSbTe
InSb	InSbTe	(GeSn)SbTe
InSe	GaSeTe	GeSb(SeTe)
Sb_2Te_3	$SnSb_2Te_4$	$Te_{81}Ge_{15}Sb_2S_2$
GeTe	$Ge_1Sb_2Te_4$	$GeSbBiTe_4$
Sb_7Te_3	$Ge_{25}As_{50}Te_{25}$	GeTeSbS
In_2Se_3	$Ge_1Sb_4Te_7$	GeTeInGa

special requirements. Luo et al. used the first principle calculation based on density function theory to identify new and possible superior phase change materials [28]. All phase change materials reported by them were characterized by a cubic or near cubic coordination, which is dominance of the p-electron bonding. The calculation results showed that the Te-based ternary materials will favor the suitable rocksalt structure if their average number of valence electrons per single atom is greater than 4.1. This criterion facilitated the search for new phase change materials and paved the way to a more fundamental understanding for phase change materials.

Kohary et al. studied the structure of amorphous InSe alloys using a first principles tight-binding molecular dynamics technique [29]. The characteristics of short-range order such as coordination numbers, radial- and bond-angle distribution functions, and electronic structure were analyzed. Similar local bonding environments were found to be present in the amorphous phase as those in InSe crystalline alloys, such as In_2Se_3, InSe, and In_4Se_3. There is a large fluctuation in coordination numbers, showing that amorphous InSe alloys cannot be considered as network-forming materials. In the future, the material properties presented in this work can serve as input parameters for continuum models that link crystallization processes to the underlying structure.

Recently Lencer et al. [30] proposed a treasure map for phase change materials on the basis of a fundamental understanding of the bonding characteristics. This map is spanned by two coordinates that can be calculated just from the composition, and represent the degree of ionicity and the tendency toward hybridization ("covalency") of the bonding. A small magnitude of both quantities is an inherent characteristic of phase change materials. This coordinate scheme enables a prediction of trends for the physical properties on changing stoichiometry.

For a high-density PCRAM array, the carrier transport between phase change materials and contact electrodes, and carrier confinement between phase change materials with isolating materials (minimizing leakage) between adjacent PCRAM cells are also important. Fundamental electronic properties such as the band alignment of GST with common microelectronic materials employed in complementary metal-oxide semiconductor (CMOS) technology could provide useful information for device design and array optimization. A method using high-resolution X-ray photoelectron spectroscopy to investigate the band alignment of phase change materials and surrounding materials was proposed [31]. The valence band offset of $Ge_2Sb_2Te_5$ on various CMOS materials; that is, Si, SiO_2, HfO_2, Si_3N_4, and NiSi, were investigated with the aid of the core-level, valence-band and energy-loss spectra. Energy band line-ups of $Ge_2Sb_2Te_5$ on these materials were thus determined as shown in Figure 13.5. This method provides an insight on phase change array integration and optimization. It can be useful to screen potential new materials even before integrating them into a PCRAM array.

13.3 PCRAM TECHNOLOGY

Scaling down the size of PCRAM cells is an important approach to the achievement of high density and low-cost memory. The more a feature size is scaled down, the higher

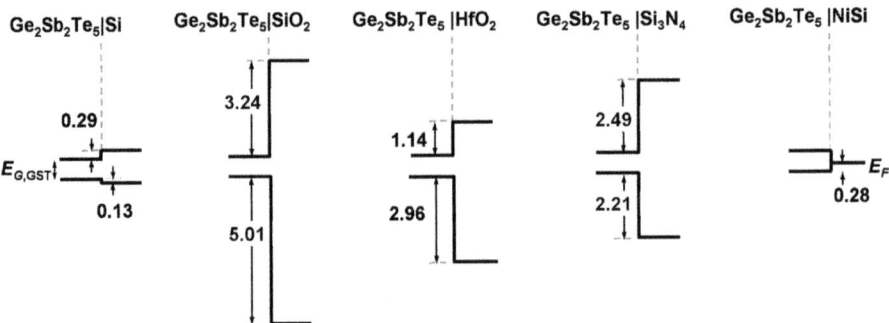

Figure 13.5. Band Alignment of GST with common CMOS materials.

the density will be. PCRAM shows potential toward high scalability. However, the scaling issues of PCRAM are not yet fully understood.

13.3.1 Scalibility of PCRAM

It used to be commonly believed that PCRAM technology is only limited by the lithography process. Hence most of the research in the past has focused on improving lithography technology. Followed by the 180-nm PCRAM fabricated by Intel in 2001, PCRAM was successfully developed at 90-nm process node by Samsung [32]. To keep extending the feature size limitation, various advanced lithography technologies such as electron beam and near-field optical microscopy [33] have been used to fabricate < 50-nm PCRAM cells.

However, with the continuous effect on minimization, it can be foreseen that the physical limitation of phase change materials will become more critical. The scaling limitations of PCRAM can arise from two aspects, which are the feature size limitation through the manufacturing process and the physical limitation of phase change materials. As lithography challenges are common for most of the memory techniques, let us discuss the physical limitation of PCRAM materials in detail.

As PCRAM is developed in the order of the nanoscale now, the interfaces play an important role and strongly cause the deviation of phase change behavior from that of bulk material behavior. In fact, the physical limitation of phase change materials is dependent on nanophase change (NPC). NPC is size dependent, interface dominated, and related to the surrounding materials, as previously reported [34]. In order to systemically study the physical limitation of phase change materials for PCRAM application, it is inevitable that the effect of the surrounding materials be taken into account. From the standard structure of the PCRAM cell shown in Figure 13.3, it can be seen that phase change materials are surrounded by metals and oxides. Considering the surrounding materials, NPC can be classified into three categories: (1) phase change in free state, (2) phase change surrounded by oxides/metals, and (3) reversible phase change surrounded by oxides/metals. In PCRAM application, the physical limitation of phase change materials is determined by the minimum volume of phase change materials that can achieve stable and reversible phase change. This classification can provide useful guidance for scaling research in PCRAM technology.

For PCRAM, the scaling of phase change materials falls into the second and third categories defined above. However, the physical limitation is a 3-dimensional (3D) issue and is difficult to study with current technologies. As the interfaces play a critical role at the nanoscale and the interface conditions are quite similar for both 2D and 3D cases, the 3D issue could be simplified into a 2D issue. Temperature-dependent electrical resistance was measured to study the NPC in phase change material sandwiched by oxide [35]. For films ≥ 20 nm, the resistance decreased sharply at about 150°C. For films with thickness < 20 nm but ≥ 3.5 nm, the sharp decrease in resistance became less obvious. Crystallization temperature Tx increased from about 150°C to about 170°C as the film became thinner. An exponential relationship can be plotted on Tx versus film thickness. However, for films ≤ 3-nm thick, the sharp decline in resistance was not observed at all. The gradual decrease in this case is due to the temperature-dependent ionization in semiconductor material rather than the crystallization process. These results indicate that there is a critical thickness of crystallization at 3 nm. A similar phenomenon has been observed in other works. Based on in-situ X-ray diffraction measurement results, it has been reported that 3.6 nm is the thickness limitation of $Ge_2Sb_2Te_5$ thin films capped by Al_2O_3 [36]. Based on current results, it can be expected that the scaling of PCRAM with $Ge_2Sb_2Te_5$ could be carried down to 2–3 nm without significant issues.

The scaling behavior of phase change nanostructures has also been investigated [37] as a method to estimate the scaling limits of PCRAM. Nanostructures with a 65-nm diameter and a 100-nm pitch have been fabricated from $Ge_{15}Sb_{85}$ and $Ge_2Sb_2Te_5$ phase change materials over large areas using electron-beam lithography. Time-resolved in-situ x-ray diffraction (XRD) was employed to study the structural properties of blanket films and the nanostructures. Blanket films and nanostructures of GST and GeSb were heated in the in-situ XRD set-up at a rate of 1°C/s, and the diffracted peak intensity was recorded with the linear detector over a 2θ range of 24–40°. This angular range contains strong diffraction peaks for both, the $Ge_2Sb_2Te_5$ and GeSb. The measurements show that the nanostructures crystallize at the same temperature as blanket films of the same material. The face-centered cubic-hexagonal phase transition that was observed at 360°C for blanket $Ge_2Sb_2Te_5$ film does not occur in the nanostructures. It was also observed that nanopatterning leads to a reduction in grain size, particularly for the $Ge_2Sb_2Te_5$ nanostructures. Both findings are encouraging for the study of the scaling of phase change materials toward NVM storage devices. The crystallization behavior studied for blanket films can be extrapolated for nanostructures down to 65-nm size, and data obtained on blanket films are useful for research regarding devices. The reduction in grain size is also favorable since smaller grains typically lead to higher resistivity of the materials in the crystalline phase, which in turn leads to a desirably smaller required current for switching the devices.

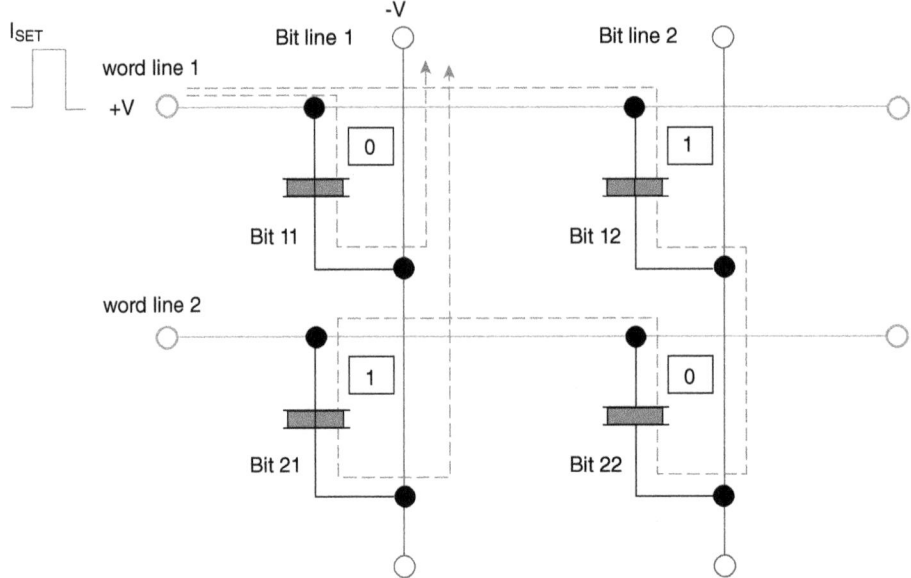

Figure 13.6. Leakage current in PCRAM array without addressing devices.

13.3.2 PCRAM Cell Structure

At the array level, PCRAM memory elements cannot be directly connected as an array due to the leakage path in the memory array as shown in Figure 13.6. Each memory element should be integrated with an addressing device, which can meet the requirements of current, leakage, and voltage of the memory cells. Programming current is a critical parameter for high density PCRAM because it determines the size of the addressing device, which is usually bigger than a PCRAM cell itself and therefore is a significant factor in the density of the PCRAM array. The programming current scales with the contact area between phase change layer and electrode, and reduces with lithography scaling. Besides scaling, an innovative approach including various cell concepts has been proposed to reduce current. The cell structures have been divided into three major catogories: scaling the contact size between the phase change material and the electrodes, scaling the size of the phase change material itself, and other methods to reduce current, such as scaling both the material and the contact [38].

13.3.2.1 Vertical Structure. The standard PCRAM structure is shown in Figure 13.7a. A phase change layer is vertically sandwiched between two electrodes. By lithographic scaling, the contact area between the phase change layer and electrode is reduced. Different vertical geometries have been proposed and are schematically shown in Figure 13.7. During operation, either the phase change layer or the bottom electrode acts as the heat source, depending on the cell structures. For PCRAM with vertical structure, the smallest cell size is normally determined by the lithography.

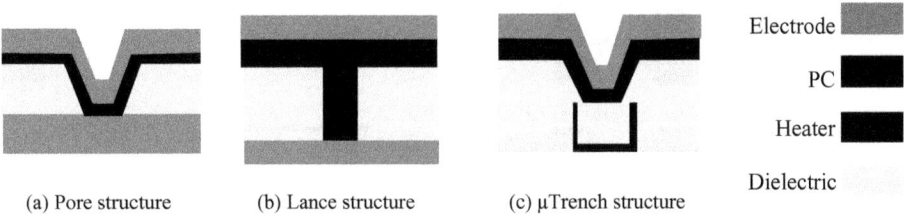

(a) Pore structure　　　　(b) Lance structure　　　　(c) μTrench structure

Electrode

PC

Heater

Dielectric

Figure 13.7. Different vertical device structures for PCRAM.

Electrode

PC

Dielectric

Figure 13.8. Edge contact PCRAM.

Figure 13.7c shows the μTrench approach introduced by Pellizzer et al. [39]. It utilizes the advantage of a thin-film process to reduce the contact size. Using a 180-nm process, a reset current of ~ 600 μA was achieved.

13.3.2.2 Side Edge Structure. One innovative idea to reduce the contact area was side edge structure proposed by Ha et al. and shown in Figure 13.8 [40]. In this case, the contact area is determined by the thickness of the thin electrode film. Scaling by reducing the film thickness is very efficient because smaller dimensions than are possible using lithography can be achieved, and the process can be very well controlled. A side edge contact PCRAM cell with a contact area of 40,000 nm^2 was fabricated and tested. For testing, four key parameters were determined: holding voltage (Vh), threshold voltage (Vth), and reset and set current. The memory cell successfully operated with 30-ns pulses of 0.20 mA for the reset state and 0.13 mA for the set state. The cycling test showed that the resistance ratio between reset and set remained larger than 20 after 10^5 cycles. Assuming the variations of photolithography process and film thickness are 10% and 1%, respectively, small and uniform contact can be expected to be manufactured with side edge contact structure using current technology. However, the writing cycle is very challenging based on the current concept and manufacturing technology.

13.3.2.3 Lateral Structure. Recently PCRAMs with lateral structures were proposed as shown in Figure 13.9 with the most investigated two lateral structures, line-type structure and bridge structure [41, 42]. In lateral structure PCRAM, the phase change material is deposited on the underlying two metal electrodes.

There are many advantages of the line-type PCRAM. First, it is conceptually simple. Second, the requirement for electrode materials is not as high as that for a PCRAM vertical contact type because for the vertical contact type, the electrode

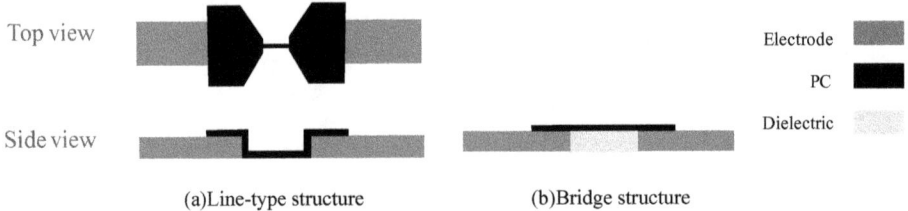

Figure 13.9. Line-type PCRAM.

materials should have appropriate resistivity, with resistivity largely maintained at high temperatures, no reaction with the phase change materials, and good adhesion to the phase change film. Third, lower programming power and current are possible because the phase change materials are surrounded only by dielectric materials, and dielectric materials have much lower thermal conductivity than the electrodes in the vertical type. Lastly the cross-section of line memory can be made very small, leading to further reduction of the programming current.

To investigate the feasibility of the phase change line concept with doped SbTe material, test devices were made of single line cells with line length in the range 80 to 1200 nm and cross-section varying between 152 and 702 nm^2.

A phase change between amorphous and crystalline states with 30 ns pulses for both the set and reset switches was demonstrated. The speed of the memory increases as the dimensions of the cell are scaled down. This feature can be explained by the growth-dominated crystallization mechanism of the doped SbTe materials, in which crystallization takes place by crystal growth from the crystalline edge of the amorphous volume toward its center. From the various crystal growth speeds measured for many doped SbTe materials, it has been estimated that the possible programming time of a line cell ranges from 5 to 100 ns.

So far, nucleation-dominated materials such as GeSbTe have been used to fabricate vertical-type PCRAM. However it was found that GeSbTe is not suitable for line-type PCRAM. Until now no growth-dominated materials have been reported on vertical-type PCRAM, but they are suitable for line-type PCRAM [41].

For the line-type PCRAM with growth-dominated crystallization, the speed of the memory increases as the dimensions of the cell are scaled down. In contrast, the crystallization time of GeSbTe materials is nearly independent of the size of the amorphous volume. reset voltages were found to be a function of line length. The overall trend is that reset voltage decreases with the line length.

It has been demonstrated that reset current can be reduced significantly by scaling down the cross-section of the line. The measured currents agree with the trend obtained from numerical calculations for relatively long lines. Further reduction of programming current is possible by using better thermal insulation material as the dielectric material surrounding the line, or by further shrinking the cross-section of the line, or both.

One million endurance cycles were achieved for line-type PCRAM. However, compared to 10^{12} cycles for vertical-type PCRAM, the overwriting capability is one of the most important challenges for line-type PCRAM.

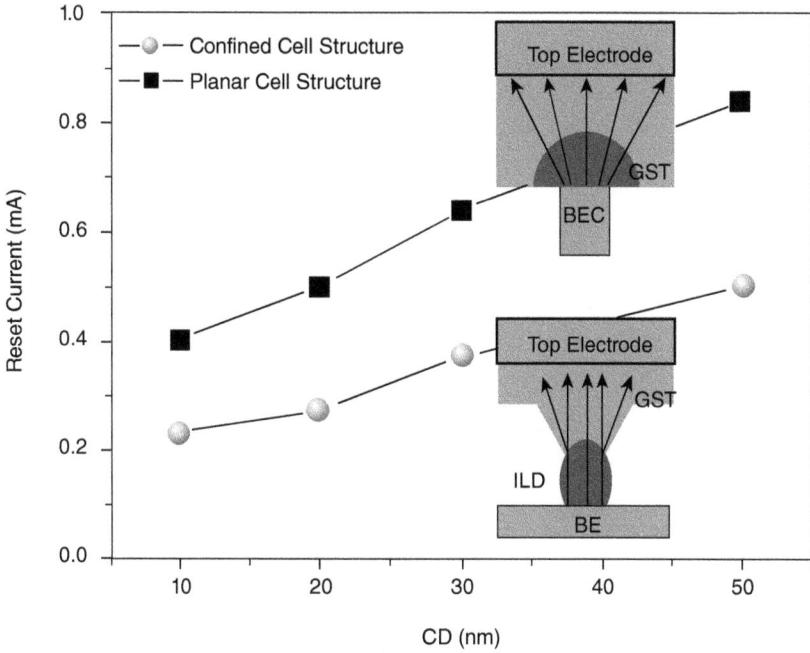

Figure 13.10. Comparison of reset current between confined and planar cell structure along with contact diameter.

13.3.2.4 Confined Structure. Another approach to reduce reset current is a confined structure for PCRAM, as shown in Figure 13.10. Lee et al. [42] first presented a PCRAM with confinement of chemically vapor-deposited GeSbTe (CVD GST) within a high aspect ratio contact of 50 nm for sub-50 nm generation PCRAMs. Thermally stable CVD $Ge_2Sb_2Te_5$ having hexagonal phase was uniformly filled within a contact having an aspect ratio of 3. By adopting confined GST, they were able to reduce the reset current below ~260 µA, and thermally stable CVD $Ge_2Sb_2Te_5$ compound having hexagonal phase was uniformly filled in a contact while maintaining constant composition along a 150-nm depth, and endurance was maintained up to 10^8 cycles without failure. In addition, no apparent drop of resistance was observed after annealing at 140°C for 48 hours. These results indicate that the confined cell structure of 50-nm contact is applicable to PCRAM devices below a 50-nm design rule owing to small GST size based on small contact and direct top-electrode contact, reduced reset current, minimized etch damage, and low thermal disturbance effect.

13.3.2.5 PCRAM with Superlattice-like Structure (SLL). The concept of SLL has also been proposed to improve PCRAM performance [43]. The basic idea is to alternatively deposit two phase change materials, one with a high crystallization speed and the other with a relatively low crystallization speed but a high stability, to form the SLL structure. It was reported that a PCRAM with such a structure can operate

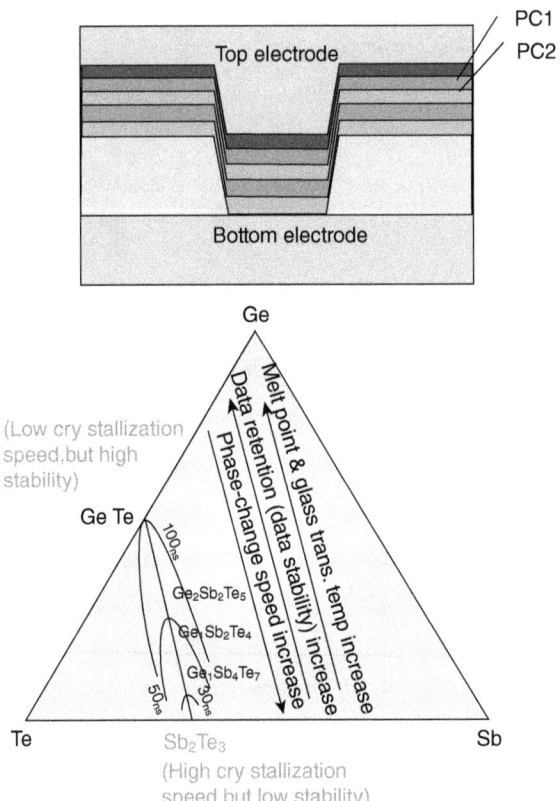

Figure 13.11. SLL PCRAM cell structure and a ternary alloy phase diagram (Ge, Sb, and Te).

at a high speed due to the presence of first material while maintaining good stability due to the second material. Figure 13.11 shows a SLL PCRAM cell structure and a ternary alloy phase diagram (Ge, Sb, and Te) with the change tendencies of the crystallization speed, the melting temperature, T_m, and the resistance difference between the amorphous and crystalline states of GeTe and Sb_2Te_3. It should be noted that GeTe and Sb_2Te_3 are not suitable for application in PCRAM individually.

Besides reducing the programming current for PCRAM, increasing its speed is also desired. The speed is highly dependent on the reversible phase change speed. It was found that SLL structure could not only reduce the programming current, but increase the switching speed of PCRAM as well. SLL PCRAM was reported to work functionally at a much shorter pulse width for both set and reset than the device with a single $Ge_2Sb_2Te_5$ layer. SLL PCRAM cells with sizes from 1 μm down to 90 nm were fabricated by a system incorporating a near-field scanner optical microscope with a femtosecond laser. It was found that the reset current is about 40% smaller than that reported in IEDM 2003 [21].

It was also shown that these differences are related to the film thickness of SLL sub-layers. A larger difference will be induced from thinner sublayers. The possible main reason for the reduced reset and set currents is related to the reduction of the thermal conductivity of SLL in comparison to that of bulk material.

It was shown by transmission electron microscopy (TEM) that the SLL structure exhibited a good interfacial quality even in the monolayer range 15 Å after deposition. Although the interface becomes not sharp after overwriting 100,000 times, the multilayer structure was still retained [43].

There are several possible reasons for the good overwrite cycle life for SLL structure. First, the active area is localized in a very small area of <1 μm^2, which is tightly surrounded and limited by the solid materials. The diffusion will be mostly realized by atomic exchange. The active area provides a closed environment, which is favorable for diffusion and interchange. Secondly, the electrical pulse applied on PCRAM is only several tenths of a nanosecond. Within this period, the phase change material will be heated up. The duration for the material above its melting point is only a few nanoseconds. This will result in a shorter time for molecular exchange and diffusion. Hence working at short pulse width is facilitated for prolonging the overwriting cycle life of the SLL structure.

13.3.3 Correlation between Phase Change Size and Speed

Fast phase change is very important for many applications, such as memory, switch, logic device, and sensor [34]. Pursuing methods to increase phase change speed has not only been of academic but also technological interest as it will enhance the speed of writing data in the PCRAM device. However, the phase change speed is mainly dominated and fundamentally limited by the intrinsic nature of the materials. The choice of phase change materials in the natural world is limited. The phase change materials that can meet the application requirement are even fewer [44]. Recently the contribution of the size effects of nanostructured phase change materials to the phase transition speed was studied experimentally [45]. When the material size shrinks, the material surface or interfaces plays an increasingly important role and may change the material properties. Figure 13.12 shows the switching speed as a function of cell size varying from 500 nm to 19 nm. Reduction of the material dimensions might be able to achieve ultrafast phase transition speed, which may lead to important applications of PCRAM.

13.3.4 Multilevel PCRAM

Besides downscaling of the cell size, multilevel recording is an efficient approach to further increase the density of memory. PCRAM has an advantage in multilevel recording because the resitance difference between the set and reset states is very high (as high as 3 orders of magnitude). A 256-Mb multilevel cell test chip in a 90-nm PCRAM was developed to explore a 2 bit/cell approach through on-chip test modes [46]. A multilevel programming algorithm has been developed based on a program-and-verify technique with the aim of creating stable intermediate regions of the cell. Each programming pulse is current-controlled, thus speeding up the Joule effect directly to the point where its efficiency is at maximum. The cell is first programmed to its low-resistance state by means of a proper set pulse. In particular, to avoid any spread due

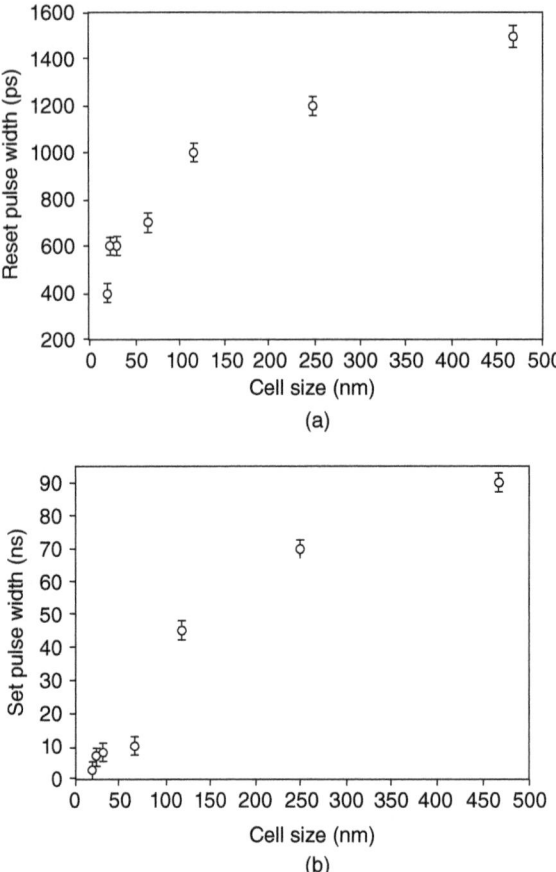

Figure 13.12. Switching speed as a function of cell size varying from 500 nm to 19 nm for (a) reset, (b) set. The pulse amplitudes are 0.8 V for set, and 4.5 V for reset.

to the previous state, a long set sweep initializes the cell to its minimum set state. This was followed by a single reset pulse to put the cell in its maximum resistance state. Then a subsequent staircase up (SCU) pulse algorithm was used to make the cell gradually more conductive as shown in Figure 13.13.

Multilevel cell technology is challenged with fitting more cell states (4 in the case of 2 bit/cell) along with distribution spreads due to process, design, and environmental variations, within a limited window.

13.3.5 PCRAM Chip

The key to make PCRAM a successful technology is to reduce its cost by increasing density. The cost of PCRAM and its capacity is determined not only by the cell size

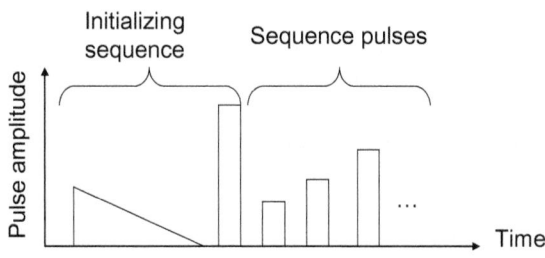

Figure 13.13. Program algorithm pulsing technique.

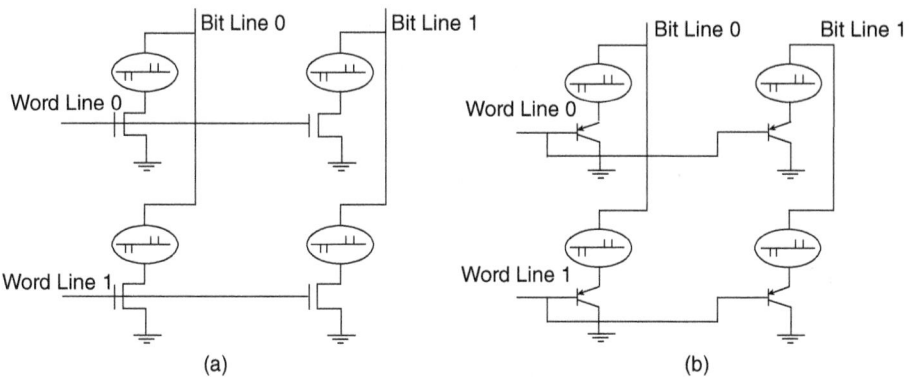

Figure 13.14. The phase change memory array is arranged in bit lines and word lines, with integration with a selecting device of (a) a CMOS transistor, or (b) a diode.

but also by the complexity of manufacturing process. PCRAM with smaller cell size and fewer processing steps will be very cost competitive.

A PCRAM array consists of a variable resistor in series with an access device. The purpose of the access device is to isolate a given memory element during programming and reading of the cell. Normally, a metal-oxide semiconductor field-effect transistor (MOSFET) or a bipolar junction transistor (BJT) is used as an addressing device to prevent leakage. When this addressing device is turned off by adding proper voltage, there is no significant current allowed to pass through the addressing device and the memory cell. Therefore, the possibility of integrating PCRAM technology with CMOS technology is an important factor to consider when evaluating its commercialization potential. Transistors are more popular in modern integrated circuit design, but diode/BJT has the advantage of providing high current. Figure 13.14 shows the schematic of a PCRAM array with the PCRAM cell integrated with MOSFET and BJT respectively. Typically BJT and diodes provide higher current density and thus smaller PCRAM size. MOSFET provides better isolation between cells.

A 90-nm, 1.8-V, 512-Mb diode-switch PCRAM has been demonstrated [32] using several key technologies such as a novel vertical diode array scheme, a self-aligned bottom electrode contact (SABEC) process scheme, and a well-optimized GST module process. The replacement of trigate MOSFET with a vertical diode provides large current. The SABEC scheme was developed for high manufacturability, which has several advantages: free-misalign margin, a reduction of critical mask layer, and a favorable correlation effect between BEC and diode. In addition, patterning the top-electrode (TE) and the GST under optimal etching conditions was proved to improve the write endurance. The vertical diode switch using a selective epitaxy growth technology has achieved a minimum cell size of 5.8 F^2 and disturbance-free core operation.

PCRAM has demonstrated good memory characteristics, such as nonvolatility, low current, good endurance, and high scalability, which shows its potential as the most promising next generation NVM. The potential applications in the near future for PCRAM could be to replace stand-alone and embedded NOR flash memory. Compared to NOR flash memory, PCRAM has a similar memory-cell size but with improved characteristics, such as faster speed and a longer lifetime. However, it would be a challenge for PCRAM to compete with NAND flash memory because NAND flash memory has achieved the smallest memory cell size and demonstrated multiple bits per cell or multiple levels per cell (MLC) capabilities. MLC and 3D stacking are the directions to further increase the density of PCRAM [46, 47].

REFERENCES

1. HDD Roadmap (2008).
2. INSIC Optical Data Storage Roadmap (2006).
3. International Technology Roadmap for Semiconductor (2009) edition.
4. N. Yamada, E. Ohno, K. Nishiuchi, and N. Akahira, J. Appl. Phys. **69**, 2849 (1991).
5. W. Brown and J. Brewer, *Nonvolatile Semiconductor Memory Technology: A Comprehensive Guide to Understand and Using NVSM Devices*. New York: IEEE press, 1998.
6. C. Y. Lu, K. Y. Hsieh, and R. Liu, Future challenges of flash memory technologies. Microelectronic Eng. **86**, 283 (2009).
7. J. S. Moodera, L. R. Kinder, T. M. Wong, and R. Meservey, Phys. Rev. Lett. **74**, 3273 (1995).
8. A. Fazio, MRS Bull. **29**, 814 (2004).
9. S. S. P. Parkin, N. More, and K. P. Roche, Phys. Rev. Lett. **64**, 2304 (1990).
10. J. Campbell Scott, Science **304**, 62 (2004).
11. J. Taylor, M. Brandbyge, and K. Stokbro, Phys. Rev. B **68**, 121101 (2003).
12. R. F. Service, Science **302**, 556 (2003).
13. Z. Liu, A. A. Yasseri, J. S. Lindsey, and D. E. Bocian, Science **302**, 1543 (2003).
14. T. A. Fulton and G. J. Dolan, Phys. Rev. Lett. **59**, 109 (1987).
15. A. Jujiwara and Y. Takahashi, Nature **410**, 560 (2001).
16. M. J. Yoo, T. A. Fulton, H. F. Hess, R. L. Willett, L. N. Dunkleberger, R. J. Chichester, L. N. Pfeiffer, and K. W. West, Science **276**, 579 (1997).
17. Y. Arimoto and H. Ishiwara, MRS Bull. **29**, 823 (2004).
18. S. R. Ovshinsky, Phys. Rev. Lett. **21**, 1450 (1968).
19. M. H. Cohen, H. Fritzsche, and S. R. Ovshinsky, Phys. Rev. Lett. **22**, 1065 (1969).

20. Y. S. Chen, H. Y. Lee, P. S. Chen, P. Y. Gu, C. W. Chen, W. P. Lin, W. H. Liu, Y. Y. Hsu, S. S. Sheu, P. C. Chiang, W. S. Chen, F. T. Chen, C. H. Lien, and M.-J. Tsai, Highly scalable hafnium oxide memory with improvements of resistive distribution and read disturb immunity. *IEDM Digest* (2009).

21. R. Bez, Chalcogenide PCM: A memory technology for next decade. *IEDM Digest* (2009).

22. S. R. Ovshinsky, The physical base of intelligence- model studies. *Detroit Physiological Society Technical Digest*, p. 17 (1959).

23. A. L. Greer, E\PCOS (2005), online publication.

24. D. Adler, H. K. Henisch, and N. F. Mott, Rev. Mod. Phys. **50**, 209 (1978).

25. D. Adler et al., J. Appl. Phys. **51**, 3289 (1980).

26. V. G. Karpova, Y. A. Kryukov, S. D. Savransky, and I. V. Karpovlya, Nucleation switching in phase change memory. Appl. Phys. Lett. **90**, 123504 (2007).

27. G. F. Zhou, H. J. Borg, J. C. N. Rijpers, and M. Lankhorst, *Tech Digest of ODS'*, p. 74 (2000), (Whistler, Canada).

28. M. Luo and M. Wuttig, Adv. Mater. **16**, 439 (2004).

29. K. Kohary, V. Burlakov, D. Nguyen-Manh, and D. Pettifor, E\PCOS (2005), online publication.

30. D. Lencer, M. Salinga, B. Grabowski, T. Hickel, J. Neugebauer, and M. Wuttig, A map for phase-change materials. Nat. Mater. **7**, 972 (2008).

31. W. W. Fang, J. S. Pan, R. Zhao, L. P. Shi, T. C. Chong, G. Samudra, and Y. C. Yeo, Band alignment between amorphous $Ge_2Sb_2Te_5$ and prevalent complementary-metal-oxide-semiconductor materials. Appl. Phys. Lett. **92**, 032107 (2008).

32. J. H. Oh, J. H. Park, Y. S. Lim, H. S. Lim, Y. T. Oh, J. S. Kim, J. M. Shin, J. H. Park, Y. J. Song, K. C. Ryoo, D. W. Lim, S. S. Park, J. I. Kim, J. H. Kim, J. Yu, F. Yeung, C. W. Jeong, J. H. Kong, D. H. Kang, G. H. Koh, G. T. Jeong, H. S. Jeong, and K. Kim, Full integration of highly manufacturable 512 Mb PRAM based on 90 nm technology. *IEDM Digest*, pp. 49–53 (2006).

33. W. J. Wang, R. Zhao, L. P. Shi, X. S. Miao, P. K. Tan, M. H. Hong, T. C. Chong, Y. H. Wu, and Y. Lin, Nonvolatile phase change memory nano-cell fabrication by femto-second laser writing assisted with near-field optical microscopy. J. Appl. Phys. **98**, 124313–124318 (2005).

34. L. P. Shi and T. C. Chong, J. Nanosci. Nanotechnol. **7**, 65–93 (2007).

35. X. Q. Wei, L. P. Shi, T. C. Chong, R. Zhao, and H. K. Lee, Thickness dependent nano-crystallization in Ge2Sb2Te5 films and its effect on devices. Jpn. J. Appl. Phys. **46**(4B), 2211 (2007).

36. D. J. Millironi, S. Raoux, R. Shelby, and J. Jordan-Sweet, Solution-phase deposition and nanopatterning of GeSbSe phase change materials. Nat. Mater. **6**, 352–356 (2007).

37. S. Raoux, C. T. Rettner, J. L. Jordan-Sweet, V. R. Deline, J. B. Philipp, and H. L. Lung, Scaling properties of phase change nanostructures and thin films. *European Phase Change and Ovonic Science Symposium* (2006).

38. Y. C. Chen, Chapter 15 of *Phase Change Materials Science and Applications*. Springer, 2008.

39. F. Pellizzer, A. Pirovano, F. Ottogalli, M. Magistretti, M. Scaravaggi, P. Zuliani, M. Tosi, R. Zonca, A. Mod-elli, E. Varesi, T. Lowrey, A. Lacaita, G. Casagrande, P. Cappelletti, and R. Bez, Novel μ-trench phase-change memory cell for embedded and stand-alone nonvolatile memory applications. *Symposium on VLSI Tech. Dig.*, pp. 18–19 (2004).

40. Y. H. Ha, J. H. Yi, H. Horii, J. H. Park, S. H. Joo, S. O. Park, U.-I. Chung, and J. T. Moon, *Symposim on VLSI Technology Digest of Technical Paper*, p. 175 (2003).

41. M. H. R. Lankhorst, B. W. S. M. M. Ketelaar, and R. A. M. Wolters, Low-cost and nanoscale non-volatile memory concept for future silicon chips. Nat. Mater. **4**, 347–352 (2005).

42. J. I. Lee, H. Park, S. L. Cho, Y. L. Park, B. J. Bae, J. H. Park, J. S. Park, H. G. An, J. S. Bae, D. H. Ahn, Y. T. Kim, H. Horii, S. A. Song, J. C. Shin, S. O. Park, H. S. Kim, U.-I. Chung, J. T. Moon, and B. I. Ryu, Highly scalable phase change memory with CVD GeSbTe for Sub 50 nm generation. *Symp. on VLSI Tech. Digest of Technical Papers*, p.102 (2007).

43. T. C. Chong, L. P. Shi, R. Zhao, P. K. Tan, J. M. Li, H. K. Lee, and X. S. Miao, Phase change random access memory cell with superlattice-like structure. Appl. Phys. Lett. **88**, 122114 (2006).

44. N. Akahira, N. Miyagawa, K. Nishiuchi, Y. Sakaue, and E. Ohno, SPIE **2524**, 294 (1995).

45. W. J. Wang, L. P. Shi, R. Zhao, K. G. Lim, H. K. Lee, T. C. Chong, and Y. H. Wu, Fast phase transitions induced by picosecond electrical pulses on phase change memory cells. Appl. Phys. Lett. **93**, 043121 (2008).

46. F. Bedeschi, R. Fackenthal, C. Resta, E. M. Donzel, M. Jagasivamani, E. Buda, F. Pellizzer, D. Chow, A. Cabrini, G. M. A. Calvi, R. Faravellil, A. Fantini, G. Torelli, D. Mills, R. Gastaldil, and G. Casagrandel, A multi-level-cell bipolar-selected phase-change memory. *IEEE International Solid-State Circuit Conference*, pp. 428–429 (2008).

47. D. C. Kau, S. Tang, I. V. Karpov, R. Dodge, B. Klehn, J. A. Kalb, J. Strand, A. Diaz, N. Leung, J. Wu, S. Lee, T. Langtry, K. W. Chang, C. Papagianni, J. Lee, J. Hirst, S. Erra, E. Flores, N. Righos, H. Castro, and G. Spadini, A stackable cross point phase change memory. *IEDM Digest* (2009).

14

NONVOLATILE SOLID-STATE MAGNETIC MEMORY

Randall Law Yaozhang and Sunny Y. H. Lua

*Agency for Science, Technology and Research (A*STAR),
Data Storage Institute, Singapore*

14.1 NONVOLATILE SOLID STATE MAGNETIC MEMORY

The increasing popularity and pervasiveness of consumer electronics with immense capabilities in computation, networking, and communications has fueled our growing appetite for high-speed, high–density, and low-power memory devices. To meet this demand, new nonvolatile storage materials and device structures are needed to overcome the limitations of existing memory technologies such as dynamic random access memory (DRAM), static random access memory (SRAM), and flash memory. The appeal of nonvolatile solid-state memory is in its mechanical robustness, access speed, random-access capability and lower power consumption compared to competing technologies. To overcome the limitations of conventional charge-based semiconductor electronics and memories, spin-based electronics (also spintronics, or magnetoelectronics) promises new device functionality, better performance, and storage density at lower power by exploiting the spin degree of freedom of electrons [1].

The giant magnetoresistive (GMR) sensor used in hard disk drive (HDD) read heads (described in Chapter 6) can be said to be the first spintronic device as well as one of the real applications of nanotechnology. The GMR effect can also be applied in memory elements for magnetoresistive random access memory (MRAM), which

Developments in Data Storage: Materials Perspective, First Edition.
Edited by S. N. Piramanayagam, Tow C. Chong.
© 2012 Institute of Electrical and Electronics Engineers. Published 2012 by John Wiley & Sons, Inc.

TABLE 14.1. Comparison of MRAM Features against Other Memory Technologies Based on ITRS 2007 [160, 161]

	SRAM	DRAM	NAND-FLASH	FRAM	ST-MRAM	PCRAM
Read (2007)	0.3 ns	1–10 ns	50 ns	45 ns	<20 ns	60 ns
Read (2022)	70 ps	0.2–10 ns	10 ns	<20 ns	<0.5 ns	<60 ns
Write (2007)	0.3 ns	0.7 ns	1 ms	10 ns	<20 ns	50 ns
Write (2022)	70 ps	0.2 ns	1 ms	1 ns	<0.5 ns	<50 ns
Retention time	Requires power	64 ms	>10 years	>10 years	>10 years	>10 years
Write endurance	$>3 \times 10^{16}$	$>3 \times 10^{16}$	10^5–10^6	10^{14}	$>3 \times 10^{16}$	10^8
Cell size	140 F^2	6–12 F^2	5 F^2	22 F^2	6–8 F^2	4.8 F^2
Read voltage (V)	1.1	2	15	0.9–3.3	<1.5	3
Write voltage (V)	1.1	2.5	2	0.9–3.3	<1.5	3
Comments			Multilevel cell	Destructive readout	Multilevel cell possible	Multilevel cell possible

promises nonvolatility, practically infinite write endurance, and short read and write times, making it a potentially superior technological possibility. Table 14.1 compares the features of MRAM against several other competing memory technologies, all of which have their own unique advantages and limitations, with MRAM being the most promising. However, controlling the resistance uniformity, switching behavior of the magnetic bits, reduction of the writing current, and integration of magnetic tunnel junctions (MTJs) with complementary metal-oxide superconductors (CMOSs) remain some of the key challenges to successful implementation and commercialization of MRAM [2–4].

In a recent review [5], J.-G. Zhu provided a broad coverage of the history and development of MRAM (such as asteroid- and toggle-mode switching), and discussed several advanced structures and materials that are under development. In this chapter, we begin by briefly describing the basic attributes, architecture, requirements, and challenges of MRAM technology. In the second and third sections, we will focus on spin-torque (ST) transfer switching in ST-MRAM and the use of magnetic layers with perpendicular magnetic anisotropy (PMA) as the benefits of PMA combined with ST-MRAM may hold the key to a practical and scalable realization of MRAM. Finally, we shall briefly describe the potential and challenges of new device schemes such as domain-wall memory and the spin-torque oscillator (STO) for future applications.

14.1.1 Fundamentals of Magnetoresistive Random Access Memory (MRAM)

A memory device requires two states to represent the bits "1" and "0." In MRAM, these are achieved by the use of "magnetoresistance." As discussed in Chapter 6, when the magnetizations of two ferromagnetic layers are aligned in an antiparallel direction, a magnetoresistive device will show a higher resistance to an electric current. Likewise, for a parallel alignment, a lower resistance will be observed. Comparing the voltages (high and low), bits 0 and 1 can be realized. By sending a current through the magnetoresistive (MR) device or by applying magnetic fields, the magnetization direction of one ferromagnetic layer can be switched, and hence two different magnetization alignments can be obtained. Therefore, a MR device is an integral part of MRAM. In addition, in a memory device, the memory has to be addressed using write and read lines, and the cross-talk between the memory elements has to be negligible. Therefore, MRAM also uses transistors to meet the electrical current and addressing requirements. There are various possible ways of writing information in MRAM devices. In one scheme, a magnetic field is produced by electrical current in electrodes running in orthogonal directions, and this method is called field-assisted writing. In another scheme, called spin-torque transfer (STT), an electrical current is sent through the MRAM devices, and the torque exhibited by the magnetization from the spin-polarized electrons is used for writing information. The following section will describe MRAM architecture and the requirements that the MR device must satisfy.

14.1.1.1 MRAM Attributes and Basic Array Architecture. Figure 14.1 shows a simple field-assisted MRAM array using cross-point architecture (XPT). The

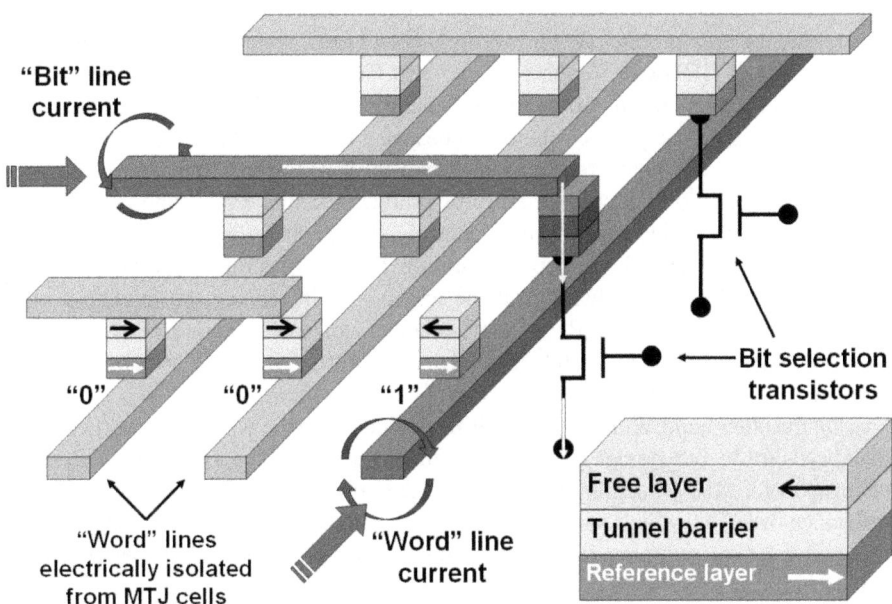

Figure 14.1. Schematic diagram of a one-transistor, one-MTJ (1T1MTJ) cell array. Each pair of bit- and word-line currents generates a combined magnetic field to switch the free layer of a single cell. In ST-MRAM, the word line is not needed.

current passing through the bit- and word-lines generates a combined ampere field to select and switch a single MTJ free layer at the wire intersection. It has to be mentioned that the MRAM element and writing strategy is designed in such a way that only the superposition of both magnetic fields from the word and bit lines at their intersection allows the MRAM element to be switched. Since this configuration provides addressability, the XPT designs attempted to avoid the selection transistor to increase the MRAM cell density by contacting the cells to the word lines [6], but as each MR device (in particular, the MTJs) introduces a resistance through which write current may be lost, it resulted in very poor read performance. In the one-transistor, one-MTJ (1T-1MTJ) architecture [7], each bit is selected by a selection transistor, and the read current flows only through the bit line and selection transistor although the write line is still required for ampere-field XPT writing. However, in the other writing scheme that uses ST transfer (to be described in the next section), the word lines are not necessary, and both read and write currents are provided by each selection transistor. Irrespective of the writing method used, the MR element in the MRAM must provide a larger MR, to obtain signals at two states that are distinguishable. Therefore, the design of MR elements with high output signals play a major role in MRAM.

In Chapter 6, an introduction to HDD read sensors based on various magnetoresistive device designs was provided. Tunneling magnetoresistance (TMR)-based sensors offer higher output signal and hence are preferred over current-in-plane (CIP)-GMR sensors in HDD read heads. However, current-perpendicular-to-plane (CPP)-GMR heads are preferred over TMR sensors for higher storage densities [8–11] due to the low resistance area product (RA) of around $0.1\ \Omega\cdot\mu m^2$, which will allow higher data transfer rates in HDDs. However, even the best CPP-GMR spin valves based on conventional ferromagnetic materials to date exhibit low ΔRA (change in resistance-area product) and giant magnetoresistance values of around $5\ m\Omega\cdot\mu m^2$ and 5% or lower respectively [12–16], hence requiring high current densities to achieve a usable signal voltage. Not only do high current densities produce thermal effects and reduce sensor lifetime, but spin-torque transfer introduced by spin-polarized current for its part will increase sensor noise and magnetic instability. The use of a dual spin-valve structure can reduce STT-induced noise but at the expense of increasing the thickness of the stack and hence the read gap. Recent success in using ferromagnetic Heusler alloys has increased CPP-GMR in all-metal spin valves to about 28.8% [17], which show some promise for future HDD read heads.

On the other hand, although CPP-GMR devices have the potential to succeed TMR read heads for higher storage densities in future, MTJs continue to outshine CPP-GMR spin valves for MRAM applications. This is due to the high magnetoresistance and high resistance of MTJs, which makes the MTJ device more compatible with CMOS technology for bit selection, reading, and writing. For example, it has been estimated that a TMR ratio of above 40% at 300 mV bias is required for a sensing time (t_{sense}) below 10 ns for a 90-nm fabrication process. At the same time, a resistance-area (RA) product below $80\ \Omega\text{-}\mu m^2$ for a CMOS write voltage of 1.2 V is required to provide a sufficient write current. These requirements are easily met by MTJs. Therefore, it is commonly accepted that a commercially viable MRAM cell will be based on TMR-based technology rather than CPP-GMR devices. The subsequent section provides a detailed view of MTJs.

14.1.1.2 Tunneling Magnetoresistance in Magnetic Tunnel Junctions.
Electrons are known to pass from one conducting electrode to another through a thin insulator layer (a few atomic layers) although the energy barrier is greater than the electron energy via a quantum mechanical transport phenomenon called "electron tunneling." With the application of a constant voltage bias across the thin insulator, a constant electron tunneling current can be set up through the tunneling barrier. When the metallic nonmagnetic spacer layer of a GMR spin valve is replaced by a thin insulator, the mechanism for MR changes from spin-dependent scattering to one of spin-dependent tunneling (or spin-selective band matching), and is called tunneling magnetoresistance (TMR). Besides being dependent on the available electronic states in the ferromagnetic electrodes similar to GMR, the tunneling process also depends on the available channels in the insulator.

TMR was theoretically described as early as 1973 by Tedrow and Meservey [18] and in 1975 by Jullière [19] in ferromagnetic-insulator-superconductor (FIS) and FIF ferromagnetic-insulator-ferromagnetic (FIF) tunneling structures, with the FIF structure becoming the most basic form of a MTJ. As tunneling current varies exponentially with barrier thickness, so does the resistance and TMR of MTJs. During the 1970s, there were experimental difficulties in obtaining high-quality pinhole-free tunneling barriers with consistent thickness. Moreover, the room temperature (RT) TMR was not sufficiently high enough to attract any attention; therefore, no one realized its technical importance. It was only in 1995, when reports of RT TMRs of 12% in $CoFe/Al_2O_3/Co$ [20, 21] and 18% in $Fe/Al_2O_3/Fe$ [22] generated a huge interest that further research into MTJs was triggered.

After over a decade of intense investigation and optimization, an amorphous AlO_x barrier from oxidized Al metal was found to achieve high TMR most easily, achieving values at RT of about 50%. This was in agreement with the prediction of Jullière's model using spin polarization data obtained experimentally for the common ferromagnetic electrodes of Co-Fe and Ni-Fe alloys [23–27]. Although this seemed to suggest that the limits of $Co-Fe/AlO_x$ MTJ had been reached, a TMR of 71.5% was obtained using a face-centered cubic (fcc) Ag bottom electrode and annealing of the sample before deposition, and oxidation of the tunnel barrier [28]. Other techniques used to improve TMR involve the use of amorphous ferromagnetic materials to reduce the interface roughness at the tunnel barrier interface to minimize pinholes [29, 30], or the use of high spin polarization materials such as the half-metallic Heusler alloy Co_2MnSi [31, 32].

A major development in recent years is the realization of "giant" TMR (GTMR) values in excess of 200% (up to 604% for CoFeB electrodes) at RT with single crystalline body-centered cubic (bcc) (001) MgO tunnel barriers and ferromagnetic electrodes [33–37], confirming predictions of ultrahigh TMR above 1000% in epitaxial Fe/MgO/Fe structures using first principles theories [38–40]. This GTMR is attributed to the dominant tunneling of only Bloch states with Δ_1 symmetry through the crystalline MgO (001) barrier because the barrier acts as a symmetry filter [41]. As the Δ_1 Bloch states in Fe- and Co-based bcc ferromagnetic metals and alloys such as Fe, CoFe, CoFeB, and some Heusler alloys are fully spin polarized in the (001) direction at their Fermi energy level, the GTMR effect is expected when a crystalline MgO (001) barrier is combined with these materials. In contrast, various Bloch states with different symmetries can tunnel incoherently through an amorphous AlO barrier in conventional MTJs, which reduces the tunneling spin polarization and hence the TMR. With further optimization of stack materials and careful control of the crystallization process, GTMRs of 138% and 50% have been achieved for RA values as low as 2.4 $\Omega \cdot \mu m^2$ and 0.4 $\Omega \cdot \mu m^2$ respectively [42, 43]. This achievement allows the production of extremely sensitive and high data rate HDD read sensors for storage densities above 500 Gb/in.^{2} (up to 1 Tb/in.^{2} is expected), exceeding the expectations of MTJs based on AlO and TiO, thus delaying (or even eliminating) the need for the difficult switch to CPP-GMR sensors mentioned in the previous section. Finally, the extremely high GTMR and spin polarization in MgO-based MTJs makes it perfectly suited for MRAM as it enables high-speed readout due to its very high output signal and relatively low current densities required for spin transfer switching.

14.1.1.3 Stability and Scalability of MRAM. Although the potential performance characteristics of MRAM such as speed and durability exceed that of several competing technologies, especially that of flash memory, the density and scalability of MRAM still need significant improvement before it becomes truly competitive above gigabit densities. Over the last decade, there has been significant industrial effort in MRAM development based on the basic ampere-field writing scheme [44–52], as well as ST-MRAM which uses STT writing [53, 54]. In June 2006, Freescale started shipping 4-Mbit MRAM chips (the 16-bit I/O MR2A16A), the first MRAM product for the market [55].

Despite these efforts and huge investments, there are several reasons why MRAM is still currently lagging behind semiconductor memory in terms of storage density. First, besides the difficulty of achieving sufficient signal levels in conventional MTJs based on AlO barriers before the advent of crystalline MgO GTMR MTJs, two major and related challenges of MRAM are in the scalability of its storage elements and writing current. Traditionally, magnetic materials with in-plane anisotropy have been used in GMR sensors and MRAM because of their low coercivity (ease of switching and higher sensitivity) and the intrinsic shape anisotropy of magnetic thin films that favor in-plane magnetization. However, in-plane ferromagnetic structures form magnetic domains for energy minimization, and the type of magnetic domains formed is strongly dependent on shape and dimension. Typical domain structures formed in patterned magnetic films are the multidomain (MD), vortex (V), and single-domain (SD) states, as shown in Figure 14.2. MD states are formed in large patterned ferromagnetic structures of various shapes as the magnetostatic energy of the structure dominates. Below a certain critical size, exchange energy dominates and results in the formation of a SD state. At intermediate dimensions between the MD and SD states, a vortex (V) state develops as a result of the approximate balance developed between the magnetostatic and exchange energies. A V state has a curling in-plane magnetization and an out-of-plane magnetization lying at the center of the vortex, as illustrated in Figure

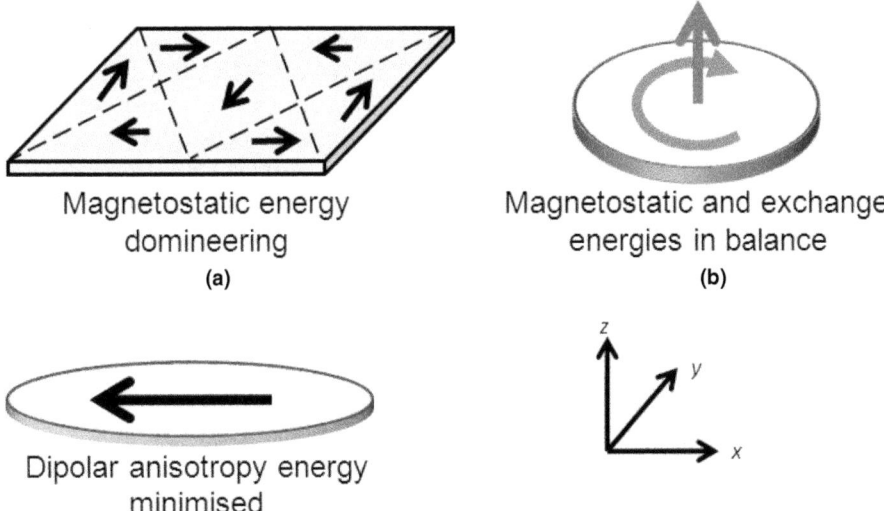

In-plane magnetic anisotropy material
(c)

Figure 14.2. Schematic diagram of (a) multidomain and (b) vortex states formed in rectangular and disk structures, respectively; (c) a single domain state is induced by shape anisotropy through increasing the aspect ratio of a disk into an ellipse. The arrows represent the magnetization distribution, and domain walls are represented by dotted lines.

14.2b. Of the above domain states, a SD state is the most preferred in MRAM applications for its controllable and repeatable magnetization behavior. By artificially elongating the disk shape along one axis (increasing its aspect ratio) into an ellipse, the dipolar anisotropy energy is minimized along the elongated axis. Therefore, due to the tendency of patterned in-plane magnetic elements to form multidomain and vortex states in submicron structures [56], an aspect ratio of two or above is usually used to maintain the magnetic layers in a single domain configuration, thereby sacrificing density. Furthermore, the strong sensitivity of the MTJ switching field distribution to defects, bit size, shape, aspect ratio, and bit-to-bit magnetic interactions makes it a challenge to minimize the spread of switching characteristics as cell dimensions shrink [56–60].

Another challenge to MRAM scalability is that as MTJ cell dimensions shrink, the thermal stability factor of the magnetic elements is reduced, resulting in the need to increase the anisotropy of the magnetic layers. This increases the required switching field of the MRAM elements, and along with smaller current lines, the writing current for field-switched MRAM increases exponentially as dimensions decrease. In a review by Ikeda et al. [61], the authors discussed the writing currents required for MRAM based on magnetic field and spin-transfer writing against the ITRS technology nodes, assuming a cell aspect ratio of 2. They showed that magnetic-field writing would clearly not be scalable toward smaller dimensions as the write current required to generate the same magnetic field magnitude increases, not decreases, with cell dimensions.

On the other hand, the reduction in write currents for ST-MRAM scales faster than CMOS technology as the current density through the device layers scales with cross-sectional area, in contrast with the CMOS gate width, which defines the current available for writing. However, for a feature size of 100 nm (100-nm transistor-gate width and MRAM cell size), spin-torque switching (STS) is possible only for devices with critical current densities below 5×10^5 A/cm^2. Therefore, one of the key challenges for MRAM research is to reduce the critical current densities below this "magic" level of 5×10^5 A/cm^2. On the other hand, one should note that for smaller feature sizes, STS becomes increasingly efficient, which relaxes the requirement for J_c.

14.1.2 Spin-Torque Magnetoresistive Random Access Memory (ST-MRAM)

Compared to field writing based MRAM, ST-based MRAM has better scalability as STS occurs at a relatively fixed threshold current density J_c, depending on the device structure. This means that for the same device structure and current density for STS, reduction in the MRAM cell size will result in corresponding reductions in the writing current, and in the dimensions of the current lines and write transistors. This section will discuss the basics of STT and advanced concepts such as STT with perpendicular magnetic anisotropy.

14.1.2.1 Basics of Spin-Torque Transfer. Due to the Zeeman splitting of their majority and minority energy bands, magnetic materials have a net spin imbalance at the Fermi level. This spin imbalance allows the generation of spin-polarized currents [62, 63], which can be used to impart some of its spin angular momentum into another magnetic layer. This exchange of spin angular momentum between an electric current and local magnetic moments results in a mutual torque, which can incite a dynamical response in the magnetization of the magnetic layer. This ST transfer effect can be used for current-induced magnetization switching (CIMS) in MRAM devices, which offers better scalability compared to magnetic field switching.

As early as 1996, Berger [64] and Slonczewski [65] predicted that a spin-polarized current could transfer its spin momentum to the magnetic layer it traverses. This spin momentum transfer could induce a STT on the magnetization of the magnetic layer, allowing the magnetic layer to switch without the application of a magnetic field, given a sufficiently high electron-current density. This STS is also called current-induced magnetization switching (CIMS), and with its first demonstration in 2000 by Katine et al. [66], STS heralded a new era of possibilities for spin-electronic devices.

STT was immediately recognized as a scalable strategy to switch MRAM elements without disturbing the neighboring cells, and quite a lot of work on the STS of CPP-GMR spin valves [67–72], AlO MTJs [73–76] and MgO MTJs [77–80] was quickly amassed. Figure 14.3 illustrates the STT mechanism of antiparallel to parallel (AP→P) and parallel to antiparallel (AP→P) transitions in a spin valve that depends on the direction of the injected electron current. The effect of damping and ST on the preces-

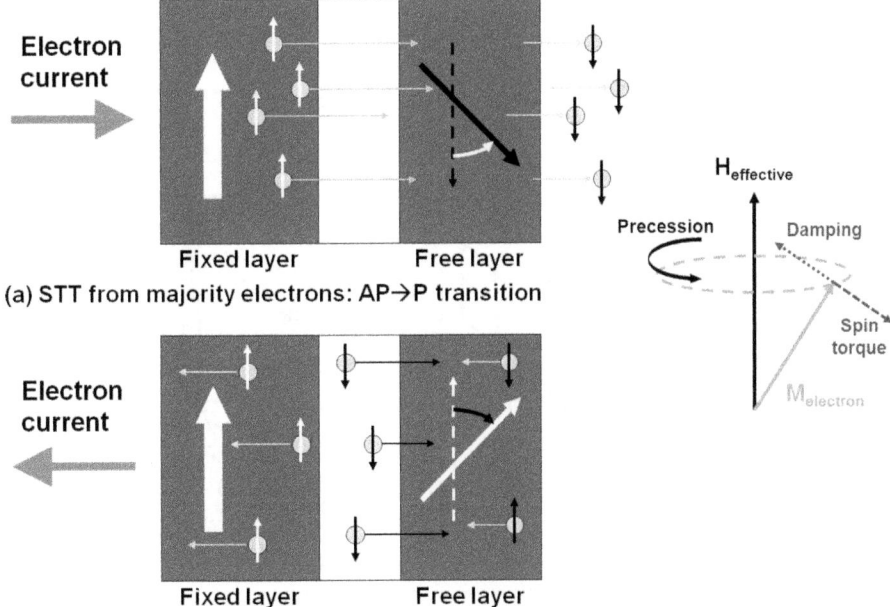

Electron current →

Fixed layer   **Free layer**

(a) STT from majority electrons: AP→P transition

Electron current ←

Fixed layer   **Free layer**

(b) STT from scattered minority electrons : P→AP transition

$H_{effective}$ — Precession — Damping — Spin torque — $M_{electron}$

<u>Figure 14.3.</u> Schematic diagram of the STS of the free layer in a spin valve upon traversal of a spin-polarized current: (a) AP→P transition occurs due to STT from majority electrons polarized by the fixed layer. (b) P→AP transition occurs due to STT from minority electrons scattered by the fixed layer.

sional motion of the electron magnetization around the effective magnetic field is also shown.

14.1.2.2 Spin-Torque Transfer in Perpendicular Anisotropy Devices.
Magnetoresistive devices with PMA are increasingly being explored for future memory applications because of their advantages over conventional in-plane magnetic devices. Compared to their in-plane anisotropy counterparts, magnetoelectronic devices with perpendicular magnetization exhibit improved thermal stability, scalability, and higher STS efficiencies for nanoscale MRAM devices.

Figure 14.4 shows a schematic of the magnetization switching paths for in-plane and perpendicular anisotropy magnetic elements. For in-plane magnetic elements, thermal agitation causes the magnetic layer to switch via rotation in the film plane due to the demagnetization field caused by shape anisotropy of the thin-film geometry. However, the mechanism of STS requires the magnetization to precess past the perpendicular direction before relaxing into the new in-plane magnetization direction. On the other hand, the thermal agitation and STS paths are the same for a perpendicular magnetic layer. Therefore, based on this simple model, we observe that demagnetization

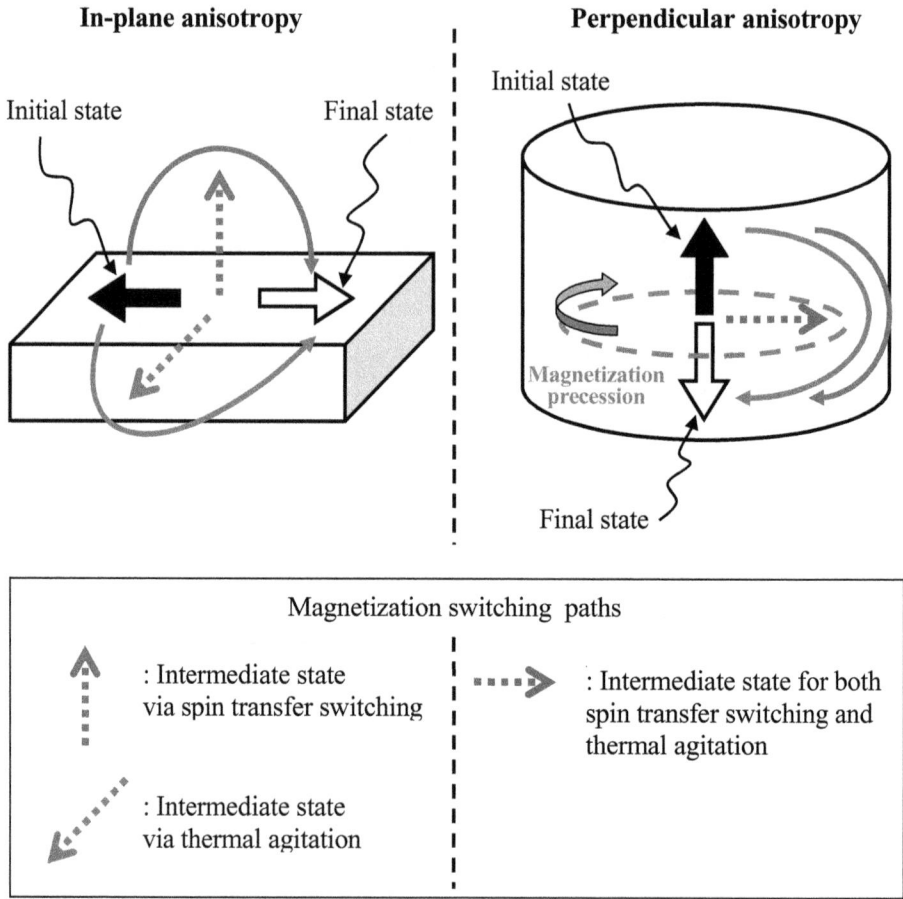

Figure 14.4. Comparison of STT and thermal agitation switching paths for in-plane and perpendicular anisotropy magnetic elements.

fields set up a barrier against STS for in-plane elements but assist STS in perpendicular elements, indicating that PMA elements indeed have higher STS efficiencies.

14.1.3 Perpendicular Magnetic Anisotropy for ST-MRAM Applications

Besides the expected efficiency enhancement in STS devices, magnetic alloys and multilayers with PMA are interesting for their high anisotropy constants (and high coercivity). This allows them to overcome the inherent shape anisotropy (demagnetization field) of thin-film geometry, as well as for their myriad of potential applications. PMA materials are most commonly studied for applications in magneto-optical (MO) recording and perpendicular HDD media [81]. Besides multilayers based on Co/Pt and

Co/Pd bilayers, rare-earth transition metal (RE-TM) alloys such as TbFeCo and GdFeCo, and alloys such as CoCr, CoPt and FePt are also widely used PMA materials.

It should be noted that the origin of PMA in these three systems are different, and will be covered only briefly in this section. In general, the magnetic anisotropy of RE-TM alloys arises from the RE single-ion anisotropy determined from crystal field anisotropy. However, these amorphous films are naturally isotropic, and therefore the easy axis cannot be determined from a local crystal field. The magnetic moments of the heavy RE elements are coupled antiparallel to the TM, and conically distributed around the easy axis of magnetization (sperimagnet) [82–84]. Although the conical distribution of RE magnetic moments seems to be important for PMA, the mechanism for it has not been completely elucidated. (Tb, Gd, Dy, Ho)-FeCo films are most commonly studied and used for MO media for their magneto-optical Kerr response, and recently for thermal-assisted magnetic recording media because of their high PMA [85, 86]. RE-TM alloy materials are also known to have poor corrosion resistance, and hence poorer device reliability compared to structures that do not incorporate RE elements.

On the other hand, alloy films with PMA such as $L1_0$ FePt, $L1_0$ CoPt, and ordered Co_3Pt exhibit extremely large magnetocrystalline anisotropy (up to 7×10^7 erg/cm^3 for FePt) due to the spin-orbit coupling of platinum, and the strong hybridization between the Pt 5d and Co or Fe 3d electronic states [87–92]. The easy axes of magnetization for these materials are along the (001) direction, and usually very high deposition and annealing temperatures (above 350°C) are required to initiate the chemical ordering that yields the required phases for large PMA. Such high process temperatures are not realistic in MRAM manufacturing due to possible interdiffusion and damage of other device layers.

14.1.3.1 PMA in Co/Pd Multilayers.

Co/Pd (and Co/Pt) multilayers have been intensively studied as promising candidates for perpendicular magnetic recording and MO recording media owing to their high perpendicular anisotropy and magneto-optical properties [93–97]. For perpendicular recording media, the crucial issue was in the reduction of grain size and minimization of the strong intergranular exchange coupling in the film in order to reduce the size of the magnetic domains, and hence medium transition noise [98–100]. This problem of strong intergranular exchange coupling in basic Co/Pd and Co/Pt multilayers has rendered them unsuitable for perpendicular recording media applications, and research is underway to combine the benefits of these layers with granular films to form coupled granular/continuous (CGC) media [101–103]. However, this same property allows such multilayer structures to be perfectly suited for GMR devices with PMA, where single domain magnetic layers with unit squareness and sharp switching are required.

PMA in magnetic superlattices of Fe, Co, and Ni with elements such as Ag, Au, Cu, Cr, Mo, Pd, and Pt have been discussed in a detailed review by Johnson et al. [104]. For Co/Pd multilayers, PMA has been attributed to Néel surface magnetic anisotropy in terms of reduced symmetry of Co atoms at the Pd/Co interface [105]. It is well known that the PMA of $(Co/Pd)_n$ increases with the number of bilayer repeats (due to increasing number of interfaces, and hence interface-induced anisotropy), and the Pd-to-Co thickness ratio. Depending on the seed layers used, Pd/Co thickness ratio, deposition conditions, and number of bilayer repeats, the anisotropy values for $(Co/Pd)_n$ are usually of the order of $1 \sim 5 \times 10^6$ erg/cm^3, and they exhibit a large negative magnetostriction coefficient λ_{111} of the order of 10^{-4} [100, 104, 106], the latter leading to a positive contribution to the PMA for an in-plane isotropic tensile stress in the multilayer [95]. Owing to the large lattice mismatch of almost 10% between Co and Pd, it has been claimed that stress-induced anisotropy plays a major role in the PMA of $(Co/Pd)_n$ [95, 107], with Victora and MacLaren showing that epitaxial strain significantly influences the interfacial anisotropy using electronic structure calculations in combination with a simple linear theory [108, 109]. It was also shown that an "alloy like Co environment" at the Co/Pd interface yields PMA through the stress-induced anisotropy [110], and in recent years, there is increasing agreement that the large magnetostriction of the CoPd alloy formed at the layer interfaces gives rise to a strong magnetoelastic anisotropy, which is a significant contributor to the PMA [106, 111]. Finally, using spin- and angle-resolved photoelectron spectroscopy (SARPES), Sawada et al. found that the hybridization between the Co 3d and the Pd 4d states causes the binding energy shift of Co 3d states, which encourages the PMA in the system [112].

14.1.3.2 Stability of Magnetic Elements with Perpendicular Anisotropy. Due to the large anisotropy constants and high coercivity of the PMA materials described above, it is clear that these materials provide higher stability and a greater potential for scaling to smaller dimensions for high-density storage when compared to in-plane anisotropy materials. Furthermore, when in-plane anisotropy materials are patterned into submicron elements, the demagnetization field results in magnetization curling at the edges, resulting in vortex magnetization [56, 113, 114] and anomalous switching [115], such that in-plane devices such as MTJs, require aspect ratios (length to width) of two or above to maintain a single domain configuration, thereby sacrificing density [116].

Figure 14.5 shows simulated magnetic force microscopy (MFM) images of patterned NiFe (using a K_u of 0 erg/cm^3) and CoPt (using a K_u of 4.9×10^7 erg/cm^3) elements with an aspect ratio of 1, which is a comparison between in-plane and PMA materials. The images show flux-closure states in the NiFe elements, which will result in the instability of stored information, compared to uniform magnetization for the PMA CoPt elements. This was also experimentally demonstrated in 2002 in the earliest report of a perpendicular anisotropy MTJ by Nishimura et al. [117], who observed for the in-plane 0.5×0.5 µm NiFe element, a flux-closed "flower pattern" remanent state resulting from vortex magnetization [56, 58]. On the other hand, the perpendicular GdFe/FeCo layer exhibited uniform perpendicular magnetization even for the smaller 0.3×0.3 µm pattern. In fact, uniform single-domain magnetization in patterned Co/Pd multilayers down to 30-nm-diameter dots have been observed from investigations of magnetic dot arrays for perpendicular patterned recording media applications [118, 119]. Furthermore, multidomain remanent states in islands with diameters below 200 nm could not be observed even upon the application of the alternating current (AC) demagnetizing field owing to the high exchange coupling of the Co/Pd multilayers, conferring further benefit for nanoscale MRAM devices. This proves that magnetoresis-

In-plane anisotropy

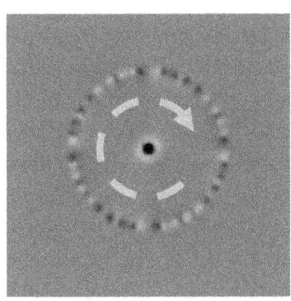 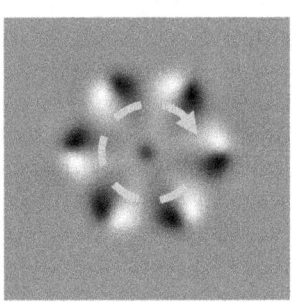 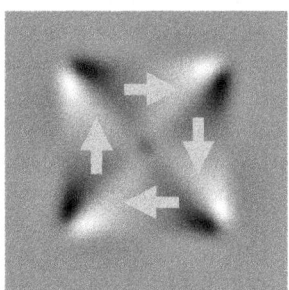

Perpendicular anisotropy

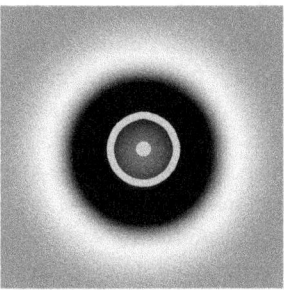  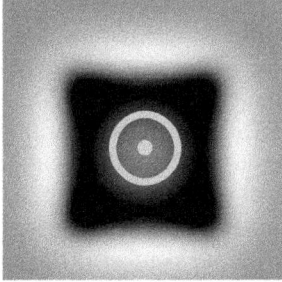

Figure 14.5. Simulated MFM images of in-plane (top) and perpendicular (bottom) anisotropy magnetic elements—Top: 500-nm-wide NiFe elements exhibiting vortex (flux-closure) states with magnetic domains heavily dependent on the shape of the magnetic element. Bottom: 500-nm-wide CoPt elements exhibiting uniform out-of-plane magnetization regardless of pattern shape.

tive devices based on magnetic layers with PMA are indeed scalable far beyond in-plane devices.

At the 52nd Magnetism and Magnetic Materials Conference (Nov 2007), several groups reported relatively high TMR in MTJs with PMA based on Co/Pt multilayers and RE-TM (GdFeCo and TbFeCo) alloys. The Co/Pt MTJs had a TMR of 8% [120] to 15% [121] using AlO tunnel barriers, while the RE-TM MTJs achieved a significant 64% TMR with a MgO tunnel barrier [122]. Another significant announcement was made at the Intermag 2008 Conference (May 2008), where a GTMR of 120% was reported in a FePt-based perpendicular MgO MTJ using Fe layers at the barrier interfaces to achieve (001) crystalline orientation [123], showing that huge TMR values can also be achieved in perpendicular systems.

14.1.3.3 Recent Progress in Perpendicular Anisotropy Spin Valves. The feasibility of STS in magnetoresistive devices was first demonstrated in February 2006 by Mangin et al., who used Co/Pt and Co/Ni multilayers in a perpendicular CPP spin valve [124]. Despite a large coercivity of 2.65 kOe in the free layer, which is more than 50 times that of in-plane MRAM devices, a reasonable switching current density in the order of 10^7 A/cm^2 was able to switch the free layer between the parallel and antiparallel states. Subsequently, rapid strides were made in the development of perpendicular MTJs based on the community's extensive experience in HDD and MO media, as well as MgO-based MRAM devices. Table 14.2 summarizes the chronological development of STS perpendicular spin valves and magnetic tunnel junctions, as reported in literature and recent conferences. So far, the current densities required to switch MgO-based MTJs with TMR of at least 60% have been reduced below 5×10^6 A/cm^2, and have maintained a thermal stability factor (K_uV/k_BT) of above 100 [125]. These results indicate the significantly higher STS efficiency of PMA devices, and that PMA materials provide a highly viable route toward high-density MRAM.

14.1.3.4 Reduction of Spin-Torque Switching Current Densities. For MRAM applications, it is of crucial importance to reduce the critical current density for STS so that the size of the write transistor can be minimized, which in turn reduces the footprint per MRAM cell and increases the storage density. An early limitation of STS in simple trilayer in-plane pseudospin valves is the high current densities (J_c, of around 10^7 to 10^8 A/cm^2) required for switching, causing undesirable device heating and subsequent failure. At the same time, the required switching current is not symmetric, with much higher J_c (about two to three times more) required for switching from the parallel (low resistance) to the antiparallel (high-resistance) state, which is due to the smaller number of minority electrons available for the parallel to antiparallel (P→AP) transition. Besides the higher write current being undesirable, this difference in writing currents for the two states also increases the complexity for writing new data.

For MR devices with in-plane anisotropy magnetic layers, several strategies have been reported for STS current reduction. One method involves sandwiching the free layer between two anti-parallel fixed layers, forming an antisymmetric spin valve [126–128]. This configuration creates a dual spin filter structure which allows both electron spins from both interfaces of the free layer to participate in STS, thus reducing the write current and improving the symmetry of the STS curve. The second method uses strongly spin-scattering insertion layers (such as Ru) at strategic locations of the spin valves, such as the capping layer of the free magnetic layer [129]. The spin-polarized electrons scatter back into the free layer by the strongly spin-scattering layer allows the electrons more opportunities to "interact" with the free layer, thus increasing the ST efficiency.

Another interesting strategy is a modification to the antisymmetric spin-valve structure, where the two fixed layers sandwiching the free layer have orthogonal anisotropies; that is, one fixed layer is in plane, and the other has PMA. The second fixed layer with PMA can also be viewed as an additional perpendicular spin polarizer, and both theoretical and experimental works have shown improved STS efficiency for in-plane spin valves with a perpendicular spin polarizer inserted adjacent to the free layer [130, 131]. For the case of perpendicular anisotropy MR devices, write current reduction becomes even more important due to the difficulty of STS in the high anisotropy

TABLE 14.2. Chronological Progress of STS in Perpendicular Anisotropy MR Devices

Reported	Authors	Stack Structure (Substrate/...)	MR	H_C (kOe)	$\mid J_C \mid$ (A/cm^2)/Write Pulse
Feb'06 Nat. Mater. [124]	HGST, Laboratoire de Physique de Matériaux, Institut d'Electronique Fondamentale	$(Co/Pt)_4/(Co/Ni)_2/Cu/$ $(Co/Ni)_4$	CPP 1%	2.65	AP→P: 2.6×10^7 P→AP: 7.5×10^7 (1000 ms)
Apr'06 APL [162]	MINT, U. of Minnesota	$(CoFe/Pt)_5/Co/Cu/$ $(CoFe/Pt)_7$	CPP 0.47%	0.17	AP→P: 1.0×10^8 P→AP: 1.3×10^8 (DC sweep)
Apr'06 APL [163]	Institute for Materials Research, Tohoku U.	$L1_0$ FePt/Au/$L1_0$ FePt	CPP 0.067%	5.4	AP→P: 1.0×10^8 $T = 77$ K, H_{ex} 6.7 kOe (100 ms)
Nov'07 MMM conf. [125] Feb'08 JAP [164]	Toshiba, Japan	TbCoFe/CoFeB/MgO/ CoFeB/TbCoFe	TMR 60% TMR 15%	1.2	AP→P: 3.5×10^6 (100 ns) AP→P: 4.7×10^6 P→AP: 4.9×10^6 (100 ns)
Nov'07 MMM conf. [165] Mar'08 APS conference [166]	AIST, Japan Toshiba, Japan	$L1_0$ FePt/Au/$L1_0$ FePt TbCoFe/CoFeB/MgO/ CoFeB/(Pd/Co)$_2$	CPP ~1% TMR 60%	1.84 0.8	J_{C0} $^{avg.}$: 1.8×10^7 (10 μs) AP→P: 2.7×10^6 (100 ns)
Apr'08 Appl. Phys. Express [167] May'08 Intermag conference [168]	AIST, Japan	$(Fe_{1ML}/Pt_{1ML})_{12}/Au/$ $(Fe_{1ML}/Pt_{1ML})_{3\ to\ 6}$	CPP 1.1% CPP 1.6%	1.2 ($H_{mls} = 1.1$)	J_{C0} $^{avg.}$: 1.1×10^7 H_{ex} 1.1 kOe J_{C0} $^{avg.}$: 1.2×10^7 H_{ex} 1.1 kOe
May'08 Intermag conference [169]	Sci. & Tech. Research Lab., Tokyo. The Inst. for Solid State Phys., The Tokyo U.	TbFeCo/CoFe /Cu/GdFe	CPP 0.06%	0.3	AP→P: 1.6×10^7 P→AP: 3.1×10^7 (1 μs)
May'08 Intermag conference [123]	Toshiba, Japan	$L1_0$ FePt /MgO/ Fe(FeCo)/$L1_0$ FePt	GTMR 120% (100%)	0.6	Not reported
Jan'09 APL [132]	Data Storage Institute, Singapore	CoFe/Cu/(CoFe/Pd)$_3$/ CoFe/Cu/Co/(Pd/Co)$_5$	CPP 1.0%	0.13	AP→P: 1.8×10^8 P→AP: 5.4×10^8 (100 ns)

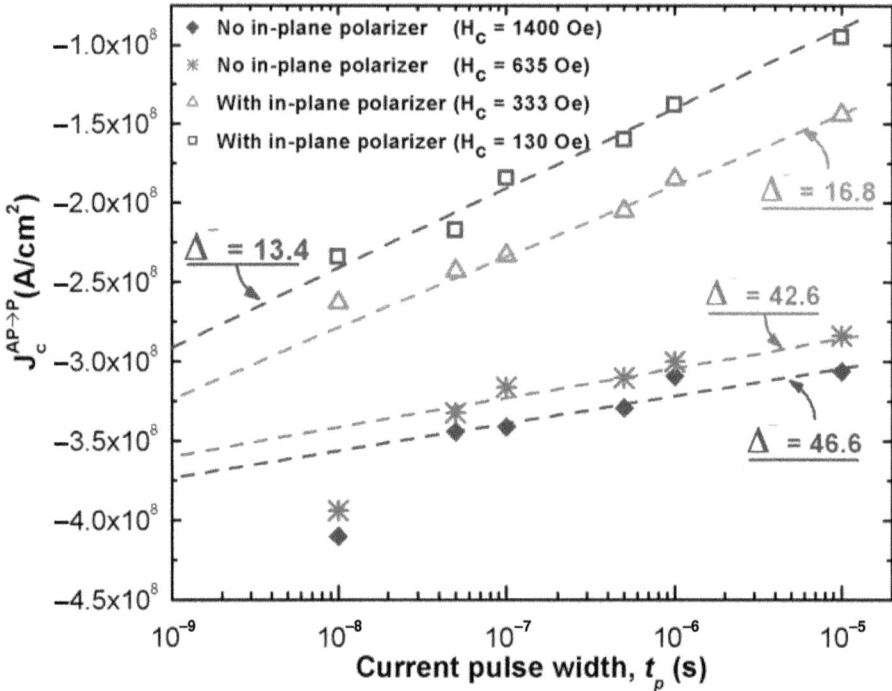

Figure 14.6. Variation of critical current densities for STS as a function of current pulse width for conventional perpendicular single-spin valves and perpendicular spin valves with an in-plane spin polarizer (free-layer coercivities are given in the Figure Legend) [132].

Co/Pd and Co/Pt multilayers commonly used as ferromagnetic layers. Furthermore, these multilayers suffer from low GMR and spin polarization owing to electron spin scattering in the Pd and Pt layers, which further increases STS critical currents. Therefore, it is necessary to design a device structure that can reduce the switching currents to practical levels. Using the idea of the perpendicular spin polarizer, it was also shown both theoretically and experimentally that the insertion of an in-plane magnetized layer adjacent to the soft layer of a PMA spin valve also reduces the switching time and critical current density for STS [132, 133]. For such a device structure, Figure 14.6 shows a 15 to 20% reduction in the intrinsic critical current density $J_{c0}^{AP \to P}$ for STS for the antiparallel-to-parallel (AP→P) transition, and a corresponding reduction in the energy barrier Δ^- for AP→P magnetization reversal by more than 60%, compared to a conventional perpendicular spin valve.

The effect of the additional in-plane or perpendicular spin polarizer layer on current injection can also be understood by the excitation of large high-frequency oscillations in the magnetization of the adjacent magnetic layer [134] in a similar fashion as in STOs, which will be discussed in the last section of this chapter. As the spin polarizer layer excites spin precession in the soft layer, it effectively lowers the energy barrier for STS, yet allows the soft layer to remain thermally stable in the absence of a write current. As the STS speed of practical ST-MRAM is of the order of 10 ns, where thermal activation becomes less significant, the excitations induced by the spin polarizer serves to replace thermal activation as a means to initiate STS. Indeed, at a pulse duration t_p of 10 ns from Figure 14.6, the $J_c^{AP \to P}$ of the conventional single spin valve devices are significantly larger than that expected from the thermal activation model, whereas the $J_c^{AP \to P}$ of devices with an in-plane spin polarizer still fit the model and are 40% lower than that of the single spin-valve devices.

14.1.4 Industrial Progress

After the demonstration of GTMR with MgO tunnel barriers in 2004, work on MgO-based ST-MRAM immediately stimulated immense research efforts and industrial interest. In December 2005 (IEDM 2005), Sony announced the demonstration of a 4-kbit 1T-1MTJ ST-MRAM with 100×150-nm elliptical storage elements [53]. This prototype chip was fabricated on a 4-level metal, 0.18-μm CMOS process, achieving TMR ratios of 100%, STS write speeds down to 2 ns, and write currents as low as 200 μA, demonstrating for the first time the potential and scalability of ST-MRAM.

In July 2006, Freescale Semiconductor became the first company to launch a full-fledged MRAM product onto the market. This pioneering magnetic field-switched 4-Mb product is based on the XPT architecture shown in Figure 14.1, and has a read/write time of 35 ns. With this success, Freescale launched their MRAM division as a spinoff company called Everspin, which currently sells 1-, 2-, 4-, and 16-Mb MRAM chips with 35 ns read/write times.

Two examples of the current industrial uses of Everspin's field-switched MRAM are Ångström Aerospace and Siemens. Ångström Aerospace uses Everspin's extended temperature range 4-Mb MRAM in its Tohoku-AAC MEMS unit (TAMU), which is a magnetometer subsystem for the Japanese research satellite SpriteSat. In this system, the MRAM chip is used to replace both flash memory and battery-backed SRAM in Ångström's module. In Siemens' Simatic Multipanel MP 277 and MP 377 platforms, the Everspin 4-Mb MRAM is used to provide a nonvolatile memory that maintains the process data for a software-programmable logic controller (SoftPLC) without battery backup.

However, despite the performance gains of MRAM compared to conventional memory technologies, the impossibility of scaling field-switched MRAM as discussed earlier has driven company research efforts by Crocus, IBM and TDK, Toshiba, Samsung and Hynix, Grandis, Everspin, and so on to focus on ST-MRAM. In December 2008 (IEDM 2008), Toshiba reported their achievement of a PMA ST-MRAM prototype with a cell size of 50 nm that can be switched within 4 ns using currents as low as 49 μA [135]. With rapid advances and intense research activities on ST-MRAM in recent years, many more prototypes and demonstrations with increasing storage densities are expected in the near future, which should bring ST-MRAM to the reliability testing phase and onto the market in the near future.

14.1.5   Emerging Device Structures and Future Applications

The prediction and experimental realization of STT has allowed great strides to be made in the development of MRAM technology and spintronics. In this section, we will briefly describe two applications of STT that are distinctly different from MRAM technology, namely the racetrack memory, which is based on magnetic domain walls, and the STO, which is based on the steady-state precessional motion of a magnetic layer when under the influence of a spin-polarized current.

14.1.5.1   Domain Walls and Racetrack Memory. In most ferromagnetic materials, small magnet ic domains are formed to lower the magnetostatic energy of the whole system for stability. The region between neighboring domains is called a domain wall (DW), inside which the magnetizations are distributed nonuniformly. The steady-state domain structures are obtained through energy minimization of the system. Bloch walls where magnetization is rotated by 180° out of plane are typically formed in bulk magnetic materials [136–138]. As one of the dimensions is reduced, and the bulk material becomes a two-dimensional thin film, Néel walls (where the magnetization changes the direction by an in-plane rotation) will be more favored than Bloch walls because of the strong demagnetizing field perpendicular to the film plane. With a further size reduction to a one dimensional case, like a nanowire, flux-closed domain structures are no longer energetically favored. Owing to its shape anisotropy, the magnetic domains are aligned along the length of the nanowire, with magnetization pointing toward (or away) from each other. In nanowires, domains are separated by head-to-head (or tail-to-tail) DWs, which can be classified as two distinct structures known as the transverse wall and the vortex wall [139].The transverse wall has its magnetization aligned transverse to the direction of the wire, and usually occurs in thin wires with widths of around 100 nm. On the other hand, the thicker vortex wall occurs in wires with larger widths of around 300 nm, and has curling magnetization forming a near flux closure in the wire.

Recently, a new scheme called racetrack memory [140, 141] was proposed for three-dimensional nonvolatile solid-state storage based on ferromagnetic nanowires. Along the nanowire, each bit of information is stored as a DW. It is claimed that racetrack memory promises to offer a 1000-fold increase in integration density and a 100-fold reduction in power dissipation as compared to the current microelectronics technology. As illustrated in Figure 14.7, a current pulse is passed along the left electrode to generate a magnetic field to magnetize and create a domain wall on the nanowire to write a bit. Subsequently, a second current pulse will be sent across wire by applying a potential difference across the two electrodes, shifting the DWs by STT [142–149]. By controlling the duration and amplitude of the current pulses, the racetrack memory structure can also function as a shift register [150]. As the DW in a nanowire with in-plane anisotropy can be a transverse wall or vortex wall, the DW widths in such nanowires are about 50 nm or more wide, which may limit the density of the DWs or bits of information that can be stored along the wire. On the other hand, materials with perpendicular anisotropy [151] may be considered for this application as PMA materials tend to form Bloch walls, which have smaller DW widths of the order of 5 nm, which will allow a tighter packing density of the DWs.

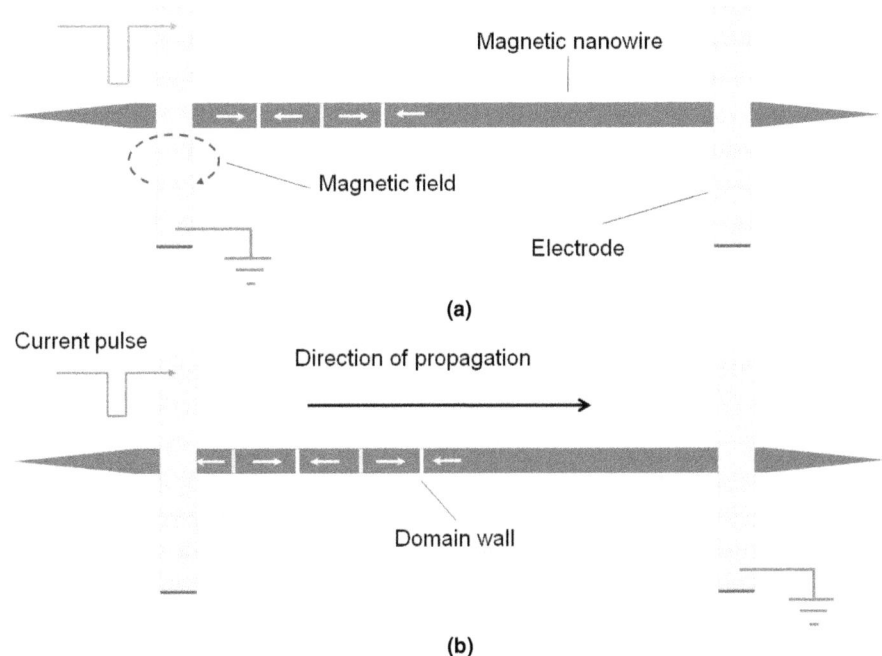

Figure 14.7. (a) A write current pulse is sent along the electrode to create a domain on the nanowire. The polarity of the write pulse will induce magnetic field to magnetize the domain formed in the nanowire. (b) A subsequent pulse is sent across the wire to shift the domain walls.

In order to realize practical information storage, the synchronization of the string of DWs along the long length of nanowire has to be controlled. Several strategies may also need to be used to prevent a DW from catching up with the one in front of it, which will result in mutual annihilation of the DWs. Finally, a deeper understanding of the ST and current-induced DW motion will be required to reduce the current densities required and reliably control the movement of the DWs.

14.1.5.2   Spin-Torque Oscillators for Microwave Generation. In 2005 another major development in STT research launched a completely new field of potential applications for spin-valve devices. In agreement with STT theory, it was reported that if a sufficiently large current pulse is applied such that the spin torque opposes the damping force, the free magnetic layer precesses in response to the driving torque from the electrons [152]. The frequency of the magnetization precession is related to the ferromagnetic resonance of the system, which is in the GHz regime. This makes it possible to design and integrate spin valves and MTJs into existing electronics for use as coherent nanoscale microwave sources. In the last few years, rapid advances in the study and design of these STOs to narrow the emission linewidths and increase the emitted microwave power have been made [153–156]. In addition, the spin-valve based oscillators have also been proposed for use in write heads to improve the writability in HDD applications [157–159].

14.1.6 Summary

By exploiting the spin degree of freedom of electrons, application of the GMR and TMR effects has enabled phenomenal increases in the storage density of HDD technology. There has been a huge research effort worldwide in applying MR devices to nonvolatile memory storage, where MRAM is expected to provide an almost universal solution to most of our storage needs. We have described the advantages of using materials with perpendicular magnetic anisotropy, which is expected to enable ST MRAM to be scalable below 20-nm cell sizes. At the same time, STS has higher efficiency in terms of torque-per-unit current compared to magnetic fields for MRAM devices below dimensions of about 250 nm, allowing for simpler device geometries and less demanding device tolerances. Furthermore, a STS writing scheme is highly scalable and does not disturb neighboring MRAM cells, and optimization of the device stack allows switching currents to be minimized while maintaining magnetic anisotropy for thermal stability, unlike field-switched MRAM. Finally, a brief introduction to racetrack memory and STOs was given, which might allow new high-density storage schemes and low-power communication devices to be possible in the future.

REFERENCES

1. S. A. Wolf, D. D. Awschalom, R. A. Buhrman et al., Spintronics: a spin-based electronics vision for the future. Science **294**, 1488 (2001).
2. W. J. Gallagher, S. S. P. Parkin, Y. Lu et al., Microstructured magnetic tunnel junctions. J. Appl. Phys. **81**, 3741 (1997).
3. S. S. P. Parkin, K. P. Roche, M. G. Samant et al., Exchange-biased magnetic tunnel junctions and application to nonvolatile magnetic random access memory. J. Appl. Phys. **85**, 5828 (1999).
4. S. Tehrani, J. M. Slaughter, E. Chen, M. Durlam, J. Shi, and M. DeHerrera, Progress and outlook for MRAM technology. IEEE Trans. Magn. **35**, 2814 (2000).
5. J.-G. Zhu, Magnetoresistive random access memory: the path to competitiveness and scalability. Proc. IEEE **96**, 1786 (2008).
6. W. Reohr, H. Honigschmid, R. Robertazzi et al., Memories of tomorrow. IEEE Circuits Devices Mag. **18**, 17 (2002).
7. J. DeBrosse, C. Arndt, C. Barwin et al., A 16Mb MRAM featuring bootstrapped write drivers, digest of technical papers, in *IEEE Symposium on VLSI Circuits*, p. 454 (2004).
8. A. Tanaka, Y. Shimizu, Y. Seyama et al., Spin-valve heads in current-perpendicular-to-plane mode for ultrahigh-density recording. IEEE Trans. Magn. **38**, 84 (2002).
9. A. Matsuzono, S. Terada, H. Ono et al., Study on requirements for shielded current perpendicular to plane spin valve heads based on dynamic read tests. J. Appl. Phys. **91**, 7267 (2002).

10. M. Takagishi, K. Koi, M. Yoshikawa, T. Funayama, H. Iwasaki, and M. Sahashi, The applicability of CPP-GMR heads for magnetic recording. IEEE Trans. Magn. **38**, 2277 (2002).

11. M. Saito, N. Hasegawa, Y. Ide et al., Narrow track current-perpendicular-to-plane spin valve GMR heads. IEEE Trans. Magn. **40**, 207 (2002).

12. M. Hosomi, E. Makino, I. Konishiike, N. Suguwara, and S. Ohkawara, Film structure dependence of the magnetoresistive properties in current perpendicular to plane spin valves and its relation with current in plane magnetoresistive properties. J. Appl. Phys. **91**, 8099 (2002).

13. H. Oshima, K. Nagasaka, Y. Seyama, Y. Shimizu, and A. Tanaka, Spin filtering effect at inserted interfaces in perpendicular spin valves. Phys. Rev. B **66**, 140404(R)-1-4 (2002).

14. H. Yuasa, M. Yoshikawa, Y. Kamiguchi, K. Koi, H. Iwasaki, M. Takagishi, and M. Sahashi, Output enhancement of spin-valve giant magnetoresistance in current-perpendicular-to-plane geometry. J. Appl. Phys. **92**, 2646 (2002).

15. H. Oshima, K. Nagasaka, Y. Seyama, A. Jogo, Y. Shimizu, A. Tanaka, and Y. Miura, Current-perpendicular spin valves with partially oxidized magnetic layers for ultrahigh-density magnetic recording. IEEE Trans. Magn. **39**, 2377 (2003).

16. H. Fukuzawa, H. Yuasa, S. Hashimoto et al., MR ratio enhancement by NOL current-confined-path structures in CPP spin valves. IEEE Trans. Magn. **40**, 2236 (2004).

17. T. Iwase, Y. Sakuraba, S. Bosu, K. Saito, S. Mitani, and K. Takanashi, Large interface spin-asymmetry and magnetoresistance in fully epitaxial Co2MnSi/Ag/Co2MnSi current-perpendicular-to-plane magnetoresistive devices. Appl. Phys. Express **2**, 063003 (2009).

18. P. M. Tedrow and R. Meservey, Spin polarization of electron tunneling from films of Fe, Co, Ni and Gd. Phys. Rev. B **7**, 318 (1973).

19. M. Jullière, Tunneling between ferromagnetic films. Phys. Lett. **54a**, 225 (1975).

20. J. S. Moodera, L. R. Kinder, T. M. Wong, and R. Meservey, Large magnetoresistance at room temperature in ferromagnetic thin film tunnel junctions. Phys. Rev. Lett. **74**, 3273 (1995).

21. J. S. Moodera and G. Mathon, Spin polarized tunneling in ferromagnetic junctions. J. Magn. Magn. Mater. **200**, 248 (1999).

22. T. Miyazaki and N. Tezuka, Giant magnetic tunneling effect in Fe/Al2O3/Fe junction. J. Magn. Magn. Mater. **139**, L231 (1995).

23. X.-F. Han, M. Oogane, H. Kubota, Y. Ando, and T. Miyazaki, Fabrication of high-magnetoresistance tunnel junctions using Co75Fe25 ferromagnetic electrodes. Appl. Phys. Lett. **77**, 283 (2000).

24. J. Yu, H. M. Lee, Y. Ando, and T. Miyazaki, Electron transport properties in magnetic tunnel junctions with epitaxial NiFe (111) ferromagnetic bottom electrodes. Appl. Phys. Lett. **82**, 4735 (2003).

25. S.-J. Ahn, T. Kato, H. Kubota, Y. Ando, and T. Miyazaki, Bias-voltage dependence of magnetoresistance in magnetic tunnel junctions grown on Al2O3 (0001) substrates. Appl. Phys. Lett. **86**, 102506 (2005).

26. K. Jun, J. H. Lee, K.-H. Shin, K. Rhie, and B. C. Lee, Enhancement of tunneling magnetoresistance by inserting an amorphous nonmagnetic FeZr layer in magnetic tunnel junctions. J. Magn. Magn. Mater. **286**, 158 (2005).

27. D. J. Monsma and S. S. P. Parkin, Spin polarization of tunneling current from ferromagnet/Al2O3 interfaces using copper-doped aluminum superconducting films. Appl. Phys. Lett. **77**, 720 (2000).

28. J. J. Yang, C. Ji, Y. A. Chang, X. Ke, and M. S. Rzchowski, Over 70% tunneling magnetoresistance at room temperature for a CoFe and AlOx based magnetic tunnel junction. APL **89**, 202502 (2006).

29. W. J. Gallagher and S. S. P. Parkin, Development of the magnetic tunnel junction MRAM at IBM: from first junctions to a 16-Mb MRAM demonstrator chip. IBM J. Res. Dev. **50**, 5 (2006).

30. D. Wang, C. Nordman, J. M. Daughton, Z. Qian, and J. Fink, 70% TMR at room temperature for SDT sandwich junctions with CoFeB as free and reference layers. IEEE Trans. Magn. **40**, 2269 (2004).

31. Y. Sakuraba, J. Nakata, M. Oogane, Y. Ando, H. Kato, A. Sakuma, T. Miyazaki, and H. Kubota, Magnetic tunnel junctions using B2-ordered Co2MnAl Heusler alloy epitaxial electrode. Appl. Phys. Lett. **88**, 022503 (2006).

32. Y. Sakuraba, M. Hattori, M. Oogane, Y. Ando, H. Kato, A. Sakuma, T. Miyazaki, and H. Kubota, Giant tunneling magnetoresistance in Co2MnSi/Al-O/Co2MnSi magnetic tunnel junctions. Appl. Phys. Lett. **88**, 192508 (2006).

33. S. Yuasa, A. Fukushima, T. Nagahama, K. Ando, and Y. Suzuki, High tunnel magnetoresistance at room temperature in fully epitaxial Fe/MgO/Fe tunnel junctions due to coherent spin-polarized tunneling. Jpn. J. Appl. Phys. **43**, L588 (2004).

34. S. Yuasa, T. Nagahama, A. Fukushima, Y. Suzuki, and K. Ando, Giant room-temperature magnetoresistance in single-crystal Fe/MgO/Fe magnetic tunnel junctions. Nat. Mater. **3**, 868 (2004).

35. S. S. P. Parkin, C. Kaiser, A. Panchula, P. M. Rice, B. Hughes, M. Samant, and S.-H. Yang, Giant tunneling magnetoresistance at room temperature with MgO (100) tunnel barriers. Nat. Mater. **3**, 862 (2004).

36. S. Yuasa and D. D. Djayaprawira, Giant tunnel magnetoresistance in magnetic tunnel junctions with a crystalline MgO(001) barrier. J. Phys. D Appl. Phys. **40**, R337 (2007).

37. S. Ikeda, J. Hayakawa, Y. Ashizawa, Y. M. Lee, K. Miura, H. Hasegawa, M. Tsunoda, F. Matsukura, and H. Ohno, Tunnel magnetoresistance of 604% at 300 K by suppression of Ta diffusion in CoFeB/MgO/CoFeB pseudo-spin-valves annealed at high temperature. Appl. Phys. Lett. **93**, 082508 (2008).

38. J. M. MacLaren, X.-G. Zhang, W. H. Butler, and X. Wang, Layer KKR approach to Bloch-wave transmission and reflection: application to spin-dependent tunneling. Phys. Rev. B **59**, 5470 (1999).

39. W. H. Butler, X.-G. Zhang, T. C. Schulthess, and J. M. MacLaren, Spin-dependent tunneling conductance of Fe/MgO/Fe sandwiches. Phys. Rev. B **63**, 054416 (2001).

40. X.-G. Zhang, W. H. Butler, and A. Bandyopadhyay, Effects of the iron-oxide layer in Fe-FeO-MgO-Fe tunneling junctions. Phys. Rev. B **68**, 092402 (2003).

41. X.-G. Zhang and W. H. Butler, Large magnetoresistance in bcc Co/MgO/Co and FeCo/MgO/FeCo tunnel junctions. Phys. Rev. B **70**, 172407 (2004).

42. K. Tsunekawa, D. D. Djayaprawira, M. Nagai et al., Giant tunneling magnetoresistance effect in low-resistance CoFeB/MgO(001)/CoFeB magnetic tunnel junctions for read-head applications. Appl. Phys. Lett. **87**, 072503 (2005).

43. Y. Nagamine, H. Maehara, K. Tsunekawa, D. D. Djayaprawira, N. Watanabe, S. Yuasa, and K. Ando, Ultralow resistance-area product of 0.4 $\Omega(\mu m)2$ and high magnetoresistance above 50% in CoFeB/MgO/CoFeB magnetic tunnel junctions. Appl. Phys. Lett. **89**, 162507 (2006).

44. R. Scheuerlein, W. Gallagher, S. Parkin, A. Lee, S. Ray, R. Robertazzi, and W. Reohr, A 10 ns read and write non-volatile memory array using a magnetic tunnel junction and FET switch in each cell, in *Proc. IEEE Int. Solid-State Circuits Conf. Dig. Tech. Papers*, p. 128 (2000).

45. M. Durlam, P. Naji, M. DeHerrera, S. Tehrani, G. Kerszykowski, and K. Kyler, Nonvolatile RAM based on magnetic tunnel junction elements, in *Proc. IEEE Int. Solid-State Circuits Conf. Dig. Tech. Papers*, p. 130 (2000).

46. H. Kano, K. Bessho, Y. Higo, K. Ohba, M. Hashimoto, and M. Hosomi, MRAM with improved magnetic tunnel junction material, in *Proc. INTERMAG Conf.*, p. BB-04 (2002).

47. H. J. Kim, W. C. Jeong, K. H. Koh et al., A process integration of high-performance 64-kb MRAM. IEEE Trans. Magn. **39**, 2851 (2003).

48. K. Ounadjela, MRAM: a new technology for the future, in NCCAVS Thin Film Users Group Proceedings, March 2004, http://www.avsusergroups.org/tfug/tfug_23proceedings.htm.

49. T. W. Andre, J. J. Nahas, C. K. Subramanian, B. J. Garni, H. S. Lin, A. Omair, and W. L. Martino Jr., A 4-Mb 0.18-μm 1T1MTJ toggle MRAM with balanced three input sensing scheme and locally mirrored unidirectional write drivers. IEEE J. Solid-State Circuits **40**, 301 (2005).

50. T. Suzuki, Y. Fukumoto, K. Mori et al., Toggling cell with four antiferromagnetically coupled ferromagnetic layers for high density MRAM with low switching current, in *VLSI Symp. Tech. Dig.*, p. 188 (2005).

51. D. Gogl, C. Arndt, J. C. Barwin et al., A 16-Mb MRAM featuring bootstrapped write drivers. IEEE J. Solid-State Circuits **40**, 902 (2005).

52. Y. Iwata, K. Tsuchida, T. Inaba et al., A 16 Mb MRAM with FORK wiring scheme and burst modes, in *Proc. IEEE Int. Solid-State Circuits Conf. Dig. Tech. Papers*, p. 477 (2006).

53. M. Hosomi, H. Yamagishi, T. Yamamoto et al., A novel nonvolatile memory with spin torque transfer magnetization switching: spin-RAM, in *IEEE International Electron Devices Meeting (IEDM 2005) Technical Digest*, p. 459 (2005).

54. T. Kawahara, R. Takemura, K. Miura et al., 2 Mb spin-transfer torque RAM (SPRAM) with bit-by-bit bidirectional current write and parallelizing-direction current read, in *Proc. IEEE Int. Solid-State Circuits Conf. Dig. Tech. Papers*, p. 480 (2007).

55. See http://www.everspin.com for more information.

56. J. Shi, S. Tehrani, and M. R. Scheinfein, Geometry dependence of magnetization vortices in patterned submicron NiFe elements. Appl. Phys. Lett. **76**, 2588 (2000).

57. J. Shi, T. Zhu, M. Durlam, E. Chen, S. Tehrani, Y. F. Zheng, and J.-G. Zhu, End domain states and magnetization reversal in submicron magnetic structures. IEEE Trans. Magn. **34**, 997 (1998).

58. J. Shi, S. Tehrani, T. Zhu, Y. F. Zheng, and J. G. Zhu, Magnetization vortices and anomalous switching in patterned NiFeCo submicron arrays. Appl. Phys. Lett. **74**, 2525 (1999).

59. J. Shi and S. Tehrani, Edge-pinned states in patterned submicron NiFeCo structures. Appl. Phys. Lett. **77**, 1692 (2000).

60. J. Janesky, N. D. Rizzo, L. Savtchenko, B. Engel, J. M. Slaughter, and S. Tehrani, Magnetostatic interactions between sub-micrometer patterned magnetic elements. IEEE Trans. Magn. **37**, 2052 (2001).

61. S. Ikeda, J. Hayakawa, Y. M. Lee, F. Matsukura, Y. Ohno, T. Hanyu, and H. Ohno, Magnetic tunnel junctions for spintronic memories and beyond. IEEE Trans. Electron Dev. **54**, 991 (2007).

62. R. Meservey and P. M. Tedrow, Spin-polarized electron tunneling. Phys. Rep. **238**, 173 (1994).

63. M. D. Stiles and A. Zangwill, Noncollinear spin transfer in Co/Cu/Co multilayers. J. Appl. Phys. **91**, 6812 (2002).

64. L. Berger, Emission of spin waves by a magnetic multilayer traversed by a current. Phys. Rev. B **54**, 9353 (1996).

65. J. C. Slonczewski, Current-driven excitation of magnetic multilayers. J. Magn. Magn. Mater. **159**, L1–L7 (1996).

66. J. A. Katine, F. J. Albert, R. A. Buhrman, E. B. Myers, and D. C. Ralph, Current-Driven Magnetization Reversal and Spin-Wave Excitations in Co/Cu/Co Pillars. Phys. Rev. Lett. **84**, 3149 (2000).

67. F. J. Albert, J. A. Katine, R. A. Buhrman, and D. C. Ralph, Spin-polarized current switching of a Co thin film nanomagnet. Appl. Phys. Lett. **77**, 3809 (2000).

68. J. Grollier, V. Cros, A. Hamzic et al., Spin-polarized current induced switching in Co/Cu/Co pillars. Appl. Phys. Lett. **78**, 3663 (2001).

69. J. Z. Sun, D. J. Monsma, D. W. Abraham, M. J. Rooks, and R. H. Koch, Batch-fabricated spin-injection magnetic switches. Appl. Phys. Lett. **81**, 2202 (2002).

70. Y. Jiang, S. Abe, T. Ochiai, T. Nozaki, A. Hirohata, N. Tezuka, and K. Inomata, Effective reduction of critical current for current-induced magnetization switching by a Ru layer insertion in an exchange-biased spin valve. Phys. Rev. Lett. **92**, 167204 (2004).

71. K. Yagami, A. A. Tulapurkar, A. Fukushima, and Y. Suzuki, Low-current spin-transfer switching and its thermal durability in a low saturation-magnetization nanomagnet. Appl. Phys. Lett. **85**, 5634 (2004).

72. J. Hayakawa, H. Takahashi, K. Ito et al., Current-driven magnetization reversal in exchange-biased spin-valve nanopillars. J. Appl. Phys. **97**, 114321 (2005).

73. Y. W. Liu, Z. Z. Zhang, P. P. Freitas, and J. L. Martins, Current-induced magnetization switching in magnetic tunnel junctions. Appl. Phys. Lett. **82**, 2871 (2003).

74. Y. Huai, F. Albert, P. Nguyen, M. Pakala, and T. Valet, Observation of spin-transfer switching in deep submicron-sized and low-resistance magnetic tunnel junctions. Appl. Phys. Lett. **84**, 3118 (2004).

75. G. D. Fuchs, N. C. Emley, I. N. Krivorotov et al., Spin-transfer effects in nanoscale magnetic tunnel junctions. Appl. Phys. Lett. **85**, 1205 (2004).

76. G. D. Fuchs, I. N. Krivorotov, P. M. Braganca, N. C. Emley, A. G. F. Garcia, D. C. Ralph, and R. A. Buhrman, Adjustable spin torque in magnetic tunnel junctions with two fixed layers. Appl. Phys. Lett. **86**, 152509 (2005).

77. H. Kubota, A. Fukushima, Y. Ootani et al., Evaluation of spin-transfer switching in CoFeB/MgO/CoFeB magnetic tunnel junctions. Jpn. J. Appl. Phys. **44**, L1237 (2005).

78. J. Hayakawa, S. Ikeda, Y. M. Lee et al., Current-driven magnetization switching in CoFeB/MgO/CoFeB magnetic tunnel junctions. Jpn. J. Appl. Phys. **44**, L1267 (2005).

79. Z. Diao, D. Apalkov, M. Pakala, Y. Ding, A. Panchula, and Y. Huai, Spin transfer switching and spin polarization in magnetic tunnel junctions with MgO and AlOx barriers. Appl. Phys. Lett. **87**, 232502 (2005).

80. H. Kubota, A. Fukushima, Y. Ootani et al., Dependence of spin-transfer switching current on free layer thickness in Co-Fe-B/MgO/Co-Fe-B magnetic tunnel junctions. Appl. Phys. Lett. **89**, 032505 (2006).

81. S. N. Piramanayagam, Perpendicular recording media for hard disk drives. J. Appl. Phys. **102**, 011301 (2007).

82. J. M. D. Coey, Amorphous magnetic order. J. Appl. Phys. **49**, 1646 (1978).

83. C. Bordel, S. Pizzini, J. Vogel et al., Microscopic origin of the macroscopic magnetic properties of TbFeCoN amorphous thin films. Phys. Rev. B **56**, 8149 (1997).

84. C. Bordel, S. Pizzini, J. C. Toussaint, B. Kervorkian, and J. Voiron, Magnetic properties of amorphous nitrogenated TbFeCo thin films. J. Magn. Magn. Mater. **193**, 170 (1999).

85. P. Hansen, C. Clausen, G. Much, M. Rosenkranz, and K. Witter, Magnetic and magneto-optical properties of rare-earth transition-metal alloys containing Gd, Tb, Fe, Co. J. Appl. Phys. **66**, 756 (1989).

86. P. Hansen, S. Klahn, C. Clausen, G. Much, and K. Witter, Magnetic and magneto-optical properties of rare-earth transition-metal alloys containing Dy, Ho, Fe, Co. J. Appl. Phys. **69**, 3194 (1991).

87. J. S. Chen, J. F. Hu, B. C. Lim, Y. K. Lim, B. Liu, G. M. Chow, and G. Ju, High coercive L10 FePt-C (001) nanocomposite films with small grain size for perpendicular recording media. J. Appl. Phys. **103**, 07F517 (2008).

88. B. C. Lim, J. S. Chen, J. F. Hu, Y. K. Lim, B. Liu, G. M. Chow, and G. Ju, Improvement of chemical ordering of FePt (001) oriented films by MgO buffer layer. J. Appl. Phys. **103**, 07E143 (2008).

89. M. Abes, J. Venuat, and A. Carvalho, Magnetic nanopatterning of CoPt thin layers. J. Magn. Magn. Mater. **286**, 297 (2005).

90. A. Christodoulides, Y. Zhang, G. C. Hadjipanayis, and C. Fountzoulas, CoPt and FePt nanoparticles for high density recording media. IEEE Trans. Magn. **36**, 2333 (2000).

91. Y. Yamada, T. Suzuki, and E. N. Abarra, Magnetic properties of electron beam evaporated CoPt alloy thin films. IEEE Trans. Magn. **33**, 3622 (1997).

92. S. Mifuji, H. Sakuma, and K. Ishii, Co-Pt/Pt thin films with perpendicular magnetization and a high coercivity prepared by gas flow sputtering. J. Appl. Phys. **97**, 10N102 (2005).

93. P. F. Carcia, A. D. Meinhaldt, and A. Suna, Perpendicular magnetic anisotropy in Pd/Co thin film layered structures. Appl. Phys. Lett. **47**, 178 (1985).

94. F. J. A. den Broeder, H. C. Donkerslot, H. J. G. Draaisma, and W. J. M. de Jonge, Magnetic properties and structure of Pd/Co and Pd/Fe multilayers. J. Appl. Phys. **61**, 4317 (1987).

95. S. Hashimoto, Y. Ochiai, and K. Aso, Perpendicular magnetic anisotropy and magnetostriction of sputtered Co/Pd and Co/Pt multilayered films. J. Appl. Phys. **66**, 4909 (1989).

96. J. V. Haezer, B. Hillebrands, R. L. Stamps, G. Guntherodt, C. D. England, and C. M. Falco, Magnetic properties of Co/Pd multilayers determined by Brillouin light scattering and SQUID magnetometry. J. Appl. Phys. **69**, 2448 (1991).

97. B. N. Engel, C. D. England, R. A. Van Leeuwen, M. H. Wiedmann, and C. M. Falco, Interface magnetic anisotropy in epitaxial superlattices. Phys. Rev. Lett. **67**, 1910 (1991).

98. L. Wu, N. Honda, and K. Ouchi, Low Noise Co/Pd Multilayer Media for Perpendicular Magnetic Recording. IEEE Trans. Magn. **35**, 2775 (1999).

99. J. Kawaji, T. Asahi, T. Onoue, J. Sayama, J. Hokkyo, T. Osaka, and K. Ouchi, Enhancement of magnetic properties of Co/Pd multilayered perpendicular magnetic recording media by using Pd/Si dual seedlayer. J. Magn. Magn. Mater. **251**, 220 (2002).

100. T. Onoue, J. Kawaji, K. Kuramochi, T. Asahi, and T. Osaka, Effect of underlayers on magnetic properties of Co/Pd multilayer perpendicular magnetic recording media. J. Magn. Magn. Mater. **235**, 82 (2001).

101. H. Muraoka, Y. Sonobe, K. Miura, A. M. Goodman, and Y. Nakamura, Analysis on magnetization transition of CGC perpendicular media. IEEE Trans. Magn. **38**, 1632 (2002).

102. Y. Sonobe, D. Weller, Y. Ikeda et al., Thermal stability and SNR of coupled granular/continuous media. IEEE Trans. Magn. **37**, 1667 (2001).

103. Y. Sonobe, H. Muraoka, K. Miura et al., Thermally stable CGC perpendicular recording media with Pt-rich CoPtCr and thin Pt layers. IEEE Trans. Magn. **38**, 2006 (2002).

104. M. T. Johnson, P. J. H. Bloemen, F. J. A. van den Broeder, and J. J. de Vries, Magnetic anisotropy in metallic multilayers. Rep. Prog. Phys. **59**, 1409 (1996).

105. F. J. A. den Broeder, W. Hoving, and P. J. H. Bloemen, Magnetic anisotropy of multilayers. J. Magn. Magn. Mater. **93**, 562 (1991).

106. H. Takahashi, S. Tsunashima, S. Iwata, and S. Uchiyama, Measurement of magnetostriction constants in (111)-oriented polycrystalline PdCo alloy and multilayered films. Jpn. J. Appl. Phys. **32**, L1328 (1993).

107. Y.-S. Kim and S.-C. Shin, Magnetoelastic effect in Co/Pd multilayer films. J. Appl. Phys. **76**, 6087 (1994).

108. R. H. Victora and J. M. MacLaren, Theory of anisotropy in strained superlattices. J. Appl. Phys. **73**, 6415 (1993).

109. R. H. Victora and J. M. MacLaren, Theory of magnetic interface anisotropy. Phys. Rev. B **47**, 11583 (1993).

110. S.-K. Kim and S.-C. Shin, Alloy-like Co environment in Co/Pd multilayer films having perpendicular magnetic anisotropy. J. Appl. Phys. **89**, 3055 (2001).

111. J. Carrey, A. E. Berkowitz, W. F. Egelhoff Jr., and D. J. Smith, Influence of interface alloying on the magnetic properties of Co/Pd multilayers. Appl. Phys. Lett. **83**, 5259 (2003).

112. M. Sawada, K. Hayashi, and A. Kakizaki, Perpendicular magnetic anisotropy of Co/Pd(111) studied by spin-resolved photoelectron spectroscopy. J. Phys. Soc. Jpn. **72**, 1161 (2003).

113. R. D. Gomez, T. V. Luu, A. O. Pak, K. J. Kirk, and J. N. Chapman, Domain configurations of nanostructured Permalloy elements. J. Appl. Phys. **85**, 6163 (1999).

114. S. Y. H. Lua, S. S. Kushvaha, Y. H. Wu, K. L. Teo, and T. C. Chong, Chirality control and switching of vortices formed in hexagonal shaped ferromagnetic elements. Appl. Phys. Lett. **93**, 122504 (2008).

115. Y. Zheng and J. Zhu, Switching field variation in patterned submicron magnetic film elements. J. Appl. Phys. **81**, 5471 (1997).

116. E. Girgis, J. Schelten, J. Sci, J. Janesky, S. Tehrani, and H. Goronkin, Switching characteristics and magnetization vortices of thin-film cobalt in nanometer-scale patterned arrays. Appl. Phys. Lett. **76**, 3780 (2000).

117. N. Nishimura, T. Hirai, A. Koganei, T. Ikeda, K. Okano, Y. Sekiguchi, and Y. Osada, Magnetic tunnel junction device with perpendicular magnetization films for high-density magnetic random access memory. J. Appl. Phys. **91**, 5246 (2002).

118. M. Albrecht, G. Hu, A. Moser, O. Hellwig, and B. D. Terris, Magnetic dot arrays with multiple storage layers. J. Appl. Phys. **97**, 103910 (2005).

119. G. Hu, T. Thomson, C. T. Rettner, S. Raoux, and B. D. Terris, Magnetization reversal in Co/Pd nanostructures and films. J. Appl. Phys. **97**, 10J702 (2005).

120. C. Ducruet, B. Carvello, B. Rodmacq, S. Auffret, G. Gaudin, and B. Dieny, Magnetoresistance in Co/Pt based magnetic tunnel junctions with out-of-plane magnetization. J. Appl. Phys. **103**, 07A918 (2008).

121. J.-H. Park, C. Park, T. Jeong, M. T. Moneck, N. T. Nufer, and J.-G. Zhu, Co/Pt multilayer based magnetic tunnel junctions using perpendicular magnetic anisotropy. J. Appl. Phys. **103**, 07A917 (2008).

122. H. Ohmori, T. Hatori, and S. Nakagawa, Perpendicular magnetic tunnel junction with tunneling magnetoresistance ratio of 64% using MgO (100) barrier layer prepared at room temperature. J. Appl. Phys. **103**, 07A911 (2008).

123. M. Yoshikawa, E. Kitagawa, T. Nagase et al., Tunnel magnetoresistance over 100% in MgO-based magnetic tunnel junction films with perpendicular magnetic L10-FePt electrodes. IEEE Trans. Magn. **44**, 2573 (2008).

124. S. Mangin, D. Ravelosona, J. A. Katine, M. J. Carey, B. D. Terris, and E. E. Fullerton, Current-induced magnetization reversal in nanopillars with perpendicular anisotropy. Nat. Mater. **5**, 210 (2006).

125. M. Nakayama, T. Kai, N. Shimomura et al., Spin transfer switching in TbCoFe/CoFeB/ MgO/CoFeB/TbCoFe magnetic tunnel junctions with perpendicular magnetic anisotropy, in *Abstract of 52nd Annual Conference on Magnetizm and Magnetic Materials, BB-09*, p. 81 (2007).

126. L. Berger, Multilayer configuration for experiments of spin precession induced by a dc current. J. Appl. Phys. **93**, 7693 (2003).

127. Y. Jiang, G. H. Yu, Y. B. Wang, J. Teng, T. Ochiai, N. Tezuka, and K. Inomata, Spin transfer in antisymmetric exchange-biased spin-valves. Appl. Phys. Lett. **86**, 192515 (2005).

128. Y. Huai, M. Pakala, Z. Diao, and Y. Ding, Spin transfer switching current reduction in magnetic tunnel junction based dual spin filter structures. Appl. Phys. Lett. **87**, 222510 (2005).

129. Y. Jiang, T. Nozaki, S. Abe, T. Ochiai, A. Hirohata, N. Tezuka, and K. Inomata, Substantial reduction of critical current for magnetization switching in an exchange-biased spin valve. Nat. Mater. **3**, 361 (2004).

130. A. D. Kent, B. Özyilmaz, and E. del Barco, Spin-transfer-induced precessional magnetization reversal. Appl. Phys. Lett. **84**, 3897 (2004).

131. T. Seki, S. Mitani, K. Yakushiji, and K. Takanashi, Magnetization reversal by spin-transfer torque in 90° configuration with a perpendicular spin polarizer. Appl. Phys. Lett. **89**, 172504 (2006).

132. R. Law, E.-L. Tan, R. Sbiaa, T. Liew, and T. C. Chong, Reduction in critical current for spin transfer switching in perpendicular anisotropy spin valves using an in-plane spin polarizer. Appl. Phys. Lett. **94**, 062516 (2009).

133. R. Sbiaa, R. Law, E.-L. Tan, and T. Liew, Spin transfer switching enhancement in perpendicular anisotropy magnetic tunnel junctions with a canted in-plane spin polarizer. J. Appl. Phys. **105**, 013910 (2009).

134. D. Houssameddine, U. Ebels, B. Delaët, B. Rodmacq, I. Firastrau, F. Ponthenier, M. Brunet, C. Thirion, J.-P. Michel, L. Prejbeanu-Buda, M.-C. Cyrille, O. Redon, and B. Dieny, Spin-torque oscillator using a perpendicular polarizer and a planar free layer. Nat. Mater. **6**, 447 (2007).

135. T. Kishi, H. Yoda, T. Kai, T. Nagase, E. Kitagawa et al., Lower-current and fast switching of a perpendicular TMR for high speed and high density spin-transfer-torque MRAM, in *IEEE International Electron Devices Meeting (IEDM 2008)*, p. 1 (2008).

136. F. Bloch, Zur Theorie des Autauschproblems und der Remanenzerscheinungen der Ferromagnetika. Z. Phys. **74**, 295 (1932).

137. L. Landau and W. Lifshitz, Theory of the dispersion of magnetic permeability in ferromagnetic bodies. Phys. Z. Sowjetunion **8**, 153 (1935).

138. A. Hubert and R. Schäfer, *Magnetics Domains*. Berlin: Springer-Verlag, 1998.

139. R. D. McMichael and M. J. Donahue, Head to head domain wall structures in thin magnetic strips. IEEE Trans. Magn. **33**, 4167 (1997).

140. S. S. P. Parkin, U.S. Patents 6,834,005, 6,898,132, 6,920,062, 7,031,178, and 7,236,386 (2004–2007).

141. S. S. P. Parkin, M. Hayashi, and L. Thomas, Science **320**, 109 (2008).

142. M. Yamanouchi, D. Chiba, F. Matsukura, and H. Ohno, Current-induced domain-wall switching in a ferromagnetic semiconductor structure. Nature **428**, 539 (2004).

143. D. Ravelosona, D. Lacour, J. A. Katine, B. D. Terris, and C. Chappert, Nanometer scale observation of high efficiency thermally assisted current-driven domain wall depinning. Phys. Rev. Lett. **95**, 117203 (2005).

144. M. Feigenson, J. W. Reiner, and L. Klein, Efficient current-induced domain-wall displacement in SrRuO3. Phys. Rev. Lett. **98**, 247204 (2007).

145. S. Laribi, V. Cros, M. Muñoz, J. Grollier, A. Hamzić, C. Deranlot, A. Fert, and E. Martínez, Reversible and irreversible current induced domain wall motion in CoFeB based spin valves stripes. Appl. Phys. Lett. **90**, 232505 (2007).

146. N. Vernier, D. A. Allwood, D. Atkinson, M. D. Cooke, and R. P. Cowburn, Domain wall propagation in magnetic nanowires by spin-polarized current injection. Europhys. Lett. **65**, 526 (2004).

147. A. Yamaguchi, T. Ono, S. Nasu, K. Miyake, K. Mibu, and T. Shinjo, Real-space observation of current-driven domain wall motion in submicron magnetic wires. Phys. Rev. Lett. **92**, 077205 (2004).

148. M. Kläui, P.-O. Jubert, R. Allenspach, A. Bischof, J. A. C. Bland, G. Faini, U. Rüdiger, C. A. F. Vaz, L. Vila, and C. Vouille, Direct observation of domain-wall configurations transformed by spin currents. Phys. Rev. Lett. **95**, 026601 (2005).

149. M. Hayashi, L. Thomas, C. Rettner, R. Moriya, Y. B. Bazaliy, and S. S. P. Parkin, Current driven domain wall velocities exceeding the spin angular momentum transfer rate in permalloy nanowires. Phys. Rev. Lett. **98**, 037204 (2007).

150. M. Hayashi, L. Thomas, R. Moriya, C. Rettner, and S. S. P. Parkin, Current-controlled magnetic domain-wall nanowire shift register. Science **320**, 209 (2008).

151. C. Burrowes, D. Ravelosona, M. Nguyen Ngoc, C. Chappert, and E. Fullerton, Role of pinning in current driven DW motion in wires with perpendicular anisotropy, in *Abstract of 53rd MMM Conference*, p. AB-03 (2008).

152. I. N. Krivorotov, N. C. Emley, J. C. Sankey, S. I. Kiselev, D. C. Ralph, and R. A. Buhrman, Time-domain measurements of nanomagnet dynamics driven by spin-transfer torques. Science **307**, 228 (2005).

153. J. C. Sankey, P. M. Braganca, A. G. F. Garcia, I. N. Krivorotov, R. A. Buhrman, and D. C. Ralph, Spin-transfer-driven ferromagnetic resonance of individual nanomagnets. Phys. Rev. Lett. **96**, 227601 (2006).

154. J.-V. Kim, Stochastic theory of spin-transfer oscillator linewidths. Phys. Rev. B **73**, 174412 (2006).

155. Q. Mistral, J.-V. Kim, T. Devolder, P. Crozat, C. Chappert, J. A. Katine, M. J. Carey, and K. Ito, Current-driven microwave oscillations in current perpendicular-to-plane spin-valve nanopillars. Appl. Phys. Lett. **88**, 192507 (2006).

156. I. N. Krivorotov, D. V. Berkov, N. L. Gorn, N. C. Emley, J. C. Sankey, D. C. Ralph, and R. A. Buhrman, Large-amplitude coherent spin waves excited by spin-polarized current in nanoscale spin valves. Phys. Rev. B **76**, 024418 (2007).

157. M. W. Covington, T. M. Crawford, T. Mclendon, G. J. Parker, and H. P. A. Van Der, Write head for high anisotropy media. U.S. Patent 6 785 092 Aug. 31 (2004).

158. J.-G. Zhu, X. Zhu, and Y. Tang, Microwave assisted magnetic recording. IEEE Trans. Magn. **44**, 125 (2008).

159. C.-K. Goh, Z.-M. Yuan, T. Zhou, L. Wang, and B. Liu, Microwave-assisted magnetic recording at lower transverse oscillating field. Appl. Phys. **105**, 07B908 (2009).

160. J. M. Slaughter, R. W. Dave, M. DeHerrera et al., Fundamentals of MRAM Technology. J. Supercond. Inc. Novel Magn. **15**, 19 (2002).

161. G. Muller, N. Nagel, C.-U. Pinnow, and T. Rohr, Emerging non-volatile memory technologies, in *Solid-State Circuits Conf. ESSCIRC'03 Proc. 29th European*, p. 37 (2003).

162. H. Meng and J. P. Wang, Spin transfer in nanomagnetic devices with perpendicular anisotropy. Appl. Phys. Lett. **88**, 172506 (2006).

163. T. Seki, S. Mitani, K. Yakushiji, and K. Takanashi, Spin-polarized current-induced magnetization reversal in perpendicularly magnetized L10-FePt layers. Appl. Phys. Lett. **88**, 172504 (2006).

164. M. Nakayama, T. Kai, N. Shimomura et al., Spin transfer switching in TbCoFe/CoFeB/MgO/CoFeB/TbCoFe magnetic tunnel junctions with perpendicular magnetic anisotropy. J. Appl. Phys. **103**, 07A710 (2008).

165. K. Yakushiji, S. Yuasa, T. Nagahama, A. Fukushima, H. Kubota, T. Katayama, and K. Ando, Spin-transfer switching and thermal stability in an epitaxial FePt/Au/FePt nanopillar with perpendicular anisotropy, in *Abstract of 52nd Annual Conference on Magnetizm and Magnetic Materials, BB-01*, p. 78 (2007).

166. T. Nagase, K. Nishiyama, M. Nakayama, N. Shimomura, M. Amano, K. Minoru, T. Kishi, and H. Yoda, Spin transfer torque switching in perpendicular magnetic tunnel junctions with Co based multilayer, in *Abstract of 2008 APS March Meeting, #C1.331* (2008).

167. K. Yakushiji, S. Yuasa, T. Nagahama, A. Fukushima, H. Kubota, T. Katayama, and K. Ando, Spin-transfer switching and thermal stability in an FePt/Au/FePt Nanopillar prepared by alternate monatomic layer deposition. Appl. Phys. Express **1**, 041302 (2008).

168. K. Yakushiji, S. Yuasa, A. Fukushima, H. Kubota, T. Nagahama, T. Katayama, and K. Ando, High thermal stability and low switching current in a perpendicular-CPP-GMR with an ultrathin epitaxial FePt free layer, in *Abstract of INTERMAG 2008 Conference, GD-09* (2008).

169. K. Aoshima, N. Funabashi, K. Machida et al., Magneto-optical and spin transfer switching properties of current-perpendicular-to plane spin valves with perpendicular magnetic anisotropy, in *Abstract of INTERMAG 2008 Conference, AA-01* (2008).

INDEX

Developments in Data Storage: Materials Perspective, First Edition.
Edited by S. N. Piramanayagam, Tow C. Chong.
© 2012 Institute of Electrical and Electronics Engineers. Published 2012 by John Wiley & Sons, Inc.

9 780470 501009